THE
CRIMINAL PROCESS

Fourth Edition

ANDREW ASHWORTH AND
MIKE REDMAYNE

OXFORD
UNIVERSITY PRESS

OXFORD
UNIVERSITY PRESS

Great Clarendon Street, Oxford OX2 6DP

Oxford University Press is a department of the University of Oxford.
It furthers the University's objective of excellence in research, scholarship,
and education by publishing worldwide in

Oxford New York

Auckland Cape Town Dar es Salaam Hong Kong Karachi
Kuala Lumpur Madrid Melbourne Mexico City Nairobi
New Delhi Shanghai Taipei Toronto

With offices in

Argentina Austria Brazil Chile Czech Republic France Greece
Guatemala Hungary Italy Japan Poland Portugal Singapore
South Korea Switzerland Thailand Turkey Ukraine Vietnam

Oxford is a registered trade mark of Oxford University Press
in the UK and in certain other countries

Published in the United States
by Oxford University Press Inc., New York

© Andrew Ashworth and Mike Redmayne 2010

The moral rights of the authors have been asserted

Crown copyright material reproduced with the permission of the
Controller, HMSO (under the terms of the Click Use licence)

Database right Oxford University Press (maker)

First edition 1994
Second edition 1998
Third edition 2005
This edition 2010

British Library Cataloguing in Publication Data

Data available

Library of Congress Cataloging in Publication Data

Data available

Typeset by Newgen Imaging Systems (P) Ltd., Chennai, India
Printed in Great Britain
on acid-free paper by
Ashford Colour Press, Gosport, Hampshire

ISBN 978-0-19-954728-9

1 3 5 7 9 10 8 6 4 2

PREFACE

Some five years have elapsed since the third edition of this work was published. That edition was published in the shadow of the Criminal Justice Act 2003, and while no legislation quite as significant as that has been passed in the intervening years, the pace of change in the criminal process has continued to be rapid. There have been significant changes to plea-bargaining with the Court of Appeal's decision in *Goodyear*, prosecutorial charging has been rolled out nationally, the range and use of out-of-court penalties have increased substantially, and the Criminal Procedure Rules have been introduced. While certain of its provisions remain unimplemented—perhaps a sign of over-hasty legislative action—the 2003 Act itself has bedded in, allowing a more detailed assessment of its significance. Thus we have seen the first convictions gained through retrials after acquittals, and the expanded admissibility of hearsay evidence has raised significant questions about compatibility of English law with the European Convention on Human Rights.

As this last example illustrates, human rights play an increasingly significant role in the criminal process, and we continue to place considerable emphasis on European human rights law. As well as developments relating to hearsay and confrontation, since the last edition there have been significant decisions from Strasbourg relating to the privilege against self-incrimination and the retention of DNA profiles. But the picture remains one of the English courts and the legislature often paying scant attention to human rights, at least until forced to act by adverse rulings in Strasbourg. The hope (or fear) that the Human Rights Act 1998 would presage the arrival of a 'rights culture' has not been realized. Indeed, so far as the criminal process is concerned, the focus has often been on finding reasons for overriding or making exceptions to the declared rights.

The aim of the book remains that of providing a thoughtful treatment of practical and normative issues in criminal processes and procedures, drawing on arguments from the law, research, policy and principle. It does not purport to be a textbook, but rather to subject a number of key issues to deeper examination than would be possible if the book were to aim for wider coverage. The structure of the work remains similar to that of the last edition, but we have added a new chapter on civil preventive orders, which highlights the problematic way in which phenomena such as ASBOs seek to avoid some of the protections offered by the criminal process.

The book opens with a chapter setting out the context of recent changes to the English criminal process. A theoretical framework is advanced in Chapter 2. This chapter retains its emphasis on the European Convention on Human Rights, and seeks to develop a human rights approach to resolving issues in the criminal process. Chapter 3 focuses on the occupational cultures of criminal justice professionals and on questions of legal ethics that arise at various stages. The book then goes on to deal with ten key issues in the criminal process, integrating and commenting upon the latest developments in law and practice. Thus Chapter 4 examines the questioning stage of the criminal process, looking at the role and powers of the police. This is followed in Chapter 5 by an analysis of powers and practices in relation to the gathering of evidence. Chapter 6 turns to the decision about whether a suspect should be prosecuted or diverted from the formal criminal process, in the light of recent changes to the role of the Crown Prosecution Service. While the emphasis in that chapter is upon diversion out of the criminal process, Chapter 7 looks at cases that are charged and then subjected to prosecutorial review, and there is detailed consideration of the functions and performance of the Crown Prosecution Service. In Chapter 8 there is an analysis of remand decisions, scrutinizing the justifications for taking away liberty before trial. Chapter 9 reviews a number of pre-trial rights and duties, including contentious issues such as the disclosure of evidence. In Chapter 10 the law and practice on plea negotiation is examined in the light of recent judicial decisions, legislative changes, and other proposals. Chapter 11 turns to the criminal trial itself, raising questions about the roles of judge and jury. Chapter 12 examines the appeals system, and the new Chapter 13 scrutinizes civil preventive orders.

The writing of the text was completed in early December 2009, and we hope to have taken into account major legal and policy changes up to that date.

A.A.,

Oxford, December 2009

M.R.,

London, November 2009

CONTENTS

TABLE OF CASES

TABLE OF STATUTES

TABLE OF INTERNATIONAL LEGISLATION

TABLE OF SECONDARY LEGISLATION, AND CODES OF PRACTICE AND CONDUCT

CODES OF PRACTICE, CODES OF CONDUCT

1

INTRODUCTION TO THE ENGLISH CRIMINAL PROCESS

Issues of criminal process are rarely out of the news. As our work on the fourth edition of this book was drawing to a close, stories on the following issues appeared in the newspapers. Stop and search powers were the subject of two stories, reflecting continuing concern about the use of these powers and, in particular, their disproportionate use against minority ethnic groups. In this respect there was some good news, in that the decision by some police forces to scale back or abandon the use of suspicionless stop and search powers under the Terrorism Act 2000 had led to a 37 per cent fall in the use of these powers.[1] But a more disturbing aspect of the use of stop and search was also highlighted in a headline reporting that 'Stop and search of ethnic minority 10-year-olds doubles in London'.[2] The use of stop and search powers raises issues of discretion in police decision making, and this was also a theme in another story. After concern about the use of cautions to deal with relatively serious offences of violence, it was announced that a review was being set up to investigate whether cautions were being given in inappropriate cases.[3] Another issue making the headlines was the retention of DNA profiles.[4] The Home Office had published its response to a consultation on the issue, which had been provoked by the decision of the European Court of Human Rights in *Marper v United Kingdom*.[5] Provisions allowing the police to retain the DNA of people who have not been convicted for six years after arrest (as opposed to the current policy of indefinite retention) were quickly inserted into the draft Crime and Security Bill. There were also stories on the treatment of victims in the criminal justice system[6] and on a major internal review of Crown Prosecution Service (CPS) policy, which promises closer engagement with communities.[7] Finally, one story about

---

[1] 'Big fall in police use of stop-and-search powers after outcry' *The Guardian* 26 November 2009.

[2] 'Stop and search of ethnic minority 10-year-olds doubles in London' *The Guardian* 17 November 2009.

[3] 'Jack Straw orders a review of police cautions for violent offences' *The Guardian* 9 November 2009.

[4] 'Police to Continue to Hold DNA of Innocent People' *The Guardian* 11 November 2009. See also Home Office, *Keeping the Right People on the DNA Database: Science and Public Protection* (2009).

[5] (2009) 48 EHRR 50.

[6] 'Sara Payne calls for major overhaul of justice system' *The Guardian* 1 November 2009.

[7] 'Outdated Crown Prosecution Service should be modernised, says DPP' *The Guardian* 30 November 2009. See also www.cps.gov.uk/news/articles/the_public_prosecution_service_—_setting_the_standard/.

mistaken conviction made a rather muted appearance. Terry Pinfold, who had had a conviction for murder quashed in 2003, was back in the Court of Appeal challenging a conviction for robbery. He was unsuccessful, and the report hints at a common criticism of the Court of Appeal: that it is often reluctant to overturn convictions, even when there is considerable evidence to cast doubt on their validity.[8]

This is a rather bewildering set of topics, but each is relevant to the criminal process. The aim of this book is to explore topics such as these and to critically assess the relevant law and practice and the debates around them. In Chapter 2, more will be said about what is understood here by 'the criminal process', what its functions are, and what principles or other criteria should be used to assess it. The present chapter gives a brief sketch of the key decision-making stages of the criminal process and their significance. It also provides the reader with some orientation by summarizing some of the main events in the reform agenda that has moulded the criminal process in the past quarter century.

1.1 KEY STAGES IN DECISION MAKING

The criminal process is part of the State response to crime, part of the mechanism by which the State applies substantive criminal law to its citizens. At its most expansive, it covers a range of decisions and procedures from the investigation and questioning of people as possible suspects through to appeals against conviction and other means of challenging convictions or acquittals. The criminal process forms part of the wider criminal justice system, which includes all the agencies and institutions (police, prosecutors, public defenders, judges, probation officers, prison officers and so on) as well as the criminal law itself and the sentencing system. In this book we focus on the criminal process, but it is not easy to define exactly what this is. Our chief concern lies with the processes and procedures whereby the system deals with potential suspects, suspects and defendants.

Before drawing attention to the key stages in the criminal process, it is important to put it in perspective. It is sometimes presented as if it were a vital tool of crime control in society, but the figures demonstrate that the majority of crime never comes to the attention of the police or other enforcement agencies, and that even when offences are brought to official attention they do not always elicit a formal response. Thus the British Crime Survey has for almost 30 years attempted to measure the amount of crime suffered by members of households. In 1999 only some 43 per cent of crimes were reported to the police, and of those, only two-thirds were recorded.[9] This means

---

[8] 'Well, it's a joke isn't it?' *The Guardian* 9 November 2009. See also *R v Pinfold* [2009] EWCA Crim 2339.

[9] Home Office, *Crime in England and Wales 2002/2003*, 9; it should be noted that the British Crime Survey does not purport to measure all crimes, and concentrates on crimes against the property or person of those aged 16 or over.

not only that figures of crimes recorded by the police may significantly under-estimate the amount of crime in society, but also that the number of offenders detected and prosecuted starts from a low base. Thus, the Home Office's 1999 estimates started with the British Crime Survey figures just mentioned; only two-thirds of the 43 per cent of reported crimes were recorded by the police, i.e. some 28 per cent; of these, fewer than a quarter were detected by the police, which means that only 6 per cent of all crimes were traced to a suspected offender; about half of those resulted in a conviction or a caution. In other words, the percentage of alleged crimes that ended up in a conviction was between 2 and 3 per cent (albeit higher for some offences, such as violent and sexual crimes, and lower for others).[10] Subsequently the Government has pressed criminal justice agencies to reduce this 'justice gap', and the latest British Crime Survey results show that the detection rate has increased to 28 per cent in 2007/08 (although it must be said that this partly reflects the 95 per cent detection rate for drug offences, which are usually discovered only when they are detected; the detection rate for robbery remains at 20 per cent, and for burglary 13 per cent).[11] However, this means that if the 1999 exercise were repeated today, the proportion of actual crimes resulting in a sentence or caution would be slightly—but not greatly—higher than 3 per cent.

The current detection rate of 28 per cent shows that, even when crime is reported to and recorded by the police, the police will not be able to identify a suspect in almost three-quarters of cases. Although it is not easy to define exactly what the criminal process is, we take it as starting with the identification of one or more suspects by the police. It is at this stage that serious issues of criminal procedure arise. If the police have identified someone who they suspect has committed a crime, they will often wish to take steps towards initiating a prosecution. In minor cases, the police are likely to proceed by issuing a summons against a suspect, which will require him to attend court. In more serious cases, the police are likely to take the course of arresting the suspect and taking him to a police station. The law on arrest was extended by the Serious Organised Crime and Police Act 2005, so that a police officer may now arrest for any one of a range of reasons, irrespective of the seriousness of the offence (see Chapter 4.2(a) below). The regime in the police station is intended to offer the suspect certain protections—for example, against unnecessary detention or unduly aggressive questioning. In all police stations where suspects may be detained, a police officer is given the role of 'custody officer'. This person should play an important role in ensuring that the protective regime operates properly. When the suspect is brought to the police station, the custody officer has to decide whether the suspect should be released without charge, charged, or (if it is thought necessary to obtain further evidence by questioning) detained for questioning.[12] That detention may be for up to six hours in the first place, and there are procedures for renewal.[13] The custody officer must record these and other decisions on a custody sheet, and the suspect must be informed of

---

[10] Home Office, *Digest 4: Information on the Criminal Justice System in England and Wales*, 29.
[11] C. Kershaw et al, *Crime in England and Wales 2007–08* (2008), 9.   [12] PACE, s 37.
[13] PACE, ss 40–4.

the right to free and confidential legal advice. The Codes of Practice issued under the Police and Criminal Evidence Act 1984 (PACE) set out standards for the conduct of police investigations. For example, they impose restrictions on the manner in which the police may question a suspect,[14] and on the handling of identification procedures. Many details of these procedures will be examined in Chapter 4, where actual practice as well as the letter of the law will be discussed. The police will seek to question the victim at an early stage, and should inform victims of violent offences of the existence of the Criminal Injuries Compensation Board. The police may also put the victim in touch with Victim Support or other similar agencies. Inquiries in a case may be completed quickly or may spread over a considerable time, in which case the police have a duty to keep the victim informed of the progress of the case.

The outline in the previous paragraph focused on police procedures. Other investigating agencies, such as HM Revenue and Customs, are subject to the Codes of Practice, although there are fewer controls over investigations by the many so-called regulatory agencies. The general principle throughout, however, is that a person may only be questioned before charge and not after charge. Once there is sufficient evidence, the suspect should be charged. However, it must not be thought that charging is the only way of commencing a prosecution. The alternative method is for a police officer to lay an information before a magistrate or justices' clerk, as a result of which a summons will be issued and served on the defendant. The summons procedure is more commonly used for minor offences: the power of arrest, which places considerable discretion in the hands of the police, is typically used for more serious offences, but can also be deployed for relatively minor offences against public order.

One of the things which is occurring at this stage of the criminal process is that the police are trying to build a case against the suspect. Even if a suspect has been caught 'red-handed', a conviction will not be probable, should the case come to court, unless the case can be made to look strong, first to the prosecutor who decides on the charge, and then to the court. In a 'red-handed' case the police will want to take statements from any witnesses and write up their own reports of the incident. A confession from the suspect will also strengthen the case. In other cases the police may want to gather further evidence by, for example, holding an identification parade, taking a DNA sample from a suspect or searching his house. Some of these evidence-gathering activities are regulated in various ways. In the case of confessions and identity parades, the regulation is largely intended to secure the reliability of any evidence produced. With DNA samples and searches of property, other values—such as privacy and bodily integrity—are at stake.

It has been assumed so far that the progression from sufficient evidence to charge or summons is natural or inevitable, but that is far from being true. An authority with the power to prosecute may decide to take no formal action at all, perhaps believing that the experience of detection or an informal warning is sufficient, or it may decide

---

[14] Taken in conjunction with ss 76, 78 and 67(1) of PACE.

that a formal caution or warning is appropriate. During the twentieth century the police developed the practice of issuing a formal caution to certain offenders, particularly the young, the elderly and those whose offences were very minor. The Crime and Disorder Act 1998 replaced police cautions for young offenders with a statutory scheme of reprimands and final warnings. The Criminal Justice Act 2003 introduced a statutory caution for adults, the 'conditional caution', which the CPS administers, but simple cautions administered by the police remain an important feature of the system (see further Chapter 6 below). Many regulatory agencies also have powers to issue formal warnings to employers, companies, farmers and others in respect of offences, and most of them prefer to adopt this approach in the hope of maximizing compliance with the law.

A significant development in the last decade has been the spread of out-of-court penalties. Some agencies have long had powers to exact financial penalties from offenders without bringing a prosecution: HM Revenue and Customs may offer citizens the opportunity to pay, say, double the amount of tax evaded as a condition of non-prosecution. The police have been given greater powers to impose Fixed Penalty Notices on road traffic offenders, and most recently the police have been given powers to impose Penalty Notices for Disorder—now running at almost a quarter of a million per year, and including many offences of theft from a shop or criminal damage.[15] These developments have considerable implications both for the place of the criminal trial and for the significant (dispositive) discretion given to the police.[16]

If the prosecution proceeds by way of summons, the defendant will be given a date for first appearance in a magistrates' court. If it proceeds by arrest, the police officer has a power to grant bail to the suspected offender without going to the police station—a power known colloquially as 'street bail'.[17] However, in many arrest cases the officer will take the suspect to the police station and, if it is decided that the suspect is to be charged, he or she must then decide whether the suspect is to be bailed or remanded in police custody after charge. There is a duty to ensure that a defendant is brought before a court as soon as practicable, which is often the morning after arrest (or on Monday morning, if the arrest takes place on a Saturday). The defendant may be bailed to appear in court or, if there are reasonable grounds for believing that detention is necessary for certain purposes, the police may keep the defendant in custody until the first court appearance.[18] At first appearance the magistrates' court must either dispose of the case or, if not (and particularly in serious cases which will be committed to the Crown Court for trial), the court must decide whether to release the defendant on bail

[15] Criminal Justice and Police Act 2001, ss 1–11, and the Police Reform Act 2002, Sch 4. These powers are discussed in detail in Ch 5.6 below.
[16] A. Ashworth and L. Zedner, 'Defending the Criminal Law: Reflections on the Changing Character of Crime, Procedure and Sanctions' (2008) 2 *Crim Law & Phil* 21.
[17] Criminal Justice Act 2003, Part 2; see A. Hucklesby, 'Not Necessarily a Trip to the Police Station: the Introduction of Street Bail' [2004] *Crim LR* 803.
[18] PACE, s 38.

or to make a custodial remand. The Bail Act 1976 proclaims a presumption in favour of bail, but also sets out various reasons for the refusal of bail: see Chapter 8 below.

Legal assistance is available at several stages in the process.[19] Not only is there a right to free legal advice at the police station, but there are duty solicitor schemes to facilitate this and to advise on representation in court. The Criminal Defence Service was established in 2001 within the Legal Services Commission, and now maintains a range of services, including a Public Defender Service,[20] but its financial basis remains a question of controversy. More generally, the Legal Aid Act 1988 provides that magistrates' courts must grant legal aid to defendants who are going to the Crown Court, and may grant legal aid for summary trials. Defendants with means are expected to make contributions, but a majority of defendants are unemployed or otherwise in receipt of State assistance. The exercise of the discretion to grant legal aid differs between courts.[21]

Until recently it was the police who took the decision whether or not to charge the defendant. However, since the advent of 'statutory charging' under the Criminal Justice Act 2003 the CPS determines the charge in most cases—sometimes working alongside the police in a local criminal justice unit, or at other times by telephone. The CPS has the power to discontinue prosecutions in magistrates' courts,[22] and may drop a case when it is brought to trial in the Crown Court, but statutory charging has had the effect of reducing the use of these powers. If it is a Crown Court case it will be necessary to draft the indictment.[23] If the defendant has been remanded in custody, time limits apply to the period between first appearance in the magistrates' court and committal (70 days), and between committal to the Crown Court and trial (112 days).[24] The prosecution may apply for an extension, but if there are insufficient grounds the accused must be released on bail until the trial.

The choice of charge determines the mode of trial. Most minor offences are triable summarily only, in the magistrates' courts. Most serious offences are triable only on indictment, in the Crown Court. The intermediate category of offences triable either way may be tried in a magistrates' court or at the Crown Court. In these cases a defendant is asked by the magistrates whether he intends to plead guilty. If he indicates his intention to plead guilty, the magistrates' court becomes seized of the case (under the 'plea before venue' procedure) and may proceed to pass sentence or, if it believes its sentencing powers are inadequate, may commit the case to the Crown Court for sentence. If, on the other hand, the defendant indicates an intention to plead not guilty, the magistrates have to decide, having heard representations, whether to commit the

---

[19] See generally E. Cape, 'The Rise (and Fall) of a Criminal Defence Profession' [2004] *Crim LR* 401.

[20] See further www.legalservices.gov.uk/criminal.asp.

[21] R. Young and A. Wilcox, 'The Merits of Legal Aid in the Magistrates' Courts Revisited' [2007] *Crim LR* 109.

[22] Prosecution of Offences Act 1985, s 23.

[23] For details, see J. Sprack, *Emmins on Criminal Procedure* (12th ed, 2008), Ch 6.

[24] Prosecution of Offences Act 1985, s 22; for analysis of the amended regulations and cases, see *Blackstone's Criminal Practice*, D10.4.

case to the Crown Court for trial. Even if they decide not to do so, taking the view that the case is suitable for summary trial, the defendant has an unfettered right to elect Crown Court trial.

If a defendant indicates an intention to plead not guilty, there may be various exchanges between prosecution and defence before the date set for trial. In some magistrates' courts there may be a pre-trial review, and in the Crown Court there will be a plea and case management hearing, intended to define the issues for trial and to facilitate rulings on the admissibility of evidence in advance of the trial.[25] In long or complex cases the Crown Court judge has the power to order a preparatory hearing, with similar powers.[26] In many cases there will be discussion between prosecuting counsel and defence counsel on the day before, or the very day of, the Crown Court trial. In some cases there may be a preliminary discussion with the judge. Defence counsel may then discuss the case with the defendant, and a change of plea to guilty may take place. This part of the process, sometimes described as 'plea-bargaining', is unregulated by statute and little regulated by the Court of Appeal. The many issues arising are discussed in Chapter 10 below.

A defendant who pleads guilty will be sentenced by the magistrates or by the Crown Court judge, after hearing a statement of facts from the prosecution and a plea in mitigation from the defence, and in non-minor cases after receiving a pre-sentence report. A defendant who pleads not guilty will be tried in the appropriate court. Magistrates' courts tend to be less formal, with less strict adherence to the law of evidence but also with a greater sense of briskness. In the Crown Court the trial will be before judge and jury, and matters are unfolded in greater detail.

A defendant convicted by a magistrates' court may appeal against conviction or sentence to the Crown Court, where the appeal takes the form of a rehearing. If either the defence or the prosecution wish to appeal on a point of law, the magistrates may be asked to state a case to the Divisional Court. A defendant convicted in the Crown Court may appeal against conviction and/or sentence to the Court of Appeal (Criminal Division). After the appeal process has been exhausted there is provision for a case to be referred to or taken up by the Criminal Cases Review Commission and, if the Commission so decides, to be referred back to the Court of Appeal. This system is intended to remedy the defects that led to the long delays in dealing with what became the notorious cases of miscarriage of justice uncovered in the late 1980s and early 1990s. These issues are further examined in Chapter 12.

The various stages in decision making outlined above apply generally, although reference was made to differences between the powers and practices of the police and of the regulatory agencies. However, there are differences of approach to cases involving certain types of suspect or defendant and certain types of alleged offence. Where the suspect or defendant is a juvenile, aged between 10 and 18, there are special procedures and safeguards. There is also special provision for mentally disordered suspects

---

[25] Criminal Procedure and Investigations Act 1996, ss 39–43.   [26] *Ibid.*, ss 28–38.

and defendants. Persons requiring interpreters or suffering from deafness, etc, should also be treated differently. As for types of offence, brief mention may be made of the different legal regimes for motoring offences and for persons suspected of terrorist offences or of serious fraud. Many motoring offences may be dealt with by a fixed penalty without a court appearance, and some of those that have to be brought to court do not require the appearance of the defendant. There are also several other differences of procedure, including particular time limits for commencing a prosecution. The Terrorism Act 2000, the Anti-Terrorism, Crime and Security Act 2001, the Prevention of Terrorism Act 2005 and other statutes give considerably greater powers to the police in the investigation of suspected terrorist offences. The Criminal Justice Act 1987 (as amended) gives enhanced powers to the Serious Fraud Office when investigating persons suspected of involvement in frauds involving millions of pounds, including a special procedure for bringing cases of serious fraud to trial.

Before leaving this outline of decisions, their context within a system needs to be emphasized. They are not discrete individual decisions taken in laboratory conditions. Rather, they should be viewed as decisions taken either by individuals or by courts, working within a given professional context. The individual police officer or Crown Prosecutor is likely to be affected, for example not only by the working practices and expectations of colleagues, but also by decisions taken by others beforehand and decisions likely to be taken at subsequent stages. The factual basis for the decision may well have been constructed by others, in a way that depends partly on selection and interpretation. This point is developed in several chapters of the book, but it is important to avoid from the outset the dominance of a 'rationalist' notion of decisions taken by individuals independently and based on objective information.[27]

1.2 DISTINGUISHING TYPES OF DECISION

The various legal procedures and practices described in the previous section combine to affect the ways in which particular suspects and defendants are processed by officials. Formal procedures do not necessarily determine that treatment, since the working practices of officials are what suspects and defendants actually experience. Those practices may be more or less faithful to the rules, and in some instances the law may leave discretion rather than imposing rules.

It is noticeable, however, that the various decisions outlined above are not all of the same kind. Most of them might be described as 'processual', in that they are decisions about the processing of the case from initial charge through to trial and appeal. But there are certain decisions that may be described more accurately as 'dispositive', in that they are concerned more with the disposal of the case. Two strong examples of this are

---

[27] Cf R. Baldwin and K. Hawkins, 'Discretionary Justice: Davis Reconsidered' [1984] *PL* 570, at 581.

the 'prosecute or divert' decision, and the decision whether to impose an out-of-court penalty. The 'prosecute or divert' decision is whether to give a police caution, conditional caution or warning or to take no formal action, rather than to prosecute. This decision, whether taken by the police, the CPS or a regulatory agency, may be regarded as analogous to sentencing. It disposes of the case, which goes no further in the system, and it may carry a form of censure. The weakness of the analogy is that no court is involved. Diversion is premised on the belief that the case does not warrant full processing and a court appearance. The second example (whether to impose an out-of-court penalty) leaves considerable discretion in the hands of the police or other law enforcement agency, and on many occasions the possibility of refusing the penalty and opting for a court appearance may be more theoretical than real. There are other stages in the criminal process which have a dispositive element—for example, the CPS decision to discontinue a case, the decision on mode of trial and, more especially, the decision to accept a guilty plea to a lesser offence or to fewer charges than originally preferred—but the 'prosecution or divert' decision and the question of imposing out-of court penalties raise deep issues of principle about the proper role of the criminal courts and the amount and type of discretion that law enforcement agencies should be allowed to wield.[28]

The point of drawing this distinction is that different considerations will apply to processual decisions and to dispositive decisions—as is clear from the analogy between dispositive decisions and sentencing, which has no application to decisions on the processing of cases. Nonetheless, in practice questions of evidential sufficiency and of public interest often intermingle in the minds of decision makers, and so the distinction may be less sharp in practice than in theory. Moreover, there is at least one type of decision that is neither processual nor dispositive: the remand decision, whether to grant bail or to remand in custody. This has no direct bearing on whether the prosecution will be continued or discontinued, nor on mode of trial or plea, although in practice it may be affected by these other decisions. Nor is it a means of taking a case out of the system and dealing with it otherwise. It is *sui generis*, and is perhaps best described as a temporizing decision, in that it arises solely if and when a case cannot be dealt with at the first court appearance. The adjective 'temporizing' refers only to why this decision is necessary rather than to the nature of the issues it raises, and these are discussed further in Chapter 8.

1.3 REFORMS OF THE CRIMINAL PROCESS

Criminal procedure reform often occurs in response to a miscarriage of justice of some sort. So it was with the Philips Royal Commission, which reported in 1981.[29] The Commission had been set up in 1977, at a time when it was becoming apparent from

---

[28] See further Ch 6 below.   [29] Royal Commission on Criminal Procedure, *Report* (1981).

the inquiry by Sir Henry Fisher into the *Confait* case that there were systemic problems that could not be examined within the confines of the review of a single case.[30] What had happened in the *Confait* case was that three young men were convicted of murder on the basis of confessions later shown to be false. The case highlighted the lack of regulation in the police station as well as the extent to which false confessions could seal an innocent defendant's fate. The Philips report ranged widely over police powers and prosecutions, and formed the basis of PACE, a piece of legislation which remains important to this day. PACE gave the police wider powers of arrest and stop and search than they had previously possessed; it also formalized the regime for detention in the police station, giving the police specific time limits in which they could detain suspects and introducing the role of the custody officer. For the first time the legislation clearly provided suspects with a right of access to legal advice while in police custody. PACE was accompanied by a series of Codes of Practice which add considerable detail to the legislative provisions, explaining how certain powers and procedures are to be given effect: examples are Code C on the detention and questioning of suspects and Code D on identification procedures. The other major piece of legislation to result from the Philips report was the Prosecution of Offences Act 1985, which took responsibility for the prosecution of offences away from the police and gave it to the newly established CPS.

The next significant event in the reform process was a series of miscarriage of justice cases, recognized as such in the late 1980s and early 1990s. The cases of the Birmingham Six, the Guildford Four, the Maguire family and Judith Ward highlighted many issues.[31] The defendants in these cases had all been convicted of offences arising out of the bombing campaign conducted by Irish nationalists during the 1970s. As in *Confait*, some of the defendants had falsely confessed. There were allegations that they had confessed because of considerable pressure—including violence—from the police. Several of the cases also involved forensic science evidence, and highlighted issues about the independence and neutrality of forensic scientists. There had also been failures to disclose evidence to the defence and, in some cases, failure by the police to disclose evidence to the prosecutor. Another disturbing feature was that in several cases the allegations of false conviction had been long-running. The Birmingham Six, for example, had had their case heard twice by the Court of Appeal before the convictions were quashed in 1991.[32] Issues about how the criminal process deals with appeals and allegations of miscarriage of justice were brought to the fore, as well as many questions about the operation of the early stages of the criminal process.

The official response to these cases was to set up another Royal Commission to consider their implications and to suggest reforms. The Runciman Commission reported

---

[30] *Report of an Inquiry by the Hon. Sir Henry Fisher into the circumstances leading to the trial of three persons on charges arising out of the death of Maxwell Confait and the fire at 27 Doggett Road, London SE6 (1977).*

[31] J. Rozenberg, 'Miscarriages of Justice' in E. Stockdale and S. Casale, *Criminal Justice under Stress* (1993).

[32] *McIlkenny* et al (1991) 93 Cr App R 287.

in 1993.[33] Its proposals were nowhere near as far-reaching as those of Philips. Perhaps this is not surprising. The miscarriage of justice cases that were generally seen as setting its agenda involved convictions secured before the protections of the PACE regime were brought in.[34] Runciman recommended new procedures for appeals against conviction and for post-appeal review of alleged miscarriages of justice, but many of its proposals involved fine-tuning the existing PACE regime rather than radical reform. Others addressed issues unconnected to the miscarriage of justice cases: there were proposals on the way cases are allocated between Crown Court and magistrates' court and on plea-bargaining, both of which were controversial.

To understand the legislation and other developments which followed the Runciman report it is important to know something about the political climate surrounding criminal justice reform. Histories of criminal justice policy suggest that for much of the twentieth century, criminal justice was not politically controversial.[35] There was a broad consensus between the main political parties as to how policy should develop. That changed at the 1979 general election, which the Conservative Party fought partly on 'Law and Order' issues. In the 1980s the police made clear their support for a Conservative rather than Labour administration, a move which helped to confirm the Conservatives as the party of law and order. The 1980s thus marked the end of the bipartisan consensus: criminal justice had become a political and therefore an electoral issue. The first major piece of criminal justice legislation after Runciman was the Criminal Justice and Public Order Act 1994. This contained provisions—advocated by the Government but not supported by the Royal Commission's report—allowing juries to draw inferences against defendants who are silent at trial or during police questioning. The following year some of the Runciman reform agenda was enacted: the Criminal Appeal Act 1995 contained reforms of the appeals and post-appeals process. The next year saw more Runciman proposals translated into legislation. The Criminal Procedure and Investigations Act 1996 made significant changes to the disclosure regime. This responded in part to a campaign by senior police officers who argued that their disclosure obligations were far too onerous—a good example of how the police will sometimes actively campaign for criminal justice reform.[36] The Act restricted prosecution disclosure obligations and at the same time introduced the requirement that the defence disclose the outline of its case before trial in the Crown Court.

Two other aspects of the political climate surrounding criminal justice reform are worth highlighting at this stage. A number of commentators on the Runciman report

---

[33] Royal Commission on Criminal Justice, *Report* (1993).

[34] There were exceptions, such as a number of cases involving the West Midlands Serious Crime Squad. See T. Kaye, '*Unsafe and Unsatisfactory'? Report of the Independent Inquiry into the Working Practices of the West Midlands Serious Crime Squad* (1991).

[35] See D. Downes and R. Morgan, 'No Turning Back: the Politics of Law and Order into the Millenium' in M. Maguire, R. Morgan and R. Reiner (eds), *The Oxford Handbook of Criminology* (4th ed, 2007); I. Loader, 'Fall of the Platonic Guardians: Liberalism, Criminology and Responses to Crime in England and Wales' (2006) 46 *Brit J Criminol* 561.

[36] See R. Morgan, 'The Process is the Rule and the Punishment is the Process' (1996) 59 *MLR* 306.

drew attention to what they perceived to be its excessive concern with increasing the efficiency of the criminal justice system: the mode of trial and plea-bargaining recommendations provided examples. This reflects a wider shift in emphasis in criminal justice policy during the 1990s, towards prioritizing managerial concerns and efficiency over respect for the basic rights of accused persons. A second issue of significance relates to what was said above about the politicization of criminal justice policy. During the 1980s, the Conservatives were able to position themselves as the party of law and order, a strategy which probably put Labour at an electoral disadvantage. When, after its electoral defeat in 1992, the Labour Party began to rethink its policies—the process from which 'New Labour' emerged—criminal justice was among them. 'Tough on crime, tough on the causes of crime' was the new Labour slogan. Labour was now prepared to embrace criminal process reforms which it would once have vehemently opposed. Its relatively muted opposition to the reforms of the right to silence in the Criminal Justice and Public Order Act 1994 was a first sign of this. In government, Labour criminal justice policy has often been presented as toughening the criminal justice system and promoting the interests of victims rather than those of defendants.[37]

Returning to the reform chronology, the mid 1990s saw other significant events. The efficiency-driven agenda could be seen in a report on aspects of the trial process written by a Home Office civil servant.[38] The Narey report highlighted the need to bring cases to trial as quickly as possible; it also endorsed Runciman's proposals on the removal of the defendant's right to elect trial by jury. Some of Narey's proposals became law in the Crime and Disorder Act 1998. Removal of the right to elect jury trial, however, proved too controversial, and after two failed attempts the Labour Government has abandoned this as a reform priority. Soon after the 1997 election, the new Government announced a review of the CPS by Sir Iain Glidewell, and the managerialist reform agenda can also be seen in his report published in 1998.[39] This review failed to examine concerns about CPS decision making and its alleged willingness to prosecute weak cases to placate the police, but for managerial reasons it proposed closer working between police and prosecutors. The 1990s also saw concern about a miscarriage of justice of a different kind, one not involving allegations of wrongful conviction. Stephen Lawrence, a young black man, had been killed in an apparently racist attack in 1993. There were police enquiries, and five young white men were interviewed, but no prosecution was brought as a result. Eventually the Lawrence family launched a private prosecution against those five individuals, but the case was stopped when the judge ruled the evidence against them insufficient. The Government set up an inquiry into the case chaired by Sir William Macpherson, a High Court judge. It reported in 1999 with the conclusion that the investigation into the murder was 'marred by a combination of professional incompetence, institutional racism and

---

[37] See, e.g., *Rebalancing the Criminal Justice System in Favour of the Law-Abiding Majority: a consultation paper* (Home Office, 2006).
[38] M. Narey, *Review of Delay in the Criminal Justice System* (1997).
[39] *Review of the Crown Prosecution Service: A Report* (1998), reviewed at [1998] *Crim LR* 517.

a failure of leadership by senior officers'.[40] Much of the report was concerned with police investigative procedures and criticisms of what took place in that particular case, but two other points are of particular importance here. First, the report found what it termed 'institutional racism' in the police: the definition of institutional racism is controversial, in that it elides racist behaviour and attitudes with practices that unintentionally have the effect of disadvantaging members of minority ethnic groups,[41] but the report succeeded in drawing attention to deep-seated problems of race in criminal justice. More will be said about these in later chapters, notably on remands (Chapter 8) and on plea (Chapter 10). Secondly, the report argued in favour of a re-examination of the double jeopardy rule that prevented the prosecution of a person already acquitted. That issue was referred to the Law Commission, which reported in favour of relaxing the double jeopardy rule,[42] and Part 10 of the Criminal Justice Act 2003 broadly implemented that report. The Macpherson report therefore showed how concern about unmerited acquittals and the treatment of victims and their families can motivate reform of the criminal process, just as much as concern about false convictions.

The growing concern about the experiences of victims and witnesses in the criminal process can also be seen in *Speaking up for Justice*, the report of a Home Office Working Party in 1998.[43] The report focused on the treatment of children and vulnerable witnesses. It raised concerns about the way in which the process of giving evidence in court may be unduly stressful for such witnesses. Many of its proposals found their way into the Youth Justice and Criminal Evidence Act 1999, subsequently developed in Part 8 of the Criminal Justice Act 2003.[44]

Perhaps the most significant legislative reform of the 1990s was one that was not specifically focused on criminal justice. The Human Rights Act 1998 gives effect to the European Convention on Human Rights in English law. More will be said about the Convention, and its importance to criminal justice, in Chapter 2. For the moment, it is worth noting that the Convention has implications for many areas of the criminal process: detention and questioning in the police station, the right to silence and the privilege against self-incrimination, remand decision making, disclosure and the rules of evidence. Assessing the actual and potential impact of the Convention on the criminal process is a major concern of this book.

However, one early sign of Government ambivalence about human rights in their application to the criminal process was the introduction of the anti-social behaviour order by s 1 of the Crime and Disorder Act 1998. The European Convention and the European Court adopt the approach that, where proceedings are in substance criminal because of what is at stake (even though the domestic law treats them as civil), they

---

[40] *The Stephen Lawrence Inquiry: Report of an Inquiry by Sir William Macpherson of Cluny* (1999): quotation at 46.1.

[41] See, e.g., the critique by M. Tonry, *Punishment and Politics* (2004), Ch 4.

[42] Law Com No 267, *Double Jeopardy and Prosecution Appeals* (2001).

[43] Home Office, *Speaking Up for Justice* (1998).

[44] For a detailed account of the background to the 1999 Act and related legislation, see P. Rock, *Constructing Victims' Rights: the Home Office, New Labour and Victims* (2004).

should be treated as criminal for the purpose of the safeguards that the Convention applies to those charged with criminal offences.[45] The whole point of the anti-social behaviour order is to circumvent this, or at least to press the point as far as it can go. Thus the Government promoted the measure as a way of avoiding the 'problem' of the criminal process: an application is made to a court under civil procedure, and if they find evidence of anti-social behaviour they may make an order imposing prohibitions on the defendant (sometimes several) restricting his behaviour in the coming years. Breach of an order is a criminal offence carrying up to six months' imprisonment in a magistrates' court or up to five years in the Crown Court. Although the House of Lords held that the standard of proof in the civil proceedings is so high as to be indistinguishable from the criminal standard, the main thrust of its decision was that the Government had succeeded in its circumvention and that the proceedings for making an order are not to be treated as criminal.[46] As elaborated in Chapter 13 below, this legislative model has been used frequently in recent years, and there are now at least 12 different forms of civil preventive order, each with a maximum penalty of five years for breach.

These developments highlight two recent tendencies affecting the criminal process. The first concerns the slippage between criminal and civil procedures. Not too long ago it was a mark of enlightenment to suggest that some forms of misconduct should be taken out of the criminal law and dealt with only through civil processes. Now it seems that that route is being exploited as a means of avoiding the protections of criminal procedure, while ensuring that, by means of making breach of the civil order an offence of strict liability with a high maximum penalty, severe sanctions are available. The second and related tendency is the increased focus on risk, and not just objective risk but also subjectively perceived risk of harm. Many of the preventive orders that can now be made—in particular, risk of sexual harm orders, anti-social behaviour orders—respond to contemporary insecurities about the risks we face and, more particularly, the risks that some people think they face (since prediction in these matters is a difficult task).

The continual process of review and reform has not abated in the first decade of the new century. The year 2001 saw the publication of the Auld review of the criminal courts.[47] The remit of the Auld review was, to say the least, wide ranging. Yet, unlike the Runciman Commission, the task was given to a single person with relatively little opportunity to commission research on the problems he was meant to solve. Auld's main recommendation was for a unified criminal court with three levels of jurisdiction, a proposal that has not survived. The report also contains a mass of detailed recommendations on aspects of evidence and criminal procedure, including prosecution appeals, double jeopardy, disclosure and several aspects of case management. It was Auld who recommended the transfer of the power to charge suspects from the police to the CPS. The Auld report also contained significant proposals on jury trial, including

---

[45] *Engel v Netherlands* (1979) 1 EHRR 647; see generally Ch 13 below.
[46] *Clingham v Kensington and Chelsea LBC* [2003] 1 AC 787.
[47] *Review of the Criminal Courts of England and Wales: Report* by Rt Hon. Lord Justice Auld (2001).

recommendations for trial by judge alone in serious and complex fraud cases and in other cases in which a defendant so elects.

Shortly after the publication of the Auld report, the world was rocked by the events of 11 September 2001. The British Government, like its American counterpart, was not slow in coming forward with new legislation extending the powers of the State in many directions. Although the Terrorism Act 2000 had consolidated and extended State powers in respect of persons suspected of 'terrorist' activities,[48] the Anti-Terrorism, Crime and Security Act 2001 introduced sweeping powers to detain without trial persons labelled as 'suspected international terrorists', in respect of which it was necessary for the Government to enter a derogation from Article 5 of the European Convention on Human Rights. In a landmark decision, the House of Lords held that these provisions and the derogation from Article 5 were incompatible with the Convention.[49] The Government's replacement device was the control order, but that has also given rise to anxious scrutiny in the courts for its compatibility with Convention rights.[50]

Reforms of the general criminal process did not cease while terrorism dominated public discussion. On the contrary, the Government pressed ahead with a number of schemes—notably two that tested the coordination of different parts of the system, the Street Crimes Initiative in early 2002[51] and various schemes targeted at persistent or prolific offenders. Some months after the Auld report, the Government published its plans on criminal justice reform in a White Paper, *Justice for All*.[52] The proposed reforms were presented as part of an ambitious plan to modernize the criminal justice system and included changes to the jurisdiction of magistrates' courts, major reform of the double jeopardy rules, provisions allowing trials without juries in the Crown Court in various circumstances, as well as very significant changes to the rules of evidence. Most of these reforms were enacted in the Criminal Justice Act 2003 and the Courts Act 2003. At the level of political rhetoric, one interesting aspect of the debates surrounding the Criminal Justice Act was a reversal of the traditional positions of the Conservative and Labour parties with respect to criminal justice. While Labour presented its reforms in the language of modernization and the promotion of victims' interests, the Conservative opposition on occasion stressed principles such as the double jeopardy rule and trial by jury as important protections for defendants against the might of the State.[53] The reforms relating to the rights of victims of crime are to be found in the Domestic Violence, Crime and Victims Act 2004: although the Government has persisted with the notion

---

[48] For a general assessment, see C. Walker, 'Terrorism and Criminal Justice—Past, Present and Future' [2004] *Crim LR* 311.

[49] *A v Secretary of State for Home Affairs* [2004] UKHL 56.

[50] Cf *Secretary of State for the Home Department v JJ* [2007] UKHL 45, with *AF v Secretary of State for the Home Department* [2009] UKHL 28. See generally C. Walker, 'The Treatment of Foreign Terror Suspects' (2007) 70 *MLR* 427.

[51] For a summary, see [2002] *Crim LR* 851.   [52] Home Office, 2002.

[53] 'Tories and Lib Dems Home in on Civil Rights' *The Guardian* 13 November 2002.

of re-balancing the criminal justice system in favour of victims,[54] that concept is riven with difficulties.[55]

In 2005 the Criminal Procedure Rules were published for the first time. This initiative, stemming from the Auld report but falling short of a code of criminal procedure, has at least drawn together a number of legal provisions and best practices on a range of topics, from investigations to witness statements, from case management to bail, from costs to international cooperation. But the Rules also offer something new, borrowing from the Woolf reforms of civil procedure the idea of specifying an 'overriding objective' of criminal trials, and binding the parties to pursuit of this objective. This has enabled the courts to emphasize the need of the defence to cooperate in the smooth running of the case, and is discussed further in Chapter 9. The Rules are available online and are updated regularly.

In the meantime, the pace of legislative change has continued unabated, with at least one major statute every year. The central thrust of the Serious Organised Crime and Police Act 2005 was to set up the Serious and Organised Crime Agency (SOCA), which has wide-ranging powers to disrupt and dislocate criminal markets, to improve intelligence-gathering (including covert surveillance) and to recover the proceeds of crime more efficiently. Among its targets are those involved in drug smuggling, in human trafficking, and in the supply of guns. The Act also includes special provisions for sentence discounts for offenders who assist the prosecution of others. The Violent Crime Reduction Act 2006 includes restrictions on drinking alcohol in certain public places, and created wider powers for the detention of sex offenders. The Serious Crime Act 2007 includes further powers to seize property in financial investigations, wider powers for HM Revenue and Customs generally, and the creation of the serious crime prevention order. Among the many changes introduced by the Criminal Justice and Immigration Act 2008 were provisions tightening the grant of bail, the creation of a violent offender order (another civil preventive order) and further expansion of the powers connected with anti-social behaviour orders. The Police and Crime Act 2009 brings changes in police accountability, extends police powers in relation to those who drink in public and extends the criminal asset recovery scheme.

1.4 PROCESS AND SYSTEM

The overview of criminal process reform sketched in the preceding paragraphs has two goals. One is to familiarize readers with some of the major reports and pieces of

---

[54] E.g. former Prime Minister Blair even went so far as to talk of the need to replace the criminal justice system with a victim justice system ('Victims Now Priority of Justice System' *The Guardian* 14 November 2002); Home Secretary Reid called for a re-balancing of the justice system in favour of victims, but this was more about increasing sentences for offenders than about improving the lot of crime victims. See also the Consultation Paper, above n 37.

[55] See further Ch 2.4(c) below.

legislation which will be discussed in later chapters. The other is to give some sense of the forces which shape criminal justice policy. The reform process is often event-driven, with proposals responding to particular problems in the criminal process which have gained publicity. The *Confait* case led on to Philips and PACE; the Birmingham Six and other miscarriage of justice cases led to Runciman and the Criminal Appeal Act 1995. At times this can make the reform process seem somewhat haphazard: if the failed prosecution of the suspects in the Stephen Lawrence case had not received the media attention that it did, it seems unlikely that the double jeopardy rule would have been the subject of provisions in the Criminal Justice Act 2003. It would be wrong, however, to suggest that there is some simple causal process whereby a failing in the system leads to reform. The account above has drawn attention to the increasingly politically charged climate in which reforms of the criminal process take place. Both major political parties seek to sell their criminal justice policies to the electorate; there is an important populist element in the way in which criminal justice policy is framed.[56] The shared assumption of the parties seems to be that being seen to be tough on crime, and claiming to promote the interests of victims rather than defendants, will bring electoral success. This assumption plays an important part in moulding the criminal process as it undergoes a seemingly continual round of reforms.

It will be evident that we refer to the criminal process, rather than to 'the criminal justice system'. This is because it is not a 'system' in the sense of a set of coordinated decision making bodies. Even from the broad survey above it will be apparent that many groups working within criminal justice are relatively autonomous and enjoy considerable discretion. Nonetheless, the inappropriateness of the term 'system' should not be allowed to obscure the practical interdependence of the various agencies.[57] Many depend on other agencies for their case load or for their information, and decisions taken by one agency can impinge on those taken by others. Thus, to take a few examples, the CPS depends largely on the police for the information on which it must take its decisions. Those CPS decisions in turn affect the case load of the courts, and may constrain the powers of magistrates' courts and of defendants to determine mode of trial. Many other examples of interdependence and influence will be found throughout the book, and in the first section of this chapter it was emphasized that decisions should be viewed in this context rather than as discrete and objectively based determinations.

References to systems and interdependence are, however, very much in the managerial mode. The criminal process impinges directly on victims, suspects and defendants. It impinges on them in the form of one or more contacts and decisions. A defendant who has been questioned by the police, charged, kept in police custody, remanded by the court, perhaps offered a plea bargain, and then tried in court is already likely to feel 'punished' irrespective of whether a guilty verdict and sentence

---

56 See further J. Pratt, *Penal Populism* (2007).

57 For discussion, see the essays by Pullinger and by Feeney in D. Moxon (ed), *Managing Criminal Justice* (1985).

follow. A person who is acquitted after such a sequence of events may well feel 'punished' by the process to which he or she has been subjected, even if relieved at the outcome. Of course this is a misuse of the term punishment, which is properly confined in the present context to sentences imposed by courts after findings of guilt. But it accords with the results of American research by Malcolm Feeley, encapsulated in the title of his book *The Process is the Punishment*.[58] Suspects and defendants often feel that the way in which they are treated is equivalent to punishment, in the sense that it inflicts on them deprivations (of liberty, of reputation) similar to those resulting from a sentence. This is particularly true for defendants who have been remanded in custody, and may flow from a single decision such as the decision to prosecute. Alternatively it may be a consequence, not so much of decisions taken in their case, but rather of what they regard as disrespect for their rights by the officials dealing with them. For present purposes, it is sufficient to make the point that the criminal process is a process to which defendants are subjected by officials who have considerable *de facto* power as well as the power of law behind them. It amounts to an exercise of State power—necessary, as part of the political system, but no less real for that. It is therefore appropriate to consider proper standards, fair procedures, accountability and other issues relevant to dealings between the State and individual citizens.

It is not just defendants but also victims and witnesses whose interests should be protected. There is no shortage of empirical research findings that victims have been and are being treated in the criminal process in ways that can be described as 'punishment'. In the language of victimologists, victims who report crimes often experience 'secondary victimization' at the hands of police, prosecutors and courts.[59] While some steps have been taken to reduce these effects (for example) by improving techniques of police questioning, by granting anonymity to victims of certain offences and by introducing video links into courts, there is little doubt that some victims still suffer psychologically and socially from their involvement in the criminal process, in addition to the crime itself. Although efforts are being made to reduce this secondary victimization—for example, through the work of the Witness Service and the provisions of the Domestic Violence, Crime and Victims Act 2004—our point here is that the criminal process can be said to be a process to which victims of crime, too, are subjected by officials.

If one adds to these processual elements the fact that the one 'temporizing' decision—remand before trial—may result in loss of liberty, and also the effects that dispositive decisions such as conditional cautions may have (as a form of sentence without trial), it is evident that there are many elements of the criminal process that call for clear and careful justification. We now move, in Chapter 2, towards an exploration of the sources of justification and of critique of the English criminal process. The

---

[58] M. Feeley, *The Process is the Punishment* (1979).

[59] See C. Hoyle and L. Zedner, 'Victims, Victimization and Criminal Justice' in M. Maguire, R. Morgan and R. Reiner (eds), *Oxford Handbook of Criminology* (4th ed, 2007), especially 468–70.

examination of principles continues in Chapter 3, where we look particularly at ethical issues in relation to the working practices of criminal justice professionals. Those general chapters are then followed by a sequence of chapters on particular stages of the criminal process—questioning; gathering evidence; diversion; charging and prosecutorial review; remands; pre-trial rights and duties; plea changing; trial procedures; and appeals.

2

TOWARDS A FRAMEWORK
FOR EVALUATION

What should we expect of a criminal process? What aims should it pursue and what values ought it to respect? In answering these questions the links between the different parts and aspects of the criminal justice system must be kept in view. The purpose and scope of the criminal law itself have a bearing on pretrial matters such as powers of arrest and even plea negotiation. The rules of evidence at trial may place some limits on the investigative powers of the police and other enforcement agencies. And the principles of sentencing are strongly related both to the criteria for diversion from the criminal process and to the system of plea negotiation. This chapter will keep those wider relationships in view while focusing on a framework for evaluating criminal procedure, chiefly in relation to pre-trial justice.

2.1 A THEORY OF CRIMINAL PROCESS

The preceding chapter has provided an outline of the criminal process. It depicts a sequential process, with suspects being identified by the police and the case then moving on to further stages. At various points suspects may drop out of the system, perhaps because the evidence is thought not to be strong enough, or it is decided that the case is suitable for diversion, or because the Crown Prosecution Service (CPS) decides on review that the case should be discontinued. The process potentially continues up to trial, which may result in conviction or acquittal. After trial, there are further stages of the process, involving appeals. More now needs to be said on what this process is about and what values should underpin it.

The sort of theory we aim to develop here is a normative one. We are trying to develop a framework which can be used to understand and evaluate the criminal process; this is different to the descriptive account of the criminal process which was given in Chapter 1. Account must be taken of the complexity of the criminal process as an institution that embodies a number of different aims and values. Another problem is that the criminal process varies between jurisdictions: some systems are inquisitorial and some adversarial (though it is not easy to pin down what these terms mean); some use juries as fact-finders and some rely on professional judges. Perhaps it would be possible to develop a single normative model of criminal process that would have sufficient detail to show that certain actual criminal processes (perhaps all adversarial ones) are in some way deficient. This would be an ambitious enterprise, and there must be doubts as to whether it would actually be possible to develop so detailed a theory—not least because some aspects of the criminal process (such as the type of fact-finder used) may reflect values which have relatively little to do with the criminal process itself. Institutions such as the jury may exist for historical and political reasons which make them more appropriate for some jurisdictions than for others.

One way of proceeding would therefore be to draw a distinction between internal and external values in the criminal process. Internal values would be the core values of criminal process, ones which all systems of criminal process should embody. One would expect such a theory to be relatively thin and lacking in detail. Something could then be said about the external values which, in a particular jurisdiction such as England and Wales, might fill in the details of this thin account. There is some merit in this approach, but there are also problems. One is that it may prove difficult to distinguish between internal and external values. The criminal process is part of the wider criminal justice system, and there are many theories of criminal justice. A theory of criminal justice may be related to some wider political theory, at which stage there are further choices of approach to be made. The situation is rather like a set of Russian dolls, where the core values of the political theory at the centre play a role in shaping the outer layers such as the criminal process. It may therefore be difficult to find agreement on internal values of criminal process that may be claimed to apply across all jurisdictions.

Because of this problem, we should say a little more about the basic values we believe should play a role in shaping the criminal process. The thin, internal account we start with reflects the values of a liberal State, where State power is limited and citizens are viewed as bearers of rights. In terms of criminal justice—and this will become important as we add detail to the thin theory—we subscribe to a retributive, or desert-based, rationale for punishment. On this view the institution of punishment is justified by the moral appropriateness of visiting censure on citizens for crimes as wrongs, and the need to reinforce that with sanctions in order that the censure be taken seriously. It is appropriate that the State should maintain a system for enforcement and adjudication, so as to ensure a public, authoritative and consistent approach to the imposition of censure. But a proper relationship between the coercive State and its citizens as rational and rights-bearing subjects means that a punishment should always be proportionate to the seriousness of the crime, and not disproportionate so as to fail to respect the offender.[1] Those principles of proportionality and respect for the suspect/defendant/offender as a rational rights-bearing subject should also underpin

---

[1] For elaboration, see A. von Hirsch and A. Ashworth, *Proportionate Sentencing* (2005), Ch 2.

the criminal process. A criminal process based on deterrence, or on principles of restorative justice, might differ significantly from one based on desert.[2]

What, then, are the purposes of the criminal process and what values should it reflect? One simple point can be made at the outset. The laws, regulations and institutions that make up the criminal process provide a set of rules, standards and areas of discretion for decision making. These rules or procedures have an immediate value, no matter what their content. Rules are intended to guide decision makers and to exert some control over their discretion. In a complex institution such as the criminal process, which involves many different actors, procedure has a coordinating function. It allows different decision makers to work together by giving them some knowledge of what other actors will have done. Set procedures also allow for transparency: they allow rules to be made accessible to the public as well as to the actors in the process. Thus procedure should serve the rule of law, by making decisions more consistent, more predictable and less arbitrary. These simple points do not say anything about the contents of the rules and standards; they merely suggest the basic value of having some set of procedures. This emphasis on proper procedures rather than arbitrariness lies, as we shall see, at the core of the European Convention on Human Rights.

Moving beyond this, it is obvious that the criminal process is part of the State response to crime. There are, however, many ways in which the State responds to crime which do not invoke criminal procedure. Much of the State's strategy against crime is preventive: it includes things as diverse as education, street lighting, and the maintenance of a visible police presence. The criminal process (as we understand the term, for the purposes of this book) is far narrower than this. It is the mechanism that authorizes the State to apply the criminal law to its citizens. It is only invoked when it is suspected that a crime has been committed. Again, though, the State can respond to suspected crime in many ways. Minor offences may be ignored, or met with a warning. Some offences, such as driving offences, are dealt with by way of fixed penalty notices. The point is even more obvious where criminal justice agencies other than the police are involved. Agencies such as the Health and Safety Executive often respond to breaches of the criminal law through processes designed to ensure future compliance; prosecution is only used as a last resort.[3] We will say more about these responses to crime in Chapter 6; the discussion of 'dispositive values' in Part 6 of this chapter is also relevant. That many of these responses are said to involve 'diversion' from the criminal process suggests that there is only a minimal sense in which the criminal process is involved. Nevertheless, the principles underlying diversion are important, in part because of the light they shed on those cases which do enter the criminal process more fully. The full criminal process becomes involved where a relatively formal response to crime is taken: where—to concentrate on the central case of the police—the police respond to a suspected offence with a view to possible prosecution. The possible end result of the process is adjudicative: a trial. Whether a trial will result will depend on

---

[2] See further Part 5 of this chapter, below.   [3] K. Hawkins, *Law as Last Resort* (2003).

many other factors. As has been emphasized, many suspects drop out of the process for a variety of reasons. But what matters is the potential, not the probability. Criminal procedure is a process that may lead to a trial.

This characterization of criminal procedure enables something to be said about its purposes. The function of criminal procedure is to regulate and facilitate the preparation of cases for trial; this suggests that the purposes of criminal trials will determine in a little more detail the functions of criminal procedure. The twin objects of the criminal trial are accurately to determine whether or not a person has committed a particular criminal offence and to do so fairly. This suggests that one important focus of criminal procedure is, broadly speaking, investigation. Criminal procedure should provide mechanisms to regulate the gathering of evidence so as to allow adjudicative decisions to be made accurately. Note that this account is already being moulded by some of the presuppositions identified earlier. The principle of proportionality in sentencing makes it especially important to obtain accurate information about the offence, so that the sentence can reflect the gravity of wrongdoing. Such detailed information might not be so important, for example, in a criminal process based on principles of restorative justice.

An investigation into a suspected criminal offence is unlikely to get very far unless the police are given certain coercive powers over suspects. Justifications may therefore be found for giving the police various powers enabling them, for example, to detain suspects in the police station and to take fingerprints and DNA samples from them. Trials, as enquiries into a defendant's guilt or innocence and as venues for sentence, are likely to be most effective if the defendant is present. This gives some basis for other coercive powers, such as the power to remand in custody, to ensure that the defendant is present at trial, and powers to summon witnesses to attend trial.

An obvious, but important, point should be made at this stage. Although criminal procedure exists to ensure a particular end result—an effective criminal trial—it is not like a mechanized assembly line in a car factory. Whether or not an assembly line is good can be judged largely in terms of its end results: whether the car it produces is of good quality. It does not matter how the metal, plastic, paint, etc is treated during the process of achieving that end. Criminal procedure is different because it deals with people. It matters how people are treated. They should be treated with dignity: in other words, their rights should be respected. Note that we are again drawing here on the wider principles of justice within which our account of the criminal process is embedded. Given that effective criminal procedure requires that prosecuting agencies be given coercive powers, it seems that a key facet of criminal procedure will be the provision of limits on those powers to ensure that the human interests connected to the respect for dignity are not unnecessarily infringed. This is in fact one of the central problems of criminal procedure: the need to reconcile a process which will bring cases to effective trial with the protection of human rights and the fundamental requirement of a fair trial. More will be said about the factors in play here later; for the moment, it is more helpful to concentrate on the relatively abstract theory of the criminal process which is being developed.

The recognition that criminal procedure infringes human interests has several implications. If cases could be brought to effective trial without affecting human interests, then it might make sense to bring all cases to trial in order to enable some definitive determination of criminal liability. However, because human interests are much affected, one function of criminal procedure should be to provide for the filtering of cases, to make sure that they are not kept in the system without good reason. Waiting for trial imposes considerable stress on people, especially those remanded in custody. The criminal process also deals with people suspected of crimes of widely varying levels of seriousness. In the least serious cases the principle of proportionality suggests that the pressures and effects of a trial may not be justified. Here, again, we can see why the topic of diversion is important in an account of the criminal process. However, the need for filtering is not just to ensure that coercive procedures are not applied more widely than they should be, or to minimize the considerable stress suffered by people awaiting trial. Filtering is also important because trials, by their nature, are fallible and somewhat unpredictable; sometimes they produce erroneous verdicts. The danger that a mistake will be made at trial provides a further reason for filtering cases during the pre-trial stage, to remove cases where there is little evidence that the suspect has committed an offence. Moreover, efficiency, the costs of procedure and trials, provide further reasons for filtering out cases which do not merit prosecution.

A convincing normative theory of the criminal process needs to be properly connected to facts about actual criminal processes. Thus, reference to the stress of waiting for trial was made in order to explain the importance of filtering cases which are in the system. There are other facts about the system which it is important to take into account. In Chapter 1, reference was made to miscarriages of justice which have played a role in shaping the system. Familiarity with these cases suggests that sometimes the police are over-eager to secure the conviction of those they believe to be guilty, and that often they will focus on an initial suspect at the expense of considering alternative lines of enquiry.[4] Police officers have been prepared to put considerable pressure on suspects in order to extract confessions from them—at one time the use of violence was not uncommon. It is known that suspects sometimes confess falsely.[5] Other sources of evidence too are fallible: eyewitness evidence is an example.[6] The frailty of such types of evidence can be difficult to detect at trial. A primary function of criminal procedure is to provide rules to ensure that reliable evidence is produced which can form the basis of an effective trial. Criminal procedure should therefore provide safeguards against especially unreliable forms of evidence. Concern for human dignity is an additional reason for this: aggressive or violent questioning infringes legitimate human interests.

This theory of criminal procedure is trial-centred; it assumes that preparation of cases for possible trial is the principal objective of the investigative and pre-trial stages. It was suggested above that the objects of the criminal trial are accurately and fairly

---

[4] See K. Findley and M. Scott, 'The Multiple Dimensions of Tunnel Vision in Criminal Cases' (2006) *Wisconsin L Rev* 291; K. Rossmo (ed), *Criminal Investigative Failures* (2008).
[5] Royal Commission on Criminal Justice, *Report* (1993), 57, and Ch 4 below.   [6] See Ch 5.3 below.

to determine whether or not a person has committed a particular criminal offence. But this may be too simple; saying a little more about trials generates a slightly richer theory of criminal process. Accurate decision making is an important function of criminal trials, but complete accuracy is unattainable: trials are fallible. Of the two sorts of errors a criminal trial can make—acquitting a guilty person or convicting an innocent person—the latter is more serious, since it involves a monstrous wrong against an individual whereas the former does not, although it reflects badly on the system and may reduce the community's confidence in it. To protect against convicting the innocent, a heavy burden of proof is placed on the prosecution. The prosecution must prove its case beyond reasonable doubt. The implication of this is that, all else being equal, of the errors that criminal courts make, more will involve acquitting the guilty than convicting the innocent. Criminal trials thus incorporate an error preference; one type of error is preferred to another. This is a cardinal value of the criminal process. This might be thought to have important implications for pre-trial criminal procedure. Perhaps this error preference should mould the pre-trial process just as it moulds the trial. In fact, it is not obvious that it should, and one should actually be wary of seeing criminal procedure as an obstacle course the purpose of which is to make it difficult for the prosecution to secure a conviction.[7] There are features of English criminal procedure which might appear to apply the error preference in the pre-trial stage: the rules protecting defendants against false confession or mistaken eyewitness identification, for example. But a perfectly good explanation for these rules was suggested above: that they help to ensure an effective trial by safeguarding the reliability of evidence. The important filtering function was also explained without reference to error preference. While it is true that the decision by the prosecution whether or not to continue a prosecution is informed by the high standard of proof at trial, this is due to the predictive nature of the CPS decision at this stage which necessarily refers to the standard of proof at trial.[8]

The trial is not just about accurate fact-finding: as we have insisted, principles of fairness lie at the heart of the trial in particular, as well as the criminal process in general. Thus, the trial is not just a diagnostic procedure, of which the sole purpose is to establish as accurately as possible (subject to the standard of proof) what happened. Ian Dennis is among those who have argued that trial verdicts must be legitimate, and that this has consequences for the use of devices such as entrapment in the pre-trial stage of criminal procedure. Indeed, he goes so far as to say that the production of legitimate verdicts is the key aim of the criminal trial, and that this takes priority over—although it usually coincides with—the aim of securing accurate verdicts.[9] Antony Duff and collaborators argue that the trial should also be seen as a communicative process, whereby the State tries to let the convicted defendant know, in terms which he can understand, why he is to be subjected to the censure of the criminal

---

[7] This obstacle course depiction of the pre-trial process is one problem with Packer's due process model, discussed further below.

[8] See Ch 7 below.   [9] I.H. Dennis, *The Law of Evidence* (3rd ed, 2007), Ch 2.

sanction. However, the State must also establish the legitimacy of its own claim to hold the defendant to account, notably by observing 'norms that require defendants to be treated as citizens of a liberal polity'.[10]

We would certainly endorse the view that the trial is not simply about accurate fact-finding. As with our account of the criminal process as a whole, we would stress the concomitant aim of respecting rights and other important values. We revisit this issue in the context of the exclusion of improperly obtained evidence in Chapter 11. For the moment, we suggest that there is some reason to be sceptical of accounts of the criminal process which stress legitimacy. It can be a rather elusive concept, unless it is confined in the ways that Duff and collaborators describe. Their central idea of calling defendants to account is certainly compatible with the kind of rights-based retributive theory of punishment that grounds our particular account.

An obvious objection to a trial-centred theory of criminal process is that in reality the criminal process in England and Wales (and, increasingly, in other jurisdictions too) is centred round trial-avoidance.[11] The guilty plea is the normal method of disposing of criminal cases. Guilty pleas are discussed in detail in Chapter 10, and the analysis there is relevant to the brief response to the 'trial avoidance' objection offered here. Guilty pleas do not avoid trial completely. Bearing in mind the retributive background to our account of criminal process, an important function of the trial is sentencing, and the court still plays a role as a sentencing venue after a guilty plea. Further, the dependence on guilty pleas does not undermine the importance of the criminal process as an investigative mechanism. A desert-based theory of sentencing emphasizes that sentences should be proportional to wrongdoing, which makes accurate investigation important, even if there will be no contested trial. In fact, one of the problems of the system of guilty pleas in England and Wales is that it may allow sentencing to be carried out without accurate knowledge of the facts of the offence: the gravity of the offending may be downplayed as part of a charge-bargain, or a defendant may plead guilty when innocent in order to take advantage of a sentence discount. But the emphasis on trials, and accurate fact-finding, allows us to criticize the systematic encouragement of guilty pleas for these very reasons. That is one of the themes of Chapter 10.

2.2 INTERNAL AND EXTERNAL VALUES

We have argued that the purposes of the criminal process are accurate determinations and fair procedures at all stages, and have suggested that the criminal trial should be

---

[10] A. Duff, L. Farmer, S. Marshall and V. Tadros, *The Trial on Trial, volume 3: Towards a Normative Theory of the Criminal Trial* (2007), 288. For discussion, see M. Redmayne, 'Theorizing the Criminal Trial' (2009) 12 *New Crim LR* 287.

[11] M. Langer, 'From Legal Transplants to Legal Translations: the Globalization of Plea-Bargaining and the Americanization Thesis in Criminal Procedure' (2004) *Harvard Int LJ* 1.

regarded as the focus of the process, even though the majority of cases do not go to trial. Our theory is partly instrumental, giving an account of the sorts of things the criminal process will need to do and the sorts of powers (to arrest and detain suspects, to filter cases) that will be needed to achieve these ends. But just as important are the values—respecting human rights—that should mould the way in which these ends are achieved. The theory is thin and relatively generic—an 'internal' theory in the sense outlined above. We now turn to consider external values, and how they inform a theory of criminal process.

Some external values are reasonably jurisdictionally specific. An example, mentioned earlier, is the use of lay fact-finders in the English criminal process (lay magistrates and juries). English criminal procedure is fairly unique in the extent to which it relies on lay fact-finders.[12] Many other systems of criminal procedure make some use of lay fact-finders, whereas some do not use them at all. Much has been written about the value that lay justice—particularly trial by jury—brings to the criminal process. The point of identifying lay justice as an external value is to suggest that those systems which rely on it do so partly for particular historical and political reasons, and that there is not necessarily anything deficient, as systems of criminal procedure, in those systems which do not.[13] Perhaps such jurisdictions can be criticized on other grounds: perhaps, as polities, they accord insufficient value to citizen involvement in decision making. But this is a much wider point than one about criminal procedure.

Another example of an external value in criminal procedure is adversarialism. Although the classification of systems of criminal procedure is a complex topic, the basic point is that adversarial systems, such as those operating in the UK and the US, give a far greater role to the parties in developing the case and conducting the trial than do 'inquisitorial' systems, such as those operating in continental Europe. In some ways, these different systems reflect competing political philosophies. In French criminal procedure, for example, the role of the State in protecting its citizens' interests is emphasized. Giving too great a role to defence lawyers is seen as disruptive and potentially inegalitarian, and also as something for which there is little need because the State can be trusted to look out for the accused.[14] This sort of view is anathema in Anglo-American criminal procedure. Damaška has also suggested that Anglo-American criminal procedure differs from continental criminal procedure in the extent to which it is 'policy-implementing'. An example is that in England and the United States, criminal procedure is prepared to forego effective fact-finding at trial, either to uphold the integrity of the system or in the hope of exerting some influence

[12] S. Doran and R. Glenn, *Lay Involvement in Adjudication* (2000).

[13] See T Hörnle, 'Democratic Accountability and Lay Participation in Criminal Trials' in A. Duff et al (eds), *The Trial on Trial Volume 2: Judgment and Calling to Account* (2006).

[14] See J. Hodgson, 'Human Rights and French Criminal Justice: Opening the Door to Pre-Trial Defence Rights' in S. Halliday and P. Schmidt (eds), *Human Rights Brought Home: Socio-Economic Perspectives on Human Rights in the National Context* (2004); J. L. Sauron, 'Les Vertus de l'inquisitoire, ou l'Etat au service des droits' (1990) 55 *Pouvoirs* 53.

over the way in which the police gather evidence. Unfairly or illegally obtained evidence may thus be ruled inadmissible at trial. Continental systems, historically at least, have tended to see control over the police as being better exercised in other ways.[15] This example will be discussed in more detail in Chapter 11. For now the point is that the way the criminal process responds to improperly obtained evidence seems best identified as an external value: there is nothing in the theory of criminal process itself which tells us whether or not courts should exclude improperly obtained evidence.[16]

We have emphasized the importance of rights in this account of criminal process. The fact that the criminal process should respect rights is an internal aspect of criminal process, but the content of the rights which the criminal process should respect is often best seen as being set externally to the criminal process. A theory of criminal process cannot always tell us very much about what rights people have. While some rights are specific to the criminal process (the presumption of innocence is an example) many rights which place important constraints on criminal process (the right to bodily integrity and the right to respect for private life, for example) have significance well beyond the criminal process. But saying that such rights are determined externally to the criminal process is not the same as saying that the rights are jurisdictionally specific. While there may be some things which we refer to as rights which have a particular significance in certain jurisdictions (the right to legal advice in the police station, for example[17]), there are many rights which any criminal process should respect. This is reflected in the fact that many international human rights documents include rights which have immense significance to the criminal process. A good way of adding more detail to our so far rather thin account of the criminal process is to examine these documents and the rights contained in them. In the next section, then, the discussion will be more descriptive. We will concentrate on the European Convention on Human Rights, which has particular significance for the criminal process in England and Wales and therefore provides a foundation for the analysis of the criminal process in the chapters which follow. The material remains relevant to a normative account of criminal process, however, for it identifies the most important of the rights which should shape the criminal process. The discussion also starts to analyse the way in which we should think about rights by showing some of the problems in the claim that rights can be balanced against other values.

---

[15] See R. Frase, 'France' in C. Bradley (ed), *Criminal Procedure: A Worldwide Study* (1999), 161–2; C. Bradley, 'The Emerging International Consensus as to Criminal Procedure Rules' (1993) 14 *Michigan J Int Law* 171.

[16] Cf Duff et al, above n 10, who tie this topic more closely to their theory of the trial.

[17] The European Court of Human Rights has held that the right of access to legal advice takes on particular importance when inferences may be drawn from silence at police interview: *Murray v United Kingdom* (1996) 22 EHRR 29. On the different attitude to legal advice in France, see n 14 above.

2.3 FUNDAMENTAL RIGHTS AND THE EUROPEAN CONVENTION

(A) HUMAN RIGHTS OBLIGATIONS

So far as this country's international obligations go, there are several international declarations of human rights to which we are subject. Three of them may be mentioned before we go on to consider the European Convention in detail. One is the International Covenant on Civil and Political Rights (ICCPR), drawn up by the United Nations and monitored by the ICCPR Human Rights Committee. The extent and formulation of rights in the ICCPR differ in some respects from those in the European Convention on Human Rights, which is considered in detail below. Although less frequently discussed in this country, the ICCPR remains a document of some importance,[18] not least because reference has been made to it (in view of its wider international status) when interpreting the European Convention.[19]

A second instrument of importance is the United Nations Convention on the Rights of the Child. This does not primarily have reference to criminal proceedings, but it does declare a number of rights of children who are either defendants in criminal cases or sentenced following a finding of guilt.[20] As with the ICCPR, the Convention on the Rights of the Child has been used by the Strasbourg Court as a source of rights applicable to young children.[21]

A third instrument, yet to exert its force, is the Charter of Fundamental Rights approved by the European Union in 2000, brought into force in 2003, and forming part of the Treaty establishing a Constitution for Europe signed in Rome in 2004. This contains several Articles devoted to safeguards in the criminal justice system, some of which go further than those currently recognized under the Convention.[22]

Those three rights instruments should be kept in mind as we turn to the European Convention on Human Rights and Fundamental Freedoms, now the foremost authoritative source of rights in this country both generally and for the criminal process. The Convention was signed in 1950, ratified by the UK in 1951, and came into force in 1953. It has been ratified by all Member States of the Council of Europe. Since 1966 the UK has allowed individual petition to Strasbourg. Thus any individual may make an application to the European Court of Human Rights, provided that domestic avenues of challenge have been exhausted. The Court will adjudicate

---

[18] See the essays in D. J. Harris and S. Joseph (eds), *The International Covenant on Civil and Political Rights and United Kingdom Law* (1995).

[19] See, e.g., *John Murray v United Kingdom* (1996) 22 EHRR 29.

[20] G. van Bueren, *Commentary on the UN Convention on the Rights of the Child* (2005).

[21] See, e.g., *V and T v United Kingdom* (2000) 30 EHRR 121.

[22] See A. Ward and S. Peers (eds), *The EU Charter of Fundamental Rights* (2004).

on whether or not the complaint is admissible. Admissible cases are then heard by a section of the Court. If the Court rules against the member state, the State will usually alter the law so as to comply with the judgment, but there is no absolute obligation to do so. The Committee of Ministers monitors State responses to findings of the Court.

(B) THE HUMAN RIGHTS ACT 1998

One reason why the UK was the subject of many adverse judgments in Strasbourg in the 1980s and 1990s was that the British courts were unable to apply the Convention when hearing domestic cases. When the Labour Government was elected in 1997, it quickly adopted the view that it was frustrating, embarrassing, and unnecessary that individuals should have to go outside the UK to secure the enforcement of rights to which the British Government committed itself long ago. The Human Rights Act was passed in 1998, and came fully into force in 2000. For present purposes, there are four principal provisions. The first is s 6, which requires all courts and public authorities (such as the police and the CPS) to conform with the Convention in all their decisions and policies. Then comes s 3, which requires courts to interpret statutes so far as possible in a way that gives effect to Convention rights—a strong interpretive duty. Sections 3 and 6 should be read together with s 2, which requires courts to take account of the decisions of the Strasbourg Court. This does not require courts always to follow decisions of the Court in interpreting the Convention, although it does suggest that good reasons should be given for not doing so.[23] Unlike some constitutions such as that of the United States, the Convention does not (under the Human Rights Act) have priority over legislation. If a higher court finds that a UK statute cannot be interpreted so as to be compatible with the Convention, the court may make a 'declaration of incompatibility' under s 4; there is then provision for the Government, if it wishes, to initiate a fast-track procedure for parliamentary amendment of legislation which falls foul of the Convention. We will note, at appropriate points in the following chapters, how the courts have adapted to the duties and powers given to them by the Human Rights Act.

(C) CONVENTION RIGHTS AND THE CRIMINAL PROCESS

For present purposes, a general overview of those Convention rights chiefly relevant to the criminal process will be given. Each of the relevant Articles will be set out, and a few illustrative comments added.

'Article 2   1. Everyone's right to life shall be protected by law. No one shall be deprived of his life intentionally save in the execution of a sentence of a court following his conviction of a crime for which this penalty is provided by law.

---

[23] As stated by the senior Law Lord, Lord Bingham, in *Anderson v Home Secretary* [2002] 4 All ER 1089, at [18].

2. Deprivation of life shall not be regarded as inflicted in contravention of this Article when it results from the use of force which is no more than absolutely necessary:

(a) in defence of any person from unlawful violence;

(b) in order to effect a lawful arrest or to prevent the escape of a person lawfully detained;

(c) in action lawfully taken for the purpose of quelling a riot or insurrection.'

This Article's relevance here resides in paragraph 2(b) and its impact on the use of force in arrest or the prevention of escape. The leading Strasbourg case is *McCann v United Kingdom*.[24] An undercover team of specially trained soldiers were keeping three IRA members under surveillance in Gibraltar, in the belief that the latter were about to carry out a bombing. When they thought that the three were about to detonate the bomb, they shot and killed them. In fact there was no detonator and no bomb. The European Court of Human Rights found that the planning of the operation was so defective that it made the killings foreseeable, although avoidable, and that this breached the victims' right to life under Article 2.1. Controversially, the majority of the Court held that the shooting did not fall within the 'absolute necessity' exception in Article 2.2, and therefore held the UK in violation of the Article. Some years earlier in *Kelly v United Kingdom*,[25] the European Commission had held that the action of a soldier in shooting at a car that had failed to stop at a checkpoint in Northern Ireland, killing one of the occupants, was 'absolutely necessary...in order to effect an arrest'. Article 2 is not well drafted in this respect: it contains no reference to the purpose of the arrest, and fails to confront the obvious point that one cannot arrest a person who has just been killed.

'Article 3 No one shall be subjected to torture or to inhuman or degrading treatment or punishment.'

Perhaps the best-known case on this Article is *Ireland v United Kingdom*,[26] in which the Court ruled that the notorious 'five techniques'[27] used in the interrogation of suspected terrorists by the authorities in Northern Ireland did not amount to 'torture', but did amount to 'inhuman and degrading treatment'. More recently, the Court has had to rule on whether the forced administration of an emetic to a suspected offender amounted to a breach of Article 3:[28] in finding a breach, the Court suggested that the 'inhuman and degrading' part of Article 3 should be treated as less powerful than the prohibition on torture. In other judgments the Court has been developing the positive duties that flow from Article 3, holding the UK to account for failing to provide proper facilities for disabled prisoners[29] and for failing to provide proper medical care for prisoners who present a known risk of suicide.[30] One difficulty is that many of

---

[24] (1996) 21 EHRR 97.

[25] (1993) 74 DR 139, on which see the critical discussion by Sir John Smith at (1994) *New LJ* 354.

[26] (1978) A.25.

[27] Wall standing, hooding, subjection to noise, deprivation of sleep and deprivation of food and drink.

[28] *Jalloh v Germany* (2007) 44 EHRR 667.   [29] *Price v United Kingdom* (2001) 34 EHRR 53.

[30] *Keenan v United Kingdom* (2001) 33 EHRR 38.

those in detention are unable to pursue claims in order to draw attention to the conditions, and so the European Committee on the Prevention of Torture and Inhuman and Degrading Treatment has been established, with authority to inspect the prisons and police stations of all Member States. It has inspected British prisons on three occasions, and has made critical reports.[31]

'Article 5   1. Everyone has the right to liberty and security of person. No one shall be deprived of his liberty save in the following cases and in accordance with a procedure prescribed by law... c) the lawful arrest or detention of a person effected for the purpose of bringing him before the competent legal authority on reasonable suspicion of having committed an offence, or when it is reasonably considered necessary to prevent his committing an offence or fleeing after having done so...

2. Everyone who is arrested shall be informed promptly, in a language which he understands, of the reasons for his arrest and of any charge against him.

3. Everyone arrested or detained in accordance with the provisions of paragraph 1(c) of this Article shall be brought promptly before a judge or other officer authorised by law to exercise judicial power and shall be entitled to trial within a reasonable time or to release pending trial. Release may be conditioned by guarantee to appear for trial.

4. Everyone who is deprived of his liberty by arrest or detention shall be entitled to take proceedings by which the lawfulness of his detention shall be decided speedily by a court and his release ordered if the detention is not lawful.

5. Everyone who has been the victim of arrest or detention in contravention of the provisions of this Article shall have an enforceable right to compensation.'

This Article covers a great deal of ground, and has been developed considerably by the Court. Since one of its purposes is to guarantee the right to liberty, it has high relevance to those stages of the pre-trial process at which liberty is curtailed—i.e. arrest, remand by the police and by a court, and trial within a reasonable time. Although Article 5 does provide (circumscribed) exceptions to deal with detention for those purposes, it makes no allowance for detention without charge or trial. For this reason the Government had to derogate from Article 5 of the Convention when Parliament enacted the Anti-Terrorism, Crime and Security Act 2001, ss 21–3 of which provide for the indefinite detention of persons certified to be 'suspected international terrorists'. The House of Lords held this provision and the derogation from Article 5 to be incompatible with the Convention,[32] and so in the Prevention of Terrorism Act 2005 the 'control order' was created. The particular use of this power by the government was held to amount to a 'deprivation of liberty' contrary to Article 5,[33] and the terms of the orders have been altered so as to reduce the number of hours of home detention; but other House of Lords decisions have held that the control order regime fails to satisfy the fair trial requirements of Article 6.[34]

---

[31] R. Morgan, 'International Controls on Sentencing and Punishment' in M. Tonry and R. Frase (eds), *Sentencing and Sanctions in Western Countries* (2001), esp at 393–9.

[32] *A v Secretary of State for Home Affairs* [2004] UKHL 56.

[33] *Secretary of State for the Home Department v JJ* [2007] UKHL 45.

[34] *Secretary of State for the Home Department v AF* [2009] UKHL 28.

That apart, Article 5 does provide for the detention of a person on reasonable suspicion of having committed an offence. In the leading case of *Fox, Campbell and
Hartley v United Kingdom*,[35] the Strasbourg Court held that:

'the exigencies of dealing with terrorist crime cannot justify stretching the notion of reasonableness to the point where the essence of the safeguard secured by Article 5(1)(c) is
impaired.'

In that case the UK was held to have violated the Article, because the only grounds
for arrest were that two of the three had previous convictions for terrorist offences.
However, in *O'Hara v United Kingdom*,[36] the Court held that the requirement of reasonable suspicion was fulfilled when the police arrested the applicant on information received, even though that information was not revealed to the Court. Article
5 requires an arrestee to be brought promptly before a court, and in *Brogan v United
Kingdom*,[37] the Court held that detention for longer than four days violated this provision. In order to determine whether it is justifiable to detain a defendant before trial,
under Article 5(3), the Court has developed an extensive jurisprudence which emphasizes the presumption of liberty and the presumption of innocence, and which requires
courts to avoid stereotypical reasoning (e.g. that someone with previous convictions
will therefore commit offences if granted bail) and to assess each case on its facts.[38] The
Court has also sought to place limits on the length of time for which a person may be
detained before trial (in conjunction with the right to trial within a reasonable time
under Article 6, below),[39] and has insisted on the importance of regular review of the
continued justification for detention.[40]

'Article 6   1. In the determination of his civil rights and obligations or of any criminal
charge against him, everyone is entitled to a fair and public hearing within a reasonable time
by an independent and impartial tribunal established by law...
    2. Everyone charged with a criminal offence shall be presumed innocent until proved
guilty according to law.
    3. Everyone charged with a criminal offence has the following minimum rights:

   (a) to be informed promptly, in a language which he understands and in detail, of the
       nature and cause of the accusation against him;

   (b) to have adequate time and facilities for the preparation of his defence;

   (c) to defend himself in person or through legal assistance of his own choosing or, if
       he has not sufficient means to pay for legal assistance, to be given it free when the
       interests of justice so require;

---

[35] (1990) 13 EHRR 157.   [36] [2002] *Crim LR* 493.
[37] (1989) 11 EHRR 117; a breach of this provision was also found in *O'Hara v United Kingdom* (last note).
[38] Discussed further in Ch 8 below; see generally the decision in *Nikolova v Bulgaria* (2000) 31 EHRR 64.
[39] See Ch 9 below on delay.
[40] E.g. *Jablonski v Poland* (2003) 36 EHRR 455; cf also Art 5(4) on review of detention.

(d) to examine or have examined witnesses against him and to obtain the attendance and examination of witnesses on his behalf under the same conditions as witnesses against him;

(e) to have the free assistance of an interpreter if he cannot understand or speak the language used in court.'

This Article has many different implications, but its central aim is to guarantee the right to a fair trial. Thus the opening words of the Article, which apply also to civil proceedings, guarantee three free-standing rights—to a fair and public hearing; to trial within a reasonable time; and to an independent and impartial tribunal. The remaining rights in Article 6 apply only to criminal proceedings, but this in itself has become a matter of controversy. The Strasbourg Court has insisted that the phrase 'charged with a criminal offence' has an autonomous meaning, thereby preventing Member States from subverting the special protections in Article 6 by framing pro-ceedings as civil.[41]

Article 6(2) declares the presumption of innocence, and this might be thought to indicate that placing burdens of proof on defendants would be very much restricted. However, this provision has been the subject of one of the loosest and least convincing judgments of the Strasbourg Court.[42] The minimum rights in Article 6.3 can be seen as non-exhaustive elaborations of the basic right to a fair trial. Many of these spe-cific rights will be discussed at the appropriate places in later chapters. The bound-aries of the right to free legal aid (Article 6.3(c)) have not yet been fully established, but it should certainly be provided when a person is in danger of being committed to prison.[43] Article 6.3(d) has a bearing not only on changes to the hearsay rule but also on the use of anonymous witnesses and of statements from witnesses unable to attend court.

No less significant have been the rights the Strasbourg Court has implied into Article 6 as concomitants of the general right to a fair trial. Probably the foremost example of this is the principle of equality of arms, which has crystallized as the right of a defendant to have disclosure of 'all material evidence for or against the accused',[44] subject to circumscribed exceptions that have attracted at least two Grand Chamber judgments in Strasbourg.[45] The Court has also implied into Article 6 the right of silence and the privilege against self-incrimination, describing them as 'generally recognised international standards which lie at the heart of the notion of fair procedure under

---

[41] Compare the leading cases of *Engel v Netherlands* (1979) 1 EHRR 647 and *Benham v United Kingdom* (1966) 22 EHRR 293 with the decision of the House of Lords in *Clingham v Kensington and Chelsea LBC; R (McCann) v Manchester Crown Court* [2003] 1 AC 787, and see the discussion in Ch 13 below.

[42] *Salabiaku v France* (1989) 13 EHRR 379; cf the stricter interpretation of Art 6.2 by the English courts in *Attorney General's Reference No 4 of 2002; Sheldrake v DPP* [2004] UKHL 43.

[43] See *Benham v United Kingdom*, above n 41.

[44] *Edwards v United Kingdom* (1993) 15 EHRR 417.

[45] Cf *Edwards and Lewis v United Kingdom* (2005) 40 EHRR 593 with *A and others v United Kingdom* (2009) 49 EHRR 625.

Article 6'.[46] In *Teixeira de Castro v Portugal*,[47] the Court confirmed that the right to a fair trial extends to the right to fair pre-trial procedures, and found a violation when a court had received and acted upon evidence obtained by entrapment. However, both express and implied rights may occasionally have to give way to countervailing rights of others involved in criminal proceedings: thus in the landmark decision in *Doorson v Netherlands*,[48] the Court held that a defendant's right of confrontation under Article 6(3)(d) may have to be somewhat curtailed in cases where witnesses have been threatened with violence and therefore ought to be questioned by the judge in the presence of counsel (but not the accused). The rights of the witnesses under Article 5 (security of person) and Article 8 (respect for private life) were rightly protected in those circumstances.

We will not give detailed consideration to Article 7, which declares the right not to be convicted or punished as a result of a law coming into force after the relevant act or omission. Suffice it to say that it has important implications for the criminal law, and that it is an aspect of the general requirement that criminal offences be defined with sufficient certainty.[49]

'Article 8.1. Everyone has the right to respect for his private and family life, his home and his correspondence.

2. There shall be no interference by a public authority with the exercise of this right except such as is in accordance with the law and is necessary in a democratic society in the interests of national security, public safety or the economic well-being of the country, for the prevention of disorder or crime, for the protection of health or morals, or for the protection of the rights and freedoms of others.'

This Article sets out the right to privacy. Once the right is engaged, it is still possible for the State to justify interfering with it, so long as the requirements of Article 8.2 are fulfilled. Innocuous as the first requirement of Article 8.2 ('in accordance with the law') may appear, the fact is that the UK has lost many cases in Strasbourg because of the absence—at least until the Regulation of Investigatory Powers Act 2000—of a proper statutory framework for electronic and other forms of surveillance.[50] Even if the 2000 Act is held to have removed the objections of 'arbitrariness' from the previous English approach, an interference with the right to privacy must also be held to be 'necessary in a democratic society' and required for one of the reasons set out in Article 8.2. The Court has developed various general principles for interpreting the exceptions to declared rights. Not only must the exception be prescribed by law, but account must also be taken of the principles of proportionality (significant intrusions into privacy only for serious offences), subsidiarity (intrusive techniques must be the last resort), accountability (prior independent authorization

[46] *John Murray v United Kingdom* (1996) 22 EHRR 29, at para 45.
[47] (1998) 28 EHRR 101, discussed below, Ch 9.4.   [48] (1996) 22 EHRR 330.
[49] See further B. Emmerson, A. Ashworth and A. Macdonald (eds), *Human Rights and Criminal Justice* (2nd ed, 2007), Ch 10.
[50] E.g. *Khan v United Kingdom* (2000) 31 EHRR 1016; *P.G. and J.H. v United Kingdom* [2002] *Crim LR* 308.

for intrusions on the declared right, supported by record-keeping and monitoring), and finality (information obtained by exceptional means should be used only for the purpose for which it was obtained).

These principles lend greater concreteness to the exceptions to the declared rights, not only to the right to respect for private life in Article 8 but also to the right of freedom of thought and religion (Article 9), the right to freedom of expression (Article 10) and the right to freedom of assembly and association (Article 11). Articles 9–11 are all followed by a second paragraph along the same lines as Article 8.2, and all have been subject to interpretation by the Court.[51]

'Article 14   The enjoyment of the rights and freedoms set forth in this Convention shall be secured without discrimination on any ground such as sex, race, colour, language, religion, political or other opinion, national or social origin, association with a national minority, property, birth or other status.'

This does not amount to a general right not to be discriminated against: its terms are restricted to discrimination in relation to Convention rights, and therefore it can only be used in a situation where a violation of one of the other Convention rights is found.

This brief introduction to the key Convention rights should be sufficient to give an outline of the interaction between the Convention and the rules of the criminal process. Detailed consideration of that interaction will be found in the relevant chapters below: what is plain from their inclusion in the Convention and from the enactment of the Human Rights Act is that they should have a special place in English law generally and in the criminal process specifically—they are more fundamental than other rights not so recognized, and have what might be termed a 'constitutional' dimension of added weight. In this context there are two other particular aspects of the Convention which are crucial to the arguments of this chapter, and to a theory of the criminal process. The first concerns the ranking of rights under the Convention, in terms of their differing strengths. The second, to which we will return later, concerns the patterns of reasoning when applying Convention rights.

(D) PRIORITY AMONG CONVENTION RIGHTS

A problem with rights-based accounts of the criminal process is that rights may conflict with each other or with other social values. Some rights may also seem to be more important, or weightier, than others. This may give the impression that rights can be traded off against one another and against other values. This, in turn, might lead one to conclude that because rights do not have an absolute value, they have no special value at all, and that a rights-based approach is in fact no different from a consequentialist

---

[51] For a full-length discussion, see Harris, O'Boyle and Warbrick, *Law of the European Convention on Human Rights* (2nd ed, 2009), Chs 8–12.

approach (discussed further below). This line of reasoning is mistaken. It is correct in
so far as rights can conflict, and can be roughly ranked in terms of importance. But
it is wrong in concluding that rights can simply be traded off against other values, or
that rights-based approaches are not distinctive. All this raises some complex issues,
but we suggest that insight on some of these questions can be gained by looking at how
they are dealt with within the framework of the European Convention on Human
Rights. This intensely practical scheme contains considerable wisdom about how to
reason about rights.

It may already have become apparent that some of the Convention rights have different strengths, or have larger or more flexible exceptions, but the key to the ranking
of Convention rights is to be found in Article 15:

'Article 15   1. In time of war or other public emergency threatening the life of the
nation any High Contracting Party may take measures derogating from its obligations
under this Convention to the extent strictly required by the exigencies of the situation,
provided that such measures are not inconsistent with its other obligations under international law.
   2. No derogation from Article 2, except in relation to deaths resulting from lawful acts of
war, or from Article 3, 4 (paragraph 1) and 7 shall be made under this provision…'

The thrust of Article 15 is that it is permissible for States to derogate from various
Convention rights if the conditions for doing so are satisfied, but that no derogation at
all is allowed from four rights. This immediately establishes an order of priority. The
non-derogable rights are:

- the right to life (Article 2),
- the right not to be subjected to torture or inhuman or degrading treatment
  (Article 3),
- the right not to be subjected to forced labour (Article 4.1), and
- the right not to be subjected to retrospective criminal laws or penalties
  (Article 7).

The fact that they are non-derogable indicates that they are the most basic of the fundamental rights in the Convention. Of course, their meaning and reach are subject to
interpretation, and in that sense they are not *absolute* rights—or, at least, not until the
scope of their application has been finally determined. But it is plain that they are not
intended to give way to 'public interest' considerations: the metaphor of 'balancing'
should not be applied here.

Another category of Convention rights might be termed qualified or prima facie
rights—the right is declared, but it is also declared that it may be interfered with on
certain grounds, to the minimum extent possible. We have already noted examples of
this in the right to respect for private life (Article 8), the right to freedom of thought
and religion (Article 9), the right to freedom of expression (Article 10) and the right to
freedom of assembly and association (Article 11). All these qualified rights are subject

to interference, if it can be established that this is 'necessary in a democratic society' on one of the stated grounds. As outlined above,[52] the Strasbourg Court has interpreted the second paragraphs of these Articles in such a way as to impose meaningful limitations on State interference with the rights.

Situated between non-derogable rights and qualified rights is an intermediate category, which is less easy to label and less easy to assess. In the European Convention this category includes the right to liberty and security of the person (Article 5) and the right to a fair trial (Article 6). One might refer to the rights in this intermediate category as 'strong rights', to demonstrate that they have a strength which is not qualified to the extent that the rights in Articles 8–11 are qualified. Indeed, the rights in Articles 5 and 6 are not at all qualified on the face of the Convention. In the internal logic of the Convention, this may prove to be quite a significant distinction. What it suggests is that, although strong rights are less fundamental than the non-derogable rights, any arguments for curtailing a strong right must at least be more powerful than the kind of 'necessary in a democratic society' argument that is needed to establish the acceptability of interference with a qualified right.

More will be said in Part 4 below about rights-based reasoning. The important point here is that it would not be accurate to state that human rights can be 'balanced' against public interest considerations, for that would be to corrupt the more demanding processes of reasoning outlined here. In the jurisprudence of the Strasbourg Court, at least, that vague notion of balancing does not dominate the interpretation of the Convention. Unfortunately, as we will see, the same is not always true of the British courts, where some judges have seized on the notion of balancing and a corrupted version of the proportionality requirement to make significant inroads into the protection of rights.

Although we have concentrated on rights in this section, there are many values which mould criminal procedure which are not to be found in documents such as the European Convention but which play an important role in shaping the criminal process. These include the values associated with the involvement of lay people in criminal justice decision making, the values associated with adversarialism, and the value of respect for victims of crime, for example. There are also the values reflected in treating defendants as an integral part of the process—as being called to account, in the terminology of Duff et al,[53] rather than as simple objects of the process, about whom judgements can be made without their being involved in the process in any significant way. Complex societies may also recognize a wide range of other values, and it is quite proper for these to be reflected in an institution such as the criminal process.

---

[52] See previous note.

[53] A. Duff, L. Farmer, S. Marshall and V. Tadros, *The Trial on Trial, volume 3: Towards a Normative Theory of the Criminal Trial* (2007).

2.4 EVALUATING THE CRIMINAL PROCESS

Thus far in this chapter we have sought to develop and to justify a theory that accords twin purposes to the criminal process—accurate determinations and fair procedures. The trial has been treated as the focus of the criminal process, and in that respect we have argued for the importance of regulating preparation for an effective criminal trial and of ensuring respect for rights and other important values. We have added a certain amount of detail to the theory by situating it in an analysis of the rights to be found in the European Convention on Human Rights. We now go on to show how and why our approach differs from certain other accounts of the criminal process.

(A) HERBERT PACKER'S TWO MODELS

The best-known framework for evaluating the criminal process is that of Herbert Packer, developed in the 1960s.[54] It has been subjected to considerable criticism and modification in subsequent years, and will not be adopted as a starting point here. It should be noted at the outset that Packer did not propose his scheme as a normative theory: he advanced two models as aids to interpreting trends in criminal procedure. Thus he suggested that tendencies in criminal justice might be evaluated by reference to two models, the Crime Control model and the Due Process model. 'The value system that underlies the Crime Control model is based on the proposition that the repression of criminal conduct is by far the most important function to be performed by the criminal process.'[55] This calls for 'a high rate of apprehension and conviction', placing a 'premium on speed and finality', and therefore preferring informal to formal procedures, with minimal opportunity for challenge. To work efficiently, the Crime Control model should ensure that weak cases are discarded at the earliest opportunity and that strong cases are taken forward to conviction and sentence as expeditiously as possible. The police are in the best position to judge guilt, and, if they form the view after their investigation that a person is guilty, the subsequent stages of the process should be as truncated as possible.

Packer contrasts with this the Due Process model, which takes cognizance of the stigma and loss of liberty that might result from the criminal process, and which insists on fairness criteria and other protections for the suspect or defendant. Thus the emphasis should be on formal and open adjudication of the facts in court, with the possibility of appeal, in order to give maximum protection to the innocent. Some proponents of the Due Process model would claim that it is a more accurate method of discovering the truth than the Crime Control model, but others would emphasize its recognition that errors do occur and its attempt to erect safeguards against mistaken judgements.

[54] H. Packer, *The Limits of the Criminal Sanction* (1968).   [55] *Ibid.*, 158.

These models are, of course, artificial constructs which list the features of a 'pure' or extreme form of a particular approach. They are designed as interpretive tools, to enable us to tell (for example) how far in a particular direction a given criminal justice system tends, and they do not of themselves suggest that one approach is preferable to the other. Stuart Macdonald, in his searching examination of Packer's legacy, argues that what he intended to produce was not models but Weberian ideal-types.[56] However, the terminology of models has been adopted widely, and various objections have been raised against Packer's approach. Five may be mentioned briefly here.

1. Packer failed to give a clear explanation of the relationship between his models. He recognized that 'the polarity of the two models is not absolute',[57] and stated that the ideology of Due Process 'is not the converse of that underlying the Crime Control model', since 'it does not rest on the idea that it is not socially desirable to repress crime'.[58] His models might be reconstructed so as to suggest that Crime Control is the underlying purpose of the system, but that pursuit of this purpose should be qualified out of respect to Due Process; or so as to suggest that Crime Control and Due Process should be recognized as the two main objectives of the system. Any such reconstruction would need to be supported by careful arguments.

2. Packer assumed that the system of pre-trial justice is capable of affecting the crime rate, since he used the term Crime Control. It is true that Packer included powers of arrest and detection rates in his discussion of pre-trial justice, but evidence is needed of a significant relationship between the extent of police powers and the crime rate.[59] Variations in the crime rate may be influenced more greatly by social and economic factors, and it would need to be established that the different styles of policing have a significant effect on the rate of convictions. The notion that different methods of processing defendants before trial might affect crime rates is not only unproven but also question-begging at a more fundamental level: surely Packer's models would be more realistic if he posited, as the primary State interest in pre-trial processes, convicting the guilty rather than controlling crime.

3. Related to this, Packer underestimated the importance of resource management as an element in the criminal process. This may have assumed greater significance in the years since Packer wrote, as governments have come under much greater financial pressure, and have brought this pressure to bear on criminal justice agencies.[60] But any contemporary model of criminal justice

---

[56] S. Macdonald, 'Constructing a Framework for Criminal Justice Research: Learning from Packer's Mistakes' (2008) 11 *New Criminal LR* 257.

[57] *Ibid.*, 154.   [58] *Ibid.*, 163.

[59] For a review of the evidence up to the mid-1990s, see D. Dixon, *Law in Policing* (1997), 81–8.

[60] However, A. E. Bottoms and J. D. McClean took this point only eight years after Packer had written: *Defendants in the Criminal Process* (1976), Ch 9.

ought to take account of the influence of targets, performance indicators and other bureaucratic goals on the workings of the main agencies (e.g. police, prosecutors).[61]

4. Packer's models make no allowance for victim-related matters. Again, this may be because there was far less consciousness of victims' interests and rights in the 1960s, but it is a significant drawback in using Packer's models today. Indeed, the models could probably not be adapted to accommodate this perspective: a new model would need to be added.

5. It is possible to mount various internal critiques of the two models. One example is the premium on speed, which Packer describes as an element in the Crime Control model. However, delays are also a source of considerable anxiety and inconvenience, and occasionally prolonged loss of liberty, to defendants. A properly developed notion of Due Process would surely insist that there be no unreasonable delay.[62]

Consideration of Packer's models begins to demonstrate the complexity of the criminal process and the problems of devising a satisfactory theoretical framework. The models may help us to identify elements of two important strands, but they neglect other, conflicting tendencies. One could try to remedy the defects by constructing further possible models: Kent Roach, for example, has developed two models incorporating victims' rights, the construction of which amply demonstrates the politicization of victims' rights rather than the rational pursuit of victim-centred objectives.[63] Macdonald has proposed a reconfiguration of the due process model as an ideal-type based on a defensive criminal law designed to protect individuals against abuses of State power; he also warns against any simplistic balancing approach, and instead emphasizes the importance of taking account of 'the competing demands of many values', including those of efficiency and reliability. In this spirit, we now leave Packer in order to examine other approaches.

(B) THE METAPHOR OF BALANCING

Much discussion of criminal justice by governments, courts and official bodies gives a central role to the notion of balance. Three clear examples in recent times are to be found in the report of the Royal Commission on Criminal Justice in 1993, in some of the leading British judgments under the Human Rights Act, and in Government claims about the rights of victims of crime. In our view, the metaphor of balancing is

---

[61] I. Loader and R. Sparks, 'Contemporary Landscapes of Crime, Order and Control' in M. Maguire, R. Morgan and R. Reiner (eds), *Oxford Handbook of Criminology* (4th ed, 2007).

[62] See the discussion in Ch 9.3 below.

[63] K. Roach, *Due Process and Victims' Rights: the New Law and Politics of Criminal Justice* (1999); for a survey of proposed re-adjustments and additions to Packer's framework, see Macdonald (above, n. 56), 263–71.

a rhetorical device of which one must be extremely wary. At worst, it is a substitute for principled argument: 'achieving a balance' is put forward as if it were self-evidently a worthy and respectable goal, rather like 'achieving justice'. Who, after all, would argue in favour of injustice or an unbalanced system? Of course it is important to recognize that the criminal process is the scene of considerable conflict between diverse aims and interests. The difficulty is that many of those who employ this terminology fail to stipulate exactly what is being balanced, what factors and interests are to be included or excluded, what weight is being assigned to particular values and interests, and so on. There were many examples of this vitiating vagueness throughout the report of the Runciman Royal Commission in 1993,[64] and this may indicate either self-delusion or intellectual dishonesty. For how can one properly invoke the notion of balance without having prepared the ground conscientiously? In this connection the most glaring omission from the Runciman report was the failure even to mention, let alone to consider and to draw upon, the rights enshrined in the European Convention on Human Rights. Nor did the Royal Commission conduct a systematic assessment of other relevant interests and claims—those of defendants, victims, potential victims, corporations, economic constraints, and so forth. By resting recommendations on the criminal justice system on notions of balance, without taking any account of human rights, the Royal Commission report laid bare its utter inadequacy on matters of principle.

A second example comes from a number of decisions of the British courts applying the Convention under the Human Rights Act 1998. By far the most significant was the first judgment handed down by the Privy Council after the 1998 Act came into force. In *Brown v Stott*,[65] an appeal from Scotland raised the question whether the privilege against self-incrimination, recognized as an implied right under Article 6,[66] protects the owner of a car from criminal conviction for failing to declare who was driving it at a given time and place. Of greater interest than the Privy Council's conclusion that the privilege should not apply in this situation was the reasoning of Lord Bingham, the senior Law Lord. Having explained that motoring laws are socially important because of the risk of death and injury from bad driving, he went on:

'If one asks whether section 172 [requiring owners to declare who was driving] represents a disproportionate response to the problem of maintaining road safety, whether the balance between the interests of the community at large and the interests of the individual is struck in a manner unduly prejudicial to the individual, whether (in short) the leading of this evidence would infringe a basic human right of the respondent, I would feel bound to give negative answers.'[67]

This is a crucial passage, setting the tone for many of the subsequent decisions under the Human Rights Act. Yet it is flawed. The plausibility of the reasoning derives from the reliance on two key concepts, 'balance' and 'proportionality', which seem to be

---

[64] Royal Commission on Criminal Justice, *Report* (1993).   [65] [2003] 1 AC 681.
[66] See n 46 above and accompanying text.   [67] [2003] 1 AC 681.

understood in terms of some kind of trade-off between a conception of the public interest (in which human rights apparently have no part) and the rights of the individual. Even if those concepts can be constructed in a defensible way, the point is that they do not belong here. As argued above, the right to a fair trial in Article 6 is a strong right under the Convention, and its component rights cannot simply be traded off by reference to the public interest. However, it must be said that the Strasbourg jurisprudence is now equivocal as to the proper place of that mode of reasoning in Article 6 cases: within a week of the decision in *Brown v Stott*, the Strasbourg Court held that the privilege against self-incrimination could not be outweighed by the social importance of anti-terrorist laws,[68] and yet more recently, on facts similar to those in *Brown v. Stott*, the Court quoted the above passage from Lord Bingham with approval.[69] There is a role for the concept of proportionality in Convention cases, but that is chiefly in respect of Articles 8–11. In that context, the concept of proportionality forms part of a specified mode of reasoning under the second paragraph of those Articles. It is relevant in considering whether the interference with the individual's right can be justified as 'necessary in a democratic society' for one of the listed reasons, and in its proper rigour should require a four-stage analysis.

(i)   Is the purpose of any rights restriction a legitimate democratic purpose?

(ii) Is the measure suitable for attaining that purpose?

(iii) Is it the least restrictive measure for attaining that purpose?

(iv) Is the measure proportionate in the strict sense, striking the proper balance between the purpose and the relevant individual rights?[70]

Lord Bingham's use of the concept in relation to Article 6 was far less disciplined and more opaque, whereas (because the Article 6 right is stronger) it should have been at least as rigorous as that four-stage analysis. We will return to this point below.

A third example involves the rights of victims. These will be discussed in more detail below, but at this point the debate about victims is a useful illustration of how the balancing metaphor is sometimes simply misleading. The Government has claimed that a major purpose of the various reforms introduced by the Criminal Justice Act 2003 was to re-balance the criminal justice system in favour of victims. It may be disputed whether any of the provisions in the Act will achieve this,[71] but the point to be made here is that this general metaphor of balancing advantages between defendants and victims is misleading in several respects. Here, the metaphor implies that the lot of defendants has to be made worse in order to make that of victims better. But many victim-centred reforms—giving victims better courtroom facilities, better support,

---

[68] *Heaney and McGuinness v Ireland* (2000) 33 EHRR 12.

[69] *O'Halloran and Francis v United Kingdom* (2008) 46 EHRR 407.

[70] This four-stage analysis is taken from the report by B. Goold, L. Lazarus and G. Swiney, *Public Protection, Proportionality and the Search for Balance* (Ministry of Justice, 2007).

[71] J. Jackson, 'Justice for All: Putting Victims at the Heart of Criminal Justice?' (2003) 30 *JLS* 309.

and keeping them properly informed of the progress of their cases—do not affect defendants in any way. Other reforms have affected defendants, for example, reforms restricting the ways in which vulnerable witnesses can be cross-examined. Here the rebalancing metaphor is more appropriate, though it may still mislead. It might be taken to suggest that there is a clash between the rights of defendants and those of witnesses when in fact there is not. The reforms centred around vulnerable witnesses are generally intended to allow such people to give their 'best evidence'. But no defendant has a legitimate interest in a witness giving unreliable evidence, or in their feeling intimidated. Even in the most controversial of these reforms, that involving a restriction on the ability of defendants to cross-examine witnesses in sexual assault cases about their sexual history, there is a shared assumption on both sides of the debate that defendants have a right to adduce all relevant evidence; the dispute has been over just what is relevant. These various reforms are not intended to affect defendants' rights, then. If there is balancing going on here, it does not involve balancing two rights. A further reason why the rebalancing metaphor may mislead is that it tends to suggest that victims have an interest in increased conviction rates, no matter how that increase is produced. One of the reforms introduced by the Criminal Justice Act 2003 was to enlarge the cirumstances in which juries can be informed of a defendant's previous convictions. Critics of this reform fear that it will lead to an increase in false convictions. If this is right, then the reform will not improve the lot of victims in any way: victims have no legitimate interest in seeing defendants falsely convicted. Reflection on this sort of example suggests that defendants share many of the interests of victims: interests in fair and dignified treatment, and in accurate fact-finding. This is something that the rebalancing metaphor only serves to obscure.

A more recent invocation of the balancing metaphor is found in the 2006 Consultation Paper, entitled *Rebalancing the Criminal Justice System in Favour of the Law Abiding Majority*. Several of the proposals, such as those involving better treatment for victims or reduction in bureaucracy, do not seem to involve any balancing at all. Even where the proposals affect defendants, there is often no balancing of rights going on: convicted defendants, for example, cannot be said to have a right not to pay compensation to victims, nor can the guilty be said to have a right to escape conviction 'on a technicality'. But the paper does contain more controversial proposals. An expansion in the use of ASBOs does raise issues about fair process; as we have noted in Chapter 1, and argue more fully in Chapter 13, ASBO-type measures seem to have been brought in partly to avoid the requirements of Article 6 of the Convention, requirements which should not simply be ignored in pursuit of crime control. But the worst deployment of the idea of balancing comes in direct criticism of a decision of the European Court of Human Rights. In *Chahal v United Kingdom*,[72] we are told, 'the Court found (by a narrow margin) that the UK Government could not consider the protection of the public as a balancing factor when arguing the case for the deportation of a dangerous

---

[72] (1997) 23 EHRR 413.

person...we are working with our partners in Europe to challenge this as vigorously as possible'.[73] What this does not tell us is that the Court was concerned at the risk that Chahal would be tortured if he was deported. It unanimously and properly held that the prohibition on torture in Article 3 was absolute, and could never be balanced against national security in domestic contexts. The minority (of 7 to 12) disagreed on a more debatable point, finding that it was proper to balance the *risk* of torture in a foreign country (which it considered to be low) against threats to national security.[74]

Our criticisms here are aimed at a vague and unprincipled use of the concept of 'balancing', a seductive notion that appears to exude fairness almost to the point of incontrovertibility. Yet talk of 'balancing' often assumes a kind of hydraulic relationship between human rights safeguards and the promotion of public safety, an assumption that should not be made in the absence of clear objective evidence. Another problem with the 'balancing' metaphor is that it may lead to restrictions on a small minority in the hope of enhancing the security of the majority.[75] A further difficulty is that too frequently no account is taken of the increase in State power that accompanies curtailments of individual rights, whereas one of the fundamental purposes of human rights is to protect individuals against arbitrary exercises of power by State officials. Moreover, even for rights in respect of which balancing is proper, the exercise should be conducted in a particular way. That is, the concept of 'balance' should be reserved for the conclusion of a lengthy and careful process, whereby rights and interests are identified; arguments for including some and excluding others are set out; appropriate weights or priorities are assigned to particular rights and interests, either generally or in specific contexts; and so forth. Above all, this must be an empirically grounded, reasoned, and principled course of argument, not simply the pronouncement of a conclusion. We will pursue this argument below. Prior to that, it will be helpful to illustrate some of the problems of balancing with reference to consequentialist theories of criminal process, which tend to rely heavily on this device.

(c) CONSEQUENTIALISM IN THE CRIMINAL PROCESS

Jeremy Bentham and John Stuart Mill are well known for their espousal of utilitarianism. The theory may take more or less sophisticated forms, but in essence social policies both generally and in respect of criminal justice should be determined by calculating what approach would conduce to the greatest happiness of the greatest

---

[73] At para 2.13.

[74] The Government's attempt to persuade the Strasbourg Court to go back on its *Chahal* judgment have met with no success. The UK Government was allowed to intervene in *Saadi v Italy* (2009) 49 EHRR 730 in order to put its balancing arguments, but they were not accepted by a unanimous Grand Chamber.

[75] For further critique of 'balancing', see J. Waldron, 'Security and Liberty: the Image of Balance' (2003) 11 *J Political Philosophy* 191; L. Zedner, 'Seeking Security by Eroding Rights: the Side-stepping of Due Process' and A. Ashworth, 'Security, Terrorism and the Value of Human Rights', both in B. Goold and L. Lazarus (eds), *Security and Human Rights* (2007).

number of people.[76] A felicific calculus, measuring pain and pleasure, would be used to determine the approach that would overall produce least pain. An obvious criticism of such a consequentialist approach is that its chief concern is with aggregate benefits, and that it may therefore ride roughshod over particular individuals (or minorities) in order to benefit the majority. The most provocative example would be torture: human rights instruments typically prohibit it absolutely, whereas utilitarians might accept it when it seems likely to yield a benefit for the majority. More prosaically, human rights instruments often proclaim the presumption of innocence in criminal proceedings, whereas on a utilitarian calculus it may often benefit the community more if defendants were required to prove, for example, any defence that they wished to raise.

Rights theories, on the other hand, are essentially anti-consequentialist: the whole point of recognizing a right is to uphold the claim of an individual to protection from treatment of certain kinds, even though such treatment may accord with the wishes of the majority or be for the overall benefit of the community. This does not mean that consequentialist reasoning is always inappropriate, but it does carve out certain spheres of activity in which it must give way to recognized rights. There has been a recent revival of consequentialist theories in criminal justice, and two may be mentioned briefly here. John Braithwaite and Phillip Pettit argue that the ultimate determinant should be the republican ideal of liberty: the difficult clashes between individual rights and public interests should be resolved by calculating which approach advances 'dominion' on a greater scale—dominion meaning non-interference by others, secured by society and the community so as to become the expectation of each individual.[77] One difficulty with this form of republican theory is that it appears not to recognize anything other than vague outer limits on State intervention in individual lives. Thus its authors refer to the need to provide reassurance to the community, and espouse incapacitative penal strategies: 'crucial to the promotion of community reassurance' is the power to 'escalate responses' as 'an offender displays more and more intransigence about offending against others'.[78] Although primarily directed at sentencing rather than at pre-trial processes, this approach provides no principled restraints on State intervention, and it is unclear whether and to what extent it would recognize individual rights. Whatever the merits of the republican ideal, the absence of principled limits means that the theory leaves individuals too much at the mercy of the State.

Andrew Sanders and Richard Young adopt a different form of consequentialism, though one that has marked similarities to Braithwaite and Pettit's. For Sanders and Young, it is 'freedom', rather than dominion, which is the value to be maximized. They argue that when human rights and other interests are being compared, the approach

---

[76] A good account of consequentialism is W. Kymlicka, *Contemporary Political Philosophy: An Introduction* (2nd ed, 2002), Ch 2.

[77] J. Braithwaite and P. Pettit, *Not Just Deserts: A Republican Theory of Criminal Justice* (1990).

[78] For brief contributions to the debate, see P. Pettit with J. Braithwaite, 'Republicanism in Sentencing: Recognition, Recompense and Reassurance', and A. Ashworth and A. von Hirsch, 'Desert and the Three Rs', both in A. von Hirsch and A. Ashworth (eds), *Principled Sentencing: Readings on Theory and Policy* (2nd ed, 1998).

that is likely to enhance freedom the most should be chosen, since the various conflicting considerations (human rights, protecting the innocent, convicting the guilty, protecting victims, maintaining public order, etc) should be seen as means to achieving the overriding goal of freedom. Thus 'all we have to do is to prioritise the goal that is likely to enhance freedom the most'.[79] Two difficulties with this approach concern the definition of freedom and the approach to balancing that it requires. The meaning of freedom is highly contestable—as the classic essay by Isaiah Berlin on negative liberty and positive liberty shows[80]—and when the authors state that they would include the freedom 'of the community at large' the glass becomes rather dark.[81] Their fundamental concept still seems to us to be under-determined, and it is not clear how they would deal with the weighting of 'competing goals, interests and rights' that is necessary.[82] They certainly recognize the need to assign weights to them, but their confidence in 'the language of freedom' to smooth the path by providing a 'common currency' may be overdone. However, we support their recognition of the sheer range of relevant interests to be considered, and their recognition that assigning weight to each of them in particular contexts is an essential precondition of any kind of 'balancing' operation.

To summarize: the principal problem with consequentialist theories is that they allow rights to be overridden in pursuit of some other value. Even the reasonably sophisticated consequentialist theories of Braithwaite and Pettit and Sanders and Young would appear to allow violations of human rights if to do so would ultimately promote dominion or freedom: Sanders and Young say not, but that suggests some kind of special protection for human rights in their freedom-based calculations, the implications of which are not spelt out. When one considers the sheer number of different values relevant to criminal justice recognized in a complex society, many of which conflict, it is difficult to believe that they can all be reduced to a single core value. To mention, once again, examples we have already used: the choice between an adversarial or inquisitorial system, or between lay or professional fact-finders, cannot sensibly be made in terms of which better promotes dominion or freedom. Or, to take another example, the value of confrontation between defendant and witness, which is contained in the US Constitution and has recently been accorded significant importance by the US Supreme Court,[83] and also features in the European Convention on Human Rights,[84] cannot easily be conceptualized or assessed in those terms either. One should be suspicious of theories that attempt, as consequentialist theories do, to reduce all human values to a single metric.

---

[79] A. Sanders and R. Young, *Criminal Justice* (3rd ed, 2007), 44.

[80] I. Berlin, 'Two Concepts of Liberty' in A. Quinton (ed), *Political Philosophy* (1967).

[81] Cf Sanders and Young, above n 79, 50, for a defence of their use of the idea of the 'freedom of the community at large'.

[82] *Ibid.*, 62.   [83] *Crawford v Washington* (2004) 124 S Ct 1354.

[84] Article 6(3)(d), the right to examine witnesses. For a recent application, see *Al-Khawaja v United Kingdom* (2009) 49 EHRR 1.

(D) DEVELOPING THE RIGHTS PERSPECTIVE

Our approach to criminal process differs from those just described in that it is rights-based. This is not to say that the purpose of the criminal process is to implement human rights, but that in the pursuit of retributive justice respect for rights is essential. Respect for rights should be seen as a concomitant aim of criminal process—not merely a side-constraint on the pursuit of accuracy or 'rectitude' in convicting the guilty and acquitting the innocent, but an objective to be attained while pursuing that aim. Thus the European Convention on Human Rights is taken to be part of the normative framework for the criminal process, as indeed it is in terms of both UK law (following the Human Rights Act) and the country's international obligations. But the Convention does not exhaust our normative arguments. We recognize that it has shortcomings: it has been supplemented by various Protocols over the years, and there are good arguments for further Protocols on, for example, discrimination. Like Packer's models it says nothing about the rights of victims and witnesses, although there are several Council of Europe recommendations dealing with those issues. The Convention also needs supplementing in respect of young suspects and defendants, and the UN Convention on the Rights of the Child is important in that respect. Furthermore, as we have noted, values beyond those contained in such documents play a legitimate role in shaping the criminal process.

The human rights perspective can make a particular contribution through its subtle weighting of different rights, and its structuring of arguments for making exceptions to rights. We noted above that certain rights do provide for interference and for a balancing process to determine whether the interference is justified. But the kind of balancing that is permitted under the Convention is a far cry from the vague and undisciplined concept often used by politicians, exemplified by Lord Bingham's landmark judgment in *Brown v Stott*.[85]

Our starting point is the hierarchy of Convention rights (sketched in Part 3(d) above) which distinguishes between non-derogable rights, strong rights, and qualified rights. The non-derogable rights permit no balancing of the public interest. For example, arguments that torturing certain people would be in the public interest cannot be entertained, as we saw the European Court of Human Rights held in *Chahal*. On the other hand, the qualified rights are self-evidently open to balancing. But what we noted was that this is not some vague exercise of trying to measure the individual's right against the wider public interest, but rather a structured process of reasoning indicated by the wording of the second paragraph of those rights and developed in the jurisprudence of the Court. This is not to deny that courts can reach different conclusions about whether an interference is 'necessary in a democratic society', or that there are grounds for contesting some judgments of this kind. The argument is that the structure of reasoning required in order to justify interference with a qualified right

---

[85] Above, p. 42.

provides a guide to the weighting of the right and the circumstances in which it can be outweighed.

More difficult are the two strong rights declared by Articles 5 and 6. It must be said that the Strasbourg Court has not been entirely consistent in its judgments. There are some decisions on Articles 5 and 6 where it has stated either that a particular right is not absolute, or that it may be necessary to balance a right against some other interest. Now this proposition must be treated with care, and not as a licence for vague and undisciplined 'balancing'. Thus the Strasbourg Court has said that both the right of silence and the privilege against self-incrimination are not absolute,[86] yet that emphatically does not mean that they can be freely 'balanced' against public interest considerations. What it means in respect of the right of silence is that there may be 'situations calling for an explanation from' the accused, in which adverse inferences may justifiably be drawn from the accused's silence: this is a significant qualification, but it refers only to the evidential situation in the case. The fact that a power is believed to be essential in the fight against terrorism has been held insufficient to justify an exception to the privilege against self-incrimination, but it remains to be seen whether the Court will continue to hold this line.[87]

As for balancing an Article 6 right against another Convention right, the principal example of this is *Doorson v Netherlands*,[88] where the Court held that the defendant's right to examine witnesses against him has to be balanced against the rights of the witnesses themselves, notably where a witness has reason to fear violent reprisals if her or his identity is revealed. But, again, this decision does not licence some vague kind of 'balancing'. In the first place, the interests 'balanced' were both rights of individuals, not any public interests. Moreover, the process of 'balancing' was quite rigidly structured: thus the Court insisted that, although it was proper to protect the identity of the witness, the rights of the defence must be curtailed as little as possible. Thus the 'handicaps under which the defence laboured [must be] sufficiently counterbalanced by the procedures followed by the judicial authorities', such as appropriate directions from the judge; and any conviction should not be based 'solely or mainly' on the evidence of the witnesses who were thus allowed to give their evidence anonymously.[89] All these requirements, indeterminate as they may be in their application, constitute an advance on general notions of 'balancing', by showing how a right can continue to exert its influence even where its application is curtailed.

Another example of a structured approach may be found in the Court's judgments on the prosecution's duty to disclose documents to the defence, and the claim of 'public

---

[86] E.g. in *John Murray v United Kingdom* (1996) 22 EHRR 29 and in *Saunders v United Kingdom* (1997) 23 EHRR 313.

[87] Compare *Heaney and McGuinness v Ireland* (2000) 33 EHRR 12 (fight against terrorism insufficient to justify exception) with *Jalloh v Germany* (2007) 44 EHRR 667 (seriousness of offence a relevant consideration). For principled discussion, see e.g. A. Ashworth, *Human Rights, Serious Crime and Criminal Procedure* (2002), 108–18; J. Waldron, 'Security and Liberty: the Image of Balance' (2003) 11 *J Political Philosophy* 191, at 203–4; L. Zedner, 'Securing Liberty in the Face of Terror' (2005) 32 *J Law & Society* 507.

[88] (1996) 22 EHRR 330.

[89] *Ibid.*, para 72; cf *Van Mechelen v Netherlands* (1997) 25 EHRR 547.

interest immunity' from having to disclose certain evidence. In the leading decision of *Rowe and Davis v United Kingdom*,[90] the Court held that the principle of equality of arms is a requirement of fairness under Article 6, but that:

'the entitlement to disclosure of relevant evidence is not an absolute right. In any criminal proceedings there may be competing interests, such as national security or the need to protect witnesses at risk of reprisals or keep secret police methods of investigating crime. In some cases it may be necessary to withhold certain evidence from the defence so as to preserve the fundamental rights of another individual or to safeguard an important public interest. However, only such measures restricting the rights of the defence which are strictly necessary are permissible under Article 6(1). Moreover, in order to ensure that the accused receives a fair trial, any difficulties caused to the defence by a limitation on its rights must be sufficiently counterbalanced by the procedures followed by the judicial authorities.'[91]

Recent judgments have re-examined the 'counterbalancing' procedures in these cases of public interest immunity, and have found that the combination of non-disclosure with the special counsel system may be insufficient to comply with the requirements of a fair trial.[92]

These examples therefore demonstrate that, on the rare occasions when the Strasbourg Court has recognized that a degree of balancing may enter into the determination of certain rights under Articles 5 and 6, it has insisted on structured reasoning. It has not allowed a right simply to be 'balanced away',[93] but has concentrated on preserving the essence of the defendant's right while giving some weight to pressing public interest considerations. If English courts and politicians are to continue to adopt the metaphor of 'balancing', it is submitted that they should at least move to a more rigorous and structured approach. As argued earlier, even the justifications for interfering with the qualified rights under Articles 8–11 of the Convention must be reasoned according to a particular structure of requirements: this renders all the more cogent the argument that rigorous and structured reasoning should be used when there is a question of 'balancing' certain rights (not all) under the stronger Articles 5 and 6 against some public interests.

Structured reasoning only takes one so far. It offers a procedure, but no ultimate criterion for making choices. Human rights standards have areas of open texture, perhaps more than some rules of domestic law. Because human rights are as much political as legal, their reach will inevitably generate controversy. But we have argued that the structure of the Convention sets certain markers and establishes an order of priority, which may be used as a basis for reasoned argument. In respect of Articles 5 and 6, which are the rights primarily relevant to the criminal process, it should be

---

[90] (2000) 30 EHRR 1.   [91] *Ibid.*, para 61.

[92] See, e.g., *A v United Kingdom* (2009) 49 EHRR 625, *Secretary of State for the Home Department v AF* [2009] UKHL 28.

[93] Even in *O'Halloran and Francis v United Kingdom* (2008) 46 EHRR 407, where the Court quoted with approval Lord Bingham's passage about balancing rights against the public interest, the Court took account of other factors in coming to its decision.

recognized that they are essentially 'trumps' over considerations of public interest. There may be limited circumstances in which certain rights may be 'over-trumped' by extreme and urgent considerations of public interest. But, even then, the Strasbourg court has shown that policies such as the fight against terrorism or the war on drugs cannot be taken as sufficient for these purposes.[94] Consequentialist approaches might well lead to other conclusions in these types of case, and that marks a significant difference in emphasis.

2.5 DEVELOPING THE RIGHTS PERSPECTIVE: THE STATE AND VICTIMS

What we have described as a theory of the criminal process—one that has the twin goals of regulating the processes for bringing suspected offenders to trial so as to produce accurate determinations, and of ensuring that fundamental rights are protected in those processes—still needs to be supplemented and adapted in several ways. Differences of approach may be necessary when dealing with young suspects, for example. It is necessary to look to the United Nations Convention on the Rights of the Child (1990), whose wide-ranging list of rights includes those in Article 40 on 'the administration of juvenile justice'. A different question is whether all the rights in the Convention ought to apply to corporate bodies as well as to individuals: how ought the right to liberty and security of the person (Article 5) or the right to a fair trial (Article 6) to apply to companies? It is also necessary to assess the relevance of what are claimed to be victims' rights. In 1985 the Council of Europe approved recommendations on *The Position of the Victim in the Framework of Criminal Law and Procedure*, and the United Nations approved a *Declaration of Basic Principles of Justice for the Victims of Crime and Abuse of Power*. No amendment was made, however, and no protocol added to the European Convention. Does that mean that victims' rights ought to be placed in some fourth, lower category of rights, beneath those enumerated above? Surely not. A more likely historical explanation, in terms of practical politics, is that no one dared to begin the process of amending the Convention for fear that it would prove counter-productive, or even so controversial as to undermine the consensus that exists around the existing rights. Victims' rights should therefore be assessed on general principles, unlimited by the restricted list of rights in the Convention, and this will inevitably raise the question of the proper role of the State in criminal procedure.

It is a commonplace that, until the final quarter of the last century, there had been a relative neglect of victims' needs for support, respect and compensation. Since then, there has been increasing recognition that the victims of crime have rights to

---

[94] E.g. *Heaney and McGuinness*, above, n 87; *Brogan v United Kingdom*, above n 37; and, on drugs, *Teixeira de Castro v Portugal* (1999) 28 EHRR 101.

respectful and sympathetic treatment from law enforcement agents; to support and help in the aftermath of the offence; to proper information about the progress of their case; to facilities at courtrooms that separate them from other members of the public; and to compensation for the crime, either from the offender or (if that is not possible) from the State, at least for crimes of violence.[95] These rights to services should be regarded as an important element in social provision for those disadvantaged by crime, and it should be the concern of people working in the criminal justice system to ensure that they are recognized and fulfilled. But completely different justifications are needed if it is claimed that victims have procedural rights in the criminal process. Should the victim have the right to be consulted on the decision whether or not to prosecute, on the bail/custody decision, on the acceptance of a plea to a lesser offence or to fewer offences, or on sentence? Some victims and victims' families want this kind of involvement, although many do not wish to have such burdens,[96] but the question here is whether there are good arguments for recognizing such claims as rights.

An essential first step is to consider what the role of the State should be in the criminal process. One familiar argument is that the State's leading role is a social necessity: if it were left to victims, their families and their supporters to deal with people who break the rules, this would open the way to revenge, retaliation, vigilantism, and serious injustice, if not anarchy. This consequentialist argument does not establish, however, why it should be the State—as opposed to local communities, for example—that should have the overall responsibility and power. For this, one needs a conception of the State's proper functions. John Gardner has argued that one of the defining roles of the State should be to facilitate peaceful living among citizens, and to safeguard the basic means by which citizens can lead good lives.[97] He argues that this requires the State to control reprisals by individuals; it also requires rules to be authoritatively established, and to be reinforced by sanctions. The State has as one of its major functions the prevention or reduction of harm, and this includes responding to wrongs done by censuring those who commit them. The State can and should do this in a way that shows respect for the offender as a rational citizen (e.g. by conforming to human rights), and which adopts a fair and consistent approach to the task.[98] These last specifications have particular resonance for the criminal process, in the investigatory, pretrial and trial stages: a major role of the State is as guarantor of the rights of all those involved, as well as providing official agencies (such as the police, public prosecutors and courts) to carry out the essential functions of law enforcement.

This may be regarded as a general argument of principle. It may have to give way, to some extent, if the reality is that a certain State is failing to perform its proper

[95] For the culmination of a lengthy process of giving statutory recognition to rights of this kind, see the Domestic Violence, Crime and Victims Act 2004, and the *Victims Code of Practice* to which it gave rise.
[96] Victim Support, *The Rights of Victims of Crime* (1995).
[97] J. Gardner, 'Punishment—in Proportion and in Perspective' in A. Ashworth and M. Wasik (eds), *Fundamentals of Sentencing Theory* (1998).
[98] See further A. von Hirsch and A. Ashworth, *Proportionality in Sentencing* (2005), Ch 2.

role—where, for example, there is widespread mistrust among the people because of long-running social divisions (perhaps Northern Ireland may still be an example); or even where it is evident that there is a vitiating gulf between provision for wealthier citizens (who can afford extra security measures) and provision for the poor, a social problem that may be no less manifest in law enforcement than in health or education.[99] But the argument of principle—the starting point, informed by the commitment to retributive justice—is that the primary interests in the application of the criminal sanction through the processes of the criminal justice system are those of the State and the suspect/defendant/offender. In respect of sentencing, the court should take a decision according to the law. The victim's personal view should be no more relevant to this than the personal view of any other individual. The rule of law, embodied in the Convention and other human rights documents, requires decisions to be taken by an independent and impartial tribunal according to settled rules announced beforehand. A particular victim may be vindictive or forgiving, demanding or afraid of the offender, and it would be an abdication of the State's responsibility to allow such individual feelings to influence the sentence. The same reasoning applies to the key stages of the criminal process, such as the decision to investigate, the decision to prosecute, and the acceptance of a plea to a different charge: the rule of law requires these decisions to be taken impartially and independently, and not influenced by the wishes of a particular individual. It is true that in practice the willingness of a victim or complainant to become involved, by making a statement or alternatively by declining to give evidence in court, can often determine whether an enquiry or prosecution is taken forward. But that fact does not alter the rights and wrongs, and indeed in some types of case (such as domestic violence) prosecutions may be brought without the victim's cooperation.[100]

The implication of this reasoning is that there are no convincing arguments for accepting that victims or victims' families have a right to influence any of the key decisions in the criminal process. Whether there is still good reason to say that the police or prosecutors should receive and 'take account of' victims' wishes before taking these decisions is a moot point: this could be criticized as a sham if at the same time we maintain that the decisions should not be *influenced* by the victim's wishes, because victims might feel they are being misled and might feel disappointed if their wishes are not followed.[101] However, this is the position reached in English law in respect of Victim Personal Statements, which may now be submitted by victims to the court, although the Lord Chief Justice's Practice Direction states that 'the opinions of the victim or victim's close relatives as to what the sentence should be are not

---

[99] For discussion and further references, see K. Roach, *Due Process and Victims' Rights: the New Law and Politics of Criminal Justice* (1999), 261; A. Ashworth, 'Responsibilities, Rights and Restorative Justice' (2002) 42 *BJ Crim.* 578, at 580–1.

[100] See the discussion in Ch 7, below.

[101] See the research into the pilot project on submitting victim statements to prosecutors, discussed by A. Sanders, C. Hoyle, R. Morgan and E. Cape, 'Victim Impact Statements: Can't Work, Won't Work' [2001] *Crim LR* 447.

relevant.'[102] Information contained in the statement may be relevant when assessing the consequences of the offence for the victim, and at the pre-trial stage the same would definitely be true at remand proceedings—there are cases where it would be important to know about the alleged victim's apprehensions about (further) violence or harassment. But this shows that a line is emerging between information from the victim (which may be relevant, subject to verification) and the opinions of the victim (which should not be relevant).

It is important now to re-assert that no part of this argument suggests that victims should be ignored or that they should be less well served. Just like defendants, they should be treated with dignity. The argument has been that they should not be granted procedural rights that enable them to influence decisions in the criminal process. This leaves untouched the need to review the rules relating to investigations, procedure and evidence in particular types of case—notably cases of sexual assault, where victims (whether male or female) remain open to questioning, in and out of court, on details of their past which are of questionable relevance to the proper interests of the defendant.[103] Similarly, all the arguments in favour of improved support, information and compensation for victims remain untouched. For example, it has been recognized for many years that victims are not always kept informed about the progress of 'their' case through the system, and sometimes hear about a plea of guilty to a lesser offence only at a much later stage. The publication of a Code of Practice for Victims of Crime under the Domestic Violence, Crime and Victims Act 2004 is a welcome step, but the Act stopped short of establishing statutory rights to services for victims.

How do these conclusions on the role of the State and on victims' rights relate to new initiatives in restorative justice? In the precise sphere of this book, the implications are limited because it is usually a precondition of a defendant entering restorative justice that he or she admits guilt. Restorative justice is not put forward as a means of resolving factual disputes or a substitute for trials. What it challenges is the view that the State should have exclusive responsibility for the administration of criminal justice, and it argues in favour of 'restorative conferences' (composed of victims and their families, offenders and their families, and community representatives) to allow victims and offenders to come to terms with what happened and to determine the response to offences.[104] Although it is said to be essential that the offender consents to participate in the conference and can walk away at any time, it is plain that the conferences take place in the shadow of the formal legal system and that any consent is therefore somewhat bounded. Victims clearly have a significant role in deciding the outcome, and this goes against the rule-of-law principles of independent and impartial judgement by making it likely that outcomes will depend

[102] See now Consolidated Practice Direction, III.28.

[103] See further J. Temkin, *Rape and the Legal Process* (2nd ed, 2002).

[104] See further G. Johnstone, *Restorative Justice* (2001); G. Johnstone, *A Reader on Restorative Justice* (2003).

to some extent on whether the victim is vindictive or forgiving.[105] For advocates of restorative justice this is less important than whether the victim comes forth with an apology to the offender and whether the victim feels better for the experience of being able to enter into a dialogue with the offender. It is evident, finally, that we have travelled a long distance from Packer's two models of the criminal process (see pp 39–41 above), and that to interpret trends and tendencies from the victim's point of view one would need an entirely different model.[106]

Insofar as restorative justice is invoked to deal with cases at the lower end of the scale of seriousness, there may be advantages in experimenting with it to see whether it yields the benefits (in terms of community reintegration and crime prevention) that tend to be claimed for it. But as the seriousness of the offences increases, so the importance of maintaining rule-of-law standards and respecting the rights of defendants in the face of sanctions imposed upon them increases. This issue is pursued further in Part 6 below.

2.6 DISPOSITIVE VALUES

The discussion thus far has focused on values in the context of a theory of the criminal process, and it is now time to return to another aspect of pre-trial decisions—'dispositive' values. The focus here is on police cautions, conditional cautions, final warnings, Fixed Penalty Notices, Penalty Notices for Disorder, restorative justice conferences and other forms of diversion from the formal process.[107] To a large extent the values relevant here reflect the purposes at the stage of sentencing, which is the best-known and most widely publicized dispositive decision, but it is important also to retain a philosophical connection with the principles discussed above in relation to process values. In particular, the right of an innocent person not to be punished is relevant to both types of decision.

(A) PREVENTION OF CRIME

The prevention of crime is among the reasons for having a criminal justice system, with police, courts, and sentences. Indeed, in Part 5 above we argued that this should be a primary function of the State. It is also an underlying reason for diversion, but this is not to say that it should be determinative in individual cases. These two points should

---

[105] See the criticisms by A. Ashworth, 'Responsibilities, Rights and Restorative Justice' (2002) 42 *BJ Crim* 578, and the reply by A. Morris, 'Critiquing the Critics: a Brief Response to Critics of Restorative Justice', *ibid.*, 596.

[106] See K. Roach, 'Criminal Process' in P. Cane and M. Tushnet (eds), *Oxford Handbook of Legal Studies* (2003), 780–1.

[107] These were introduced in Ch 1 above, and will be discussed in detail in Ch 6 below.

be kept separate. It is one thing to argue that the system of diversion should operate in such a way that it contributes to the overall prevention of crime, at least by dealing with offenders in ways that do not increase the chances of further law-breaking by them or by others. It is another thing to maintain that the prospect of a particular person not reoffending should be a necessary or sufficient reason for diverting that offender from the formal criminal process: that might conflict with the principle of proportionality (see (d) below). The point here is that, since dispositive decisions without trial may be regarded as part of or analogous to the sentencing system, they should certainly not be invoked in a way that increases the probability of people committing offences.

(B) CONSENT AND FAIRNESS

This principle has a direct connection with process values. The system should ensure that, as far as possible, a person's decision whether or not to accept diversion is a free and informed one, and that there is a right of access to a court if guilt is disputed.[108] The idea of a completely free decision may be regarded as illusory, in the sense that the alternative of going to court will often be perceived as more stressful, but there are ways of maximizing this freedom. For example, legal advice should be available so as to help a suspect with this decision, not least because cautions, final warnings and PNDs are recorded and may be cited in subsequent proceedings, and also because restorative justice conferences may sometimes be less benign than they might seem.[109] Penalty Notices for Disorder, unlike other out-of-court disposals, do not require an admission of guilt by the ticketed person; they do not rank as convictions, yet they are recorded on the Police National Computer and may be used against a person in various circumstances. This underlines the need to ensure that methods of diversion do not become methods of subversion, so far as fairness and the protection of the innocent are concerned.

(C) VICTIM COMPENSATION

Any arrangement for diversion should ensure that the victim does not thereby lose a right to compensation. The system should remain committed to victims' rights to support and services, for the reasons elaborated at p 52 above. This does not necessarily mean that offenders should be required to pay full compensation to their victims in order to be eligible for diversion: as in formal sentencing proceedings, compensation should reflect the offender's means too. Again, the statutory requirements for conditional cautions appear to deal properly with this question, but for informal processes such as restorative conferences there is no legal framework.

---

[108] As required under Art 6: *Ozturk v Germany* (1984) 6 EHRR 409.

[109] This is not to imply that legal advice necessarily leads to the best outcome for an accused person: see Ch 3 on the ethics of defence lawyers, and Ch 10 on lawyers' advice on plea.

(D) PROPORTIONALITY OF IMPOSITION

There should be a sense of proportion between the seriousness of the offence and that to which the offender is asked to agree as part of the diversion. This is not merely a means of ensuring that consent is as voluntary as it can be. It is also a basic element of desert in sentencing: a person who has committed an offence only deserves to be punished to an extent that may be described as appropriate to the seriousness of the offence committed, in terms of harm and culpability. Thus the impositions on those who are 'diverted' must be proportionate to one another, in the sense that more serious cases should involve more onerous requirements and less serious cases should involve less onerous requirements. The impositions should also be of modest severity overall, so that they can appropriately be ranked below court-imposed penalties.

In terms of the human rights discussed in Part 3(c) above, why is proportionality of sentencing so important? Apart from the strong arguments of principle for ensuring that punishment is proportionate so as to deal fairly with individuals,[110] the European Court of Human Rights has insisted that punishments must not be so disproportionate as to constitute 'inhuman and degrading' punishment under Article 3;[111] the Charter of Fundamental Rights in the European Union, in force since 2003, declares in Article 49(3) that 'the severity of penalties should not be disproportionate to the criminal offence'; and there are other examples of human rights documents insisting on this limitation of State punishment.[112] In terms of human rights law, therefore, the right not to be punished disproportionately to the seriousness of the offence committed seems well established.

One emergent difficulty, as suggested above, is that some processes which are intended to be beneficial to the offender will in fact be more onerous, in terms of the requirements they impose, than is justified by reference to the seriousness of the offence. This may be a problem with the outcomes of some restorative conferences, and there is therefore an argument in favour of taking steps to limit the impositions that may be made or 'agreed', or to require court approval of the outcome. The same difficulty may arise with some rehabilitative programmes offered as part of diversion: there is a developing range of programmes to tackle alcohol or substance abuse, to manage anger, etc, and the degree of commitment required may be considerable. Proponents of these programmes often claim that it is no use if offenders participate in them for less than the full course; but if this means months of attendance, and therefore considerable impositions by comparison with the seriousness of the offence, there are urgent questions of disproportionality to be addressed.

---

[110] For elaboration, see A. von Hirsch and A. Ashworth, *Proportionate Sentencing* (2005), Chs 1 and 2.

[111] *Weeks v United Kingdom* (1988) 10 EHRR 293, and other authorities discussed in Emmerson, Ashworth and Macdonald (eds), *Human Rights and Criminal Justice* (2nd ed, 2007), Ch 16.

[112] See D. van Zyl Smit and A. Ashworth, 'Disproportionate Sentences as Human Rights Violations' (2004) 67 *MLR* 541.

2.7 CONCLUSION: THE CRIMINAL PROCESS AND THE LIMITATIONS OF HUMAN RIGHTS

In this chapter we have begun to sketch a rights-based theory of the criminal process—that the process should have the twin goals of regulating the procedures for bringing suspected offenders to trial so as to produce accurate determinations, and of ensuring that fundamental rights are protected in those processes. We have offered arguments for our belief that this approach should be adopted in England and Wales—both on principle and because it is implicit in international documents such as the European Convention on Human Rights that now play a fundamental role in English law. However, we have also recognized the need to supplement the Convention rights and to develop a fuller statement of rights that would include (for example) the rights of young people and the rights of victims. We have also proposed separate objectives for dispositive decisions, notably the decision to divert a person from the criminal process without trial. We have not overlooked the many conflicts that inevitably occur in the criminal process and the many difficult decisions those require: the human rights framework has been offered as a way of dealing with those conflicts that has a firmer moral and political foundation than consequentialist theories and has greater integrity and transparency than approaches that simply refer to 'balancing'. However, two limitations of rights theories must be kept firmly in view—the gap between the law in action and the law in the books, and the political volatility of criminal justice systems.

(A) RIGHTS, RHETORIC AND REALITY

Theories of rights are essentially normative: they indicate what should or should not be done, what should be protected and when. To recognize a right is important, but to ensure that it is respected in practice is something different. Our approach to the criminal process based on human rights does not purport to be a description of the present system in operation. Thus we do not overlook the variable gap, sometimes small and sometimes large, between passing a law that recognizes and protects a right and ensuring that the right-holders are in a position to exercise that right as intended. Wherever relevant in this book we refer to empirical evidence that sheds light on whether certain rights or procedures are properly implemented in practice. We will argue that there are respects in which police decisions, decisions by Crown Prosecutors, decisions by magistrates at remand proceedings and decisions on the acceptance of pleas of guilty (to take just four examples) fail to give due protection to established rights. When we refer with approval to the statutory framework for conditional cautions under the Criminal Justice Act 2003, there is no assumption that the requirements are being observed in all cases in practice (see p 179 below). That remains to be seen, once there has been an opportunity for empirical research on conditional cautions.

Generally speaking, what is required to ensure that declared rights are actually respected is not only an ethical commitment on behalf of the relevant agency to respecting those rights (see Chapter 3 below), but also proper information to suspects/defendants about their rights and ready access to legal advice relating to their predicament. The same applies to information about victims' rights, and access to support or information through Victim Support or the Witness Service. There have been several improvements in recent years, but it is a longstanding complaint that neither suspects nor victims and witnesses have all the information they are entitled to expect about their rights and how to exercise them. If they do not, it is likely that there will be a significant gap between the law as declared and the law in practice.

(B) THE POLITICAL VOLATILITY OF THE CRIMINAL PROCESS

In recent years the criminal justice system has increasingly become a focus for political posturing.[113] It is not so much that the two leading political parties have conflicting approaches, but rather that they are trying to outdo one another in the 'toughness' of their rhetoric. In the mid-1990s the Conservatives bolstered their political cause through the words and policies of the then Home Secretary, Michael Howard, who proclaimed that 'prison works'. As the re-shaping of 'New Labour' began around that time, 'weak' policies on law and order were identified as a potential threat to its other policies and to electoral success: even after the 1997 election victory, by a margin of some 180 seats, the Labour Government continued to regard any 'weakness' in its criminal justice policies as a danger to its popularity—an analysis that attributes considerable influence to the media, sections of which would seize on any apparently 'weak' policies.

The Government knows, from its own research, that a prison-led policy of public protection is highly unlikely to succeed, even if it were defensible on other grounds. So few offences are reported, so few detected, and so few prosecuted, that increasing the use of imprisonment for the 2 or 3 per cent of offenders who fall to be sentenced by the courts is a far less propitious route to public protection than investment in crime prevention policies.[114] Yet the Government's pronouncements, for example in the White Paper of 2002 that preceded the Criminal Justice Act 2003[115] and in the more recent re-statement of its criminal justice priorities,[116] lay the greatest emphasis on the 'heavy end' of criminal justice—longer sentences for persistent criminals and for 'dangerous' offenders—and, while they mention community-based measures, fail to set out and publicize a truly evidence-based policy.

---

[113] See D. Downes and R. Morgan, 'No Turning Back: the Politics of Law and Order into the Millenium' in M. Maguire, R. Morgan and R. Reiner (eds), *The Oxford Handbook of Criminology* (4th ed, 2007); M. Tonry, *Punishment and Politics* (2004).

[114] A. Ashworth, 'Criminal Justice Reform: Principles, Human Rights and Public Protection' [2004] *Crim LR* 516.

[115] Home Office, *Justice for All* (2002).

[116] Ministry of Justice, *Punishment and Reform: our Approach to Managing Offenders* (2008).

Moreover, the Government's pronouncements rarely contain any reference to human rights issues. Although the Labour Government introduced the Human Rights Act, its criminal policy statements have tended to pay no attention to the issue, and often seem to make a virtue out of avoiding or minimizing human rights protections. A succession of reports from the Joint Committee on Human Rights have forced the government to be explicit about the relationship between legislative proposals and relevant human rights, which they have typically not done in policy statements. For example, when the Joint Committee on Human Rights examined the Criminal Justice Bill presented to Parliament in late 2002, it found many respects in which the Bill appeared to have been put together either in ignorance or in defiance of the Convention.[117] Similarly, its more recent scrutiny of provisions in the Policing and Crime Bill 2009 found various points on which human rights arguments had been either not considered or too lightly dismissed.[118]

If the Government were to try to defend this approach, it would probably be on the ground that it is well aware of the human rights issues, but that the challenge facing contemporary society is of a different order and therefore calls for exceptional measures. Rarely do the media or the Government talk about criminal policy in general. More commonly, they identify particular types of crime and criminal. More stringent or tougher measures are needed (we are told) for the fight against terrorism, for the war on drugs, to combat organized crime, and so forth. This might sound convincing if it were not placed in the context of a society that aspires to the rule of law and which has long proclaimed its adherence to various international treaties on human rights. It is, as we argued at p 43 above, a complete misconception to argue that human rights become less important whenever the detection and prosecution of serious crime is the objective. On the contrary, at a theoretical level human rights are safeguards against arbitrary action by governments, e.g. by failing to observe proper procedural protections when dealing with suspects and defendants. And in terms of the jurisprudence of the Strasbourg Court, there are many pronouncements showing that governments cannot simply remove safeguards under Articles 5 and 6 in the name of the fight against terrorism or other serious crimes.[119] No Government statements on the criminal process discuss these issues in relation to new policies. The rhetoric is all about taking tough measures and protecting victims. There is nothing about upholding human rights (which is also in the public interest), and the rhetoric of protecting victims would not be sustainable on a proper analysis of the ways of protecting people that are likely to be most effective on the available evidence. Our rights approach indicates a framework for dealing with apparent conflicts between individual rights and 'the public interest'—one that urges greater transparency about the weighting of

---

[117] Joint Committee on Human Rights, *Criminal Justice Bill: Further Report* (11th Report of Session 2002–03), paras 40–54.

[118] Joint Committee on Human Rights, *Legislative Scrutiny: Policing and Crime Bill (gangs injunctions)* (15th Report of Session 2008–09).

[119] See the cases cited in nn 86 and 87 above.

rights, and closer attention to claims about the need to diminish rights and the outcome of doing so, but no meta-principle that purports to resolve all difficult cases.[120]

FURTHER READING

DUFF A., FARMER, L., MARSHALL, S., and TADROS, V., *The Trial on Trial, volume 3: Towards a Normative Theory of the Criminal Trial*, Oxford: Hart Publishing, 2007.

REDMAYNE, M., 'Theorizing the Criminal Trial' (2009) 12 *New Criminal LR* 287.

ROACH, K., 'Criminal Process' in P. Cane and M. Tushnet (eds), *Oxford Handbook of Legal Studies*, Oxford: Oxford University Press, 2003.

Questions for Discussion

1. Do Packer's models of the criminal process still have a valuable role to play?
2. What is the purpose, or what are the purposes, of the criminal trial?
3. What should be the role of victims in decision making in the criminal process?
4. How should one decide which theory of the criminal process is the most satisfactory?

---

[120] See also Waldron, above n 87.

3

ETHICS, CONFLICTS
AND CONDUCT

Chapter 2 sketched a normative model of the criminal process in which the pursuit of a particular end—retributive justice—was constituted and constrained by respect for rights and other values. This chapter examines one way in which the demands of this rather abstract model can be put into practice: through the consideration of ethics. Ethics are important for a number of interconnected reasons: first, as we have just noted, ethical principles can help to close the gap between our aspirations and our day-to-day actions. This is reflected in the fact that ethical codes now exist to guide the conduct of a number of actors in the criminal process. Secondly, while the criminal process is structured by a framework of rules, discretionary decision making plays a crucial role. Rules always leave room for interpretation, and often deliberately preserve discretion. Such discretion should be exercised in an ethical way. A third reason why ethics are important is that the question of just what conduct is ethically right is often not a simple one to answer. It is not much use responding to someone who asks how to exercise their discretion by telling them to do so in a way that both pursues retributive justice and respects rights. This is in part because different actors in the criminal process play different roles, and we expect these roles to mould the way in which they act. Thus, to take the most obvious example, we expect the defence lawyer advising his client to act differently to the police officers who are questioning him. The consideration of ethics involves considering how such roles should guide conduct, and there is room for debate about the correct principles.[1] Finally, ethics are important because actors in the criminal process are constantly tempted to subvert the rules and principles intended to govern their conduct, even when the rules leave little room for interpretation. The criminal process deals with people who have done, or—the qualification is significant—are alleged to have done, all manner of unattractive things, and judgements of 'moral character' may lure officials into bending the rules in order to ensure that such people are convicted, or treated harshly.[2] This is perhaps the greatest challenge to the pursuit of justice in the criminal process—the

---

[1] Cf the classic articles by W. H. Simon, 'The Ethics of Criminal Defense' (1993) 91 *Mich LR* 1703 and D. Luban, 'Are Criminal Defenders Different?' (1993) 91 *Mich LR* 1729.

[2] On judgements of moral character, see, e.g., K. Hawkins, *Law as Last Resort* (2003), at 183, 243 and 334–5 on Health and Safety inspectors, and H. Parker, M. Sumner and G. Jarvis, *Unmasking the Magistrates* (1989) on the magistracy.

temptation to seek justice summarily. It is not only police officers who are inclined to subvert the rules or to act in a way inappropriate to their role; as we will see, defence lawyers, prosecutors and judges all face the same temptation. A strong commitment to ethics, and a clear understanding of the ethical implications of one's role in the system, are therefore cornerstones of the criminal process.

The chapter opens with a brief discussion of the idea of ethical conduct. Next it outlines some *un*ethical practices, and then attempts to examine and reconstruct some possible justifications for such practices. Consideration is then given to the problems of displacing the occupational cultures and other influences which may lead to resistance against change. Formal accountability systems are also discussed, and the chapter concludes with a consideration of the prospects for bringing about changes in the conduct of practitioners within the system.

3.1 RULES, ROLES AND ETHICS

Is there any need to discuss ethics when there are so many legal rules, codes, and guidelines impinging on the work of law enforcement agents? Is there really any room for moral disputation when we have such documents as the Police and Criminal Evidence Act 1984 (PACE) and its Codes of Practice, the Code for Crown Prosecutors, the Code of Practice for Victims of Crime, and countless recent statutes on criminal justice? Three good reasons may be offered for pressing ahead with ethical inquiries.

First, ethical principles should apply to those who lay down rules and guidelines as well as to those who are subject to them. Thus there should be no suggestion that ethical issues affect only the lower ranks: the decisions of members of the legislature, the Home Secretary, the Director of Public Prosecutions (the DPP), and the Lord Chief Justice should be equally subject to appraisal on ethical grounds. However, there should be no confusion between legal rules and moral or ethical principles. It is good that legal rules should be based on ethical principles, rather than (say) on short-term pragmatism, but the function of ethical principles is to supply strong reasons for adopting a particular rule. Insofar as incorporation of the European Convention on Human Rights into English law imports a kind of higher law, which even legislators should respect, this constitutes one formal source of ethical principles for policy-makers. But, as we saw in Chapter 2, the Convention does not contain all the rights and principles that ought properly to be upheld.

Secondly, there is no warrant for the view that the criminal justice system is entirely covered by rules and clear-cut guidance. Recent years have seen greater efforts to introduce various forms of guidance and accountability, but there are still vast tracts of discretion, some of it deliberate so as to enable flexibility, some eked out by practitioners to allow them to follow their preferred practices. Wherever there is discretion, and even where there are rules, there may be choices between following ethical principles and following other policies or preferences.

Thirdly, it is well known that there are strong occupational cultures among the various professional groups in the criminal justice system. The point is clearest in relation to the police. For example, a study of detectives for the Royal Commission on Criminal Justice concluded that a necessary step towards improving the situation would be 'raising CID officers' awareness of the faults in the traditional "detective cul-ture" ("macho" and "elitist" attitudes, belief that "rules are there to be bent", excessive secrecy and suspicion of outsiders, and so on) and the ease with which young officers are sucked into it, almost without realising it'.[3] In its report, the Royal Commission referred to 'the culture and approach of the Criminal Bar' as a possible obstacle to the success of some of its proposals for streamlining pre-trial procedure.[4] Research into the conduct of criminal defence lawyers has also shown how the culture of many solicitors' firms operates so as to adapt the law and the lawyer's role, in ways that differ from the formal rhetoric and procedures, and which result in less than full protec-tion for suspect-defendants.[5] There is also evidence that judges sitting in the Court of Appeal were received into an occupational culture which, for many years, resulted in a particularly restrictive approach to the exercise of the court's statutory powers.[6] In the face of such well-entrenched cultures, what are the prospects for rules, let alone guidelines or unfettered discretion? In practical terms these cultures seem to be direct competitors with ethical principles, partly because they often put sectional interests first, but partly also because they sometimes challenge the values of those who argue for the recognition of rights. Exploration of these occupational cultures will be one of the principal tasks in this chapter.

What kind of principle may be described as ethical? It should be a principle that is impartial as between persons, and for which one can give reasons which show a respect for the rights and interests that have a good claim to be protected. Impartiality in this context requires that no preference should be shown towards persons (whether sus-pects, victims, defendants, or whatever) on extraneous grounds such as wealth, social connections, sex, race, and so forth. It also forbids conduct based on the self-interest of the official or criminal justice practitioner, who ought to act out the ethical commit-ments attached to the assigned role (e.g. investigating officer, defence lawyer) and set aside personal convenience, profit or other extraneous motivation. As for rights and interests, this refers not merely to the interests discussed in Chapter 2 above, but also to the fundamental orientation of the criminal process towards either an inquisitorial or an adversarial approach. Although several of the procedures in English criminal justice blur the line between the two, there is little doubt that the fundamental orienta-tion is towards an adversarial model. This, in turn, invests various actors with certain role responsibilities.

---

[3] M. Maguire and C. Norris, *The Conduct and Supervision of Criminal Investigations* (1992).

[4] Royal Commission on Criminal Justice, *Report* (1993), para 7.36 on preparatory hearings.

[5] M. McConville, J. Hodgson, L. Bridges and A. Pavlovic, *Standing Accused* (1994); M. Travers, *The Reality of Law* (1997).

[6] R. Nobles and D. Schiff, *Understanding Miscarriages of Justice* (2000), Ch 3.

Thus the duty of the defence lawyer is 'to promote and protect fearlessly and by all lawful and proper means the lay client's best interests'.[7] In relation specifically to criminal defence, the lawyer must endeavour to protect the defendant 'from conviction except by a competent tribunal and upon legally admissible evidence sufficient to support conviction for the offence charged':[8] this requires the defence lawyer to contest all arguable issues, but not necessarily to take advantage of favourable errors made by the prosecutor or the court.[9] This is where the countervailing duty of the lawyer to the court, particularly the duty not to mislead the court, comes into play.[10] Thus when it is said that the defence lawyer's duty is that of 'obtaining an acquittal within the limits of lawful procedure',[11] the last six words demonstrate how the lawyer's duty to the court may override the duty to the client. The extent of the duty to the client is also bounded by the lawyer's personal responsibility for the way in which the defence is run (although the Court of Appeal will only overturn a conviction if the defence advocate was 'flagrantly incompetent').[12] There are several controversial issues in the ethics of defence lawyering, including those relating to the defence of someone who has admitted guilt, to defending where the prosecution or the court has made an error,[13] and to attacking the character of prosecution witnesses.[14] However, in this chapter we are concerned not only with the conflicts within the lawyer's role but also with the conflict between ethical principles and occupational cultures, as we will see in Part 2 below.

Whereas the defence lawyer's role is essentially partisan, that of the prosecuting lawyer should be impartial, not seeking convictions as such but taking on the role of a 'minister of justice'.[15] The prosecutor's goal should be to conduct the case dispassionately, seeking justice according to the law (not relying, for example, on inadmissible evidence) and disclosing to the defence all evidence that should be disclosed. As noted on pp 67–8 below, the failure of prosecuting lawyers to disclose evidence to the defence lay at the root of some of the notorious cases of miscarriage of justice. In the present context, the point about disclosure illustrates the way in which roles and ethics may be subject to alteration by statute: the disclosure rules were altered by the Criminal Procedure and Investigations Act 1996 and again by the Criminal Justice Act 2003,

---

[7] General Council of the Bar, *Code of Conduct*, para 203(a).   [8] *Ibid.*, Annex H, para 12.1.

[9] It appears that the distinction lies between errors of law (which the defence lawyer should draw to the court's attention) and errors of fact (which may be allowed to persist): for references and discussion, see M. Blake and A. Ashworth, 'Some Ethical Issues in Prosecuting and Defending Criminal Cases' [1998] *Crim LR* 16; M. Blake and A. Ashworth, 'Ethics and the Criminal Defence Lawyer' (2004) 7 *Legal Ethics* 167; E. Cape, 'Rebalancing the Criminal Justice Process: Ethical Challenges for Criminal Defence Lawyers' (2006) 9 *Legal Ethics* 56.

[10] General Council of the Bar, *Code of Conduct*, para 202.

[11] C. Humphreys, 'The Duties and Responsibilities of Prosecuting Counsel' [1955] *Crim LR* 739, at 746.

[12] E.g. *Nangle* [2001] *Crim LR* 506.   [13] See further the materials above, n 9.

[14] See the research by J. Temkin, 'Prosecuting and Defending Rape: Perspectives from the Bar' (2000) 27 *J Law & Soc* 219.

[15] General Council of the Bar, *Code of Conduct*, Annex H, para 11; R. J. Buxton, 'The Prosecutor as Minister of Justice' [2009] *Crim LR*.

and the roles (and ethical duties) of both prosecuting and defending lawyers must change with them.

3.2 IDENTIFYING 'UNETHICAL' PRACTICES

In order to provide a factual basis for the discussion in the rest of the chapter, it is now proposed to identify fairly briefly some seven presumptively unethical practices. Many of them are discussed in greater detail later in the book, but it is important at this early stage to illustrate the context in which ethical arguments take place. Whether the practices can properly be termed 'unethical' will not be determined until we have discussed the explanations for them, but they are discussed here because they appear to be unethical. There is no suggestion that all the practices are widespread, but it is believed that they occur on some occasions, and references are given to support this belief.

(A) 'HELPING THE POLICE WITH THEIR INQUIRIES'

One of the purposes of introducing new rules on detention in police stations under the Police and Criminal Evidence Act 1984 was to ensure that persons brought to police stations under arrest were only detained if it was necessary to do so, and if there was sufficient evidence for a charge.[16] Early research by McKenzie, Morgan and Reiner showed that custody officers routinely authorized detention without an examination of the sufficiency of evidence, and did so by reference to the need 'to secure or preserve evidence or to obtain evidence by questioning'.[17] A subsequent Home Office study found the same situation: 'it was exceptional for detention not to be authorised', and this happened in only one of some 4,000 cases.[18] This practice is unethical because it deprives suspects of protection against being detained unless that is absolutely necessary, a protection that Parliament intended to give them.[19]

(B) RIGHTS OF SUSPECTS

The 1984 Act and its Codes of Practice were also designed to lay down standards of fair treatment and to restate the courts' discretion to exclude evidence obtained in contravention of the standards. The reason behind these protections is to spare defendants

---

[16] Police and Criminal Evidence Act 1984, s 37.

[17] I. McKenzie, R. Morgan and R. Reiner, 'Helping the Police with their Inquiries: the Necessity Principle and Voluntary Attendance at the Police Station' [1990] *Crim LR* 22.

[18] C. Phillips and D. Brown, *Entry into the Criminal Justice System* (1998), 49.

[19] E. Cape, *Defending Suspects at Police Stations* (5th ed, 2006), 58–9, and citing (at 61) the statement of the Home Office Minister in 1984 that the detention must be necessary, 'not desirable, convenient or a good idea but necessary'.

intimidation, and to enhance the reliability of any evidence that is obtained. Yet the years since 1986 have seen a steady stream of cases in which police officers have been found to have departed from the Codes of Practice on Questioning and on Identification.[20]

(C) FAILURE TO INFORM SUSPECTS OF RIGHTS

Another purpose of the 1984 Act was to require the police to inform each suspect/ defendant of certain rights—the right to make a telephone call from the police station, the right to have someone informed of one's detention, and the right to have legal advice that is free, independent, and given in a private consultation. After the implementation of the new law in 1986 it was found that not all suspects were being informed of these rights.[21] The relevant Code of Practice was altered in 1991, and further research showed that the rate of informing suspects had increased but was still less than complete; almost all suspects were told of the right to legal advice, but only 73 per cent were told that it is free, 56 per cent were told that it is independent, and hardly any were told that the consultation would be private.[22] A subsequent Home Office study confirmed that the statement of rights was made in different ways at different police stations, suggesting that this might be connected to the differing rates of take-up of legal advice that were found.[23] Insofar as police officers give the statement in an unclear or unduly rapid fashion, or emphasize the possible problems (such as delay) in summoning legal advice, they probably engage in unethical conduct. The motivation may be that they regard the law as impeding the most effective approach to investigation.

(D) FAILURE TO DISCLOSE RELEVANT EVIDENCE

Similar motivation may underlie the failure by the police to disclose to the prosecution or the defence certain evidence in favour of the defence, which was a reason for quashing the convictions in the cases of the Maguire Seven, the Birmingham Six, and Judith Ward.[24] The Attorney-General's Guidelines on disclosure were not in force at the time of the original trials in these cases, but the principle of disclosure did exist. Similarly, in the case of the Maguire Seven, the outcome of certain tests carried out by the Forensic Science Service, with results favourable to the defendants, was not notified to the defence. Non-disclosure of forensic evidence also occurred in the cases of

---

[20] See generally Cape, *ibid.*, Ch 8; among the examples are *Forbes* [2001] 1 AC 473 and *Harris* [2003] EWCA Crim 174.

[21] A. Sanders and L. Bridges, 'Access to Legal Advice and Police Malpractice' [1990] *Crim LR* 494.

[22] D. Brown, T. Ellis and K. Larcombe, *Changing the Code: Police Detention under the Revised PACE Codes of Practice* (1993).

[23] Phillips and Brown, above n 18, 61.

[24] For further details, see J. Rozenberg, 'Miscarriages of Justice' in E. Stockdale and S. Casale (eds), *Criminal Justice under Stress* (1993).

the Birmingham Six and Judith Ward. These omissions can be regarded as unethical. Breaches of the disclosure rules were not confined to the 1970s, as subsequent appellate decisions demonstrate.[25] The rules on disclosure have since been changed twice, in 1996 and 2003.[26] Failure to follow statutory requirements conscientiously is unethical, whether it is the police, the prosecution, or the defence that is at fault.

(E) FAILURE TO PROTECT A CLIENT AT INTERVIEW

One of the reasons for allowing suspects the right to consult a lawyer at a police station is to ensure that the conduct of the police towards the suspect is scrupulously fair. However, in some cases legal advisers are reluctant to intervene to protect their client, allowing hostile and hectoring modes of questioning to pass without comment.[27] In clear cases this is unethical conduct by the legal adviser, particularly where the lawyer's motivation for failing to intervene is not related to advancing the interests of the particular lay client.

(F) FAILURE TO DISCONTINUE A WEAK CASE

A primary reason for introducing the Crown Prosecution Service (CPS) was to bring a professional prosecutorial review into the system, to prevent weak or inappropriate cases from going to court.[28] The CPS was given a power of discontinuance,[29] and was subsequently given the power to charge suspects ('statutory charging', discussed in Chapter 7 below). Insofar as there are still cases which the CPS pursue even though they know that there is insufficient evidence, perhaps to retain good relations with the police or out of a pro-conviction motivation inconsistent with the 'minister of justice' role that prosecutors are meant to adopt,[30] this is unethical.

(G) AVOIDANCE OF 'PRESUMPTIVE' MODE OF TRIAL

Under the existing system for determining mode of trial, various cases have arisen in which the prosecution has preferred an either-way charge, the defendant has elected Crown Court trial, and the prosecution has thereupon dropped the either-way charge and brought a charge that is triable summarily only, in a magistrates' court. Defendants have challenged these tactics by means of judicial review, and the Divisional Court has held that in general the choice of charge lies within the discretion of the prosecutor so long as the substituted charge is not inappropriate and there is no bad faith,

---

[25] E.g. *Fergus* (1994) 98 Cr App R 313.   [26] For discussion, see Ch 9.2 below.

[27] See, e.g., D. Roberts, 'Questioning the Suspect: the Solicitor's Role' [1993] *Crim LR* 368, and J. Baldwin, 'Legal Advice at the Police Station' [1993] *Crim LR* 371.

[28] Royal Commission on Criminal Procedure, *Report* (1981), para 7.6.

[29] Prosecution of Offences Act 1985, s 23, discussed in Ch 7 below.

[30] J. Baldwin, 'Understanding Judge Ordered and Directed Acquittals in the Crown Court' [1997] *Crim LR* 536, esp at 550–2; see further Ch 7 below.

oppression, or prejudice.[31] The CPS Code now instructs prosecutors not to prefer a higher charge in this situation, save in exceptional circumstances. It remains possible to alter the charges before the mode of trial proceedings have begun, which also raises ethical issues. It is one thing to lower the charge to ensure that the case is heard quickly (avoiding the waiting time for the Crown Court) if there are good reasons for this, perhaps connected with victims or other witnesses; it is quite another thing to do this in the hope of taking advantage of the higher conviction rate in magistrates' courts. Admittedly the ethical argument here is complex, but the temptations for prosecutors require careful assessment.

3.3 UNDERSTANDING 'UNETHICAL' BEHAVIOUR

The preceding section has set out some examples of behaviour that might be described as 'unethical', in the sense that it fails to show proper respect for citizens and often removes, circumvents or weakens certain rights that should be accorded to the suspect or defendant. There may be other sources of miscarriages of justice, but the focus here is on conduct that may be said to involve some conscious circumvention of the rules. Suspending final judgement on whether these practices are to be termed unethical, we must first inquire into the reasons for them.

There is often a tendency to regard practices of this kind as the product of individuals, exercising a discretion unconstrained by context or by colleagues. This is the 'rotten apple' theory, assuming that a small number of 'rogue' individuals decide to defy the rules. This ignores the fact that these individuals work in a professional context in which several influences such as organizational rules and occupational pressures operate, sometimes fuelled by the unrealistic expectations of the public and others.[32] Thus research into the police has often concluded that much police behaviour is influenced by a 'cop culture' that is spread widely through the organization. There is no need here to enter into an extensive analysis of the findings of the various researchers. It is sufficient to mention four elements that seem to be at the core of 'cop culture':

(a) support for colleagues' decisions and the inappropriateness of close supervision;

(b) what is termed 'the macho image', which includes heavy drinking and physical presence, and may extend to sexist and racist attitudes;

---

[31] *R v Liverpool Stipendiary Magistrate, ex p Ellison* [1989] *Crim LR* 369; cf the similar legal and ethical problems raised by preferring a new charge and thereby obtaining an extension of time limits, *R v Leeds Crown Court, ex p Wardle* [2001] UKHL 12 and *R v J* [2005] 1 AC 562.

[32] K. Hawkins, 'The Use of Legal Discretion: Perspectives from Law and Social Science' in K. Hawkins (ed), *The Uses of Discretion* (1992), at 22.

(c) the sense of mission in police work; and

(d) the idea that rules are there to be used creatively and 'bent' if necessary to achieve 'justice'.[33]

The suggestion is that these and similar attitudes are widespread, not that they are universal. There may be differences from division to division, particularly between rural and urban areas. There may be individuals or groups, particularly women and some younger police officers, who accept few or no aspects of the culture. Senior officers may argue that changes are taking place, but the stronghold of the culture has always been in the lower ranks. That there are negative elements in police cultures has been observed so frequently that their existence (even dominance)[34] in some quarters cannot be doubted, but the cultures are diverse and complex and certainly not monolithic.[35]

In an attempt to unravel the reasons which underlie the culture, we may begin by considering (a) support for colleagues' decisions and the inappropriateness of close supervision. Two research studies for the Royal Commission on Criminal Justice in the 1990s found that the supervision of junior officers in the conduct of inquiries and in questioning was not the norm and was often regarded as a breach of the trust that should be shown in every officer's skills.[36] This is linked to the idea of police solidarity and the duty to support a fellow officer, although it may have a darker side, as the Royal Commission recognized in its reference to officers and civilian staff being 'deterred by the prevailing culture from complaining openly about malpractice'.[37] To some extent the isolated position of the police in society may breed a form of solidarity and defensiveness and the culture may reflect the differing perspectives of police officers 'at the sharp end' and those officers who are managers, with the lower ranks covering for one another and trying to shield from senior officers various deviations from the rules.[38]

There is well-established evidence of the existence in the British police of (b), what is termed the 'macho image', manifest in the physical dangers of the job, 'the alcoholic and sexual indulgences' of male police officers, and the struggle of women police officers to gain acceptance.[39] There are, however, important points to be made about this aspect of 'cop culture'. First, it does not follow that there is a precise correlation between the way the police talk and behave when off-duty, and their conduct of their

---

[33] For detailed discussion, see, e.g., J. Skolnick, *Justice without Trial* (1966); J. Chan, 'Changing Police Culture' (1996) 36 *BJ Crim* 109; D. Dixon, *Law in Policing: Legal Regulation and Police Practices* (1997); S. Choongh, 'Policing the Dross: a Social Disciplinary Model of Policing' (1998) 38 *BJ Crim* 623.

[34] B. Loftus, 'Dominant Culture Interrupted' (2008) 48 *BJ Crim* 756, and B. Loftus, *Police Culture in a Changing World* (2009).

[35] See the review by J. Foster, 'Police Cultures' in T. Newburn (ed), *Handbook of Policing* (2003), and now Loftus (above n 34).

[36] J. Baldwin, *Supervision of Police Investigations in Serious Criminal Cases* (1992); Maguire and Norris, above n 3.

[37] Royal Commission on Criminal Justice, *Report*, para 2.65.

[38] R. Reiner, *The Politics of the Police* (3rd ed, 2000), 101–3.

[39] *Ibid.*, 97–8, for the evidence.

duties.[40] The demanding nature of police work may be said to make it necessary to 'let off steam' when off-duty or in the canteen, and it does not necessarily mean that this translates into conduct at work.[41] Secondly, on the allegation that racism forms part of the police culture, Robert Reiner suggests that some interpretations fail to take proper account of the nature of police work in a society that places ethnic minorities at a disadvantage in many respects.[42] Indeed, Reiner argues more generally that, just as it is unrealistic to regard police malpractices as stemming from isolated individuals without reference to the wider police culture, it is equally unrealistic to focus on the culture without reference to the social structures that contribute to and sustain it. Account must be taken of the role assigned to the police in society—as a form of social service that has to deal with the least advantaged people, as well as meeting targets that often imply a degree of control over social events that they simply cannot exert.

In a sense the typical elements of 'cop culture' may appear to be odd bedfellows of (c), the sense of mission in police work. This is a serious-minded, socially conservative cluster of attitudes which celebrate the position of the police as a 'thin blue line' standing between order and chaos. Of course it is not claimed that the mission, any more than the culture, is monolithic. Indeed, the conflict in police ideologies between advocates of 'zero tolerance' and advocates of the 'problem-solving' approach demonstrates one clear difference. The research evidence regards the mission as strengthened by seeing the police as being on the side of the right, serving society and ranged against offenders and other miscreants who are in the wrong. Reiner describes the subtle interplay of three themes: 'of mission, hedonistic love of action, and pessimistic cynicism' that constitute the core of the police outlook.[43] Many officers join the police with a sense of mission, in terms of defending society and its institutions against attack and disorder, and then develop a kind of cynicism about social trends that seem to threaten existing ways of doing things. The Royal Commission appeared to accept some such view:

'We recognize that police malpractice, where it occurs, may often be motivated by an over-zealous determination to secure the conviction of suspects believed to be guilty in the face of rules and procedures which seem to those charged with the investigation to be weighted in favour of the defence.'[44]

To be sceptical about the moral quality of this police mission would be easy: it certainly contains its contradictions, in that it purports to emphasize established moral values when there is evidence that some officers rejoice in various sexual exploits, and in that it adopts a puritanical attitude towards drug-users when police alcoholism is a long-standing problem.[45] Yet, these contradictions apart, there is a true sense in which

---

[40] C. Hoyle, *Negotiating Domestic Violence* (1998), Ch 4, for a sustained discussion of both empirical evidence and theoretical interpretations.

[41] P. A. J. Waddington, 'Police (Canteen) Culture: an Appreciation' (1999) 39 *BJ Crim* 286.

[42] Reiner, above n 38, 98–9 and 124–34; cf Foster (above n 35), 215–18.

[43] Reiner, above n 38, 90.   [44] Royal Commission on Criminal Justice, *Report*, para 1.24.

[45] Reiner, above, n 38, 98.

the police are performing an essential and central social function. To this extent both the term 'police force' and its modern successor, 'police service', contain elements of realism. There is nothing unhealthy in having a sense of mission about that, any more than it is unhealthy for doctors, nurses, or even lawyers to have a sense of mission. Just as people are right to expect committed medical care when ill or injured, so citizens are entitled to expect committed official action when they fall victim to a crime or in the face of threats to good order. Often, this amounts to the protection of the weak against the predatory. But while the vital nature of this social function cannot be disputed, its definition can be—not least when it leads to forms of so-called 'noble cause corruption', with officers succumbing to the temptation to seek justice summarily, and to regard outcomes as more important than processes.[46] Similar conflicts may arise in the context of 'consumer demand' for certain services from the police, which leads to government targets and to dilemmas for officers.[47] Elements of police culture evidently define the police mission differently from Parliament, for example, since police officers often express contempt for 'legal restrictions'. There is no question that the maintenance of good order counts, but there is room for debate about what counts as the maintenance of good order.

This leads us directly to (d): the idea that rules are there to be used creatively and bent. The sense of mission may be so powerful that it displaces respect for the laws. There are two strands to this. The first emphasizes the use of the criminal law as a resource for legitimating or reinforcing police handling of a situation: the police officer has available a range of offences with which to support his or her authority, and may decide whether or not to invoke one of them as a reason for arrest and charge.[48] Of course this is hardly applicable to crimes such as murder, rape, and armed robbery, but it can be applied to the range of public order offences, obstruction and assault on police officers, and a number of other charges. The primary objective of the police may be to keep the peace and to manage situations; in this they use and exert authority; anyone who resists that authority may be arrested and even charged. The second strand concerns the various procedural rules about questioning, notably the Codes of Practice under PACE. One reason these rules are broken from time to time may be that they are seen as unwise impediments to proper police work, standing in the way of vigorous questioning which will get at the truth, or (sometimes) will produce the results which senior police officers or the media seem to want. On the one hand there is pressure arising from the high expectations of others; on the other there is a belief that those expectations cannot be met when lawmakers fail to understand the realities of police work.

Compared with the police, rather less is known about the occupational cultures of other groups within the criminal justice system. But it should not be thought that

---

[46] See P. Neyroud, 'Policing and Ethics' in T. Newburn (ed), *Handbook of Policing* (2003), 587.

[47] See P. Neyroud, 'Ethics in Policing: Performance and the Personalization of Accountability in British Policing and Criminal Justice' (2006) 9 *Legal Ethics* 16.

[48] For a classic study on this, see E. Bittner, 'The Police on Skid Row: a Study in Peacekeeping' (1967) 32 *American Sociological Review* 699.

other groups do not have working cultures which pull against the ethical discharge of their role responsibilities, and a few words can be said here about defence solicitors and crown prosecutors. In the detailed study some 20 years ago of a number of criminal defence practices in England and Wales by McConville, Hodgson, Bridges and Pavlovic, several unethical practices were discovered at various stages. Once again, the researchers did not claim that all criminal defence practices operated in this way: indeed, they pointed out that some practices were well run and properly orientated. But they drew attention to some defence lawyers' failure to protect clients in police stations from improper questioning,[49] encouraging or even engineering a plea of guilty in spite of the client's inclinations,[50] 'selling out' clients in court by using a particular phraseology that made it clear to magistrates that the lawyer believed that the client's instructions were unworthy of belief.[51] Why might defence lawyers and their staff indulge in these and other kinds of unethical behaviour? The research led to various suggestions. One of these is that some of the practices are driven by financial considerations, arising from the structure of the legal aid system. There was also evidence that some defence lawyers subscribed to what, in police language, may be termed 'toe-rag theory': that particular clients (or clients of a particular kind, or from a certain family or housing estate) are guilty anyway, are always committing crimes, and therefore it is pointless to go through the motions of a 'full and fearless defence'.[52] This approach may be underpinned by a desire to keep 'on the right side' of the police and the courts where possible, rather than losing credibility by mounting a vigorous defence of a presumptively guilty villain. This led the authors to suggest that one of the defects may be in the training of solicitors, in that it fails to emphasize the centrality of human rights to the defence lawyer's role responsibilities. In other words, the adversarial system of criminal justice cannot work properly if and to the extent that lawyers fail to provide 'full and fearless' defence of their clients,[53] let alone if they allow their moral judgement of certain clients to detract from their proper role responsibility. On the other hand, as Ed Cape has argued, some recent reforms have tended to undermine the proper adversarial elements in criminal justice, therefore requiring more from the defence lawyer in order to protect the defendant's rights.[54] Moreover, ethical constraints do not pull in a single direction: thus some defence lawyers may use cross-examination to attack witnesses in a way or to a degree that strains the boundaries of ethics, sometimes to create a good impression with the client rather than because there really is a material inconsistency in a witness's story.[55]

---

[49] McConville et al, above n 5, 61–2, 112–5 and 124.

[50] *Ibid.*, 70 and 194ff; also Travers, above n 5, Chs 5 and 6.

[51] *Ibid.*, 180–1; see also A. Hucklesby, 'Remand Decision Makers' [1997] *Crim LR* 269, at 278–9.

[52] A. Mulcahy, 'The Justifications of "Justice"' (1994) 34 *BJ Crim* 411.

[53] See further M. McConville, 'Plea Bargaining: Ethics and Politics' in S. Doran and J. Jackson (eds), *The Judicial Role in Criminal Proceedings* (2000); L. Bridges, 'Ethics of Representation on Guilty Pleas' (2006) 9 *Legal Ethics* 80.

[54] E. Cape (above n 9).

[55] McConville et al, above n 5, 219; also P. Rock, *The Social World of an English Crown Court* (1993), Ch 2.

What about unethical behaviour by crown prosecutors? In this sphere there is considerably less research to draw upon, but there is some evidence that crown prosecutors sometimes resolve the conflicting pressures upon them by indulging in unethical conduct. One example already given is that prosecutors may pursue a weak case, even though aware of the weakness, for reasons which can only be described as unethical—for example, a desire to keep 'on the right side' of the police, or even agreement with the police view that the defendant deserves to be put through a trial.[56] A closely-related example might be where a key exhibit or a vital witness goes missing at the eleventh hour: the ethical approach might be to discontinue, or at least to draw the predicament to the attention of the defence, whereas continuing with the case in the hope that the loss will not come to light is surely unethical. If it is accepted that the role of the prosecutor, even in an adversarial system, is to act as a minister of justice, these and related practices should be condemned as unethical.

3.4 JUSTIFYING 'UNETHICAL' BEHAVIOUR BY CHALLENGING THE ETHICS

In the foregoing paragraphs we have discussed possible reasons for the occupational cultures of various criminal justice agencies and for resulting conduct which appears unethical. One element running through these explorations is that some, even many, of those who act in the ways described may argue that their behaviour is ultimately ethical. In other words, they may claim the moral high ground, and argue that the notions of ethics being relied upon here are flawed, limited and inappropriate.

(A) ARGUMENTS FOR CIRCUMVENTING RULES

In order to establish the context for any such redefining of the ethical, we might consider three standpoints that appear to ooze practicality and good sense, particularly among those who work in particular parts of the criminal justice system. The first, already mentioned in one context, is the argument that certain rules should be circumvented because the rule makers do not understand the practical problems. The second is that it is wrong to expect police, prosecutors, etc to operate with 'their hands tied behind their backs'. And the third is that, when the CPS drops a case, or when a court gives a lenient sentence, or even when the Court of Appeal quashes a conviction, this is bad for morale in the criminal justice system. All these standpoints are connected, but they deserve brief discussion individually.

---

[56] Baldwin, above n 30; see also J. Jackson, 'Ethical Implications of the Enhanced Role of the Crown Prosecutor' (2006) 9 *Legal Ethics* 35.

Is it right to circumvent rules on the ground that the rule makers do not understand the day-to-day, on-the-ground problems of the criminal process? The claim is heard in various quarters. It is heard among some police officers in relation to PACE and its Codes of Practice: these are restrictions imposed by people who expect 'results' and yet do not understand the difficulties the police have to encounter. A similar claim might be heard among barristers who resent the procedural imperatives and preparation times associated with plea and case management hearings and other pre-trial assessments.[57] There are three problems with a claim of this kind. First, there is the constitutional argument: any official or public organization that substitutes its own judgement for one reached through the appropriate democratic channels is behaving unconstitutionally. Both the police and lawyers' groups are well able to put their points in political debate, and should therefore accept the outcome in their work. Secondly, there is the values argument: the claim assumes that crime control, in a fairly absolute form, is the only value that is in the public interest. It gives no weight to the protection of the rights of suspects, particularly in terms of the importance of procedures rather than merely outcomes. And thirdly, there is the evidential argument: is it really true that 'the job' cannot be done if the restrictions are observed? In fact this is less likely to be a matter of evidence than a question of values again, since the claim that the job cannot be done suppresses the unarticulated clause, 'within the prevailing culture'. If a different culture prevailed, perhaps the job could be done. One can only plausibly assert that it cannot be done if one assumes no change in the culture. These three arguments expose the weaknesses of the claim that it may be justifiable to circumvent rules made by out-of-touch rule makers. They apply no less to the view said to obtain among some magistrates' clerks some years ago, that High Court rulings were there to be circumvented because 'the judges did not understand the practicalities, e.g. of dealing with truculent, often regular, customers, or a busy court schedule'.[58] This, again, seems to have been based on the assumption that the conviction of the 'guilty' is important above all else.

The second claim is similar in some respects. It is that society expects the police to combat crime with their hands tied behind their backs, or that society expects prosecutors to obtain convictions with one hand tied behind their backs. The precise formulation varies, but the target is always the 'restrictions' imposed, usually by the legislature but sometimes by the higher judiciary. The claim could be countered by means of the three arguments deployed above—the constitutional point, the values argument, and the question of evidence. However, another argument is worth raising here: the assumption that respecting the rights of suspects significantly diminishes the number of convictions and therefore the protection of the public and of victims. This is a complicated argument, requiring considerable space to develop and to rebut. Suffice it to say here that no clear evidence has been found that the adverse inferences

---

[57] Royal Commission on Criminal Justice, *Report*, para 7.36; Auld Report, *Review of the Criminal Courts* (2001), 490–2.

[58] The words of a magistrates' clerk, quoted by A. Rutherford, *Criminal Justice and the Pursuit of Decency* (1993), 62.

from silence permitted for some 15 years since the Criminal Justice and Public Order Act 1994 have produced a significant increase in convictions. They have produced changes in working practices within the criminal process, as Home Office research demonstrates,[59] but the failure to meet the objectives of increasing the number of convictions—and critics always argued that this might mean an increase in wrongful convictions—suggests that the rather complicated legal distinctions that have grown up around the 1994 Act are simply not worthwhile and that the adverse inference provisions should be abolished.[60] Thus giving protection to suspects does not necessarily mean fewer convictions: it is not a zero-sum game, as it were.

The third claim is that it is bad for police morale when the CPS decides against pursuing a particular case, contrary to the wishes of the police. Parallel claims are sometimes heard when a court gives a low sentence on conviction, and there is also the suggestion that one reason why station sergeants tend not to refuse charges from officers who bring in arrestees is that it might affect morale. Now as an empirical proposition this claim may well be correct. Such events may reduce police morale, as may new restrictions on their questioning of suspects, changes in their pay and conditions, and several other matters. The problem here is whether one should defer to the conservatism that underlies the morale of many professions, including the police, a conservatism no doubt linked with a sturdy defence of the police mission. The police mission is therefore a crucial element in any attempt to redefine the ethical approach. What kind of ethics, it might be asked, could call into question the vigorous pursuit of the fundamental social functions of crime prevention and conviction of the guilty?

(B) RE-ASSESSING THE ETHICAL APPROACH

To answer this question, we might begin by constructing a model version of the mission. Some of the main elements have been described above, but there is a need for a rounded version that could fit the words and opinions of police officers. The key element is crime control: this is surely a primary objective of the criminal justice system. It means that law observance should be maximized. In this the police are inevitably in the front line, having peacekeeping functions that (in terms of time spent) outstrip the processing of suspected offenders. A second element is that, where the interests of the defendant conflict with those of the victim or society, priority should be given to the latter. A third and connected element, following from the first two, is that the police should pursue this society-centred approach so far as is possible, exploiting any discretion left by the criminal justice system to further the conviction of those whom they believe to be guilty. Taken together, these elements of crime control and the protection of society may be treated as establishing a powerful

---

[59] T. Bucke, R. Street and D. Brown, *The Right of Silence: The Impact of the Criminal Justice and Public Order Act 1994* (2000).

[60] D. Birch, 'Suffering in Silence: a Cost-Benefit Analysis of section 34 of the Criminal Justice and Public Order Act 1994' [1999] *Crim LR* 769.

case in favour of the police mission. If we are not to descend into anarchy, someone has to do it. Better that it be done in a committed way than without any sense of its social importance.

Assuming that there is some truth in this account, is it defensible? Almost every step suffers from confusion which, when examined, mixes overstatement with understatement and neglects important features of social life. It would be easy to claim that this is because this version of the police mission has been formulated in a way favourable to the thesis being advanced: but the counter-arguments below can be ranged against any other version of the police mission that keeps faith with what has been found by on-the-ground research.[61] The counter-arguments are these.

The first element refers to crime control as if it were to be pursued without regard to any other values. Is it plausible to advance such an uncomplicated notion? To take an extreme but telling example, does it suggest that the police should be free to use repressive measures wherever they regard them as appropriate, or that torture should be available for use on those suspected of serious crimes? If the answers are negative, as they should be, then we need to adopt a more sophisticated and sensitive notion than 'crime control'. Many people might accept at first blush that crime control is the ultimate aim of the criminal justice system, but on reflection they would surely recognize that it ought not to be pursued without qualification. That would lead to a police state.

The second element is that priority should be given to the victim or society over the interests of the suspect/defendant. In the vernacular this might be called 'toe-rag theory', since its essence is that the interests of the 'innocent and good' should be preferred over those of the suspect or defendant. As one constable stated some years ago, 'Speaking from a policeman's point of view it doesn't give a damn if we oppress law-breakers, because they're oppressors in their own right.'[62] This seems to suggest that accused persons should have no rights, or few rights, or at least rights that can be overridden when that is necessary in the public interest (as interpreted by the police). This is to turn the idea of rights on its head. The whole idea of rights is that they respect the individual's autonomy and ensure that the individual is protected from certain kinds of inappropriate behaviour and is furnished with certain assistance when he or she is in the hands of public officials. As we saw in Chapter 2 above, rights are essentially anti-utilitarian claims, in the sense that they represent claims that the individual not be treated in certain ways even if that might handicap pursuit of some collective good. However, the idea of priority for 'the interests of society' seems to accord the individual suspect or defendant no particular rights, and to deny the whole legitimacy of human rights such as those incorporated in the European Convention and discussed at pp 30–6 above.[63] Moreover, it does so at a stage before the suspect or

---

[61] E.g. the findings of Maguire and Norris, above n 3.   [62] Quoted by Reiner, above n 38, 89.

[63] This is not to overlook the importance of victims' rights, which may on occasion conflict with those of suspects and defendants. But, again, there is a difference between victims' interests and the public interest: for further discussion, see pp 51–4 above.

defendant has been convicted, thereby affirming a strong presumption of guilt arising from the investigating officer's belief. Is it really acceptable to place so much emphasis on the judgement of one or more police officers, especially if one element in the cop culture is a mutual support and respect for the skills of others which frowns on routine supervision?

These arguments also show the weakness of the third element, always seeking to promote the interests of society against those of the suspect. This is flawed for various reasons. Suspects are members of society. Even members of society who are unlikely to be suspected of crime might accept that those who are suspected should be accorded some rights. Few would agree that it should be for the police to decide which suspects should be accorded rights and which not. The notorious cases of miscarriage of justice make us well aware that police officers' judgements of someone's guilt or innocence should not be determinative. Surely the ethical approach for the police is to ensure that evidence is collected fairly and then presented to the court for its adjudication. Upholding the right to a fair trial requires procedural fairness in the gathering of evidence and in the construction of the case.

The conclusion is therefore irresistible that the 'police mission' described above cannot claim the moral high ground: it is not a 'noble cause,' and does not justify officers in seeking to do justice summarily. It overstates the notion of crime control by assuming that this should be pursued either without qualification or with only such qualifications as the police deem appropriate. It assumes that respect for the rights of suspects is bound to detract from crime control, and does so for insufficient reason. In this it understates the importance of respect for human rights, in terms of fair procedures for those suspected of crime. And, like the 'balancing' approaches criticized in Chapter 2, it shows no appreciation of the subtlety and structures of arguments about the reach of human rights, and rather tends to assume that human rights should be overridden whenever it can be said to be in the public interest to do so.

Any challenge by prosecutors to the ethical approach might take a similar form: the essence would be that certain rules and procedures stand in the way of what is right in terms of crime control. For example, John Baldwin found that some crown prosecutors would run a relatively weak case where the charge was a serious one: he quotes one as saying that 'the more serious the case and the more finely balanced it is, the more you stretch the point'. He concludes that 'some CPS lawyers share a common value system with the police, a core element of which is that serious cases ought to be prosecuted, almost irrespective of considerations as to evidential strength'.[64] The supporting argument would be, therefore, that this is necessary to ensure that wrong-doers are brought to book, and that the 'stretching' of the rules is justified by that end. The counter-arguments are (a) that this is not the prosecutor's function in an adversarial system, since the prosecutor should act as a minister of justice who is not concerned to maximize the number of convictions but to ensure

---

[64] Baldwin, above n 30, 551.

that the due process of the law is carried through; and (b) that the purported justification that 'there is a lot more at stake in letting a potential rapist, murderer or child abuser off the hook'[65] overlooks what is at stake for the individual defendant, which is why the Royal Commission of 1981 insisted that 'a realistic prospect of conviction', not simply a prima facie case, should be required before a defendant is put through a trial.[66] No doubt the CPS would regard Baldwin's findings as outdated, but unfortunately there has been no independent research into prosecutors' working practices since then.

3.5 DISCRETION AND ACCOUNTABILITY

It will be evident from the foregoing paragraphs that many of the decisions to be taken by criminal justice agencies are characterized by discretion rather than by binding rules. As Keith Hawkins puts it:

'Discretion arising from a number of sources suffuses the processes of law enforcement and regulation. Discretion is plastic, shaped and given form to some extent by the institutions of law and legal arrangements and more substantially by decision-makers' framing behaviour. Systems of formal rules, for all their appearance of precision and specificity, work in only imprecise ways. Indeed, precision and consistent practice are not necessarily assisted by the drafting of ever more elaborate schemes of rules. The legal system is not neatly carved up by smoothly functioning institutional arrangements, but in reality, as a loosely coupled set of subsystems, is more messy, with internal inefficiencies and conflicts. Those enforcing rules may seek to attain the broad aim of a legal mandate in general terms, but the specific question of whether and how a particular rule applies in a particular circumstance will inevitably be reserved for, or assumed within, the discretion of the legal actor concerned.'[67]

Thus, as we have seen in this chapter, whether there are rules or areas of discretion, occupational cultures and working practices may exert an influence on how people with power in the criminal process actually operate. One way of trying to combat this is through codes of ethics, but their prospects of success are variable. One institutional approach to ensuring that the various authorities fulfil their functions and exercise their powers as they ought to is through systems of accountability. We have already seen how values such as the protection of declared rights (of victims and suspects or offenders) and the prevention of abuse of power by officials might be threatened if the policies or the practices of a law enforcement agency diverge from the purposes of the system. Methods of accountability should include proper scrutiny of general policies, rules, and/or guidelines for decision making, active supervision of practice, avenues for challenging decisions and openness rather than secrecy at key stages.

---

[65] A senior crown prosecutor, quoted by Baldwin, *ibid.*   [66] For further discussion, see Ch 7 below.
[67] K. Hawkins, *Law as Last Resort* (2003), 424–5.

In a democratic form of society, issues of public policy should be decided by the legislature. However, in matters of law enforcement the tendency has been for Parliament to avoid such issues and to leave them to each agency itself, usually without any check other than the formal requirement to submit annual reports to the House of Commons. Thus agencies such as the HM Revenue and Customs, the Environment Agency and the Health and Safety Commission are relatively free to determine their own policies: although some of their procedures are authorized by statute, there is no overall body that reviews the policies and practices of these agencies, despite their tremendous significance for the reach of the criminal process. On the other hand, the tendency has been to draw the police increasingly under a system of central control. Although there remains a considerable degree of local accountability, the thrust of the first part of the Police Reform Act 2002 is to give statutory authority for increased central control, giving greater powers to the Home Secretary and maintaining the role of HM Inspectorate of Constabulary as a principal means of accountability.

More generally, law enforcement bodies are subject to scrutiny from various government and parliamentary sources. The Select Committee procedure applies, and thus the Justice Committee examines the performance of such organizations as the police, the CPS, the Forensic Science Service and the Prison Service. Within Government, there is also the role of the Audit Commission in assessing the performance of agencies. The existence of these bodies adds to accountability, even though their direct powers are limited. Perhaps of greater operational impact are the inspectorates in the criminal justice system. The Probation Service, the Prison Service and the CPS (as well as the police) are overseen by Her Majesty's Inspectors, who issue annual reports that receive considerable publicity. However, there are other major law enforcement agencies that stand outside any such system of independent inspection: neither HM Revenue and Customs, nor the Environment Agency, Health and Safety Commission or any of the other so-called regulatory agencies is subject to inspection, and there is certainly no such body to oversee the work of defence lawyers who receive criminal legal aid money, let alone the work of the judiciary.

Are law enforcement agencies accountable to the courts? There is a number of public law doctrines available, but the tendency has been to confine judicial review to the outer limits of unreasonableness (by applying the *Wednesbury* principle).[68] In recent years there have been some cases of successful judicial review of certain policies for and against prosecution,[69] but the prevailing attitude remains one of reluctance.

Accountability is an important feature of a criminal justice system. It encourages transparency, it may enhance the protection of the rights of individuals, and it helps to ensure that the power entrusted to law enforcement authorities is not abused. However, it is wrong to rely on *post hoc* accountability methods to secure these desirable goals.

---

[68] See P. Craig, 'Grounds for Judicial Review: Substantive Control over Discretion' in D. J. Feldman (ed), *English Public Law* (2nd ed, 2009).

[69] See Chs 6 and 7 below.

If more members of the public can be drawn into the criminal process, whether as lay visitors in police stations or through jury service, that increases transparency. But the key objective is to ensure that rules and guidelines are applied faithfully, and not limited in their practical effect because their purpose and spirit are not accepted by those who are supposed to apply them. It will therefore be argued that there is a key role for training and for ethical orientation.

3.6 CRIMINAL JUSTICE REFORM THROUGH ETHICS

Law enforcement agencies and the administration of criminal justice are governed by masses of legislative rules, and yet it is well established that: (i) even rules can be adapted, (ii) there are wide areas of discretion, and (iii) there must continue to be some areas of discretion. One step, to promote respect for 'rule of law' ideals and to avoid the kind of arbitrariness against which Articles 5 and 6 of the Convention are intended as safeguards, is to attempt to structure discretion by the use of guidance and guidelines. Other common features of reform proposals are better training of criminal justice personnel and better lines of accountability. Measures of this kind, espoused in various forms by such politically disparate groups as the 1993 Royal Commission on Criminal Justice after their review of criminal justice processes and by Michael McConville, Andrew Sanders and Roger Leng at the end of their sharply critical research report on police and prosecution services 20 years ago,[70] are now recognized to be far more promising than mere changes in legal rules.

The reason for this is the strength of occupational cultures within such key agencies as the police, the CPS, the various regulatory inspectorates, defence solicitors, the criminal Bar, the Forensic Science Service, and so on. More has been said here about the occupational culture of the police, to some extent justifiably since they form the principal filter into the criminal justice system, but we have also reviewed evidence on occupational cultures within the CPS, among defence lawyers, and even among appellate judges. What is noticeable about at least some of the occupational cultures in criminal justice is that their concern is not simply to preserve established working practices or to defend traditional territories of influence, but also to see that 'justice' is done. This is the sense of mission. Everything turns, of course, on what one takes to be 'justice' in this context. We must refuse to accept references to 'the interests of justice', 'the public interest', and even (more emotively) 'the interests of victims'—unless it is carefully spelt out how exactly these rather sweeping claims have been arrived at. We need to identify the values that underlie such statements, and then consider what values should be recognized in criminal justice. But this essential part of the ethical approach cannot be treated in isolation: one cannot expect changes in

---

[70] M. McConville, A. Sanders and R. Leng, *The Case for the Prosecution* (1991), Ch 10.

the culture of lawyers, let alone in the culture of the police, so long as politicians and other key figures fail to show respect for the value of human rights and other ethical precepts.[71]

To expect those working in criminal justice to adopt an ethical approach, it is necessary to have some kind of code of ethics. To expect rules alone to change behaviour may be naïve, but without some rules or guidance it is unlikely that behaviour will be changed at all. Then the priority must be to formulate and to develop codes of ethics that not only set out the proper spirit and orientation of those performing certain functions, but also give examples of points at which an ethical approach might differ from an unethical approach. In this respect, both the General Council of the Bar's *Code of Conduct for Barristers* and the Law Society's *Code for Advocacy* stand in need of some reconsideration: the use of examples could improve them significantly. Although the Bar's *Code of Conduct* includes some ethical principles for prosecutors, these should be reconsidered and an ethical code for crown prosecutors developed in parallel.[72]

To formulate such principles, reflection on the proper roles of the various groups and agencies within the criminal justice system would be needed. The literature of English criminal procedure is replete with statements about the proper role of the prosecutor. In the nineteenth century it was said that the motivation of a prosecutor should be that of a Minister of Justice,[73] and this was elaborated by Sir Herbert Stephen when he wrote that the object of the prosecutor should be 'not to get a conviction, without qualification, but to get a conviction only if justice requires it'.[74] The rhetoric of this position recognizes that obtaining convictions should not be regarded as the sole or dominant aim of the prosecutor, and that the concept of justice also includes recognition of certain rights of defendants and of victims.[75] The CPS' overall aim includes a commitment not just to fair and independent review of cases but also to 'their fair, thorough and firm presentation at court',[76] but the documents on the website stop short of giving guidelines or even examples of practices this would favour or disfavour. Somewhere the CPS should articulate guidance on ethical approaches to situations where, for example, the prosecutor realizes that the court has made an error in favour of the prosecution, or realizes that certain evidence may have been obtained unfairly, or enters into plea negotiations despite doubts that the charge(s) can be sustained in court, or is tempted to make representations at remand

---

[71] See the powerful argument of J. Chan, 'Changing Police Culture' (1996) 36 *BJ Crim* 109 on the link between police culture and prevailing socio-political attitudes.

[72] For general analysis of these codes and their professional context, see D. Nicolson and J. Webb, *Professional Legal Ethics* (1999), Ch 4.

[73] Crompton J in *Puddick* (1865) 1 F & F 497.

[74] H. Stephen, *The Conduct of an English Criminal Trial* (1926), 11.

[75] Cf the somewhat ambivalent statement in the American book by C. M. Nissman and E. Hagen, *The Prosecution Function* (1982), 2: 'In pursuing his goal to seek justice, the prosecutor must punch through the tiresome criminal defender, whose goals are necessarily in conflict with the search for truth and justice.' The concept of justice carries much freight here.

[76] From 'The CPS Aim and Vision', at www.cps.gov.uk (accessed 16 November 2009).

proceedings even though it is unclear that the statutory requirements for a custodial remand are fulfilled.[77]

In respect of defence lawyers the reasons for spelling out the ethical approach are no less pressing. It is insufficient to state, in a broad way, that the lawyer should seek to protect the client while not misleading the court. There must be a sharper statement of the defence lawyer's guiding function: where the objective of providing a 'full and fearless' defence conflicts with the lawyer's duty to the court, it is essential to spell out what course this indicates in a range of common situations. Among those would be the problems of defending a person believed to be guilty, particularly where the lawyer believes that perjury has been or will be committed; where the defence lawyer knows of an error of law, or alternatively an error of fact, in the proceedings which favours the defence; where advice has to be offered to a client who wishes to plead not guilty; where the client wishes the lawyer to make an application for bail against the lawyer's professional judgement; when the lawyer believes that the client is innocent, despite indicating an intention to plead guilty; and so on.[78]

The reason for emphasizing the importance of giving examples is to try to give the ethical principles the greatest chance of practical success. While many lawyers are dismissive of principles of this kind, on the basis that 'each case depends on its own facts', this is not entirely true. Some situations and ethical dilemmas are common, and for those an orientation can be given; for unusual and controversial situations, only general ethical principles may be offered. However, ethical guidance that is as detailed as possible would help to confront those elements of occupational culture that are known to give priority to unethical motivations such as financial reward, preserving contacts and distaste for particular suspect/defendants. Defining the role responsibility of a defence lawyer, prosecutor, or police officer is the first step. But no less essential is the further step of putting together examples of situations where there may be a divergence between the ethical and other approaches.

Once this has been done, the next step would be to inculcate the principles through training and other means, in a way that engages with the new policing agenda (including human rights).[79] The main task would be to convey the reasons why these principles are worth adhering to, whether by abstract instruction or by means of role-play exercises, debates, etc. This approach must be integrated into a programme for retraining personnel at all levels, from senior management down to new recruits. The struggle towards consistency in areas of discretionary decision making should involve training, supervision and review: as Field concluded from his study of diversionary decisions in youth justice, 'reshaping the professional culture of decision-making may be as important protection for young people as the procedural values

---

[77] See further Blake and Ashworth, above n 9, and R. Young and A. Sanders, 'The Ethics of Prosecution Lawyers' (2004) 7 *Legal Ethics* 167.

[78] Bridges, above n 53; cf Nicolson and Webb, above n 72, Ch 7, and Legal Services Commission, *Code for the Criminal Defence Service* (2005).

[79] See Neyroud, above n 46.

of due process.'[80] Even if the training is well done, a statement of ethical principles would be a poor match for a well-entrenched occupational culture, as recent research by Loftus bears out.[81] The key questions must be addressed convincingly: why must I show respect towards someone who admits to a dreadful crime? If I feel that I can solve a difficult case only by deviating from the rules, is it not in the interests of society that I should do so? Both the democratic argument and ethical principles should be elaborated in reply.

These broad prescriptions should be no less applicable to other groups such as judges, court clerks, the Forensic Science Service, the so-called regulatory agencies and so on. No doubt some will be sceptical of the claims of the ethical approach, particularly when pitted against entrenched occupational cultures in certain spheres. Certainly no claim is being made here that, even if successfully defined and then inculcated, it would solve the problems of the pre-trial process. Rather the argument is that it ought to be recognized as a worthwhile part of altering the orientation of the system towards the ideals and values set out in Chapter 2 above. Simply declaring those principles, or other legal rules, is unlikely to work, for reasons that have been explained. The gap between the law in the books and the law in practice will become ever more visible in the chapters that follow, and it is the value-systems of those people who dominate practice that emerge as the key element.

FURTHER READING

YOUNG, R. and SANDERS, A., 'The Ethics of Prosecution Lawyers' (2004) 7 *Legal Ethics* 167.

CAPE, E., 'Rebalancing the Criminal Justice Process: Ethical Challenges for Criminal Defence Lawyers' (2006) 9 *Legal Ethics* 56.

BRIDGES, L., 'Ethics of Representation on Guilty Pleas' (2006) 9 *Legal Ethics* 80.

LOFTUS, B., 'Dominant Culture Interrupted' (2008) 48 *BJ Criminol* 756.

Questions for Discussion

1. To what extent are the findings of research on 'cop culture' generalizable to other decision makers in the criminal process?

2. Are ethical conflicts inherent in the role of criminal defence lawyer in the English system?

3. Should every criminal justice agency have a code of ethics? What good would this do?

---

[80] S. Field, 'Early Intervention and the "New" Youth Justice: a Study of Initial Decision-making' [2008] *Crim LR* 177, at 189.

[81] See Loftus, above n 34.

4

QUESTIONING

In 1992, the Court of Appeal quashed the convictions of the 'Cardiff Three', three young men who had been convicted of murder. There is no doubt that the men were innocent: the actual killer was later located through a DNA match and pleaded guilty at his trial in 2003.[1] One of the pieces of evidence against the Cardiff Three was the confession of one of them, Stephen Miller. Quashing the convictions, the Court of Appeal commented on the way in which Miller had been questioned by the police: 'Miller was bullied and hectored.... Short of physical violence, it is hard to conceive of a more hostile and intimidating approach by officers to a suspect.'[2] The case highlights one of the key problems that criminal procedure must address, which was identified in the previous chapter. In police detention, suspects like Miller can be subjected to serious abuses. Such abuses are unacceptable in themselves, but also undermine one of the key aims of the criminal process, which is to produce reliable evidence. Faced with police bullying, Miller confessed falsely, and this was one factor accounting for the wrongful convictions at trial.

Police questioning is a key pressure point in criminal procedure partly because it is central to police investigative practices. Over the years, the powers of arrest available to the police have been extended, allowing the police to rely on detention for questioning in a greater proportion of cases. During questioning, it is perhaps not surprising that the aim of the police will be to produce a confession. The majority of suspects—around 60 per cent—do make some form of confession, and confessions are powerful evidence, likely to secure a conviction at trial.[3] Suspects who are not forthcoming about their guilt may be seen as obstructing the police investigation. The reaction of the police may then be to put more pressure on the suspect, by detaining and questioning him for longer and by adopting a harsher tone.[4] This

---

[1] 'Real Killer Jailed in Case of Cardiff 3' *The Guardian* 5 July 2003.

[2] *R v Paris, Abdullahi and Miller* (1992) 97 Cr App R 99, 103.

[3] M. McConville, *Corroboration and Confessions: The Impact of a Rule Requiring that No Conviction Can Be Sustained on the Basis of Confession Evidence Alone* (1993), 32–3. In 98 per cent of cases where a confession was secured, the suspect pleaded or was found guilty. More recent research found that admissions were made in 66 per cent of cases: C. Clarke and R. Milne, *National Evaluation of the PEACE Investigative Interviewing Course* (2001), 33.

[4] See S. Kassin et al, 'Behavioral Confirmation in the Interrogation Room: On the Dangers of Presuming Guilt' (2003) 27 *Law & Human Behavior* 187.

is doubtless the sort of process that led to the oppressive questioning of Miller. A further possibility is that, given that confessions are good evidence, police officers may 'verbal' suspects by falsely attributing incriminating statements to them. These occurrences are constant dangers, ones which criminal procedure needs to erect safeguards against.

During the 1990s there were significant changes to the context of police questioning. The beginning of that decade saw considerable concern about false confessions. Although the regulation of police detention through the Police and Criminal Evidence Act 1984 (PACE) was often said to have made such concerns redundant, the Cardiff Three case, and others, showed that serious abuses and false confessions could still occur.[5] Post-PACE there has, however, been considerable effort put into training police in less aggressive interviewing practices.[6] Police investigative practices were also said to be changing in another way, becoming less reliant on confessions and more so on proactive policing, using intelligence and sting operations.[7] Some of these practices have problems of their own (see the discussion of surveillance in Chapter 5 and entrapment in Chapter 9) and it is not evident that they have led to much change in the emphasis on questioning suspects.[8] Even if there has been a move away from aggressive interviewing, the 1990s saw other changes which have contributed to making the police interview room a more pressurized environment. In spite of the recommendation of the Royal Commission on Criminal Justice that the 'right to silence'—the rule that adverse inferences should not be drawn from a suspect's silence—be retained, soon after the Commission reported the Conservative Government announced that it would be seeking to abolish the right. Important changes to the right to silence were then introduced by the Criminal Justice and Public Order Act 1994 (CJPOA). The legislation will be discussed in more detail below, but at this stage it is worth explaining that one of the key provisions is that, where a defendant relies at trial on a fact not mentioned to the police during interview, a court or jury may draw adverse inferences against him.[9] It is against this background that this chapter examines issues connected to police questioning.

---

[5] For other examples, see the case of George Heron, discussed in G. Gudjonsson, *The Psychology of Interrogations and Confessions: A Handbook* (2003), 96–106; and the case reported in 'Judge Brands Detectives as Liars after Collapse of Robbery Trial' *The Guardian*, 8 October 2003. For further allegations of police violence, see 'Metropolitan Police Officers Flushed my Head in Toilet, Says Suspect' *The Guardian* 10 June 2009; 'Met Police May Face Charges Over Violent Arrest of Terror Suspect' *The Guardian* 9 November 2009. See also *R v Smith* [2003] EWCA Crim 927.

[6] See T. Williamson, 'Towards Greater Professionalism: Minimizing Miscarriages of Justice' in T. Williamson (ed), *Investigative Interviewing: Rights, Research, Regulation* (2006); G Gudjonsson, 'Investigative Interviewing' in T. Newburn, T. Williamson and A. Wright (eds), *Handbook of Criminal Investigation* (2007).

[7] M. Maguire and T. John, 'Covert and Deceptive Policing in England and Wales: Issues in Regulation and Practice' (1996) 4 *Eur J Crime, Criminal L & Criminal Justice* 316.

[8] Research conducted in 1993–4 found that the majority of arrests were still based on reactive policing, with only 13 per cent based on 'surveillance/enquiries'. C. Phillips and D. Brown, *Entry into the Criminal Justice System: A Survey of Police Arrests and Their Outcomes* (1998).

[9] CJPOA, s 34.

4.1 QUESTIONING AND CONFESSIONS: PSYCHOLOGICAL RESEARCH

One of the most important advances in the understanding of the process by which the police elicit confessions has been the development of a sophisticated body of psychological research on questioning. Such research has become increasingly important in the practice of the courts, with psychologists and psychiatrists often called to give expert evidence about the reliability of confession evidence in individual cases.[10] Psychological research also offers more general lessons to the legal system as to how it should deal with the questioning process and the evidence that results from it.

Research on police questioning tells us something about the circumstances in which suspects confess to crime. A significant finding is that the questioning process itself often does little to elicit confessions. Most suspects who confess do so at the outset of the police interview, rather than in response to being challenged by the police.[11] As to why some suspects but not others decide to confess, the most significant factor appears to be the strength of evidence against them. A suspect who knows that the police are likely to be able to prove his guilt has little to lose by confessing.[12] Are some types of defendant more likely to confess than others? Gudjonsson has attempted to answer this question. One, perhaps surprising, finding was that the mental characteristics of defendants do not appear to be linked to the likelihood of confession. Although many police suspects are intellectually disadvantaged, this does not necessarily make them more likely to confess to the police.[13] The only individual factor which was identified as being a good predictor of whether a suspect would confess was whether that person had taken illegal drugs in the 24 hours before arrest. 'The most likely explanation', Gudjonsson concludes, 'is that suspects who are dependent on illicit drugs are motivated by factors that they perceive as expediting their release from custody.'[14]

The factors described above do not distinguish between true and false confessions. It is obviously very difficult to conduct research into the reasons why people confess falsely, because the truth or falsity of a confession is often impossible to establish. Notorious cases such as that of Stephen Miller, described in the introduction, can provide some pointers. A study of 125 proven false confession cases in the US concluded that coercive interrogation practices were the major cause of false confessions.[15] False confessions tended to occur in serious cases, where the stakes were high and where often there was little other evidence against a suspect.[16] In such circumstances, the

---

[10] See, e.g., *R v Antar* [2004] EWCA Crim 2708; *R v Nolan* [2006] EWCA Crim 2983.

[11] Gudjonsson, above n 5, 70, 133. But cf S. Soukara et al, 'What Really Happens in Police Interviews of Suspects? Tactics and Confessions' (2009) 15 *Psychology, Crime & Law* 493, 500–1.

[12] *Ibid.*, 153.   [13] *Ibid.*, 73.   [14] *Ibid.*, 71.

[15] S. Drizin and R. Leo, 'The Problem of False Confessions in the Post-DNA World' (2004) 82 *North Carolina L Rev* 891.

[16] R. Ofshe and R. Leo, 'The Decision to Confess Falsely: Rational Choice and Irrational Action' (1997) 74 *Denver University L Rev* 979.

police may put a large amount of pressure on a suspect who—the lack of evidence suggests—could well be innocent. Gudjonsson has explored the explanations given by prisoners who claim to have confessed falsely. His findings again identify the pressure exerted by the police as a significant factor. But prisoners also claimed to have confessed falsely for reasons over which the police would have less control: out of fear of custody, and to protect other people.[17] Finally, psychological factors may contribute to false confession. Some people will confess to crime even when they are faced with no external pressure to confess, perhaps as a form of attention seeking.[18] The young, and the mentally disordered are over-represented in false confession cases.[19] But Gudjonsson stresses that 'false confessions are not confined to the mentally ill and those with learning disability. . . . The view that apparently normal individuals would not seriously incriminate themselves when interrogated by the police is wrong.'[20] Gudjonsson has, however, pioneered research on the way in which the psychological factors of compliance and suggestibility can contribute to false confessions. Some people, who are not necessarily intellectually disadvantaged, may be particularly likely to comply with those in authority, or to accept suggestions (e.g. 'you hit him') put to them by other people. It may not be obvious to the police whether an individual is compliant or suggestible, though these characteristics can be measured by psychological tests.[21] These various findings should be borne in mind during the discussion that follows.

4.2 THE CONTEXT OF QUESTIONING

(A) ARREST AND DETENTION

In order to gain a full understanding of police questioning, we need to know something about the context in which it takes place. One reason for this should already be apparent: as has been noted, research suggests that it is in serious cases where there is little evidence against suspects that the danger of false confession is greatest. Ensuring that the police can only question suspects against whom there is reasonable evidence of guilt will reduce the risk of false confession. On the other hand, if it is made too difficult for the police to question suspects, they may be unduly impeded in the investigation of crime. We therefore begin by considering the circumstances in which suspects can be arrested and detained in police custody. Of course, there are other issues at stake here than the reliability of evidence gained through questioning: arrest and detention is an intrusion on the liberty of suspects and there is therefore potential for breach of Article 5 of the European Convention on Human Rights (ECHR). There

---

[17] Gudjonsson, above n 5, 176.
[18] See *R v Flanagan* [2005] EWCA Crim 2286; *R v Lawless* [2009] EWCA Crim 1308.
[19] Drizin and Leo, above n 15.   [20] Above n 5, 626.   [21] *Ibid.*, Chs 13–14.

are good reasons to minimize arrest and detention apart from the risks they pose in terms of false confessions.

The usual process is that a suspect will be arrested and then taken to the police station where questioning is likely to ensue.[22] PACE has always given the police fairly wide arrest powers, and these have recently been expanded by the Serious Organised Crime and Police Act 2005.[23] Under the previous law, a distinction was drawn between 'arrestable offences' and other, less serious, 'non-arrestable offences'. The distinction embodied a basic idea of proportionality, the idea being that arrest would not normally be appropriate where the least serious offences were concerned. Here, the police could usually proceed by way of summons, requiring the person concerned to attend court at some later date.[24] But now this distinction has gone, and the police are able to arrest for any offence, no matter how trivial, so long as they reasonably believe that one of the reasons in s 24(5) of PACE applies. The reasons include enabling the person's name or address to be ascertained; preventing loss, damage or injury; preventing the person from disappearing, and 'to allow the prompt and effective investigation of the offence or of the conduct of the person in question'. Arrest remains discretionary, and the police may still proceed by way of summons in any case, but the criterion of allowing 'prompt and effective investigation' is sufficiently vague that it is little more than a rubber stamp which could justify arrest in any situation where the police wish to question a suspect. A Code of Practice, Code G , has been issued under PACE, and this does note that officers should consider whether their objectives 'can be met by other, less intrusive means. Arrest must never be used simply because it can be used.'[25] An important question is whether a suspect's willingness to attend the police station on a voluntary basis means that arrest is not needed for this purpose, but the Divisional Court did not find it necessary to rule on this issue in the one case where it has been raised.[26] Without empirical research, it is difficult to know whether this expansion of arrest powers has led to an increased number of arrests. One hint is that, after the new provision was introduced,[27] the number of arrests for notifiable offences (a category which includes many minor offences which were not previously 'arrestable', such as the various offences of causing alarm or distress under the Public Order Act 1986[28]) increased by 6 per cent in 2005–6, and by 4 per cent

---

[22] Another possibility now is that a suspect will be arrested, and then bailed, the condition of bail being to report to the police station where they may be questioned. On 'street bail', see A. Hucklesby, 'Not Necessarily a Trip to the Police Station: The Introduction of Street Bail' (2004) *Crim LR* 803.

[23] For an overview of the new provisions, see R. C. Austin, 'The New Powers of Arrest' [2007] *Crim LR* 459.

[24] PACE, s 25 did allow the police to arrest for non-arrestable offences where the issue of a summons was not practicable, for example if they could not be sure of the person's name and address.

[25] PACE Code G, para 1.3.

[26] *R on the Application of 'C' v Chief Constable 'A' Police, 'A' Magistrates' Court* [2006] EWHC 2352 (Admin). See J. R. Spencer, 'Arrest for Questioning' (2007) 66 CLJ 282.

[27] On 1 January 2006.

[28] The full list of notifiable offences can be found at: www.homeoffice.gov.uk/rds/pdfs09/countnotif09. xls. 'Arrestable offences' were defined in the old PACE, s 24 and Sch 1A.

in 2006–7, rates which contrast with the smaller rates of increase in previous years (usually 1 or 2 per cent).[29]

Putting to one side the question of whether arrest powers should have been widened, and any affects this might have had, it is difficult to say how widely or justifiably arrest powers are used. Research on police decision making 'on the street' emphasizes the flexibility of police powers, which allow coercive measures such as arrest to be used for a variety of purposes, some with little connection to crime investigation.[30] There has long been an increasing number of arrests year on year, even during periods of falling crime rates, and as we have seen the rate of increase has recently grown.[31] Some commentators suggest that PACE has led to arrests being carried out on a firmer evidential basis than was previously the case, but others doubt this.[32] As for the outcome of arrest, Phillips and Brown found that 40 per cent of arrestees were eventually convicted; 50 per cent were charged, 17 per cent cautioned, 20 per cent had no further action taken against them and 13 per cent were dealt with in other ways.[33] They also found evidence that black and Asian suspects were arrested on weaker evidence than white suspects.[34] More recent statistics show that there is ethnic disproportion in arrest rates, though they cannot speak to the extent to which these arrests are justified. In 2007/8, blacks were nearly four times as likely to be arrested as whites.[35]

On being arrested, a suspect should be told that he is under arrest, and the grounds for the arrest.[36] He should also be cautioned, and taken to a police station.[37] At the police station detention is not, in theory, automatic: it must be authorized by the custody officer. PACE provides that a suspect can be detained where the custody officer reasonably believes that detention is necessary 'to secure or preserve evidence…or to obtain evidence by questioning him'.[38] Though the 'necessity' criterion might be thought to be relatively demanding, research shows that it is not. It is very rare for custody officers to refuse to permit the detention of suspects.[39] It will be apparent that both this provision, and the law on the discretion to arrest for arrestable offences, empower the police to detain suspects in order to question them even if there is little evidence against the suspect, or if there is sufficient evidence to permit the case to proceed to court without questioning.

---

[29] See the various annual publications, now published by the Ministry of Justice, entitled *Arrests for Recorded Crime (Notifiable Offences) and the Operation of Certain Police Powers Under PACE*.

[30] See A. Sanders and R. Young, 'From Suspect to Trial' in M. Maguire, R. Morgan and R. Reiner (eds), *The Oxford Handbook of Criminology* (4th ed, 2007).

[31] The most recent figures can be found in *Arrests for Notifiable Offences and the Operation of Certain Police Powers Under PACE, England and Wales 2006/07* (2008).

[32] D. Brown, *PACE Ten Years On: A Review of the Research* (1997), 51–5.

[33] C. Phillips and D. Brown, *Entry into the Criminal Justice System: A Survey of Police Arrests and Their Outcomes* (1998), xiv.

[34] *Ibid.*, 44.

[35] Ministry of Justice, *Statistics on Race and the Criminal Justice System 2007/8* (2009), Table 5.2a.

[36] PACE, s 28, Code C, 10.3 and note 10B.   [37] PACE, s 30, Code C, 10.4.   [38] PACE, s 37(2).

[39] D. Brown, above n 32, 57–62.

Once arrested and taken to a police station, suspects can be detained for a considerable period before being charged. As with arrest, recent changes to PACE have expanded powers of detention.[40] All arrestees can be detained for an initial period of 24 hours.[41] After this, a police officer of at least the rank of superintendent can authorize detention for a further 12 hours, taking the total to 36, so long as the person concerned is under arrest for an indictable offence. 'Indictable' is a broad category, comprising all offences other than those which can only be tried in the magistrates' court; it includes offences such as minor theft. During this period detention should be reviewed periodically by a senior officer: after an initial period of six hours, and then at nine hour intervals.[42] The evidence suggests that, especially during the initial 24 hours, the process of review is routinized and is not a very effective means of limiting detention to what is necessary.[43] After 36 hours further detention can only be authorized by the magistrates' court. The magistrates can authorize further detention, 36 hours at a time, up to a maximum of 96 hours.[44] In practice, detention is usually for a relatively short period: the average is around seven hours.[45] It should be noted that there are wider powers of detention for terrorist offences.[46]

It is possible for suspects to be questioned at the police station even if they have not been formally arrested. Some attend the police station 'voluntarily'. Research has found that voluntary attendance may be used quite frequently: at one police station a third of all suspects were dealt with as voluntary attenders.[47] This process avoids some of the regulations imposed by PACE, such as the detention time limits.[48]

(B) LEGAL ADVICE

The Royal Commission on Criminal Procedure saw access to legal advice in the police station as a fundamental part of its proposed regime for regulating the police station. Legal advice, it was hoped, would go some way to 'minimising the effects of arrest and custody on the suspect'.[49] The right to legal advice is guaranteed by s 58 of PACE, which provides that 'A person arrested and held in custody in a police station or other premises shall be entitled, if he so requests, to consult a solicitor privately at any time.' Clearly, this right would be of little value if few suspects could afford legal advice, or if they did not know whom to contact, so when PACE was introduced a system of duty solicitors was put in place, providing free legal advice on

[40] See E. Cape, 'Modernising Police Powers—Again?' [2007] *Crim LR* 934.   [41] PACE, s 41.
[42] PACE, s 40.
[43] D. Dixon et al, 'Safeguarding the Rights of Suspects in Police Custody' (1990) 1 *Policing & Society* 115.
[44] PACE, ss 43, 44.   [45] Phillips and Brown, above n 33, 109.   [46] Terrorism Act 2000, Sch 8.
[47] I. McKenzie, R. Morgan and R. Reiner, 'Helping the Police with their Enquiries: The Necessity Principle and Voluntary Attendance at the Police Station' [1990] *Crim LR* 22; D. Dixon, *Law in Policing: Legal Regulation and Police Practices* (1997), 113–15.
[48] There are some protections in PACE, s 29 and Code C, 3.21–2.
[49] Royal Commission on Criminal Procedure, *The Investigation and Prosecution of Criminal Offences in England and Wales: The Law and Procedure* (1981), para 4.77.

a 24-hour basis—though suspects could also contact a nominated solicitor, as many did. While it has never been perfect, and had to be improved over the years in the light of research uncovering various failings, the system for delivering legal advice to those detained in the police station is one of the successes of PACE. However, recent attempts to control spending on legal aid raise the threat of the scheme being undermined.

On arrival at the police station, an arrestee will be booked in and at this point should be offered access to legal advice. The right is absolute, in that it cannot legally be denied, though in strictly defined circumstances s 58 allows the police to delay access to legal advice. The courts have enforced a strict reading of s 58,[50] and it now seems to be rare for the police to delay access. Before PACE was introduced, around 10 per cent of suspects may have asked for legal advice.[51] Post-PACE the figure has crept up. Research in the 1990s found that around 40 per cent of suspects asked for legal advice;[52] the most recent figure, based on research at two police stations, is that 60 per cent of suspects asked for legal advice.[53] It has been found that the police have some ability to manipulate suspects' requests for legal advice in the manner in which they inform them of it.[54] Not all suspects are told that legal advice is free, nor informed of their rights clearly, factors that are likely to influence uptake of legal advice.[55] But requesting advice does not always mean that advice is received. The 1990s research found that of the nearly 38 per cent requesting advice, 34 per cent received it.[56] Skinns' more recent study found that while 60 per cent requested legal advice, 48 per cent received it.[57] Although suspects who have requested legal advice should not be interviewed until they have received it, some may drop their requests, and this may well happen because of concerns about the delay that waiting for contact with a solicitor entails. Skinns found that suspects were concerned about delay, and on average had to wait nearly four hours for legal advice;[58] other research has found

---

[50] *R v Samuel* [1988] 1 QB 615.

[51] The figures in the literature vary considerably: see D. Brown, *PACE Ten Years On: A Review of the Research* (1997), 95.

[52] T. Bucke and D. Brown, *In Police Custody: Police Powers and Suspects' Rights under the Revised PACE Codes of Practice* (1997), 19; T. Bucke, R. Street and D. Brown, *The Right of Silence: The Impact of the CJPOA 1994* (2000), 21.

[53] L. Skinns, 'I'm a Detainee; Get me Out of Here' (2009) 49 *Brit J Criminol* 399, 407. There was noticeable variation between the two research sites, with more requests for advice at the privately managed police station.

[54] A. Sanders and L. Bridges, 'Access to Legal Advice and Police Malpractice' (1990) *Crim LR* 494. Skinns, *ibid.*, also found claims that police would use conversations during transit to the police station as a means of dissuading suspects from accessing legal advice.

[55] D. Brown, T. Ellis and K. Larcombe, *Changing the Code: Police Detention Under the Revised PACE Codes of Practice* (1992), 26, 31, problems which Skinns confirms still exist: above n 53, 66.

[56] Bucke and Brown, above n 52, 23.

[57] Skinns, above n 53, 407.

[58] L. Skinns, '"Let's Get it Over With": Early Findings on the Factors Affecting Detainees' Access to Custodial Legal Advice' (2009) 19 *Policing and Society* 58.

that those arrested during the night, when delays are likely to be longest, are more likely to cancel requests.[59] Some advice is given over the telephone, and some advisers attend the police station but not the interview.[60]

There have been problems with the quality of legal advice offered to suspects in detention. Some solicitors' firms have used representatives who are not legally qualified to give advice.[61] A qualification scheme has been introduced, and the quality of advice now seems to have improved.[62] But even solicitors are sometimes not particularly zealous in defence of their clients. The most telling example of this is that a solicitor sat through the abusive interviews of Stephen Miller (described in the introduction to this chapter) without objecting to them. There was also remarkably little intervention during the oppressive interviewing of George Heron.[63] In a more recent case, a confession was excluded on account of a solicitor's hostile and sarcastic interventions at interview.[64]

Pressure to reduce spending on legal aid has recently had a number of effects on police station legal advice.[65] Free legal advice for certain less serious offences, including driving with excess alcohol and all non-imprisonable offences, is now restricted to advice delivered over the telephone. If detainees wish to consult a solicitor in person, they will not receive legal aid for any fees incurred. It may well be that the category of 'telephone only' matters will be expanded in the future. Solicitors are also now paid a fixed fee for attending the police station, rather than being paid per hour, and this may obviously encourage them to offer advice over the telephone rather than in person. There is also a new system for the delivery of legal advice. Rather than the police attempting to contact the suspect's chosen solicitor or the duty solicitor, all calls are now made to the Defence Solicitor Call Centre (DSCC). If DSCC staff determine that the request involves a telephone only matter, they will contact CDS Direct, a body set up by the Legal Services Commission to deliver police station advice efficiently.[66] Otherwise, DSCC will attempt to contact the nominated solicitor or the duty solicitor.

There are various concerns about these new arrangements. In minor matters, suspects who want free legal advice no longer have a choice of solicitor, but must use CDS Direct. CDS Direct may offer perfectly good advice, and may have the advantage of doing so more quickly than would another legal adviser, thus potentially minimizing time spent

---

[59]   Phillips and Brown, above n 33, 64.

[60]   Bucke and Brown, above n 52, at 32, found that a legal adviser was present at all interviews in 37 per cent of cases where suspects were interviewed. The figure was almost identical in Clarke and Milne's more recent study: above n 3, 32.

[61]   J. Hodgson, 'Adding Injury to Injustice: The Suspect at the Police Station' (1994) 21 *J Law & Soc* 85.

[62]   L. Bridges and S. Choongh, *Improving Police Station Legal Advice* (1998).

[63]   Gudjonsson, above n 5, 105.   [64]   *M* [2000] 8 *Archbold News* 2.

[65]   For a critical analysis, underlining the lack of independent research on how the changes affect detainees, see L. Bridges and E. Cape, *CDS Direct: Flying in the Face of the Evidence* (2008).

[66]   CDS stands for Criminal Defence Service.

in custody.[67] However, it is known that suspects value being able to choose a legal adviser[68] and they may well be suspicious of a source of advice which appears so closely controlled by the State. The strategic shift to delivering as much advice as possible by telephone raises further potential problems. While such advice may offer the advantage of reducing delay, without proper research we do not know how effective it is or how it is perceived by suspects. It also appears that police stations are not well set up to cope with the delivery of large amounts of advice by telephone, because there are few areas where such advice can be delivered in privacy.[69] Speaker phones in the cells and the use of a telephone at the custody desk are plainly unsatisfactory arrangements, which in all probability breach various provisions of the ECHR. Finally, there are concerns that the new arrangements, whereby calls are routed through DSCC rather than being made direct to a nominated solicitor, will increase delays. Given the connection between delay and cancelled requests for legal advice, this is a significant issue. Skinns' research did find that a higher proportion of requests for legal advice are withdrawn than had previous research,[70] and while it is not known what the reason for this is, there is cause for concern here.

To return now to the primary focus of this chapter, which is the process of police questioning, the lesson to draw from the foregoing is that, while legal advice is undoubtedly an important safeguard for suspects, it would be a mistake to exaggerate its impact. The majority of suspects do not receive legal advice and do not have a legal adviser with them during police questioning.

4.3 INTERVIEWS

(A) THE RULES

The legal regime governing the questioning of suspects is to be found in PACE, Code C and to a lesser extent in case law. The first rule worthy of note is that interviews should take place in the police station.[71] To allow suspects to be questioned outside the police station would be to provide a loophole through which the police station regime—including access to legal advice and the recording of interviews—could be evaded. There are exceptions to the basic rule to allow the police to ask questions if gaining information from a suspect is urgent.[72]

The rule against interviewing outside the police station depends on having a definition of 'interview'. Sometimes the police will question a person regarding an incident

---

[67] An evaluation in 2008 found that CDS called the police station within 15 minutes of receiving a request for advice in 98 per cent of cases: Legal Services Commission, *Evaluation of CDS Direct First Phase Expansion* (2008), 3. Whether the police answer the call is another matter: see Bridges and Cape, above n 65, 29.

[68] V. Kemp and A. Balmer, *Criminal Defence Services: Users' Perspectives* (2008), 35.

[69] See R. Pattenden and L. Skinns, 'Choice, Privacy, and Publicly Funded Legal Advice at Police Stations' (2010) 73 *MLR* (forthcoming).

[70] Above n 53.   [71] Code C, 11.1.   [72] *Ibid.*

and have their suspicions raised through the response to their questions. If questioning continues, at some point a dividing line will be crossed and the questioning will become an interview. Code C defines an interview in terms of whether the questions asked are about involvement in an offence.[73] Nevertheless, there may be claims that a suspect has freely made admissions before arriving at the police station. In these circumstances, anything said should be put to the suspect at the beginning of the formal interview, giving him an opportunity to confirm or deny it.[74]

It is unclear how often suspects are interviewed outside the police station. One study conducted for the Royal Commission on Criminal Justice found a figure of 10 per cent, but this is not regarded as a reliable estimate:[75] the real figure is probably larger. The courts are alive to the problems in this area, and enforce the Code C definition of interview relatively strictly.[76] Nevertheless, the admission in court of statements made outside the police station is still a possibility.[77] Given the concerns here, and the fact that an admission denied by the defendant will have little evidential value, this seems to be an area where a strict rule of inadmissibility—unless the statement is either recorded or later confirmed by the suspect—would be appropriate.[78] Any decision to admit such evidence would create incentives for the police to try to gain admissions outside the police station regime, or to verbal suspects.

The suspect should be cautioned at the start of the interview.[79] After the changes to the right to silence were introduced, the caution has been in the form: 'You do not have to say anything. But it may harm your defence if you do not mention when questioned something which you later rely on in court. Anything you do say may be given in evidence.'[80] The caution is relatively complex and, given the level of intellectual disadvantage among police suspects, there are considerable doubts about how well it is understood. One study found that none among a group of 30 suspects could give a correct explanation of the caution;[81] indeed, even police officers have difficulty in explaining the caution correctly.[82] Some officers attempt to explain the caution to suspects, but there is a fear that a technically inexact explanation, or an attempt to explain which reveals that the suspect really does not understand the consequences of not mentioning facts, might harm the case in court. Some training sessions have therefore

---

[73] Code C, 11.1A, 10.1.   [74] Code C, 11.4.

[75] S. Moston and G. Stephenson, *The Questioning and Interviewing of Suspects Outside the Police Station* (1993).

[76] E.g. *Okafor* [1994] 3 All ER 741; cf *R v Senior and Senior* [2004] Cr App R 215; *R v Bhambra* [2008] EWCA Crim 2317; *R v Shillibier* [2006] EWCA Crim 793.

[77] Statements might also be made inside the police station, before the formal interviewing process has begun: *R v Van Gelderen* [2008] EWCA Crim 422.

[78] Cf *Van Gelderen*, *ibid.* A statement attributed to the suspect by various police officers was held admissible, despite the fact that the statement was quickly denied when put to him at interview.

[79] Code C, 10.1.   [80] Code C, 10.5.

[81] S. Fenner, G. Gudjonsson and I. Clare, 'Understanding of the Current Police Caution (England and Wales) Among Suspects in Police Detention' (2002) 12 *J Community & Applied Social Psychology* 83.

[82] I. Clare, G. Gudjonsson and M. Harari, 'Understanding of the Current Police Caution (England and Wales)' (1998) 8 *J Community & Applied Social Psychology* 323.

advised officers not to attempt an explanation,[83] a good example of how concern about the admissibility of evidence can override ethical concerns. If there is evidence that a suspect does not understand the caution, then surely it is proper not to hold facts not mentioned in interview against him in court.

The issue of the caution has been further complicated by the decision of the European Court of Human Rights in *Murray v United Kingdom*.[84] Here it was held that a suspect's Article 6 right to a fair trial was breached when he was denied access to legal advice in a situation where adverse inferences could be drawn from his failure to mention facts at interview.[85] The right to silence provisions have therefore been amended to prevent the drawing of adverse inferences from suspects who have not had access to legal advice, but this means that the standard caution will sometimes be misleading. Thus, if the suspect is to be interviewed outside the police station, or before consulting with a legal adviser who he has requested, or after he has been charged, the 'old' caution must be given: 'You do not have to say anything, but anything you do say may be given in evidence.' Some suspects, at different points in time, will be given first one caution and then the other. Code C contains a form of words to explain the change,[86] but there must again be doubts about comprehensibility.

An accurate record should be made of all interviews.[87] This is an important safeguard against verballing. The introduction of tape recorders in interview rooms has facilitated this process, and tape recording is now standard practice.[88] In recent years the video-taping of interviews with suspects has also become common, especially in more serious cases.[89] Video offers the advantage of a more complete record of what occurred. But the process does bring some new dangers. In an Australian study, Dixon found that judges were keen to play the tapes in court, and that judges and prosecutors believed that much could be read into the suspect's demeanour.[90] But demeanour is a poor guide to veracity at the best of times, and will be even more so when the subject is seen under the stressful conditions of police questioning.[91] Whichever form of recording is used, there is the problem of producing a transcript or summary of the tape. The process is time consuming and often introduces inaccuracies.[92]

---

[83] Bucke, Street and Brown, above n 52, 28.   [84] (1996) 22 EHRR 29.

[85] Cf *R v Ibrahim* [2008] EWCA Crim 880, holding that confessions made during an interview where legal advice has been denied, as well as inferences from lies, are admissible. This might raise issues under Art 6: see the ECtHR decision in *Salduz v Turkey*, App No 36391/02 (2008).

[86] Code C, Annex C.   [87] Code C, 11.7.   [88] See generally PACE, Code E.

[89] PACE Code F covers video-taping of interviews.

[90] D. Dixon with G. Travers, *Interrogating Images: Audio-Visually Recorded Police Questioning of Suspects* (2007), 233–6. See also G. Lassiter et al, 'The Potential for Bias in Videotaped Confessions' (2006) 22 *J Applied Social Psychol* 1838, for discussion of the impact of camera angle on how coercive questioning is judged to be.

[91] S. Kassin and C. Fong, ' "I'm Innocent": Effects of Training on Judgments of Truth and Deception in the Interrogation Room' (1999) 23 *Law & Human Behavior* 499.

[92] See Royal Commission on Criminal Justice, *Report* (1993), Ch 4 paras 73–80; Gudjonsson, above n 5, 85.

Another limitation to the recording of interviews is that in some cases the police may rehearse what is to be said on tape, or exert pressure on suspects, before the formal interview begins. This is a further reason for concern about what is said outside the police station. Inside the station, cell visits by officers are meant to be recorded, but it is difficult completely to ensure against rule-breaking.[93] As an antidote, the Royal Commission on Criminal Justice recommended video-taping custody areas, so that in the event of a dispute the movements of police officers could be checked.[94] Most custody suites are now covered by CCTV, but coverage is unlikely to be absolute. In her recent research Skinns found evidence that 'off the record' conversations still took place, both during the journey to the police station and within it, for example when suspects were taken out to the exercise yard for a cigarette.[95]

Prolonged interviewing of suspects is problematic. In a difficult or complex case it may be justified, but in some cases prolongation of the interview process may wear down and confuse the suspect. Stephen Miller was interviewed for 13 hours, and this doubtless contributed to his confessing falsely. Drizin and Leo's study of false confessions in the US found that extremely long sessions of interviewing were common in their sample of false confessions: the average length was over 16 hours.[96] Code C contains rules on breaks between interviews for refreshments and requires suspects to have at least eight hours rest in 24, free from questioning, but there is no cap on the cumulative length of questioning, other than the time limits on detention. These are not inconsiderable, as was seen above. Even with rules on the police station environment, the potential effects of custody on suspects should not be underestimated. Suspects are likely to be nervous and uncertain. They have little control over the environment in which they find themselves. Many complain of lack of sleep—something which has been found to impair the ability to cope with questioning.[97]

Code C does provide that questioning should end when the police have gathered a certain amount of information. The interview process should cease when the officer in charge of the investigation:

(a) 'Is satisfied all the questions they consider relevant to obtaining accurate and reliable information from the suspect about the offence have been put to the suspect, this includes allowing the suspect an opportunity to give an innocent explanation and asking questions to test if the explanation is accurate and reliable, eg to clear up ambiguities or clarify what the suspect said;

(b) has taken account of any other evidence which is available; and

(c) …the custody officer reasonably believes there is sufficient evidence to provide a realistic prospect of conviction….'[98]

---

[93] M. McConville, 'Videotaping Interrogations: Police Behaviour on and off Camera' [1992] *Crim LR* 532.
[94] Above n 92, Ch 4, para 37.   [95] Skinns, above n 53, 409 and above n 58, 66–7.
[96] Above n 15.   [97] Gudjonsson, above n 5, 31.   [98] Code C, 11.6.

This provision was modified in 2003; previously the Code had said little, other than that questioning should end when the officer believes that a prosecution should be brought and that there is sufficient evidence for it to succeed. Under this provision, courts had held that inferences could not be drawn from silence where questioning continued after the cut-off point.[99] The 2003 revision is doubtless a response to this; it appears to provide for a longer period of questioning than the earlier version. Questioning can continue beyond the point at which there is sufficient evidence to justify prosecution, in order to test the suspect's version of events and obtain accurate information from him. This might be said to signify a change in the nature of the questioning process, from an investigative one, where the aim of the police is largely to find out what happened, to a case-building one, where the suspect's version of events can be tested in more detail and his response, or lack of it, to the evidence against him will be significant. More will be said about the significance of this in the discussion of the right to silence, below.

PACE and the codes regulate the environment in which interviewing takes place. They say little, however, about how interviews should be conducted. Code C lays down some basic rules: questioning should not be oppressive, and the police should not offer inducements such as release on bail in return for a confession.[100] However, the situation as regards the sentence discount for a plea of guilty is unclear. As we will see in Chapter 10, those who plead guilty can obtain a sentence discount of up to a third. Under the most recent guidelines, the full sentence discount is only available to those who 'indicate willingness to admit guilt at the first reasonable opportunity'.[101] The first reasonable opportunity can include the police interview.[102] If the police bring the sentence discount to the suspect's attention, does this constitute an inducement that would breach Code C, and potentially render any confession inadmissible? While it is not obvious why a statement that the full discount will only be forthcoming if the suspect confesses should be different to an offer to release on bail, a court that reached this conclusion would be faced with difficult questions about the voluntary nature of *any* guilty plea tendered in the hope of a discount, and about the current policy of making the discount as widely known as possible. What we do know is that some police forces have brought the sentence discount to the attention of suspects at interview. In *Attorney General's References Nos 14 and 15 of 2006*, the Court of Appeal observed:

'There is a further reason why it would not be just to reduce Webster's discount in order to reflect the strength of the case against him. When being interviewed by the Hertfordshire constabulary, according to the practice then prevailing in that district, he was shown a notice that stated that if he admitted guilt at that interview, which was the first reasonable

---

[99] See E. Cape, 'The Revised PACE Codes of Practice: A Further Step Towards Inquisitorialism' [2003] *Crim LR* 355, 364.

[100] Code C, 11.5.

[101] Sentencing Guidelines Council, *Reduction in Sentence for a Guilty Plea* (2004), para 4.3.

[102] *Ibid.*, Annex 2.

opportunity, he would receive a maximum reduction of sentence of one third. He confirmed in answer to questions that he understood this to be the position and then went on to admit his participation in the offences.'[103]

Hertfordshire Police had presumably concluded that their policy complied with Code C, and the Court of Appeal offered no criticism—though in this case the defendant did not challenge his confession. However inconsistent this seems, it may be that the sentence discount constitutes a legal inducement. In this context it is worth noting that similar questions arise under s 73 of the Serious Organised Crime and Police Act 2005, which recognizes that defendants may be offered a reduced sentence in return for assisting the prosecution. We know that this was brought to a suspect's attention during police questioning in *Ibrahim*,[104] but the admissibility of any resulting confession has not yet been raised in court.

A few further guidelines on the interview process may be found in the case law. As under Code C, oppression is outlawed, but the definition of oppression is pitched fairly high: confronting the suspect with disturbing information is not regarded as oppressive.[105] The repeated bullying questioning of Stephen Miller, though, was held to be oppressive. In addition, a confession may be excluded if it was obtained in conditions likely to lead to its being unreliable, or if admitting it is likely to make the trial unfair.[106] These requirements—discussed in more detail below—offer limited guidance to questioners. To gain more idea of how interviews are actually conducted, it is necessary to turn to the empirical research.

After the miscarriages of justice of the 1980s and early 1990s, much effort was put into training officers to use less aggressive, 'investigative' interviewing styles.[107] The current model, which is informed by psychological research, goes under the mnemonic PEACE: Planning and preparation; Engage and explain; Account, clarification and challenge; Closure; Evaluate. In essence, the idea is not simply to seek the suspect's assent to the police version of events, but to obtain an account from the suspect which is then challenged on the basis of any evidence the police have. Emphasis is placed on open questions, rather than closed or leading ones. The lack of recent research on police interviews makes it very difficult to know how far the shift to the PEACE model has changed things. There is evidence from the 1990s to suggest that aggressive interviewing is now rare. Pearse and Gudjonsson concluded that the interviews for non-serious crimes that they studied differed markedly from those described in the pre-PACE research, where manipulation and persuasion was common. In fact, they felt that police officers were too reluctant to challenge the suspect's version of events,

---

[103] [2006] EWCA Crim 1335, [54].

[104] Above n 85, [66]. This was in the context of a 'safety interview' with a terrorist suspect.

[105] PACE, s 76, interpreted in *Fulling* [1987] 2 All ER 75; see also *Foster* [2003] EWCA Crim 178.

[106] PACE, ss 76, 78.

[107] For current training policy, see National Policing Improvement Agency, *National Investigative Interviewing Strategy* (2009).

and that training needed to address this.[108] A study of the PEACE model by Clarke and Milne, involving interviews which probably date from the late 1990s, concluded that compliance with PEACE was uneven. Closed and leading questions remained common, an approach which 'is not conducive to obtaining a complete account'.[109] While the researchers concluded that interviewing had improved since the early 1990s, the most worrying finding was that 10 per cent of interviews may have breached PACE requirements, and this included several which involved oppression: 'instances of undue pressure, bullying and continual challenge'.[110] Other problems involved the treatment of suspects with mental health problems and failure to caution or explain the position as to legal advice.[111] Further training was recommended.[112] In further research on the impact of training, Griffiths and Milne found that interviewers who had been trained in the PEACE model fell below the expected standard when tested. However, advanced training, which is given to officers dealing with the most serious cases, had a dramatic effect on interview skills, though there was some drop off in ability over time.[113] Most recently, Soukara et al studied tape recordings of 80 interviews provided to them by the police; the interviews probably date from the early 2000s.[114] They found that 'ethical' interviewing tactics predominated. Problematic tactics, such as police attempts to minimize the seriousness of the crime, did not occur. Confessions were obtained in 31 of the 80 cases, leading the researchers to conclude that ethical tactics may even be more productive than more aggressive ones.[115] However, while there is much to reassure here, we lack a comprehensive picture of current interviewing tactics. It has always been in serious cases, where the police may be under significant pressure to get results, that interviewing has been most problematic. Such cases are rare enough that they may not have been represented in the recent research studies reviewed here. Gudjonsson's conclusion, based mainly on cases up to the early 1990s, was that in serious cases the police will resort to a number of pressurizing and manipulative tactics to gain a confession. This can result in confessions of dubious quality and censure by the courts.[116]

(B) THE RIGHT TO SILENCE

It was noted earlier that, despite the recommendations of the Royal Commission on Criminal Justice, major changes to the right to silence were introduced by the Criminal

---

[108] J. Pearse and G. Gudjonsson, 'Police Interviewing Techniques at Two South London Police Stations' (1996) 3 *Psychology, Crime & Law* 63.

[109] Above n 3, 102.   [110] *Ibid.*, 40.   [111] *Ibid.*, 40.   [112] *Ibid.*, 102.

[113] A. Griffiths and B. Milne, 'Will it All End in Tiers? Police Interviews with Suspects in Britain' in Williamson, above n 6.

[114] Soukara et al, above n 11.

[115] This theory has apparently been confirmed by empirical research: see S. Kassin et al, 'Police-Induced Confessions: Risk Factors and Recommendations' in *Law & Human Behavior* (forthcoming), 26, referring to unpublished research by Rigoni and Meissner.

[116] Gudjonsson, above n 5, Ch 4.

Justice and Public Order Act 1994. This legislation does not require suspects to answer questions, either during interview or at trial: in that sense a right to silence remains. What the legislation does do is allow a court or jury to draw adverse inferences from silence in four situations. One of them—where a defendant does not testify at trial—will not be discussed here. Two of the other situations are relatively well defined. Under s 36, where a suspect fails to account for objects, substances or marks on him or in his possession, an adverse inference can be drawn against him at trial. Under s 37, the failure to account for his presence at a particular place is treated the same way. With these sections, an inference can only be drawn if a specific question about the object/mark/presence is put to the suspect. In contrast, s 34 is much more open-ended. Adverse inferences can be drawn where a defendant relies on a fact in his defence at trial which he failed to mention during police questioning. The fact must be one which he could reasonably have been expected to have mentioned during questioning. The discussion here will concentrate on s 34, although many of the points are also applicable to ss 36 and 37.

There are a number of arguments for and against allowing adverse inferences.[117] To start with some of the reasons why these provisions were introduced, it is often said that silence, of the sort targeted by s 34, is suspicious, and that it is only right to draw it to the attention of the fact-finder. There can of course be innocent reasons for not mentioning facts during police interview, which include feeling ill or intimidated, not trusting the police, and wanting to protect someone else.[118] But, so long as these possibilities can be effectively brought to the attention of the jury, and weighted in the evaluation of the evidence, there does not seem anything inherently wrong in asking it to consider drawing an inference from silence. Another reason given for reform was that defendants might gain acquittal at trial by producing an 'ambush' defence—one that the prosecution had no inkling of, and would not be able to rebut at trial. There was little evidence of ambush defences being a significant problem,[119] and in any case new provisions on defence disclosure—which were recommended by the Royal Commission on Criminal Justice—offer an equally appropriate way of dealing with defence ambush.[120] All the same, the argument that ambush defences were not a significant problem was hardly an argument for the status quo, unless some positive reasons for retaining the traditional scope of the right to silence could be mustered.

What reasons are there, then, for not permitting inferences from silence? Strong reasons of principle are sometimes mentioned, such as that adverse inferences conflict with the privilege against self-incrimination. That claim raises a number of

---

[117] See the discussion in D. Morgan and G. Stephenson, *Suspicion and Silence: The Right to Silence in Police Investigations* (1994).

[118] See M. McConville and J. Hodgson, *Custodial Legal Advice and the Right to Silence* (1993).

[119] R. Leng, *The Right to Silence in Police Interrogation: A Study of Some of the Issues Underlying the Debate* (1993).

[120] The provisions are to be found in the Criminal Procedure and Investigations Act 1996, discussed further in Ch 9.

complex issues which will be dealt with in Chapter 5. One problem with adverse inferences is that they put pressure on suspects to talk. This was something of concern to the Royal Commission on Criminal Justice, which worried that the pressure might lead to innocent suspects making incriminating statements. Here it quoted from the Report of the Royal Commission on Criminal Procedure, which had argued that adverse inferences 'might put strong (and additional) psychological pressure upon some suspects to answer questions without knowing precisely what was the substance of any evidence for the accusations against them.... This in our view might well increase the risk of innocent people, particularly those under suspicion for the first time, making damaging statements.'[121] Two comments can be made about this. First, the passage notes that any pressure brought to bear by the possibility of inferences will be additional to the existing pressures of police interview. There is little doubt that many suspects find detention and questioning an intimidating process. However, it is sometimes noted that those who are especially vulnerable to making false confessions are likely to do so anyway, even with the full protection of the right to silence. While there is some truth in this, the traditional right to silence allows legal advisers to counsel vulnerable suspects to remain silent without worrying that this may jeopardize the case in court. Allowing adverse inferences also gives an additional tool to the police, who might use inferences as a particular threat in some cases. There seems to be some merit, then, to the argument about the dangers of pressurizing suspects. A second point to make about the passage just quoted is that it gestures towards another reason for the traditional right to silence: it highlights the fact that at police interview, the suspect may not know the details of the evidence against him. At trial, most people would think it unfair to ask a defendant to defend himself without full knowledge of the prosecution case. It is arguable that similar concerns apply at interview, and that here suspects should not be asked to engage in discussion of the case against them unless they know its details.[122] Thus the Royal Commission on Criminal Procedure worried that a suspect would be required to 'answer questions based upon possibly unsubstantiated and unspecific allegations or suspicion, even though he is not required to do that at the trial. Such a change could be regarded as acceptable only if, at a minimum, the suspect were to be provided at all stages of the investigation with full knowledge of his rights, complete information about the evidence available to the police at the time, and an exact understanding of the consequences of silence.'[123] The principle here might be linked to a more theoretical defence of aspects of the right to silence made by Kent Greenawalt. According to Greenawalt, it is a basic moral principle that

---

[121] Quoted in Royal Commission on Criminal Justice, above n 92, Ch 2, para 23.

[122] A. Zuckerman, *The Principles of Criminal Evidence* (1989), 330.

[123] Royal Commission on Criminal Procedure, *The Investigation and Prosecution of Criminal Offences in England and Wales* (1981), 4.52.

one should not be expected to respond to accusations in the absence of reasonable suspicion.[124]

These, then, are some of the arguments for and against the changes to the right to silence brought in by the CJPOA. The actual provisions in the Act were not the last word on just when adverse inferences could be drawn from silence. The provisions left considerable scope to the courts to interpret them and to add additional safeguards. It is therefore important to look at the case law before examining how the Act has changed the context of police interview.[125] This is an area in which the European Court of Human Rights has been involved: it has cautiously accepted that the new law is compatible with the Convention. In *Murray*,[126] a decision on similar provisions in Northern Ireland, the Court found that the right to silence is not absolute. It found it permissible that the accused's silence, 'in situations which clearly call for an explanation from him, be taken into account in assessing the evidence adduced by the prosecution.'[127] It did, however, observe that in that case the question of what inferences to draw had been left to a professional judge, and that a number of other safeguards restricted the use of silence as evidence of guilt. It also held that the fact that Murray had been denied access to legal advice before police questioning led to a breach of Article 6: legal advice was seen as taking on particular importance in cases where inferences could be drawn from silence. This, as was seen earlier, led to changes in English law and to a new caution which has to be given where a suspect is questioned without access to legal advice. The Court considered the English silence provisions in more detail in *Condron v United Kingdom*.[128] Again, the provisions were found to pass muster so long as they were handled carefully. In particular, it was held to be crucial to instruct the jury in some detail on the nature of inferences that can be drawn from silence. The Court endorsed the model direction on inferences from silence given by the Court of Appeal, and found that the fact that part of it had not been given by the trial judge in *Condron* led to a breach of Article 6. A similar conclusion was reached in *Beckles v United Kingdom*.[129]

Under the current case law of the European Court of Human Rights and the Court of Appeal, then, a jury in an inferences from silence case must be given a number of directions.[130] It should be told that the defendant cannot be convicted solely or mainly on the basis of an inference from silence, and that an inference can only be drawn if it is satisfied that: when interviewed, the defendant could reasonably have been expected to mention the fact in question; that the only sensible explanation for his failure to do so is that he had no answer at the time or none that would stand up

---

[124] K. Greenawalt, 'Silence as a Moral and Constitutional Right' (1981) 23 *William & Mary L Rev* 15.

[125] For a more detailed analysis, see M. Redmayne, 'English Warnings' (2008) 30 *Cardozo L Rev* 1047, 1054–71.

[126] Above n 84.   [127] *Ibid.*, [47].   [128] (2001) 31 EHRR 1.   [129] [2002] *Crim LR* 917.

[130] See *R v Argent* [1997] 2 Cr App R 27; Judicial Studies Board Specimen Direction 40 (at www.jsboard. co.uk).

to scrutiny; and that without the inference from silence, the prosecution's case is so strong that it clearly calls for an answer by the defendant.[131] The usual inference to be drawn is that the fact in question is false.

The most unsatisfactory case law from the Court of Appeal has been on the subject of legal advice. The court has doubtless felt that it has had to be cautious here. It expressed a concern that ruling that legal advice not to answer police questions is a bar to adverse inferences would render s 34 'wholly nugatory'.[132] Initially, it seemed that in a case where a suspect had remained silent on legal advice, the jury would have to consider whether the reasons for the advice were good ones.[133] The Court of Appeal rethought its position in *Betts and Hall*, where it noted that what really mattered was whether the defendant had remained silent because of legal advice, not whether his decision was wise or whether the advice was good.[134] But later decisions have now doubted this. In *Howell*, the defendant claimed that he would have been only too happy to explain himself to the police, but his legal adviser had counselled silence, and he had decided to follow this advice.[135] The Court of Appeal now held that an adverse inference could be drawn even if the defendant genuinely relied on his solicitor's advice. What was important, instead, was whether the suspect was behaving reasonably. 'There must always be soundly based objective reasons for silence, sufficiently cogent and telling to weigh in the balance against the clear public interest in an account being given by the suspect to the police.'[136] This was followed by *Hoare*, where some attempt was made to reconcile the judgments, but with the bottom line being that a jury can still draw an inference where a suspect has been advised to stay silent by his solicitor.[137] Both *Howell* and *Hoare* are marred by some very poor reasoning.[138] As the reference to the public interest in *Howell* indicates, these judgments are driven by policy concerns; the courts want suspects to talk to the police. But even if it is in the public interest that suspects should talk to the police, this goes no way to justify drawing an adverse inference in the individual case. That depends, in simple terms, on whether silence is suspicious. And where a legal advisor has counselled silence, it is surely difficult to conclude that silence is suspicious, ie that the suspect's real reason for silence is that he has no good explanation for the evidence against him rather than that he is relying on his solicitor's advice that silence is in his best interests. The most depressing thing in these judgments is Auld LJ's rhetorical question: 'if [an innocent] defendant is advised to remain silent, why on earth should he do so...?',[139] a question which can only make one wonder why we bother going to such

---

[131] The notes to the JSB directions observe that there is some uncertainty as to the last of these requirements. Its endorsement by the European Court of Human Rights in *Beckles*, and by the Court of Appeal in *Chenia* [2003] 2 Cr App R 6, point to its being mandatory.

[132] *Condron and Condron* [1997] 1 Cr App R 185, 191.

[133] A good discussion is I. Dennis, *The Law of Evidence* (3rd ed, 2007), 182–8.

[134] [2001] 2 Cr App R 257; see also *Chenia*, above n 131.

[135] [2003] *Crim LR* 405, confirmed in *Knight* [2004] 1 Cr App R 9.   [136] *Ibid.*, 24.

[137] [2005] 1 Cr App R 22.   [138] See Redmayne, above n 125, 1066–71.

[139] *Hoare*, above n 137, [53].

trouble giving suspects access to legal advice. Insofar as there is a wider lesson to draw here, it is that there is an inevitable tension between promoting legal advice to suspects and allowing juries to draw inferences from silence. But to resolve this tension by allowing juries to draw inferences where there is no rational basis for doing so is unprincipled.

A further tension in the adverse inferences scheme concerns disclosure. We noted above that there are questions about whether it is fair to draw an inference from silence where a suspect does not know the details of the case against him. While the police may be under a duty not to actively mislead a suspect, for example by telling him that evidence exists where it does not,[140] they are under no obligation to inform suspects of what evidence there is against them. As the Court of Appeal put it in *R v W*, 'there is simply no rule of law or practice requiring the police to disclose the full extent of their relevant evidence before questioning a suspect'.[141] There may be good reasons for not disclosing too much at the start of an interview. The police worry that full disclosure of the evidence—for example, of a DNA match between suspect and scene of crime—will allow the suspect to fabricate an exculpatory story.[142] One of the themes of investigative interviewing is that the suspect should give an account which should then be challenged in terms of its fit with the evidence. Here, partial disclosure may be helpful; indeed, psychological research suggests that while it is very difficult to tell whether a suspect is lying by observing his demeanour, selective disclosure of evidence may be an effective way of detecting deceit.[143] So far, however, the courts have done little to indicate that lack of disclosure should block an inference from silence; it is simply one factor that might be put to the jury.[144] There is a hint that the European Court of Human Rights might see non-disclosure as more significant. In *Murray* it noted that inferences from silence were permissible 'in situations which clearly call for an explanation from'[145] the suspect, but this point has never been expanded on. The tension, then, is between what may be a useful police tactic of withholding evidence at interview, and drawing inferences from silence. In *Kirk*, the police did not inform the suspect that the victim of a mugging had died, leading the Court of Appeal to rule that evidence of the ensuing confession should have been excluded, because *Kirk* had not been able to make informed decisions about whether to answer questions and whether to consult a lawyer.[146] The courts now need to give more thought to the question whether similar concerns should block inferences from silence in cases where little evidence has been disclosed.

---

[140] *R v Mason* [1988] 1 WLR 139.   [141] [2006] EWCA Crim 1292, [8].

[142] See HMIC, *Under the Microscope Refocused: A Revisit to the Thematic Inspection Report on Scientific and Technical Support* (2002), 10–11.

[143] See M. Hartwig et al, 'Detecting Deception via Strategic Disclosure of Evidence' (2005) 29 *Law & Human Behavior* 469; M. Hartwig et al, 'Strategic Use of Evidence During Police Interviews: When Training to Detect Deception Works' (2006) 30 *Law & Human Behavior* 603.

[144] See *Argent*, above n 130; cf *R v Beckles* [2005] 1 WLR 2829, [51].

[145] Above n 84, 47.   [146] [2000] 1 WLR 567.

What effect has s 34 had on suspects in practice? Research allows a number of con-clusions to be drawn.[147] Changes to the right to silence may have led to fewer suspects refusing to answer some or all of the questions put to them by the police: one study found that the number of suspects refusing to answer all questions had fallen from 10 to 6 per cent.[148] But this has not led to more confessions: some police officers feel they are just getting more lies from suspects.[149] This may be helpful if the lie can be shown to be false, but it is not necessarily an easy route to conviction. And where the convic-tion rate is concerned, the new provisions have made no discernible impact.[150] One concern highlighted by the research is that the new law, and the caution that goes with it, can be used as a weapon by the police. If a suspect has been advised to stay silent, the police can repeatedly refer to the terms of the caution to persuade the suspect to rethink his position, thus driving a wedge between the suspect and his adviser.[151] Finally, some legal advisers have expressed concern about how the new law can bring pressure to bear on the vulnerable.[152]

There are, then, reasons for concern about the changes to the right to silence brought in by the CJPOA. While the Court of Appeal and European Court of Human Rights have gone some way to erecting safeguards to prevent the jury putting too much weight on silence, rather less has been done to ensure that the inferences from silence regime does not operate unfairly in the police station. Requirements of dis-closure before interview remain—perhaps with good reason—minimal and, by not taking a firmer stand on the issue of legal advice, the courts have effectively diluted its authority, strengthening the hand of the police in cases where suspects are advised to stay silent. In *Murray* the European Court of Human Rights took a strong stand on the issue of access to legal advice before interview. In giving judgment, the Court noted that

'at the beginning of police interrogation, an accused is confronted with a fundamental dilemma relating to his defence. If he chooses to remain silent, adverse inferences may be drawn against him.... On the other hand, if the accused opts to break his silence during the course of interrogation, he runs the risk of prejudicing his defence without necessarily re-moving the possibility of inferences being drawn against him. Under such conditions the concept of fairness enshrined in Article 6 requires that the accused has the benefit of assist-ance of a lawyer already at the initial stages of police interrogation.'[153]

Yet most suspects still face this dilemma without the benefit of legal advice; all that is required is that they be given access to advice, something which, for various rea-sons, the majority still do not take up. In *Howell*, the Court of Appeal also observed

---

[147] T. Bucke, R. Street and D. Brown, *The Right of Silence: The Impact of the CJPOA 1994* (2000). Broadly similar conclusions about the operation of Northern Irish law are drawn in J. Jackson, M. Wolfe and K. Quinn, *Legislating Against Silence: The Northern Ireland Experience* (2000).

[148] Bucke, Street and Brown, *ibid.*, 31; but cf Clarke and Milne's study of 177 interviews with suspects which found that 10 per cent involved 'no comment' interviews: above n 3, 33.

[149] *Ibid.*, 34.   [150] *Ibid.*, 67; for some complications, see Redmayne, above n 125, 1081–2.

[151] Bucke, Street and Brown, above n 147, 27–30.   [152] *Ibid.*, 37–8.   [153] See n 84 above, 67.

that s 34 changes the context of police questioning: '[n]ow, the police interview and trial are to be seen as part of a continuous process in which the suspect is engaged from the beginning.'[154] More recently, as was noted earlier, the Code C rules on when questioning should end have been changed: under the revised Code, questioning—which can continue so as to test the suspect's account and can capitalize on this by using non-responses as evidence—might be thought to have taken on some of the nature of cross-examination. Given the new significance of questioning, it would seem right to strengthen the suspect's due process protections in the police station.[155] This would include stronger requirements on disclosure of the police case before interview—or, if disclosure is minimal, a bar on adverse inferences—and perhaps better access to legal advice. Suspects cannot be forced to consult lawyers if they do not want to, but it is known that some refuse legal advice so as not to prolong their detention. Having legal advisers on hand in police stations has been suggested as a way to overcome this problem, and it is perhaps now time to give it more thought.[156]

The point, then, is not that a regime which involves drawing inferences from silence in the police station is inevitably unfair. Its fairness is conditional on the environment in which questioning takes place   The other problem that has emerged in the wake of the CJPOA is the way in which the courts deal with the issue of legal advice as a reason for silence. The judiciary are doubtless concerned that allowing legal advice to be a reason for silence that prevents adverse inferences would result in all solicitors counselling suspects to remain silent. This seems unlikely: after all, it was not what happened prior to the introduction of the CJPOA provisions. But even if this concern is realistic, it does not follow that the courts should take it into account. If they do—as seen in *Howell*—they will penalize defendants who follow legal advice. If that is the only way to make s 34 workable, then it would be better not to have the section at all. Again, the point is not that there is anything wrong in theory with drawing inferences from silence, but that if the scheme cannot be made to work fairly in practice, it would be preferable to abandon it.

4.4 INTERVIEWING VICTIMS

While the focus of this chapter is on the questioning of suspects, it is worth noting briefly that similar concerns apply to police questioning of victims and witnesses. Like

---

[154] See n 135 above, 23.

[155] See J. Jackson, 'Silence and Proof: Extending the Boundaries of Criminal Proceedings in the United Kingdom' (2001) 5 *E & P* 145; J. Jackson, 'Re-Conceptualizing the Right of Silence as an Effective Fair Trial Standard' (2009) 58 *ICLQ* 835.

[156] See A. Sanders, 'Can Coercive Powers be Effectively Controlled or Regulated? The Case for Anchored Pluralism' in E. Cape and R. Young, *Regulating Policing: The Police and Criminal Evidence Act 1984, Past, Present and Future* (2008), 71.

suspects, victims and witnesses can be suggestible and compliant; they need to be questioned carefully. Whereas suspects have an interest in ensuring that what they say is not distorted by the police, victims and witnesses will often have less incentive to do so. They may feel that the best way they can help the police is by agreeing with any suggestions put to them, or by being as definite as possible about what they saw. It is therefore important to avoid putting leading questions to witnesses, or to disclose to them too much of the investigator's theory of the case.

For the police, the purpose of questioning victims and witnesses is generally to produce a statement—a written summary of their evidence. The statement plays an important part in the processing of the case: it will form part of the case file reviewed by the Crown Prosecution Service (CPS) in deciding whether to continue the prosecution. Cases often come to court some months after the event in question. Witnesses may then have little memory about what they saw at the time. A witness's earlier statement is often used to 'refresh' memory—which raises the possibility that inaccuracies in the statement will then be repeated in the witness's testimony. And increasingly witness statements themselves can be admitted as evidence under various exceptions to the hearsay rule.[157]

What is known about the questioning of victims and witnesses suggests that standards here are worse than where suspects are concerned. Studies have indicated that police officers use questioning tactics which shape the evidence gained from witnesses.[158] As with the questioning of suspects, there is now much emphasis on training and the PEACE model is emphasized. Specialist training is given to those interviewing sensitive witnesses, such as children. But there is little evidence that the training has had much impact. Clarke and Milne found that in run of the mill cases leading questions were common, and the 'predominant use of closed questions and the view that interviewers were "just taking a statement" indicates that interviews were clearly highly interviewer driven, with a confirmatory bias.'[159] The majority of interviews succeeded in gaining only a partial account from the interviewee. Shepherd and Milne conclude: 'Officers are apt to interview witnesses in ways that are wholly improper and ineffective'.[160]

As Shepherd and Milne point out, one measure would go a long way towards addressing these problems. If interviews with witnesses were recorded, it would be possible to check exactly what had been said and to judge whether the interviewer had used inappropriate methods. Recording would also allow effective supervision,

---

[157] See A. Heaton-Armstrong, D. Wolchover and A. Maxwell-Scott, 'Obtaining, Recording and Admissibility of Out-of-Court Witness Statements' in A. Heaton-Armstrong et al, *Witness Testimony: Psychological, Investigative and Evidential Perspectives* (2006).

[158] E. Shepherd and R. Milne, 'Full and Faithful: Ensuring Quality, Practice and Integrity of Outcome in Witness Interviews' in A. Heaton-Armstrong, D. Wolchover and E. Shepherd (eds), *Analysing Witness Testimony* (1999).

[159] See Clarke and Milne, above n 3, 58–9.

[160] E. Shepherd and R. Milne, ' "Have you Told Management about this?": Bringing Witness Interviewing Into the Twenty-First Century' in *Witness Testimony*, above n 157.

giving teeth to the efforts at training; after all, recording of interviews with suspects is doubtless one factor which has contributed to improvements in this area. Current policy is that interviews with vulnerable witnesses, and significant witnesses in major enquiries, will be recorded. But, ever mindful of resources, the Government has not been keen to extend recording.[161] As Shepherd and Milne point out, though, cheap portable recording devices are now available.[162] It is surely time to require recording of all interviews which lead to the production of witness statements.

4.5 CONFESSIONS IN COURT

It has been seen that there remain concerns about the way in which suspects are interviewed by the police, especially given changes to the right to silence. In the worst case scenario, a false confession will be the result of the interviewing process. Research suggests that confessions exert a powerful influence on juries.[163] It is therefore important to have safeguards at court which will guard against a false confession leading to a conviction.

The key legal provision in this regard is s 76 of PACE. Under this section, a confession should be ruled inadmissible if it has been obtained by oppression (s 76(2)(a)), or 'in consequence of anything said or done which was likely, in the circumstances existing at the time, to render unreliable any confession which might have been made by him in consequence thereof' (s 76(2)(b)). There is a degree of overlap between this section and s 78, which applies to confessions as well as to other prosecution evidence. Section 78 allows evidence to be excluded where its admission would render the proceedings unfair; this provision is discussed in detail in Chapter 11. Section 77 requires a court to caution a jury about relying on confessions made by the mentally handicapped. Here, the focus will be on s 76(2)(b).[164]

The wording of this provision is convoluted. It is not a simple 'exclude if unreliable' rule, but instead requires the court to consider *hypothetical* unreliability: the confession should be excluded, 'notwithstanding that it may be true',[165] if it was obtained in circumstances conducive to unreliability. The reason for this is presumably that the provision is intended to sanction bad questioning practices, even if they produce a confession which can be proved to be reliable, for example by evidence corroborating

---

[161] *The Conduct of Investigations into Past Cases of Abuse in Children's Homes—Government Response* (2003), paras 29–35.

[162] Above n 160.

[163] See I. Blandon Gitlin, K. Sperry and R. A. Leo, 'Jurors Believe Interrogation Tactics are not Likely to Elicit False Confessions: Will Expert Witness Testimony Inform them Otherwise?' *Psychology, Crime and Law* (forthcoming).

[164] The oppression safeguard is important, but appears to be rarely applied. The confession of Stephen Miller seems to be the only example of an appeal court finding interviewing conduct oppressive.

[165] Section 76(2).

it or even a further admission by the defendant.[166] For the most part, then, the case law is clear: 'one cannot overcome problems about the reliability of a confession by using extrinsic evidence to show that it is likely to be true.'[167] But in *Proulx*, a case where a suspect had confessed in an undercover operation that dangled financial and romantic rewards in front of him, particular stress was put on the concept 'any confession'. This was held to mean 'any such confession', and to require examination of exactly what had been said by the suspect: 'the relevant confession is thus to involvement in...a killing about which the applicant had already volunteered knowledge'.[168] Combined with the emphasis on the original court's assessment of the applicant, this approach comes close to looking at actual rather than hypothetical unreliability.

If a reliable confession may be excluded under s 76 because of the way in which it was obtained, it may also be true that an unreliable confession may be admitted if it was not procured by wrongdoing. The wording 'anything said or done' hints that only if the police do something wrong will the confession be excluded. There is a certain amount of uncertainty in the case law here, revolving around the question of how much emphasis should be placed on these words. For example, in *Goldenberg* the defendant had requested an interview with the police but claimed that the result-ing confession was potentially unreliable because he was desperate to be bailed so as to be able to obtain heroin.[169] The Court of Appeal held that this could be ignored because he had not confessed in consequence of anything said or done by the police, but on his own initiative. This rather restrictive view was supported in *Crampton*[170] and *Wahab*,[171] but in a number of other cases factors such as a low mental age have been taken into account.[172] In *Foster*, however, the suspect's vulnerability was down-played by the Court of Appeal because while it may have been known to the police, it had not been shown that the interviewing officers were aware of it.[173] *Crampton* also highlights the causal test in the section: the words 'in consequence of' appear twice in s 76(2)(b), and this again tends to focus the test on the role of misconduct in securing confessions. The Court of Appeal in *Crampton* referred to the pre-PACE case law, quoting from *Rennie*: 'very few confessions are inspired solely by remorse. Often the motives of an accused are mixed and include a hope that an early admis-sion may lead to an earlier release or to a lighter sentence. If it were the law that the mere presence of such a motive, even if prompted by something said or done..., led inexorably to the exclusion of a confession, nearly every confession would be ren-dered inadmissible.'[174] In this way, the background factors, which put some pressure on all suspects to confess, can be ignored. The approach of the courts seems to be that only if the police draw the prospect of bail and the like to the suspect's attention

---

[166] As in *McGovern* (1991) 92 Cr App R 228.   [167] *R v Blackburn* [2005] EWCA Crim 1349, [62].

[168] *R v Bow St Magistrates' Court, ex p Proulx* [2001] 1 All ER 57, [46].

[169] (1989) 88 Cr App R 285.   [170] (1991) 92 Cr App R 369.   [171] [2003] 1 Cr App R 15.

[172] E.g. *Everett* [1988] *Crim LR* 826; *McGovern*, above n 166.   [173] [2003] EWCA Crim 178, [63].

[174] (1982) 74 Cr App R 207, 212.

will a confession be excluded.[175] As we saw above, it is not clear what the status of the sentence discount is, but given the degree of promotion it gets nowadays it may be that even if the police draw it to the suspect's attention it will be treated as a background factor.

One criticism of s 76 and its case law is that the courts have retained a reasonable degree of latitude in individual cases by never settling on a definitive interpretation of the section. In *Proulx*, it is actual reliability which is highlighted. In cases such as *Goldenberg* and *Crampton*, the focus shifts away from reliability and towards wrongdoing. It was noted above that illicit drug taking is a factor predictive of confession, the likely explanation being that drug takers are anxious to escape from custody. It does not seem right, then, that this very real factor is ignored in the reliability determination. The emphasis on wrongdoing in the s 76 case law is not necessarily a bad thing: breach of the Code C rules will often disadvantage a suspect in some way. But a better way to scrutinize confessions would surely be for s 76(2)(b) to be focused purely on reliability, leaving concerns about fairness and wrongdoing to be dealt with through the application of s 78.

It has been seen that PACE and the Codes give little detailed guidance on what is and is not appropriate questioning. It should now be apparent that the s 76 case law adds little in the way of detail. Could more detailed guidelines be given? This is something which it is probably very difficult to do. It is not easy to say what degree of pressure it is appropriate to apply to suspects in order to gain admissions; and there are so many different ways in which pressure can be applied that creating guidelines is difficult.[176] However, one rule which has been suggested is a prohibition on deception in police interviews.[177] Research on questioning in the US reveals that deception, in the form of exaggerating the strength of evidence, or inventing the existence of evidence, is common;[178] it is also associated with false confessions.[179] Deception is in fact a tactic recommended by the leading US interrogation manual.[180] Such deception was found to be a common ploy in police questioning prior to PACE,[181] but it now seems to meet with judicial disfavour.[182] It seems right that it should be clearly outlawed. Not only is police deception ethically problematic,[183] it also puts inappro-

---

[175] See *Barry* (1992) 95 Cr App R 384; Code C, 11.5.

[176] For various examples of pressurizing tactics, see Gudjonsson, above n 3, Ch 4.

[177] A. Alschuler, 'Constraint and Confession' (1997) 74 *Denver U L Rev* 957.

[178] Ofshe and Leo, above n 16.

[179] See Drizin and Leo, above n 15; R. A. Nash and K. A. Wade, 'Innocent But Proven Guilty: Using False Video Evidence to Elicit False Confessions and Create False Beliefs' (2009) 23 *Applied Cognitive Psychology* 624.

[180] Gudjonsson, above n 3, Ch 1.

[181] B. Irving, *Police Interrogation: A Study of Current Practice* (1980).

[182] See *R v Mason* [1988] 1 WLR 139, and the case of George Heron discussed in Gudjonsson, above n 3, 98. *R v Imran and Hussain* [1997] *Crim LR* 754 holds that there is a duty on the police not to actively mislead a suspect.

[183] For further discussion of the ethical issues, see A. Ashworth, 'Should the Police be Allowed to Use Deceptive Practices' (1998) 114 *LQR* 108.

priate pressure on suspects to confess. If the evidence against a suspect is in reality thin, this points towards innocence, and pressuring tactics should not be used. Of course, if there really is strong evidence incriminating a defendant it is appropriate to confront him with it; although this constitutes pressure to confess, the degree of pressure is calibrated with the degree to which we have reason to believe that the suspect is guilty.

There is another rule which can be applied to confessions and which has similar merits: a rule requiring that confessions be corroborated by supporting evidence. This would mean that a defendant could not be convicted on the basis of a confession alone. A majority of the Royal Commission on Criminal Justice rejected such a rule, settling instead for a requirement to warn the jury about the dangers of relying on a confession alone.[184] One reason given against a corroboration rule was that it would lead to the collapse of some cases which are at present successfully prosecuted. This 'would lead to some defendants walking free who would rightly be found guilty under the present rules. This could only be regarded as acceptable if it could be shown that the proposed corroboration rule gave sufficiently greater safeguards against wrong convictions than are now available.'[185] The problem with this way of putting things is that it focuses on right and wrong convictions. It is of course very difficult to know whether a conviction based on no more than a confession is right or wrong in the sense of true to the facts. A more principled way of resolving the debate is to ask whether unsupported confessions are, by their nature, sufficiently strong as evidence to warrant conviction. Even a guilty person is not 'rightly found guilty' if that finding is based on weak evidence. Despite the improvements brought in by PACE and the awareness of the problems of false confessions, confessions remain a problematic sort of evidence. Given the context of detention in the police station, police questioning is always a process which applies pressure to suspects to confess. There are also the factors highlighted in *Rennie*: confessions will often be made in the hope that they will bring some advantage. Although a confession will probably be excluded if it can be shown to have been made as the result of an explicit offer to grant bail or the like, research suggests that offers of lenient treatment can be communicated implicitly.[186] Suspects who are addicted to drugs may be particularly keen to bring their detention to an end. And the increasing emphasis on sentence discounts for guilty pleas and other forms of cooperation make it increasingly likely that suspects will expect to gain some advantage from confessing. The court in *Rennie* is right that such factors alone should not result in the exclusion of a confession, but they do help to make the case for a corroboration rule. In sum, there are simply too many doubts about the processes which lead suspects to confess for a conviction on a confession alone ever to be justified.

---

[184] Above n 92, Ch 4, para 87.   [185] *Ibid.*, Ch 4, para 71.
[186] S. Kassin and K. McNall, 'Police Interrogation and Confession: Communicating Promises and Threats by Pragmatic Implication' (1991) 5 *Law & Human Behavior* 233.

4.6 CONCLUSIONS

Two recent reviews of confessions and the processes that produce them, written by psychologists who have long taken an interest in false confessions, conclude with a series of recommendations for regulation of the police questioning process.[187] The proposals focus on the situation in the US, and it is striking that on the whole the recommendations reflect what is already standard practice in the UK. In the UK confessions are recorded, there are rules giving suspects some respite from very lengthy questioning sessions, the presentation of false evidence is probably frowned upon, police are trained in 'investigative' interviewing techniques, and research suggests that tactics such as minimization (where the police downplay the gravity of the crime) are rare. While in this chapter we have been critical of various aspects of the detention and questioning process, it is important to underline how much progress there has been since the 1980s,[188] and how favourably the situation in the UK compares with that in the US where, remarkably, many jurisdictions do not require that police questioning be recorded.

Nevertheless, it is important to underline that, however well regulated the police questioning process is, confessions remain a suspect type of evidence. Police detention will always be stressful, and innocent suspects will always have some incentives for confessing. This is why there is a case to be made for the corroboration of confessions. It is also crucial that the gains there have been since PACE are not undermined by Government initiatives to cut costs by reducing the amount and quality of legal advice available to suspects. Finally, looking beyond confessions, we have seen that it is time to bring the new questioning culture to interviews with witnesses as well as suspects.

FURTHER READING

SKINNS, L., 'I'm a Detainee; Get me Out of Here' (2009) 49 *Brit J Criminol* 399.

KASSIN, S. and GUDJONSSON, G., 'The Psychology of Confessions: A Review of the Literature and Issues' (2004) 5 *Psychological Science in the Public Interest* 33.

REDMAYNE, M., 'English Warnings' (2008) 30 *Cardozo L Rev* 1047.

---

[187] S. M. Kassin et al, 'Police-Induced Confessions: Risk Factors and Recommendations' in *Law & Human Behavior* (forthcoming); S. Kassin and G. Gudjonsson, 'The Psychology of Confessions: A Review of the Literature and Issues' (2004) 5 *Psychological Science in the Public Interest* 33.

[188] See also D. Dixon, 'Authorise and Regulate: A Comparative Perspective on the Rise and Fall of a Regulatory Strategy' in Cape and Young, above n 156.

Questions for Discussion

1. Should inferences be drawn at trial from a suspect's failure to mention facts at a police interview?

2. Are defendants given sufficient protection against false conviction by (a) the rules governing detention and questioning and (b) the courts?

5

GATHERING EVIDENCE: RELIABILITY, PRIVACY AND BODILY INTEGRITY

The criminal process is, in large measure, an investigative process. It exists to prepare cases for effective trial. To this end, prosecuting authorities are given powers enabling them to gather evidence. But these powers can infringe various interests. Some may be the interests of the criminal process itself: the purposes of the process are undermined if unreliable evidence is gathered. Others will be values external to criminal process, such as liberty, privacy, freedom from humiliation and bodily integrity. This chapter examines the ways in which these concerns do, and should, mould the process of gathering evidence against suspects. The sections of this chapter are relatively unconnected, more freestanding than those in other chapters of this book. However, from this rather fragmented set of topics we hope there emerges a picture of the complexity of criminal process, showing the varied interests and constraints that affect it.

5.1 STOP AND SEARCH

Stop and search is one of the most controversial police powers. This is primarily because of long-standing concern that the power is used in a racially discriminatory manner.[1] Commenting on the evidence it heard from minority ethnic communities, the Stephen Lawrence Inquiry observed: 'If there was one area of complaint which was universal it was the issue of "stop and search"'.[2] While the Lawrence Inquiry highlighted the racial sensitivity of stop and search and gave impetus to efforts to improve the way in which the power is used, it seems that little has changed. As various reviews of the situation ten years on from the Lawrence Inquiry note, the disproportionate use of stop and search against blacks has grown rather than diminished and the power

---

[1] See, e.g., B. Bowling and C. Phillips, *Racism, Crime and Justice* (2002), Ch 5.
[2] *The Stephen Lawrence Inquiry* (1999), para 45.8.

remains a sensitive issue with minority ethnic communities.[3] Even ignoring the race issue, there is concern that the majority of stops and searches are carried out on flimsy grounds and that stop and search is a generally ineffective means of investigating and disrupting crime.

Section 1 of the Police and Criminal Evidence Act 1984 (PACE) provides a police officer with a power to stop and search persons and vehicles if he reasonably suspects that he will find stolen or prohibited articles—prohibited articles being weapons or items which can be used to commit offences of dishonesty or criminal damage.[4] A number of other statutes provide similar powers for other offences, most notably the Misuse of Drugs Act 1971, which permits searches for controlled drugs.[5] There are also significant stop and search powers under the Criminal Justice and Public Order Act 1994 (CJPOA), s 60 and the Terrorism Act 2000, s 44. Under the former, an area may be designated as one within which a general power of stop and search for offensive weapons will exist for 24 hours. When this occurs, a police officer may stop and search persons and vehicles for weapons 'whether or not he has any grounds for suspecting that the person or vehicle is carrying weapons'.[6] The power can only be used where a senior officer reasonably believes that serious violence will take place within the area. A similar power exists to designate an area and carry out searches for items connected with terrorism under the Terrorism Act 2000.[7] Again, reasonable suspicion is not required. This power has been used widely, with the whole of the Metropolitan police area designated for 'suspicionless' stops for terrorist items since 2003.[8] A code of practice issued under PACE, Code A, governs the use of all stop and search powers.

Stop and search involves detaining a suspect in a public place for a short period in order to search his or her outer clothing.[9] The suspect can be made to remove a jacket and gloves, but any more intrusive search should be carried out by an officer of the same sex as the suspect and in private—for example, in a police van.[10] The most intrusive searches should only be carried out at a police station, and only if the suspect can be taken there quickly.[11] The distinction between the stop and the search is significant: the officer may question the suspect before carrying out the search: questioning may be used to dispel suspicion (as when the suspect gives an explanation for his suspicious behaviour), but it should not be used to generate reasonable suspicion where none already exists.[12] Many people will be stopped but not searched; a stop which does not result in a search is much less intrusive and humiliating than one that does. It is obvious that, in general, stop and search potentially impacts on two rights found in the European Convention on Human Rights (ECHR). Article 5 guarantees the right to liberty and security of person and Article 8 the

---

[3] Home Affairs Committee, *The Macpherson Report—Ten Years On* (2009), 4–5; N. Rollock/Runnymede Trust, *The Stephen Lawrence Inquiry 10 Years On: An Analysis of the Literature* (2009), 56–60. See also J. Foster, T. Newburn and A. Souhami, *Assessing the Impact of the Stephen Lawrence Inquiry* (2005).

[4] Criminal Damage was added by the Criminal Justice Act 2003, s 1.   [5] Section 23.

[6] CJPOA 1994, s 60(5).   [7] Sections 44–7. See also s 43.

[8] See *R (Gillan) v Commissioner of Police of the Metropolis* [2006] UKHL 12.

[9] Code A, 1.2, 3.3, 3.5.   [10] Code A, 3.6; PACE, s 2(9)(a).   [11] Code A, 3.7, note 6.

[12] Code A, 2.11.

right to private life. Article 5 does list a series of circumstances in which 'detention' will be permitted, but in the context of investigating crime reasonable suspicion is required. In *Gillan*, however, the House of Lords held that stop and search did not involve 'detention'; it followed from this that Article 5 did not apply and that suspicionless searches under the CJPOA were prima facie Human Rights Act compliant.[13] The majority also considered that Article 8 was not engaged, though Lord Brown did consider that in certain circumstances a search would be sufficiently intrusive to raise Article 8 issues.[14]

One of the key concerns about stop and search is that it is used on the basis of stereotypes, and over the years the definition of reasonable suspicion in Code A has been expanded to make it as clear as possible that this is unacceptable. There must be an 'objective basis' for the suspicion, 'based on facts, information, and/or intelligence'.[15] 'Reasonable suspicion can never be supported on the basis of personal factors alone'— for example, race, age, appearance, previous convictions.[16] 'Reasonable suspicion cannot be based on generalisations or stereotypical images of certain groups or categories of people as more likely to be involved in criminal activity;' and 'a person's religion cannot be considered as reasonable grounds for suspicion and should never be considered as a reason to stop or search.'[17] But a generalization based on the suspect's behaviour, as when the suspect appears to be hiding something, is permissible.[18] The latest version of the Code advises that reasonable suspicion 'should normally be linked to accurate and current intelligence', and that searches are most effective when targeted 'in a particular area at specified crime problems'.[19] 'The overall use of these powers is more likely to be effective when up to date and accurate intelligence or information is communicated to officers and they are well-informed about local crime patterns.'[20] No one reading the Code could be left in doubt about the sensitivity of the issues involved in stop and search.

The police are required to make a record of the search—including the basis for reasonable suspicion—and to provide the suspect with a copy. Researchers have found that officers often resorted to 'voluntary' or 'consensual' searches to avoid the Code requirements—including that of recording.[21] Code A now provides that 'An officer must not search a person, even with his or her consent, where no power to search is applicable'.[22] A record should be made of even consensual searches. The police will, however, often ask a person to account for themselves, asking what they are doing in a particular street, or why they are carrying a particular object. Just as anyone can ask a question of a person on the street, no legal power is needed to enable the police to ask such questions. While citizens are under no legal duty to answer such questions, the fact that police officers are figures of authority makes such encounters of dubious consensuality. A recommendation of the Lawrence Inquiry was therefore that instances of 'stop and account' should be recorded, with a copy of the record given to the person

---

[13] Above n 8.   [14] *Ibid*, [74].   [15] Code A, 2.2.   [16] *Ibid*.   [17] *Ibid*.
[18] Code A, 2.3.   [19] Code A, 2.4.   [20] Code A, 2.5.
[21] See D. Dixon, *Law in Policing: Legal Regulation and Police Practices* (1997), 93–104.
[22] Code A, 1.5.

questioned.[23] Under concerns about excessive police paperwork, this requirement is now being rethought.[24]

On the basis of the records made by police officers, the Home Office compiles statistics on the use of stop and search powers, including information on the race of those stopped. The figures are doubtless inaccurate owing to under-recording by the police (data from the British Crime Survey suggest that a quarter of stops go unrecorded),[25] but they tell us something about trends and about the racial disparity in the application of the power. In 2007–8 there were 1,035,438 recorded stops in England and Wales under PACE and other legislation requiring reasonable suspicion.[26] This is the highest level since 1998–9. In the early 2000s, the number of stops declined, probably as a result of criticisms of the power made by the Lawrence inquiry; police officers certainly reported sensitivity about use of the power against people from minority ethnic groups.[27] The renewed upward drift suggests that police sensitivity over the power is wearing off; it may also reflect concerns over knife crime and the belief that stop and search is an effective means of tackling it.[28] PACE Code A explains that 'the primary purpose of stop and search powers is to allow officers to allay or confirm suspicions about individuals without using their power of arrest.'[29] Most often, suspicions turn out to be unfounded. In 2007–8 only 11 per cent of stop and searches led to an arrest.[30] As often in the criminal process, the overall figures mark considerable regional variation. Cheshire stopped only six per thousand of its population in 2007–8, and Essex only eight per thousand, while the Metropolitan Police searched 60 per thousand and Merseyside 35.[31] Production of arrests also varies; for the Metropolitan Police, 11 per cent of stops led to an arrest while in Cheshire the figure was 24 per cent.[32] But there is not always a correlation between the amount the power is used and its success rate; while Essex searched many fewer of its population, it shared an 11 per cent arrest rate with London; Merseyside was more successful in this respect with a 17 per cent arrest rate.[33]

The figures on race and stop and search are initially stark. In 2007–8 blacks were nearly eight times more likely to be searched than whites, a slightly greater racial disparity than in the previous year,[34] and a situation that on its face is worse than it was

[23] See now Code A, 4.12. For criticism, see M. Fitzgerald, 'Stop and Think' *The Guardian* 26 March 2002.

[24] See K. Reid, 'Race issues and Stop and Search: Looking Behind the Statistics' (2009) 73 *J Crim L* 165.

[25] *Arrests for Notifiable Offences and the Operation of Certain Police Powers Under PACE: England and Wales, 2002/03*HOSB 17/03, paras 23–4.

[26] Ministry of Justice, *Statistics on Race and the Criminal Justice System 2007/8* (2009), 27.

[27] Foster et al, above n 3.

[28] This was the spin put on one piece of research: see 'Stop and Search Cuts Gun and Knife Crime' *The Times* 16 March 2009. This finding was denied by the authors of the report cited in the article; See Centre for Crime and Justice Studies Press Release, 16 March 2009. For the actual report, see Silvestri et al, *Young People, Knives and Guns* (2009). More recently, the Metropolitan police have claimed that stop and search has reduced knife crime: 'Knife Crime Down as Police Hail Stop and Search' *The Times* 18 May 2009.

[29] Code A, 1.4.   [30] *Satistics on Race*, above n 26, 28.

[31] *Statistics on Race*, above n 26, Table 4.2a.   [32] *Ibid.*, Table 4.4a.   [33] *Ibid.*

[34] *Ibid.*, 28. 'Black' is the term used in this report; figures for Asians are given separately. The figures given here are for 'ethnic appearance', as determined by police officers. Officers must also ask those stopped to provide their 'self-defined' ethnicity.

at the time of the Stephen Lawrence inquiry when blacks were five times more likely to be stopped.[35] In 2007–8 Asians were more than twice as likely to be stopped as were whites. There is again some regional variation, but all forces stopped a higher proportion of whites than blacks.[36] Many black people are searched more than once in a year.

These figures on race need careful interpretation, however. The Home Office figures showing that blacks are several times more likely to be stopped than whites reflect the proportion of black and white people in the national or local population. It can be argued, however, that taking the proportion of blacks and whites in the residential population as a whole as the basis for calculating the stop and search rate is not a good way of judging whether stop and search powers are being used in a discriminatory manner. The people most likely to be targeted for stop and search are young people who appear in public in areas with a high police presence. If blacks outnumber whites in this 'pool', then there may not be as much racial disparity as appears on the face of the figures. Research has been conducted on the population 'available' for stop and search, which tries to take this into account.[37] The general conclusion of this study is that when the population available for stop and search is used as the basis for the calculation, much of the disparity disappears. In fact, one general trend across the research areas was for whites to be stopped at a rate higher than their proportion in the available population.[38] This raises an obvious question: if stop and search is being targeted on particular areas—areas with large numbers of young black men on the streets—can this targeting be justified, or is it in itself discriminatory? The conclusion of the research was that stop and search was generally targeted on areas with high crime rates, and to that extent the targeting was justified. Beneath this general picture of racial equity, however, were found 'examples where those from minority ethnic backgrounds were stopped and searched more often than would have been expected from their numbers in the available population.' And 'stops and searches were targeted at some areas where there [were] disproportionate numbers of those from minority ethnic backgrounds, yet where the local crime rates did not appear to justify this attention.'[39]

There are other ways of looking beyond the population statistics. One is to look at arrest rates. Here it turns out that the same proportion of whites as blacks is arrested following a stop, which might suggest that the police stop each group on the basis of a similar level of suspicion (Asians, though, are slightly less likely to be arrested).[40] However, as Bowling and Phillips point out, this statistic is not all that meaningful.[41] As we saw in Chapter 4, the police have very wide powers of arrest and there is no guarantee that these are not used in a biased manner; indeed, a stop and search may

[35] Above n 2, 45.9.   [36] Above n 26, Table 4.2a.

[37] MVA and J. Miller, *Profiling Populations Available for Stops and Searches* (2000). See also P. Waddington, K. Stenson and D. Don, 'In Proportion: Race, and Police Stop and Search' (2004) 44 *B J Criminol* 889.

[38] *Ibid.*, 84–5.   [39] *Ibid.*, 87.   [40] *Ibid.*, Table 4.4a.

[41] B. Bowling and C. Phillips, 'Disproportionate and Discriminatory: Reviewing the Evidence on Police Stop and Search' (2007) 70 *MLR* 936.

generate an arrest because of the way the person being searched interacts with the police. There is some research evidence that, in general, blacks are arrested on less evidence than whites.[42] A little more light is shed on the debate about race and stop and search by a study which found that in the research area the racial imbalance in stops was no more pronounced in situations where police were likely to be able to distinguish the person's race before a decision to sop was made than in situations where the race of the target was not obvious (such as in stops of vehicles or stops at night).[43] This study concluded that the racial imbalance in the use of the power reflected the racial make up of the areas where the power was being used, and that the use of the power in those areas was generally justified by crime rates. But even though high crime areas seem to be the ones targeted for high levels of stop and search, there may still be bias of some sort at work if stop and search itself is a power which is difficult to justify because, for example, it makes a minimal contribution to crime prevention and detection.[44] We turn to this issue shortly.

So far we have concentrated on stop and search under PACE and other statutes which require reasonable suspicion. The Home Office also collects statistics on stop and search powers which do not require reasonable suspicion: the general powers to search for weapons or terrorist equipment which we noted above. In 2007–8 there were 53,125 recorded weapons stops under the CJPOA, s 60, and 117,278 terrorist stops under the Terrorism Act 2000, s 44 (compared to 37,197 terrorist stops in the previous year).[45] As would be expected, these stops generate fewer arrests than stops that do require reasonable suspicion. In 2006–7 (the latest year for which there are figures) the CJPOA power led to arrests in 3.6 per cent of cases; only a quarter of these arrests were for weapons.[46] In 2007–8 stops of people and vehicles under the Terrorism Act led to arrests in just 1 per cent of cases, and of this small number of arrests only 6 per cent were for terrorism offences.[47] No one has ever been convicted of a terrorist offence as a result of one of these arrests.[48] Racial disparity is marked for the CJPOA power. In the Metropolitan Police area, blacks are nine times more likely to be searched under this power than whites, and Asians twice as likely.[49] Under the Terrorism Act powers, blacks are only marginally more likely to be searched than whites, and Asians a little less than twice as likely.[50] The annual review of anti-terrorist legislation by Lord Carlile has noted concerns about 'compensation stops' where whites are stopped for

[42] C. Phillips and D. Brown, *Entry into the Criminal Justice System: A Survey of Police Arrests and Their Outcomes* (1998), 44.

[43] Waddington et al, above n 37.

[44] L. Lustgarten, 'The Future of Stop and Search' [2002] *Crim LR* 603, 616–17.

[45] *Statistics on Race*, above n 26, 29.

[46] *Arrests for Recorded Crime (Notifiable Offences) and the Operation of Certain Police Powers Under PACE: England and Wales 2006/07* (2008), 14.

[47] *Statistics on Race*, above n 26, Tables 4.7a, 4.8a.

[48] Lord Carlile, *Report on the Operation in 2008 of the Terrorism Act 2000 and of Part I of the Terrorism Act 2006* (2009), para 148.

[49] Above n 26, Table 4.5a.   [50] *Ibid.*, Table 4.7a.

no reason other than to balance the statistics,[51] and the Metropolitan Police Authority refers to anecdotal evidence of misreporting of these stops in order to thwart attempts to monitor any bias in their use.[52]

If stop and search under the Terrorism Act does not require reasonable suspicion, on what basis should stops be made? The Act itself is quite cryptic. The power may be exercised 'only for the purpose of searching for articles of a kind which could be used in connection with terrorism' (s 45(1)(a)), but 'may be exercised whether or not the constable has grounds for suspecting the presence of articles of that kind'.[53] This implies that the power might be used randomly, but the House of Lords in *Gillan* thought that stopping people on a random basis—people whom there was no reason to suspect of being involved in terrorism—would be pointless and even counter-productive.[54] It thought that searches would be based on some sort of suspicion, re-ferring to 'a professional's intuition' and the fact that 'the person selected conforms to some extent in the mind of the police officer to the stereotype of a person who might possibly be in possession' of terrorist articles.[55] For its part, PACE Code A states that:

'The selection of persons stopped…should reflect an objective assessment of the threat posed by the various terrorist groups active in Great Britain.…Officers must take particular care not to discriminate against members of minority ethnic groups in the exercise of these powers. There may be circumstances, however, where it is appropriate for officers to take account of a person's ethnic origin in selecting persons to be stopped in response to a spe-cific terrorist threat (for example, some international terrorist groups are associated with particular ethnic identities).'[56]

In practice, it seems that this power sometimes is used inappropriately. As noted above, Lord Carlile observes that 'compensation stops' may take place; he is also critical of the fact that s 44 is used to aid non-terrorism policy on some occasions.[57] Section 44 was used prominently against a heckler at the Labour Party conference in 2005. The Police Complaints Authority is currently investigating the use of the power to search chil-dren aged 11 and 6 years,[58] and the Metropolitan Police Authority has complained of 'arbitrary and discretionary practice [that] can only leave the door wide open to offic-ers to base their selection of whom to stop on prejudice, unconscious or otherwise.'[59]

While it is no surprise that a power as widely drafted as that in s 44 should be abused on some occasions, the more difficult question is the one raised by the guidance in Code A: to what extent should race play a role in decisions to stop under the Terrorism

[51] Above n 48, 140.
[52] Metropolitan Police Authority, *Counter-Terrorism: The London Debate* (2007), 50.
[53] Section 45(1)(a)–(b).
[54] Above n 8, [41], [67]. Lord Carlile has noted that stops have sometimes been carried out on a suspicion-less, numerical basis: above n 48, para 140.
[55] *Ibid.*, [67].   [56] Code A, para 2.25.   [57] Above n 48, para 147.
[58] Press release 10 September 2009. See also 'Stop-and-Search of Ethnic Minority 10-Year-Olds Doubles in London' *The Guardian* 17 November 2009.
[59] Above n 52, 52.

Act?[60] The House of Lords considered this issue in *Gillan*.[61] The question was pertinent because, in its earlier decision in the *Roma Rights* case, the House had held that a policy among immigration officers of being more suspicious of potential immigrants who were Roma constituted unlawful discrimination under the Race Relations Act.[62] The response of the House of Lords to this problem in *Gillan* was that stop and search would be lawful so long as it was not based solely on race. As Moeckli argues, this is a not very convincing response to the problem.[63] If stopping all Asians constitutes illegal discrimination, can it really be permissible to stop, say, all Asian males or all Asians wearing dark glasses? So long as there is differential treatment on the basis of race, a problematic form of discrimination would appear to remain.

Returning now to the broader question of racial disparity in the use of stop and search, we have seen that, while there is some debate, research on populations 'available' for stop and search has generally found that the police do not discriminate in their use of the power in those areas where it is used, i.e. the power is used proportionately with respect to the racial make up of the population on the street in particular areas. All the same, the headline figure of blacks being nearly eight times as likely to be stopped as whites indicates that the experience of the black community is still one of being far more vulnerable to stop and search than is the white community, a form of targeting that may draw more blacks into the criminal justice system and helps to lead to their pronounced over-representation on the DNA database (see Part 5 of this chapter). Unsurprisingly, then, there is considerable evidence that stop and search is corrosive of good relations between the police and the black community. The Police Complaints Authority found that while only 10 per cent of people making complaints against the police were black, 40 per cent of complaints about stop and search made by black people.[64] The Authority found that 'black people experience a different kind of dissatisfaction about stop and searches than do white people, and that the incidents they complain about are intrinsically different'.[65] Other research on the experience of stop and search has found that those from minority ethnic communities do not feel that the power is being used fairly: some feel that they are stopped in situations where white people would not be, and some complain of racist language during the stop.[66] In 2004 the Metropolitan Police Authority found considerable dissatisfaction—even anger—among minority ethnic communities about the use of stop and search.[67] More

[60] There is a large literature on the general question of 'racial profiling'. See, e.g., B. Harcourt, *Against Prediction: Profiling, Policing and Punishing in an Actuarial Age* (2007), Chs 4–7; K. Lippert-Rasmussen, 'Racial Profiling Versus Community' (2006) 23 *J Applied Philosophy* 191; M. Risse and R. Zeckhauser, 'Racial Profiling' (2004) 32 *Philosophy & Public Affairs* 131; O. De Schutter and J. Ringelheim, 'Ethnic Profiling: A Rising Challenge for European Human Rights Law' (2008) 71 *MLR* 358.

[61] Above n 8.

[62] *R (European Roma Rights Centre) v Immigration Officer at Prague Airport* [2004] 2 WLR 147.

[63] D. Moeckli, 'Stop and Search Under the Terrorism Act 2000' (2007) 70 *MLR* 654.

[64] Police Complaints Authority, *Stop and Search Complaints 2000–2001, Summary Report* (2004), 12.

[65] *Ibid.*, 21.

[66] V. Stone and N. Pettigrew, *The Views of the Public on Stops and Searches* (2000), 17–19, 26.

[67] Above n 26.

recently it has commented on the Terrorism Act power: 'the damage to community relations is significant and the deterrent effect is dubious'.[68] Being a target of stop and search has been found to be correlated with having less confidence in the police.[69] By alienating young people, stop and search may actually be counter-productive.[70]

Stop and search makes some contribution to crime control, but not a very significant one. There has been speculation as to whether the rate of stop and search has a general deterrent effect on crime, but studies of the connection between crime rates and stop rates find no strong connection.[71] A visible police presence on the streets no doubt deters some crime, but beyond this the actual use of stop and search probably adds little. Stop and search does, however, play some role in detecting crime: as noted above, currently around 11 per cent of PACE stops result in an arrest. About 30 per cent of these arrests are for drugs offences, probably most often for cannabis, and about 20 per cent are for handling stolen property.[72] It is questionable whether tackling such low level offending is worth the cost to police-community relations that is extracted by stop and search.[73] More generally, and ignoring drugs offences, it has been estimated that for every 106 crimes committed which are susceptible to arrest via stop and search, one stop and search arrest is made.[74] Some crimes are prevented by stop and search—for example a person may be arrested on their way to commit burglary, or car theft, via stop and search. But it is thought that only 0.1 per cent of crime is disrupted by use of the power.[75]

Stop and search powers can be used by the police in better and worse ways. As noted above, some forces have higher arrest rates from stop and search than do others. If stop and search is carefully targeted, there will be fewer stops and a higher arrest rate, though a lower number of arrests overall (that is because the police sometimes 'get lucky' when conducting a poorly targeted search).[76] A well targeted stop is also less likely to alienate the person involved. People who are stopped are sensitive to the manner in which the stop is carried out: when the police act politely and respectfully—as Code A requires[77]—there is again less damage to community relations: a 27 per cent increase in complaints about stop and search this year is therefore worrying.[78] The overall arrest rate of 11 per cent is a clear indication that the grounds for stops are often flimsy. An 11 per cent chance of finding evidence of a crime would seem to fall some way below the standard of 'reasonable suspicion'. Research evidence confirms that stops often are carried out on the basis of hunches and poorly supported

---

[68] Above n 52, 53.

[69] J. Miller, N. Bland and P. Quinton, *The Impact of Stops and Searches on Crime and the Community* (2000), 51–2.

[70] See M. Fitzgerald, *Final Report into Stop and Search* (1999), and 'Stop and Search Makes Gangs Stronger, Says Former Met Boss' *The Guardian* 28 August 2008.

[71] Miller et al, above n 69, Ch 3; cf Fitzgerald, *ibid.*

[72] *Arrests for Recorded Crime*, above n 46, Table PA.   [73] See Fitzgerald, above n 70.

[74] Miller et al, above, n 69, 23.   [75] *Ibid.*, 30.   [76] See, e.g., Fitzgerald, above n 70.

[77] Code A, 3.1.

[78] Independent Police Complaints Commission, *Police Complaints: Statistics for England and Wales 2008/09*, 6.

generalizations.[79] Indeed, everything we know about the way police discretion is used on the streets suggests that stop and search will be used in circumstances outwith the requirements of PACE. It will be used by the police to assert authority over particular sections of the community, to break up groups of youths, and to gather intelligence.[80]

As currently practised, stop and search is objectionable for many reasons.[81] Yet the public generally support the existence of stop and search powers, and do not wish to see them abolished.[82] If the power to stop and search was taken away from the police there would probably be minimal impact on the prevention and detection of crime. But there might be other negative effects. Arrest can be justified on very similar grounds to stop and search—both powers hinge on reasonable suspicion.[83] The arrest power allows the police to take a suspect to a police station and to detain him for a considerable length of time. The greatest negative impact of removing stop and search powers, then, would probably be an increase in the number of low suspicion arrests.

There are some signs that the police are becoming aware of the heavy costs and minor gains associated with indiscriminate use of stop and search powers. Some police forces have announced that they will no longer use the power to conduct suspicionless searches under the Terrorism Act.[84] Even the Metropolitan Police, which uses them massively— over 100,000 stops in 2007–8—has announced plans to cut them back, relying primarily on reasonable suspicion searches to combat terrorism.[85] The latest figures (2008–9) on stop and search under the Terrorism Acts show a 37 per cent fall in their use across the country, which is welcome, though there has been an 82 per cent increase in London, which is not.[86] Given the availability of reasonable suspicion searches, there seems little justification for the powers in the Terrorism Act and the CJPOA. There is some justification for retaining reasonable suspicion searches, but given the low arrest rate there is a strong case for focusing them more carefully and using them far less. However, police discretion on the street is difficult to control, and once the power to stop and search is given it is almost inevitable that it will be used more widely than envisaged. If we are to retain stop and search we probably have to accept that the power will continue to cause problems, especially in relation to minority ethnic communities.

Update: in January 2010, the ECtHR held that the exercise of stop and search powers under s 44 of the Terrorism Act 2000 was in breach of Article 8 (privacy) of the Convention (*Gillan and Quinton v United Kingdom*, Appln 4158/05). The wide discretion given to the police, reflected in the sheer number of stops, meant that the interference with privacy involved was not 'in accordance with the law', as required by Article 8(2).

---

[79] Most recently, P. Quinton, N. Bland and J. Miller, *Police Stops, Decision-Making and Practice* (2000).
[80] See *ibid.* and Fitzgerald, above n 70.   [81] See generally Lustgarten, above n 44.
[82] Stone and Pettigrew, above n 66, 41.   [83] See Ch 4.
[84] 'Hampshire Police Suspends Use of Terrorism Act Stop and Search Powers' *The Guardian* 15 July 2009.
[85] 'Police to Severely Curtail Use of Stop and Search Powers' *The Guardian* 6 May 2009.
[86] Home Office, *Operation of Police Powers Under the Terrorism Act 2000 and Subsequent Legislation* (2009), 43 and Table 2.1.

5.2 SURVEILLANCE

It is widely agreed that the use of surveillance techniques by law enforcement agencies has increased considerably and is likely to increase further. Not only are more offences being committed by electronic means, but also the range of techniques and devices for the surveillance of citizens becomes ever wider and it is natural that law enforcement agencies should wish to take advantage of this technology in order to improve the detection of crimes. Surveillance techniques that involve (for example) electronic eavesdropping or imaging may promise a high degree of reliability. However, they also raise a number of human rights concerns, and it is these concerns that have led to some recent changes in English law.

The general approach of the common law to matters such as the interception of communications is that this is permissible unless specifically made unlawful. Thus until the 1980s, telephone-tapping was authorized by the Home Secretary, and there was no relevant law. When this was challenged in *Malone v United Kingdom*,[87] it was found to be in breach of Article 8 of the ECHR. Paragraph 1 of that Article safeguards an individual's right to respect for private life, home and correspondence. Paragraph 2 permits interference with the right on certain grounds that make it 'necessary in a democratic society', but the interference must be 'in accordance with the law'—so as to ensure that interference is not arbitrary but has procedural safeguards built in. The UK had no relevant law, and soon after the decision the Interception of Communications Act 1985 was passed. This introduced a statutory authorization scheme for telephone-tapping, but failed to deal with surveillance generally. Other methods remained unregulated, save for Home Office guidelines.

Among the subsequent challenges was that in *Khan v United Kingdom*,[88] where police officers had placed a listening device on the wall of a private house and recorded incriminating conversations. The police officers had followed the procedure of obtaining the chief constable's authority, but there was no legislative framework in England and so the interference with the targeted person's right to respect for private life was not 'in accordance with the law'. The Government anticipated this ruling by promoting the provisions that became Part III of the Police Act 1997, which provides an authorization procedure for surveillance involving entry on to property. However, this piecemeal approach to legislation still failed to provide a general framework for all forms of intrusive surveillance, and adverse decisions from Strasbourg continued to come.[89]

Many of the points of principle about safeguarding human rights in the process of using surveillance were accepted in a White Paper that proposed new legislation,[90] and the result is the Regulation of Investigatory Powers Act 2000. Although much more

---

[87] (1985) 7 EHRR 14.   [88] (2000) 31 EHRR 1016.

[89] E.g. *Govell v United Kingdom* [1999] EHRLR 121; *Halford v United Kingdom* (1997) 24 EHRR 523; and, also relating to an investigation in the 1990s, *PG and JH v United Kingdom* [2002] *Crim LR* 308.

[90] Home Office, *Interception of Communications in the United Kingdom* (Cm 4368 of 1999), prompted by JUSTICE, *Under Surveillance* (1998).

general than previous legislation, it fails to integrate or incorporate the provisions in Part III of the Police Act 1997, which remain in force. In outline,[91] the first part of the 2000 Act replaces the Interception of Communications Act 1985 with a new framework that extends to communications on public and private networks. It provides a procedure whereby the Home Secretary may issue a warrant, and ss 5(2) and 5(3) reflect the language of Article 8(2) of the Convention in referring to proportionality and to the various reasons for which interference may be held necessary in a democratic society. The second part of the 2000 Act, in outline, introduces a regulatory framework for three forms of surveillance. *Directed surveillance* is covert surveillance that is not intrusive in its method but is likely to reveal matters within the protection of Article 8(1). *Intrusive surveillance* is covert surveillance that does involve intrusion into private premises or a vehicle. *Covert human intelligence sources* are persons who maintain a close relationship with a target suspect and thereby obtain information falling within the ambit of Article 8(1). What the Act does is to require authorization by a senior police officer, on the statutory grounds, before directed surveillance or covert human intelligence sources are deployed; and to require authorization of intrusive surveillance at the level of chief constable or, if the matter is urgent, by a senior police officer. The Act establishes a Commissioner to review warrants issued and a Tribunal to deal with complaints; the most intrusive forms of surveillance require prior authorization by a Commissioner. Commissioners also carry out regular inspections in order to audit compliance. This is more or less a continuation of the previous system, and it is doubtful whether it is Convention-compliant. The Strasbourg Court has held more than once that a procedure for interference with Article 8 rights must require judicial authorization,[92] and it must be highly doubtful whether the procedures for authorization by middle-ranking police officers (in respect of directed surveillance, covert human sources and, in some circumstances, intrusive surveillance) satisfy this requirement. Moreover, there is room for argument about the vagueness of some key terms in the Act—such as 'serious crime'—now that the Strasbourg Court is taking a more stringent approach to cases of State interference with Article 8 rights.[93]

One flaw in the scheme of the new legislation is that the hierarchy of levels of surveillance was drafted in rather simple terms. 'Intrusive surveillance', which generally requires prior approval by a Commissioner, involves surveillance of residential premises or a private vehicle,[94] but people may engage in highly sensitive communications, with expectations of privacy, outside such areas. In *McE v Prison Service of Northern Ireland* the House

---

[91] For discussion of the 2000 Act, see S. Bailey and N. Taylor, *Civil Liberties: Cases, Materials and Commentary* (6th ed, 2009), 578–600.

[92] E.g. most clearly in *Kopp v Switzerland* (1999) 27 EHRR 91, at para 74; cf the reasoning of the Home Office in the White Paper (above, n 4) at para 7.2, which is unpersuasive insofar as many other European and Commonwealth countries require judicial authorization, as the JUSTICE report (above, n 4) points out.

[93] The Government relied on two decisions of the Commission, *Hewitt and Harman v United Kingdom* App No 20317/92 and *Christie v United Kingdom* (1994) 78–A DR 119, as confirming that the phrases 'in the interests of national security' and 'the economic well-being of the country' are sufficiently certain; but in recent years the Court itself has signalled a greater emphasis on certainty in decisions such as *Valenzuela v Spain* (1998) 28 EHRR 483 and *Amann v Switzerland* (2000) 30 EHRR 843.

[94] Regulation of Investigatory Powers Act 2000, s 26(3).

of Lords considered appeals by detainees who complained about the possibility that their discussions with legal advisers and doctors might be subject to surveillance.[95] The House of Lords held that while such surveillance was permissible under the Act—and that the Act's provision of authority to carry out covert surveillance overrode a suspect's right to consult a solicitor in private guaranteed in s 58 of PACE[96]—to comply with Article 8 of the ECHR it needed to be authorized at the higher level required for intrusive surveillance, rather than at the internal police level deemed appropriate for directed surveillance.

While it has now been in force for several years, no independent research on the operation of the Regulation of Investigatory Powers Act 2000 (RIPA) has been conducted. It is therefore difficult to tell how well the scheme is working. The most useful source of information is the annual reports by the Surveillance Commissioner.[97] The limited information provided here suggests that requests for authorization by the Commissioner are seldom refused: appeals against refusals are extremely rare, there being one or none each year. And while there are over 2,000 authorizations for property interferences granted by the police each year, very few (usually six or less) are quashed by the Commissioner. This suggests a reasonably permissive regime. While the Commissioner's monitoring reveals various unauthorized instances of surveillance, those examples that come to his attention usually seem to involve surveillance equipment being left in a premises after an operation has ended. The case law reveals occasional more serious abuses of surveillance powers.[98] One notable trend has been a decline over the years in the number of 'Covert Human Intelligence Sources'—informers—registered by the police. Whether this is because of a drift away from this sort of operation—puzzling, as the Commissioner notes, given the modern emphasis on 'intelligence led' policing[99]—or because some informers are redesignated as 'tasked witnesses' in order to evade the regulatory scheme,[100] is hard to say. Overall, though, the Commissioner, while keen to press for best practice and better training, suggests that the RIPA scheme is working well.

The Government is currently considering some changes to the RIPA scheme. While this is mainly driven by public concern about local authorities using surveillance to investigate such minor matters as dog-fouling, the consultation paper contains a modish reference to cutting police paperwork, asking: 'what more should we do to reduce bureaucracy for the police so they can use RIPA more easily to protect the public against criminals?'[101] The Commissioner has been rightly critical of this:

'It should not be acceptable that the use of covert powers is made 'easy' for any public authority. The fundamental purpose of the legislation is to ensure that covert surveillance is necessary, proportionate and carried out in a way which is compliant with human

---

[95] [2009] UKHL 15.

[96] Lord Phillips dissented on this point: see at [24]–[25].

[97] Available at www.surveillancecommissioners.gov.uk/about_annual.html.

[98] *R v Grant* [2005] 2 Cr App R 28.   [99] Above n 97, 2005–6 Report, 7.4.

[100] *Ibid.*, 2006–7 Report, 2.3.

[101] Home Office, *Regulation of Investigatory Powers Act 2000: Consolidating Orders and Codes of Practice: A Public Consultation Paper* (2009), 8.

rights.... [T]he bureaucracy some complain about is often self-inflicted and due to police officers' failure to construct their documents concisely and with clarity.'[102]

In conclusion, RIPA represents a significant step towards protecting human rights in the process of gathering evidence through surveillance methods. While it is unfortunate that the Government adopted such a minimalist view of the requirements of Article 8 on such questions as judicial authorization, defining the grounds for interference, and informing individuals that they have been subject to surveillance, surveillance by law enforcement officers is now much more fully regulated than it was ten years ago.

5.3 EYEWITNESS IDENTIFICATION EVIDENCE

(A) BACKGROUND ISSUES

Eyewitness identification evidence plays a significant role in the criminal process. An analysis of cases in the Crown Court found it to be very or fairly important in around a quarter of cases;[103] it is used more often in certain types of crime, such as robbery and burglary.[104] Yet eyewitness identification is a relatively frail type of evidence: it has played a significant role in a number of miscarriages of justice. Laszlo Virag, for example, was convicted of murder after eight witnesses picked him out at an identification parade. He was later exonerated and the case led to a review of identification procedures.[105] Writing in 1972, the Criminal Law Revision Committee suggested that mistaken eyewitness identifications were 'by far the greatest cause of actual or possible wrong convictions'.[106] In the US, the Innocence Project has used DNA evidence to overturn a number of convictions secured before DNA technology was widely available. A review of the exoneration cases suggests that eyewitness identification played an important role in about 75 per cent of these wrong convictions.[107]

The primary concern of the criminal process where eyewitness identification evidence is concerned is to secure reliable evidence. There are a number of factors that may affect the accuracy of a particular eyewitness identification. Some of these relate to the witness, such as eyesight, memory, the conditions in which the offence was observed: distance from the offender, duration of the incident, quality of light (the psychological literature refers to these as 'estimator variables').[108] These are factors

---

[102] Above n 97, 2008–9 Report, para 5.32.

[103] M. Zander and P. Henderson, *Crown Court Study* (1993), para 3.3.1.

[104] G. Pike, N. Brace and S. Kynan, *The Visual Identification of Suspects: Procedures and Practice* (Home Office Briefing Note 2/02).

[105] P. Devlin, *Report to the Secretary of State for the Home Department of the Departmental Committee on Evidence of Identification in Criminal Cases* HC 338 (1976).

[106] Criminal Law Revision Committee, *Eleventh Report: Evidence (General)* Cmnd 4991 (1972), para 196.

[107] See www.innocenceproject.org/understand/Eyewitness-Misidentification.php.

[108] A good overview of the literature is G. Wells, A. Memon and S. Penrod, 'Eyewitness Evidence: Improving its Probative Value' (2006) 7 *Psychological Science in the Public Interest* 45.

that the criminal process has relatively little control over, though at the trial stage the court should obviously do its best to draw their importance to the fact-finder's attention. There are other factors, though, over which the criminal process has much more control ('system variables'). The most obvious of these relate to the way in which any identification procedure is carried out, for example whether an identification parade is held or whether the witness is simply asked to identify the suspect as the offender at trial, when he is standing in the dock. There are more subtle factors, too, which the process has some influence over, such as the amount of time that elapses between the crime and the identification procedure, and whether the witness might have seen pictures of the suspect in the press before being asked to make an identification.

Because of the importance of eyewitness identification evidence, and the recognition of its potential frailty, there is a considerable body of psychological research which examines in some detail the criteria that affect its quality.[109] It is worth highlighting some of the more obvious factors that have been shown to influence eyewitness identification. In the typical situation, a person has observed a crime being committed, and is later shown a suspect by the police and asked whether the suspect is the person seen earlier. Memory plays a crucial role in this process: the witness is being asked to compare a remembered image with the person shown to her. Memory decays over time, so in general the earlier the procedure is held, the better. Memory, and therefore the identification process, are also open to suggestion. The significance of this point cannot be over-emphasized. We saw in Chapter 4 that suggestion can sometimes lead to false confessions. We would expect most people to have a relatively clear memory of whether or not they committed a crime, so if suggestion can lead to a person confessing to a crime they did not commit, it is no surprise that suggestion is easily capable of affecting people's visual memories. Indeed, a good example of the power of suggestion is that experiments have shown that fingerprint examiners, who make visual comparisons between prints without having to rely on memory, can be manipulated by suggestion into being more or less likely to declare a match between prints.[110] And suggestion can be an unconscious process. Scientists conducting medical trials on new drugs know the importance of making the processes 'double blind', so that the person giving the drug to the subject does not know whether she is handing out the trial drug or a placebo. Otherwise, the person administering the drug can unconsciously influence the subject, making her health more likely to improve even if she is only receiving a placebo. It is therefore crucial that, so far as possible, identification procedures which might suggest to the witness that a particular person is suspected to be the offender should be avoided. For example, confronting the witness with a suspect and saying

---

[109] See, e.g., Wells et al, *ibid.*; B. Cutler and S. Penrod, *Mistaken Identification: The Eyewitness, Psychology and the Law* (1995); G. Wells and E. Olson, 'Eyewitness Identification' (2003) 54 *Annual Review of Psychology* 277.

[110] I. Dror and R. Rosenthal, 'Meta-Analytically Quantifying the Reliability and Biasability of Forensic Experts' (2008) 53 *J Forensic Sciences* 900; I. Dror and P. Fraser-Mackenzie, 'Cognitive Biases in Human Perception, Judgement, and Decision Making: Bridging Theory and the Real World' in D. Rossmo (ed), *Criminal Investigative Failures* (2009).

'we think this is the person who attacked you' will rarely be appropriate, because such a process is very suggestive. It is better to provide the witness with an identification process which involves a choice being made between several people. Thus the usual process for identification in England and Wales is now a video identification procedure, where the witness sees images of the suspect along with various other people (known as 'fillers' or 'foils'). Even with this process, it is important to avoid suggestion. If the person conducting the parade holds their breath when the image of the suspect appears, there is a risk of suggestion and therefore the best procedures will, like medical trials, be double blind, so that the administrator is either unaware of who the suspect is or cannot tell when the witness is looking at the suspect's image.[111]

The degree of suggestion involved in an identification process, then, is one important system variable. Psychological research also points to another important, and rather more subtle, system variable, which involves the extent to which an identification process is simultaneous or sequential. In a simultaneous process, like the classic identification parade we are all familiar with from film and television, the witness sees the suspect and fillers all at the same time. In a sequential process, the witness sees them one at a time. The theory behind this distinction is that simultaneous processes prompt the witness to make a relative judgement, answering the question 'which of these people looks most like the person I saw?', while a sequential process is more likely to engage an absolute judgement: 'is this the person I saw?' The theory is that the latter type of judgement is preferable because it protects an innocent suspect against mistaken identification. Wells' description of one experiment, involving a traditional, simultaneous identification procedure, is a good illustration of the dangers involved:

'...a crime was staged 200 times for 200 separate witnesses. All of the witnesses were shown one of two lineups. Every witness was warned that the offender might not be in the lineup. Half of the witnesses viewed a six-person lineup in which the offender was present. Of these 100 witnesses, 21% made no selection at all, 54% picked the offender, 13% picked a particular filler, and the remaining witnesses spread their choices across other lineup members. The other half of the witnesses viewed a lineup in which the offender was removed and was not replaced. The critical question in this scenario is what happened to the 54% of witnesses who would have chosen the offender had he been present: did they shift to the no-choice category, thereby causing 75% per cent to make no choice? No. Of these 100 witnesses, the no-choice rate increased to only 32% whereas the person who was previously picked only 13% of the time was now picked 38% of the time. In other words...removing the offender from the lineup led witnesses to shift to the 'next best choice', nearly tripling the jeopardy of that person.'[112]

This suggests that simultaneous procedures are best avoided, and indeed, research suggests that sequential procedures produce fewer false identifications.[113] However,

---

[111] M. Phillips et al, 'Double-blind Photoarray Administration as a Safeguard Against Investigator Bias' (1999) 84 *J Applied Psychology* 940.

[112] G. Wells, 'Eyewitness Identification: Systemic Reforms' [2006] *Wisconsin L Rev* 617, 619.

[113] *Ibid.*, 626.

there is an interesting complication here. It seems that by prompting absolute judge-ment, a simultaneous procedure is a harder test for the witness, so that if the perpet-rator is present among the images, he is less likely to be picked by the witness. Thus while sequential procedures protect innocent suspects, it seems that they may also protect guilty ones. Potentially, then, questions about how to design identification procedures raise difficult issues about appropriate trade-offs in criminal process.

While the foregoing suggests that some identification procedures pose greater risks to innocent suspects than do others, it is very difficult to generalise about what level of risk actual procedures pose. Research in England and Wales suggests that in actual cases witnesses picked fillers about 20 per cent of the time.[114] If identifi-cation procedures involve 8 fillers in addition to the suspect,[115] then an innocent suspect would bear a risk of being identified of just over 2 per cent. However, this assumes that an innocent suspect is no more likely to be picked than any of the fill-ers. It is plausible that an innocent suspect will often have been arrested because of his resemblance to the perpetrator, and it may be difficult to find fillers who look like the perpetrator to a similar degree, so that if innocent suspects often look more like the perpetrator than does anyone else in the array they may bear a considerably higher risk of false incrimination than 2 per cent. The experiment described by Wells indicates how some people are especially at risk of being chosen. In a review of a range of studies, it was found that a filler who resembled the 'perpetrator' was chosen 27 per cent of the time.[116] Suggestive processes will obviously pose additional risks for innocent suspects.

(B) REGULATING IDENTIFICATION PROCEDURES

Identification procedures are governed by Code D, issued under PACE.[117] The basic requirement of the Code is that where a witness may be able to identify the perpetrator of a crime, an identification procedure should be held.[118] Responsibility for organizing identification procedures is given to an identification officer, who must be of at least the rank of inspector and must not be involved with the relevant investigation.[119] Since its introduction in the early 2000s, video identification has become the standard pro-cedure. Here, the witness is shown images of the suspect and several—usually eight—fillers. The video images show each person looking at the camera and turning their head in each direction to present side views. The fillers are selected from a large data-base.[120] This procedure has a number of advantages over traditional live identification

---

[114] See T. Valentine, 'Forensic Facial Identification' in A. Heaton-Armstrong et al, *Witness Testimony: Psychological, Investigative and Evidential Perspectives* (2006), 290–1. Note that this research involved live identification parades, rather than the currently used video identification.

[115] This is the minimum number required by Code D.

[116] N. Steblay et al, 'Eyewitness Accuracy Rates in Sequential and Simultaneous Lineup Presentations: A Meta-Analytic Comparison' (2001) 25 *Law & Human Behavior* 459.

[117] The latest version, to which we refer, came into force in February 2008.   [118] Code D, 3.12.

[119] Code D, 3.11.   [120] See Valentine, above n 114.

parades;[121] video identifications can be arranged far more quickly and easily than live parades, and video identifications proceed sequentially. Use of a database makes it easier to find fillers who resemble the suspect, and research has found that video identifications are fairer in this respect than live parades: observers provided with the witness's description of the suspect could guess who the suspect was 15 per cent of the time when viewing video arrays, as opposed to 25 per cent of the time with live parades (one would expect 11 per cent of guesses to be correct by chance alone).[122] So while Code D does allow for some discretion to use other procedures, the primary rule—'the suspect shall initially be offered a video identification'—and the fact that video identification is simpler and fairer, means that in practice video identification is prioritized.

There are, however, criticisms of the way video identifications are conducted in practice. While the Code lays down important safeguards, such as recording the witness' description of the perpetrator before any identification procedure is conducted, and warning the witness that the person they saw may not be present in the set of images, there is no requirement that video identifications be double blind, so it is possible for the identification officer, consciously or not, to alert the witness to the identity of the suspect. Relatively simple arrangements could solve this problem (the witness could view the images on a screen out of the identification officer's sight and with the suspect's position among the video clips selected at random); a double blind requirement would therefore be a sensible addition to Code D.[123] Another potential problem is that, while video identification is a sequential process, Code D contains provisions which undermine some of the advantages sequential procedures are thought to offer in promoting absolute over relative judgements. In a strict sequential procedure, the witness would only see each image once and would have to make a 'yes' or 'no' decision, without knowing how many images they would see. A positive response would bring the procedure to an end, and revisiting images would not be possible. Code D, however, provides that the witness 'should be asked not to make any decision as to whether the person they saw is on the set of images until they have seen the whole set at least twice.'[124] The witness can also ask to view particular images repeatedly; these provisions obviously make it easier for the witness to rely on a judgement of relative likeness. In an interesting study, however, Valentine et al compared the Code D provisions to a strict sequential procedure and found that, contrary to expectations, a strict procedure offered no advantages.[125] While, in line with previous research, strict procedures led to fewer correct identifications, unlike in previous research they offered no benefits in terms of a reduced risk of false identification. Earlier, we noted that the adoption of sequential identification procedures might pose difficult questions about

[121] See T. Valentine, S. Darling and A. Memon, 'Do Strict Rules and Moving Images Increase the Reliability of Sequential Identification Procedures?' (2006) 21 *Applied Cognitive Psychology* 933, 934.

[122] T. Valentine and P. Heaton, 'An Evaluation of the Fairness of Police Lineups and Video Identifications' (1999) 13 *Applied Cognitive Psychology* 59.

[123] See Valentine, above n 114.   [124] Code D, Annex A.11.   [125] Above n 121.

appropriate trade-offs in criminal process—should we sacrifice some true identifications in order better to protect innocent suspects? It seems that we may not be faced
with this dilemma when it comes to the question whether Code D should be tightened
up to make video identification a stricter sequential process, because such a move
would not in fact further protect the innocent. The issues explored by Valentine et
al certainly deserve further research. It may be, for example, that when an innocent
suspect bears a particular resemblance to the perpetrator, stricter procedures would
provide some benefit. But at the moment the research gives some reassurance that
Code D—more by accident than by design—strikes an appropriate balance between
protecting the innocent and allowing identification of the guilty.

So far we have examined the Code D provisions where the police have a suspect
whom they can involve in an identification procedure. However, the police will not
always be in this position. If they arrive at the scene of a street robbery shortly after
the incident occurred, they may know that the perpetrator will still be in the vicinity,
but not know whom to suspect among the various people in the area. In this situation,
it will be tempting to involve the victim in picking out the perpetrator on the street.
If the victim does identify someone, the police will then have a suspect whom they
can arrest. However, there are obvious problems in this situation. Code D and the
identification procedures available in the police station are intended to give suspects
some protection from biased and suggestive practices. It will be very difficult to avoid
bias and suggestion where identification takes place on the street. Code D does contain provisions on this situation, referring to 'cases where the suspect's identity is not
known'.[126] Here:

'a witness may be taken to a particular neighbourhood, or place to see whether they can
identify the person they saw.... the principles applicable to the formal procedures...should
be followed as far as practicable, for example...care must be taken not to direct the witness'
attention to any individual unless, taking into account all the circumstances, this cannot be
avoided. However, this does not prevent a witness being asked to look carefully at the people
around at the time or to look towards a group or in a particular direction.'[127]

The police should keep a record of what takes place and, as in all cases, the witness
should be asked to provide a description of the perpetrator before any identification
is attempted.

Given the increased risk of false identification in this situation, the question of the
distinction between cases where the suspect's identity is known and where it is not
is an important one. It seems that once the police have sufficient evidence to arrest
a particular suspect, the suspect's identity will be known and a formal identification
procedure—usually video identification—should take place if he disputes the identification. Arrest requires reasonable suspicion, a criterion sufficiently vague that the
known/not known distinction is imprecise, and there is room for argument about just
where the distinction should lie. Although there is normally good reason to minimize

---

[126] Code D, 3.2.   [127] *Ibid.*

the use of arrest, because, as Code G notes, arrest involves a significant interference with the right to liberty,[128] in cases where identity is potentially an issue arrest, by engaging the requirement of formal identification procedures, might be in the suspect's interest. Indeed, it has been suggested that wider use of arrest powers could be used to more or less eliminate the need for street identifications.[129] This is probably unrealistic, as there will often be more than one potential suspect in the vicinity of the crime. For its part, the case law is, perhaps inevitably, unclear as to when arrest should take place. According to the House of Lords in *Forbes*, there needs to be 'some apparently reliable evidence implicating' the person arrested.[130] In *K v DPP*,[131] the police arrived at the scene of a street robbery shortly after it had been committed. A sniffer dog was used to follow the trail of the perpetrators; D was found nearby, and was brought towards the police car where he was identified by V. The Court of Appeal was concerned by the use of this extremely suggestive procedure. It found that here there was sufficient evidence to arrest D and that this would have been the proper course. In *Toth*,[132] however, customs officers observed a car being used for a drug deal. One of the officers who had witnessed the transaction then went to the address of the vehicle's registered keeper. The keeper was identified by the officer and then arrested. The Court of Appeal thought that this was appropriate, and that there was not sufficient evidence to arrest the vehicle's registered keeper without an identification of him as having been present at the scene. While the facts of the cases are very different, it is not obvious that *Toth* can be reconciled with the less permissive approach in *K*, where all that was known seems to have been that D was standing on the street somewhere in the direction the perpetrators had run off in.

If a suspect is identified through a process of street identification, then the situation will be that a suspect is known and the PACE safeguards will apply. As we have seen, this means that if the suspect disputes the identification, then an identification procedure, usually video identification, should be held. However, the Code contains a significant caveat to this requirement: 'unless it is not practicable or it would serve no useful purpose in proving or disproving whether the suspect was involved in committing the offence. For example, when it is not disputed that the suspect is already well known to the witness.'[133] The 'no useful purpose' qualification was added to the Code after the House of Lords' decision in *Forbes*,[134] which held that the previous language of the Code made identifications procedures mandatory so long as the suspect disputed identity. *Forbes* involved the situation where a suspect had become known to the police through a street identification, and it was rather odd that a formal identification procedure should be required in this

---

[128] Code G, 1.2.

[129] D. Wolchover and A. Heaton-Armstrong, 'Ending the Farce of Staged Street Identifications' (2004) 3 *Archbold News* 5. See also *id.*, 'Improving Visual Identification Procedures Under PACE Code D' in *Witness Testimony*, above n 114.

[130] *R v Forbes* [2001] 1 AC 473, 482.   [131] [2003] EWHC 351 (Admin).

[132] [2005] EWCA Crim 754.   [133] Code D, 3.12.   [134] Above n 130.

situation, because once a witness has picked out someone on the street an identification procedure does not seem to offer very much in terms of testing their recollection of who they saw committing the offence (as opposed to their memory of whom they later picked out). The 'no useful purpose' language was doubtless intended to give the police more discretion in this situation. It seems to have resulted in some uncertainty as to when an identification procedure should be held,[135] but the courts have continued to hold that the requirement is a strict one, and they have continued to cite *Forbes* as authority that an identification procedure is a mandatory requirement in this situation.[136] As it was put in *R v Callie*, the words 'no useful purpose' 'are strong and the Code is mandatory. They do not allow a proportionality exercise so that the Code . . . would not apply if some, but very limited, purpose would be served.'[137] As for the specific example given by the Code—where it is not disputed that the suspect is already well known to the witness—the courts have taken a fairly strict line here too, holding that someone last seem some years ago is not 'well known'.[138] As we will see, though, the courts rarely hold that breaches of the Code in these situations are grounds for excluding identification evidence, and this has doubtless contributed to there being a steady stream of cases where the Code has been breached.

Suspects have some rights in relation to identification procedures. Paragraph 3.17 of Code D specifies a series of pieces of information they must be told, which includes the fact that they need not consent to an identification procedure. However, if they do not consent then the police may attempt to hold an identification procedure without their consent, for example by using an image from CCTV or holding a group identification, where the suspect is seen as part of an informal group such as among people leaving his place of work. A refusal to consent can also be given in evidence at any subsequent trial. If the police reasonably suspect that the suspect will not cooperate, they can proceed to capture his image covertly without giving the notice of rights in 3.17. Once this is done, however, the suspect should be given the opportunity to cooperate in providing more suitable images for use in a video identification.[139] The suspect and his adviser can view the set of images compiled for video identification, and make objections which should be taken into account 'if practicable'.[140] The suspect's representative can be present at the video identification procedure. There are currently plans to remove this right; so long as a comprehensive video recording is made of proceedings, this is probably not objectionable.[141]

---

[135] See *Streets Ahead: A Joint Inspection of the Street Crime Initiative* (2003), 60–1.

[136] E.g. *R v Harris* [2003] EWCA Crim 174, [26]; *R v Darren B* [2005] EWCA Crim 538, [12]; *R v Muhidiniz* [2005] EWCA Crim 2464, [14].

[137] [2009] EWCA Crim 283, [22].

[138] E.g. *Harris*, above n 136; *Darren B*, above n 136; *McKenna v DPP* [2005] EWHC 677 (Admin).

[139] Code D, 3.20.   [140] Code D, Annex A.7.

[141] Home Office, *Government Proposals in Response to the Review of the Police and Criminal Evidence Act 1984* (2008), 33. For commentary, see D. Wolchover, 'Viper Disappointments in the PACE Review' (2008) 10 *Archbold News* 4.

(C) EYEWITNESS EVIDENCE IN COURT

When a case involving identification evidence comes to court, two important issues arise: what should happen if Code D has been breached? What should the jury be told about identification evidence, given its evident frailties? If there has been a breach of Code D, a defendant will often argue that identification evidence should be excluded (if the breach involved no identification procedure being held, the argument will usually be that a prior street identification or recognition should be excluded, or, if there is no eyewitness identification, that proceedings should be stayed as an abuse of process).[142] However, exclusion is by no means automatic. The case law here is part of the wider case law on s 78 of PACE, under which evidence may be excluded if it would render the proceedings unfair. Section 78 is discussed in more detail in Chapter 11; as far as Code D is concerned, the cases suggest that evidence will be excluded if there has been a 'significant and substantial' breach of its provisions. Factors taken into consideration include whether the police have acted in bad faith, and whether the defendant has been disadvantaged by the breach.[143] Even then, exclusion is by no means automatic. In *Wellington*, a 'non-technical' breach of the Code, which was held to have deprived D of one means of challenging the evidence against him, was held not to lead to exclusion.[144] One reason for this is that the courts emphasize the overall state of the evidence against D—exclusion is less likely if the identification is corroborated.[145] Thus in *Forbes*, while the House of Lords interpreted Code D strictly, it held that the evidence obtained in breach of Code D was properly admitted in court. It endorsed the Court of Appeal's observation that:

'The evidence was compelling and untainted, and was supported by the evidence (which it was open to the jury to accept) of what the appellant had said at the scene. It did not suffer from such problems or weaknesses as sometimes attend evidence of this kind: as, for example, where the suspect is already visibly in the hands of the police at the moment he is identified to them by the complainant.'[146]

The House of Lords did hold, though, that in cases where an identification procedure had not been held in breach of Code D the jury should be told that such a procedure 'enables a suspect to put the reliability of an eyewitness's evidence to the test, that the suspect has lost the benefit of that safeguard and that the jury should take account of that fact in its assessment of the whole case, giving it such weight as it thinks fair.'[147] The courts now seem to put considerable emphasis on whether or not a 'Forbes warning' was given; often this will be seen as sufficient remedy even where D has suffered some

---

[142] See generally A. Roberts, 'Pre-Trial Defence Rights and the Fair Use of Eyewitness Identification Procedures' (2008) 71 *MLR* 331.

[143] For reviews of the case law, see I. Dennis, *The Law of Evidence* (3rd ed, 2007), 271–4.

[144] *R on the Application of Wellington v DPP* [2007] EWHC 1061 (Admin).

[145] See *McKenna*, above n 138, at [16]: 'when one comes to consider the fairness of the position under s 78, one looks at all the evidence.' See also *R v B* [2008] EWCA Crim 1524.

[146] Above n 130, [32].   [147] *Ibid.*, [27].

disadvantage through the breach.[148] This is not a convincing approach. Although often not deliberate, in these cases the actions of the police have deprived the defendant of one means of testing the evidence against him, such as by denying him a video identification or failing to record the witness's first description of the suspect, making the trial as a whole a less reliable means of establishing guilt. A *Forbes* warning appears to be a rather ineffectual response to this: how is the jury to take into account, for example, the fact that, had it been recorded, the witness's description might have been a poor fit for D? The proper response in most of these cases would be to exclude the identification evidence.[149]

Moving on from breaches of Code D, the remaining question is how the courts warn juries about the inherent frailties of eyewitness identification evidence. In the wake of the Devlin Committee's report, the Court of Appeal laid down guidelines on this issue in *R v Turnbull*.[150] *Turnbull* requires judges to warn juries about the dangers of mistaken identification. Whenever a case depends 'wholly or substantially' on identification evidence, the judge should warn the jury of the special need for caution before convicting on such evidence. The warning should go into a reasonable amount of detail, informing jurors that even convincing witnesses, or more than one witness, can be mistaken, that innocent people have been convicted on the basis of mistaken eyewitness evidence, and drawing their attention to the details of the identification in issue.[151] In cases where the quality of identification evidence is poor—for example, an identification based on a fleeting glance 'or on a longer observation made in difficult conditions'—the judge should go further. The case should be withdrawn from the jury unless there is evidence to support the identification. If there is supporting evidence, then the judge should bring it to the jury's attention; oddly, though, there is no requirement for the jury to accept the supporting evidence before convicting: thus a jury can still, in theory, convict on poor quality identification evidence alone.[152]

Turnbull is a welcome safeguard, though it is not without its problems. The courts have considerable leeway in deciding just how *Turnbull* applies, especially when it comes to the distinction between good and poor quality evidence. According to *Turnbull*, quality is good 'for example when the identification is made after a long period of observation, or in satisfactory conditions by a relative, a neighbour, a close friend, a workmate and the like.'[153] The example of poor quality evidence that is given is 'a fleeting glance or...a longer observation made in difficult conditions'.[154] There is quite a gap between these examples: should a short, but not fleeting, observation in good conditions be classified as good or poor quality? It is not surprising to find in

---

[148] See, e.g., *Muhidiniz*, above n 136; *Darren B*, above n 136; *Harris*, above n 136; *R v Lewis and Thomas* [2006] EWCA Crim 2895.

[149] For more detailed discussion of possible remedies, see Roberts, above n 142.

[150] [1977] QB 224.

[151] On the importance of covering all of the elements in *Turnbull*, see *R v Nash* [2004] EWCA Crim 2696.

[152] This point, always apparent on a literal reading of *Turnbull*, is confirmed in *R v Ley* [2006] EWCA Crim 3063.

[153] Above n 150, 229.   [154] *Ibid.*

the case law some inconsistency as to when the *Turnbull* requirements on supporting evidence apply.[155] And the standard for 'good quality' can be rather low. In *Williams*, a two-second observation of a person in a moving vehicle was held not to be poor quality because it was made by a police officer.[156] Despite the Devlin Committee's observation that cross examination is little use as a means of testing identification evidence,[157] there remains a tendency to put much trust in the jury. Thus in *Waterfield*, the victim of a stressful sexual assault, who had been tired and had been drinking before the incident, identified D at a video identification 22 days later.[158] The Court of Appeal did not think that these factors made the identification 'inherently unreliable', and considered that the jury was in the best position to consider the impact of the various factors on the identification evidence. Two other cases demonstrate some of the problems here. In *Banks*, D's identification procedure was compromised when the witness turned up at the police station and found herself in the same room as D.[159] She said that she did no more than register the presence of another person in the room, but it is of course impossible to tell whether her later identification of D was influenced by having glimpsed him on that occasion. In *R v I*, the victim's mother took him to the school which they had been told the person who had assaulted him attended.[160] The headmaster presented the victim with two photographs, one of which the victim picked out. This very suggestive procedure compromised the video identification held shortly afterwards. In both these cases the courts seem to have accepted that the identification evidence was good and could stand alone, which implies that problems with identification procedures are not considered to impact on the distinction between good and poor quality evidence. It is true that the emphasis in *Turnbull* is on the conditions in which the witness saw the crime take place, rather than on subsequent procedures, but there is no logical reason for drawing this distinction when considering whether identification evidence can stand alone. The decisions in these cases also show considerable faith being put in the jury to divine what impact the errors may have had on the quality of the evidence.

It has been questioned whether the courts should rely at all here on the good/poor quality distinction. The Devlin Committee had not distinguished between good and poor evidence, and had recommended directing juries in all cases that 'it is not safe to convict upon eye-witness evidence unless the circumstances of the identification are exceptional or the eye-witness evidence is supported by substantial evidence of another sort.'[161] There is something to be said for this approach. All the evidence suggests that there are limits to the strength of eyewitness evidence: the figures, reviewed earlier, on the likelihood of an innocent suspect being picked out on an identification procedure are a graphic illustration of this. Most defendants plead guilty, and if it is likely that few innocents plead guilty, the proportion of cases involving mistaken identification at trial will be much higher than the proportion of mistaken

---

[155] Cf *Oakwell* [1978] 1 All ER 1223; *Curry* [1983] *Crim LR* 737; *Bowden* [1993] *Crim LR* 379.
[156] *The Times* 7 October 1994.   [157] Above n 105, 4.25.   [158] [2009] EWCA Crim 1815.
[159] [2005] EWCA Crim 1858.   [160] [2007] EWCA Crim 923.   [161] Above n 105, para 8.4.

identifications occurring at identification procedures.[162] The basic fact is that some types of evidence are simply not powerful enough to justify conviction unless there is supporting evidence. Of course, even the Devlin committee recognized that a rule with too bright a line might be problematic: exceptional circumstances would justify conviction on an eyewitness identification alone. The sorts of situations described in *Turnbull* as constituting good quality evidence might be thought to justify a conviction when standing alone. But in all other cases, the Devlin committee's approach seems appropriate.

In conclusion, as with confession evidence, the system for regulating the production of eyewitness evidence in England and Wales is relatively impressive. The use of video identification, and the detailed rules in Code D, offer significant safeguards to suspects, far superior to arrangements in many jurisdictions. Various points of detail can be criticized, most obviously the absence of a requirement for procedures to be double blind, but apart from this Code D stands up well.[163] If there is criticism of the current system, much of it would be directed at the courts. While the courts may have done well to emphasize the importance of identification procedures in the face of the ambiguous language of Code D ('no useful purpose'), they have done less well in giving clear guidance on the admittedly difficult question of when street identifications are appropriate. There is also room for concern that, despite the difficulties that juries must face in gauging the accuracy of eyewitness identifications, the courts continue to put too much faith in juries, both when it comes to responding to breaches of Code D—over-reliance on *Forbes* warnings—and in letting juries convict on eyewitness evidence alone in too wide a range of cases.

5.4 VOICE IDENTIFICATION

In some cases, a witness may not have seen the offender's face, but only heard his voice. There is little doubt that voice identification raises many of the same concerns as visual identification: mistakes can occur, and even confident witnesses can make them. In fact, the psychological research suggests that voice identification is even less reliable then visual identification.[164] Code D, however, says almost nothing about voice identification, simply noting that 'while this code concentrates on visual identification procedures, it does not preclude the police making use of aural identification procedures such as a "voice identification parade", where they judge that appropriate.'[165] It is initially disappointing to read this in the 2008 version of the Code, given that the problems here have been known for many years. However,

---

[162] This is the 'pleading effect', discussed in Wells et al, above n 108, 51–2.

[163] For other suggestions, see Valentine, above n 114.

[164] See D. Ormerod, 'Sounds Familiar?—Voice Identification Evidence' [2001] *Crim LR* 595.

[165] Code D, 1.2. See also 1.8.

the Home office has issued a circular, endorsing guidance first developed by the Metropolitan Police for use in a particular case.[166] While this lacks the mandatory force of Code D, and makes no requirement that an identification procedure be held in a particular case, the guidelines, which have obviously been developed with help from experts in the field, are impressive, and it is hoped that the courts will hold the police to the standards in them in appropriate cases. The guidelines outline how to set up a voice identification parade, avoiding potential pitfalls such as having participants read a set text (which can apparently lead to unnatural vocal inflection), by using interview tapes. It is suggested that experts be involved in selecting appropriate excerpts to be used. One valuable suggestion is that the selection of recordings be played to a number of mock witnesses, who know nothing more than what can be gleaned from a description of the crime, to see if the suspect's voice stands out. The procedures outlined in the guidelines are resource intensive, and it might be difficult to implement them if voice identification became as common as visual identification, but the idea of using naïve subjects to test the array of images used in video identifications so as to see whether the suspect stands out would be worth implementing in eyewitness cases, if only as a quality audit in selected cases. If a person who had read only the witness's description of the perpetrator was able to pick out the suspect from among the fillers, this would be a useful indication that the video identification procedure was unfair.

The courts are reasonably alert to the dangers posed by voice identification. A suitably modified *Turnbull* direction is recommended—though one might wonder if a stronger warning is appropriate—and the Court of Appeal is critical where this is not given.[167] The majority of cases seem to involve voice recognition: witnesses who claim to recognize the perpetrator's voice. While this may well be more reliable than the identification of a voice only heard during the crime, it is worth noting that in visual identification cases involving recognition, the courts often hold that an identification procedure is required.[168] This might well be appropriate in cases of voice recognition, even ones involving recent familiarity (as the Court of Appeal has noted, in experiments people can fail to recognize the voices of intimates speaking over a telephone[169]), so it is disappointing that neither the courts, nor the Home Office through Code D, have taken the initiative here. The courts have done better where the police have purported to recognize recorded voices, being very critical of this move.[170] In summary, while there is awareness of the difficulties involved in voice identification and voice recognition, more needs to be done to hold the police to best practice in this area.

[166] Home Office Circular 057/2003.
[167] *R v Hersey* [1988] *Crim LR* 281; *R v Phillips* [2007] EWCA Crim 1042.   [168] See n 138 above.
[169] *R v Flynn* [2008] 2 Cr App R 20, [16].
[170] *Flynn, ibid.* For similar concerns about police visual identification from CCTV, see *R v Smith* [2009] 1 Cr App R 36.

5.5 DNA SAMPLES

In the last 20 years, DNA evidence has become an important part of the criminal justice landscape in England and Wales. No one can doubt the utility of DNA evidence in identifying offenders and building a powerful case against them. What has been more controversial has been the growth of a large DNA database against which samples of DNA found at crime scenes can be checked. The database currently holds the DNA profiles of more than 4.2 million people, or some 7 per cent of the population.[171] The database has grown so large in part because of regular expansion of police powers to take DNA samples from suspects.[172] Under the original version of PACE, samples could only be obtained from those suspected of involvement in serious arrestable offences, and when the DNA database was first established DNA profiles could not be retained unless a person was convicted. But after changes introduced by the Criminal Justice Act 2003, DNA samples could be taken, without consent, from anyone *arrested* for involvement in a recordable offence, irrespective of whether they were convicted or even prosecuted, and whether or not the sample would be useful in investigating the offence for which they had been arrested.[173] The sample, as well as a DNA profile obtained from it and entered on the database, could be retained indefinitely. These wide powers of retention led to the UK being held in breach of the Article 8 right to privacy by the European Court of Human Rights (ECtHR) in *Marper v United Kingdom*.[174] As a result, restrictions on the power to retain DNA profiles on the database were included in the Crime and Security Bill 2009.

DNA obviously contains sensitive personal information, such as information about our ancestry and susceptibility to disease. DNA profiles, however, contain information taken from very small portions of the genome. The relevant portions are 'non-coding', in other words they do not play a role in determining the features or development (the 'phenotype') of the person concerned; they are sometimes referred to as 'junk' DNA. But it is not quite right to say that DNA profiles contain no significant information at all. Because even non-coding DNA is inherited, DNA profiles contain some information about who is related to whom. It is also possible to make limited inferences about a person's ethnicity on the basis of a DNA profile.[175]

DNA samples (the actual biological material, as opposed to the profile, which, as explained, is the non-coding information drawn from the sample) were retained in case changes in technology mean that a new set of DNA profiles needed to be generated from them at some point in time, but the technology is now good enough—and the work involved in re-analysing the samples so enormous—that this is unlikely

---

171 Hansard, 10 November 2008, col 799W (Alan Campbell MP, written answer).

172 For the history of the expansion of the relevant powers, see C. McCartney, *Forensic Identification and Criminal Justice: Forensic Science, Justice and Risk* (2006), Ch 1.

173 PACE, s 63.   174 *S and Marper v United Kingdom* (2009) 48 EHRR 50.

175 See Nuffield Council on Bioethics, *The Forensic Use of Bioinformation: Ethical Issues* (2007), 2.15–2.21.

ever to be considered. While it would be illegal to use the retained samples to discover genetic information about a particular individual, their retention has been
sensitive, and following the ECtHR's decision in *Marper*,[176] the Government has
now accepted that all samples should be destroyed.[177] The discussion here will
therefore concentrate on DNA profiles, which raise more difficult issues than do
samples.

When the House of Lords had considered *Marper*, a majority held that retention
of DNA profiles raised no privacy issues.[178] The ECtHR, however, came to the opposite conclusion, finding that the ability to explore genetic relationships and make
inferences about ethnicity meant that DNA profiles enable 'the authorities to go well
beyond neutral identification.'[179] One might quibble with some of this. Inferences
about ethnicity would not be drawn from the profiles in issue in *Marper*, because these
are taken from known people and details about the person's ethnic appearance will
be recorded along with other relevant information such as name and date of birth.
Inferences about ethnicity will only be made where a DNA sample is found at a crime
scene, and in the absence of a match to the database the police want information
about the offender's possible ethnic appearance. This practice was simply not in issue
in *Marper*. The point about genetic relationships is a sounder one, but it is still important to understand just what occurs. If a crime scene sample is checked against the
database, but no match is reported, a search may be conducted for near matches, on
the assumption that these may involve the offender's relatives. The police might then
approach the source of a close match, and ask this person to name close relatives, who
might then come under suspicion. So while the database provides a lead, information
about relatedness will come, if at all, from the person approached by the police, who
is under no legal obligation to comply. Nevertheless, as a report issued by the Nuffield
Council on Bioethics notes, familial searching needs to be carried out with great sensitivity.[180] While the ECtHR's concerns about DNA may have been overstated, it seems
that even had there been no concerns about sensitive information it would still have
held that DNA profiles raise issues under Article 8, for in the same judgement it also
considered the retention of fingerprints, finding that 'fingerprints objectively contain
unique information about the individual concerned allowing his or her identification
with precision in a wide range of circumstances. They are thus capable of affecting his
or her private life.'[181]

This led the Court to a consideration of whether retention of DNA profiles and
fingerprints was justified under Article 8(2). While all European jurisdictions allow
the retention of such material in some circumstances, *Marper* highlighted the exceptionally wide powers available in England and Wales—neither applicant had

---

[176] Above n 174.

[177] This was conceded in the original consultation paper: Home Office, *Keeping the Right People on the
DNA Database: Science and Public Protection* (2009), 5.2. It is confirmed in the post-consultation proposals:
Home Office, *Written Minsterial Statement: DNA and Fingerprint Retention* (2009).

[178] [2004] UKHL 39. Baroness Hale dissented on this point: see at [67]–[79].

[179] Above n 174, [75].   [180] Above n 175, 6.11.   [181] Above n 174, [84].

been convicted of a criminal offence, and yet their profiles would be retained indefinitely. The Court found that the 'blanket and indiscriminate nature' of the powers 'fails to strike a fair balance between the competing public and private interests.'[182] While the Government had provided some evidence that retention of DNA from those arrested but not convicted contributed to identifying offenders, the court thought that insufficient detail was given to make the Government's case for wide retention.

The Government responded with a rather rushed consultation paper outlining its response to the judgement in *Marper*.[183] The institute that produced the empirical research on reoffending which was said to provide the evidence base for the proposals quickly distanced itself from the research published in the report.[184] As far as the unconvicted were concerned, the main proposal was that profiles should be retained for six years, except in the case of offences involving serious violence, terrorism and sexual offending, where the limit would be 12 years. In the final proposals, this distinction was dropped, with a six year limit proposed for all crimes. In outline, the final recommendations, which form the basis for the provisions in the Crime and Security Bill, are that arrest for a recordable offence should continue to be the threshold for obtaining a DNA profile. Those who are convicted will continue to have their profiles retained indefinitely. The non-convicted will have their profiles removed from the database after six years. For those under 18, the situation is more complex. Those convicted of a serious offence will, like adults, have their profiles retained indefinitely. For other convictions, the limit is five years, but retention is indefinite if there is a second conviction. Unconvicted 16- and 17-year-olds will have their profiles retained for six years if the arrest was for a serious offence. Otherwise, the limit is three years for all juveniles. Currently, anyone who has been profiled but not convicted can ask the Chief Constable of the relevant police force to destroy the profile, and the profile might be destroyed in 'exceptional' circumstances, for example if it is agreed that no crime was committed. This will continue to be possible, but it is proposed to introduce clearer guidelines to regulate this practice. In all cases, fingerprints would be treated in the same way as DNA profiles.

These proposals are a fairly minimalist response to the judgement in *Marper*, but the Government hopes to avoid the 'blanket and indiscriminate' charge by claiming that the proposals are based on research. A short paper published alongside the proposals compares the likelihood of arrest for those arrested but not convicted with the likelihood of arrest for the general population; the former likelihood is said to equal the latter one six years after the initial arrest, hence the six-year retention period.[185] There are various uncertainties involved in this calculation, and the Home Secretary has admitted that the evidence for the six year limit is 'sparse'.[186]

---

[182] *Ibid.*, [35]   [183] Home Office, above n 177.
[184] 'DNA Storage Proposals "Incomplete"' www.news.bbc.co.uk/1/hi/uk/8273882.stm.
[185] Home Office, *DNA Retention Policy: Re-Arrest Hazard Rate Analysis* (2009).
[186] 'My DNA Dilemma' *The Guardian* 25 November 2009.

Arguments about who should be included on the DNA database and for how long are complex.[187] In thinking about the issues it is probably helpful to equate DNA profiles to fingerprints; with both types of biometric data, the principal concern in terms of privacy is that inclusion on the database can lead to being the subject of criminal investigation in the future. Unfortunately, beyond various anecdotes, we have little reliable information about how important the DNA database is in securing convictions against people in various groups: the convicted and the unconvicted, and those arrested for more and less serious crimes. We also have limited information about the attitudes of the general public.[188] The most contentious issue in the debate is whether DNA profiles and fingerprints should be retained from those who have not been convicted of an offence, but the question of how long the profiles of the convicted should be retained for is significant too. It might be argued that if the convicted remain at a higher risk of offending, then they are likely to be rearrested at some point, in which case a new profile can be taken.[189] When it comes to the unconvicted, in the response to the consultation it seems that a majority were opposed to retention.[190] This purist stance is initially attractive, but it does have its problems. Police forces often keep records about those they arrest, detailing names, reason for arrest and the like, and it might be questioned why there is such concern about DNA profiles but not about these other forms of recorded information. Further, if it is conceded that the profiles of the convicted should be retained for at least some period, and if this concession is based on risk of reoffending, then 'purists' would need to consider arguments that the arrested but not convicted have a higher risk of offending than the general population.[191]

A popular position on the retention of profiles of the unconvicted is the 'Scottish model', which a 'large volume' of respondents to the consultation agreed with, and which has the support of the Conservative party and was endorsed by the Nuffield Council on Bioethics.[192] Under this approach, profiles are only retained from those arrested for violent and sexual offences, and for a limited period (three years in Scotland, though the police can apply for a two-year extension). It is not clear what the argument for this position is, especially as it might be said to stigmatize a certain group of arrestees. More serious offences tend to have lower recidivism rates than less serious ones, so in terms of risk of reoffending the Scottish policy might even be said

---

[187] See generally D. Lazer (ed), *DNA and the Criminal Justice System: The Technology of Justice* (2004).

[188] The Human Genetics Commission (*Nothing to Hide, Nothing to Fear? Balancing Individual Rights and the Public Interest in the Governance and Use of the National DNA Database* (2009)) carried out what appears to be very impressive research on public attitudes using focus groups and citizens' juries. They apparently found that informed opinions were reasonably evenly split between various proposals, but the report does not give a clear summary of the public's conclusions.

[189] See K. Soothill, 'Keeping the DNA Link' (2009) 159 *NLJ* 1021.

[190] Home Office, *Keeping the Right People on the DNA Database: Science and Public Protection, Summary of Responses, Public Consultation 7 May–7 August 2009* (2009), 2.1.

[191] See above n 185. One very striking piece of research found that those acquitted of rape were very similar to those convicted in terms of subsequent criminal careers. K. Soothill, C. Way and T. Gibbens, 'Rape Acquittals' (1980) 43 *MLR* 159.

[192] Above n 175, xv.

to target the wrong people. Obviously it is more important to convict people of serious offences, but this does not provide a straightforward case for singling out those who have been arrested for sexual and violent offences. Versatility in offending—offenders who commit serious crimes tend to commit less serious ones as well—means that there is a case for retaining profiles of those arrested for minor crimes in order later to gain convictions for more serious ones.[193]

One serious omission in the Government's proposals on the DNA database is equality. Ethnic disproportion on the database is marked: one in three young black males has a profile on the database, compared to one in eight young white males. This results from the ability of the police to take profiles on arrest, and as we saw in Chapter 4, there is evidence that blacks are arrested on a lower evidence base than whites. The equality issue was highlighted as a cause for concern in the Nuffield report,[194] but was not mentioned in the Consultation Paper, nor in the later ministerial statement despite having been raised by consultees. Evidently, the database is not a direct cause of inequality; police decision making is. But to argue that the database simply reflects problems elsewhere in the criminal process is to ignore the fact that whites have significantly less chance of being arrested as a result of a database match to a crime scene profile than do blacks. In this way, by putting blacks at a greater risk of conviction, the database is prone to amplify black over-representation in the criminal justice system. This is sometimes used as an argument for having a truly universal database, with people included at birth.[195] The Human Genetics Commission found considerable public support for this idea, but was not itself convinced that equality provided good reasons for a universal database.[196]

In summary, there is no obvious place to draw the line when it comes to deciding whose DNA profiles and fingerprints should be retained on databases. The Government's current proposals can at least be said to be based on some research evidence, which is more than can be said for the 'Scottish model'. But once the debate moves on to degrees of risk, as it now seems to have done, questions are raised about whether there is a strong case for retaining the profiles of the convicted for an indefinite period when those of the unconvicted are not.

5.6 THE PRIVILEGE AGAINST SELF-INCRIMINATION

Our final example of a principled constraint on the ability of the State to gather and use evidence against suspects is the privilege against self-incrimination. This example

---

[193] See M. Gottfredson and T. Hirschi, *A General Theory of Crime* (1990); Home Office, above n 177, 34–5.

[194] Above n 175, 4.63–4.66.

[195] See D. Kaye and M. Smith, 'DNA Databases for Law Enforcement: The Coverage Question and the Case for a Population-Wide Database' in Lazer, above n 187.

[196] Human Genetics Commission, above n 188, paras 3.40–3.45.

is in many ways more complex than those considered so far. While the privilege is recognized in international human rights documents,[197] and has been implied into the ECHR by the Court in Strasbourg, its scope and underlying justification are difficult to pin down. Historical studies suggest that our understanding of the privilege has shifted over time.[198] While acknowledging those points, we should begin by noting that certain aspects of the privilege do appear to have universal support. In English law, the most fundamental application of the privilege occurs at trial, in the form of the rule that the defendant is not a compellable witness at his own trial. The significance of this is that the defendant can refuse to testify, and cannot be held in contempt of court for this refusal. Witnesses other than the accused benefit from certain immunities,[199] but, in general, they can be held in contempt if they do not attend court and testify when summonsed. Different jurisdictions deal with the accused's position at trial in different ways, but, while the accused may not be able to escape being questioned, it would appear to be a general principle that he cannot be punished for refusing to answer questions.[200] In the discussion to follow, we will try to show some of the values that underpin the privilege against self-incrimination, concentrating on the way the privilege has been developed under the ECHR.[201]

(A) WHEN DOES THE PRIVILEGE APPLY?

In 1993, in *Funke v France*,[202] the ECtHR recognized the privilege as being part of the fair trial guarantee in Article 6. The applicant was suspected of tax evasion. The authorities demanded that he provide them with details of his bank accounts; when Funke did not do so the French court fined him 50 francs a day. The Court found that: 'The special features of customs law…cannot justify such an infringement of the right of anyone "charged with a criminal offence"…to remain silent and not to contribute to incriminating himself.'[203] Some years later, in *Saunders v United Kingdom*, it expanded on these rather cryptic comments.[204] Saunders had been investigated under the Companies Act 1985 after he had been suspected of illegally boosting the price of shares in his company. Under the Act, inspectors had the power to require that he produce documents and answer questions put to him. Refusal could be punished as contempt of court

[197] International Covenant on Civil and Political Rights, Art 14; Inter-American Convention on Human Rights, Art 8.
[198] See R. Helmholz et al, *The Privilege Against Self Incrimination: Its Origins and Development* (1997); M. MacNair, 'The Early Development of the Privilege Against Self-Incrimination' (1990) 10 *OJLS* 66.
[199] Most significantly, spousal immunity: see Dennis, above n 143, 539–42.
[200] For example, in China the accused need not give sworn evidence; in France, the defendant cannot avoid being questioned, but, again, need not take an oath and need not answer. See C. Bradley, *Criminal Procedure: A Worldwide Study* (1999), 88, 176.
[201] For a more detailed review of the ECHR case law, see A. Ashworth, 'Self-Incrimination in European Human Rights Law—A Pregnant Pragmatism?' (2008) 30 *Cardozo L Rev* 751.
[202] (1993) 16 EHRR 297.   [203] *Ibid.*, [44].   [204] (1997) 23 EHRR 313.

and any information gained through this process could be used against Saunders at trial. The ECtHR found the latter point significant: its 'sole concern', it explained, was 'with the use made of the relevant statements made at the applicant's criminal trial'.[205] The fact that his statements had been used against him at trial put those proceedings in breach of Article 6. This time the Court said something more about the justification for the privilege against self-incrimination:

'[The] rationale lies, *inter alia*, in the protection of the accused against improper compulsion by the authorities thereby contributing to the avoidance of miscarriages of justice and to the fulfilment of the aims of Art 6. The right not to incriminate oneself, in particular, presupposes that the prosecution in a criminal case seek to prove their case against the accused without resort to evidence obtained through methods of coercion or oppression in defiance of the will of the accused. In this sense the right is closely linked to the presumption of innocence.... The right not to incriminate oneself is primarily concerned, however, with respecting the will of an accused person to remain silent. As commonly understood in the legal systems of the Contracting Parties to the Convention and elsewhere, it does not extend to the use in criminal proceedings of material which may be obtained from the accused through the use of compulsory powers but which has an existence independent of the will of the suspect such as, *inter alia*, documents acquired pursuant to a warrant, breath, blood and urine samples and bodily tissue for the purposes of DNA testing.'[206]

This passage has been repeated, with minor variations, in several other cases.[207]

The effect of *Saunders* in English law was that a number of statutes giving similar 'inquisitorial' powers to investigators were modified by the introduction of 'use immunity'.[208] Use immunity means that, although a suspect can be subjected to sanctions—such as a fine, or being held in contempt of court[209]—for refusing to answer questions or provide information, the information so obtained cannot then be used in court. (This position, whereby investigators can gain information but not use it to gain a conviction, has been described as 'the worst of all possible worlds' by one commentator.[210]) Use immunity has received some emphasis in later ECtHR decisions. In *Heaney and McGuiness v Ireland*, the defendants had been found close to the scene of a terrorist bombing.[211] Under Irish law, they could be asked to provide an account of their movements in the preceding 24 hours; refusal to do so was a criminal offence. The Court again found a breach of the convention, noting that the situation as to whether or not the applicants' answers to such questions could be used at a trial for the offence under investigation was unclear. And in *Marttinnen*,[212] the defendant faced criminal liability for refusing to disclose details of his assets in debt enforcement proceedings; this was held to breach Article 6 because again there was no guarantee

---

[205] *Ibid.*, 67.   [206] *Ibid.*, 68–9.   [207] E.g. *JB v Switzerland* [2001] *Crim LR* 748.

[208] Youth Justice and Criminal Evidence Act 1999, s 59.

[209] *IJL and others v United Kingdom*, Appln 29522/95, 19 September 2000.

[210] S. Sedley, 'Wringing Out the Fault: Self-Incrimination in the 21st Century' (2001) 52 *NILQ* 107, 120.

[211] (2000) 33 EHRR 12.   [212] *Marttinnen v Finland*, ECtHR, 21 April 2009.

that information disclosed could not be used against him in proceedings for debt fraud, an investigation of which was under way.

That use immunity should play a role in the case law is perhaps not surprising. The privilege protects against self-incrimination. If information provided carries no risk of self-incrimination, the privilege does not apply. This means that some requests by the State for information are perfectly legitimate so far as the privilege is concerned. Thus in *King v United Kingdom*,[213] King was held to have been properly fined for failing to provide information about his tax liability, because he was not being prosecuted for a tax offence beyond the one involving his refusal to provide information. Similarly, in *Weh v Austria* the applicant was asked to provide details of who was driving his car on a particular date when it was seen to break the speed limit; when he gave vague details he was fined for providing inaccurate information.[214] As criminal proceedings had not been commenced against Weh in respect of the speeding offence (the authorities had charged 'unknown offenders'), he was held not to benefit from the privilege against self-incrimination. This is a rather fine distinction, and it is in tension with some of the reasoning in *Marttinnen*.[215]

The scope of the privilege against self-incrimination is limited in another way: in the view of the ECtHR in *Saunders* it does not apply to material which has an existence 'independent of the will' of the subject 'such as, *inter alia*, documents acquired pursuant to a warrant, breath, blood and urine samples and bodily tissue for the purposes of DNA testing'. This pronouncement has caused much bemusement. After all, many of the cases where the Court has held that the privilege does apply involve material which appears to have an existence independent of the will: *Funke* and *Marttinnen* involved financial details. In *Jalloh*,[216] the German police took a suspected drug dealer to hospital, where he was administered an emetic which made him regurgitate drugs. The drugs surely had an existence independent of the will, yet the ECtHR held that the privilege applied. The not very satisfactory reasoning used to distinguish 'breath blood and urine samples' from the swallowed drugs was that the situation in *Jalloh* involved real evidence, as opposed to material which would be examined for the presence of alcohol or drugs, and that the degree of force used in *Jalloh* was greater than in the case of a simple blood etc test.[217] The former point received a little elucidation in *Gäfgen v Germany*, where the real evidence in *Jalloh* was said to have been elicited as a direct result of a breach of Article 3, and was contrasted with real evidence discovered as the indirect effect of a threat of violence.[218]

An interesting English case has recently probed the question of what material the privilege applies to. *R v S and A* involved investigation into suspected terrorism.[219] The police wanted to access encrypted files on the defendants' computer, but were unable to do so without an encryption key. Under s 49 of the Regulation of Investigatory Powers Act 2000 the defendants were asked to provide the key either orally or in writing.

---

[213] (2004) STC 911.   [214] (2005) 40 EHRR 37.   [215] See above n 212, esp at [64].
[216] *Jalloh v Germany* (2007) 44 EHRR 32.   [217] *Ibid.*, [113]–[114].
[218] (2009) 48 EHRR 13, [104].   [219] [2008] EWCA Crim 2177.

Failure to do so was a criminal offence, punishable by a term of imprisonment. The Court of Appeal held that the key had an existence independent of the will:

'Once created, the key to the data, remains independent of the appellant's "will" even when it is retained only in his memory.... In this sense the key to the computer equipment is no different to the key to a locked drawer. The contents of the drawer exist independently of the suspect: so does the key to it. The contents may or may not be incriminating: the key is neutral.'[220]

The point about the neutrality of the material received further emphasis:

'The actual answers, that is to say the product of the defendants' minds, could not be in-criminating. The keys themselves simply opened the locked drawer, revealing its contents. In much the same way that a blood or urine sample provided by a car driver is a fact inde-pendent of the driver, which may or may not reveal that his alcohol level exceeds the per-mitted maximum, whether the defendants' computers contain incriminating material or not, the keys to them are and remain an independent fact.'[221]

So far we have seen that, under the ECtHR's jurisprudence, the privilege against self-incrimination applies to information which may incriminate the defendant in criminal proceedings, and which does not exist independently of his will. A further question about the privilege is whether it is absolute, or whether its breach might be justified in some situations. Here, the ECtHR's jurisprudence is not entirely satisfac-tory.[222] In cases such as *Saunders* and *Heaney*, the court denied that the need to inves-tigate complex financial transactions or serious crime—a terrorist bombing—could justify a breach of the privilege. While *Heaney* did allow that the privilege was not absolute, it suggested that any abrogation of the privilege must not destroy its 'very essence'.[223] In *Jalloh*, however, the Court slipped into the language of balancing, sug-gesting that 'the weight of public interest in the investigation and punishment of the offence at issue' was a relevant consideration in determining whether Article 6 had been breached.[224] But because the case involved only a minor drug dealing offence, with the applicant receiving a suspended sentence, the breach was not justified. The real test case for breaches of the privilege has been the regulation of road traffic offences. As we have seen, in *Weh* the applicant was asked to identify who had been driving his car, and his unhelpful response gained him a criminal conviction. Powers such as this are a common way of dealing with car ownership, and have received extended dis-cussion in the UK in *Brown v Stott*[225] and in Strasbourg in *O'Halloran and Francis v United Kingdom*.[226] In the latter case, the applicants' cars had been filmed breaking the speed limit. Section 172 of the Road Traffic Act 1988 required them to provide details of who was driving the car at the relevant time. They alleged that this breached their

---

[220] *Ibid.*, [20].   [221] *Ibid.*, [21].

[222] See J. Jackson, 'Re-Conceptualizing the Right of Silence as an Effective Fair Trial Standard' (2009) 58 *ICLQ* 1.

[223] Above n 211, 55.   [224] Above n 216, [117].   [225] [2001] 2 WLR 817.

[226] (2008) 46 EHRR 21.

privilege against self-incrimination. The ECtHR found no breach; it seemed to accept that the privilege against self-incrimination is not absolute,[227] and offered several reasons why, on the facts, 'the very essence' of the right was not negated. It noted that the compulsion involved—'a moderate and non-custodial penalty'[228]—was minor, and that the applicants had only been asked to provide a limited amount of information.[229] Both of these points are problematic.[230] As noted above, in *Jalloh* the level of penalty was used as evidence that the offence was not a very serious one and thus that coercive measures were not appropriate; if penalty level can be used to argue in either direction, it is hardly a principle that can restrain breach of the privilege. As for the complexity of the information sought, what is surely more significant is that the answer to the question is capable of incriminating the subject.

The Court in *O'Halloran* was on firmer ground when, quoting from the Privy Council's decision in *Brown v Stott*, it noted that:

'"All who own or drive motor cars know that by doing so they subject themselves to a regulatory regime. This regime is imposed not because owning or driving cars is a privilege or indulgence granted by the State but because the possession and use of cars (like, for example, shotguns...) are recognised to have the potential to cause grave injury". Those who choose to keep and drive motor cars can be taken to have accepted certain responsibilities and obligations as part of the regulatory regime relating to motor vehicles, and in the legal framework of the United Kingdom, these responsibilities include the obligation, in the event of suspected commission of road traffic offences, to inform the authorities of the identity of the driver on that occasion.'[231]

In other words, this is not so much a case of the privilege being outbalanced by the need to regulate vehicle ownership, as that there is here a clear regulatory regime, involving licensing, registration, number plates and the like, which vehicle owners voluntary enter into. While this reasoning is perhaps not entirely satisfactory (in rural areas, vehicle ownership may be something of a necessity), it has some pedigree in the criminal law where it is an argument that sometimes features in the justification of strict liability offences.[232] It is certainly preferable to a plain balancing argument; accepting that the harm caused by cars outbalanced the applicants' rights would have obvious repercussions for cases like *Heaney*, where the privilege would easily be outbalanced by arguments about the need to respond to terrorism.[233]

---

[227] There is some ambiguity in the judgement, e.g. at [53] it is not clear whether the Court accepts that the privilege is non-absolute as opposed to that some forms of compulsion may not breach the right in the first place.

[228] *Ibid.*, [58], quoting from *Brown v Stott* [2001] 2 WLR 817.   [229] *Ibid.*, [58].

[230] See Ashworth, above n 201, 762–5.   [231] Above n 226, [57].

[232] See R. Duff, 'Strict Liability, Legal Presumptions and the Presumption of Innocence' in A. Simester (ed), *Appraising Strict Liability* (2005), 138–41.

[233] It might, though, be argued that the privilege has more value in serious cases, and thus that the weights on either side of the balance are greater in a case like *Heaney*. That is an interesting possibility, but the argument remains to be made.

(B) SCOPE OF THE PRIVILEGE

By describing the case law, with an emphasis on ECtHR decisions, we have given some idea of what the privilege against self-incrimination involves. It should be emphasised, however, that the privilege is a controversial principle, with a number of writers questioning whether it is possible to justify it.[234] One way of approaching these more normative issues is to return to one of the questions that surfaces in the case law: to what sort of information does the privilege apply? The ECtHR has tried to delimit the privilege by arguing that it does not apply to material which has an existence independent of the subject's will, but it has been criticized for applying this criterion inconsistently by finding breaches of the privilege in cases involving the production of documents and drugs.[235] It is possible to argue that there is more consistency in the case law than might at first appear. The critical passage in *Saunders* refers to 'documents acquired pursuant to a warrant' as being outside the scope of the privilege, and in the earliest case, *Funke*, there was criticism that the authorities, 'Being unable or unwilling to procure [the documents] by some other means, ... attempted to compel the applicant himself to provide the evidence of offences he had allegedly committed.'[236] It may be that there would have been no criticism had the authorities used their powers to find the relevant information themselves, such as by executing a search warrant. On this view, what was objectionable was that Funke and other applicants in cases involving documents were placed under a legal obligation to cooperate with the authorities by handing over incriminating information. The privilege, it could be said, is means and not material based, prohibiting a particular means of acquiring information rather than protecting a particular type of material.[237] This way of viewing the privilege would avoid some rather odd distinctions that have been drawn in the case law. For example, in *S and A*, the case involving the encryption key, the Court of Appeal suggested that the key existed independently of the appellants' will, equating it to a physical key or a blood or urine sample. There is a sense in which this is true, but the distinction is probably not conducive to a principled case law. Any information stored in the memory, such as Heaney's memory of what he had been doing in the preceding 24 hours, might similarly be said to have an independent existence. This would be even more obvious if Heaney kept a diary which the police asked him to hand over to them; it would seem perverse to differentiate between obliging Heaney to hand over the diary and obliging him to give a verbal account of his movements.[238] To be fair, the

---

[234] See, e.g., D. Dolinko, 'Is there a Rationale for the Privilege Against Self-Incrimination?' (1986) 33 *UCLA L Rev* 1063; R. Allen, 'Theorizing About Self-Incrimination' (2008) 30 *Cardozo L Rev* 751.

[235] See, e.g., T. Ward and P. Gardner, 'The Privilege Against Self-Incrimination: In Search of Legal Certainty (2003) *EHRLR* 387; Dennis, above n 143, 161–5.

[236] Above n 202, [44].

[237] See M. Redmayne, 'Rethinking the Privilege Against Self-Incrimination' (2007) 27 *OJLS* 209.

[238] But for a theory that would draw a distinction here, on the grounds that Heaney is able to lie when responding verbally but not when handing over the diary, see D. Seidmann and A. Stein, 'The Right to Silence Helps the Innocent' (2000) 114 *Harvard L Rev* 430.

Court of Appeal in *S and A* did not over-emphasize the argument that the key existed independently of the will, putting rather more weight on the argument that knowledge of the key was not in itself incriminating (and allowing that in some circumstances it might be, as where knowing the key could be used to prove the defendant's knowledge of the contents of a computer file). The court used this distinction to explain why blood and urine samples are not protected by the privilege, an argument we also find in *Jalloh*, where a distinction between directly and indirectly incriminating material appears to be drawn. Again, though, these distinctions are unappealing. There is very little difference between the drugs in *Jalloh* and a blood sample, and little too between asking the appellants in *S and A* to disclose the encryption key and to disclose the contents of the file. It is better to say that in all these situations the privilege is breached, at least prima facie, because the subject has been placed under a legal obligation to cooperate with the prosecution.

If the scope of the privilege against self-incrimination is defined in terms of whether the subject is placed under an obligation to cooperate, things such as blood and DNA samples will fall outside the protection of the privilege when they are taken by force, because this involves no cooperation. In this situation they will be taken independently of the will, just like documents found during a search of the suspect's house. This is not, of course, to say that there is nothing problematic in taking blood by force; this would be an act of violence and a significant breach of the right to bodily integrity. It may well be better to breach the privilege against self-incrimination than the right to bodily integrity, and in fact in English law it is an offence under the Road Traffic Act to refuse to supply a breath or blood sample[239] (a breach of the privilege, in terms of the account developed here), but the police have no power to take blood without consent.[240] A further implication of the argument is that in *Jalloh* there was no breach of the privilege against self-incrimination; not because the case involved real evidence, but because Jalloh was not placed under an obligation to cooperate; in fact he refused to cooperate and was held down while the emetic was administered by force. The ECtHR, though, was quite right to find a breach of Article 3 on these facts.

Another question about the scope of the privilege concerns its connection with the right to silence, which was discussed in the previous chapter. Terminology is one problem here. To this point, we have described the privilege against self-incrimination as a principle under which the State should not place a suspect under a duty to cooperate with a prosecution which is being brought against him. For the purposes of the discussion here, we would distinguish the right to silence as being the rule that inferences should not be drawn from a suspect's failure to mention facts at police interview or failure to testify at trial. The European Court has held that this rule is not required as part of a fair trial; in other words, inferences can be drawn from silence, as under the Criminal Justice and Public Order Act 1994, without conflict with Article 6 (see Chapter 4). The court has, however, emphasized the need to draw such

---

[239] Road Traffic Act 1988, ss 6, 7.   [240] PACE, s 62(1)(b).

inferences with care, and to offer legal advice to those held in the police station in a regime where their failure to mention facts can be used against them at trial.[241] As a matter of theory, this approach is fruitful: there is a good argument that there is no strong relationship between the right to silence, as just defined, and the privilege against self-incrimination. Drawing inferences from silence does not place a suspect under an obligation to speak; indeed, the words of the new caution begin: 'you do not have to say anything'. The Criminal Justice and Public Order Act may put a certain amount of pressure on suspects to speak, but this is not the same as obliging them to. However, as the Strasbourg Court notes, it is important that the regime of inferences from silence is handled carefully. To the extent that silence is suspicious, it is appropriate to draw inferences from silence. But if inferences are drawn too readily, or given too much weight, the scheme of drawing inferences from silence will change from being one where suspects face the natural consequences of their suspicious behaviour, to one where the only rational explanation for inferences is that they are being used to encourage suspects to speak by penalizing non-cooperation. Once the inferences from silence regime operates in this manner, it does appear to be in tension with the privilege against self-incrimination.[242] We also saw in Chapter 4 that there is evidence that the current caution is difficult to understand. If it is interpreted by suspects as meaning that they are required to speak, then in practice there would again be a conflict with the privilege against self-incrimination.

(C) A FUNDAMENTAL RIGHT?

To this point, we have outlined the ECtHR jurisprudence on the privilege against self-incrimination and suggested how it might be reinterpreted. In the process, something has been said about the scope of the privilege. But the hardest question remains: why should the criminal process respect a principle which places limits on its ability to obtain evidence from suspects? What principles underpin the privilege? There is no agreed theory of the privilege's value; indeed, as noted above, an influential position is that no coherent normative theory of the privilege can be developed.[243] On the account developed here, the privilege protects people from being placed under an obligation to cooperate with the prosecution. At a fairly general level, then, the privilege says something about the proper relationship between citizens and the State. Criminal prosecution is often controversial, and involves the State in one of its most powerful guises. The privilege allows citizens to keep some distance between themselves and the State, and avoids them having to make what will often be a significant personal sacrifice. Placing people under an obligation to cooperate would usually involve criminal sanctions, and this would often be an excessive response to a suspect's non-cooperation.[244]

---

[241] *Murray v United Kingdom* (1996) 22 EHRR 29; *Condron v United Kingdom* (2001) 31 EHRR 1.

[242] See M. Redmayne, 'English Warnings' (2008) 30 *Cardozo L Rev* 1047, 1082–3.

[243] See n 234 above.   [244] For an elaboration of this account, see Redmayne, above n 237.

The passage from *Saunders*, quoted above, mentions various values that justify the privilege, including that the privilege is connected to the presumption of innocence. This point is worth brief discussion, in part to disambiguate some of the points often made in this context. In Chapter 4 we drew attention to Greenawalt's argument that, as a matter of basic morality, one should not be expected to respond to accusations unless they are backed up with evidence.[245] This means that it is wrong to draw inferences from silence where there is not a reasonable basis for suspecting the person involved of wrongdoing. This principle might be said to reflect the presumption of innocence, where the presumption is understood not, as evidence lawyers tend to understand it, as a rule about the standard of proof in criminal cases, but as a rule about how the State should treat citizens. The State should not treat its citizens as suspects unless it can provide reasons for doing so; it should treat people with civility.[246] This principle might be seen as connected to the privilege against self-incrimination, in that at a deeper level both principles are about the relationship between citizen and State. But for many purposes it is useful to separate the principles. The privilege is more fundamental in that even when it is appropriate to draw an inference from silence—when there is sufficient evidence against the suspect to justify doing so—the privilege holds that it is still inappropriate to require cooperation. For example, at trial an inference may be drawn from the fact that the accused does not testify after the prosecution has made out a prima facie case, but it would still be wrong to hold the accused in contempt of court for not testifying. The principles, however, overlap to this extent: if there is a situation where breach of the privilege might be justified—for example, in the situation at issue in *O'Halloran*—cooperation should not be required unless the person involved is reasonably suspected of wrongdoing.

The account of the privilege against self-incrimination developed here is broad in two respects. First, it applies to real evidence such as blood and documents as much as to answers to questions, so long as they are obtained by placing the suspect under a duty to cooperate. While this creates a prima facie conflict between the privilege and the provisions of the Road Traffic Act, requiring the owners of vehicles to provide samples and to answer questions, we have suggested how one strand of the reasoning in *O'Halloran* might be used to create an exception to the privilege in this situation without engaging in unruly balancing of rights against social interests. A second way in which the account here is broad is that the values underpinning it seem to apply to duties to incriminate other people as much as to duties to incriminate oneself, because both involve the State imposing itself on a very personal realm.[247] To some extent the law recognizes this parallel, for there are provisions relating to spousal immunity which mean that in many cases a person cannot be required to testify against their spouse,[248] just as they cannot be required to testify against themselves. But consider s 38B of the Terrorism Act 2000. Under this provision it is a criminal offence, punishable by up

---

[245] K. Greenawalt, 'Silence as a Moral and Constitutional Right' (1981) 23 *William & Mary L Rev* 15.

[246] See D. Nance, 'Civility and the Burden of Proof' (1994) 17 *Harvard J Law & Public Policy* 647.

[247] See further Redmayne, above n 237.   [248] See n 199 above.

to five years' imprisonment, to fail to inform the authorities that another person is engaged in terrorist activity, when that other person is known or reasonably suspected to be engaged in such activity. That other person might, of course, be a spouse or sibling.[249] If we regard it as important to maintain some distance between ourselves and the State, so that the State's ends cannot be made to become our ends, then this wide-ranging provision is as objectionable as many of those discussed above.

FURTHER READING

BOWLING, B. and PHILLIPS, C., 'Disproportionate and Discriminatory: Reviewing the Evidence on Police Stop and Search' (2007) 70 *MLR* 936.

WELLS, G., MEMON, A. and PENROD, S., 'Eyewitness Evidence: Improving its Probative Value' (2006) 7 *Psychological Science in the Public Interest* 45.

NUFFIELD COUNCIL ON BIOETHICS, *The Forensic Use of Bioinformation: Ethical Issues*, London: Nuffield Council on Bioethics, 2007.

JACKSON, J., 'Re-Conceptualizing the Right of Silence as an Effective Fair Trial Standard' (2009) 58 *ICLQ* 1.

Questions for Discussion

1. Should: (a) powers to stop and search without reasonable suspicion and (b) powers to stop and search with reasonable suspicion be abolished?

2. How well are defendants protected against the risk of false eyewitness identification by (a) Code D and (b) the courts? Could defendants be given increased protection without unduly obstructing the conviction of the guilty?

3. In what circumstances should DNA profiles and fingerprints be taken and retained from those suspected of crime?

4. What is the value, if any, of the privilege against self-incrimination?

---

[249] See 'Bomb Suspect's Relatives Remanded in Custody' *The Guardian* 9 May 2003; 'Student on Bristol Terror Plot Charge Goes on Trial' *The Guardian* 2 September 2009.

6

GATEKEEPING AND DIVERSION

The concern of this chapter is with those decisions that determine whether or not a case enters the criminal justice system and, if so, what course it is set upon. These decisions were described in the first chapter as dispositive, which indicates that decisions to divert a case from prosecution (by preferring one of the alternatives discussed in this chapter) are likely to dispose of the case and be the final way of dealing with the offender for this offence. Some of these offenders may breach the conditions of their diversion and be brought back into the criminal process, but in the vast majority of cases the diversion has a practical finality. This makes it particularly appropriate to explore the reasons why some cases are diverted and others are not; and to question whether diversion is always the most appropriate course for the public, the defendant, and the victim.

Out of all the criminal offences committed in any one year, only a very low proportion result in formal proceedings being taken against a suspect/defendant. The process of attrition, as it has come to be known, is gradual and substantial. Figures derived from the British Crime Survey a decade ago, dealing with eight of the most frequently committed types of indictable offences, suggested that no more than 2 per cent result in a conviction.[1] Starting with those offences actually committed, around half of them are never reported to the police. Members of the public may choose not to report an offence because they think the police unable to help, because they regard the offence as too minor to report, because the offence is regarded as a private or domestic matter, because of fear of reprisals, or for other reasons. Of the 43 per cent that were reported to the police, a significant proportion were not recorded as crimes. A variety of reasons may come into play here: the offence may be attributed to a child below the age of criminal responsibility, or the police may not accept the victim's account, or the incident may have been resolved quickly and informally. This reduced the number of offences remaining in the system to 28 per cent. The next difficulty is that only a proportion of recorded offences were 'cleared up', in the sense of being detected or otherwise resolved. In relation to the eight types of crime studied in the British Crime

---

[1] G. C. Barclay (ed), *Digest 4: information on the Criminal Justice System in England and Wales* (1999), 29. The offences are criminal damage, theft of a motor vehicle; theft from a motor vehicle; bicycle theft; burglary, wounding, robbery, and theft from the person.

Survey, about one-fifth were cleared up and this reduced the percentage remaining in the system from 28 to 5.5 per cent. Some of the offences that were cleared up resulted in nothing more than an informal warning or no further action at all, particularly when traced to young offenders. Thus only 3 per cent of the offences resulted in a formal caution or in prosecution. Almost one-third of those are cautions, which (in the form of reprimands and warnings) remain widely used for younger offenders, leaving some 2.2 per cent to be sentenced by the courts.

This startling rate of attrition does not apply equally to all crimes: in particular, more serious crimes, particularly those where the victim sees the assailant, more often end in conviction. Among those studied in the British Crime Survey, offences of wounding resulted in a much higher rate of court appearance. A higher proportion of recorded offences were cleared up and were then dealt with formally, so that some 10 per cent of offenders were sentenced by the courts. The attrition rape of rape has long been a source of concern, and many surveys suggest that fewer than 10 per cent of cases end with a conviction for rape, although a higher percentage end in a conviction of some kind.[2]

What are the implications of the rate of attrition? One is that it demonstrates the naïveté of expecting the sentences passed by the courts to act as a significant control on crime. Those sentences deal with a small proportion of offenders—although, for the most part, they will be the most serious offenders—and, even making allowances for the probability that the symbolic effect of those (few) sentences will be greater than their proportionate size, this suggests that a strategy for the prevention of crime should not place great emphasis on sentencing. This is not to deny that sometimes sentences may exert a specific and/or general deterrent effect, but it is to counsel caution against overestimating those effects in the context of low rates of reporting, detection, and so on. A second implication is that decisions taken by law enforcement agents have a considerable influence on the selection of cases that go forward into the criminal process. As we shall see, a major revolution in diversion has taken place in recent years, with a range of out-of-court disposals (including fixed penalty notices, penalty notices for disorder and cannabis warnings) becoming at the disposal of law enforcement agents such as police officers. In relation to cases that go forward to prosecution, the decisions of police and prosecutors have a qualitative as well as a quantitative effect: the offenders who find themselves convicted in court are not a random group of the totality of offenders, nor necessarily are they the most serious group.[3] They are chosen, when others are not, for a variety of reasons that will be explored below.

The focus of this chapter will be upon the decisions taken by the gatekeepers of the criminal process. The discussion of different types of gatekeeper will be less detailed

---

[2] Cf J. Harris and S. Grace, *A Question of Evidence? Investigating and Prosecuting Rape in the 1990s* (1999); S. Lea, U. Lanvers and S. Shaw, 'Attrition in Rape Cases' (2003) 43 *BJ Crim* 583; J. Temkin and B. Krahe, *Sexual Assault and the Justice Gap: a Question of Attitude* (2008), esp at 9–23.

[3] Although it is probably true to say that many cases are not reported because they are thought too minor, one study of the victims of violence found that the probability of an offender being brought to court and convicted was not related to the objective seriousness of the assault: C. Clarkson et al, 'Assaults: the Relationship between Seriousness, Criminalisation and Punishment' [1994] *Crim LR* 4.

than the extensive literature would permit, in order to facilitate the analysis of general issues. The role of the police will be outlined first, followed by a comparison with the approach of regulatory bodies as agencies that select for official action certain types of person or situation, a selection that may lead either to prosecution and trial or to a form of diversion. The second section considers the range of formal responses to those who are believed to be offenders. The third section focuses on police cautions and other out-of-court disposals, and the fourth on the role of the CPS. The fifth section examines accountability, and the sixth analyses the values behind some of the differing policies.

6.1 REPORTING AND ENFORCING

There is a real sense in which society is self-policing. The vast majority of offences are brought to the attention of the police by members of the public, and so the police operate in a reactive role. The decision to report probably means that the victim or witness expects something to be done about the offence. However, as we saw earlier, about one-half of the eight common types of offence studied in the British Crime Survey are not reported, and prominent among the reasons are a belief that the crime was insufficiently serious to report, and a belief that the police would not be able to do anything about it. The latter reason may betray a pessimism about police effectiveness rather than a genuine judgement that no formal response is necessary. In practice, however, many of these cases will also involve the first reason—that the formal invocation of law enforcement machinery is not really necessary. To that extent, then, members of the public may be said to filter out of the system, at the earliest stage, many non-serious offences. However, the notion of society as self-policing cannot be pressed too far. The police are not simply the agents of the public, reacting whenever requested and not otherwise. There are at least three respects in which the police or other agencies exert a powerful influence. First, we have seen that the police do not record as crimes all incidents that are reported to them as crimes. As many as two-fifths of all incidents reported as thefts, robberies, woundings, etc are not recorded by the police as such.[4] Some of these incidents may be dealt with by invoking minor public order charges, such as breach of the peace, which are not recorded crimes. But many of them will not be recorded or will be 'no-crimed'. The result is that, although the police are largely dependent on the public to report offences, they do not always record what is reported. The police operate as a significant filter on public reports, and even though members

---

[4] The counting rules changed in 2002, as a result of the introduction of the National Crime Recording Standard, but the evidence shows that since 1995 there has been a steady increase in the proportion of reported crimes that are recorded as crimes by the police: J. Simmons and T. Dodd, *Crime in England and Wales 2002–2003*, 32.

of the public may want official action (and, implicitly, official recording of the offence), this may not be what occurs.

Secondly, the idea of society as self-policing does not account for the many offences, perhaps one-quarter of indictable crimes, that are discovered by the police themselves. Here the argument becomes complicated. Sometimes, when the police have a 'crack-down' on certain forms of offences, such as soliciting for sex or drug-dealing in a particular locality, this is a response to complaints from the public. Such cases may be regarded, partly at least, as examples of social self-policing. On the other hand there may be many cases in which the police themselves decide to have a 'campaign' against a particular form of offending: drug-dealing in clubs would be more likely to fall into this category, as would drink-driving. The police are operating proactively here, to some extent because the crimes are victimless and therefore there is no victim to make a complaint. In this context the patterns of law enforcement may largely reflect the availability of police officers and the preferences of those in operational control: the police can only mount 'proactive' campaigns if they are not overwhelmed by the 'reactive' demands of crimes reported to them, and when they do adopt a proactive strategy there may be a choice of what type of offence to target.

A third difficulty with the idea of society as self-policing is that this overlooks, or at least over-simplifies, the nature of the police function. Thus far we have referred to police work as if its focus is enforcing the law by catching criminals, whether as a result of prompting by a member of the public or as a result of a police campaign. Research shows that these kinds of activity do not dominate everyday policing. Much of what the police do is to perform a kind of service function, attending to a wide range of incidents that require something to be done about them—from road accidents and rowdy parties to stray cattle and barking dogs. Into all these situations the police officer brings authority and the ability to draw upon coercive powers if needed. These powers become even more prominent when there is thought to be a risk of public disorder—for example, at a demonstration or march or football match. These are the occasions on which the function of the police as maintainers of order comes to the fore. Whether the police use their coercive powers depends on a number of contingencies. If there is a genuine threat to good order they may intervene to make one or more arrests. Studies of police behaviour have long maintained that a police officer is more likely to arrest and charge someone who threatens the officer's authority by means of insults or failure to comply with the officer's commands or requests.[5] This forms part of the working culture of the police, discussed in Chapter 3. Significant as that proposition is in explaining why certain types of person come to be arrested and charged, it should not be allowed to overshadow the probability that some people clearly threaten to cause public disorder and should therefore be prevented from

---

[5] The classic study is by E. Bittner, 'The Police on Skid Row: a Study in Peacekeeping' (1967) 32 *Amer Soc Rev* 699; cf the more recent research reported by S. Choongh, *Policing as Social Discipline* (1997).

going further.[6] In other words, the use of arrest and criminal charges or out-of-court disposals by the police in incidents thought to threaten good order is likely to be an amalgam of some clearly justifiable cases and others that turn more on the disposition, pride, or self-image of particular officers. Any description that ignores one or the other lacks realism. The notion that Parliament makes the laws and the police 'merely' enforce them finds no echo here. The police manage situations so as to maintain order, using the offences in the Police Act 1996 and the Public Order Act 1986 as resources to draw upon, to be invoked against those who threaten the police conception of what constitutes good order and how it should be achieved. There is a considerable amount of low-level discretion, the significance of which will become clear as the chapter progresses.

Perhaps as many as one-quarter of all prosecutions are brought by agencies other than the Crown Prosecution Service (CPS). Of those, research ten years ago showed that some 80 per cent of non-police prosecutions were brought by four agencies—local authorities, the Driver and Vehicle Licensing Authority, the Television Licensing Office and the Department of Social Security.[7] Among the many others, the Health and Safety Commission brings prosecutions for offences concerning safety at work and in transport systems; HM Revenue and Customs bring prosecutions for offences relating to the evasion or attempted evasion of tax and customs duties; the Environment Agency brings prosecutions for offences of pollution; the Department of Trade and Industry brings prosecutions for financial offences; local consumer protection officers bring prosecutions for trading offences committed by shops and businesses; and so on. One major difference is that all these agencies (unlike the CPS) have both an investigatory function and the power to prosecute. Each of them therefore has control over all the relevant decisions. Another major difference between these agencies and the CPS is that there is no accountability structure for the various agencies. Each of them follows its own policies and practices, with no attempt at an overall strategy among different agencies, and few attempts to harmonize their policies with those of the police and the CPS.

Cranston's research into consumer protection departments found that prosecution is usually regarded as a last resort, after informal settlements and warnings.[8] A similar finding emerged from the study of the Pollution Inspectorate by Richardson, Ogus and Burrows,[9] from the research by Hawkins into environmental health officers[10] and later into the Health and Safety Commission,[11] and from the research by Hutter into the approaches of the Factory Inspectorate, the Industrial Air Pollution Inspectorate and environmental health officers.[12] HM Revenue and

---

[6] See R. Reiner, *The Politics of the Police* (3rd ed, 2000), Ch 4.

[7] G. Slapper, *Organisational Prosecutions* (2001).

[8] R. Cranston, *Regulating Business* (1979), 107 and 168.

[9] G. Richardson, A. Ogus and P. Burrows, *Policing Pollution* (1982).

[10] K. Hawkins, *Environment and Enforcement* (1984).   [11] K. Hawkins, *Law as Last Resort* (2003).

[12] B. Hutter, *The Reasonable Arm of the Law* (1988).

Customs has long pursued its aim, of the maximization of public revenue, by means of settlements and penalties outside the criminal process, with relatively rare resort to the courts.[13]

The Environment Agency may be examined by way of illustration. The functions of the Agency include the regulation of pollution, waste disposal, wildlife conservation, fisheries and water resources. The Agency publishes its 'Enforcement and Prosecution Policy' and also a more detailed document on the functions of the Agency with respect to particular types of offence.[14] The reader is immediately struck by the difference in emphasis from the CPS:

'The Agency regards prevention as better than cure…The purpose of enforcement is to ensure that preventative or remedial action is taken to protect the environment or to secure compliance with a regulatory system.'[15]

Combined with this difference in outlook is a difference in powers. Unlike the CPS, the Environment Agency has full investigative powers, and also many powers short of prosecution—such as the power to issue enforcement notices and/or prohibition notices, the power to suspend or revoke environmental licences and a power to issue fixed penalty notices. 'Where a criminal offence has been committed, in addition to any other enforcement action, the Agency will consider instituting a prosecution, administering a caution or issuing a warning.'[16] The guidance then goes on to list various 'public interest factors' which the Agency regards as relevant to the decision to prosecute.[17] In addition, the 'Guidance for Enforcement and Prosecution Policy'[18] includes detailed guidance on enforcement action in respect of particular activities (e.g. water quality, waste management, flood defence, radioactive substances). It spells out a 'Common Incident Classification Scheme', with three levels of environmental effect for which there would normally be different levels of enforcement action. Breaches in category 3 would normally attract no more than a formal warning, for example. Where prosecution is being considered, usually in a category 1 case and sometimes in a category 2 case, a range of relevant factors is set out for consideration (e.g. impact, intent, previous history, offender's attitude).

Similar policies and practices are to be found in the work of the Health and Safety Executive. One part of its mission statement sets the tone: 'to secure compliance with the law in line with the principles of proportionality, consistency, transparency and targeting on a risk-related basis.' The difference of emphasis from the police and CPS is soon apparent: 'while the primary purpose of the enforcing authorities is to ensure that

---

[13] J. Roording, 'The Punishment of Tax Fraud' [1996] *Crim LR* 240.

[14] Access to these is simple through the Agency's website at www.environment-agency.gov.uk.

[15] Environment Agency (issued 7 August 2008), paras 4 and 6.   [16] *Ibid.*, para 8.

[17] *Ibid.*, para 23. These factors are similar to those stated in the Code for Crown Prosecutors. Paragraph 21 of the document states that 'the Agency recognises that the institution of a prosecution is a serious matter that should only be taken after full consideration of the implications and consequences. Decisions about prosecution will take account of the Code for Crown Prosecutors.'

[18] www.environment-agency.gov.uk, version 20, issued 18 February 2009.

dutyholders manage and control risks effectively, thus preventing harm, prosecution is an essential part of enforcement.'[19] This statement, and those of the Environment Agency (above), show that the regulatory agencies are pervaded by a culture of diversion. Prosecution is regarded very much as a last resort: the priority is to ensure compliance with the appropriate standards of safety. The result is that prosecutions are relatively rare, and this in turn gives rise to criticisms of unevenness and consequent unfairness in the use of the criminal law. Some argue that the infrequency of prosecutions and the predominance of warnings and other remedial measures indicates that regulatory agencies have been 'captured' by big business, or that the structure of regulation is an attempt to persuade the public that enforcement is being taken seriously when it is not. The written policies of the various agencies do show that the approach to prosecution differs markedly from that of the police.

Empirical research into the working practices of regulatory agencies goes some way to explaining why the difference in approach has evolved and is sustained. The leading study by Keith Hawkins argues that Health and Safety inspectors are motivated, in their enforcement decisions, by considerations of morality (bad cases justify prosecution) and by considerations of commensurability (non-serious deviations from the required standards call for lesser responses than prosecution),[20] as well as being affected by staffing levels, workloads and inspectors' perceptions of public reactions. Hawkins also confirms that individual inspectors differ in their approaches, some being more willing to bring a prosecution than others. Robert Baldwin has argued that there has been a significant shift towards readier resort to punitive sanctions in recent years, especially in financial and business regulation.[21] However, this punitive drift does not destroy the contrast between the police and the regulatory agencies: the latter are still predominantly orientated towards ensuring compliance through negotiation, with their inspectors dealing on a long-term basis with businesspeople, and regarding the background threat of prosecution as more effective than its frequent use. Moreover, their staffing resources would not permit them to prosecute suspected offenders to the extent that the police resort to prosecution: bringing a prosecution is a significant drain on an inspector's time.[22]

The Environment Agency and the Health and Safety Commission have been chosen as examples of the many agencies which pursue a preventive or 'compliance' approach to enforcement, as distinct from a 'deterrence' or 'sanctioning' strategy which places greater emphasis on prosecution.[23] Compared with the approach of the police and CPS, their much greater emphasis on diversion rather than prosecution raises acute questions of social justice. Companies, wealthy offenders, and middle-class offenders

---

[19] Health and Safety Executive, *Enforcement Policy Statement* (accessed 28 July 2009), para 37.
[20] K. Hawkins, *Law as Last Resort* (2003), 243 and 220–6.
[21] R. Baldwin, 'The New Punitive Regulation' (2004) 67 *MLR* 351; the main concern of the article is to show how and why the change of policy is not having the desired effect on corporate behaviour.
[22] Hawkins, above n 20, 46, 300, 421–2.
[23] For further discussion, see the works at nn 10–11 above.

are more often dealt with by regulatory agencies, and benefit from the alternatives approaches to dishonesty used (for example) by HM Revenue and Customs,[24] whereas the more disadvantaged dishonest members of society are more likely to find their conduct defined as a police matter, with prosecution for theft or fraud. Yet the offences may be no different in terms of seriousness. This might be defended on the principles of parsimony, of minimum intervention, and of assigning greater priority to the goal of securing maximum compliance than to equality of treatment; if effectiveness is the goal, it is often argued that regulatory approaches are superior to prosecutions in this area.[25] However, the effect is unacceptable in terms of social justice—allowing middle-class or white-collar offenders to benefit from diversion and other alternatives to prosecution, while lower-class or blue-collar offenders are processed in the 'normal' way.

How should this inequality be tackled? To assimilate the treatment of the clients of regulatory agencies to that of the clients of the police would increase overall suffering, and some argue that it is wrong to insist on equality if it results in equality of misery.[26] However, there are surely other ways of tackling this inequality of treatment. Initiatives to decriminalize minor offences or to reduce penalties for them should be devised. More fundamentally, fresh thought needs to be given to the approach of the police and prosecution service to the cases that come to their attention. It is not enough to develop restorative justice responses, because there are prior questions about the effectiveness of warnings (police cautions appear to be relatively effective), about the need for such strong sanctions for non-compliance with conditional and/or preventive orders (the regulatory agencies have a more open approach to repeated non-compliance), and about the treatment of offenders with whom the police interact regularly (as do regulatory inspectors in their work). There are strong objections to any system that allows different investigative and prosecution agencies to pursue such divergent policies in respect of offences of similar levels of seriousness, without any attempt to address the inherent issues of social injustice.

6.2 THE RANGE OF DIVERSIONARY RESPONSES

The criminal law provides the framework for formal responses to alleged lawbreaking, and yet we have also seen that it functions as a resource to be invoked in situations where this is thought necessary so as to enforce compliance or to maintain order or

---

[24] We do not enter into detail about the powers and practices of HMRC; but see J. Newth, *HMRC Investigations and Enquiries* (2008), Ch 14, on HMRC's use of penalties.

[25] Cf M. Levi, *The Investigation, Prosecution and Trail of Serious Fraud* (1993), and D. J.Middleton, 'The Legal and Regulatory Response to Solicitors Involved in Serious Fraud' (2005) 45 *BJ Crim* 810, G. Slapper and S. Tombs, *Corporate Crime* (2000), Ch 8.

[26] The argument of N. Morris and M. Tonry, *Between Prison and Probation* (1990) in respect of equality of treatment in sentencing, criticized by A. Ashworth, *Sentencing and Criminal Justice* (5th ed, 2010), Ch 7.

respect.[27] Discretion appears to be a key element in what actually happens—whether a case is diverted or sent for prosecution; and, if it is diverted, what form of diversion is chosen. The main focus in the following paragraphs is on the police and their approach to suspected offenders, but there will be intermittent reference to the approach of the regulatory agencies.

What is diversion, and why has its use increased in recent years? The concept of diversion means diverting cases away from the criminal courts and dealing with them in other ways. In his recent report, Rod Morgan refers to the phenomenon as 'summary justice' or 'pre-court summary justice';[28] the Government's term, 'out-of-court disposals', will be used here, in conjunction with the criminological term 'diversion'.[29] Formerly diversion had a non-punitive flavour, but this appears no longer to be a necessary feature. The attractions of diversion are that it aims to be simpler, cheaper, less bureaucratic (cutting police paperwork); it is a more proportionate and less stigmatic response to many minor offences; and it appears to be no less effective, in terms of reconvictions, than conviction and sentence. Against this, however, it must be said that many European systems of law maintain a doctrinal contrast between the principle of compulsory prosecution (sometimes called the principle of legality) and the principle of expediency (sometimes called the opportunity principle). The principle of compulsory prosecution is respected because it is said to promote the principles of legality and equal treatment, to prevent political interference with the process of justice, and also to heighten general deterrence.[30] In theory all those who commit offences are brought before the courts for an open determination of guilt and (if convicted) for sentencing, and there is no broad discretionary power to avoid prosecution—on the grounds that this might lead to local variations, allegations of political motivation or discrimination, or the undermining of law by expediency. If the administration of the criminal law produces unjust results, it is for the legislature to amend it and not for prosecutors to make their own policies. Thus s 152 of the German Code of Criminal Procedure requires the public prosecutor to bring a prosecution in respect of all punishable conduct, to the extent that there is sufficient evidence. In practice, of course, there are various exceptions to this, including s 153a, which allows conditional termination of proceedings.[31] There are financial pressures towards the

---

[27] Above, n 7; see also D. Brown and T. Ellis, *Policing Low-Level Disorder* (Home Office Research Study 135, 1994), 42–3.

[28] R. Morgan, *Summary Justice: Fast– but Fair?* (2008); the same term is used by Young (see n 35 below), but it will not be adopted here because, although it evokes the lack of solemnity in the imposition of the sanction, it invites a confusion with two established terms, summary offences and summary jurisdiction.

[29] Office for Criminal Justice Reform, *Out-of-court Disposals for Adults: a Guide to Alternatives to Prosecution* (2007).

[30] See, e.g., J. Herrmann, 'The Rule of Compulsory Prosecution and the Scope of Prosecutorial Discretion in Germany' (1974) 41 *U Chi LR* 468; P. J. P. Tak, *The Legal Scope of Non-Prosecution in Europe* (1986).

[31] Herrmann, above, n 27; J. Herrmann, 'Bargaining Justice: a Bargain for German Criminal Justice?', (1992) 53 *U Pittsburgh LR* 755. For the somewhat similar situation in Italy (principle of compulsory pros-

streamlining of criminal justice systems, as well as an increasing realization that prosecution and sentence in court are stressful for all participants and are not necessarily more effective (in terms of reconviction rates) than forms of diversion. Another well-established system of prosecutorial waiver is that whereby Dutch prosecutors may ask defendants to pay a *transactie* in return for a promise of non-prosecution.[32] Prosecutor fines also operate in Scotland, where procurators fiscal have the powers. The Council of Europe has developed this theme in its recommendations for the simplification of criminal justice.[33]

The number of exceptions to the principle of compulsory prosecution might be thought to support an argument that systems such as the German are really little different from the English. The one proclaims a principle of compulsory prosecution and then derogates from it in several ways, whereas the other recognizes from the outset that prosecution policy must be a question of expediency.[34] However, there is a substantial difference: whereas the German and other systems explicitly recognize the principle of compulsory prosecution because of the values (the principles of legality and equal treatment) it upholds, those fundamental values and principles have little explicit recognition, even as starting points, in the heavily pragmatic English system. Instead, the alternatives to prosecution have developed one by one, often without statutory foundations, and hardly constitute a 'system' of diversion. However, they are used in large numbers, and their form and their justifications need careful scrutiny.

The context for the English system is set by two major changes in the role of the police in the last quarter of a century. On the one hand, the police lost their dominance of decisions to prosecute when the CPS was introduced in 1986, and more recently they lost their dominance of charging decisions when the statutory charging scheme transferred much power to the CPS in 2003. On the other hand, the police were encouraged in the 1980s to increase their use of police cautions to deal with less serious cases, and they have done so, exercising a dispositive discretion in relation to significant numbers of defendants; and there has also been what Richard Young describes as 'a drift towards summary justice' in on-the-street policing,[35] with police officers acquiring and using a range of non-criminal measures and also Penalty Notices for Disorder, which are explicitly punitive. More will be said about these trends and their implications, but first we should show the extent to which diversionary measures are now used by the police:

AQ:

---

ecution, with practical derogations) see S. Maffei, 'Negotiations on Evidence and Negotiations on Sentence: Adversarial Experiments in Italian Criminal Procedure' (2004) 2 *J Int Crim J* 1050.

[32] C. Brants and S. Field, 'Discretion and Accountability in Prosecution' in C. Harding et al, *Criminal Justice in Europe* (1995), esp 134–6.

[33] Council of Europe, *The Simplification of Criminal Justice*, Recommendation R(87)18 (1987).

[34] Cf H. Jung, 'Criminal Justice: a European Perspective' [1993] *Crim LR* 237, at 241.

[35] R. Young, 'Street Policing after PACE: the Drift to Summary Justice' in E. Cape and R. Young (eds), *Regulating Policing: the Police and Criminal Evidence Act 1984, Past, Present and Future* (2008).

Table 6.1 Numbers of detections and detection rate by method, 2006/07 and 2007/08

	Recorded crime					
	2006/07	2007/08	% change	2006/07	2007/08	% point change in rate
	Number of detections			Detection rates[1]		
Charge/summons	693,811	674,592	−3	12.8	13.6	0.8
Cautions	357,306	358,016	0	6.6	7.2	0.6
Offences taken into consideration	121,417	107,213	−12	2.2	2.2	−0.1
Penalty notices for disorder	139,735	129,037	−8	2.6	2.6	0.0
Cannabis warnings	81,311	104,207	28	1.5	2.1	0.6
Total sanction detections	**1,393,580**	**1,373,065**	**−1**	**25.7**	**27.7**	**2.1**
Non-sanction detections[2]	81,840	868	−99	1.5	0.0	−1.5
All detections	**1,475,420**	**1,373,933**	**−7**	**27.2**	**27.8**	**0.6**
Total number of offences[3]	**5,427,559**	**4,950,671**	**−9**			

[1] The number of crimes that are cleared up by method divided by total number of recorded offences.
[2] The rules governing the recording of non-sanction detections changed from 1 April 2007 to substantially reduce the range of offences and circumstances in which a non-sanction detection could be claimed.
[3] Total recorded crime whether cleared up or not.

This table does not include conditional cautions authorized by the CPS, although they are a form of (non-police) diversion. Nor does it refer to the range of diversionary measures available to and used by the various regulatory agencies. We can briefly introduce seven forms of diversion, assuming a case in which there is sufficient evidence that a person has committed an offence.

(A) NO FURTHER ACTION

The police may decide to take no further action. Examples would be cases where the defendant has already been sentenced to custody, or indicates a willingness to have the offence 'taken into consideration' in sentencing for another crime, or the offender is very young, or the offence is non-serious.

(B) INFORMAL WARNING

A second alternative is an informal warning, given by a police officer in circumstances where a formal caution is considered unnecessary or inappropriate. Such a warning might be given by an individual officer on the beat, so that the offender is not even taken to a police station. Motorists have often benefited from informal warnings of this kind. However, the use of informal warnings for other crimes varies between areas, with only between 11 and 18 of the 43 police forces using them regularly,[36] although the overall trend seems to be upwards. Inspectors working for the various regulatory agencies may also use informal warnings in some cases: for example, in the Guidance issued by the Environment Agency, there is recognition that inspectors may occasionally give informal warnings, and there is an intermediate form of warning called a 'site warning' that is noted on the site inspection report but does not result in the sending of a warning letter.[37]

(C) CANNABIS WARNING

When cannabis was re-classified from class B to class C in 2004, the cannabis warning was introduced. It may be used where a person is found in possession of a small amount of cannabis, and it is a spoken warning delivered by a police officer on the street or at a police station.[38] When cannabis was returned to class B in January 2009, the cannabis warning was retained. For persons under 18 the first offence of possessing cannabis for personal use may be followed by a cannabis warning; the second offence should be followed by a Penalty Notice for Disorder; for third or subsequent offences, there is a presumption in favour of prosecution. It is not clear to what extent this policy of escalation will exclude informal warnings: before 2004 the police dealt with many cases in this way,[39] but they now seem to be encouraged to use and record a cannabis warning.

(D) SIMPLE POLICE CAUTIONS, REPRIMANDS AND WARNINGS

A third alternative is the formal police caution, now known as the simple caution to distinguish it from the conditional caution (see (e) below). The police should only offer to caution an offender when there is sufficient evidence to prosecute: this is a caution for an offence, and should be distinguished from informal warnings given by individual officers. The police caution is usually delivered by a senior officer in uniform at a police station. There is no legislative basis for this kind of cautioning, but cautions should be recorded by the police and disclosed to the court in an antecedents statement when relevant.[40] A caution for a sex offence results in the offender being placed on the Sex Offender Register and subjected to the various notification requirements under the Sexual Offences Act 2003. Cautions for young offenders were replaced,

---

[36] Audit Commission, *Misspent Youth: Young People and Crimes* (1996), para 30; R. Evans and R. Ellis, *Police Cautioning in the 1990s* (1997), 3; Warburton et al, below, n 39.

[37] Guidance, above n 19, para 2.4.

[38] Office for Criminal Justice Reform, *Out-of-court Disposals for Adults: a Guide to Alternatives to Prosecution* (2007), 6; see also Morgan, *Summary Justice*, 13.

[39] H. Warburton, T. May and M. Hough, 'Looking the Other Way: the Impact of Reclassifying Cannabis on Police Warnings' (2005) 45 *BJ Crim* 113.

[40] See the discussion in Part 6.3(a) below.

under the Crime and Disorder Act 1998, by a statutory scheme of reprimands and final warnings.[41]

(E) CONDITIONAL CAUTIONS

Sections 22–27 of the Criminal Justice Act 2003 introduce a new form of diversion, the conditional caution. Such a caution may only be given to a person aged 18 or over, against whom the CPS decides that there is sufficient evidence of guilt, and who has admitted guilt. The conditions will usually be related to participation in a rehabilitative programme or the making of reparation. Further details of this new measure are given in Part 4 of this chapter. Like the measures in some of the continental European systems described earlier, the conditional caution may include a financial condition such as paying compensation to the victim or making a payment to a relevant charity. Some agencies, notably HM Revenue and Customs, have long possessed a power to require compounded penalties as an alternative to prosecution.[42] This means that a person may be required to pay, say, twice the under-paid tax under threat of being prosecuted otherwise.

(F) FIXED PENALTY NOTICES

Since the Road Traffic Act 1988 the police have been able to use a fixed penalty notice to deal with various motoring offences, starting with the most minor and now encompassing a wide range of road traffic offences. The scheme has been extended to a number of other offences, such as litter, dog fouling and a range of environmental offences. An fixed penalty notice can be issued by the police, local authority officers or the Environment Agency, and may range from £50 to £500 as stipulated in the relevant statute. The ticketed person may challenge the notice, in which case the matter goes to court, as does any instance of non-payment.[43]

(G) PENALTY NOTICES FOR DISORDER

Since 2003 it has been possible for the police to issue a Penalty Notice for Disorder to anyone aged 16 or over committing what was originally described as 'low-level, anti-social and nuisance offending'. The list of offences carrying an £80 penalty includes drunk and disorderly, theft of property up to £200, and various public order offences; some minor offences carry a £50 penalty. This gives the police considerable on-the-street power, although 'payment involves no admission of guilt'. Further details are given in Part 6.4(d) below.

---

[41] For discussion of their use, see S. Field, 'Early Intervention and the "New" Youth Justice' [2008] *Crim LR* 177.

[42] See Newth, n 24 above.   [43] See Morgan, *Summary Justice*, 13.

In one important respect all the forms of diversion mentioned here, both in this country and in others, are the same. All of them allow the defendant the alternative of contesting guilt in court, by declining to accept the official offer and leaving the authorities to prosecute. This is in accordance with the European Convention on Human Rights, Article 6(1) of which has been interpreted so as to require the possibility of recourse to a court for a person who contests the decision to impose a penalty.[44]

6.3 THE POLICE AND SELECTIVE ENFORCEMENT

Once the police have sufficient evidence against an offender, they may (in conjunction with the CPS) consider prosecution, or may consider one of the other alternatives just set out. This 'prosecute or divert' decision remains a crucial stage in responding to offences and suspected offenders, but the advent of conditional cautions, Fixed Penalty Notices (FPN) and Penalty Notices for Disorder (PND) means that the line is more blurred than previously. Those forms of 'diversion' require something of the offender, and may be seen without difficulty as a form of punishment. The powers of the police on the street have been enhanced significantly by the arrival of the PND and the cannabis warning. Yet even genuine diversion can have its coercive side: the Government's new (2006) strategy for dealing with prostitution includes various measures aimed at the 'welfare' of prostitutes, focused on the reduction of exploitation of sex workers but imposing a coercive framework that may prove to be no less controlling than the straightforward use of the criminal sanction.[45] In particular—and this is a general point, not confined to the policing of sex workers—there is now a considerable array of civil preventive orders for which the police can apply, including the anti-social behaviour order and several others, and there are the less formal Acceptable Behaviour Contracts. As we shall see in Chapter 13 below, all of these are coercive and controlling in themselves, and they have the criminal sanction as enforcement. The terms of each form of diversion from the criminal courts must therefore be scrutinized with care. The great push towards wider use of cautioning came in the 1980s: the Home Office made several attempts, in circulars in 1983, 1985 and 1990, to persuade the police to increase diversion and to reduce the proportionate use of prosecutions. These had considerable success, and not just in respect of juveniles. For adult males the cautioning rate rose from 5 per cent in 1984 to 18 per cent in 1991, and for adult females from 14 to 40 per cent.[46] The circular of 1990 went so far as to state 'that the courts should

[44] *Le Compte, Van Leuven and De Meyere* (1981), A.43, para 23; *De Weer* (1980) A.35, para 23.

[45] See the analysis by J. Scoular and M. O'Neill, 'Regulating Prostitution: Social Inclusion, Responsibilization and the Politics of Prostitution Reform' (2007) 47 *BJ Crim* 764.

[46] *Criminal Statistics, England and Wales* (1986 and 1991), Table 5.5.

only be used as a last resort, particularly for juveniles and young adults'.[47] However, there was a hardening of policy in the mid-1990s, and a Home Office circular of 1994—promoted by the then Home Secretary, Michael Howard, with the phrase 'your first chance is your last chance'—aimed to bring about significant reductions in repeat cautioning and in cautioning for indictable-only offences. The result was a significant downturn in the use of cautions for indictable offences, from almost 250,000 in 1993 to 192,000 in 1998, reaching a low point of 143,000 in 2002. Since then the use of cautions has increased for indictable offences to 205,000 in 2007, and the use of cautions for summary offences has increased steadily from 96,000 in 1998 to 158,000 in 2007.[48]

(A) THE FORMAL PRINCIPLES FOR POLICE CAUTIONING

The principles on which the police should take their gatekeeping decisions are set out in Home Office Circular 16/2008, entitled 'Simple Cautioning of Adult Offenders'. This document has no legal standing; indeed, police cautioning remains almost entirely a set of extra-legal practices. However, the aim of the circular is to structure the discretion of the police. It states that 'a simple caution should be used for low-level offending', and suggests that officers should refer to the Gravity Factors Matrix developed by the Association of Chief Police Officers in order to check the gravity of the offence in question: that matrix grades offence types from 1 (least serious) to 4 (most serious).[49] The guidance emphasizes the need for 'a clear and reliable admission of the offence', which should be recorded;[50] it should be 'in the public interest' to use a simple caution; and it should be 'appropriate to the offender', taking account of aggravating or mitigating factors, but inclining against a caution for an offender who has received a previous caution, conditional caution or conviction, unless a period of time has elapsed.[51] The views of the victim (if any) should be sought, but should not be determinative; but the guidance still states that 'whether the offender has made any form of reparation or has paid compensation' is a relevant factor.[52] The offender should be allowed access to legal advice, and should be made aware of the consequences of a caution—notably, that it will be recorded and cited in court, and that it may trigger notification requirements if it is given for a sexual offence. A caution may only be given for an indictable-only offence if it is referred to the CPS. Otherwise, if it has been reviewed by a police officer of the rank of sergeant or above, the caution should be administered at a police station by a police officer.

---

[47] Home Office Circular 59/1990, para 7.

[48] *Criminal Statistics England and Wales 2007*, Table 3.2.

[49] Originally published in 1995; excerpts from the Metropolitan Police guidance are to be found in the judgement of Schiemann LJ in *R v Metropolitan Police Commissioner, ex p Thompson* [1997] 1 WLR 1519.

[50] HOC 16/2008, *Simple Cautioning of Adult Offenders*, paras 9 and 19.

[51] *Ibid.*, paras 15 and 23.   [52] *Ibid.*, para 20.

(B) FOR AND AGAINST CAUTIONING

It seems clear that, despite the downturn in the late 1990s and the advent of conditional cautions, the simple caution is here to stay as a form of dispositive diversion. What are the advantages claimed for cautioning, rather than prosecuting? The Home Office states that the simple caution aims to:

(a) deal quickly and simply with less serious offenders where the offender has admitted the offence;

(b) divert offenders where appropriate from appearing in the criminal courts;

(c) record an individual's criminal conduct for possible reference in future criminal proceedings or relevant security checks; and

(d) reduce the likelihood of re-offending.[53]

The first purpose refers to proportionality, implying that quicker and simpler responses are more appropriate for less serious offences, although the words 'and more cheaply' are implicit. The 2008 version brings the offender's admission of guilt into the primary justification for the caution, which is an important step. The second aim seems to subscribe to the principle of minimum intervention, and perhaps to the idea that court appearances have a labelling effect that may confirm offenders in their deviance.[54] The third aim is to support the recording system, so that where an offender has made an admission of offending this is recorded and available when security checks are done or subsequent proceedings brought. The fourth aim makes a bold claim about effectiveness. Statistics show that some 85 per cent of those cautioned in 1985 and 1988 were not convicted of a serious offence within two years of their caution.[55] This reconviction rate of 15 per cent is much lower than that for offenders convicted at court, at least for first offenders, which is 29 per cent for those without any previous convictions.[56] It could be commented that any such comparison is flawed because the court group is likely to have a higher proportion of people with previous cautions, who are more likely to be reconvicted anyway. A small matched study of juveniles by Mott suggests that those cautioned are still less likely to reoffend than those sentenced in court.[57] However, those who adopt the principle of minimum intervention do not need to establish that cautions are more effective, in terms of reconvictions. It is sufficient to argue that they have not been shown to be less effective than conviction and sentence.

What are the disadvantages of cautioning? Four possible disadvantages merit brief discussion—the danger of net-widening, pressure on defendants to admit to offences, unfairness to victims and failure to discourage repeat offenders.

---

[53] *Ibid.*, para 8.

[54] Properly speaking, diversion from the criminal courts cannot be an aim of cautioning. It is simply its effect. An 'aim' would be a reason why offenders should be diverted in this way.

[55] Home Office Statistical Bulletin 8/94, *The Criminal Histories of those Cautioned in 1985, 1988 and 1991*.

[56] G. Philpotts and L. Lancucki, *Previous Convictions, Sentence and Reconviction* (1979), 16.

[57] J. Mott, 'Police Decisions for Dealing with Juvenile Offenders' (1983) 23 *BJ Crim* 249.

Table 6.2 Offenders cautioned as a percentage of offenders found guilty or cautioned by type of offence, sex and age group, 1992–2007

England and Wales

Percentages

Year	All offenders All ages	Males						Females				
		Aged 10–11	Aged 12–14	Aged 15–17	Aged 18–20	Aged 21 and over	All ages	Aged 10–11	Aged 12–14	Aged 15–17	Aged 18–20	Aged 21 and over
Indictable offences												
1992	41	96	86	59	29	23	61	99	96	81	50	46
1993	41	96	83	59	32	26	60	99	95	80	52	46
1994	41	95	81	56	34	25	59	100	94	77	50	44
1995	41	94	79	54	35	26	59	99	93	76	51	44
1996	40	94	77	51	35	26	56	99	91	72	50	44
1997	38	93	74	49	35	26	52	98	89	68	48	42
1998	37	91	72	48	34	24	51	97	88	67	46	39
1999	34	87	69	45	31	22	48	96	87	64	43	36
2000	32	86	68	43	29	20	47	95	86	63	41	34
2001	31	86	66	42	28	19	46	95	85	64	41	32
2002	30	83	63	41	29	19	44	94	84	62	41	32
2003	32	85	66	44	31	20	45	92	83	65	44	33
2004	34	85	67	45	30	21	49	93	86	68	48	36
2005	38	87	69	47	34	26	54	95	87	72	52	41
2006	41	89	70	49	38	29	56	96	88	71	56	44
2007	40	87	68	46	37	30	56	96	87	70	57	43

Summary offences

Year													
1992	18	22	96	84	57	26	16	9	99	91	68	25	6
1993	18	22	97	85	63	30	16	10	95	89	74	28	7
1994	18	21	97	82	60	29	15	9	99	86	67	27	6
1995	18	20	94	78	56	28	13	11	95	80	65	25	7
1996	16	19	95	79	55	29	12	10	97	82	60	23	6
1997	18	19	94	77	50	28	12	14	94	78	52	28	10
1998	17	18	92	73	47	26	11	15	98	79	53	28	10
1999	18	18	88	70	46	26	11	17	92	75	56	32	11
2000	15	16	86	67	44	24	9	12	92	75	56	26	7
2001	16	17	88	67	44	23	10	13	86	75	55	25	8
2002	14	15	85	63	41	22	9	13	92	72	54	25	8
2003	16	16	86	65	44	24	10	14	82	72	56	25	8
2004	16	16	86	66	45	24	10	15	82	73	57	26	8
2005	19	19	88	68	47	25	12	16	95	75	59	27	10
2006	23	24	90	72	50	28	17	19	95	77	60	30	12
2007	24	26	90	70	48	29	19	20	94	75	58	32	13

(i) Net-widening

Net-widening is the process of using a new measure, not (or not only) to encompass the target group of offenders who would otherwise have been prosecuted, but also to drag into the net people who might otherwise have benefited from a lesser response. This danger was pointed out to the police in the 1985 circular, and there is little evidence that the considerable increases in cautioning during the 1980s were achieved through any significant net-widening.[58] Whilst there may have been some cases of this kind, the figures suggest a genuine transfer of offenders away from prosecution towards cautioning.

(ii) Pressure on defendants

Where a caution is offered this may put pressure on a suspect to admit to an offence when it is not clear that he or she committed it. If the suspect denies knowledge of a certain fact, he or she might wish to decline a caution and have the point adjudicated in court; and yet the disincentives to taking that course are so great (delay, risk of not being believed, risk of conviction) that acceptance of the caution is likely. Despite the prominence now given in the Home Office Circular to the need to obtain a 'clear and reliable admission', it remains possible that the alternative prospect of prosecution may be used to obtain an 'admission' that is not genuine.[59] It would take a strong person to refuse a caution and implicitly to challenge the police to prosecute, but such cases do occasionally happen and refusals to accept a caution may be vindicated.[60] In effect, whenever a person knows or believes that there will be a choice between accepting a caution and risking a prosecution, there is bound to be pressure to accept the caution. The disadvantages of this must be minimized by ensuring that legal advice is always available,[61] and that there is adequate supervision from senior police officers. The issue of safeguards is particularly important now that cautions are cited in court and relied upon for other purposes.

(iii) Unfairness to victims

Unfairness to victims has probably been one unfortunate consequence of cautioning. The number of offenders ordered to pay compensation by criminal courts increased by one-half between 2002 and 2007, mostly for summary offences,[62] but for those who are cautioned there is no prospect of a binding order for compensation. It may still be true that the relatively high level of police cautioning operates to deprive some victims of compensation from their offenders. However, as we will see below, the scheme

---

[58] M. McMahon, 'Net-Widening: Vagaries in the Use of a Concept' (1990) 30 *BJ Crim* 121.

[59] *R v Metropolitan Police Commissioner, ex p Thompson* [1997] 1 WLR 1519.

[60] In one case a doctor who used force to defend himself refused to accept a caution for assault, was prosecuted, and was acquitted: *The Times* 17 June 1998.

[61] See *DPP v McAra* [2002] 1 Cr App R 159, discussed in Part 6.7 below.

[62] *Sentencing Statistics 2007*, Table 4.9.

of conditional cautions embodies an attempt to address this problem by making the payment of reparation an enforceable condition.

(iv) Repeat cautioning

A fourth argument, increasingly heard in recent years, is that cautioning (in particular, repeat cautioning) sends the wrong message to some offenders. The idea that a caution standing alone was insufficient was a major force behind the system of reprimands and warnings for young offenders under the Crime and Disorder Act 1998. The system allows no more than one reprimand, and no more than one final warning (which will 'usually be followed by a community intervention programme, involving the offender and his or her family to address the causes of the offending and so reduce the risk of further crime'), and then prescribes prosecution. This three-step approach applies even where the next offence may not otherwise be serious enough to warrant prosecution. Some will regard this as a significant increase in legality, in reducing the discretionary elements of the system and bringing the response to young offenders more into the open forum of the courts. Others will insist that discretion remains abundant, notably in giving informal warnings which do not invoke the statutory system, and may regard the stepwise approach as an unfortunate move away from a proportionality principle in youth justice. Indeed, Stewart Field's research led him to conclude that 'pre-charge decision-making in youth justice remains a highly discretionary process rooted in personal judgement', despite the more elaborate statutory framework introduced by the 1998 Act.[63] The same may well be true of the impact of the Home Office Circulars on simple cautions.

(C) LOCAL VARIATIONS

One manifestation of the predominance of discretion is the apparent gap between national standards and local practices, leading to so-called 'justice by geography'. Despite the guidance set out in the three Home Office circulars of 1985, 1990 and 1994, Evans and Ellis concluded, on the basis of research in late 1995, that 'the circulars have not been successful in achieving greater consistency between forces'.[64] On the face of it, there are still significant differences in cautioning rates among police areas. Thus the 2007 figures show a national average cautioning rate of 30 per cent for adult males, and variations from 49 per cent in Northamptonshire, 47 per cent in Warwickshire, and 42 per cent in Essex and in Hertfordshire, 35 per cent in the Metropolitan Police area, and then down to 15 per cent in North Yorkshire, 16 per cent in Greater Manchester, 17 per cent in Merseyside. For adult women the national average cautioning rate is 43 per cent, but police forces vary from 65 per cent in Northamptonshire and 59 per cent in Staffordshire down to 19 per cent in Merseyside and 27 per cent in North Yorkshire.[65]

---

[63] S. Field, 'Early Intervention and the New Youth Justice' [2008] *Crim LR* 177, at 189.
[64] Evans and Ellis, *Police Cautioning in the 1990s* (1996), 2.
[65] *Criminal Statistics England and Wales 2007*, Table 3.5.

Although these variations may in part reflect different offence mixes and different proportions of first offenders, it is unlikely that those factors will provide a complete explanation. Clearly the differing policies adopted by different police forces still play a role.[66]

When criticisms of variations in criminal justice are voiced, the reply is often that police forces are responding to local conditions and particular problems. It is certainly true that many worthwhile initiatives in criminal justice have come about through local attempts to address local problems; but there is also the probability that some local variations stem from a stubborn and insular unwillingness to absorb new national policies and to change working practices. Discretion thus opens the way to various practices, overt or covert. Two studies of the police in the 1990s strongly suggest that on some occasions the Home Office instructions on cautioning are used to legitimate or rationalize decisions already made on other grounds.[67] Thus the probability is that some decisions result from a simple following of the guidelines, whereas others are motivated more by assessment of the 'moral character' of the offender or victim or by concerns related to the police mission.[68]

(D) PENALTY NOTICES FOR DISORDER

The Criminal Justice and Police Act 2001 introduced a new dispositive power for the police—issuing a PND. The police themselves were the prime movers in this innovation, lobbying for a measure that would enhance on-the-street control and yet cut paperwork and police time too.[69] The PND was piloted from 2002 and rolled out nationally in 2004. A PND can be issued by a police officer or community support officer for one of a list of possible offences: at the higher tier of £80 are the more serious offences, including wasting police time, being drunk and disorderly, shop theft under £200, criminal damage less than £500 and using threatening or abusive words contrary to s 5 of the Public Order Act; at the lower tier of £50 are the less serious offences, including railway trespass and consuming alcohol in a prohibited zone. A PND may be issued to a person aged 16 or over, but the fines for those under 18 are £40 and £30 respectively. The penalty should be paid within 21 days, or alternatively the person may request to have the case brought to court. If the person does neither, the penalty is increased by 50 per cent and registered at court as an unpaid fine, to be enforced accordingly. The statistics show that some 52 per cent are paid in full, 43 per cent registered as a fine and court hearings are requested in just 1 per cent of cases.[70]

---

[66] R. Evans and C. Wilkinson, 'Variations in Police Cautioning' (1990) 29 *Howard JCJ* 155.

[67] See M. McConville, A. Sanders and R. Leng, *The Case for the Prosecution* (1991), 122 and Ch 6 generally; and R. Evans, 'Evaluating Young Adult Diversion Schemes'[1993] *Crim LR* 490.

[68] See above, Ch 3.

[69] Young, 'Street Policing after PACE', 178.

[70] *Criminal Statistics England and Wales 2007*, Table 7.2.

The stated aims of the PND scheme are fourfold:[71]

(i)   offer operational officers a new, effective alternative means of dealing with low-level, anti-social and nuisance offending;

(ii)   deliver swift, simple and effective justice that carries a deterrent effect;

(iii) reduce the amount of time that police officers spend completing paperwork and attending court, while simultaneously reducing the burden on the courts;

(iv)   increase the amount of time officers spend on the street and dealing with more serious crime and to free the courts to deal with more serious offending.

The last two aims seem to amount to the same thing. We must now ask whether these aims should be supported, and whether they are being achieved.

There are several possible problems with PNDs as introduced and operated. First, it is plain that they are mislabelled. Theft from a shop and criminal damage are not necessarily forms of disorder. The truth is that they have been brought into the scheme in order to solve practical problems for the police, largely that of dealing with shop thefts. The first aim has accordingly been worded so as not to focus on disorder (as does the title PND), and to include 'nuisance offending'. Secondly, the implications of the PND seem to run too far. The officer who issues the PND must be satisfied that there is sufficient evidence to prosecute for the crime, but in an on-the-street encounter there may be questions about this.[72] No admission from the ticketed person is required, but the PND discharges all liability to be prosecuted for that offence and it does not rank as a conviction. However, it may be recorded on the Police National Computer, may be cited in court as evidence of bad character, and is evidence in civil proceedings such as ASBO applications.[73] It may be true that a ticketed person who wishes to dispute the evidence can request to be brought to court, but since a PND is not a conviction and requires no admission of guilt, there is an incentive to 'cut one's losses' and 'get it all over with'. It is therefore questionable to rely on it as evidence of guilt. However, the features of the PND (not an admission, no criminal record, no prosecution for that offence) have been held not to prevent a prosecution for a more serious offence arising out of the same facts, if the grounds for doing so subsequently come to light. Thus in *Gore and Maher* (2009)[74] the defendants had punched and kicked a man in a drunken fight; the victim said he was all right, the two men were arrested and were given PNDs, one for drunk and disorderly and the other for causing harassment, alarm or distress. It later emerged that the victim's arm was broken, and a CCTV recording showed the force of the blows delivered, so the two defendants were prosecuted for inflicting

[71] See 'Penalty Notices for Disorder' at www.police.homeoffice.gov.uk/operational-policing/crime-disorder/index.html; and generally Office for Criminal Justice Reform, *Out-of-Court Disposals for Adults*, 12–13.

[72] C. Kraina and L. Carroll, *Penalty Notices for Disorder: Review of Practice across Police Forces* (2006), 11.

[73] Office for Criminal Justice Reform, *Out-of-Court Disposals for Adults*, 13.

[74] [2009] EWCA Crim 1424.

grievous bodily harm. The Court of Appeal held that the prosecutions were not an abuse of process, because payment of a PND merely prevents prosecution for the offence for which the PND was given; there was no implied undertaking not to prosecute for a more serious offence, if appropriate facts came to light.

Thirdly, the emphasis on reducing the workload of the lower courts raises questions about the proper function of those courts. The choice here is between police law, where the police are themselves judge and jury in relation to PNDs, and resort to an independent and impartial tribunal. It is not a clinching argument to say that the ticketed person always has the option of going to court, because there may be other pressures, particularly the fear of a heavier sentence. Nor is it sufficient to argue that the PND is not a conviction, because we have shown how ambiguous its status and implications are. The simplification of criminal justice comes at a price: in most other countries it is the quasi-judicial figure of the public prosecutor who decides on diversionary financial penalties, and it is questionable whether such power should be given to the police on the street (with little supervision, as the research shows).[75]

The extent to which the police have embraced the PND—a power that they requested—is evident from the statistics. Some 64,000 were issued in the first year (2004), and the total reached some 200,000 in both 2006 and 2007. The most frequent offence was causing harassment, alarm or distress contrary to s 5 of the Public Order Act (about 40 per cent), followed by drunk and disorderly (22 per cent) and theft from a shop (21 per cent). All but 3 per cent of PNDs were issued for higher tier offences.[76] These figures suggests that the emphasis is on on-the-street policing, but we do not know whether PNDs are being issued appropriately or inappropriately, or whether there is any racial or other over-representation. In relation to shop theft (and criminal damage), the victim's perspective appears not to have been assessed. The Home Office instructions require the consent of the victim or retailer to the issue of a PND for shop theft over £100 and criminal damage over £300,[77] but further research on this is required.

6.4 THE ROLE OF PROSECUTORS

Some of the objections to simple cautions and to PNDs—their largely discretionary nature; the conferral of considerable disciplinary power on the police; the absence of a legal basis for cautions; the disadvantage to some victims—may appear to have been remedied by the introduction of conditional cautions under the Criminal Justice Act 2003. Much depends, however, on how the new arrangements are operated. Simple cautions, PNDs, cannabis warnings and other diversionary measures will remain available, and so there are important practical choices to be made. The Revised Code

[75] Kraina and Carroll, *Penalty Notices for Disorder*, 12.
[76] *Criminal Statistics England and Wales 2007*, Table 7.3.
[77] Office for Criminal Justice Reform, *Out-of-Court Disposals for Adults*, 12.

of Practice for Conditional Cautions states that the objective of conditional cautions is to provide 'an opportunity to achieve an early positive response to low-level offending behaviour for those persons willing to admit their offending and to comply with certain conditions'.[78]

One major difference is that the CPS determines whether a conditional caution is appropriate.[79] Although conditional cautions (like simple cautions) are administered by a police officer, and although the police may pass a case to the CPS with a recommendation for a conditional caution, it is for a prosecutor to decide that there is sufficient evidence to charge the offender with an offence, and that a conditional caution should be given in the case. Section 23 of the Criminal Justice Act 2003 sets out five requirements that must be met before a conditional caution (for a person aged 18 or over) can be given. In summary they are:

(a) that a constable or other 'authorised person' must have evidence that the offender has committed the offence;

(b) that the prosecutor should decide that there is sufficient evidence to charge, and that a conditional caution should be given;

(c) that the offender admits the offence;

(d) that the effect of the conditional caution is explained to the offender, together with the consequence of breach; and

(e) that the offender signs a document containing the details of the offence, his admission, his consent to the conditional caution, and the conditions attached.

These statutory requirements are welcome. The Revised Code of Practice reinforces them by, for example, stating that it should be made clear 'that the offender has the opportunity to receive free and independent legal advice', 'that an admission should never be made merely to receive a conditional caution', and that 'the offender may decide at any stage to withdraw from the conditional caution'.[80] These are among the steps necessary to bring rule-of-law protections into this key area of dispositive decision-making, where a decision to divert (and a person's acceptance of that diversion) may have significant consequences. What conditions may be set? A person's decision to accept a conditional caution may well depend on the nature and onerousness of the conditions. Section 22(3) stated originally that the condition(s) must have as their objective either the rehabilitation of the offender or the making of reparation for the offence or both, but the section has been amended to introduce a third objective, the punishment of the offender. This has been followed by the introduction, as a pilot

---

[78] *Revised Code of Practice for Conditional Cautions—Adults*, laid before Parliament on 8 July 2009, para 2.1.

[79] Applying CPS, *The Director's Guidance on Conditional Cautioning* (5th ed, 2007).

[80] *Revised Code of Practice for Conditional Cautions*, para 11.3.

in three CPS areas from 2009, of the power to add a fine to a conditional caution. The Revised Code of Practice makes it clear that the aims of rehabilitation and repa- ration should be given priority, and that 'punitive conditions should only be used where there are no appropriate reparative or rehabilitative conditions (or where those conditions do not provide a proportionate response to the offending behaviour).'[81] Reparation may involve doing actual repairs or paying compensation to the victim. Rehabilitation may involve taking courses on behaviour modification, participation in a form of restorative justice, etc. Much will depend on the local availability of rel- evant schemes. If the condition is financial (i.e. payment of compensation or, where available, a fine), the prosecutor should take account of the means of the offender and the circumstances of the case in determining the amount to be paid.[82] What are the consequences of non-compliance? Section 24 provides that failure without reasonable cause to comply with any of the conditions may result in the institution of criminal proceedings for the original offence. The caution is therefore confirmed as a form of conditional non-prosecution. There remains an element of prosecutorial discretion, and there may be circumstances (perhaps where the breach is relatively minor) in which it is decided not to revoke the conditional caution. If a prosecution is brought, however, this terminates the conditional caution. Section 24(2) also provides that the document signed by the offender when accepting the conditional caution is admis- sible in the proceedings. A conditional caution will be recorded and can be cited in subsequent proceedings, thus emphasizing the significance of the choice made by the defendant and the need to ensure that this is not the product of pressure.

6.5 ACCOUNTABILITY

It is apparent from the discussion of the gatekeeping practices of the police, the regu- latory agencies and the CPS that discretion is the dominant characteristic. Codes of Practice have been created, but these are so generally phrased and so lightly enforced that their impact is muted—they can readily be used so as to justify decisions taken on other grounds. To what extent, if at all, are these decision makers accountable? The question has to be answered on two different levels: accountability for general policy, and accountability for individual decisions.

The CPS has a primary role in the scheme of conditional cautions, and the next chapter examines the framework of its accountability (including the Inspectorate). The main decision makers on cautioning have always been the police, and there have been significant changes to their accountability. The traditional concept of constabu- lary independence, in which local Chief Constables have been answerable to the law and also subject to HM Inspectorate of Constabulary, was considerably watered down by the provisions in Part 1 of the Police Reform Act 2002. That Act gave statutory

---

[81] *Ibid.*, para 7.2.   [82] *Ibid.*, para 8.2.

authority for far greater central direction in policing, although there remains considerable discretion in the hands of Chief Constables.[83] However, in respect of decisions on diversion from prosecution, the framework remains rather weak. No doubt the terms of the Home Office circular on cautioning are used as a basis for inspections by Her Majesty's Inspector of Constabulary. No doubt, also, there are possible financial implications for refusal to comply. However, as far as the law is concerned, the Chief Constable of each area is solely responsible for decisions on law enforcement in that area. Since the Court of Appeal has held that 'No Minister of the Crown can tell him that he must or must not prosecute this man or that one',[84] the Home Office Circular cannot be binding in law.

Although the Crime and Disorder Act 1998 introduced a statutory scheme of reprimands and warnings for young offenders, and the Criminal Justice Act 2003 introduced conditional cautions, there is still no legislative regulation of simple police cautions.[85] A legislative framework would be important in terms of human rights and rule-of-law values, but it is not clear whether it would have much effect in curbing local variations.

Accountability for individual decisions depends largely on the internal structure of the agency. Within the police, there may be local police traditions or cultures that lead to variations in interpretation, even if there is a clear force policy. It is a well-known characteristic of the police that the amount of supervision of constables is not great, and that they have much *de facto* discretion.[86] Historically this has not been true of cautioning decisions, and cases for caution must still be referred to sergeant level for approval. But the interaction between the arresting officer and the station sergeant remains influential in determining what happens subsequently. And the effect of force policy on those interactions is likely to be variable. The extent of a police force's commitment to cautioning will determine whether or not it can overpower certain aspects of the occupational culture.

To what extent can police decisions at this stage of the process be challenged in the courts? The answer differs according to whether the decision is to prosecute or not to prosecute. If a person is charged, despite falling within one of the categories for cautioning outlined in the Home Office Circular, it seems that judicial review may be possible but that this would be judicial review of the CPS if they decide to continue the prosecution rather than discontinuing it. This, the Divisional Court held,[87] was because the police are merely the initiators of proceedings, and the 'last and decisive word' on the issue lies with the CPS.[88] The CPS would take this decision within the

---

[83] D. Ormerod and A. Roberts, 'The Police Reform Act 2002' [2003] *Crim LR* 141.

[84] *R v Metropolitan Police Commissioner, ex p Blackburn* [1968] 2 QB 118, *per* Lord Denning MR.

[85] This was recommended by the Royal Commission on Criminal Justice, *Report* (1993), para 5.57.

[86] M. Maguire and C. Norris, *The Conduct and Supervision of Police Investigations* (1992); B. Irving and C. Dunnighan, *Human Factors in the Quality Control of CID Investigations* (1993).

[87] *R v Chief Constable of Kent, ex p L* (1991) 93 Cr App R 416, *per* Watkins LJ at 426.

[88] As mentioned above, the Criminal Justice Act 2003 transfers the power to charge from the police to the CPS in most non-minor cases.

framework of the Code for Crown Prosecutors (to be discussed in Chapter 7 below), which is similar in terms to the Home Office Circular. However, the leading case of L[89] was expressly limited to decisions to prosecute juveniles and, although there is some authority in favour of extending the principle to decisions to prosecute adults,[90] the House of Lords has decided that judicial review of decisions to prosecute should be confined to cases of dishonesty, bad faith or some other exceptional circumstance.[91] It remains possible to allege that a particular prosecution amounts to an abuse of process, and to apply for it to be stayed on that ground.[92]

What of the reverse situation, where the police decide not to prosecute a suspected offender but to administer a caution? It is established that in these circumstances an application for judicial review may succeed if it can be shown that the appropriate principles were not followed, whether the case concerns a juvenile or an adult.[93] Thus in the case of P,[94] judicial review of a juvenile caution was granted when the police had failed to explain the role of appropriate adult to the child's mother and had failed to explain the consequences of an admission. In the case of C,[95] judicial review of a decision not to prosecute an adult was granted to the alleged victim when it was shown that the CPS had failed to have regard to a material consideration.

The caution itself may be challenged if the procedure leading up to the decision was unfair. Thus in *R v Metropolitan Police Commissioner, ex parte Thompson*[96] the Divisional Court granted an order of *certiorari* quashing a caution. Counsel for the defendant argued that, where the police appear to be offering a caution if the defendant were to admit the offence, this is an unfair inducement which, on an analogy with the exclusion of confessions, should nullify the acceptance of the caution. The Divisional Court agreed with this proposition. The ruling is significant in two ways: first, it emphasizes the need to ensure that cautions are only offered and accepted in appropriate cases; and secondly, it is important when cautions are recorded and may be relied upon subsequently. The ruling also shows why it is desirable to have access to legal advice before accepting a caution, a point reinforced by the decision in *DPP v Ara*.[97] In this case the police decided that a defendant was suitable for a caution as a result of what he had said during an interview. The defendant took legal advice subsequently, but his solicitor was not allowed by the police to have access to the tape

[89] *R v Chief Constable of Kent, ex p L* (1991) 93 Cr App R 416.

[90] *R v Inland Revenue Commissioner, ex p Mead* [1993] 1 All ER 772, *per* Stuart-Smith LJ at 780. In principle, the availability of diversion for adults following the introduction of conditional cautions constitutes a strong reason for permitting judicial review of decisions to prosecute instead.

[91] *R v Director of Public Prosecutions, ex p Kebilene* [2000] 2 AC 326; see also *R (Mondelly) v Metropolitan Police Commissioner* [2006] EWHC 2390 (Admin).

[92] For discussion of the doctrine of abuse of process, see Ch 12 below.

[93] *R v General Council of the Bar, ex p Percival* [1990] 3 All ER 137, discussed by C. Hilson, 'Discretion to Prosecute and Judicial Review' [1993] *Crim LR* 639.

[94] *R v Metropolitan Police Commissioner, ex p P* (1995) 160 JP 367, discussed by R. Evans, 'Challenging a Police Caution using Judicial Review' [1996] *Crim LR* 104.

[95] *R v Director of Public Prosecutions, ex p C* [1995] 1 Cr App R 136.   [96] [1997] 1 WLR 1519.

[97] [2002] 1 Cr App R 159.

recording of the interview. The Divisional Court upheld the decision of the justices to stay the prosecution on grounds of abuse of process, on the basis that a person should have access to legal advice before deciding whether to accept a caution, and the refusal to disclose the interview tape rendered informed legal advice impossible. Both the Code of Practice for Conditional Cautions and the Home Office Circular on simple cautions incorporate the implications of these two decisions.

To what extent are the various regulatory agencies accountable for their very different enforcement policies? We have noted that the annual report is practically the only means of being called to account for policy. There is no inspectorate for the regulatory agencies, no steering committee for the policies of the regulatory sector, and certainly no body charged with reviewing the relationship between regulatory policies and the approach of the police to law enforcement. As for accountability for individual decisions, research suggests that there are variations in the local culture of different parts of a single agency—one familiar finding is a divergence of approach between rural areas and urban areas.[98] In his study of Health and Safety inspectors Hawkins emphasizes 'the centrality of organizations', their norms, their goals and their culture, in determining the approach taken by individual inspectors.[99] Individual inspectors may vary in their preparedness to bring a prosecution on given facts, but part of the explanation for their behaviour may be organizational pressures. Moreover, an individual decision not to prosecute is unlikely to be reviewed, within most agencies, unless it is a case of particular sensitivity to which the attention of senior officials has been drawn. Judicial review of a decision not to prosecute would be available in theory, since most of these agencies have the 'last and decisive word' within their own sphere of operation, but there are few examples of challenges being brought in this way.

The prospects for some consistency in the regulatory sphere have been improved by the enactment of the Regulatory Enforcement and Sanctions Act 2008. This establishes Local Better Regulation Offices, charged particularly with coordinating the enforcement activities of local authorities. More significantly, the Act introduces a range of 'civil sanctions' for use by a wide range of bodies, including the Environment Agency, Financial Services Authority and Food Standards Authority, as well as local authorities. More will be said about the implications of this Act below.

6.6 VALUES AND PRINCIPLES

In this chapter we have described a significant trend towards diversion and away from prosecution-conviction-sentence, but the developing forms of diversion (notably conditional cautions and PNDs) incorporate penalties and must be characterized as forms of non-judicial punishment. This makes it all the more important to ask questions

---

[98] See, e.g., B. Hutter, *The Reasonable Arm of the Law* (1988).   [99] Hawkins, above n 19, 330.

about values. Is equality of treatment ensured? Are the interests of victims properly respected? Are the rights of defendants respected? Do these developments represent an extension or a sacrifice of crime control?

(A) EQUALITY OF TREATMENT

In the previous section we saw that the due execution of stated policies is not buttressed by an effective framework of legal accountability. There is no legislation on simple cautions, and the legal frameworks for reprimands and warnings for young offenders under the Crime and Disorder Act 1998, for conditional cautions under the Criminal Justice Act 2003, and for PNDs under the Criminal Justice and Police Act 2001 are largely permissive and leave a large swath of discretion that is only slightly narrowed by the various codes of practice.

The predominance of discretion might be regarded as a contradiction of the principle of equality before the law and equal treatment. In many European countries, the considerable weight given to the principle of compulsory prosecution shows awareness of the values at stake. It is true that most countries do not regard this as an absolute principle, and in recent years have sought to allow scope to the principle of expediency whereby certain cases are diverted from the courts, usually by prosecutors. But these can be regarded as circumscribed exceptions to the principle that criminal justice should be dispensed in open court, after a full consideration of the issues, with reasons given.[100] The major difference in this country is that the issues are not even discussed in terms of the principles at stake. These decisions may profoundly affect the course of a suspect/ offender's life: not only may prosecution itself be highly significant for the defendant in terms of anxiety and stress, damage to reputation, and possible loss of employment, but the choice of method of diversion may have significant implications for the offender. If discretion is to be bestowed on certain authorities, it should be carefully structured so as to achieve desired policies and properly controlled through channels of accountability. Do cautioning practices and diversion accord appropriately favourable treatment to vulnerable groups such as the mentally disturbed? The diversion of mentally disordered offenders is a well-established practice, although it has been argued that the ready referral of mentally disturbed suspects to the mental health services and hospitals may sometimes be a disproportionately severe response, or may deprive them of rights they would have if prosecuted, or both.[101] There is evidence that in some cases the incidence of mental disorder is not recognized by the police, or indeed by the police surgeon, and that therefore appropriate safeguards are not put in place.[102] Of those whose disorder is

---

[100] See, e.g., H. Lensing and L. Rayar, 'Notes on Criminal Procedure in the Netherlands' [1992] *Crim LR* 623; J. Hodgson, 'Codified Criminal Procedure and Human Rights: Some Observations on the French Experience' [2003] *Crim LR* 165.

[101] D. Carson, 'Prosecuting People with Mental Handicaps' [1989] *Crim LR* 87.

[102] See C. Phillips and D. Brown, *Entry into the Criminal Justice System* (1998), 188–9; Bradley Report, *Mentally Disordered People in the Criminal Justice System* (2009), para 16.

recognized, the rate of diversion and no further action is relatively high.[103] Mentally dis-ordered people who come into contact with the police may be taken to a 'place of safety' under ss 135–136 of the Mental Health Act 1983, and the Bradley Report recommends tightening the protocols for joint working with the health service on this issue. For those taken to court, there is a scattering of court-based assessment and diversion schemes, one purpose of which is to identify and assess mentally disordered defendants and to see whether a form of diversion (such as immediate hospital admission) is possible and desirable.[104] A preliminary study of an Islington scheme showed that many of the men-tally disordered defendants had problems with living accommodation, problems of sub-stance abuse, and that there was an apparent over-representation of black people with psychotic illness.[105]

A second problem of equality of treatment concerns racial discrimination. Several studies suggest that there is some discrimination against black people in respect of decisions to prosecute or caution. For example, Tony Jefferson and Monica Walker found that Asians were much more likely to be cautioned than any others, but that black people were less likely than whites to receive a caution.[106] The Commission for Racial Equality monitored the cautioning of juveniles in seven police forces and found that black people were more likely to be referred for prosecution than whites.[107] It seems likely that part of the difference in prosecution rates revealed by these stud-ies would disappear if account were taken of whether the individual was willing to admit the offence: more black people decline to admit the allegations against them, which removes their eligibility for a caution.[108] However, there are other studies indicating a lower cautioning rate for African-Caribbean people, notably a study of juvenile cautioning by Evans[109] and the broader Home Office study by Phillips and Brown.[110] The picture is complicated by the fact that 'no further action' was taken against a higher proportion of black and Asian suspects, because of 'their lower admission rate and their involvement in certain types of offence which typically have above average NFA rates'. More recently, Martina Feilzer and Roger Hood conducted a large survey for the Youth Justice Board which found that the chances of a case involving a mixed-parentage young male being prosecuted were 2.7 times greater than that of a white young male with similar case characteristics, and that the chances of

---

[103] Phillips and Brown, 'Entry into the CJS', 188–9.

[104] See J. Peay, 'Mentally Disordered Offenders' in M. Maguire, R. Morgan and R. Reiner, *Oxford Handbook of Criminology* (4th ed, 2007), at 506–8.

[105] E. Burney and G. Pearson, 'Mentally Disordered Offenders: Finding a Focus for Diversion' (1995) 34 *Howard JCJ* 291.

[106] T. Jefferson and N. Walker, 'Ethnic Minorities in the Criminal Justice System' [1992] *Crim LR* 83, at 88.

[107] Commission for Racial Equality, *Juvenile Cautioning: Ethnic Monitoring in Practice* (1992).

[108] M. Fitzgerald, *Ethnic Minorities and the Criminal Justice System* (1993), 18; see also C. Phillips and B. Bowling, 'Ethnicities, Racism, Crime and Criminal Justice' in M. Maguire, R. Morgan and R. Reiner (eds), *Oxford Handbook of Criminology* (4th ed, 2007), 440.

[109] R. Evans, 'Comparing Young Adult and Juvenile Cautioning in the Metropolitan Police District' [1993] *Crim LR* 572.

[110] Phillips and Brown, *Entry into the Criminal Justice System* (1998), 92.

a mixed-parentage young female being prosecuted were six times that of a similarly placed white female.[111] This evidence is, as the report puts it, 'consistent with discriminatory treatment.'

A third problem is posed by the differential cautioning rates (indictable offences) for females, which are much higher than those for males—in 2007, 87 per cent for girls aged 15–17 compared with 68 per cent for boys, and 43 per cent for women aged 21 or over compared with 30 per cent for men.[112] The face-value interpretation would be that females are receiving unduly favourable treatment, but this fails to take account of the probability that offences of different types and different levels of seriousness would be found in the different groups. Thus Phillips and Brown found that 'females were more likely to be cautioned because they were far more likely than men to admit their offences and more likely to be arrested for less serious offences (typically shoplifting).'[113] However, research in the early 1990s found that, whereas a majority of both sexes had no previous criminal history, cautioned males were twice as likely as females to have been previously convicted[114]—suggesting that some men were being treated more leniently than women, perhaps benefiting from repeat cautioning when women were not. Again the picture is far from clear, but it would be unwise to assume that women are typically treated more leniently.

(B) VICTIMS' RIGHTS

Are the existing arrangements for diversion effective in securing the rights of victims? In relation to simple cautions, the Home Office Circular refers to the views of the victim as a factor in the decision whether or not to caution, adding that victims should be made aware that 'although their views will be taken into account, they will not necessarily be conclusive to the outcome'.[115] As noted above, the simple caution is not well adapted to ensuring the payment of compensation to the victim. However, reprimands and warnings for young offenders under the Crime and Disorder Act 1998 can include requirements to make reparation. Turning to conditional cautions, they can be offered on the condition that the offender makes reparation or pays compensation to the victim. The Revised Code of Practice makes it clear that the views of the victim 'should be taken into account in deciding whether a conditional caution is appropriate and in determining suitable conditions', but that the decision itself 'lies with the prosecutor'. Thus, 'care must be taken not to raise the expectations of the victim whilst seeking their views'. Moreover, 'the victim's consent must be obtained in any case where direct reparation or restorative justice processes are being

---

[111] M. Feilzer and R. Hood, *Differences or Discrimination?* (2004).
[112] *Criminal Statistics, England and Wales 2002*, Table 5.5.
[113] Phillips and Brown, above n 102, 92.
[114] C. Hedderman and M. Hough, *Does the Criminal Justice System Treat Men and Women Differently?* (1994), 2.
[115] HOC 16/2008, *Simple Cautioning of Adult Offenders*, para 20.

considered', and the victim should be informed 'where the conditions attached to a caution have a direct impact on the victim', e.g. where compensation is to be paid or the offender is required to stay out of a designated area.[116] The rules for the issue of PNDs are rather different—'the victim is consulted on the issuing of the disposal' and 'a PND mshould not be issued where the victim is opposed to this'.[117] It should be borne in mind that many PNDs are issued for public order offences with no direct victims: the different rule for PNDs seems to stem from the fact that issuing a PND removes the possibility of a compensation order being made, and where it is proposed to issue a PND for retail theft of over £100 or criminal damage of over £300 the victim's consent is required.

(C) DEFENDANTS' RIGHTS

One common feature of diversion schemes is that the defendant can decline the offer made by the police or prosecution if guilt is disputed, leaving them to prosecute in court and have the matter decided there. This is one reason why access to legal advice is important before a caution or conditional caution is issued, and why there is a 21-day period after the issue of a PND in which the ticketed person can decide to opt for a court hearing. Whilst these defendant options are sufficient to comply with the European Convention on Human Rights,[118] it nonetheless leaves to the defendant a choice that is not without pressure. The making of an offer of a caution before the defendant had admitted guilt of the offence constituted the unfair procedure in the *Thompson* case,[119] although it is true that some suspects may know or be advised of the possibility of a caution or conditional caution if they admit the offence. In principle, however, the police should first decide what action is appropriate, and only then ask the defendant whether he admits the offence and is prepared to accept a caution. In substantive terms, it appears that neither a caution nor a conditional caution amounts to a 'criminal charge' such that all the extra safeguards in Article 6(2) and (3) of the Convention apply, and the House of Lords so held in a decision on reprimands and final warnings for young defendants.[120] However, Ian Brownlee has argued that the position might be different in the case of a conditional caution with the payment of a financial penalty as the condition,[121] a point that remains to be settled.

(D) CRIME CONTROL

Does the expansion of diversionary and non-judicial penalties amount to an increase or a decrease in effective crime control? Sufficient research to answer this question

---

[116] *Revised Code of Practice for Conditional Cautions—Adults* (2009), paras 9.1–9.3.
[117] OCJR, *Out-of-Court Disposals for Adults* (2007), 12–13.   [118] Above, n 39.
[119] Above, p. 182.   [120] *R (on application of R) v Durham Constabulary* [2005] UKHL 21.
[121] I. Brownlee, 'Conditional Cautions and Fair Trial Rights: Form versus Substance in the Diversionary Agenda' [2007] *Crim LR* 129.

has not been carried out, not least because PNDs and conditional cautions are recent innovations. However, it should not be forgotten that the reconviction figures for cautions have generally been more favourable than those for convictions in court, and that according to Government figures—cited at a time when the diversionary regime for young offenders was being formalized by the introduction of reprimands and final warnings—it is only after three offences that a prosecution is less likely to be followed by reconviction than a caution.[122] It is therefore important to resist the temptation to equate greater severity with greater crime control: cautions and other forms of diversion may have no less preventive efficacy, and possibly greater preventive efficacy, than the prosecution-conviction-sentence approach. Indeed, as we saw in Part 2 of this chapter, it is beliefs of this kind that make many regulatory agencies confident that their compliance-oriented approach is more effective than ready resort to the criminal courts. On the other hand, one implication of this may be that diversionary and non-judicial penalties actually extend and deepen social control over certain groups: this has been argued in the context of the change from punitive to welfare-oriented approaches to tackling prostitution,[123] and Richard Young has argued more generally that the 'drift to summary justice' penalizes the poor and marginalized.[124]

6.7 CONCLUSIONS

The diversion of non-serious offenders away from the criminal courts has been advocated across Europe as a necessary and desirable way of simplifying criminal justice.[125] The strongest arguments in favour of diversion are that prosecution-conviction-sentence may be a disproportionate response to some less serious forms of law breaking, and that in general the prosecution approach may be a less effective response in terms of reoffending and therefore prevention. A secondary argument—though often powerful with governments—is that diversion may hold out the prospect of saving time and money. The courts are not involved, and less preparatory work is required of the police and prosecutors, so that the police (in particular) have more time to pursue serious criminals. However, we have noted above that a drive towards cost-cutting and simplification may lead to neglect of the rights of victims and the rights of defendants, and it remains important to ensure that this does not occur in practice even when the formal rules are designed to safeguard rights.

What, for these purposes, is diversion? It is a semi-formal alternative to sending a case down the prosecution-conviction-sentence track. It is, therefore, a non-judicial form of disposal: but a form of disposal it certainly is. Thus it empowers law enforcement

[122] Home Office, *No More Excuses* (1997), para 5.9, referring to research by the Audit Commission.
[123] J. Scoular and M. O'Neill, 'Regulating Prostitution' (2007) 47 *BJ Crim* 764.
[124] Young, 'Street Policing after PACE'.
[125] Council of Europe, *The Simplification of Criminal Justice* (1987).

agents, such as the police, community support officers, and officers of the various regulatory agencies (such as HM Revenue and Customs, the Environment Agency and others), to impose punishment. Whether a simple caution or formal warning amounts to punishment may be debated, since there are usually no obligations attached, even though the simple caution can be cited in court subsequently as evidence that the offence was committed. But FPNs and PNDs plainly involve punishment, in the form of payment of the penalty; and conditional cautions may involve punishment—even if it is thought that requiring reparation or participation in some rehabilitative scheme does not amount to punishment, payment of a financial penalty certainly does. The powers bestowed on regulatory agencies by the Part 3 of the Regulatory Enforcement and Sanctions Act 2008 are termed civil sanctions, but the 'fixed monetary penalties' are clearly punitive, and some of the other powers may be.

One possible objection to these references to punishment is that all the forms of diversion discussed here are voluntary, in the sense that the citizen always has the possibility of refusing. Consent is inconsistent with State punishment. This view must be dismissed as naïve: it is well known that in practice there is an element of coercion, sometimes in the background and sometimes (at least so far as it appears to the defendant) in the foreground, that renders this form of consent a rather impoverished species of the genus. The House of Lords in the *Durham* case recognized that explicit pressure to 'admit it and we'll let you off with a caution' would invalidate a subsequent admission;[126] the question is whether implicit pressure of the same kind should also be recognized. The alternative is prosecution in court, which may be considered more severe. Moreover, methods of diversion (other than no further action) may have adverse consequences: although FPNs are not recorded for use, any PND, simple caution or conditional caution can be cited in subsequent proceedings (although a PND may be treated as evidence of bad character but not as evidence of guilt), and any caution for a sex offence entails the notification requirements of the Sexual Offences Act 2003.

It is unfortunate that there is no proper hierarchy of methods of diversion. It may well be that the threefold hierarchy of diversion measures for young offenders—no further action, reprimand, final warning—is not always followed by the police,[127] but that can be regarded as a problem of supervision and monitoring. Where there is uncertainty concerns the relationship between simple cautions, conditional cautions and PNDs. To some extent this is resolved by the separate spheres in which PNDs operate, but not entirely: many PNDs are given for public order offences, but cautions could be considered for them, and certainly cautions or conditional cautions could be considered for many of the thefts from shops and criminal damage offences than now attract PNDs. Issuing a PND may be simpler for the police, but it is questionable whether that should be the foremost consideration. More attention should be given to the proper relationship between these three forms of diversion, if the aspirations to

---

[126] *R (on application of R) v Durham Constabulary* [2005] UKHL 21.
[127] S. Field, 'Early Intervention and the New Youth Justice: a Study of Initial Decision-Making' [2008] *Crim LR* 177.

proportionality and transparency that now suffuse the various codes of practice and policy statements are to be given real purchase. If it is said that the appropriateness of a particular form of diversion is always a matter for judgement, then this revives the question whether enforcement officers should have such power in these matters. The CPS is at least a quasi-judicial body, and is not directly involved in law enforcement. The CPS is therefore a much more appropriate body to be determining these extra-judicial punishments, if we are to have them.[128] But that is unlikely to be applicable to PNDs, which are often issued on the street, unless what is issued becomes merely a notice of a PND, to be ratified subsequently by the CPS after reviewing the case. That would call for some police paperwork, however, and is likely to be dismissed as undermining the imperatives behind the introduction of the PND.

These uncertainties about the relationship between the various forms of diversion illustrate the considerable amount of on-the-ground discretion that remains in the system. It is not enough for codes of practice and circulars to state that proportionality and transparency are at the heart of diversionary measures. What is needed is greater accountability and, in particular, better supervision and inspection systems. One justification for this is to assess the merits of the kinds of local variations that inevitably develop when there is so little concrete guidance: in relation to PNDs it should now be possible to determine best practice, and the interface between simple cautions and conditional cautions will soon develop to the extent that it can be evaluated nationally.

The predominant justifications for diversion by out-of-court disposals are in terms of simplification, speed, cost and effectiveness. These are worthy objectives, but each of them should be evaluated fully rather than assumed; but even if diversion does further those goals, there are six other issues to be considered. First, proportionality of response (minor penalties for minor offences) is a splendid principle, but it is important to know how the various out-of-court disposals are being employed by the police and others. This is not just a question of monitoring by the inspectorates, but rather it calls for carefully empirical research. Secondly, Rod Morgan shows that there is evidence of net-widening, and asks pertinent questions about the additional people being dragged into the criminal justice net by the expansion of out-of-court disposals: is that 'offenders who were previously able to offend with virtual impunity for want of police and criminal justice attention [are] now being brought effectively to book', or 'does it involve the criminalisation of marginally criminal behaviour which in the past was dealt with ... through the application of various informal community sanctions'?[129] Thirdly, in the absence of evidence it is quite possible that some relatively serious cases are being dealt with informally, perhaps without full understanding of the consequences. The magistracy has raised this question: there may be pressures felt by the person who accepts a PND or caution, and yet if that person is to gain the equivalent of a criminal record the matter should really be ventilated in open court, not

---

[128] An argument made some years ago in A. Sanders, 'The Limits of Diversion from Prosecution' (1988) 28 *BJ Crim* 513.

[129] Morgan, *Summary Justice*, 30.

in a police station or on the street.[130] Fourthly, even if one can dispel fears that the use of out-of-court disposals is target-driven or is a means of raising revenue,[131] there are genuine questions about the level at which penalties are set, and their comparability.

Those four points emerge from Rod Morgan's forthright report, which shows how little is really known about the actual application of out-of-court disposals. But there are two further issues to be considered. One is power relations between the police (and other enforcement agents) and the public: measures such as PNDs give police considerable *de facto* power, and there is a need for authoritative study of its effects on the rights of citizens. The second is social justice: in principle, the criminal justice system should respond consistently and proportionately to alleged offenders in a way that reflects the amount of harm foreseeably done and their culpability, and this principle should apply across the boundaries between the many different enforcement agencies. Why should there be differences in response to someone who pollutes a river, someone who defrauds the Revenue, someone who fails to take proper precautions for the safety of employees, someone who steals property from another, someone who sells unsound meat, and so on? One reply is that it is impossible to compare the relative seriousness of these different offences, and hence each of them must be viewed in its separate context. That is an unsatisfactory reply, since it is possible to make some progress towards a ranking of the relative seriousness of offences,[132] and to identify rankings of offences that are clearly inappropriate. The difficulty of settling on comprehensive criteria of offence-seriousness should not be deployed as an excuse for avoiding the broader questions of social justice that arise when relatively poor and powerless people are subjected to PNDs or prosecuted whereas the better connected are enabled to pay their way out of trouble without the stigma of a criminal conviction.[133]

One example of the case for differential treatment concerns fraud: the Royal Commission on Criminal Justice did not accept Levi's suggestion that regulatory mechanisms be used quite widely in fraud cases,[134] but it did recommend that some fraud cases and some of those handled by the Securities and Investments Board might receive different treatment:

'Where the offence is of a technical nature, there has been no specific loss or risk to any member of the public (or if there has, where restitution can be made), and the predominant issues relate to the protection of the integrity of the markets rather than to serious dishonesty as such, then it may be that regulatory action is both appropriate and sufficient'.[135]

The Commission insisted that the penalties 'must be sufficiently severe that it could not be alleged that so-called "white-collar crime" was being more leniently handled than

---

[130] *Ibid.*, 20–1.   [131] *Ibid.*, 27–9.

[132] For discussion, see A. Ashworth, *Sentencing and Criminal Justice* (5th ed, 2010), Ch 4.

[133] Cf A. Sanders, 'Class Bias in Prosecutions', (1985) 24 *Howard JCJ* 176.

[134] M. Levi, *The Investigation, Prosecution and Trial of Serious Fraud* (1993).

[135] Royal Commission on Criminal Justice, *Report*, para 7.63.

other equivalent offences'. That recognizes the point of principle, in terms of consistent treatment, but hardly deals with it in a manner that convinces across the whole spectrum of crimes. Nor does the argument that diversionary or civil measures are more effective in dealing with 'white collar crime' necessarily conclude the argument:[136] What is necessary is a thorough review of the prosecution policies of the various regulatory agencies. At present there is little accountability, and certainly no overall accountability to a single body that can oversee consistency in matters of prosecution. It is one thing to argue that the different contexts in which some agencies work make different approaches appropriate. It is quite another thing to argue that there should be no attempt at a common starting point, and no concern with broader issues of social justice and the apparent unfairness of these differing arrangements. These fundamental issues of social justice are taken further in the next chapter, on prosecutions.

FURTHER READING

YOUNG, R., 'Street Policing after PACE: the Drift to Summary Justice' in E. Cape and R. Young (eds), *Regulating Policing: the Police and Criminal Evidence Act 1984, Past, Present and Future*, Oxford: Hart Publishing, 2008.

MORGAN, R., *Summary Justice: Fast—but Fair?*, London: CCJS, King's College, 2008.

Questions for Discussion

1. Are there good arguments for expanding the use of diversion from the criminal justice process?
2. Are there sufficient safeguards against the misuse of out-of-court penalties?
3. Should there be greater regulation of the enforcement powers of the so-called regulatory agencies?

---

[136] See D. J. Middleton, 'The Legal and Regulatory Response to Solicitors involved in Serious Fraud' (2005) 45 *BJ Crim* 810.

7
PROSECUTIONS

For many years the prosecution system in England and Wales has been organized differently from almost any other. The police exerted considerable control over prosecutions until the creation of the Crown Prosecution Service (CPS) in 1986, and even after that the police retained the initial decision whether or not to prosecute, with the CPS having the role of prosecutorial review. From 2004 a system of 'statutory charging' has removed decisions to prosecute from the police to the CPS for most offences (save a few less serious ones). The next step is likely to be the creation of a broader-based public prosecution service, combining the CPS with the RCPO (Revenue and Customs Prosecutions Office) to create an organization that 'will provide advice and prosecution services not only to the police but also to the Serious Organised Crime Agency, Her Majesty's Revenue and Customs and the UK Border Agency.'[1] This is an important step, although it will be apparent that it does not extend to any of the regulatory agencies discussed in Chapter 6 that retain both investigative and enforcement functions.[2] This chapter begins by outlining the origins and functions of the CPS. It then moves on to a discussion of several aspects of the prosecutorial function in the criminal process, in the belief that the decision to prosecute someone is in itself a form of imposition by the State that requires justification: not only must there be sufficient evidence to warrant putting the person to the trouble of mounting a defence, but there should also be a professional system for weeding out evidentially weak cases so as to protect the innocent by removing the possibility of miscarriages of justice in such cases. Moreover, there must be good policy reasons for considering and deciding that it is in the public interest to bring the prosecution (i.e. this must be both a proportionate and an appropriate response). In the course of exploring these issues we raise questions about the standards and the performance of the CPS and other agencies in this respect. We also ask about the ethical orientation of English prosecutors: are they committed to the appropriate ethical standards, and how (if at all) is compliance with ethical principles monitored? How committed are prosecutors to ensuring that human rights are respected in their decision making? The principle of equality of treatment is

---

[1] CPS, *The Public Prosecution Service—Setting the Standard* (July 2009), www.cps.gov.uk.
[2] See the review by the House of Commons Justice Committee, *The Crown Prosecution Service: Gatekeeper of the Criminal Justice System* (2009), Ch 5, discussed in Part 7.9 below.

discussed throughout the chapter, not least in relation to the differences of approach taken by different prosecuting agencies. Of all the offences in English criminal law, some are treated as the business of the police and others are treated as the business of various 'regulatory' agencies, as noted above. It cannot be said that the former are invariably more serious than the latter. Questions therefore arise about the justifications for different treatment, at the stage of prosecution or diversion, of offences of similar gravity that are committed in different types of situation and therefore policed and prosecuted by different agencies.

7.1 THE CROWN PROSECUTION SERVICE

Whose task should it be to prosecute alleged offenders? For many centuries the victim of the alleged offence had to be the motivating force behind the decision to prosecute, largely because there was no other agency to do this. There was no organized police force and no other body appointed by central or local government to initiate or organize prosecutions. Eventually the police became more and more involved in prosecuting, and as the regular police force was formed in the early part of the nineteenth century, it became natural to expect them not only to detect and arrest suspected offenders but also to initiate their prosecution. Doubts were expressed at the time about the propriety of giving this power to the police,[3] but these were not voices in favour of the status quo. On the contrary, the task of prosecuting was a burden on victims, and even where there were prosecution associations at work the result would still be inconsistencies of practice and inefficiencies in criminal justice. There were some arguments in favour of an independent prosecuting service, for the constitutional reason that it was inappropriate to bestow this task on a group (the police) whose principal tasks were keeping order and investigating alleged crimes.[4] Those arguments did not prevail, and the police appear to have taken over prosecutions almost by default. However, there was little doubt about the propriety of ensuring that this task was borne by a public body rather than by victims, whether individually or in association with one another: as part of its role in protecting people from crime, the State should make arrangements for the prosecution of those whose (alleged) conduct is judged to warrant that response.

Prosecution arrangements in England and Wales were altered in the mid-1980s. Until then there were three principal prosecuting agencies. The police, as just mentioned, had brought most prosecutions since the mid-nineteenth century. By the early 1980s, many police forces had developed or begun to develop a prosecuting solicitors' department, but it was still the police who took most of the decisions since the prosecuting

[3] See G. Dingwall and C. Harding, *Diversion in the Criminal Process* (1998), Ch 2, for a brief history and further references.
[4] *Ibid.*, 32.

solicitors were in their employ. Secondly, the Director of Public Prosecutions had a small department in London, dealing with all murder prosecutions, and with a spread of other cases concerned with such matters as national security, public figures, and alleged offences by police officers. And thirdly, there were the various agencies such as the Inland Revenue, the Post Office, the Health and Safety Commission (including the Factory Inspectorate), the Pollution Inspectorate, local authorities (including, for example, their environmental health officers), and so forth. These so-called 'regulatory agencies' (already mentioned in Chapter 6 in the context of law enforcement) mostly had their own prosecutors.

Arguments in favour of changing the system were heard at various times, but perhaps the most influential event was the publication in 1970 of a report by the British section of the International Commission of Jurists.[5] This report drew upon arguments of principle (that it was wrong for the police, who investigated crimes, to take decisions in relation to prosecution, which require impartiality and independence) and also more pragmatic arguments (that the police were experts at investigation, and it would be a better use of their time to focus on this rather than to undertake all these prosecutorial duties). This report was constantly referred to in the 1970s, but it took a spectacular miscarriage of justice to provide the impetus for reform. The report on the *Confait* case, published in 1977, made criticisms of several aspects of the criminal justice system, and proposed that changes in the prosecution system should be considered.[6] The arguments for and against change were then considered by the Royal Commission on Criminal Procedure, chaired by Sir Cyril Phillips. There was much discussion of the Scottish system, in which each area has a procurator-fiscal who directs the police in the investigation of crime, who interviews suspects and witnesses, and who has several powers similar to those of a continental examining judge.[7] On the other side there were vigorous arguments from the police that they should retain control over prosecutions, using their experience and local knowledge.

The Royal Commission reported in 1981 in favour of the establishment of an independent public prosecutor system, endorsing a division of functions between investigators and prosecutors but placing the dividing line in a different place than the Scots system, giving fewer powers to the prosecutor.[8] After debates about whether the system should be locally accountable or national,[9] the Prosecution of Offences Act 1985 created a national Crown Prosecution Service, headed by the Director of Public Prosecutions and formally accountable to the Attorney-General. The CPS has a duty to take over all prosecutions instituted by the police (except for certain minor

---

[5] JUSTICE, 'The Prosecution Process in England and Wales' [1970] *Crim LR* 668.

[6] *Report of an Inquiry by the Hon. Sir Henry Fisher into the circumstances leading to the trial of three persons on charges arising out of the death of Maxwell Confait and the fire at 27 Doggett Road, London SE6* (1977).

[7] Cf Royal Commission on Criminal Procedure, *Report* (1981), Ch 7, with R. M. White, 'Investigators or Prosecutors or, Desperately Seeking Scotland: Re-Formulation of the "Philips Principle"' (2006) 69 *MLR* 143.

[8] White, *ibid.*, 153–7 and *passim*.

[9] See the White Paper, *An Independent Prosecution Service for England and Wales* (1983).

offences), and has a power to take over other prosecutions. The CPS was therefore accorded a status independent of the police. Section 10 of the Prosecution of Offences Act 1985 lays upon it the duty to publish a Code for Crown Prosecutors and to report annually to Parliament on its work and the use of its powers. Notable among these is its power to discontinue prosecutions in the magistrates' courts.[10] Unlike public prosecutors in many other jurisdictions, it was not given powers to institute proceedings itself, to direct the police to investigate any matter, or to put questions to any person.[11] However, since the advent of statutory charging in 2004, the CPS has had greater powers, to be discussed below.

The CPS has carried out its statutory obligation to publish its *Code for Crown Prosecutors*, and has revised it five times since. The Code was first published in 1986, with subsequent editions in 1992, 1994, 2000, 2004 and 2010. The revision in 1994 was intended to ensure that the Code was phrased in plain English suitable for lay persons to read, as well as making some changes of substance which will be referred to below. The changes made in the 2000 version were relatively minor. In the last few years there has been a welcome step towards openness, with the publication on the CPS website of considerable amounts of prosecutorial guidance previously confidential to crown prosecutors.[12] Much of what appeared in the five Prosecution Manuals in former years is now available, most notably lists of factors relevant to decisions whether or not to prosecute for specific offences. This increases transparency, and should enable greater public understanding as well as affording possible grounds for challenge where it appears that the guidance has not been followed. Integrated into this guidance are the various sets of 'Charging Standards', established jointly by CPS lawyers and the police in the late 1990s with a view to assisting the police in setting the charge at the right level initially and ensuring that the CPS has a common starting point when reviewing case files. It is fair to say that when the three sets of Charging Standards—on offences against the person (now revised), on motoring offences, and on public order offences—were first issued the reaction was mixed. Some regarded them as part of a cost-cutting exercise rather than as a mere attempt to foster greater consistency: thus it was argued that the borderline between the summary offence of common assault and the indictable offence of assault occasioning actual bodily harm has been set in a way that is legally debatable and is designed to ensure that as many cases as possible remain in the magistrates' courts. Certainly the legal definition of assault occasioning actual bodily harm would encompass some of the harms now stated to fall into common assault for prosecution purposes.[13] It should be added that the movement towards greater transparency in matters of policy has resulted in a wide range of other guidance documents being placed on the CPS website, dealing

---

[10] Prosecution of Offences Act 1985, s 23.

[11] For the early history of the CPS, see Lord Windlesham, *Responses to Crime: Volume 4* (2001), Ch 4.

[12] See the second edition of this work, at 179.

[13] See F. G. Davies, 'CPS Charging Standards: a Cynic's View' (1995) 159 *JP* 203, and 'Ten Years of the Crown Prosecution Service: the Verdict' (1997) 161 *JP* 207.

with such matters as consents to prosecution, international cooperation, domestic violence, the reinstitution of proceedings, evidential considerations, case preparation, witnesses, disclosure, and many others. This is much to be welcomed: reference to the guidance is made at appropriate points below, and there is further discussion in Part 7.6 below.

The crucial question, however, is whether the guidance is faithfully applied. Research findings on this are discussed as appropriate throughout the chapter. However, there have been significant changes in the organization and working of the CPS in recent years. When the Labour Government came to power in 1997, one of its earliest initiatives was to set up a review of the CPS, chaired by Sir Iain (formerly Lord Justice) Glidewell. The emphasis of that review turned out to be largely managerial, and there was a disappointing reluctance to discuss major issues of policy on prosecutions.[14] The significant changes in working practices that have resulted include the introduction of many CPS caseworkers, not legally qualified, to deal not only with the preparation of cases but also with the presentation of 'straightforward' guilty plea cases in magistrates' courts. The range of their potential duties was increased in April 2004 to include appearing at early administrative hearings and at hearings after a guilty plea where the court had ordered a pre-sentence report. These changes were said to form part of the 'modernization' of the CPS,[15] but they also mean that many roles that were originally intended to be fulfilled by qualified lawyers are now being carried out by (trained) laypeople.

This could be defended as part of a strategy to deploy CPS lawyers for more important tasks. In 2001 the Auld Review called for major changes in the powers and duties of the CPS, to allow them to take a more direct and proactive role by determining the charge and preparing the case for trial. Thus Lord Justice Auld recommended that the CPS 'should determine the charge in all but minor, routine offences or where, because of the circumstances, there is a need for a holding charge before seeking the advice of the Service.'[16] The relevant law was changed accordingly by ss 28, 29 and 30 of the Criminal Justice Act 2003, in combination with Schedule 2.

These provisions introduced what is known as the 'statutory charging scheme', whereby the CPS take all charging decisions at the outset in respect of all indictable only and triable-either-way offences, whereas many lesser offences may be charged by the police (although they may seek advice from the CPS).

'The specific aims of the new charging arrangements may be summarised as follows: the elimination at the earliest opportunity of hopeless cases, the production of more robust prosecution cases, the elimination of unnecessary or unwarranted delays in the period between

---

[14] Glidewell, *The Review of the Crown Prosecution Service: a Report* (1998), reviewed at [1998] *Crim LR* 517.

[15] 'Extended Role for CPS Caseworkers', press release of 29 April 2004, www.cps.gov.uk.

[16] Auld LJ, *Review of the Criminal Courts of England and Wales* (2001), 412.

charge and disposal, and the reduction of the number of trials that "crack" through the offering and acceptance of guilty pleas to reduced charges at a late stage in the process.'[17]

A joint inspection of the statutory charging arrangements by the Inspectorates of Constabulary and the CPS was generally supportive of the new arrangements. Discontinuance of weak cases was happening earlier, and final charging decisions by prosecutors were of good quality. The review identified a number of respects in which the arrangements could be improved, including a simplification of the varying processes adopted for statutory charging by different areas, greater consistency of approach by prosecutors, improved file preparation by the police, and improved methods for the actual giving of advice by the CPS to the police.[18] Working relationships between police and CPS were said to have improved more at national level than at local level, and both organizations favour greater flexibility in local arrangements.[19] Efforts to reduce the rate of discontinuance had met with some successs, but by 2007–08 had still not reached the target figure in either magistrates' courts or the Crown Court. However, the guilty plea rate at both courts was higher than the target figure, which might be said to reflect better case preparation.[20] The arrangements have led to the presence of a duty prosecutor in larger police stations, and CPS Direct has been developed simultaneously to provide out-of-hours advice by telephone. A recent review of CPS Direct found that this was a particularly successful part of the new arrangements, often more flexible and more responsive to police requirements, delivering good quality advice but with an appeal process where there was disagreement. Most of the recommendations for improvement relate to technology and resources rather than to the service itself.[21] This discussion of statutory charging should not be taken to suggest that the police bring a case file to the CPS, who then reach a determinative judgement on it. One of the anticipated benefits of statutory charging is a close working relationship between police and CPS, leading to 'joint investigation' (with the CPS involved from an early stage) and 'proactive prosecuting' (which means thinking of trial issues from an early stage).[22]

In late 2009, two changes in the joint working arrangements were announced.[23] The CPS Direct service, which allows the police out-of-hours access to CPS advice on charging, is to be extended so as to become a 24-hour service, available also during the working day in order to provide easier access to advice for the police. At the same time, there will be a pilot study in which the boundary of statutory charging will be changed, and all summary-only offences will become the responsibility of the police

---

[17] I. Brownlee, 'The Statutory Charging Scheme in England and Wales: Towards a Unified Prosecution System?' [2004] *Crim LR* 896, at 897.

[18] HMCPSI and HMIC, *Joint Thematic Review of the New Charging Arrangements* (2008), Ch 3.

[19] *Ibid.*, para 3.35.

[20] *Ibid.*, para 15.21.

[21] HMCPSI, *Inspection of CPS Direct* (2008), Ch 3.

[22] Y. Moreno and P. Hughes, *Effective Prosecution* (2008), Ch 2.

[23] 'CPS and ACPO announce charging developments': www.cps.gov.uk (10 November 2009).

to charge. The supporting argument is that this will allow the CPS to concentrate on the more serious cases; but it is a further step back to the pre-CPS days, and, given the seriousness of some summary-only offences (such as common assault, assaulting a police officer, taking a vehicle without the owner's consent), it revives arguments of fairness, impartiality and legal knowledge against allowing the police to be both investigators and prosecutors in the same case.

7.2 EVIDENTIAL SUFFICIENCY

It is wrong for a person to be prosecuted if the evidence is insufficient. The essence of the wrongness lies in the protection of the innocent: if this principle is taken seriously, it should mean not merely that innocent people are not convicted, but also that innocent people should not be prosecuted. That is important for two reasons: first, as a method of ensuring that innocent people are not subsequently convicted, by weeding out weak cases at an early stage; and secondly, because being prosecuted is a considerable inconvenience (as expressed in the dictum that 'the process is the punishment'),[24] often a source of profound worry, and sometimes a considerable expense, and it may also lead to an element of stigma and loss of social esteem. The homely phrase, 'no smoke without fire', might well be applied. There are therefore sound moral reasons for not prosecuting someone against whom the evidence is insufficient. There are also good economic reasons: it is a waste of police time in compiling a full file on the case, of prosecution time in reviewing the case, and of court time in dealing with the case. It is therefore desirable in general that weak cases should be eliminated as early as possible: it was for this purpose that the Royal Commission on Criminal Procedure recommended the introduction of a public prosecution service to provide independent review, and that the Auld Review recommended the extension of CPS powers to the initial laying of the charge.

There are at least three major issues to be discussed before the principle of evidential sufficiency can be translated into practice. One is the test of sufficiency—what should it be? Closely intertwined with this is the second question—should the test vary according to the stage the case has reached? And third, how can prosecutors, at the stage of prosecutorial review, be expected to assess cases on the basis of a written file? In discussing these issues, it must constantly be borne in mind that evidential sufficiency is only one of the factors relevant in prosecutions. Another is the lawfulness of the prosecution in procedural terms—have the appropriate formalities been completed? Have the time limits been observed? Has there been a previous prosecution arising out of the incident, so as to raise considerations of double jeopardy? A further

---

[24] M. Feeley, *The Process is the Punishment* (1979), Ch 1; particular emphasis is placed on this by J. Rogers, 'Restructuring the Exercise of Prosecutorial Discretion in England' (2006) 26 *OJLS* 775.

factor is the policy of diversion, discussed in the previous chapter in the context of the cautioning of offenders. Thus, even if a case satisfies the test of evidential sufficiency, there may be strong reasons of public policy or, as it is termed in England and Wales, 'public interest' in favour of dealing with the case by means other than prosecution. In practice, questions of evidential sufficiency and public interest often interact, but for clarity of exposition this part of the chapter is devoted chiefly to evidential sufficiency, and the issue of 'public interest' is left over until the following part.

(A) FORMULATING THE TEST OF EVIDENTIAL SUFFICIENCY

Until the early 1980s the test that the police were said to apply in deciding whether the evidence was strong enough for prosecution was the '*prima facie* test': is there 'evidence on the basis of which, if it were accepted, a reasonable jury or magistrates' court would be justified in convicting'?[25] This often seemed to mean that as long as there was some evidence on the main points that need to be proved the defendant ought to be brought to court to answer the charge.[26] The weakness of the test was that it made no explicit reference to the strength and credibility of the evidence, nor to probable lines of defence. In his submission to the 1981 Royal Commission on Criminal Procedure, the then Director of Public Prosecutions denounced this test as inadequate: it was wrong, he argued, that a person could be prosecuted when an acquittal was more likely than a conviction, and the minimum standard should require that conviction is more probable than acquittal.[27] The Director's approach was commended by the Royal Commission on the basis that a lower standard would be 'both unfair to the accused and a waste of the restricted resources of the criminal justice system'.[28] When the CPS came into existence, the first edition of the Code for Crown Prosecutors in 1986 required a 'realistic prospect of conviction', a test that remains unchanged today.

Paragraph 4.5 of the 2010 Code for Crown Prosecutors requires crown prosecutors to take account of 'what the defence case may be and how that is likely to affect the prospects of conviction', and to consider 'whether the evidence can be used and is reliable'. The admissibility of evidence is a matter of legal judgement: paragraph 4.7a suggests that decisions to prosecute should not be based on evidence that is likely to be excluded by the court, such as unfairly obtained evidence or some hearsay. If there is doubt about whether the evidence would be included, the CPS should obtain a ruling in court.[29] The reliability of evidence is said to turn on such matters as 'the defendant's age, intelligence or lack of understanding' (where a confession is relied upon), the background of prosecution witnesses (in terms of dubious motives or relevant previous convictions), and the strength of any identification evidence.[30]

---

[25] Royal Commission on Criminal Procedure, *Report*, para 8.8.
[26] Provided, of course, that the 'public interest' test was also satisfied: see below.
[27] Royal Commission on Criminal Procedure, vol ii, *The Law and the Procedure* (1981), Appendix 25.
[28] Royal Commission on Criminal Procedure, *Report*, para 8.9.
[29] CPS, *Explanatory Memorandum* (1996), para 4.20.
[30] For detailed discussion, see Moreno and Hughes, *Effective Prosecution*, Ch 3.

What is the legal basis for the 'realistic prospects' test, and what are its theoretical justifications? It is clearly predictive in nature: it requires the prosecutor to assess whether, on the evidence likely to be given at the trial, a conviction is more probable than an acquittal. This includes matters such as the admissibility of the evidence and the likely defence. Paragraph 4.6 of the Code states that 'a realistic prospect of conviction is an objective test'. There are two different ways in which this might be interpreted. One is a straight predictive approach (sometimes termed 'the bookmaker's approach'):[31] the crown prosecutor's task would be to predict how the court in which the case would be tried would react to the evidence. This might require the prosecutor to take account of the different conviction rates of magistrates' courts and the Crown Court, and of any local trends in willingness or unwillingness to convict in certain types of case. An alternative would be an 'intrinsic merits' approach, according to which the task of the prosecutor would be to judge the strength of evidence and to apply the law to it faithfully. On this approach, prosecutors would exercise the function of keeping cases away from the lay tribunal when they judge that the evidence is insufficient, even though they think that the tribunal might well convict, and correspondingly prosecutors would persevere with a case when they believe that the evidence is sufficient, even though they recognize that the local court is unlikely to convict. Thus on the predictive view the disposition of the local courts sets the standard, whereas on the 'intrinsic merits' view it is a legal standard applied by various prosecutors to case files that determines decisions.

Those who believe in the supreme importance of lay adjudications would favour the predictive view. Magistrates and juries should be the central figures, and prosecutors should merely attempt to anticipate their decisions rather than to neutralize or even bypass them. On the other hand, fidelity to law would favour the 'intrinsic merits' approach, since one might doubt whether there could be sufficient reason why a local bench or justices' clerk, or the juries of a particular neighbourhood, should be allowed to distort or disregard the law of the country as a whole. Thus the American Bar Association has stated that: 'In cases which involve a serious threat to the community, the prosecutor should not be deterred from prosecution by the fact that in his jurisdiction juries have tended to acquit persons accused of the particular kind of criminal act in question.'[32] This is also consistent with paragraph 4.6 of the Code: a 'realistic prospect of conviction' means that 'a jury or bench of magistrates, properly directed in accordance with the law, is more likely than not to convict the defendant of the charge alleged'. In the Explanatory Memorandum of 1996 a straight predictive view was rejected explicitly:

'Crown Prosecutors should not take into account any perceived local views of the bench or juries when considering whether there is a realistic prospect of conviction. The reason for this is simple: if local considerations of this nature were allowed to influence the decision to prosecute, the goal of consistent decision-making would be lost.'[33]

---

[31] See *R (on the application of B) v Director of Public Prosecutions* [2009] *Crim LR* 652.

[32] ABA, *Standards Relating to the Prosecution Function* (1980), 3–3.9.

[33] CPS, *Explanatory Memorandum*, para 4.10.

The Explanatory Memorandum went on to set out some of the points to be taken into account when making these judgements. It also included the extraordinary assertion that 'the quality of justice does not vary from courtroom to courtroom or between tiers of court'.[34] There is considerable evidence that it does, and that many crown prosecutors believe that it does.[35] In particular, it is widely believed to differ between magistrates' courts and the Crown Court, in which the acquittal rates are certainly different. The Memorandum would have been on firmer ground in saying that the quality of justice dispensed by the two levels of court ought not to differ.

The 'intrinsic merits' approach has now been endorsed by the Divisional Court in *R (on the application of B) v Director of Public Prosecutions* (2009).[36] The victim of a serious assault identified his attacker and gave an account of the attack to the police. When it emerged that the victim suffered from a psychosis that sometimes led to paranoid beliefs and hallucinations, a psychiatric report was commissioned. The report concluded that the victim's condition might affect the reliability of his perceptions and recollections. The CPS therefore discontinued the case, but the Divisional Court granted judicial review of that decision. Toulson LJ held that it was premature and unsatisfactory to drop the case without further discussion with either the victim or the psychiatrist about the actual reliability of his evidence. The CPS decision appears to have proceeded from either a misreading of the psychiatric report or unfounded stereotyping of the victim because of his mental disorder. The Court went on to find a breach of Article 3 of the Convention, holding that the dropping of the prosecution violated the State's obligation to protect citizens from serious assaults and increased the victim's sense of being outside the law's protection, and the Court awarded the victim £8,000 damages for the inhuman and degrading treatment suffered. This is a strong decision in respect of those with forms of mental disturbance,[37] and it has the wide significance of endorsing a version of the 'intrinsic merits' approach that insists on close attention to the actual evidence in the particular case. Such an approach places considerable weight on prosecutors' judgements, but it should be supported since it aspires to advance the purpose of the law rather than deferring to the reaction of the (local) courts.

Since the inception of the CPS prosecutors have been heavily reliant on the police for information and assessments of the statements and the evidence, but two changes have now taken place. First, joint working and 'collocation' of police and prosecutors should increase the accuracy of information exchanged between them. Secondly, prosecutors are now allowed, within certain protocols, to undertake pre-trial witness interviews of prosecution witnesses. This innovation was the subject of a pilot study,[38]

---

[34] *Ibid.*, para 4.13.

[35] A. Hoyano et al, 'A Study of the Impact of the Revised Code for Crown Prosecutors' [1997] *Crim LR* 556, at 563.

[36] [2009] EWHC 106 (Admin), [2009] *Crim LR* 652.

[37] See now the CPS document, *Supporting Victims and Witnesses with Mental Health Issues* (July 2009), available at www.cps.gov.uk.

[38] P. Roberts and C. Saunders, 'Introducing Pre-Trial Witness Interviews—a Flexible New Fixture in the Crown Prosecutor's Toolkit' [2008] *Crim LR* 831; cf now para 48 of the 2010 Code.

and is now becoming available nationally. This may help to fill gaps in the prosecution case or otherwise strengthen it, but the danger of an accusation of coaching witnesses is never far away.

(B) EVIDENTIAL SUFFICIENCY AND THE STAGES OF THE CRIMINAL PROCESS

The Code for Crown Prosecutors formerly stated a single test of evidential sufficiency: whether there is a 'realistic prospect of conviction'. As argued in previous editions of this book, that test is not suitable for practical application at all stages of the criminal process.[39] For example, at the end of questioning the police may believe that they have sufficient evidence to justify remanding a defendant in custody before first appearance at court, and the CPS may take the same view at that stage; but it may not be possible to say that there is a realistic prospect of a conviction. Similarly, in many cases the prosecutor receives a file for the first time just before remand proceedings are due to begin. This may be the morning after the defendant's arrest. The prosecutor will have had no time to listen to any interview tapes, and so it is likely that the police summary will dominate. Both the police and the crown prosecutor may believe that they have (or will have) sufficient evidence to justify the charge, but they may still have witnesses to interview and forensic reports to receive. In strict terms, there may not yet be a realistic prospect of conviction. Can a remand in custody be justified in these circumstances? Even one week's loss of liberty—often spent in an overcrowded prison, with poor facilities, away from family, friends, and employment (if any), and without unrestricted access to legal advice—is a serious deprivation. As we shall see in Chapter 8, the Bail Act 1976 directs a magistrates' court to have regard to the strength of the evidence; but, again, this is usually taken on trust from the CPS, who in turn may take it on trust from the police.

The CPS took this point in the 2004 version of the Code, and the 2010 Code distinguishes between the Full Code Test, applicable in normal situations, and the Threshold Test, applicable in cases where it would not be appropriate to release a suspect on bail after charge, but the evidence to apply the Full Code Test is not yet available. The new guidance is based on Article 5(1)(c) of the Convention, which states that no one shall be deprived of their liberty except on reasonable suspicion of having committed an offence. According to paragraph 5.6 of the 2010 Code, the prosecutor should consider whether there is 'at least a reasonable suspicion that the suspect has committed an offence.' This should be done by reference to:[40]

(a) the nature, extent and admissibility of any likely further evidence, and the impact it will have upon the case;

---

[39] See the second edition of this work, p. 184.

[40] 2010 version of the Code, para 5.11. See also para 5.3 for four conditions that must be met before the threshold test may be applied.

(b) the charges that all the evidence will support;

(c) the reasons why the evidence is not available;

(d) the time required to obtain the further evidence and whether any
     consequential delay is reasonable in all the circumstances.

Recognition of the need for this threshold test is a significant step, but how robust
the 'reasonable suspicion' standard is may be doubted. Indeed, the Inspectorates suggest that the test should be clearer about the prosecutorial judgement on which it is
based, namely that it will in due course be 'possible to mount a viable case against the
suspect'.[41] Moreno and Hughes emphasize that the threshold test is merely an interim
measure, 'to be used by prosecutors in exceptional circumstances in order to manage high risk offenders [sic] whilst significant outstanding evidence is obtained by the
police within a reasonable time.' Thus the test 'is about managing substantial bail risks
where all of the evidence is not available' and should not be regarded as a short-cut for
a charging decision.[42] However, although paragraph 5.13 recognizes these concerns:

'A decision to charge and withhold bail must be kept under review. The evidence gathered must be regularly assessed to ensure the charge is still appropriate and that continued objection to bail is justified. The Full Code Test must be applied as soon as reasonably
practicable.'

its wording ought to be stronger. The defendant's right to liberty under Article 5
should only be withheld temporarily on these grounds, and it would be better to see
open recognition of the principle of urgency and of the importance of ensuring that
a suspect should not be kept in custody any longer than absolutely necessary under
the Threshold Test. The inspectorate's finding that in 57 per cent of cases where the
Threshold Test was used there was not a timely review applying the full code test therefore gives cause for concern.[43]

7.3 THE PUBLIC INTEREST

The discussion of regulatory agencies in Part 2 of Chapter 6 has already demonstrated that there are different conceptions of the public interest at work across the
broad sphere of law enforcement. Most of these agencies, which have both investigative and prosecution powers, regard their primary role as one of securing compliance with the standards laid down by law. They are often willing to take time to
achieve this, and many agencies adopt an approach that may be termed accommo-
dative or conciliatory—using persuasion, education and negotiation as the principal

---

[41] HMCPSI and HMIC, *Joint Thematic Review of the New Charging Arrangements* (2008), para 5.21.
[42] Moreno and Hughes, *Effective Prosecution*, 48–50.
[43] HMCPSI and HMIC, *Thematic Review of the New Charging Arrangements* (2008), para 12.9.

methods, and leaving the power to prosecute as a background threat which is rarely invoked. There is evidence that some regulatory agencies are becoming more punitive in recent years,[44] but the prevailing orientation is still towards persuasion and negotiation.

The position of the CPS has been rather less constant. The 1986 and 1992 editions of the Code for Crown Prosecutors were phrased so as to suggest that a prosecution should only be brought if 'the public interest requires' it, a formulation which suggested that there should be a presumption in favour of diversion from prosecution, and that a good reason was needed for prosecuting. It is not clear whether this emphasis was intended, or indeed whether it was thus interpreted in practice. However, in the 1994 version of the Code there was a distinct shift in the language, reflecting the then Home Secretary's determination to reduce the frequency of cautioning,[45] and this was repeated in the 2000 edition.[46] However, the advent of conditional cautioning has led to a further change, since the CPS is now in the business of considering and giving effect to diversion through out-of-court disposals (as we saw in Chapter 6.4 above). Thus paragraph 4.12 of the 2010 Code States:

'A prosecution will usually take place unless the prosecutor is sure that there are public interest factors tending against prosecution which outweigh those tending in favour, or unless the prosecutor is satisfied that the public interest may be properly served, in the first instance, by offering the offender the opportunity to have the matter dealt with by an out-of-court disposal. The more serious the offence or the offender's record of criminal behaviour, the more likely it is that a prosecution will be required in the public interest.'

Rather little is said, in the Code itself, about the factors that should dispose a prosecutor to select an out-of-court disposal. There are some general descriptive statements in paragraph 7 of the Code. The only prescriptive statement is that 'prosecutors will offer a conditional caution where it is a proportionate response to the seriousness and the consequences of the offending and where the conditions offered meet the aims of rehabilitation, reparation or punishment within the terms of the Criminal Justice Act 2003' (paragraph 7.1). Although there is more in the DPP's Guidance on Conditional Cautioning, it is disappointing that this paragraph says nothing about the criteria for the various out-of-court diposals.

The 2010 version of the Code follows its predecessors in setting out lists of common factors for and against prosecution. Among the factors in favour of prosecution (paragraph 4.16) are the fact that the victim was vulnerable, or the offence was motivated by any form of discrimination, or the defendant has relevant previous convictions or cautions, or the defendant was a ringleader or organizer of the offence, and so on. Many of these are well known as factors which militate in aggravation of sentence.[47] Similarly many of the 'common public interest factors against prosecution'

[44] R. Baldwin, 'The New Punitive Regulation' (2004) 67 *MLR* 351.

[45] A. Ashworth and J. Fionda, 'The New Code for Crown Prosecutors: Prosecution, Accountability and the Public Interest' [1994] *Crim LR* 894; cf R. Daw, 'A Response' [1994] *Crim LR* 904.

[46] Code for Crown Prosecutors (2000), para 6.2.

[47] See A. Ashworth, *Sentencing and Criminal Justice* (5th ed, 2010), Ch 5.

listed in paragraph 4.17 are circumstances which might otherwise mitigate sentence. Some of these are factors personal to the offender which make it likely that prosecution and conviction will have a disproportionately severe effect: old age, mental or physical ill health, mental disorder, and cases where there is evidence that the strain of criminal proceedings may lead to a considerable worsening of the accused's mental health. The justification for tipping the scales against prosecution in these cases is presumably some notion of equity or mercy, in the sense that it would be unfair to continue with a prosecution if that would have an impact on the particular offender far greater than is warranted by the offence.[48]

What justifications may be suggested for the other 'public interest factors against prosecution'? Several of them seem to be related to the notion of proportionality, since they refer to types of case in which prosecution and sentence might be an inappropriately severe response to the offence committed. Where the offence is so minor that a court is only likely to impose 'a nominal penalty', prosecution might not be 'in the public interest'. This refers to cases where a discharge or low value fine seems likely: the wording of the Code indicates that this involves a predictive judgement about the courts' sentencing practice,[49] although in line with the 'intrinsic merits' approach to evidential sufficiency it ought to be a principled judgement, not a predictive one. The cases envisaged are ones in which the harmfulness of the conduct was relatively low, or where the offender's culpability was low, including cases of 'genuine mistake or misunderstanding' or minor harm 'caused by a misjudgement', and some cases where the offender is elderly or suffering from mental illness. These, then, are cases lying towards the foot of any scale of offence-seriousness. The argument is that many of them do not warrant the bringing of formal proceedings, and might be dealt with more appropriately by an informal warning, or no action at all, and perhaps not even a police caution or conditional caution. The theory of desert or proportionality,[50] combined with the established finding that the process of being prosecuted may itself involve inconvenience, anxiety, or pain,[51] supports the proposition that a line should be drawn beneath which prosecution as a response is disproportionate and heavy-handed. Jonathan Rogers argues that it would be clearer, in terms of criteria for the prosecutor and communication to others, if the 'public interest' test were divided into two, and in particular if the 'harms of prosecution' (in terms of age, health, consequential lossess, etc) were set out and considered separately.[52]

---

[48] For discussion of this principle in sentencing, see *ibid.*, 151–5 and 208–11.

[49] CPS, *Explanatory Memorandum*, para 4.37. Both here and in the first factor in favour of prosecution in para 4.16a of the Code ('a conviction is likely to result in a significant sentence'), the language of the Code is based on prediction rather than on the 'intrinsic merits'.

[50] See A. von Hirsch and A. Ashworth (eds), *Principled Sentencing* (2nd ed, 1998), Ch 4.

[51] Royal Commission on Criminal Procedure, *Report*, para 8.7; M. McConville and J. Baldwin, *Prosecution, Courts and Conviction* (1981).

[52] J. Rogers, 'Restructuring the Exercise of Prosecutorial Discretion' (2006) 26 *OJLS* 775; see also n 24 above and accompanying text.

7.4 CPS POLICIES AND THEIR IMPLEMENTATION

Parts 2 and 3 of this chapter have concentrated on the Code for Crown Prosecutors, as the basic CPS policy document. However, research has suggested that prosecutors do not frequently consult the Code itself,[53] but rather rely on the large amount of guidance relating to specific issues in prosecuting, now available on the CPS website.[54] Among the detailed documents are those relating to domestic violence, sexual offences, racially and religiously aggravated offences, mentally disordered offenders, and youth offenders and child witnesses. There are also fact-sheets summarizing CPS policy on such matters as prosecuting for manslaughter, driving offences involving a fatality, and sexual offences. The CPS 'Instructions for Prosecuting Advocates' runs to over 100 pages and cover a wide range of procedural and substantive issues. In this part of the chapter we examine some of the principal CPS policies in the light of evidence about their implementation.

(A) PROSECUTING CASES OF DOMESTIC VIOLENCE

The investigation and prosecution of domestic violence has become a major area of re-assessment in recent years.[55] Several studies have drawn attention to the high rate of attrition of these offences, and the concern that a complainant's withdrawal of the original statement may be due to pressure or threats from the abuser which make it inappropriate to drop the case.[56] The CPS Policy for Prosecuting Cases of Domestic Violence (3rd edition)[57] emphasizes that prosecutors may go ahead with the case even if the complainant wishes the case to be stopped. An experienced prosecutor will look at the causes of the complainant's change of mind, and will also look at the broader implications for family, children, etc. Prosecution is more likely if the offence was serious. Thus:

'We always think very carefully about the interests and safety of the victim when we decide where the public interest lies. But we prosecute cases on behalf of the public and not just in the interests of any particular individual.'[58]

In 2004 the CPS Inspectorate published the report of a joint thematic inspection with the Inspectorate of Constabulary, *Violence at Home*. This report showed an extremely high attrition rate (463 initial reports, 13 convictions), and found that in a number of

---

[53] A. Hoyano et al, 'A Study of the Impact of the Revised Code for Crown Prosecutors' [1997] *Crim LR* 556.

[54] www.cps.gov.uk.

[55] See C. Hoyle, *Negotiating Domestic Violence* (1998); M. M. Dempsey, *Prosecuting Domestic Violence* (2009).

[56] A similar phenomenon is also to be found in reported rape cases where victim and perpetrator had previously been in an intimate relationship, and where intimidation or economic dependence appear to be the reasons for victim withdrawal: S. Lea, U. Lanvers and S. Shaw, 'Attrition in Rape Cases' (2003) 43 *BJ Crim* 583, at 596.

[57] Accessed 4 August 2009.   [58] *Ibid.*, para 6.1.

cases the CPS guidance had not been followed.[59] That was several years ago, but it is fair to note that the recent thematic review of Discontinuance reveals some evidence of similar problems. The discontinuance rate for domestic violence cases was 24 per cent, more than double the 11 per cent for all cases, and the Inspectorate suggests that prosecutors should be identifying more of the weak cases at an earlier stage ('be realistic about the future viability of cases').[60]

(B) PROSECUTING RACIALLY AGGRAVATED OFFENCES

Sections 29–32 of the Crime and Disorder Act 1998 introduced a number of racially aggravated versions of existing offences, with higher maximum penalties. At the time of their introduction concern was expressed that there would be few convictions of these offences because the CPS would accept a guilty plea to the ordinary (non-aggravated) version of the offence. The CPS soon asserted its intention not to do this, and its 'Guidance on Prosecuting Cases of Racial and Religious Crime' states in bold type that 'it is CPS policy not to accept pleas to lesser offences, or omit or minimise admissible evidence of racial or religious aggravation for the sake of expediency'.[61] Apart from that, the Guidance document emphasizes the social importance of enforcing the legislation. The Inspectorate's thematic report on these cases emphasized the need to flag racially aggravated offences for special scrutiny, and to train specialist prosecutors who could supervise the processing of these cases.[62]

The empirical evidence shows how these ideals might come to be compromised in practice. Burney and Rose studied the operation of racially aggravated offences, and their report demonstrates the relatively high level of discontinuance for these offences—over 40 per cent in 1999. CPS data cited insufficiency of evidence as the reason for 41 per cent of terminations, and witness refusal or non-appearance as the reason for 35 per cent.[63] Their conclusion was that 'the CPS is caught between the desire to be seen to be doing justice to the victims of racism, and a legal structure which increases the pressure to drop the racial aspect of the case when the substantive offence is admitted.'[64] The time-honoured response to research findings of this kind, in all criminal justice agencies, is to say that that might have been a correct description at the time but that practices have moved on since the research was completed. That response is not available here, because of the publication of subsequent reports. Appearing in late 2003 was the John Report, *Race for Justice*, which looked again at similar areas of decision making. The report included 33 case studies of racially aggravated incidents, and found that 25 of them were either discontinued or downgraded

[59] HMCPSI and HMIC, *Violence at Home: A Joint Thematic Inspection of the Investigation and Prosecution of Cases Involving Domestic Violence* (2004).

[60] HMCPSI, *Discontinuance* (2007), para 3.14.

[61] CPS, *Guidance on Prosecuting Cases of Racist and Religious Crime* (accessed 4 August 2009). For present purposes, the category of religiously aggravated offences will not be discussed separately.

[62] HMCPSI, *Casework having a Minority Ethnic Dimension* (2002).

[63] E. Burney and G. Rose, *Racist Offences—How is the Law Working?* (2002), 77.   [64] *Ibid.*, 85.

(by acceptance of a guilty plea) to a lesser offence. Acceptance of a plea to a non-racially aggravated offence:

'...occurred in no less than 12 of the 33 cases. The plea bargaining process in some cases involved an offer (that could be from either prosecution or defence) to plead guilty to another, usually less serious, charge if the race dimension is removed altogether. In the 12 cases mentioned, "public interest" was given as the main reason for the CPS decision. However, in some of these cases the assessment of the public interest made by prosecutors seemed questionable.'[65]

Significantly, the John Report went on to praise the CPS Guidance whilst casting strong doubt on the Service's ability to ensure that it is implemented:

'Without structural changes to build in management accountability for the way racist and religious crime is prosecuted and recorded across the Service, there is no reason to believe that, excellent though it is, the Guidance will be followed such that there are consistent and common standards for the prosecution and recording of these offences.'[66]

The John Report admitted that the cases it examined were dealt with up to two years earlier, but made the point that initiatives that are impressive on paper may simply not translate into practice. The CPS cannot be sure that what the John Report found 'is not being repeated in the day to day practice of prosecutors'.[67] This is a vital point that has been reiterated in several contexts in this book: having the law or the guidance right is a necessary first step, but there are powerful reasons for believing that policies announced at the top of large organizations are not always implemented by those who deal with matters on a day-to-day basis. It is naïve to assume that rules are followed to the letter in everyday practice, and thereby to discount the effect of occupational cultures, pressures from others and a simple desire to ease one's working life.

The CPS Inspectorate published in April 2004 its follow-up report on cases with a minority ethnic dimension.[68] Although it concluded that CPS performance had improved in the preceding two years, it still found a considerable number of racially aggravated cases 'in which we considered that the charge was reduced inappropriately... We still disagreed with the decision in more than one-fifth of cases in which the charge was reduced.'[69] The Inspectorate also noted variations in the willingness of prosecutors to take such offences to trial, and found that some areas had not yet designated and trained specialist prosecutors for these cases. Moreover, the Inspectorate was not convinced that there would be rapid progress at a time when the new arrangements statutory charging were claiming experienced staff and considerable resources.

---

[65] The Gus John Partnership, *Race for Justice: a review of CPS decision making for possible racial bias at each stage of the prosecution process* (2003), para 95; details of some of the questionable decisions are given in the subsequent paragraphs of the report.

[66] *Ibid.*, para 143.   [67] *Ibid.*, para 170.

[68] HMCPSI, *A Follow Up Review of CPS Casework with a Minority Ethnic Dimension* (2004).

[69] *Ibid.*, para 6.52.

(C) RECORDING DECISIONS AND REASONS

One finding common to the John Report and to the various HMCPSI reports is the poor quality of endorsements on CPS files. Thus the John Report questions whether prosecutors in their case studies were unaware of the Guidance or whether there were other factors influencing their prosecutorial review decisions: 'the file endorsements do not allow researchers to answer basic questions that are begged by such practices'.[70] The same considerations, of course, apply to internal supervision of prosecutors: if the files are not fully written up, how can there be proper monitoring of the quality of decisions? The Inspectorate's report on cases of domestic violence makes the same points. In relation to decisions not to prosecute, the Inspectorate observed that 'public interest considerations should be recorded, but in many cases they were not and there was little to show which factors had been considered, or the weight given to them, during decision-making.'[71] The Inspectorate devoted four paragraphs to this issue, of which this is the first:

'File endorsements were of inconsistent quality and in many cases inadequate. It was often difficult to ascertain the factors taken into account at various stages of the process, whether there had been compliance with the Code and the Policy, and sometimes the actual decision made.'[72]

While it remains possible that all these decisions were correctly taken and that these are merely failures of record-keeping, the reports suggest strongly that this was not the case. The poor quality of file endorsement not only makes internal monitoring difficult, but also casts doubt on the training and the ethos of those taking these crucial decisions. The thematic inspection on discontinuance described as disappointing the finding that as many as 17.5 per cent of files on discontinued cases did not contain a proper record of the reasons for the decision.[73]

(D) DOWNGRADING OF CHARGES

The Glidewell Review was specifically asked to examine the criticism that the CPS were 'downgrading' too many charges, either by reducing the charge to a lower level or by accepting a guilty plea to a lesser offence. In the event its examination of this issue was rather lame, since it failed to discuss the available research and simply concluded that there was a suspicion 'that charges, particularly in relation to offences of violence and associated offences, are downgraded on occasions when they should not be.'[74] It is well known that the ladder of offences of violence, provided by the Offences Against the Person Act 1861, gives ample opportunity for downgrading and charge bargaining: in the 1990s research by Moxon and Hedderman found that only one-fifth

---

[70] *Ibid.*, para 99. The report makes similar points at paras 22, 31, 92 and 115.
[71] HMCPSI, *Violence at Home* (2004), para 7.18.   [72] *Ibid.*, para 7.77.
[73] HMCPSI, *Discontinuance* (2007), para 4.11.
[74] I. Glidewell, *Review of the Crown Prosecution Service* (1998), 85.

of cases initially charged under s 18 were eventually dealt with under that section,[75] and Cretney and Davis found an even lower proportion of section 18 cases that were not downgraded.[76] We have also seen that downgrading remains a matter for concern in relation to racially aggravated offences.

One reason for some downgradings may relate to mode of trial. When the CPS has received a case file from the police, it may conclude that the case ought to be tried in the magistrates' court. To achieve this it may drop the higher charge and substitute a lower one, although it is not supposed to do this after a defendant has elected Crown Court trial on an either-way charge. Paragraph 9.2 of the Code for Crown Prosecutors states that speed should never be the only reason for trying to keep a case in the magistrates' court, whereas any greater delays and stress on witnesses might be an adequate reason. As for the allegedly high rate of acceptance of guilty pleas by the CPS in exchange for reducing the charge(s),[77] it is difficult to find general evidence on this, although we saw that the John Report identified this tendency in respect of racially aggravated offences,[78] and it is quite possible that detailed analysis of other offences might yield similar results. This would hardly be surprising, since the structure of the English criminal justice system is such as to place considerable pressure on defendants to plead guilty, and the relatively high acquittal rate in the Crown Court may also incline prosecutors to accept a plea to a lesser offence. Paragraph 10.2 of the 2010 Code declares that:

'Crown Prosecutors should only accept the defendant's plea if they think the court is able to pass a sentence that matches the seriousness of the offending, particularly where there are aggravating features. Crown Prosecutors must never accept a guilty plea just because it is convenient.'

David Jeremy rightly castigates this provision as 'opaque to the point of being unhelpful'.[79] The reference to sentencing is disingenuous, since either the defendant has the intent for s 18 or has not. The court cannot pass sentence for a lesser offence, such as s 20, on the basis of that intent; and the sentencing ranges for s 20 are considerably below those for s 18.[80] In practice, the opaqueness of paragraph 10.1 allows the known hazards of trials and the cost-effectiveness of guilty pleas combined with the significant structural pressure within the whole system (see Chapter 10 below) to enter into CPS decisions, and thereby produces rates of downgrading for section 18 cases that are distinctly higher than those for murder.[81]

---

[75] D. Moxon and C. Hedderman, 'Mode of Trial Decisions and Sentencing Differences between Courts' (1994) 33 *Howard JCJ* 97; similarly E. Genders, 'Reform of the Offences against the Person Act: Lessons from the Law in Action' [1999] *Crim LR* 689, only 19 per cent eventually dealt with under s 18.

[76] A. Cretney and G. Davis, *Punishing Violence* (1995), 137; cf also research R. Henham, 'Further Evidence on the Significance of Plea in the Crown Court' (2002) 41 *Howard JCJ* 151, revealing differences by circuit.

[77] For general discussion of 'charge-bargaining', see Ch 10.3 below.

[78] Above, n 64 and accompanying text.

[79] D. Jeremy, 'The Prosecutor's Rock and Hard Place' [2008] *Crim LR* 925, at 935; see also 931.

[80] Sentencing Guidelines Council, *Assault and Other Offences against the Person* (2008), 14–15.

[81] The priority of obtaining a conviction, above obtaining a conviction for the most appropriate offence, was also found by E. Burney and G. Rose, *Racist Offences—How is the Law Working?* (2002), 78.

Reduction of charges may be justified if the defendant has originally been over-charged: the CPS would be performing their correct review function if they insisted on this. But this does not always happen. The HMCPSI report on domestic violence cases found that after CPS review the vast majority of cases proceeded on the correct charge, but they concluded that some 9 per cent of cases had not proceeded on the correct charge even after CPS review of the file:

'Overcharging by the police, and no action by the CPS to address it in the early stages of the case, can raise the expectations of victims unnecessarily. It can have a particularly negative effect if the charge is reduced at a later stage, in terms of retaining the commitment of the victim to the prosecution.'[82]

One of the expectations of the statutory charging arrangements was that they would reduce the amounts of overcharging and downgrading by ensuring that the correct charge is laid in the first place. There is no research on this, but when the 2008 review by the Inspectorates examined file quality it assessed 25 per cent as good, 45 per cent as adequate, and 30 per cent as poor, adding that file quality appeared to have some correlation with the success of the outcome.[83] This is hardly a ringing endorsement of statutory charging, and may be thought to lend some credence to the fears of those who have suggested that closer working between police and prosecutor might increase rather than reduce the tendency to pursue a weak case if the incident is serious. 'The momentum towards trial builds. The expectation of all parties including victims tend to support the continuance of the case,'[84] but eventually the pressure to accept a plea to a lesser offence may persuade the reviewing lawyer that a bird in the hand is worth two in the bush.

(E) DISCONTINUANCE

Section 23 of the Prosecution of Offences Act 1985 gives the CPS the power to discontinue charges brought in the magistrates' courts. However, ever since the CPS was founded there has been criticism that the CPS discontinues too high a proportion of cases, and the White Paper of 2002 referred to the 13 per cent discontinuance rate in the context of 'what is not working' in the system.[85] If one consults the annual reports of the CPS, the percentage of cases discontinued in the magistrates' courts (including bind-overs)[86] stood at 16.2 per cent in 2001–02 but declined to 13.8 per cent by 2003–04, to 10.9 per cent in 2006–07 and then to 8.7 per cent by 2008–09.[87] The straightforward interpretation of this substantial change is that, prior to 2004, the police laid the ori-

---

[82] HMCPSI, *Violence at Home* (2004), para 7.54.

[83] HMCPSI and HMIC, *Review of the New Charging Arrangements* (2008), paras 12.11–12.16.

[84] Jeremy, 'The Prosecutor's Rock and a Hard Place', at 935.

[85] Home Office, *Justice for All* (2002), 51.

[86] That is, the figure now includes cases that were discontinued when the defendant agreed to be bound over to keep the peace for, usually, a year. This shadowy practice calls for principled examination.

[87] CPS, *Annual Report 2003–2004*, Annex A, 5; CPS, *Annual Report 2008–2009*, Annex B, 5.

ginal charge, often without consulting the CPS, and that was why a higher proportion of them had to be discontinued on subsequent review by the CPS; and that since
2004, as statutory charging has become embedded in police and prosecutorial practices, the initial charge is more likely to be accurate and there should be fewer occasions on which it proves necessary to discontinue. Why were cases discontinued? The
Inspectorate's 2007 review of discontinuance found that 43 per cent were discontinued because of insufficient evidence, 24 per cent on public interest grounds, and 26 per
cent 'unable to proceed' (which usually means that a key witnesses refused to give evidence). The discontinuance rate for domestic violence rates was higher than for most
other offences, as discussed in Part 4(a) above. Many of the discontinuances were also
for motoring or public order offences that were charged initially by the police, since
they fall outside the statutory charging scheme. Nonetheless, the Inspectorate raises
some doubts about the quality of pre-charge decisions by prosecutors, over 10 per cent
of which were found not to have complied with the full code test, and also about delays
in decision making about discontinuance, which affected more than a quarter of the
discontinued cases.[88] These are important findings, but it is now necessary to have a
fuller programme of academic research into these key CPS decisions.

For example, Mhlanga's research showed that a much higher proportion of prosecutions brought against non-white defendants were discontinued than against white
defendants, and that the grounds were mostly evidential, suggesting that more charges
were brought against non-white defendants when the evidence was weak:[89] is statutory
charging and collocation likely to result in more of those cases being charged correctly
in the first instance?

This discussion of discontinuance should not omit reference to 'public interest' factors, which account for around 30 per cent of all discontinuances in the magistrates'
courts. On CPS figures from the mid-1990s, half of these were cases in which a very
small or nominal penalty was thought likely, and a further quarter were cases in which
a caution was thought more appropriate.[90] One comparative measure here is the proportion of sentences in court that are 'very small or nominal'. It is difficult to find a
precise figure for this, since there is no record of the number of small fines handed
down by the courts; equally, it could be argued that in some circumstances a conditional discharge is neither very small nor nominal.[91] But it is worth pointing out that
the use of discharges for indictable offences has increased considerably since the CPS
was created, so that in 2007 some 53,000 adult male offenders received a discharge

[88] HMCPSI, *Discontinuance* (2007), paras 4.7–4.16.

[89] G. Barclay and B. Mhlanga, *Ethnic Differences in Decisions on Young Defendants Dealt With by the Crown Prosecution Service* (2000). See further HMCPSI, *A Follow Up Review of CPS Casework with a Minority Ethnic Dimension* (2004), paras 11.13–11.23, suggesting that the over-charging of minority ethnic defendants remains an issue.

[90] National Audit Office, *Crown Prosecution Service* (1997), 42.

[91] A conditional discharge may be for a period of up to three years: if the offender commits a further offence during the specified period, he is liable to be sentenced for both the new offence and the offence for which the conditional discharge was granted.

and some 17,000 adult female offenders.[92] Whether the arrival of conditional cautions will have an effect on these figures remains to be seen, but they might be taken to suggest that fewer cases (even of indictable offences) need to be prosecuted. However, as argued in Chapter 6 above, that depends on agreement as to which cases should be diverted from court and which should be dealt with judicially.

(f) ACQUITTALS BY THE JUDGE

Whereas discontinuance rates have (not always rightly) been taken as a measure of CPS performance in summary cases, so in Crown Court cases the performance of the CPS has sometimes been measured according to how frequently cases end in an acquittal by the judge. Acquittals by judge are of two different types. A judge-ordered acquittal occurs where the prosecutor informs the court that the CPS does not wish to proceed, and the judge formally orders the jury to acquit. A directed acquittal occurs during or at the end of the prosecution's case in court, if the judge decides that there is insufficient evidence on one or more elements of the offence. Research by Block, Corbett and Peay in the early 1990s suggested that dispassionate scrutineers could identify weak cases among those that ended in acquittals by the judge: a minimum of 22 per cent of acquittals occurred in cases that were regarded as foreseeably flawed in the opinion of a trained prosecutor,[93] and the researchers' own assessments led them to state that:

'although fewer than half of ordered acquittals were considered definitely or possibly foreseeable, three quarters of directed acquittals were so classified. This supports our view, derived from the study, that directed acquittals result largely from weak cases that should have been discontinued, whereas ordered acquittals result largely from unforeseeable circumstances.'[94]

Baldwin conducted a somewhat similar enquiry for the CPS in 1995, with a sample of around 100 cases ending in acquittal by judge and some 70 other cases. He found that the ordered acquittals occurred chiefly where a key witness retracted a statement or failed to arrive at court (48 per cent), the judge took the view at the outset that the case was too weak (16 per cent), or the case was terminated following the convictions of other people (14 per cent). The directed acquittals occurred chiefly because a key witness failed to come up to proof (34 per cent), or there were problems of law or admissibility of evidence (32 per cent) or the judge ruled the evidence insufficient (12 per cent).[95] The important question is how many of these were foreseeable and ought to have led to earlier discontinuance. Baldwin found that around 41 per cent of all cases resulting in acquittal had reservations of a prosecutor entered upon the file at an early stage, and a further 35 per cent of files mentioned reservations but dis-

[92] *Sentencing Statistics England and Wales 2007*, Table 1.5.
[93] B. Block, C. Corbett and J. Peay, *Ordered and Directed Acquittals in the Crown Court* (1993).
[94] *Ibid.*, 100.   [95] Baldwin, above n 91, 539.

counted them. His conclusions ran along two main lines. One was the acute difficulty of judging witness credibility and reliability, on the basis of either case files or discussions with police officers on the case. The advent of pre-trial witness interviews might improve matters here.[96] The other was that three characteristics of some prosecutors—inexperience, lack of self-confidence, and the sharing of values with the police—meant that some cases were not terminated as early as they should have been.[97] In particular, Baldwin found that:

'some prosecutors share a common value system with the police, a core element of which is that serious cases ought to be prosecuted, almost irrespective of considerations as to evidential strength. Cases have developed a considerable momentum by the time of committal, and expectations build up that cases will proceed to the Crown Court. In such circumstances, it is easy to understand why some prosecutors, particularly when lacking in experience or self-confidence, hesitate in making hard decisions in complex or serious cases.'[98]

Too often, therefore, cases were allowed to 'run'. To the extent that some of these characteristics remain, judgement must be reserved on expectations that statutory charging, with police and prosecutors working together, will lead to significant changes.[99]

Baldwin also found that, especially in serious cases, some prosecutors were reluctant to make the 'tough' decision of terminating a weak case, but would rather pass the responsibility for the decision to the court. As one prosecutor commented, 'the proper forum for deciding whether a person is telling the truth is the jury'.[100] Baldwin comments that this attitude 'can often be a superficial cop-out', but it is at least worth acknowledging that the jury system can make this sort of reasoning attractive. A similar attitude surfaced in the Stephen Lawrence Inquiry.

The initial prosecution of the murder of Stephen Lawrence was discontinued, largely owing to problems with the eyewitness evidence in the case. The prosecutor's decision was challenged during the inquiry by counsel for the Lawrence family, who argued that in making the decision the prosecutor was taking over the role 'of the judge or the jury', but the inquiry found that the decision had been perfectly proper.[101] One might find some support for the 'leave it to the jury' approach in the law of evidence: as we will see in Chapter 11, the *Galbraith* test does depict questions of credibility as being exclusively within the domain of the jury. When this is coupled with the ambiguity of the evidential sufficiency test (as between a predictive or intrinsic merits test), it is not surprising that prosecutors should allude to the role of the jury when continuing with a borderline case. Our view is that, however difficult the decision, the paramount principle is that weak cases should not go to court. Prosecutors should not dodge their

96 P. Roberts and C. Saunders, 'Introducing Pre-Trial Witness Interviews' [2008] *Crim LR* 831.
97 Baldwin, 551.   98 *Ibid.*, 551.
99 Anecdotal evidence given to the House of Commons Justice Committee led it to insist that the different responsibilities of police and CPS should not become blurred as a result of working more closely together: *Crown Prosecution Service* (2009), paras 26 and 31.
100 *Ibid.*   101 Sir W. Macpherson, *The Stephen Lawrence Inquiry* (1999), paras 39–30 to 39–32.

responsibility by arguing that the decision is for the jury, since it is their prior decision whether the evidence is strong enough to justify putting the defendant on trial.

Returning to acquittals by judge, is it right to regard these as a measure of CPS efficiency? The CPS resists this on the ground that judge-directed acquittals may simply mean that a key witness failed to come up to proof when the prosecution believed that they would. Thus the CPS Inspectorate found in 1999 that some 78 per cent of cases in which a magistrates' court or judge dismissed the prosecution were cases which 'failed for reasons that the CPS could not have foreseen'.[102] It seems that judge-directed acquittals fell from 12 per cent of contested trials in 1991–92 to 7 per cent of contested hearings in 2002–03.[103] It is difficult to assess the current position: the latest CPS statistics show a continuing decline in judge-directed acquittals in the Crown Court, from 1,254 in 2006–07 to 990 in 2008–09,[104] whereas the *Judicial Statistics* show a fairly steady number of acquittals by judge from 2004 (1,536) through 2006 (1,698), dropping slightly in 2008 (1,497).[105] It is therefore unclear whether this represents an improvement in the quality of preparation of cases and assessments of whether witnesses will come up to proof. In 2003–04 some 15 per cent of cases sent to the Crown Court resulted in a judge-ordered acquittal when the CPS offered no evidence because the realistic prospect of conviction had gone, or where a defendant had serious medical problems; or when witnesses went missing; or where the defendant has already been dealt with for other offences; CPS figures indicate that the percentage had declined to 11.7 by 2008–09,[106] whereas the *Judicial Statistics* show a steady rise in the number of cases discharged by the judge, from 9,036 in 2004 through 9,919 in 2006 to 10,245 in 2008.[107] It is a great pity that neither the statistics nor even the trends are consistent. In cases which are to be heard in the Crown Court the CPS has no other opportunity to drop the charges save by offering no evidence. Whether the weakness that leads to a change of mind should have been identified earlier is a matter on which the research by Baldwin and by Block, Corbett and Peay casts light, but the proportion of cases in which this is so cannot be estimated with confidence.

7.5 THE ROLE OF THE VICTIM

To reflect 'the increasing importance attached to the role of the victim in the criminal justice system', CPS documents now refer more explicitly to the 'views of victims' rather than simply to the 'interests of victims'. However, the Code for Crown Prosecutors

---

[102] CPSI, *Adverse Cases* (1999), para 2.4.

[103] CPS, *Annual Report 2002–03*, 34; the figures are presented differently in the *Annual Report 2003–2004*, Annex A, 8, but the total numbers of judge-directed acquittals are certainly not declining.

[104] CPS, *Annual Report 2008–09*, Annex B, 10.   [105] *Judicial Statistics 2008*, Table 6.8.

[106] CPS, *Annual Report 2003–04.*, Annex A, 8; and CPS, *Annual Report 2008–09*, Annex B, 10. These figures include defendants bound over to keep the peace, some of whom would be persons already dealt with for other offences.

[107] *Judicial Statistics 2008*, Table 6.8.

now adopts somewhat confusing language, stating that 'prosecutors should take into account any views expressed by the victim regarding the impact that the offence has had'.[108] Slightly differently, the CPS statement on 'Care and Treatment of Victims and Witnesses' refers to views as well as interests:

'The CPS acts in the public interest and not just in the interests of any one individual. The interests of the victim are nonetheless important when deciding where the public interest lies, and the CPS will take account of the consequences for the victim of the decision whether or not to prosecute and will consider any views expressed by the victim or victim's family.'[109]

There is now a contrast with the Lord Chief Justice's guidance to courts on dealing with Victim Personal Statements: 'the opinions of the victim or the victim's close relatives as to what the sentence should be are therefore not relevant, unlike the consequence of the offence on them.'[110] It is not clear why the CPS should promise to consider the views of the victim or victim's family if the decision is to be taken on public interest grounds, and this form of guidance may create expectations among victims that the CPS should not create. Indeed, the Justice Committee of the House of Commons rightly detected a confusion in the CPS's statements on this, deriving from some of the Government's claims to be 'rebalancing the criminal justice system in favour of the victim.' The Committee's recommendation is clear and strong:

'Telling a victim that their views are central to the criminal justice system, or that the prosecutor is their champion, is a damaging misrepresentation of reality. Expectations have been raised that will inevitably be disappointed. Furthermore, the criminal justice system is set up to represent the public rather than individuals, and there are good reasons for this. The CPS's role as independent arbiter of decisions about prosecution is critical. Explaining this role clearly to victims such that their expectations are managed realistically, rather than raised then disappointed, is vital.'[111]

This receives a particular application in domestic violence cases in which a victim withdraws a complaint or statement, and wants the prosecution to be dropped. In her 1990s research Carolyn Hoyle found that 'the CPS rarely proceeded with a case once the victim had withdrawn'.[112] The CPS Inspectorate concluded in 1998 that, in cases of victim withdrawal, 'we are not satisfied that the policy is being applied correctly or, on occasions, at all'—the policy being to proceed if possible, without reference to the victim's wishes.[113] When Her Majesty's Crown Prosecution Service Inspectorate (HMCPSI) conducted its further review in 2004 to monitor progress in dealing with domestic violence, it found that around 44 per cent of withdrawal

---

[108] Code for Crown Prosecutors (2010), para 4.18.
[109] CPS, *Care and Treatment of Victims and Witnesses* (amended 8 April 2009).
[110] *Practice Direction (Victim Personal Statements)* [2002] 1 Cr App R 69, at para 3(c).
[111] House of Commons Justice Committee, *The Crown Prosecution Service* (2009), para 83.
[112] C. Hoyle, *Negotiating Domestic Violence* (1998), 170.
[113] HMCPSI, *Cases involving Domestic Violence* (1998), para 12.3.

cases were proceeded with, but commented that this left 'scope for improvement' and
that 'appropriate consultation with the police was not commonplace.'[114] As stated in
Part 7.4(a) above, the Inspectorate's 2007 report on discontinuance again raised questions about the high discontinuance rate of domestic violence cases, and argued for
improved pre-charge decision making.[115] In these cases, then, it is clear that the victim's (expressed) wishes should certainly not hold sway. Michelle Dempsey advances
strong reasons in favour of this response, as promoting the effective prosecution of
domestic violence in the context of a public prosecution system.[116] She also argues that
victims cannot claim a moral right to be a party in the criminal trial, not least because
this would transform the public element in criminal trials, in terms of 'the political
community call[ing] the defendant to account'.[117] This is a further indication that the
CPS, in its various statements on the treatment of victims, has gone too far.

However, there is one situation in which the victim's views ought to be heeded—
where the victim wants compensation from the offender. The CPS has a duty to press
for compensation where the victim expresses a wish for it, and to make sure that the
necessary information is available. The advent of conditional cautions (discussed in
Chapter 6.4 above) provides prosecutors with a possible means of securing compensation to the victim without prosecuting, and the CPS publication 'Conditional Cautions
for Victims' claims that 'significant numbers of victims are receiving compensation
far quicker than if they had to wait for a criminal process'.[118]

The Domestic Violence, Crime and Victims Act 2004 introduced a statutory Code
of Practice for Victims of Crime that imposes various duties on the CPS in relation to
communication with victims and victims' families. Additionally, the CPS has published 'The Prosecutor's Pledge', which includes direct promises to victims relating to
their care and treatment during the prosecution process.

7.6 DISCRETION: REFINING THE CRIMINAL LAW

We have already noted that there is a great deal of 'Legal Guidance' on the CPS
website. Prosecutors have to reach judgements on evidential sufficiency and on the
public interest, as discussed in Parts 7.2 and 7.3 above, but there are also broader

---

[114] HMCPSI, *Violence at Home* (2004), Appendix 5, R12.

[115] HMCPSI and HMIC, *Discontinuance* (2007), paras 3.11–3.14 and 4.15. See further, in the somewhat
analogous field of rape prosecutions, the comparative research of L. Ellison, 'Promoting Effective Case-
Building in Rape Cases: a Comparative Perspective' [2007] *Crim LR* 691.

[116] M. M. Dempsey, *Prosecuting Domestic Violence* (2009), esp Ch 8; Dempsey argues strongly for a further reason, that the State and public prosecutors should act so as to denounce the patriarchy evident in
domestic violence cases.

[117] *Ibid.*, 196.

[118] Unfortunately, at least one case reveals that procedures to consult victims on compensation are not
always observed: *R (on the application of Guest) v Director of Public Prosecutions* [2009] *Crim LR* 730.

policy questions that are left to the CPS. A new offence, such as causing death by careless driving (Road Safety Act 2006) or corporate manslaughter (Corporate Manslaughter and Corporate Homicide Act 2007), requires a sentencing policy for the courts to apply—supplied by the Sentencing Guidelines Council—and also a prosecution policy for the CPS to follow. The CPS creates these policies for itself, no doubt after discussion with relevant law officers, and they have particular importance. They effectively define the ambit of the offence, insofar as they include some factual variations and exclude others. Moreover, there are questions of the ambit of the criminal law that are deliberately left to the CPS to decide. A recent high-profile example concerns the offence of aiding and abetting suicide: in *R (on the application of Purdy) v Director of Public Prosecutions*,[119] the House of Lords allowed an application that called for the Director of Public Prosecutions to set out the factors considered relevant for and against prosecuting someone who renders assistance to another person who is terminally ill or severely and incurably disabled and who intends to commit suicide.[120] Another example is provided by the extensive list of offences against children created by the Sexual Offences Act 2003. In broad terms the Act criminalizes all consensual sexual touching between children, so that two 15-year-olds who kiss or fondle each other commit an offence. At the time the Government's argument was that CPS guidance would prevent inappropriate prosecutions, but that a strict law is necessary to ensure that anyone who takes advantage of a child sexually can be prosecuted to conviction. The difficulty with this argument is that provisions in many other jurisdictions (and, soon, in Scotland)[121] frame the law so as to exclude many interactions between children, usually by stating that the offence is not committed where the ages of the two young people are no more than two years apart. English law leaves this question to the CPS, whose guidance contains no such clear rule but sets out various considerations that will point in the direction of non-prosecution or prosecution. The structure of this part of sexual offences law is open to criticism, and may indeed be contrary to the European Convention on Human Rights;[122] the important point in the present context, however, is that a considerable amount of discretion has been left to the CPS deliberately by the legislators. Whereas it might be said that the charging standards and legal guidance issued by the CPS on most offences amounts merely to refining the law, the significance of the discretion in some areas (such as sexual offences involving the young) amounts to a power, for all practical purposes, to define the law.

---

[119] [2009] UKHL 45.

[120] *Ibid.*, at para 55 *per* Lord Hope. The speech of his Lordship contains a detailed examination of the history and structure of prosecutorial discretion in this country.

[121] See J. R. Spencer, 'Child and Family Offences' [2004] *Crim LR* 347, and Sexual Offences (Scotland) Act 2009.

[122] The House of Lords held that it is compatible with the Convention, in *G* [2008] UKHL 37; cf the critical comments at [2008] *Crim LR* 819.

7.7 ACCOUNTABILITY

To what authorities and to what extent are prosecutors accountable? The absence of clear and effective lines of accountability for many regulatory agencies was discussed in the previous chapter. The focus here will be chiefly upon the CPS.

(A) ACCOUNTABILITY TO PARLIAMENT

The CPS is organized hierarchically, with its local branches (42 areas, and CPS Direct), and a headquarters. Internal lines of accountability end with the Director of Public Prosecutions. He or she is answerable to the Attorney General, who has ministerial responsibility for the general policies pursued by the CPS but not in respect of decisions taken in individual cases. There is thus no accountability to Parliament for decisions in individual cases, but it is the practice of Members of Parliament to refer to the Director of Public Prosecutions individual cases brought to their attention by constituents or others. The Director will usually reply by letter, giving some reason for the decision (often, a decision to discontinue a prosecution). There is, however, no independent complaints mechanism.[123] The CPS is also open to scrutiny by the Justice Committee of the House of Commons and by the National Audit Office.[124] As we saw earlier, the Prosecution of Offences Act 1985 imposes on the Director a statutory responsibility to issue a code, and to report annually to Parliament. The annual reports now have to record the CPS's performance in relation to Government targets, but apart from that they have always tended to be written in the style of Voltaire's Dr Pangloss, and omit certain important topics such as conditional cautions (for which no statistics are given).

That marks a significant contrast to the reports of the principal source of CPS accountability, HMCPSI. By the mid-1990s there was still no inspectorate of the CPS, unlike the established inspectorates of constabulary, probation and then the prisons, and it is to the credit of the CPS that it set up its own internal inspectorate, which issued several critical reports.[125] In 2000, HMCPSI was formally established, and it has continued to issue searching reports on the performance of local CPS areas and on a number of general themes across areas. We have quoted from its report on *Violence at Home* in Part 4 of this chapter, and also from its recent reports on Discontinuance and on the New Charging Arrangements. Attention should also be drawn to the thematic review of rape cases, where the Inspectorate was critical of the quality of file endorsements (absence of reasons

---

[123] The House of Commons Justice Committee describes this as a 'serious weakness': *The Crown Prosecution Service* (2009), para 98.

[124] *Ibid.*; and National Audit Office, *Crown Prosecution Service: Effective Use of Magistrates' Courts Hearings* (2006).

[125] E.g. the report on *Cases involving Domestic Violence* (n 115 above and accompanying text), and its report on *Central Casework Section* (1999).

for decisions) and also detected elements of inconsistency in key decisions which led to a recommendation that all decisions to drop or substantially to reduce the charge should be discussed with a second specialist lawyer.[126] The report also notes plenty of good practice in dealing with these sensitive cases, but it certainly does not give the impression that everything is for the best, as the CPS annual reports tend to do.

(B) ACCOUNTABILITY TO THE COURTS

The courts have stated many times their willingness to review decisions not to prosecute. It was established in the first *Blackburn* case[127] that the courts would be prepared judicially to review a general policy not to prosecute for certain classes of offence, for example, all thefts with a value below £100. In the third *Blackburn* case,[128] Lord Denning MR suggested that the courts would also be prepared to review an individual decision not to prosecute, and this dictum has received subsequent judicial support.[129] The primary basis for judicial review would be that either the policy or the individual decision not to prosecute was unreasonable in a *Wednesbury* sense, that is, was such that no reasonable prosecuting authority would have adopted the policy or taken the decision.[130]

We saw in the last chapter that the Divisional Court has upheld such challenges to the decision not to prosecute and the decision to caution in several decisions.[131] In the *Manning* case,[132] the Divisional Court quashed a CPS decision not to bring a prosecution arising out of a death in custody. Lord Bingham CJ stated that the standard of review must not be set too high, on the ground that judicial review is the only means by which the citizen can seek redress against a decision not to prosecute. That is not entirely true, since it remains possible to mount a private prosecution (on which see (c) below). But such a prosecution requires considerable time and energy, and the whole purpose of a public prosecution system is to prevent citizens from having thus to exert themselves. The greater difficulty with the *Manning* decision is that it is confined to cases of death in custody: while Lord Bingham made it clear that the CPS ought to give reasons for not bringing a prosecution in such circumstances, there remains no obligation to give specific reasons for non-prosecution. Where reasons are given, the path to judicial review (and therefore effective accountability) is much easier. Thus in the *Jones* case,[133] judicial

---

[126] HMCPSI, *Report on the Joint Investigation into the Investigation and Prosecution of Cases Involving Allegations of Rape* (2002), para 8.54 and paras 8.69–8.78.

[127] *R v Metropolitan Police Commissioner, ex p Blackburn* [1968] 2 QB 118.

[128] *R v Metropolitan Police Commissioner, ex p Blackburn (No 3)* [1973] 1 QB 241.

[129] *R v General Council of the Bar, ex p Percival* [1990] 3 All ER 137.

[130] *Associated Provincial Picture Houses v Wednesbury Corporation* [1948] 1 KB 223.

[131] See Ch 6.5 above.

[132] *R v DPP, ex p Manning* [2001] QB 330, analysed by M. Burton, 'Reviewing Crown Prosecution Service Decisions not to Prosecute' [2001] *Crim LR* 374; see also *R (on application of Joseph) v Director of Public Prosecutions* [2001] *Crim LR* 489.

[133] *R v DPP, ex p Jones* [2000] *Crim LR* 858.

review of a decision not to bring a manslaughter charge was granted on the ground that the Director of Public Prosecutions had failed to apply the law correctly to the facts. However, in *R (on the application of Guest) v Director of Public Prosecutions*[134] the court quashed a decision to administer a conditional caution (and, with it, the decision not to prosecute) in a case where the Code for Crown Prosecutors had clearly been misapplied—failing to prosecute for a serious assault—and the Director's Guidance on Conditional Cautions had also been misapplied. Whether a subsequent prosecution (by the CPS or a private prosecutor) would then be quashed for abuse of process was left open.

Accountability for decisions to prosecute raises different issues. In *R v Chief Constable of Kent and another, ex parte L*,[135] the Divisional Court accepted that an individual decision to prosecute a juvenile could be subject to judicial review if it were clearly contrary to a settled policy of the Director of Public Prosecutions, i.e. the Code for Crown Prosecutors. Stuart-Smith LJ in the Divisional Court in *R v Inland Revenue Commissioners, ex parte Mead*,[136] accepted that judicial review of a decision to prosecute would also be possible where the applicant was an adult; the other member of the court, Popplewell J, disagreed with this. The House of Lords in the *Kebilene* case[137] held that an action for judicial review of a decision to prosecute should not be entertained unless there is evidence of dishonesty, bad faith or other exceptional circumstances—an approach that accords little significance to the pains of being prosecuted.[138]

Finally, the courts are willing to stay proceedings for abuse of process where the prosecutor is found to have manipulated the criminal process in some way.[139] The leading case is *Abu Hamza*,[140] where the Court of Appeal emphasized that it would rarely be in the public interest to stay proceedings, but that it was prepared to do so where there had been an unequivocal representation by a prosecutor, on which the defendant had acted to his detriment. It seems that the requirement of detriment may not be insisted on, where a clear decision not to prosecute has been communicated to a defendant.[141]

(C) ACCOUNTABILITY AND PRIVATE PROSECUTIONS

The right to bring a private prosecution still exists and, although the Director of Public Prosecutions has a statutory power to take over a private prosecution (and then to

---

[134] [2009] *Crim LR* 730. See also *R (on the application of Omar) v Chief Constable of Bedfordshire* [2002] EWHC 3060 (Admin).

[135] (1991) 93 Cr App R 416.   [136] [1993] 1 All ER 772.   [137] [2000] 2 AC 326.

[138] On which see Rogers, 'Restructuring the Exercise of Prosecutorial Discretion'.

[139] For detailed analysis, see A. Choo, *Abuse of Process and Judicial Stays of Criminal Proceedings* (2nd ed, 2008), Ch 2.

[140] [2007] QB 659.

[141] *H v Guildford Youth Court* [2008] EWHC 506 (Admin).

discontinue it, if this is thought advisable),[142] private prosecutions come before the courts each year in a small but not insignificant number of cases.[143] The rationale for retaining the right was that it serves as a safeguard against unjustified or unfair prosecutorial decisions, particularly inertia on the part of either police or CPS. Their Lordships were divided in *Jones v Whalley*,[144] Lord Bingham regarding the right of private prosecution as 'of questionable value' but Lord Mance regarding it as potentially significant. In *Jones v Whalley* itself the House of Lords held that a private prosecution may not be brought when the police or CPS have decided to issue a simple caution for an offence (and that would apply *a fortiori* to a conditional caution). Some would argue that the possibility of a judicial review of decisions by the CPS and police should be sufficient (see (b) above). There is also a strong argument that the nature of a private prosecution differs from that of a public prosecution, since a private prosecutor is bringing the case in order to achieve a particular end whereas a public prosecutor should act as a Minister of Justice (see Part 7.8 below). Sir Richard Buxton has therefore argued that private prosecutions in the Crown Court should always be conducted by counsel, and not by the applicant in person; and that in deciding whether to issue a summons to a private prosecutor, magistrates should take into account whether the prosecution is to be 'managed by counsel.'[145]

7.8 PROSECUTORIAL ETHICS

The CPS Code spells out the objective of impartiality:

'Prosecutors must be fair, independent and objective. They must not let any personal views about the ethnic or national origin, gender, disability, age, religion or belief, political views, sexual orientation, or gender identity of the suspect, victim or any witness influence their decisions. Neither must prosecutors be affected by improper or undue pressure from any source.'[146]

This aspect of an ethical orientation to prosecuting concerns fairness as impartiality, in terms of non-discrimination and non-susceptibility to pressures from others. It will be no less important in the context of the statutory charging, where prosecutors work more closely with the police, and where prosecutors for the first time have direct responsibility for a form of diversion from prosecution (conditional cautions).

What about the specific ethical principles of prosecuting cases that have been charged? It may be claimed that each crown prosecutor, as a solicitor or barrister, is

---

[142] Prosecution of Offences Act 1985, s 6(2), as interpreted in *R v Director of Public Prosecutions, ex p Duckenfield* [2000] 1 WLR 55.

[143] L. H. Leigh, 'Private Prosecutions and Diversionary Justice' [2007] *Crim LR* 289, at 293–5.

[144] [2006] UKHL 41.

[145] R. Buxton, 'The Private Prosecutor as Minister of Justice' [2009] *Crim LR* 427, at 431.

[146] Code for Crown Prosecutors (2010), para 2.4.

governed by the ethical code of the relevant professional organization.[147] In Chapter 3 we reviewed the various formulations of the prosecutor's role, as a kind of 'Minister of Justice' concerned with obtaining convictions without unfairness to defendants. Various international documents now deal with these broader questions about the prosecutor's role, including the United Nations Guidelines on the Role of Prosecutors (1990), the standards agreed in 1999 by the International Association of Prosecutors, and the Council of Europe's recommendation on the role of public prosecutors (2000).[148] The role has been characterized in the US Supreme Court by stating that the prosecutor:

'is in a peculiar and very definite sense the servant of the law, the twofold aim of which is that guilt shall not escape or innocence suffer...It is as much his duty to refrain from improper methods calculated to produce a wrongful conviction as it is to use every legitimate means to bring about a just one.'[149]

The importance of these statements lies in their endorsement of the argument, developed in Chapter 3 above, that the protection of rights should be regarded as part of the law, and not as standing in opposition to the proper role of police or prosecutors. Whilst it is true that defence lawyers have the primary task of securing the defendant's rights, prosecutors should neither indulge in nor condone unlawful or unethical practices. They should show no less respect for fairness and human rights, as embodied in principles such as those set out in Chapter 2, than for the obtaining of convictions of the guilty. Paragraph 2.6 of the Code enjoins prosecutors to apply the principles of the European Convention on Human Rights; but we have seen, particularly in Parts 3 and 4 of this chapter, that an organization that works closely with the police may—on some occasions at least—become 'prosecution-minded' to an extent that compromises this broader ethical position. One way of tackling this would be to draw up some practical ethical guidance directed at the kinds of situation in which conflicts of this kind are likely to arise. Guidance cannot always overwhelm occupational cultures and other more subtle pressures, but it is one step in that direction.

7.9 CONCLUSIONS

This chapter has outlined the purpose and functions of the CPS, evaluated some of the principles they proclaim, and examined empirical evidence of their performance of their various tasks. We have noted that, as with other large organizations, formulating

---

[147] See M. Blake and A. Ashworth, 'Some Ethical Issues in Prosecuting and Defending Criminal Cases' [1998] *Crim LR* 16.

[148] Council of Europe, Recommendation R 19 (2000), *The Role of Public Prosecution in the Criminal Justice System*. See generally International Association of Prosecutors, *Standards for Prosecutors: an Analysis of the United Kingdom National Prosecuting Agencies* (2006).

[149] *Berger v United States* 294 US 78 (1935), *per* Sutherland J at 88.

the principles and the guidance satisfactorily is not sufficient to ensure that they are implemented in practice. Frank recognition of the gap between rhetoric and reality is rare in the CPS's own documents, but the presence of the Inspectorate (and the publication of a small number of research reports)[150] ensures that a more realistic view of the prosecution system can be obtained.

In this concluding section we raise four general issues. First, are the new charging arrangements leading prosecutors to reach judgements more or less independently than under the previous system? It has always been a problem for the CPS that their information comes almost entirely from the police,[151] who may construct a case in a way designed to dispose the prosecutor towards a particular outcome. There seem to be two key questions: first, is there a danger that prosecutors who have to deal with police officers on a day-by-day basis come to adopt an anti-defendant and pro-prosecution philosophy, of the kind that leads them to 'run' cases where in truth the evidence is weak? We have noted that Baldwin's research suggested this, and that anecdotal evidence presented to the Justice Committee raised the issue again.[152] The related question is whether, on the other hand, prosecutors are now tending to under-charge because of the pressure of targets, which count any conviction rather than a conviction for the most appropriate offence as a positive outcome. Again, the Justice Committee heard this raised by police officers as a possibility, and the Director of Public Prosecutions' response was that there is no evidence of under-charging. But, as the Justice Committee pointed out, the position is just that—no evidence—and it is unsatisfactory that there is no monitoring or evaluation of this crucial issue.[153] The complexity of these issues is increased by the recent announcement of a pilot study that will assess the effects of moving more charging decisions back to the police (see Part 7.1 above).

Secondly, what should be the role of the CPS in relation to out-of-court disposals? In Chapter 6 we saw that the increase in diversion through out-of-court disposals is a major feature of contemporary criminal justice, but that the central role of the police and other agencies with law enforcement duties is questionable. This suggests that the Criminal Justice Act 2003 was right to bestow on the CPS the power to offer conditional cautions to offenders, although evaluation of their use is awaited, and it is disturbing to find that in some areas conditional cautions are being authorized by lay caseworkers without proper supervision from CPS lawyers.[154] That could undermine the whole initiative, since part of its rationale is that legal qualified prosecutors may be seen as quasi-judicial officials who can rightly be trusted to exercise these powers fairly. Public prosecutors in many other countries have had similar powers for some

---

[150] The CPS has published on its own website the fairly critical John Report on possible racial bias: see n 64 above.

[151] Cf however the consultation paper on CPS interviews of witnesses, above, nn 37 and 38.

[152] See the references in nn 97–9 above.

[153] House of Commons Justice Committee, *Crown Prosecution Service* (2009), paras 34–45.

[154] *R (on the application of Guest) v Director of Public Prosecutions* [2009] *Crim LR* 730 (caseworker grossly misapplied guidance on conditional cautions and prosecutions, evidently without supervision).

years[155]—even in Scotland, where the 'fiscal fine' established itself in the 1990s.[156] It is a dispositive power, akin to sentencing, and that is why both the CPS guidance and actual practices (including the deployment of law caseworkers) need to be assessed at an early stage. The problem at the moment, as identified in Chapter 6 above and by the Justice Committee, is that there is no overall scheme or consistency. One indication of the absence of a scheme or rationale is the Director of Public Prosecutions' statement to the Justice Committee that it is wrong to assume that all or most cases attracting a caution or conditional caution, for example, would otherwise have gone to court;[157] yet the idea of taking cases away from courts was one of the motivating forces behind the increase in these powers, as we saw in Chapter 6, and some would regard it as an alarming example of net-widening that the powers are being used otherwise. The problem is that the powers have mushroomed without any overall plan or control. The Justice Committee is right to recommend a thorough review.[158] Thirdly, the tension between the CPS as a national organization and as a local service needs to be managed with care. The national model was embraced by the original reforms, but there has long been evidence of local variations. More importantly, the Government now envisages greater community engagement and has announced the introduction of 'community prosecutors' in certain areas in 2009–10. The Justice Committee is right to question this development, asking 'what kind of local discretion is desirable and beneficial to the public interest'. It questions 'how local responsiveness can be made compatible with the demands of natural justice for system-wide consistency.'[159]

Fourthly, there remains the need urgently to confront the fundamental issues of social fairness raised by the different enforcement and prosecution policies of the CPS and the so-called regulatory agencies. The arrival of conditional cautions gives the CPS the opportunity to re-assess its own role in diversion. However, there remain broader issues of fairness that need to be tackled on a wider criminal justice canvas. The different policies of the CPS and the various regulatory agencies (which tend not to prosecute frequently, but to prefer forms of diversion) mean that citizens who commit offences that are of roughly equivalent seriousness may receive a very different response according to the agency that deals with enforcement. There is a need for a general review of the proper policies to be pursued by the so-called regulatory agencies, as well as the CPS, and also for a new system of accountability that applies the same standards to the CPS and the other agencies.[160] If equality before the law and equal treatment are to be realistic aspirations, this glaring anomaly in English criminal justice must no longer be left unchallenged. The Justice Committee noted the disparities and commended the Attorney General for starting work on bringing together

---

[155] J. Fionda, *Public Prosecutors and Discretion: a Comparative Study* (1995); A. Selih, 'The Prosecution Process' in Council of Europe, *Crime and Criminal Justice in Europe* (2000), 103.

[156] For discussion, see P. Duff and N. Hutton (eds), *Criminal Justice in Scotland* (1999), Ch 7.

[157] House of Commons Justice Committee, *Crown Prosecution Service* (2009), para 51.

[158] *Ibid.*, para 59.   [159] *Ibid.*, para 114.

[160] See White, 'Investigators and Prosecutors', at 159–60.

the diverse prosecuting agencies. But the Committee did not recommend that the CPS should become the single prosecuting authority for all agencies, as in Scotland,[161] and more importantly it failed to highlight the social justice implications of the current situation.

FURTHER READING

ROGERS, J., 'Restructuring the Exercise of Prosecutorial Discretion in England' (2006) 26 *Oxford JLS* 775.

JEREMY, D., 'The Prosecutor's Rock and Hard Place' [2008] *Crim LR* 925.

HOUSE OF COMMONS JUSTICE COMMITTEE, *The Crown Prosecution Service: Gatekeeper of the Criminal Justice System*, London: The Stationery Office, 2009.

Questions for Discussion

1. Are the evidential tests in the Code for Crown Prosecutors satisfactory both in principle and in their operation?

2. Is the public interest test in the Code for Crown Prosecutors satisfactory both in principle and in its operation?

3. Is there a strong case for making the CPS responsible for all prosecutorial decision making, including prosecutions that regulatory agencies and local authorities wish to initiate?

---

[161] *Ibid.*, paras 134–6, where the Committee did at least recommend that the remit of the Crown Prosecution Service Inspectorate should be extended to cover all other prosecuting agencies.

8

REMANDS BEFORE TRIAL

The bail/custody decision raises some of the most acute conflicts in the whole criminal process. On the one hand there is the individual's right to liberty, safeguarded by Article 5 of the Convention, and the interest of a person arrested and charged with an offence in remaining at liberty until the trial has taken place. On the other hand, there is a public interest in security and in ensuring protection from crime. Some practitioners, politicians, and others have concluded that the way to deal with this conflict is in each case to balance the defendant's rights with the public interests. However, the vague notion of 'balancing' that is usually advanced in this context is manifestly inadequate. No judgement of balance can be properly reached until there is a clear appreciation of what rights defendants (and actual or potential victims) have at this stage, as well as fuller analysis of the content and legitimacy of the claimed public interests, and of the evidential foundations for predictions of risk. As will appear during the course of this chapter, there is a wide range of relevant considerations, combined with a dearth of practical information at some crucial stages. Because of the impact on the liberty of the defendant, the issues are too important to leave to wide expanses of little-regulated discretion, whether in the hands of police officers, magistrates or judges. The focus in this chapter will be on the issues of principle raised by the law and practice.[1]

To grant a person bail is to accept their claim to liberty in the period before the next official proceedings; bail may be unconditional or conditional. To refuse bail means that the consequence is likely to be a remand in custody, i.e. in prison. Questions of remand on bail or in custody arise at various stages in the criminal process. First, there is 'street bail', that is, the power of an officer who arrests a person for an offence to release the arrestee on bail, to report to a police station at a specified time.[2] Secondly, there is the possibility of police bail, granted at the police station, pending the first court appearance. Thirdly, there is the court's decision on remand between the first and the final court appearance. Fourthly, there is the question of remand after conviction and before sentence is passed, for example to allow

---

[1] For full accounts of the law and practice, see N. Corre and D. Wolchover, *Bail in Criminal Proceedings* (3rd ed, 2004).

[2] See the discussion in Part 2 of this chapter, below.

time for the preparation of a report on the defendant. And fifthly, there is the question of remand pending an appeal against verdict or sentence, which is the subject of a Practice Direction.[3] The fourth and fifth decisions will not be discussed here, and there will be only a few references to police bail and street bail. The principal focus is upon the court's decision whether to remand on bail or in custody between first appearance and trial.

8.1 REMANDS, RIGHTS AND RISK

What rights of a defendant are at stake here? Article 5(1) of the Convention declares the general right to liberty, but allows liberty to be taken away in six distinct situations, the third of which (in Article 5(1)(c)) is the lawful arrest or detention of a person in order to bring him before a competent legal authority on reasonable suspicion of having committed an offence.[4] Article 5(3) goes on to provide that persons detained under that paragraph shall be brought promptly before a court, and shall be entitled to trial within a reasonable time.[5] In applying these provisions, the European Court of Human Rights in Strasbourg has developed several distinct requirements. Its decisions have recognized four grounds for the refusal of bail: risk of absconding before trial, risk of interfering with the course of justice, risk of committing offences and risk to public order.[6] More importantly, the Strasbourg organs have insisted on a number of procedural guarantees during remand proceedings, and we will see later in the chapter how these have affected or might affect English law.

For the present, our starting point is provided by three principles that stand out in the Strasbourg jurisprudence. The first is that the basis for considering the application of Article 5 should always be a presumption of liberty and a presumption of innocence (taken, of course, from Article 6(2)). Thus in *Caballero v United Kingdom*,[7] the Commission stated that the judge:

'having heard the accused himself, must examine all the facts arguing for and against the interest of a genuine requirement of public interest justifying, with due regard to the presumption of innocence, a departure from the rule of respect for the accused's liberty.'

---

[3] *Practice Direction: Bail Pending Appeal* [1983] 1 WLR 1292.

[4] On 'reasonable suspicion', see Ch 4 above.

[5] For discussion of the rather clumsy drafting of Art 5(3) and the Court's interpretation of it, see B. Emmerson, A. Ashworth and A. Macdonald (eds), *Human Rights and Criminal Justice* (2nd ed, 2007), Ch 13B.

[6] For elaboration, see *ibid.*, Ch 13C, and E. Player, 'Remanding Women in Custody: Concerns for Human Rights' (2007) 70 *MLR* 402.

[7] (2000) 30 EHRR 643, at 652, endorsed by the Court at [21]. (The Commission decision was originally referred to as *CC v United Kingdom*, see [1999] *Crim LR* 228.)

The same passage goes on to articulate the second major principle prominent in the case law—the need to avoid stereotypical reasoning and to assess each case individually:

'For example, the danger of an accused's absconding cannot be gauged solely on the basis of the severity of the sentence risked.[8] As far as the danger of re-offending is concerned, a reference to a person's antecedents cannot suffice to justify refusing release.'[9]

There is also authority for a third principle, evident in both the remand decisions and the decisions on trial within a reasonable time—that courts should take care to impose the least restrictive regime on a defendant pending trial. Before depriving a defendant of liberty, courts must consider 'whether there [is] another way of safeguarding public security and preventing him from committing further offences',[10] an injunction that points in English law towards conditional bail in one of its forms. Other judgments emphasize the need for 'special diligence' and speed where a defendant is remanded in custody, rather than on bail.[11]

It is not difficult to understand the reasons for the rights declared in the Convention. In principle, it is quite wrong that anyone, including agents of law enforcement, should be able to make an arrest, bring a charge, and then, without proving that charge in court, secure the immediate detention of the defendant.[12] Detention without trial is widely regarded as an incident of totalitarianism, or at least an expedient to be contemplated only in an extreme kind of national emergency.[13] It therefore follows that any argument for depriving unconvicted individuals of their liberty in civil society ought to have peculiar strength. Indeed, that point is reinforced when one considers the potential consequences for the defendant of a loss of liberty before trial—not just the deprivation of freedom to live a normal life, often compounded by incarceration under the worst conditions in the prison system, but also restricted ability to prepare a defence to the charge, loss of job, strain on family relations and friendships, and often appearance in court in a deteriorated or demoralized condition. The higher rates of suicide and self-injury for unconvicted rather than convicted prisoners may have much to do with these adversities.[14]

No doubt it was considerations of this kind that led the Supreme Court of the United States to declare that:

'this traditional right to freedom before conviction permits the unhampered preparation of a defence and serves to prevent the infliction of punishment prior to conviction. Unless

---

[8] Citing *Yagci and Sargin v Turkey* (1992) 20 EHRR 505, para 52.

[9] Citing *Muller v France* (17 March 1997), para 44.

[10] *Clooth v Belgium* (1991) 14 EHRR 717, Commission at para 75; reiterated by the Court in *Jablonski v Poland* (2003) 36 EHRR 455, at [84].

[11] *Punzelt v Czech Republic* (2001) 33 EHRR 1159, at [73].

[12] See R. A. Duff, *Trials and Punishments* (1986), 140, arguing that in principle custodial remands before trial are utterly inconsistent with respect for individual citizens as rational agents.

[13] This, of course, is a major reason why the provisions in ss 21–29 of the Anti-Terrorism, Crime and Security Act 2001, authorizing the detention without trial of 'suspected international terrorists', were held inconsistent with the Convention in *A v Home Secretary* [2004] UKHL 56.

[14] A. Liebling and H. Krarup, *Suicide Attempts and Self-Injury in Male Prisons* (1993), 52.

this right to bail before trial is preserved, the presumption of innocence, secured only after centuries of struggle, would lose its meaning.'[15]

Thus in the years following this fine statement US law and practice tended to concentrate on the problem of securing the attendance of defendants at trial. However, surveys showed that courts were mostly using financial bonds (sureties) as the means to this end, and that the result was the pre-trial imprisonment of people too poor to raise the money for such a bond.[16] Congress passed the Federal Bail Reform Act in 1966, legislating for 'release on recognisance' rather than financial bonds as the normal pre-trial order.[17] The second phase was marked by a growing anxiety about the commission of offences by people on bail, a concern that culminated in Congress passing the Bail Reform Act of 1984. The main thrust of this Act was to move the rationale to prediction of future danger, allowing a court to authorise pre-trial detention if there was clear and convincing evidence that 'no condition or combination of conditions of pre-trial release will reasonably assure the safety of any other person and the community'.[18] When this was challenged in *United States v Salerno*,[19] the majority held that pre-trial detention on these grounds was essentially regulatory, since the intent of Congress was not to impose punishment on dangerous people but rather to protect 'the safety of the community';[20] thus, as pre-trial detention is intended to manage risks rather than inflict punishment, due process standards are not applicable.[21] The minority retorted that this approach 'merely redefine[s] any measure which is claimed to be punishment as "regulation" and, magically, the Constitution no longer prohibits its imposition'.[22] This kind of argument, which we will meet again in Chapter 13, raises two questions. First, what are the proper criteria for determining whether or not a measure amounts to punishment or a penalty? One element in that question is whether a measure can be classified as punishment as well as something else (e.g. prevention, regulation), or whether the categories should be regarded as mutually exclusive. Measures such as the detention of the mentally disordered, of persons subject to quarantine, of illegal immigrants pending deportation (as set out in Article 5.1 of the European Convention) are circumstances in which the State is justified in depriving a person of liberty even though that person has not been convicted of an offence—indeed, is not even suspected of one. Secondly, if a measure is classified as something different from punishment,

---

[15] *Stack v Boyle* 342 US 1 (1951), *per* Vinson CJ at 4.

[16] See C. Foote, 'Compelling Appearance in Court: Administration of Bail in Philadelphia' 102 *U Pa LR* 1031 (1954); on the subsequent research by the Vera Institute that led to the change in federal law, D. J. Freed and P. Wald, *Bail in the United States* (1964).

[17] For an outline, see P. R. Jones and J. S. Goldkamp, 'Judicial Guidelines for Pre-Trial Release: Research and Policy Developments in the United States' (1991) 30 *Howard JCJ* 140.

[18] See n 17 above and accompanying text.   [19] 481 US 739 (1987).

[20] Cf the reasoning of the Strasbourg Court on theconcept of punishment in *Welch v United Kingdom* (1995) 20 EHRR 247, holding that a measure can be punitive in effect even if it is preventive in intent.

[21] See the discussion by M. Feeley and J. Simon, 'Actuarial Justice: The New Emerging Criminal Law' in D. Nelken (ed), *The Futures of Criminology* (1994), 175–81.

[22] *United States v Salerno*, at 760 *per* Marshall and Brennan JJ; for discussion, see A Dershowitz, *Pre-Emption* (2006), 240–50.

what principles should be applied? In other words, we know the additional safeguards that apply to criminal proceedings involving punishment; but 'is it possible to articulate a consistent and workable jurisprudence of anticipatory governmental action'[23] or are we left with a jurisprudential black hole?[24] Whatever the classification of pre-trial detention, the justification must be strong and pressing in view of the deprivation of liberty involved. This shift from securing the defendant's attendance at trial to protecting the safety of the community occurred elsewhere at the same time,[25] raising deep questions about the presumption of innocence and detention without trial. In practice, however strong the presumption of liberty at the pre-trial stage, in all judicial systems there is some provision for that presumption to be rebutted. Typical grounds for refusing bail are the risk that the defendant will not appear for trial; the risk that the defendant will commit offences unless placed in detention; and the risk that the defendant might interfere with witnesses or otherwise obstruct justice. All these grounds for pre-trial detention are phrased in terms of risk: the State is using its power by authorizing the detention of certain people to reduce certain risks to other citizens and to the criminal justice system. Are these separate grounds justifiable reasons for depriving a person of liberty? If they are, do we have sufficient knowledge to be able to assess the risks accurately?

Let us consider the first of the three main grounds for refusing bail—that otherwise the defendant is unlikely to stand trial or, alternatively put, that there is a significant risk of absconding. In terms of justification, one key question concerns the relative social importance of ensuring that persons charged with offences attend their trial on the due date. Courts are rightly reluctant to hold a trial in a defendant's absence.[26] Presumably the police could be dispatched to arrest someone who failed to attend without offering a reasonable excuse, but there might be a greater anxiety over certain defendants who seem likely to flee the country or to hide themselves away. In principle, there is a greater public interest in securing the trial of those charged with more serious rather than less serious offences. As for the assessment of risk, we saw that the Strasbourg jurisprudence counsels against simply assuming that persons charged with serious offences will fail to appear at trial. There must be some ground for identifying a significant risk—perhaps that the defendant had on previous occasions failed to attend trial. Even then, the court must be satisfied that no other method of securing attendance at trial would be effective (deprivation of liberty must be a last resort).

A second main ground is the probability of committing offences if granted bail. In terms of justification, it is often asserted that there is a public interest in ensuring

---

[23] Derschowitz, *ibid.*, 244.

[24] A. Ashworth, 'Criminal Law, Human Rights and Preventative Justice' in B. McSherry, A. Norrie and S. Bronitt (eds), *Regulating Deviance* (2009).

[25] For the change in Ireland, including a referendum, see C. Fennell, *The Law of Evidence in Ireland* (2nd ed, 2003), 53–9; for Canada, see N. Padfield, 'The Right to Bail: a Canadian Perspective' [1993] *Crim LR* 510.

[26] But there may be circumstances in which this is permissible consistently with Art 6 of the Convention: see *Jones* [2002] UKHL 5, and B. Emmerson, A. Ashworth and A. Macdonald (eds), *Human Rights and Criminal Justice* (2nd ed, 2007), 574–8.

that people already charged with an offence do not commit offences during the period before their trial. The exact basis for this is unclear. Is it that the State is somehow responsible for the conduct of persons who have been charged but not yet tried, perhaps because it is the slowness of the machinery of criminal justice that creates the opportunities? Otherwise, in what way do remandees differ from, say, people with previous convictions who are walking the streets? Surely it cannot be that anyone who has been charged may be presumed guilty, and for that reason may be thought likely to commit a further offence if left at large before the formal trial: that reasoning, with its presumption of guilt, would contradict the presumption of innocence. Indeed, this was one of the grounds on which the Irish Supreme Court refused to recognize this as a legitimate ground for pre-trial detention, commenting that 'this is a form of preventative justice which...is quite alien to the true purpose of bail'.[27] Yet the trend undoubtedly is to deny this, and for governments to regard the period between arrest and trial as a time at which they must take action to control risks to citizens, and must endeavour to promote public safety by providing for some defendants to be deprived of their liberty.[28] One argument may be that the fact that a person has been charged with an offence is crucial. In some cases the defendant may well have confessed guilt and indicated an intention to plead guilty, which may be taken to contradict the presumption of innocence; but defendants may change their intentions when the prosecution evidence becomes clear and they have received legal advice, so it would be unwise to build too much on those foundations. More generally, it could be argued that the laying of a charge ought to be attributed significance now that the Crown Prosecution Service (CPS) has primary responsibility for such decisions; but that overlooks the need for the CPS frequently to take the charging decision before all the evidence is available. As we saw in Chapter 7, the 2004 version of the Code for Crown Prosecutors now propounds a 'threshold test' for cases where 'the suspect presents as a substantial bail risk if released from custody', that test being one of reasonable grounds to suspect the defendant of having committed the offence.[29] That standard is, as argued in Chapter 7, significantly below the 'reasonable prospect of conviction' test that is normally required. The arguments here, then, are much weaker than is commonly supposed; and none of them is compatible with the fundamental presumption of innocence, since they tend in the direction of assuming guilt. The Strasbourg Court has indeed insisted that the existence of reasonable suspicion of the offence is a necessary precondition for any custodial remand,[30] and that there must be persuasive evidence for concluding that there is a significant risk of serious offences

---

[27] *People (Attorney-General) v Callaghan* [1966] IR 426, *per* Walsh J at 516. In 1996 the Irish Constitution was amended so as to provide for pre-trial detention where reasonably necessary 'to prevent the commission of a serious offence by that person'. See further U. ni Raifeartaigh, 'Reconciling Bail Law with the Presumption of Innocence' (1997) 17 *Oxford JLS* 1, and 25 above.

[28] The Supreme Court of Canada reached a similar conclusion in *Morales* (1993) 77 CCC (3d) 91.

[29] See Ch 7.2(b) above.

[30] 'The persistence of a reasonable suspicion that the person arrested has committed an offence is a condition *sine qua non* for the lawfulness of the continued detention': *Assenov v Bulgaria* (1999) 29 EHRR 652, at [154].

being committed. That does not confront the question of why liberty should be taken away before trial, but offers a procedure that gives some recognition to the presumption of liberty, if less to the presumption of innocence.

A third ground is the probability that the defendant might interfere with witnesses or otherwise obstruct the course of justice if released on bail. In some of these cases there is a distinct justification: the risk to the security of another person. Where the rights of another citizen are shown to be at risk, perhaps in a domestic violence case or some other instance of ongoing attacks, the protection of those rights may well provide a justification for restrictions and, in some circumstances, for the deprivation of liberty. The uttering of threats by the defendant towards the victim would be one way of demonstrating the risk. In contrast to the situation in the previous paragraph, threats offer evidence of a specific risk to a particular person. Therefore, if it appears to be a choice between the defendant's liberty or the victim's freedom from probable harm, detention pending trial may be easier to justify.[31] If there is thought to be a more general risk of interfering with witnesses or obstructing the course of justice, the justification for restricting the defendant's liberty is to secure the integrity of the criminal justice system. But for any such restriction, and particularly for a deprivation of liberty, there must be persuasive evidence of the risk—perhaps evidence that the defendant may have been involved in such incidents before, or evidence of threats uttered.

The fourth ground for the refusal of bail recognized by the Strasbourg Court is where the nature of the crime and the probable public reaction to it are such that the release of the defendant might lead to public disorder. This justification may apply where it is considered right, exceptionally, to detain a defendant for his own protection.[32]

All these grounds for the refusal of bail turn on questions of predicted risk. In relation to the most frequent ground for refusal of bail—the risk of offences being committed in the period before trial—the 'risk' consists of the probability of an offence being committed if the defendant is granted bail, and the seriousness of any likely offence. A low probability of a very serious offence ought to have more weight than a high probability of a minor offence. Indeed, for non-serious offences, it will be argued, custodial remands should simply be ruled out. However, what we have seen in this section and will continue to see throughout this chapter is that the crucial issues are conspicuously under-determined. We have failed to identify a persuasive reason for the State to take power over defendants in the pre-trial period, to the extent of depriving them of liberty. We have argued that the well-known fallibility of predictions of dangerous conduct applies no less in the pre-trial sphere. These themes will now be developed more specifically in relation to the relevant English law.

---

[31] See the considerations set out in Part 7 of the *CPS Policy on Prosecuting Cases of Domestic Violence*, at www.cps.gov.uk. On the positive duty of a State to protect individuals under threat, see *Osman v United Kingdom* (1998) 29 EHRR 245, and B. Emmerson, A. Ashworth and A. Macdonald, *Human Rights and Criminal Justice* (2nd ed, 2007), Ch 18.

[32] *Letellier v France* (1992) 14 EHRR 83.

8.2 THE LAW RELATING TO REMANDS

This part of the chapter considers the history and current form of the law relating to remands, first in relation to court remands, and then in relation to remand decisions taken by the police.

(A) COURT REMANDS

In England and Wales the law relating to remands has developed in two distinct phases. The first phase focused chiefly on the problem of securing the attendance of the defendant at the trial. In *Robinson* (1854), Coleridge J held that this was the sole point to which the magistrates should give attention.[33] In *Rose* (1898),[34] Lord Russell stated that 'it cannot be too strongly impressed on the magistracy that bail is not to be withheld as a punishment but that the requirements as to bail are merely to secure the attendance of the prisoner at his trial'. It was not until the 1940s and 1950s that the English courts, with Lord Goddard as Lord Chief Justice, began to establish that an alternative ground for remanding in custody is that the defendant is likely to commit an offence if granted bail.[35] The Home Office took the unusual step of circulating to all magistrates the text of Lord Goddard's remarks in *Wharton* (1955).[36] Statutory confirmation came in the provisions of the Criminal Justice Act 1967, an Act which also introduced the possibility of granting conditional bail. So, roughly in parallel to the United States and ahead of Ireland and Canada,[37] the emphasis in English law changed to prevention. The relevant law for England and Wales is now contained chiefly in the Bail Act 1976, as amended. In essence, a court has four main alternatives: release on unconditional bail, release on conditional bail, release on bail subject to a surety or security, and remand in custody.

Little needs to be said about unconditional bail. As for conditional bail, the Act makes provision for this in s 3(6). It appears that around one-quarter to one-third of defendants granted bail are placed under conditions:[38] Raine and Willson found that the most common condition is residence at a specified address (78 per cent of conditional cases), followed by not contacting named persons (46 per cent), not going to a certain address (24 per cent), curfew (21 per cent), and reporting at a police station (18 per cent).[39] They found that many conditions are proposed by the defence, in the

---

[33] (1854) 23 LJQB 286. For summaries of the history, see A.K. Bottomley, 'The Granting of Bail: Principles and Practice' (1968) 31 *MLR* 40, and Corre and Wolchover (above, n 1), 11–19.

[34] (1898) 78 LT 119.

[35] See *Phillips* (1947) 32 Cr App R 47; *Wharton* [1955] *Crim LR* 565 ('unless the justices felt real doubt as to the result of the case, men with bad criminal records should not be granted bail'); and *Gentry* [1956] *Crim LR* 120 (same policy reiterated).

[36] See Bottomley, above n 33, at 52.   [37] See nn 16–25 above and accompanying text.

[38] P. M. Morgan and P. Henderson, *Remand Decisions and Offending on Bail* (1998), Ch 4.

[39] J. Raine and M. Willson, 'The Imposition of Conditions in Bail Decisions' (1996) 35 *Howard JCJ* 256; very similar percentages were found by Morgan and Henderson (previous note), at 42.

hope of deflecting the court from a custodial remand, rather than by the magistrates themselves; sometimes it seems that bail conditions are offered when unconditional bail might have been the outcome otherwise. They also found that half their interviewees believed that bail conditions would not be enforced, a perception that clearly weakens the efficacy of conditional bail. Amendments introduced by the Criminal Justice and Immigration Act 2008 provide for conditional bail with electronic monitoring, if the court is satisfied that the defendant would not be granted bail without electronic monitoring.[40] The Bail Act also provides that a court may, subject to certain restrictions, require a surety to secure the defendant's attendance at court. It may also require a defendant to give security for surrender to custody before release on bail. The danger with financial conditions, as the American experience shows, is that they may tend to exclude the less well-off from bail, and insofar as some remands in custody occur because the levels of surety set by the courts are unrealistic, this is quite wrong, being unfair discrimination against people of modest means.

The centrepiece of the Bail Act is s 4, which proclaims what has been described as a general right to bail or a presumption in favour of bail. Thus s 4(1) provides that 'a person to whom this section applies shall be granted bail except as provided in Schedule 1 to this Act'.[41] Paragraphs 2–6 of Part I of that Schedule[42] list a number of 'exceptions to the right to bail', including custodial remands for the defendant's own protection[43] and (more doubtfully) custodial remands because the court does not yet have sufficient information to take a decision on bail. The main provision is paragraph 2, which must be quoted in full:

'The defendant need not be granted bail if the court is satisfied that there are substantial grounds for believing that the defendant, if released on bail (whether subject to conditions or not), would–

(a) fail to surrender to custody, or

(b) commit an offence while on bail, or

(c) interfere with witnesses or otherwise obstruct the course of justice, whether in relation to himself or any other person.'

These three grounds correspond broadly with those approved by the European Court of Human Rights in its development of Article 5(3), and have a loose affinity with those subsequently incorporated in the Bail Reform Act of 1984 in the US.[44] The Schedule to the English Act goes on to set out various considerations to which regard should

---

[40] By s 51 and Sch 11; the power was previously available only in respect of persons under 18.

[41] Cf the amendments relating to summary offences punishable with imprisonment, in the Criminal Justice and Immigration Act 2008, s 52 and Sch 12.

[42] Part II of the Schedule deals separately with non-imprisonable offences, which will not be discussed here.

[43] See above, n 26, for a relevant Strasbourg decision. Section 13 of the Criminal Justice Act 2003 introduces the possibility of alternatively granting conditional bail in such cases.

[44] The US Act refers to a serious risk that the defendant will flee or will obstruct justice; or where the case involves a crime of violence (very broadly defined), a major drug offence or any crime punishable by

be had when taking bail/custody decisions. Among those is 'the defendant's record as respects the fulfilment of his obligations under previous grants of bail in criminal proceedings', a matter plainly relevant when the court is considering exception (a) to the right to bail.

Another consideration is 'the character, antecedents, associations and community ties of the defendant'. Community ties may be relevant to the probability that a defendant will attend his trial (exception (a)), since it may be argued that a person who is homeless or in temporary accommodation is more likely to abscond than someone with a permanent address (and a family) in the locality. However, it has been urged repeatedly that homelessness should not lead to a custodial remand without thorough exploration of other alternatives.[45] The 'character and antecedents' of the offender may give grounds for a prediction of whether he or she is likely to offend if given bail (exception (b)). This question has attracted surprisingly little legal analysis or empirical inquiry. One oft-quoted statement is that of Atkinson J in the Court of Criminal Appeal in *Phillips*,[46] where he warned courts against granting bail to defendants with a 'record of housebreaking', and added that 'in 19 out of 20 cases it is a mistake [to] release young housebreakers on bail'. Statistical studies suggest that this is a considerable exaggeration.[47] The Strasbourg Court has signalled the need for courts to avoid stereotypical reasoning and therefore not to make assumptions simply on the basis of a criminal record:[48] previous convictions must be recent, relevant and of a certain seriousness before it will be proper to contemplate rebutting the presumption of liberty on this ground.

A further consideration listed in paragraph 9 is 'the nature and seriousness of the offence or default (and the probable method of dealing with the offender for it)'. The Strasbourg Court has warned against a general assumption that the seriousness of the charge increases the risk of non-appearance at trial, and there must be further and specific evidence of a risk of this defendant absconding.[49] The seriousness of the charge ought to be relevant to custodial remands on the second ground, in recognition that it would be wrong to remand in custody a person whose charge (if proved) would be unlikely to result in a custodial sentence. However, on the face of the Bail Act, and the exceptions to bail that it enumerates, the probability of further minor offences such as shoplifting could justify a custodial remand. The Act should be amended so that exception (b) refers to the likelihood of committing a *serious* offence whilst on bail, as does the law on custodial remands of juveniles, so as to make this principle clear.

The Convention had some effect in curtailing attempts to 'toughen up' the law of bail in the 1990s. Section 25 of the Criminal Justice and Public Order Act 1994 sought to remove a court's powers to remand on bail any person charged with murder, attempted murder, manslaughter, rape or attempted rape who already has a conviction for such

---

life imprisonment; or where the case involves a felony charge against someone previously convicted of two offences in the above categories.

[45] E.g. in Home Office Circular 155/1975, *Bail Procedures.*   [46] (1947) 32 Cr App R 47.

[47] E.g. P. M. Morgan, *Offending Whilst on Bail* (1992).   [48] Above, n 7 and accompanying text.

[49] Above, n 8 and accompanying text.

an offence. In *Caballero v United Kingdom*,[50] the Strasbourg Court confirmed that this was in breach of Article 5(3), because, as the Commission had put it, 'the exclusion from the risk assessment of a consideration of all the particular circumstances and facts of each accused's case (other than the two facts contained in s 25) exposes, of itself, accused persons to arbitrary deprivation of liberty.' Section 25 was amended[51] so as to provide that a court may only grant bail to such persons if satisfied that 'there are exceptional circumstances which justify it'. This may still be thought inconsistent with the presumption of liberty implicit in Article 5(3), since the re-worded s 25 establishes a presumption in these cases in favour of deprivation of liberty,[52] and the Strasbourg Court has held that the authorities, not the defendant, must bear the burden of proving the need for detention.[53] By adopting an interpretative approach that treats as an 'exceptional circumstance' the view that the defendant appears unlikely to commit a serious offence if not remanded in custody,[54] a court could find the substance of s 25 compatible, but not the burden of proof.

Following the Law Commission's report, two other provisions of the Bail Act have been amended in an attempt to produce Convention compatibility. Thus s 26 of the Criminal Justice and Public Order Act 1994 has been amended by s 14 of the Criminal Justice Act 2003, so as to establish a presumption that a person should not be granted bail if it appears that he has committed an offence whilst on bail for another charge, 'unless the court is satisfied that there is no significant risk of his committing an offence' if granted bail. Similarly, the 2003 Act provides a presumption that a person who has failed to appear at court without reasonable cause should not be granted bail, and similarly a person who tests positive for a class A drug, again unless the court is satisfied that there is no significant risk of a further failure to surrender to bail. The 'no significant risk' formula is more directly linked to the rationale of each provision than 'exceptional circumstances', but it still reverses the general presumption of liberty. It also places great weight on assessments of risk, and ought to be interpreted as calling for sound, evidence-based reasons in favour of detention whereas, by virtue of the presumption, the defendant has to produce evidence-based reasons why there is no significant risk in granting him bail.

(B) POLICE REMANDS

The powers of the police to remand persons whom they have interviewed and may wish to interview again, and persons whom they have charged, pending their first court appearance, are contained in the Police and Criminal Evidence Act 1984, as

---

[50] (2000) 30 EHRR 643 (above n 7); the Government conceded after the Commission's opinion, and so the Court did not deliver a full judgment.

[51] By s 56 of the Crime and Disorder Act 1998.

[52] Cf the unsatisfactory decision in *R v Crown Court at Harrow* [2003] 1 WLR 2756, criticized by A. Ashworth and M. Strange, 'Criminal Law and Human Rights' [2004] *EHRLR* 121, at 128–9.

[53] *Reid v United Kingdom* (2003) 37 EHRR 9, at [70].

[54] Adapting the Court of Appeal's sentencing judgment in *Offen (No 2)* [2001] 1 WLR 253; see Law Commission, *Bail and the Human Rights Act 1998* (2001), Part VIII.

amended by the Criminal Justice and Public Order Act 1994.[55] The principal change in the 1994 Act was to confer on the police the power to grant bail with conditions: previously, they were only able to grant unconditional bail or to keep the suspect in custody overnight pending court appearance. One danger of granting such a power, well known to criminologists, is that it may be used in a net-widening manner. That is, a power intended to reduce the number of remands in custody can actually be used in cases where unconditional bail was previously allowed. In Raine and Willson's research at six police stations towards the end of 1995 this seems to have been the result. The introduction of conditional bail led to a small overall reduction in over-night detention of suspects by the police, but a significant drop in cases of unconditional bail. Where conditional bail was granted, the most frequent conditions were to keep away from a named place or a named person, sometimes for the protection of a witness or complainant. In view of the relatively slight drop in overnight detentions followed by court proceedings, it appears that the change has not contributed to a reduction in costs to the extent that was anticipated.[56] Raine and Willson also found that in some cases the police were using their bail powers as bargaining chips in their dealings with suspects, a finding that is hardly surprising[57] but which raises again the question whether such extensive powers over the liberty of individuals should be granted to the police.

The Criminal Justice Act 2003 introduced the concept of 'bail elsewhere than at a police station', known as street bail. These powers are discretionary, and the provisions on 'the right to bail' in the Bail Act 1976 do not apply here: police officers *may* release an arrested person on bail, and require that person to attend at a police station. No other requirement may be imposed, which means that other forms of conditional bail are not possible 'on the street.' It is not clear how these new powers will be used, and whether they will succeed in avoiding unnecessary processing of suspects at police stations and therefore in contributing to an increased police presence on the streets.

8.3 THE TREATMENT OF UNCONVICTED DEFENDANTS

The vast majority of cases in magistrates' courts do not involve any remand of the defendant, whether on bail or in custody, although the figures show a drift towards dealing with fewer cases at the first appearance.

---

[55] For the detailed procedures, see Y. Moreno and P. Hughes, *Effective Prosecution* (2008), 44–6.

[56] J. Raine and M. Willson, 'Police Bail with Conditions' (1997) 37 *BJ Crim* 593.

[57] See the similar findings from Canada reported by G. Kellough and S. Wortley, 'Remand for Plea: Bail Decisions and Plea Bargaining as Commensurate Decisions' (2002) 42 *BJ Crim* 186.

Table 8.1 Cases dealt with in magistrates' courts at first appearance[58]

	Summary motoring offences	Other summary offences	Indictable offences
1986	97%	92%	47%
1996	89%	82%	36%
2002	89%	80%	39%
2007	88%	75%	42%

This shows an overall decline in the proportion of cases dealt with at first appearance, although the figures for indictable offences appear to have stabilized in recent years. The vast majority of the indictable defendants in 2007 had been arrested (90 per cent) rather than summoned (10 per cent).[59] Turning to those not dealt with on first appearance, custodial remands of those charged with indictable offences who were ultimately dealt with in a magistrates' court have varied little over the years, standing at 10 per cent in 2002 and 8 per cent in 2007. Among those committed by magistrates for trial in the Crown Court, the proportion remanded in custody has risen from 22 per cent in 1986 to 31 per cent in 2002 and 32 per cent in 2007. Research in the 1980s by Jones (1985) and in the 1990s by Hucklesby (1997) revealed wide variations in the use of custodial remands by courts in different areas, suggesting the persistence of local cultures on this issue.[60]

What is the position in the prisons? Remand prisoners have always tended to be placed in the most overcrowded conditions in the system, since they are sent to local prisons. When the Woolf Inquiry reported on conditions in Strangeways and other prisons which had seen disturbances in 1990, a considerable proportion of the report was devoted to improving the lot of remand prisoners—unconvicted, but bearing the brunt of poor conditions.[61] Moreover, the provision of legal advice to defendants remanded in custody is difficult and may impair their defence.[62] All of this is certainly inconsistent with the proper treatment of people who have not yet been convicted, even if it is not formally in breach of the presumption of innocence and the right to legal assistance. The number of people in prison on remand has been fairly constant for the last 15 years: the total stood at 13,400 in 2007, of which 8,000 were awaiting trial and the remainder convicted and awaiting sentence.[63] This constitutes a much lower

[58] *Criminal Statistics England and Wales* 1986, 1996, 2002 and 2007.

[59] *Criminal Statistics England and Wales 2007*, Table 4.2.

[60] P. Jones, 'Remand Decisions at Magistrates' Courts' in D. Moxon (ed), *Managing Criminal Justice* (1985); and A. Hucklesby, 'Court Culture: an Explanation of Variations in the Use of Bail at Magistrates' Courts' (1997) 36 *Howard JCJ* 129.

[61] *Prison Disturbances April 1990: Report of an Inquiry by Rt. Hon. Lord Justice Woolf and His Honour Judge Tumin* (1991), particularly Ch 10.

[62] See the study of young remand prisoners by F. Brookman and H. Pierpoint, 'Access to Legal Advice for Young Suspects and Remand Prisoners' (2003) 42 *Howard JCJ* 452.

[63] See Jacobson, Player et al, 'Remanded in Custody: Recent Trends in England and Wales' (2010) forthcoming, Table 3. This article contains a wealth of recent statistics on remands.

proportion of the total prison population than a decade earlier, but that is because the number of convicted and sentenced offenders in prison has risen so steeply to some 84,000. The remand population remains high, particularly in respect of those who have not yet had their trial. Average waiting time for those remanded in custody in 2007 was 55 days, some three days fewer than the previous year.[64]

Some improvements in the remand system may have taken place, but in the light of the fundamental right to liberty enshrined in Article 5 we must continue to examine whether it is necessary to have as many as 8,000 people in prison at any one time awaiting trial—a figure that represents some 75,000 people remanded in custody each year.[65] One way of examining this issue is to consider the outcomes of the cases against those remanded in custody. For 2007, the figures show that of all persons remanded in custody some 15 per cent were acquitted, 29 per cent received a non-custodial sentence, and 52 per cent were sent to custody.[66]

These figures raise a number of serious questions. In the cases of those remanded in custody and subsequently acquitted or not proceeded against, the loss of liberty is particularly hard on the individuals concerned. It could be argued that these are not necessarily cases of malfunction in the criminal justice system: if a conscientious judgement was made about the probability that, if not remanded in custody, they would fail to attend trial, commit offences whilst on bail, or interfere with witnesses, none of those matters bears directly on the probability of conviction. However, the importance of these decisions for defendants means that two aspects of custodial remands require special attention. First, the Strasbourg Court has made it clear that the remanding magistrates must be satisfied of the continued existence of 'reasonable suspicion' (i.e. substantial evidence) against the defendant,[67] and paragraph 9 of Schedule 1 to the Bail Act states that the strength of the evidence should be considered. To what extent are magistrates able to do this meaningfully? It is well known that decisions by magistrates tend to correspond with recommendations by the CPS, which in turn correspond with decisions by the police. The correlations are strong, but not invariable, and therefore do not necessarily lead to inferences of undue influence or failure of decision makers to examine issues independently. Thus Morgan and Henderson found that, in respect of those held in police custody, the CPS recommended custody for only 48 per cent, and 76 per cent of those recommendations were accepted; the CPS recommended conditional bail for a further 46 per cent, and magistrates accepted 90 per cent of those recommendations.[68] Since one-fifth of those remanded in custody are acquitted or not proceeded against, this ought to prompt inquiries into the reasons why they were remanded in custody. Morgan and Henderson identify a number of characteristics that are strongly associated with decisions to remand in custody, notably the absence of a fixed address, seriousness of charge and bail history. It is also important to know why cases were dropped, where that was the outcome, and why this could not have

---

[64] *Ibid.*   [65] *Ibid.*, Table 2.   [66] *Ibid.*, Table 4.

[67] Above n 30 and accompanying text.

[68] P. Morgan and P. Henderson, *Remand Decisions and Offending on Bail* (1998), 37.

happened at an earlier stage. At the very least, the figures suggest that the pain of custodial remand, felt so acutely by those subject to it, does not always weigh so heavily with those who take decisions in respect of defendants.[69]

What about those who receive non-custodial sentences after being remanded in custody? This is the outcome for about a quarter of males and nearly one-third of all females remanded in custody before trial. Does it mean that they were unnecessarily remanded in custody in the first place?

At least four lines of argument cast doubt on this. The first is the one that most sentencers hasten to offer: that a court passing sentence must recognize the fact that the offender has already spent time in custody, and that a court may properly take this into account and impose a non-custodial sentence in a case where, if there had been no custodial remand, it would probably have imposed custody. The magistrates who pass sentence will rarely be the same individuals who refused bail and ordered the custodial remand, so the sentencing decision will be taken entirely *de novo*. There can be no objection to the court taking account of what has already happened: indeed, this may allow the court to adopt a more constructive approach than it might otherwise have felt able to do, by making a community order rather than imposing a custodial sentence. The implication of this argument is that the imposition of a non-custodial sentence does not necessarily suggest that the custodial remand was wrong, since in many cases if there had not been a custodial remand there would have been a custodial sentence. In theory this argument seems plausible. It is difficult, however, to determine how much substance it has in practice, since no research has been carried out into the reasoning of magistrates when sentencing offenders who have been in custody on remand. No one knows what proportion of the cases resulting in a non-custodial sentence are a response to the custodial remand, and what proportion imply that there need have been no custodial remand in the first place.

Moreover, this first argument may prove rather more than was intended. If it is true that sentencers tend to take account of the fact that an offender has spent time in custody on remand, it may be the case that some of those given custodial sentences are sentenced in that way simply so as to facilitate their immediate release. If the court learns that an offender has been in prison for two months awaiting trial, it may feel that he or she has already been punished quite sufficiently (or even too heavily) for the offence, and may therefore impose a sentence of four months' imprisonment so as to ensure immediate release.[70] Otherwise, the court might have chosen some kind of community order as a suitable sentence. It is not known how many courts would react in this way—some might grant a conditional discharge or other sentence in these

---

[69] It should also be added that this country, unlike many of its European neighbours, does not have a statutory scheme for compensating those who are remanded in custody and then acquitted, although Art 5(5) of the Convention mandates 'an enforceable right to compensation'.

[70] This is said to be the approach of some courts in other European countries: see, e.g. W. Heinz, 'The Problems of Imprisonment' in R. Hood (ed), *Crime and Criminal Policy in Europe: Proceedings of a European Colloquium* (1989).

circumstances. But the point is that the numbers of people remanded in custody who are subsequently given custodial sentences by magistrates' courts may also include some cases (we know not how many) where the court would not have imposed custody if there had been no custodial remand. To take the further step and assert that the numbers of those given non-custodial sentences who would have received custody but for the custodial remand are far greater than the numbers of those given custodial sentences who would have received non-custodial sentences but for the custodial remand is to advance into the realms of speculation. The proportions are not known.

A second argument against taking the figures at face value is that the criteria for granting or withholding bail are not directly related to the probability of a custodial sentence. The three criteria in para 2 of the Schedule to the Bail Act focus only on the period between first court appearance and trial. It is true that para 9 of that Schedule suggests that courts should also have regard to 'the nature and seriousness of the offence and the probable method of dealing with the offender for it', but it is not clear how much separate attention has been given to this provision. Where a defendant is remanded in custody because there are substantial grounds for believing that otherwise he or she may not attend the trial, or for believing that otherwise witnesses may be threatened, these reasons have nothing to do with the likely sentence in the case. The statistics are not sharp enough to determine the relative proportions of cases: in the Home Office's 1978 survey, the probability of committing an offence was given as a reason in 63 per cent of cases, and the probability of the defendant absconding was given as a reason in 51 per cent of cases. Exactly how many cases depended only on one or the other reason is unclear, but some evidently bear no relationship to the probability of a custodial sentence on conviction.

A third argument points to the divergence between the bail provisions and the relevant sentencing law. Section 152(2) of the Criminal Justice Act 2003 states that a court 'must not pass a custodial sentence' unless satisfied that the offence 'was so serious that neither a fine alone nor a community sentence can be justified for the offence'.[71] No such restrictions are to be found in the Bail Act and, except with reference to juvenile remands, there is no clear injunction that the court should adopt the least restrictive form of remand (unconditional bail; conditional bail) unless satisfied that the defendant would receive a custodial sentence if convicted as charged.

A fourth argument raises questions about whether the remand decisions taken in court really are considered and rounded determinations. We have already noted the findings of Morgan and Henderson that, in the majority of cases, magistrates tend to adopt the same course as that recommended by the CPS.[72] Hucklesby found that the vast majority of remand hearings were uncontested: only in 9 per cent of cases was there a different view advanced by prosecution and defence. In most cases the CPS did not oppose bail, and in almost half of the cases where bail was opposed the defence did

---

[71] A similar provision has been part of the law since 1991: see Criminal Justice Act 1991, s 1(2).

[72] Morgan and Henderson, above n 68; for experimental evidence to the same effect, see M. Dhami, 'Conditional Bail Decision-Making in the Magistrates' Court' (2004) 43 *Howard JCJ* 27, at 40.

not contest this. At least two processes appear to be at work here. One is the influence of the police: if they grant bail from the police station, it is highly unlikely that a court is going to find that a custodial remand is needed, and the CPS would have difficulty in sustaining such an argument.[73] The other is the influence of court culture, which sustains different rates of remand in custody in different courts over prolonged periods of years.[74] Both influences tend to suggest that in some cases the CPS does not make the recommendation it might think appropriate, and Hucklesby's finding that generally nearly nine out of ten CPS recommendations are accepted by the court[75] shows that the CPS makes different recommendations on similar cases because they are to be heard in different courts, or even by differently constituted benches. Moreover, this process of anticipating the decisions of other parties is also evident in the approach of some defence solicitors, who admit both to adapting their representations to the particular bench (sometimes not applying for bail if it would be 'hopeless' in view of the constitution of the bench), and to using various tactics or coded language in order to distinguish bail applications which they believe in from those which they make purely because the client has insisted. This is a clear example of unethical behaviour, with defence lawyers failing to do their best to advance a defendant's case or, as Hucklesby puts it, ranking 'their credibility and status with the court above the interests of their clients'.[76] Hucklesby found that the CPS usually failed to give reasons for its representations: indeed, in 60 per cent of cases where the CPS requested a custodial remand, no reasons were stated, and even in cases where the defence contested the hearing the CPS failed to give its reason (e.g. by referring to a reason in the Bail Act) in many cases.[77] Insofar as these practices persist, they constitute a clear demonstration of the way in which apparently open and formal processes mask the reality of informal decision making, anticipation of the decisions of others, and the drive to maintain professional respect. In the present context, the implication is that decisions result from possibly tacit or even unconscious local coalitions between police practice and bench traditions, with the CPS and defence solicitors operating in a way that sees them anticipating the decisions of others in many cases and only rarely standing up for a view that differs from that of other key participants. Of course, a high rate of concordance in decisions does not conclusively prove undue influence, since it remains possible that the police, the CPS, and then the courts are applying the same criteria independently and reaching mostly the same conclusions, but the evidence of the criminal justice practitioners interviewed by Hucklesby strongly suggests otherwise.[78]

Consideration of the four lines of argument against a face-value interpretation of the statistics on trial and sentence therefore demonstrates a pervasive uncertainty about

---

[73] J. Burrows, P. Henderson and P. Morgan, *Improving Bail Decisions: the Bail Process Project* (1994); for similar findings in Canada, see Kellough and Wortley, above n 57, at 204.

[74] Hucklesby, above n 60; A. Hucklesby, 'Remand Decision Makers' [1997] *Crim LR* 269.

[75] *Ibid.*, 276; also Morgan and Henderson, above n 68, 35–6.

[76] Hucklesby [1997] *Crim LR* 269, at 279.   [77] *Ibid.*, 280–1.

[78] Hucklesby, above n 60, at 137–40.

the use of bail and of remands in custody. We lack the detailed research necessary to establish which explanations account for what percentage of cases: Mandeep Dhami's experimental research suggests that divergences of approach are at their greatest in high-risk cases,[79] and closer monitoring of actual decisions is now needed. At the same time, however, the terms of the law on remands ought to be re-examined. In principle, as the Strasbourg Court has emphasized, the strength of the case ought to be a primary factor, before one of the specific grounds for deprivation of liberty is considered. In practice this creates difficulties in cases where the full evidence may not have arrived by the first (or even subsequent) remand hearing, especially if the results of a forensic science test are being awaited. We saw earlier that the CPS has now acknowledged this point by lowering the standard of evidence required,[80] but it remains a key issue in custodial remands. In principle, too, the probable penalty, if the defendant is convicted as charged, ought to be a factor. The Bail Act should require the court to be satisfied that a custodial sentence would be appropriate, if the case were proved as alleged; and it should re-write the 'future offences' ground so as to state expressly that there should be no remand in custody unless there is a substantial risk of *serious* offences being committed if the defendant were left at liberty.[81] If risk is to be a criterion, there must be legislative guidance not only on the seriousness of the probable offence but on the degree of risk and the basis for inferring it. This raises the issue of the information provided to bail decision makers, a topic taken up in Part 5 of this chapter.

8.4 THE TREATMENT OF VICTIMS AND POTENTIAL VICTIMS

This is a provocative heading, intended to raise starkly the question whether the public in general or victims in particular have received any benefit from having larger numbers of defendants in custody at any one time. It would be almost impossible to trace any effects on the crime rate, largely because (1) the 'crime rate' is itself an elusive phenomenon which even surveys of victims (which are more complete than official records) have difficulty in charting,[82] and (2) even if we had a reliable measure of the number of crimes committed each year, it would necessarily be a product of several interacting influences, and it would rarely be possible to attribute particular trends to particular causes. But the question can be approached from other angles. One is to inquire into the volume of offences committed by persons who have been granted bail,

---

[79] M. Dhami, 'From Discretion to Disagreement: Explaining Disparities in Judges' Pre-Trial Decisions' (2005) 23 *Behavioural Sciences and the Law* 367.

[80] See the 2004 edition of the Code for Crown Prosecutors, discussed in Ch 7.2(b) above.

[81] The 1996 amendment to the Irish Constitution insists on risk of a serious offence (see n 27 above), and this is also evident in the Strasbourg jurisprudence (see n 31 above).

[82] See M. Maguire, 'Crime Data and Statistics' in M. Maguire, R. Morgan and R. Reiner (eds), *Oxford Handbook of Criminology* (4th ed, 2007).

perhaps with a view to suggesting that either too few people or the wrong people are remanded in custody. Another is to inquire into the proportion of those remanded in custody who are subsequently given non-custodial sentences, with a view to suggesting that it was unnecessary to order their pre-trial detention to secure public protection.

The most direct sense of public protection is to protect someone who has been threatened with violence by the defendant or who has a well-grounded fear of violence. Such issues may arise in neighbourhood disputes or intra-family offences. The *Code of Practice for Victims of Crime* (2005) sets out the entitlements of victims, witnesses, and others from various service providers, such as the police, the CPS and the court service. In relation to the release on bail of persons arrested or charged, for example, the Code sets out various duties of the police to keep victims informed.[83] The CPS policy on domestic violence cases refers to the duty of the CPS to make representations to the court in favour of a custodial remand to avoid danger, threats or pressure for victims, and in lesser cases to propose conditions for bail.[84] There is also a prosecution right to appeal against the grant of bail, in respect of all imprisonable offences.[85]

Turning to public protection in a more general sense, let us begin by considering possible bail failures. Of those bailed to appear at court for indictable offences, the percentage failing to appear on the due date at a magistrates' court declined from 19 in 2002 to 14 in 2007, and at the Crown Court it declined from nine in 2002 to five in 2007.[86] These may be regarded as wrong decisions in the sense that the court evidently thought that there were no substantial grounds for believing that they would fail to surrender to custody. However, no such grounds may have been apparent at the time, and in any event the courts could be said to have decided correctly in the vast majority of cases. Moreover, it does not follow that these remandees should have been placed in custody: for some of them, conditional bail may have proved effective, and for many of the absconders from magistrates' courts their offending behaviour would not be particularly serious.

Of greater public concern are those defendants remanded on bail who are found to have committed offences during the period of remand. A study by Morgan and Henderson of some 2,300 bail cases in 1993–94 found that 17 per cent of those bailed by the courts were convicted of an offence committed during the period of bail.[87] Most of them were convicted of only one offence committed on bail, and the factors most closely connected with offending on bail were:

(a) a wait of more than six months before trial;

(b) a charge of car crime, burglary or robbery;

---

[83] Home Office, *Code of Practice for Victims of Crime* (2005), paras 5.14–5.17 and 5.21–5.25.

[84] CPS, *Policy on Prosecuting Cases of Domestic Violence*, Part 7.

[85] Criminal Justice Act 2003, s 18, amending the Bail (Amendment) Act 1993.

[86] *Criminal Statistics England and Wales 2002*, Table 5.9; *Criminal Statistics England and Wales 2007*, Table 4.10.

[87] Morgan and Henderson, above n 68, 44.

(c) a previous custodial sentence;

(d) age under 18; and

(e) a previous breach of bail.

Where an offence was committed on bail, it was particularly likely to be the same type of offence as originally charged if that charge was theft or handling (54 per cent), burglary (46 per cent), or a serious motoring offence (35 per cent).[88] If public protection is to be an important purpose of the bail/custody decision, then there is a need to focus on two distinct issues. The first is whether we can predict with sufficient accuracy which offenders are more likely to offend on bail than not: the Home Office is not optimistic about this,[89] and in view of the relatively low percentage of bailed defendants proved to offend on bail (17 per cent) this is hardly surprising. Even if the general predictive tools were more accurate, the focus ought then to be on the offences committed on bail. If the majority happen to be offences of theft or car crime, this prompts the question whether custodial remands are appropriate in these cases. It has been argued above that other means of restricting those whose offending behaviour is not conspicuously serious should be tried. It is important not to move directly from regarding 'offending on bail' as a problem, which it is, to regarding the use of custody as an appropriate or (in more than the short term) effective remedy. Indeed, it seems that the easiest offences to predict are likely to be lower on the scale of seriousness, raising doubts about the justification for remands in custody to prevent them.

This makes the connection between the failures of remands on bail and the failures of remands in custody. Is the public best protected by the extensive use of custodial remands? It is true that custodial remand represents a guarantee that the defendant will not commit offences against most members of the public (except, of course, those who are in prison either on conviction or on remand themselves). But deprivation of liberty remains, in principle, an incursion into a person's rights and that requires strong justification. Protecting a person against threats of violence may (in the absence of conditions that would be effective) be a sufficient reason for custodial remand. But we should ask whether protecting the public against theft or car crime is sufficient to outweigh this fundamental right. Moreover, we should recall the discussion in Part 3 of this chapter, where it was shown that one-quarter of those remanded in custody are not convicted, and that around one-quarter receive non-custodial sentences. For the reasons there discussed, this raises serious questions about the need, from the point of view of public safety, to remand so many people in custody before trial.

---

[88] *Ibid.*, 46.

[89] *Ibid.*, 60; Morgan and Henderson's study reports on an initiative to reduce offending on bail which had only mixed results.

8.5 PROCEDURAL JUSTICE AND REMAND DECISIONS

We now move on to consider four aspects of procedure relevant to the fairness of remand decisions—access to legal advice; bail information schemes; the speed of court hearings; and appeals.

(A) ACCESS TO LEGAL ADVICE AND ASSISTANCE

The European Court of Human Rights has insisted that a person should have a right to legal assistance before being deprived of liberty, especially before trial.[90] English law contains various provisions to ensure access to legal advice, both on arrest and detention and then during any custodial remand. But research shows that in practice the path towards provision of this access is not always smooth. Young remand prisoners have practical difficulties contacting their lawyers, and the lawyers have practical difficulties in arranging visits to prisons, particularly within the constraints of their other obligations.[91] The geographical dispersal of women's prisons creates difficulties in meeting solicitors.[92] In view of the importance of such contacts to the preparation of a defence, and thus to respecting the right declared in Article 6(3)(b), this may amount to a significant handicap to those remanded in custody. The provision of legal advice at the police station is generally better, but the conditions for giving and receiving legal advice are not always sufficient to satisfy the Convention (e.g. by telephone within earshot of police officers).[93] Strasbourg decisions on the Convention have helped to produce a recognition that there is a duty on the prosecution to make some disclosure to the defence before bail hearings, in order to satisfy the principle of equality of arms that is established as an element of the right to a fair trial.[94] The Attorney General's Guidelines on Disclosure state that 'disclosure ought to be made of significant information that might affect a bail decision,'[95] although the extent of compliance with this guidance is not known.

(B) BAIL INFORMATION SCHEMES

The problem of obtaining relevant and verified information for remand courts has been recognized for some time. If remand decision makers have insufficient information

---

[90] Emmerson, Ashworth and Macdonald, above n 5, 13–50.

[91] See the research summarized in F. Brookman and H. Pierpoint, 'Access to Legal Advice for Young Suspects and Remand Prisoners' (2003) 42 *Howard JCJ* 452, at 460–3.

[92] Player, 'Remanding Women in Custody', 423–5.

[93] Compare the strong statement of principle and its application in *Brennan v United Kingdom* (2002) 34 EHRR 18, with the unsatisfactory domestic decision in *M and La Rose v Metropolitan Police Commissioner* [2002] *Crim LR* 215.

[94] E.g. *Nikolova v Bulgaria* (1999) 31 EHRR 64; *R v DPP, ex p Lee* [1999] 2 All ER 237.

[95] Attorney General, *Disclosure of Information in Criminal Proceedings* (2000); see also Law Com 269, *Bail and the Human Rights Act 1998*.

on the defendant's personal and social situation, the possibility of advancing cogent grounds for conditional or unconditional bail is diminished. The Vera Institute of Justice began programmes in the US in the early 1960s, aimed at supplying courts with some objective data on which they could base their decisions, in particular data about the defendant's 'community ties'.[96] The idea was taken up in England and Wales by the London office of the Vera Institute of Justice.[97] Since then, bail information schemes have spread slowly to become part of the system, in both prisons and courts. Not surprisingly, however, the quality of provision is variable.[98]

Bail information schemes have a limited bearing on remand decisions. The reason behind the majority of decisions to remand in custody is the second statutory ground, the likelihood that the defendant would commit an offence whilst on bail. Bail information schemes are not concerned principally with this ground or this group of defendants, although they may sometimes yield information that enables a case to be made for conditional bail. Given the many other elements in bail decisions, it may be that bail information schemes have limited added value, but increase the confidence of courts in their chosen outcomes.[99]

(C) SPEED AND DELAY

The police are the first agency to deal with all those who are arrested, and, as we have seen, they take an initial decision whether to detain the defendant in custody pending the court appearance or to grant police bail. The CPS is responsible for making representations to the court about bail, but in many cases the crown prosecutor is likely to receive a large pile of case files on arrival at work in the morning (consisting of 'overnight arrests' by the police) and will have to present these cases to the court that very morning. The prosecutor is therefore reliant on form MG7 prepared by the police, which makes it particularly important that the police record details of the grounds for any objection to bail that is proposed.[100] Prior to the remand hearing there is unlikely to be much time for a detached review of the evidence in the case. However, there is evidence that the CPS do not merely follow police decision making: research by Morgan and Henderson in 1993–94 shows that, in respect of some 1,500 defendants refused police bail and held in custody overnight, the CPS recommended a custodial remand in only 48 per cent of cases, conditional bail in a further 46 per cent of cases, and unconditional bail in 6 per cent.[101] This suggests that, despite the speed at which decisions have to be taken, a degree of independent judgement is brought to bear.

---

[96] See Jones and Goldkamp, above n 32, 1404.

[97] C. Stone, *Bail Information for the Crown Prosecution Service* (1988).

[98] See the discussion of schemes in women's prisons by Player, 'Remanding Women in Custody', 424.

[99] See the experimental research by M. Dhami, 'Do Bail Information Schemes Really Affect Bail Decisions?' (2002) 41 *Howard JCJ* 245.

[100] Moreno and Hughes, *Effective Prosecution*, 233–9.

[101] Morgan and Henderson, above n 68, 37.

The brevity of the hearings themselves has long given cause for concern, in view of the momentous consequence of loss of liberty in some cases. Doherty and East's Cardiff study in 1981 found that cases were processed in court with great rapidity, the clerk setting the tone by rattling through the necessary words. Even in cases where defendants were remanded in custody, some 38 per cent were concluded within two minutes and 87 per cent within ten minutes.[102] No doubt some of the former were remands of persons already in prison, whereas most of those taking longer than ten minutes were probably first hearings, but the figures still raise concerns in view of the seriousness of taking away liberty. It seems that many magistrates still make bail decisions in a few minutes,[103] and it is not known whether the extra emphasis on procedural justice resulting from training under the Human Rights Act has altered practice in this respect.

No less important is the time taken to complete cases: the Strasbourg jurisprudence requires 'particular expedition' where a person is being held in custody.[104] Figures from 2002 showed 450 prisoners on remand for more than 12 months, and a further 900 on remand for 6–12 months.[105] Comparable figures appear not to be given in the 2007 statistics;[106] but insofar as some remand prisoners are held for such periods, this may involve breaches of Article 5(3).

(D) APPEALS AND REAPPLICATIONS

When a court refuses bail or attaches conditions to it, there is an obligation to state the ground(s) on which the court relies and to give reasons for bringing the case within that ground.[107] A defendant who is refused bail by a magistrates' court may make a reapplication to a judge in chambers. Correspondingly, the Bail (Amendment) Act 1993 introduced a prosecution power to appeal to a judge against the grant of bail by a magistrates' court in the face of representations by the prosecution, and the Criminal Justice Act 2003 extended that power to all imprisonable offences. The case for a defence right of reapplication is unanswerable in view of the enormity of the consequences of a decision to remand in custody. The case for a prosecution power of appeal is strong in cases where there is thought to be a clear danger to individuals if the defendant is granted liberty. Unless the power is shown to be used oppressively, it surely has a proper place in criminal procedure.

---

[102] C. Doherty and R. East, 'Bail Decisions in Magistrates' Courts' (1985) 25 *BJ Crim* 251.

[103] M. Dhami, 'Conditional Bail Decision-Making in the Magistrates' Court' (2004) 43 *Howard JCJ* 27, at 28.

[104] E.g. *Reid v United Kingdom* (2003) 37 EHRR 9, at [78].

[105] *Prison Statistics 2002*, Table 2.5.

[106] Ministry of Justice, *Offender Management Caseload Statistics 2007* (2008).

[107] Bail Act 1976, s 5(3); for low rates of compliance in the early 1990s, see A. Hucklesby, 'Bail or Jail? The Practical Operation of the Bail Act 1976' (1996) 23 *JLS* 213—reasons only given for custodial remands in 47 per cent of cases.

8.6 EQUAL TREATMENT IN REMAND DECISIONS

To what extent do remand decisions appear to discriminate against certain sections of the population? To what extent do they fail to recognize the special needs of certain groups? These questions warrant considerable discussion in their own right, and it is possible only to give some general indications here.

The findings of research into the impact of race on remand decisions prompt questions about discrimination. In his study of over 3,000 cases Roger Hood found that a higher proportion of defendants from an Afro-Caribbean background (26 per cent) than whites (20 per cent) were remanded in custody pending trial and that, even after taking account of variations in the key facts of individual cases, some apparent discrimination remained.[108] The John Report on racial elements in CPS decision making found that the CPS opposed bail more frequently for African-Caribbeans than for other groups of defendants, especially on the ground of the risk of obstructing justice. File endorsements did not disclose the evidential foundations for many of the recommendations, suggesting that information from the police may have been passed on orally. The report concludes that it is probable that racial stereotyping was influencing some of these decisions.[109] In relation to young arrestees, Feilzer and Hood found higher rates of remand into secure conditions among black (10 per cent) and mixed parentage (13 per cent) young males than among those who were white (8 per cent) or from Asian or other ethnic groups (6 per cent). Moreover, 'as many as a third of cases where a black male had been remanded in custody failed to result in conviction, compared with one in five cases involving white males.'[110] A related issue is that the proportion of foreign nationals is significantly higher among remand prisoners (19 per cent) than sentenced prisoners (11 per cent).[111]

Whereas the numbers of males on remand have remained relatively steady over the last 15 years, the number of women held on remand has increased by some 80 per cent.[112] A higher proportion of the female prison population is on remand than the male prison population (19 compared with 16 per cent). Can these figures be justified by reference to the relative seriousness of the offences? Apparently not: some 20 per cent of women remandees were charged with offences of sex or violence, compared with 33 per cent for men. The largest single category for remanded women was drugs offences; also some 9 per cent of women were remanded for theft or handling, compared with 7 per cent of men. It seems unlikely that these alleged offences were all so serious as to call for a custodial sentence on conviction. Indeed, the figures

---

[108] R. Hood, *Race and Sentencing* (1992), 146–50; see also M. Fitzgerald, *Ethnic Minorities and the Criminal Justice System* (1993), 19–21.

[109] The Gus John Partnership, *Race for Justice: A review of CPS decision making for possible racial bias at each stage of the prosecution process* (2003), paras 16 and 28; for similar suggestions in Canada, see G. Kellough and S. Wortley, above n 57, 196.

[110] M. Feilzer and R. Hood, *Differences or Discrimination?* (Youth Justice Board, 2004).

[111] Jacobson, Player et al, 'Remanded in Custody'.

[112] *Ibid.*, from which all figures in this paragraph are taken.

suggest this: whereas 54 per cent of remanded men were sentenced to custody, only 45 per cent of remanded women received imprisonment.[113] Even bearing in mind the points raised in Part 3 above, it is a serious cause for concern that fewer than a half of women remanded in custody are thought to require a custodial sentence. The 'culture of neglect' to which Elaine Player has referred needs to be addressed with urgency.[114]

Special arrangements for the remand of mentally disordered defendants were introduced by the Mental Health Act 1983. However, the power to remand defendants to hospital for a psychiatric report, rather than to prison, appears not to have been widely used. Courts still remand defendants to prison for reports in large numbers. A study by Robertson and others in 1989 found that many custodial remands were made in cases where the offence was minor and the defendant had no fixed address. There were then delays before an assessment by an outside psychiatrist could take place, and often delays in hospital admission thereafter, although about a half of those seen by psychiatrists were offered a hospital bed. The authors comment that 'remands in custody [are] not only an inhumane, but an ineffective way of securing help and care for disturbed people'.[115] A 1993 survey by Kennedy and others confirmed that many mentally disturbed people remanded in custody did not have stable housing arrangements, and the authors argue that at least one-fifth of them could and should be accommodated in probation hostels rather than placed in prison.[116] Mentally disturbed people are still represented in disproportionately large numbers among the remand population in prisons, and mental problems connected with substance abuse are a growing concern.[117] Recent research by Plugge, Douglas and Fitzpatrick found high levels of drug misuse among women remand prisoners, with half of them using heroin daily prior to their remand to prison.[118] They also found that the health of addicts improved during their stay in prison, raising the possibility that courts were remanding some of these women in custody not by applying the statutory criteria but in order to give them access to healthcare which was unavailable or less effective in the community. This is deeply problematic.[119]

8.7 CONCLUSIONS

The starting point for discussion of remands should be Article 5 of the Convention, which declares the right to liberty, and Article 6.2, which declares the presumption

---

[113] *Ibid.*   [114] Player, 'Remanding Women in Custody', 403, 425.

[115] G. Robertson, S. Dell, A. Grounds and K. James, 'Mentally Disordered Remand Prisoners' (1992) 32 *Home Office Research Bulletin* 1.

[116] M. Kennedy, C. Truman, S. Keyes and A. Cameron, 'Supported Bail for Mentally Vulnerable Defendants' (1997) 36 *Howard JCJ* 158.

[117] D. Brooke, C. Taylor, J. Gunn and A. Maden, 'Substance Misuse as a Marker of Vulnerability Among Male Prisoners on Remand' (2000) 177 *BJ Psychiatry* 248.

[118] E. Plugge, N. Douglas and R. Fitzpatrick, *The Health of Women in Prison* (2006).

[119] As argued by Jacobson, Player et al, 'Remanded in Custody'.

of innocence.[120] Detention without trial is objectionable in principle, because it negatives these rights. In principle there are two ways of constructing a justification for
depriving a defendant of these rights. The first is to argue that there is a distinct risk to
the rights of another citizen: this may arise if the defendant has already been charged
with assaulting a person and there is evidence to suggest a risk of further violence
(as is sometimes the case following incidents of 'domestic violence'). Alternatively it
may arise where there is reason to believe that the defendant will threaten someone,
especially a victim-complainant or witness. Previous threats could provide sufficient
evidence. What emerges clearly is that such decisions should involve both principled
reasoning and an assessment of risk. Although in practice much attention is often
focused on risk, on the basis of submissions made by the prosecution or police, the
issue of principle is no less critical. If the right to liberty is to be taken seriously, courts
that do find a significant risk must still strive to preserve the defendant's liberty by
seeking non-custodial means of responding to the risk through conditional bail.

A second strand of justification refers to overwhelming reasons of public interest.
We have questioned the origins, nature and strength of this public interest in the possible pre-trial conduct of persons who are presumed innocent,[121] but it seems to be
a feature of many legal systems that the presumption of innocence weakens once a
person has been charged by a public prosecutor. One element is the public interest in
ensuring that defendants who have been charged attend their trials. Although it would
be difficult to deny some such interest, it is questionable whether it is strong enough to
justify taking away a person's liberty, particularly when the offence charged is not of
the highest seriousness and absconding is not a certainty but a greater or lesser probability. This is, *par excellence*, a sphere in which non-custodial methods of securing
attendance should be developed, particularly bail hostels and electronic tagging.[122]
And it should certainly be a precondition that the offence as alleged is 'worth imprisonment', before there is any question of imprisoning someone so as to ensure that the
trial takes place.

Another element of public interest may be that of minimizing the number of offences
committed by persons on bail. The foundations of this interest were discussed critically in Part 1 of this chapter, and the re-enactment of a provision requiring courts to
treat offending on bail as an aggravating factor in sentencing demonstrates the political force of this concern.[123] However, the Bail Act's reference simply to the probability
of committing 'an offence' whilst on bail is much too weak. At the very least, the law
should insist that (a) the prosecution has satisfied the court that there is sufficient
evidence against the defendant on the charge laid; (b) that the person is granted conditional bail only if there are good reasons against unconditional bail; and (c) that,
before the person can be remanded in custody, there is good reason to believe that,

---

[120] See Player, 'Remanding Women in Custody'.   [121] Above, p 233.
[122] See the provisions for electronic monitoring introduced by the Criminal Justice and Immigration Act
2008, at n 40 above.
[123] Criminal Justice Act 2003, s 143(3).

if convicted as charged, the defendant would probably receive a custodial sentence. Some oblique recognition of the latter point may be found in the Practice Direction on failure to surrender to bail.[124]

Once again, however, interacting with these issues of principle is the practical problem of risk assessment. In order to determine whether it is more likely than not that this defendant will commit an offence likely to result in imprisonment if granted bail, there is a need for a database for the prediction of offending, the like of which appears not to exist in England and Wales. There is a database for the probability of keeping the conditions of parole if released from prison, and there are some data on the probability of certain offenders committing so-called 'dangerous' offences. But here, unlike in the US, there is no database that can be used to predict offending, let alone serious offending, whilst on bail. The American research by Goldkamp and Gottfredson does contain some useful pointers—for example, that reoffending and non-appearance at trial are highly correlated so that to predict one is usually to predict the other; and that bailees are more likely to offend the longer the period awaiting trial[125]—but it remains true that the numbers of false positives would be high. The scattered research in England suggests the same, as we saw above: it is easy to say that people charged with taking cars are the group most likely to offend on bail, but most of them are not in fact detected in law-breaking whilst on bail. Similarly, it is easy to claim that courts should have greater regard to objections to bail advanced by the police, but the vast majority of those to whom the court grants bail in the face of police objections are not detected in law-breaking whilst on bail.[126]

None of these observations breaks new ground, and yet their significance for bail has been accorded little attention. Thousands of people are being deprived of their liberty every year on the basis of predictions which have insecure statistical foundations. All the criminological evidence in analogous fields points to the likelihood of considerable over-prediction. If, as argued here, the primary concern is to prevent the commission of *serious* crimes in the period between arrest and trial, that makes the problem of protection harder, not easier. Serious crimes are rarer and therefore more difficult to predict than law-breaking in general, and the rate of false positives may well be very high.[127]

At a time when governments have shown an attraction to tougher policies on remands, it is essential to reassert fundamental principles: the courts should operate with a strong presumption in favour of liberty and innocence; this ought not to be displaced unless the court is satisfied that there is sufficient evidence to continue with the charge, a test which should become stricter as time progresses and should require

---

[124] Practice Direction, *Bail: Failure to surrender and trial in absence*, available in the Consolidated Criminal Practice Direction at www.hmcourts-service.gov.uk.

[125] J. Goldkamp and M. R. Gottfredson, *Policy Guidelines for Bail: An Exercise in Court Reform* (1985), based on research in Philadelphia courts.

[126] Above, n 87 and accompanying text.

[127] For a brief summary of the research on identifying dangerous offenders, see Ashworth, *Sentencing and Criminal Justice* (5th ed, 2010), Ch 6.8.

careful judgements by the CPS. The court's decision on the form of remand should be governed by a statutory framework or by guidelines similar to those for sentencing.[128] In principle, there should be progressive levels of justification, and preferred disposals with reasons required for departing from them.[129] The preferred disposal should be unconditional bail. There should be evidence-based reasons for moved to the next level, conditional bail. The next step up, to remand in custody, should only be taken where the court is satisfied that the charge, if proved at the trial, would be likely to result in the imposition of a custodial sentence, and where the evidence for the chosen ground for refusing bail is clear and convincing. Even then, the court should first consider whether conditional bail with a requirement of electronic monitoring would not be adequate. If a court decides that a custodial remand is unavoidable, it should be for as short a period as possible. English law does have mechanisms to ensure this, including time limits for cases where the defendant is remanded in custody,[130] but some defendants still spend more than six months (and a few more than 12 months) awaiting their trials in custody.[131] Although waiting times are longer in most other European countries, this does not excuse long delays when they occur.

In conclusion, we make five points about remand decisions. First, they rely to a large extent on predictions, and the evidential foundations are rarely strong. That ought to counsel great caution: although it is common these days to refer to risk, public protection and public safety, this should not be allowed to conceal the fragility of many of these predictions. Secondly, the Convention framework as developed by the Strasbourg Court ought to be used instead of the more common references to 'balancing' the defendant's right to liberty against the need for public protection. In principle, the right to liberty should be respected, and only if there is strong evidence should one of the recognized exceptions be allowed to prevail. Moreover, the Strasbourg Court has emphasized the evidential basis for and the seriousness of the charge. As argued here, English law should be amended so as to require courts to consider the probability of a prison sentence being imposed if the facts alleged are proved, before a custodial remand is made. That requires the court to make a prediction of a different kind, but one that should be possible if there is coherent guidance on sentencing. This leads on to the third factor: there must be greater willingness among decision makers to question the decisions taken previously in each case, and to re-appraise the evidence and the approach to be taken. In particular, the CPS must be prepared to conduct a meaningful review of the police conclusion, and the court should likewise conduct a meaningful review of the CPS recommendation. Defence lawyers, too, must be prepared to offer a 'full and fearless' defence rather than trying to curry favour with the court or CPS, as Hucklesby's research suggests in some cases. Such changes will require alterations to the system, since decision makers cannot be expected to reach different

---

[128] For similar proposals, see Dhami (above, n 79) and Player (above, n 6).

[129] Cf P. Robinson, 'Punishing Dangerousness: Cloaking Preventive Detention as Criminal Justice' (2001) 114 *Harvard LR* 1429, at 1447.

[130] Corre and Wolchover, above n 1, Ch 12.   [131] Above n 99 and accompanying text.

decisions without (a) a little more time and (b) fresh information. Fourthly, the question of police remands must be revisited. It seems to be assumed that the only practical approach to deciding bail/custody decisions prior to a court appearance is to leave these to the police. However, that gives them considerable (bargaining) power over suspects, and a decision to refuse bail has strong correlations with subsequent decisions about loss of liberty. The question of conferring this power on a senior member of the CPS should be revisited urgently. And fifthly, courts must (continue to) adopt a more legalistic and rights-responsive approach to remand decisions. The right to liberty and the presumption of innocence should become part of the everyday currency of the courts, to make it clear how exceptional a remand in custody should be. This has little to do with overcrowding in the prisons: even if there were many available places in the prisons, the argument for remanding an accused person in custody ought to be a strong one. The remand issue is not a prisons problem, so much as a justice problem. At the same time, and for the same reason, efforts to develop non-custodial facilities for holding defendants in the community must be re-doubled.

FURTHER READING

HUCKLESBY, A., 'Remand Decision-Makers' [1997] *Crim LR* 269.

DHAMI, M., 'From Discretion to Disagreement: Explaining Disparities in Judges' Pre-Trial Decisions' (2005) 23 *Behavioural Sciences and the Law* 367.

PLAYER, E., 'Remanding Women in Custody: Concerns for Human Rights' (2007) 70 *MLR* 402.

Questions for Discussion

1. Are there grounds for concern about the number of people remanded in custody who are subsequently acquitted or convicted and given a non-custodial sentence?

2. Does the English system respect the rights of defendants who have been charged but not convicted?

3. Should bail be refused in cases where a custodial sentence on conviction would be unlikely?

9

PRE-TRIAL ISSUES: DISCLOSURE, DELAY AND ABUSE OF PROCESS

As a case proceeds to court, mechanisms need to be in place to ensure that an effective trial can take place. Much of this will be the business of the parties, who will prepare their trial strategies, ensure that witnesses are called and so on. But not everything can be left to the parties: in the run up to the trial, there are various procedural mechanisms to ensure that the eventual trial runs smoothly and fairly. In this chapter, we consider some of these processes. In terms of facilitating the smooth running of the trial, we concentrate on ways of screening cases and clarifying some of the issues prior to trial. In terms of ensuring that the defendant is not subjected to an unfair trial, we examine some question that arise under the broad heading of abuse of process, concentrating on issues of delay and the entrapment doctrine.

9.1 FILTERING CASES PRIOR TO TRIAL

In preceding chapters it has been stressed that defendants should not face trial unless there is good justification for their doing so. This is partly because of the cost of trial procedures; partly because of the distress and inconvenience they impose on defendants; and partly to protect the innocent from mistaken conviction. Thus, at various stages of the criminal process, there are evidential barriers to filter out weak cases. There must be 'sufficient evidence' before a defendant is charged,[1] and the Crown Prosecution Service (CPS) must determine that there is a reasonable prospect of conviction before taking a case to court. As we saw in Chapter 7, the CPS should also ensure that prosecution is in the public interest. Even when the trial has commenced, there are evidential barriers to ensure that the defendant is not put in jeopardy of conviction without good reason. In the Crown Court the judge should not let the case go

---

[1] See Ch 4 and E. Cape, 'Sufficient Evidence to Charge?' [1999] *Crim LR* 874.

to the jury unless there is sufficient evidence to enable a jury to find the crime charged
to be proved beyond reasonable doubt;[2] there is a similar test in summary trial.

A further filtering mechanism exists in the pre-trial stage. All cases start their lives
in the magistrates' court, where issues such as bail can be given a speedy initial determination (see Chapter 8). But the more serious criminal cases are tried in the Crown
Court. Historically, the process of 'committal' has been used to give defendants an
opportunity to claim that there is insufficient evidence to justify bringing their case to
trial. The mechanism for doing so used to be the institution of the grand jury, but the
grand jury was abolished in 1930. For much of the last century defendants were able
to use 'committal proceedings' before the magistrates to argue against the case proceeding to jury trial. Various committees and commissions recommended the abolition of committal proceedings, on the basis that 'paper committals' served no useful
purpose and 'full committals' put victims and witnesses under stress by requiring
them to give their evidence twice,[3] and they were eventually abolished for cases triable only on indictment in 2001.[4] Abolition was extended to either way offences by the
Criminal Justice Act 2003,[5] under provisions which are expected to be brought into
force in 2010.[6] Cases are now transferred to the jurisdiction of the Crown Court by a
relatively simple administrative mechanism, and defendants are likely to wait for the
trial proper before arguing that the prosecution case is weak. It is not easy to say why
the filtering process operated by the magistrates gradually came to lose its significance
in the criminal process. There may be a number of factors. A dry run of the case during
committal would once have been the major opportunity for a defendant to discover
the details of the case against him. But improvements in disclosure rules—as well,
perhaps, as something as banal as the invention of the photocopying machine—has
meant that committal proceedings are no longer needed for this purpose. The creation of the CPS which, whatever its flaws, does review the strength of the case and does
discontinue a considerable number of prosecutions (see Chapter 7), may also be part
of the explanation.

The current procedures for transferring cases to the Crown Court are, in outline,
as follows. There is an initial hearing in the magistrates' court to decide the question
of bail. In either way offences there will also be a mode of trial hearing, and then,
if the case is to be tried on indictment, it is simply transferred to the Crown Court
without committal. This does not deprive the defendant of all means of challenging
the case prior to trial. He can apply to the Crown Court to have the case against him
dismissed.[7] The judge has discretion whether or not to hear oral evidence on the application. He should dismiss the case against the accused if he considers the prosecution

---

[2] *R v Galbraith* [1981] 1 WLR 1039, discussed in Ch 11.

[3] See Royal Commission on Criminal Justice, *Report* (1993), 89–91, discussing similar recommendations
by the Royal Commission on Criminal Procedure (1981) and the Fraud Trials Committee (1987).

[4] Under the Crime and Disorder Act 1998, s 51.   [5] Section 41 and Sch 3.

[6] *Blackstone's Criminal Practice 2010*, D10.4.

[7] Crime and Disorder Act 1988, Sch 3; Crime and Disorder Act 1998 (Dismissal of Charges Sent) Rules
1998 (SI 1998 No 3048).

does not have enough evidence to enable a reasonable jury to convict.[8] Applications to dismiss the case are probably rare.

9.2 PRE-TRIAL DISCLOSURE

(A) PROSECUTION DISCLOSURE

Disclosure of evidence before trial is a matter of some importance. From the point of view of efficiency, trials will run most smoothly when each side has some notice of the evidence and arguments that the opposing side will present at trial. But there are also more serious issues of justice at stake here. Non-disclosure of prosecution evidence was a common factor in many of the miscarriage of justice cases of the late 1980s and early 1990s. Failures in prosecution disclosure continue to be a frequent ground of appeal to the Court of Appeal, which has noted that it hears 'countless' cases on the issue.[9] Many cases referred to the Court by the Criminal Cases Review Commission involve disclosure issues.[10]

As far as the prosecution is concerned, there is a basic requirement that it disclose its case prior to trial. This will usually take the form of a bundle of witness statements presented after the case has been transferred to the Crown Court. Evidence not disclosed in this manner may not be admissible at trial. In the magistrates' court, there is a similar requirement of advance notice of the evidence as far as either way offences are concerned.[11] Remarkably, there is no legal requirement that the defence be advised of the prosecution case in advance in summary cases. Although the Divisional Court has held otherwise,[12] it is quite possible that this breaches Article 6 of the European Convention on Human rights (ECHR), which has been held to require equality of arms.[13] In light of this, guidelines on disclosure issued by the Attorney General now state that the prosecution should disclose its case in all summary proceedings.[14]

The foregoing deals with advance notice of the evidence the prosecution intends to call at trial. What of evidence that it does not intend to call? If, for example, a witness interviewed by the police fails to support the prosecution's version of events, it is unlikely that the prosecution would choose to call that person at trial. Yet knowledge of

---

[8] For more detail, see *Blackstone's Criminal Practice 2010*, D10.22.

[9] *R v Pomfrett* [2009] EWCA Crim 1471, [4]. See, e.g., *R v Giles* [2009] EWCA Crim 1388; *R v Zengeya* [2009] EWCA Crim 1369; *Tucker v CPS* [2008] EWCA Crim 1368.

[10] See L. Elks, *Righting Miscarriages of Justice? Ten Years of the Criminal Cases Review Commission* (2008), 309–11.

[11] Magistrates' Courts (Advance Information) Rules 1985.

[12] *R v Stratford JJ, ex p Imbert* [1999] 2 Cr App R 276.

[13] For further discussion, see B. Emmerson, A. Ashworth and A. Macdonald, *Human Rights and Criminal Justice* (2nd ed, 2007), 549–60.

[14] *Attorney General's Guidelines on Disclosure* (2005), para 57.

what the witness said might be of considerable importance to the defence. Rules requiring disclosure of such unused material were gradually developed by the courts.[15] In
1996 they were put on a statutory footing. The Criminal Procedure and Investigations
Act 1996 (CPIA), along with the Code of Practice issued under it, lay out in some detail
how prosecution disclosure should be managed and what tests should be applied to
determine whether material should be disclosed. Aspects of the regime were modified
by the Criminal Justice Act 2003.[16] The first thing to say about prosecution disclosure
of unused material is that it has long been controversial. This is partly because, as
noted above, failures in prosecution disclosure are a common element in many well-
known miscarriage of justice cases; it is perhaps hardly surprising that the prosecution
should sometimes be reluctant to disclose to the defence material which may undermine its case. It is also because the 1996 reforms were introduced as a result of claims
by the police that the common law disclosure regime imposed too heavy a burden on
them; the reforms were thus widely perceived as having restricted the defence's ability
to access important information.

The principles that should apply to prosecution disclosure are reasonably
straightforward. The defence has a right to disclosure of all relevant evidence; as
the principle is sometimes put, the prosecution should be seen as the trustee, rather
than the owner, of any information gathered during the police investigation.[17] The
European Commission of Human Rights has expressed a similar idea in terms of
equality of arms: the State's superior resources mean that the defence should have
access to all relevant evidence that has been or could be gathered by the prosecution.[18] The CPIA regime attempts to put these principles into effect by placing an
obligation on the police to list and describe unused material in a 'schedule'.[19] The
schedule is crucial to the operation of the disclosure scheme. It forms the basis
on which the CPS will make decisions as to what material should be disclosed to
the defence; the schedule itself is disclosed to the defence, and is thus the primary
means by which the defence can make a claim that material relevant to it has not
been disclosed. Any material which 'might reasonably be considered capable of
undermining the case for the prosecution or of assisting the case for the accused'[20]
should be disclosed to the defence. This test should be kept under review.[21] Thus,
as the facts change, and as more is learned about the defence case, further material may fall within the test and require disclosure. Prosecutors should continue to
consider disclosure during the course of the trial. There are exceptions for sensitive
material (material which carries a 'real risk of serious prejudice to an important
public interest'[22]). This is recorded on a separate schedule, which is not disclosed

---

[15] For an overview of the history, see R. Leng, 'The Exchange of Information and Disclosure' in
M. McConville and G. Wilson (eds), *The Handbook of the Criminal Justice Process* (2002).

[16] See generally M. Redmayne, 'Disclosure and its Discontents' [2004] *Crim LR* 441.

[17] P. O'Connor, 'Prosecution Disclosure: Principle, Practice and Justice' [1992] *Crim LR* 464.

[18] *Jespers v Belgium* (1981) 27 DR 61.   [19] CPIA, s 24.   [20] CPIA, s 3(1)(a).

[21] CPIA, s 9.   [22] *R v H & C* [2004] UKHL 3, [36].

to the defence. The framework for disclosing sensitive information is considered further below.

In practice, as various research studies have shown, there are a number of problems with the way this scheme works.[23] Some of the Criminal Justice Act 2003 reforms were intended to address these shortcomings, in particular by simplifying the test for prosecution disclosure, but the most recent survey by the Crown Prosecution Service Inspectorate (CPSI) identifies continuing problems.[24] A major problem is that decisions about disclosure are made by prosecutors (and, in some cases, at trial by appointed counsel), who are to a large extent reliant on information provided to them by the police. But the schedules prepared by the police are poor: they often contain insufficient detail to enable prosecutors to make informed decisions about what should be disclosed (about half of cases), and sometimes fail to mention significant information altogether.[25] Ideally, the CPS should scrutinize the schedules carefully, and ask for more information from the police where detail is lacking. But the CPSI found that this happened in less than half of cases where descriptions were inadequate.[26] Sometimes the response of prosecutors, often prompted by judges who have little faith in the disclosure regime, is to make 'blanket' disclosure, allowing the defence access to any information it wishes, or all information in a particular category (e.g. witness statements), rather than making a considered application of the test in the Act.[27]

It is not surprising to find these problems in the disclosure regime. The police have little incentive to make the schedules transparent. While the CPSI found no evidence of deliberate non-disclosure by the police,[28] Quirk's interview based study found that police officers admitted that they were reluctant to help the defence through disclosure.[29] One officer noted the possibility of listing potentially disclosable material on the sensitive schedule, so that defendants would not have access to it and be in a position to request disclosure, and the CPSI noted its concerns about this. In its view, only 20 per cent of cases judged by the police to involve sensitive material were properly categorized as such; and inadequate descriptions of material on the sensitive schedules were again rarely questioned by prosecutors. The Inspectorate therefore felt unable to provide an 'assurance as to the appropriateness of CPS handling of material categorised as sensitive', noting that 'there is a significant risk that miscarriages of justice may occur'.[30] While some of the problems with the disclosure regime are caused by lack of training and resources—compiling the schedules, reviewing them, and chasing up inadequate descriptions is time consuming—it is likely that, as Quirk

---

[23] CPSI, *The Inspectorate's Report on the Thematic Review of the Disclosure of Unused Material* (2000); J. Plotnikoff and R. Woolfson, *'A Fair Balance'? Evaluation of the Operation of Disclosure Law* (2001).

[24] HMCPSI, *Disclosure: A Thematic Review of the Duties of Disclosure of Unused Material Undertaken by the CPS* (2008).

[25] *Ibid.*, 32–4.   [26] *Ibid.*, 33.   [27] *Ibid.*, 34–5, 67–8.   [28] *Ibid.*, 63.

[29] H. Quirk, 'The Significance of Culture in Criminal Procedure Reform: Why the Revised Disclosure Scheme Cannot Work' (2006) 10 *E & P* 42, 48–50.

[30] HMCPSI, above n 24, 51.

notes, adversarial attitudes and the wish not to help defendants escape conviction (especially when it can be assumed that the majority will plead guilty) plays a role. Indeed, prosecutors are not immune from taking an overly adversarial attitude. Elks, a former member of the Criminal Cases Review Commission, has highlighted the case of *Blackburn*[31] in this respect, where the prosecution did not disclose the fact that the complainant had a history of false complaints, and notes that this is an example of a miscarriage of justice that may well have been caused by the original provisions of the original Criminal Procedure and Investigations Act.[32]

There are no obvious solutions to the shortcomings of the disclosure regime. Plotnikoff and Woolfson concluded that the answer lay in training and funding of prosecutors, to enable them to make informed decisions about the material gathered during the police investigation. The most recent CPSI report echoes this, making various recommendations to promote better scrutiny of schedules and transparency of decision making in relation to them. While the CPSI notes that the practice of blanket disclosure is fairly common, it does not endorse it as a solution, partly because it goes against the existing legal framework and partly because, if large amounts of material are simply handed to the defence, resources will still be needed to cover defence claims on legal aid in relation to the scrutiny of the material.[33] Its most radical suggestion is that in cases tried in the magistrates' courts, unused material should simply be handed to prosecutors who would then make their own decisions about disclosability, thus avoiding the need to rely on schedules.[34] This proposal has some merit, so long as the CPS can be given adequate resources to do a proper job. It might, though, be questioned why this innovation should be confined to summary cases. While these cases will generally involve less potentially disclosable material, there is some irony in leaving prosecutors reliant on police compiled schedules in the more serious cases heard in the Crown Court.

While the regime introduced by the CPIA has had some benefits, such as the provision of schedules to the defence which help it to monitor what has not been disclosed, it is obvious the prosecution disclosure remains a problematic area. While greater involvement of prosecutors in decision making about disclosure, as suggested by the CPSI, holds out some promise, it is doubtful that there are any easy solutions here. To some extent, the system will always be reliant on the police, and the police are inevitably reluctant to disclose unused material that may be helpful to defendants.

(B) DEFENCE DISCLOSURE

When it comes to defence disclosure, different principles apply. Before 1996, there was no general obligation on the defence to disclose details of its case before trial.

---

[31] [2005] EWCA Crim 1349.   [32] Elks, above n 10, 315–17.

[33] See also the very strong criticism of this practice in Court of Appeal, *Protocol for the Control and Management of Unused Material in the Crown Court* (2006), paras 30–1.

[34] HMCPSI, above n 24, 40–1.

There were limited exceptions to this general rule, applying to alibis, expert evidence, and serious fraud trials. The CPIA changed this, imposing an obligation on the defence, in trials on indictment, to disclose details of its case following initial disclosure by the prosecution. There is no statutory requirement of defence disclosure in summary trials, though disclosure will sometimes be beneficial to the defence because, by alerting the prosecution to the issues to be raised, it may trigger further prosecution disclosure. Defence disclosure was expanded by the Criminal Justice Act 2003 (CJA).[35] As the law now stands, in the Crown Court the defence should provide a defence statement, setting out the details of its case, including any defences and points of law to be raised, and the matters on which it takes issue with the prosecution, as well as the reasons why it does so.[36] The CJA contains provisions which would go even further than this, requiring the defence to disclose the names and addresses of the witnesses it intends to call and details of any expert witnesses it has consulted.[37] These provisions were controversial[38] and would have been difficult to enforce. They have not yet been implemented and it now seems doubtful that they ever will be.

Defence disclosure has certain parallels with the changes to the right to silence introduced by the Criminal Justice and Public Order Act 1994 (see Chapter 4). Both are enforced by adverse inferences. If a defendant fails to issue a defence statement, or if his defence at trial departs from what was disclosed, an adverse inference may be drawn against him. It must be said, however, that adverse inferences from non-disclosure are even less straightforward than those from silence. The defendant's failure to disclose a defence before trial is only suspicious because the law places an obligation on him to do so, and in that situation the inference that the defence is fabricated is surely a weak one. Indeed, where the defendant fails to disclose a point of law on which he relies, it is difficult to see how any adverse inference could be drawn at all. Further, if disclosure is inadequate, it will often be difficult to judge whether this is the defendant's fault or that of his legal team. These problems no doubt partly explain why the defence disclosure provisions in the CPIA have had such little impact. In contrast to the mass of case law on the inferences from silence provisions, there are barely any reported cases on the conditions in which an inference from faulty disclosure can be drawn.[39] The research suggests that the majority of defence statements are insufficiently detailed to meet the requirements of the Act, yet that judges and prosecutors are reluctant to make much of such failings. The changes brought in by the CJA 2003 did give sharper teeth to the enforcement mechanisms,[40] but despite the scolding delivered in the Court of Appeal's Disclosure Protocol—calling for a

---

[35] See Redmayne, above n 16. The provisions were further modified by the Criminal Justice and Immigration Act 2008, s 60.

[36] CPIA, s 6A.   [37] CJA 2003, ss 34–35.   [38] See Redmayne, above n 16.

[39] The principal decision is *Tibbs* [2000] 2 Cr App R 309. See also *Wheeler* [2001] 1 Cr App R 10; *R (Sullivan) v Crown Court at Maidstone* [2002] 1 WLR 2747.

[40] CPIA, ss 6E, 11.

'complete change in the culture' relating to defence disclosure[41]—there are no signs that things have changed.[42]

(C) THE DEFENDANT'S OBLIGATIONS

Defence disclosure raises issues of principle. Some commentators consider that it goes against the grain of the adversarial system for defendants to have to perform duties which may be helpful to the prosecution. These issues are best considered in the context of wider changes in criminal procedure, which emphasize the need for defendants to cooperate with the courts. A useful starting point is the Court of Appeal's decision in *R v Gleeson*.[43] Here, the defence realized it had a technical defence to the charge made in the indictment. It waited until the end of the prosecution case, and then made a submission of no case to answer on the basis that the common law conspiracy charged by the prosecution was impossible (i.e. it claimed that the defendant had conspired to do something which was not actually an offence). The judge agreed that this was a sound defence, but permitted the prosecution to redraft the indictment so that the charge was statutory conspiracy (to which impossibility is not a defence). The defence appealed on the basis that the judge should not have permitted this course of action. In dismissing the appeal, the Court of Appeal commented on the duties of the defence:

'A prosecution [should] not be frustrated by errors of the prosecutor, unless such errors have irremediably rendered a fair trial for the defendant impossible. For defence advocates to seek to take advantage of such errors by deliberately delaying identification of an issue of fact or law in the case until the last possible moment is, in our view, no longer acceptable, given the legislative and procedural changes to our criminal justice process in recent years.'[44]

The CJA amendments make defence obligations somewhat clearer than they were at the time of *Gleeson*. The CPIA now specifies that, in the Crown Court, the defence should disclose any points of law to be relied on, though the sanction specified for failure is the drawing of adverse inferences rather than, as in *Gleeson*, the loss of a watertight defence.

Shortly after *Gleeson* was decided, the Criminal Procedure Rules (CPR) were introduced.[45] These rules set out the duties of the parties and the courts in relation to the conduct of criminal proceedings. Rule 1.1 sets out the 'overriding objective' of the rules, which is 'that criminal cases be dealt with justly'.

---

[41] Above n 33, paras 32–46.

[42] The CPSI review, above n 24 at 48, judged that less than half of defence statements met the criteria in the CPIA. See also R Denyer, 'The Defence Statement' [2009] *Crim LR* 340, noting that he is 'still waiting' to see effective defence statements.

[43] [2004] *Crim LR* 579.   [44] *Ibid.*, [35].

[45] An up-to-date version of the rules can be found at: www.justice.gov.uk/criminal/procrules_fin/rulesmenu.htm.

'Dealing with a criminal case justly includes—

    (a) acquitting the innocent and convicting the guilty;

    (b) dealing with the prosecution and the defence fairly;

    (c) recognising the rights of a defendant, particularly those under Article 6 of the European Convention on Human Rights;

    (d) respecting the interests of witnesses, victims and jurors and keeping them informed of the progress of the case;

    (e) dealing with the case efficiently and expeditiously;

    (f) ensuring that appropriate information is available to the court when bail and sentence are considered; and

    (g) dealing with the case in ways that take into account—

        (i) the gravity of the offence alleged,

        (ii) the complexity of what is in issue,

        (iii) the severity of the consequences for the defendant and others affected, and

        (iv) the needs of other cases.[46]

Rule 1.2 places a duty on the parties to 'prepare and conduct the case in accordance with the overrriding objective', and rule 1.3 requires the courts to further the objective when dealing with cases. Rule 3.2 further specifies the duty of the courts:

'(1)   The court must further the overriding objective by actively managing the case.
(2)   Active case management includes—

    (a) the early identification of the real issues;

    (b) the early identification of the needs of witnesses;

    (c) achieving certainty as to what must be done, by whom, and when, in particular by the early setting of a timetable for the progress of the case;

    (d) monitoring the progress of the case and compliance with directions;

    (e) ensuring that evidence, whether disputed or not, is presented in the shortest and clearest way;

    (f) discouraging delay, dealing with as many aspects of the case as possible on the same occasion, and avoiding unnecessary hearings;

    (g) encouraging the participants to cooperate in the progression of the case; and

    (h) making use of technology.

(3)   The court must actively manage the case by giving any direction appropriate to the needs of that case as early as possible.'

Rule 3.3 obliges the parties to assist the court in its pursuit of the overriding objective. After these general pronouncements, the rules descend to the level of procedural detail, setting out how various stages of litigation should proceed.[47]

---

[46] CPR 2005, 1.1(2).

[47] Though there are more radical tinges to some sections of the rules, e.g. Part 33 on Expert Evidence.

The Criminal Procedure Rules are significant in that they indicate that the defence's concern should not just be to win its own case, but to ensure that the case is dealt with justly, where justice includes the conviction of the guilty. While *Gleeson* suggests that a new vision of criminal adjudication was emerging prior to the introduction of the rules, the rules have been referred to on various occasions as marking a 'fundamental change' in criminal procedure.[48] The comments of the Divisional Court in *Malcolm v Director of Public Prosecutions* are failrly typical:

'Miss Calder's submissions, which emphasised the obligation of the prosecution to prove its case in its entirety before closing its case, and certainly before end of the final speech for the defence, had an anachronistic, and obsolete, ring. Criminal trials are no longer to be treated as a game, in which each move is final and any omission by the prosecution leads to its failure. It is the duty of the defence to make its defence and the issues it raises clear to the prosecution and to the court at an early stage. That duty is implicit in r.3.3 of the Criminal Procedure Rules 2005, which requires the parties actively to assist the exercise by the court of its case management powers, the exercise of which requires early identification of the *real* issues. Even in a relatively straightforward trial such as the present, in the magistrates' court (where there is not yet any requirement of a defence statement or a pre-trial review), it is the duty of the defence to make the real issues clear *at the latest* before the prosecution closes its case.'[49]

As we have seen, in the Crown Court the defence is under a statutory obligartion to disclose its defence to the prosecution before trial. Although there is no such statutory obligation in the magistrates' court, an implication of CPR 3.2 and 3.3 is that the defence may be asked to reveal details of its case prior to trial. Thus in *Robinson v Abergavenny Magistrates' Court*,[50] when the defence raised an unanticipated issue at a late stage, the prosecution was granted an adjournment to give it time to respond to the new point. The Divisional Court rejected an application for judicial review of the decision to grant an adjournment, finding that *Gleeson* applied to the magistrates' court as much as to the Crown Court. The defence lawyer was said to have lost sight of his obligations under the CPR, and to be out of touch with the 'modern approach' to litigation.[51] In *R (on the application of DPP) v Chorley Magistrates' Court*, it was suggested that defendant should have been asked to identify the issues to be raised, and the witnesses needed, at a pre-trial hearing. That he had not done so meant that he should gain no advantage from taking the prosecution by surprise.[52]

However, there may be limits to what the defence can be required to do in pursuit of the overriding objective. In *Kelly v Warley Magistrates' Court* the District Judge asked the defence to produce a list of its witnesses prior to trial, to enable the prosecution to check their criminal records.[53] As we have seen, the CJA 2003 amended

    [48] *Lawson v Stafford Magistrates' Court* [2007] EWHC 2490 (Admin), [30].
    [49] [2007] EWHC 363 (Admin), [31]. For a very useful review of case law in this area, see P. Fields, 'Clarke and McDaid: A Technical Triumph' [2008] *Crim LR* 612.
    [50] [2007] EWHC 2005 (Admin).   [51] *Ibid.*, [27].   [52] [2006] EWHC 1795 (Admin), [26].
    [53] [2007] EWHC 1836 (Admin).

the disclosure provisions of the Criminal Procedure and Investigations Act, adding a requirement that the defence provide a list of its witnesses to the prosecution. But this provision has not yet been implemented, and in any case would only apply in the Crown Court. In *Kelly* it was argued that it would be odd if the CPR could introduce a requirement which the Government has so far decided not to implement, but this contention did not find favour, Laws LJ doubting 'whether this inchoate legislation can of itself bear the inference that the CPR provide no power to do what the deputy district judge did.'[54] It was nevertheless held that the District Judge had gone too far. Details of defence witnesses were subject to litigation privilege, and the court was concerned that unless the sanctions for failure to comply with a direction to reveal witness details were moderate and proportionate, the judge's direction would amount to an attempt to interfere with privilege rather than simply to regulate proceedings.[55] This would be the case, for example, if the judge had threatened to prohibit the defence from calling a witness whose details had not been provided to the prosecution before trial. However, the CPR have been amended in response to *Kelly*. Under rule 3.10 parties can be asked to provide details of the witnesses they wish to call, and rule 3.5(6) now provides a wide power to order any appropriate sanction. This probably now overrides litigation privilege.[56]

Perhaps the most radical application of the CPR has been in *R v Musone*, where they were used to justify the exclusion of defence evidence of 'substantial probative value'.[57] Musone had attempted to ambush a co-defendant, by introducing evidence of the co-defendant's bad character at a late stage; this was in breach of a provision requiring early notice of an intention to introduce bad character evidence. It seems that Musone could not have been prevented from doing this had the CPR not been in force. But in order to give the co-defendant a fair trial, the overriding objective was held to allow the judge to exclude the evidence.

What is one to make of these developments? Some might argue that the defence should not have to be helpful to the prosecution and that disclosure obligations, as well as some of the developments under the CPR, are therefore unprincipled. While the relevant principles are no doubt complex,[58] the uncompromising position just outlined has little to be said for it. Exceptions to the old rule that the defence does not have to disclose its case have long been recognized, thus an alibi notice provision was introduced as early as 1967, and appears to have been uncontroversial. And as a matter of theory, it is not evident that the defence could be said to have a right to win a case by taking the prosecution by surprise. As the CPR's overriding objective recognizes, trials are at least in part a search for the truth, and ambush has no part to play in this. However, in the previous chapter we noted that the privilege against self-incrimination is a widely

---

[54] *Ibid.*, [14].   [55] *Ibid.*, [32]–[35].
[56] See Law Society, *Criminal Procedure Rules: Impact on Solicitors' Duties to the Client* (2008).
[57] [2007] EWCA Crim 1237.
[58] See R. Mosteller, 'Discovery Against the Defense: Tilting the Adversarial Balance' (1986) 74 *California L Rev* 1567.

recognized principle of criminal procedure, and the privilege was characterized in terms of a defendant's immunity from being placed under a duty to cooperate. Do disclosure obligations and the like infringe this principle? It is arguable that they do not. Decisions such as *Gleeson*, *Robinson* and *Chorley Magistrates' Court* do not not state that defendants have to cooperate; they merely decide that defendants should not be able to gain an advantage, such as an acquittal on technical grounds, through doing so. And the statutory disclosure regime is enforced through adverse inferences, which like inferences from silence, can be said not to infringe the privilege. While the courts in cases such as *Malcolm* have been reasonably creative in dealing with procedure—for example, allowing the prosecution to recall a witness to address a late defence point after the justices had retired to decide the case—courts have not used the CPR to undermine aspects of procedure which might be said to embody substantive values. Thus in *Shaw v Director of Public Prosecutions* the prosecution, realising that it had made a mistake, changed the charge on which the defendant was to be tried at a late stage of proceedings. *Gleeson* was distinguished; the change, which suddenly put the defendant in jeopardy of imprisonment, was held to be inappropriate.[59] While *Musone* did involve the use of the CPR to exclude significant defence evidence, the Court of Appeal did note that this outcome should be rare,[60] and stressed that the exclusion was in pursuit of a fair trial for both defendants.

(D) PUBLIC INTEREST IMMUNITY

So far, we have considered the disclosure of non-sensitive material. There are further complexities in the disclosure regime where sensitive material is involved. If the police investigation involved an informer, for example, the prosecution might well be reluctant to disclose this information to the defence. In this situation the prosecution can make a claim of 'public interest immunity' (PII). This area of the law has caused various problems. The basic principle is that PII claims need to be judged by the courts; the prosecution should not decide that relevant material is sensitive and therefore not to be disclosed; non-disclosure needs the approval of the trial judge. Beyond this, the courts recognize three different types of PII claim. In type 1 claims, the defence will be alerted to the fact that a claim is being made and to the general nature of the material involved: for example that it relates to an informer but not the identity of the informer. In type 2 claims the defence will be notified of nothing more than that an application is being made; this might occur where telling the defence that the claim relates to an informer would make it obvious who the informer is. In type 3 claims the defence will not even be told that a PII application is being made.

The English courts, as well as the European Court of Human Rights, stress the importance of informing the judge whenever material is not being disclosed for PII reasons. The judge can then look out for the defence's interests during the trial. At

---

[59] [2007] EWHC 207 (Admin).   [60] Above n 57, [60].

the start of the trial, for example, it might seem that PII material is not relevant to the defence case; but the case might develop at trial in such a way that the material does become relevant and the decision to withhold it needs to be reassessed. There is less consensus on other issues. Type 2 PII hearings raise particular problems, for here the defence is not able directly to present argument on the key issue: the importance of the sensitive material to its case. In *Jasper v United Kingdom*,[61] the defence argued that in this situation the judge should appoint a 'special counsel', who could represent the defence during the PII hearing, being privy to the nature of the sensitive material but not reporting back to the defence on its exact nature.[62] A majority of the court thought the English courts did not need to go this far to comply with Article 6, but a substantial minority dissented on this point. In *Edwards and Lewis v United Kingdom*,[63] the court seems to have come close to reversing its decision in *Jasper*. Both defendants made entrapment claims at their respective trials. Here the European Court of Human Rights (ECtHR) thought it especially important that the defence should have some say about certain information that was not disclosed on PII grounds. This was because it was thought unfair to have the judge decide an issue—the validity of the entrapment claim—while in possession of information relevant to that claim about which the defence was not able to present adversarial argument. The solution, it was thought, was to appoint special counsel. This shows rather less trust in the impartiality of the judiciary than did the decision in *Jasper*.

Unsurprisingly, the decision in *Edwards and Lewis* threw the English courts into some turmoil. A few trial judges appointed special counsel, and the issue quickly came before the House of Lords. Its decision in *R v H and C*[64] is in some ways unhelpful. Rather than giving clear guidance on when special counsel should be appointed, it suggests that the issue should rarely arise because prosecutors can simply apply the test of disclosure found in the CPIA: if sensitive material assists the defence case or undermines the prosecution case, then it should (probably) be disclosed. If the prosecution cannot accept disclosure, it should terminate the prosecution. Where sensitive material does not meet the test in the CPIA, then it need not be disclosed. In neither case should the judge normally be troubled with the decision. While this may sound very sensible, it does not really confront the difficulty that prosecutors seem to encounter in practice. That they often do bring PII issues to the judge's attention suggests that they do not find the basic CPIA test a simple one; rightly or wrongly, they do not trust their own judgement and would rather involve the judge. Keeping the judge out of the picture may make things simpler from the point of view of the appearance of justice and the concerns expressed by the ECtHR, but it may not be the fairest way of dealing with the issues. Beyond this, the House of Lords was prepared to say little more than that the appointment of special counsel should be exceptional. Its reticence

---

[61] (2000) 30 EHRR 1.
[62] For a discussion of special counsel, and the difficulties they face, see J. Ip, 'The Rise and Spread of the Special Advocate' [2008] *PL* 717.
[63] (2005) 40 EHRR 24. See also *Botmeh v United Kingdom* (2008) 46 EHRR 31.
[64] [2004] 2 WLR 335.

may have been due, in part, to the knowledge that the Government had requested a referral of the decision in *Edwards and Lewis* to the Grand Chamber of the European Court of Human Rights. This request, however, was later withdrawn. In practice, the courts may find more useful guidance in the judgment of the Court of Appeal, which held that special counsel should be appointed whenever sensitive material is relevant to a 'preliminary determinative ruling', such as an application to stay proceedings, or where it is prejudicial to a defendant so that the judge does not feel able to make a decision involving the material without adversarial argument.[65] Later cases confirm that judges should never make rulings on the basis of material which, because it is subject to PII, the defence are unaware of and thus cannot contribute argument on.[66] However, the Court of Appeal has rejected the contention that judges are unable to put relevant material out of their minds when considering a point of law; this 'compart-mentalisation of the judicial mind' avoids the need for special counsel.[67]

There is another matter relating to PII on which judicial guidance has been dis-appointing. So far we have said nothing about the test the judge should apply when ruling on a PII claim. The basic question here is whether the judge should withhold rel-evant evidence from the defence in order to protect sensitive information. The ECtHR has suggested that this approach may be acceptable: 'The entitlement to disclosure of relevant evidence is not an absolute right. In any criminal proceedings there may be competing interests, such as national security or the need to protect witnesses at risk of reprisals or keep secret police methods of investigation of crime, which must be weighed against the rights of the accused.'[68] This view is a familiar one; it supposes that the defendant's rights are subject to being traded off against other values. The importance of those other values should not be slighted. An informer whose identity is revealed may be put in danger, and if they are to be protected this may involve very sig-nificant disruption to their life. Ordered to disclose the identity of such a person, the prosecution may feel it has no choice but to abandon the prosecution. Yet it is hardly palatable to withhold relevant evidence from the defence. There is obviously a difficult dilemma here, but given that non-prosecution—rather than the endangerment of the informer—is an option, one should be very wary of using the sort of balancing lan-guage that the ECtHR appears to espouse. Another point to bear in mind is that the prosecution may be able to avoid the dilemma described here by not bringing a pros-ecution which depends crucially on an informer in the first place. If a balancing test is to be used, then it is important to take a wide view of the issues (Could the situation have been avoided? Why not abandon the prosecution?) rather than one which simply weighs the importance of sensitivity against the defendant's rights.

Where PII is concerned, the English courts have tended to distance themselves from the sort of balancing language used by the ECtHR. Yet they have managed to

---

[65] [2004] 1 Cr App R 17.
[66] *Ali and Hussain v Revenue and Customs Prosecutions Office* [2008] EWCA Crim 1466.
[67] *R v May* [2005] EWCA Crim 97, [20]–[21].
[68] *Edwards and Lewis v United Kingdom*, above n 49, 53.

leave considerable ambiguity as to the nature of the test to be applied. In *Keane* it was suggested that material should be disclosed if it 'may prove the defendant's innocence or avoid a miscarriage of justice'.[69] Of course, the basic rule is that the defendant does not have to prove innocence. It is difficult to know whether this is just a careless choice of words, or whether the test is intended to set a reasonably high threshold. In favour of the latter interpretation, one might suppose that, had the court intended a simple test of relevance to be applied, it would have said so. Things are not clarified by the House of Lords in *H and C*. While the general thrust of the judgment is that relevant evidence should be disclosed to the defence, there are dicta which suggest that it is acceptable to withhold information so long as it will not be of significant help.[70]

There may be good reason for some caution in setting the test for disclosure of PII material. If the test is too wide—including, for example, material which '*may* be relevant' to the defence case—then the judge at a preliminary hearing may feel the need to disclose evidence which turns out not to be relevant to the defence case as it is developed at trial. But the current test for disclosure in the CPIA—'material which might reasonably be considered capable of undermining the case for the prosecution or of assisting the case for the accused'—is sufficiently robust to avoid this problem. Given the difficulty of justifying a balancing test where the defendant's ability to defend himself is concerned, there is a good argument for applying this test at the PII stage. Any material which meets this test should be disclosed. As for the vexed question of special counsel, the Court of Appeal's guidance in *H and C* appears to ensure that special counsel will be appointed in cases where they are most needed, that is, where the judge has a difficult decision to make and will benefit from adversarial argument. The contention in later cases, however, that judges can simply put sensitive material out of their mind when deciding certain issues, is dubious, and should be treated with caution.[71]

9.3 ABUSE OF PROCESS: AN OVERVIEW

In the remainder of this chapter, we will make frequent reference to the doctrine of abuse of process and its use to control criminal proceedings. We therefore begin with a brief overview of abuse of process before considering its application to two particular areas: delay and entrapment.[72]

The courts, both civil and criminal, have an inherent power to regulate their own process. This extends to being able to stop a case from proceeding in order to prevent

---

[69] [1994] 1 WLR 746, 751–2.   [70] Above n 50, [18], [37].

[71] See A. Wistrich, C. Guthrie and J. Rachlinski, 'Can Judges Ignore Inadmissible Information? The Difficulty of Deliberately Disregarding' (2005) 153 *U Pennsylvania L Rev* 1251.

[72] See generally A. Choo, *Abuse of Process and Judicial Stays of Criminal Proceedings* (2nd ed, 2008); J. Rogers, 'The Boundaries of Abuse of Process in Criminal Trials' [2008] *Current Legal Problems* 289.

the judicial process from being abused; in more technical terms, the case is 'stayed' as an abuse of process. A stay is not equivalent to an acquittal, and it is possible that the authorities could attempt to prosecute the defendant again for the same offence. However, any such prosecution would almost certainly be stayed as itself an abuse of process.

There are two broad situations in which proceedings may be stayed.[73] The first is where the defendant cannot receive a fair trial; an example would be where adverse media publicity has undermined the ability of the trial to proceed in an unbiased manner.[74] The second is where, although the defendant can still receive a fair trial in that he does not face an undue risk of false conviction, it would nevertheless be unfair to try him. A good flavour of the thinking behind this second type of abuse of process is provided by Lord Griffiths in one of the leading authorities, *R v Horseferry Road Magistrates' Court, ex parte Bennett*.[75] Here, the defendant had been brought to Britain to stand trial, not through formal extradition procedures, but by being arrested and handcuffed to the seat of an aeroplane bound for London:

'In the present case there is no suggestion that the appellant cannot have a fair trial, nor could it have been suggested that it would have been unfair to try him if he had been returned to this country through extradition procedures. If the court is to have the power to interfere with the prosecution in the present circumstances it must be because the judiciary accept a responsibility for the maintenance of the rule of law that embraces a willingness to oversee executive action and to refuse to countenance behaviour that threatens either basic human rights or the rule of law.... The courts, of course, have no power to apply direct discipline to the police or the prosecuting authorities, but they can refuse to allow them to take advantage of abuse of power by regarding their behaviour as an abuse of process and thus preventing a prosecution.'[76]

A striking example of the application of the doctrine is *R v Grant*,[77] where the police installed a listening device in the exercise yard of the police station where Grant was held. In this way they were able to overhear privileged conversations between the defendant and his solicitor, however, they apparently learned nothing of relevance to the case against Grant. Despite this, the Court of Appeal held that the trial should have been stayed as an abuse of process:

'we are in no doubt but that in general unlawful acts of the kind done in this case, amounting to a deliberate violation of a suspected person's right to legal professional privilege, are so great an affront to the integrity of the justice system , and therefore the rule of law, that the associated prosecution is rendered abusive and ought not to be countenanced by the court.'[78]

The court continued by noting that the police's action 'seriously undermines the rule of law'.[79]

---

[73] Choo, *ibid.*, 18; *R v Beckford* [1996] 1 Cr App R 94.
[74] E.g. *R v McCann* (1991) 92 Cr App R 239.   [75] [1994] 1 AC 42.   [76] *Ibid.*, 150.
[77] [2005] EWCA Crim 1089.   [78] *Ibid.*, [54].   [79] *Ibid.*, [57].

In Chapter 11 we consider the criminal trial in more detail. One of the topics covered there is the exclusion of improperly obtained evidence, where we argue that the appropriate rationale for exclusion is generally remedial: excluding evidence obtained in breach of the defendant's rights puts the defendant back in the position he ought to have been in, had his rights not been breached. While a remedial rationale might be used to explain many abuse of process cases, it cannot be stretched to fit the situation in *Grant*—Grant has not been disadvantaged by the breach of his right—and it is a poor fit for the way the court talks about abuse of process in that case. The court talks about the integrity of the justice system, a principle which reflects a principle of integrity, or legitimacy, that features prominently in scholarship about the criminal process.[80] If the court was to associate itself with the wrongdoing in *Grant*, it would undermine its integrity as a forum for dispensing justice and upholding the rule of law.

9.4 DELAY

Cases should generally be brought to trial as quickly as possible. There are several reasons why delay should be avoided. First, as we have observed on several occasions, the pre-trial stage involves considerable stress and uncertainty for defendants, as well as for victims. The case should be resolved as soon as possible so that all involved can get on with their lives. Where defendants are concerned, things are even more serious where bail has been denied. Every day between remand and trial is an extra day in custody; while time served on remand can be taken into account at the sentencing phase if the defendant is found guilty, no compensation is offered in the event of an acquittal. Secondly, human memory declines over time. The longer the period between the alleged crime and the trial, the less likely witnesses are to remember events clearly. Delay therefore makes the trial a less accurate means of adjudicating guilt and innocence. A third possible reason for avoiding delay has been highlighted in recent Government initiatives to bring defendants to trial as quickly as possible—sometimes within days of the alleged crime. It is thought that a speedy response to offending reinforces the connection between the crime and its punishment, bringing home to offenders the consequences of their offending behaviour. Thus the latest in a series of efficiency-based initiatives is 'Simple, Speedy, Summary Justice', which aims to deal with simple cases as quickly as possible in the magistrates' courts, with fewer pre-trial hearings and earlier guilty pleas.[81] Pilot projects suggest that this initiative has been largely successful.[82] Of course, it is possible for justice to be too quick, and earlier initiatives in expediting cases to trial have raised concerns that the defence has been

---

[80] See Choo, n 72 above; I. Dennis, *The Law of Evidence* (3rd ed, 2007), Ch 2.

[81] See Home Office, *Delivering Simple, Speedy, Summary Justice* (2006).

[82] Criminal Justice System, *Delivering Simple, Speedy, Summary Justice: An Evaluation of the Magistrates' Courts Tests* (2007).

given insufficient time to prepare for court.[83] The recent pilots provide some evidence that things are now working better, with fewer defence requests for adjournments suggesting that initiatives to deliver evidence to the defence in a timely manner have been successful.[84] Overall, adult cases in the magistrates' courts are now dealt with on average within seven weeks of charge.[85] The more complex cases in the Crown Court inevitably take longer. In 2008 in the more serious, indictable-only cases, defendants sent for trial in the Crown Court and who pleaded not guilty waited 29 weeks before trial. Cases where the defendant is remanded in custody are expedited, and on average these defendants wait for seven weeks less than those on bail.[86]

In the rest of this section, we concentrate on how the courts respond to cases in which, for various reasons, there has been considerable delay in bringing a case to trial. There are three main contexts in which pre-trial delay becomes an issue. The first is where a number of years have elapsed between the alleged crime and its prosecution; this may happen, for example, in child abuse cases where the victim does not feel able to report the crime until adulthood. Secondly, where a defendant is remanded in custody, there are various time limits imposed to ensure that the case does not take too long to come to trial. The courts often have to deal with situations where the prosecution argues that there are good reasons for extending the time limits. Finally, the courts also concern themselves with delay between charge and trial, whether or not the defendant has been on remand. If the prosecution does not bring the case to trial within a reasonable time, the court may stop the prosecution as an abuse of process. Each of these contexts will be dealt with in turn.

(A) DELAY AND 'STALE' OFFENCES

As far as stale offences are concerned, there is a very different approach between summary and indictable offences. For summary offences—the least serious offences, which can only be tried in the magistrates' courts—proceedings must be started within six months of the alleged offence having taken place.[87] Apart from such cases, in English criminal law, there is no statute of limitations.[88] There is thus no bar to bringing a case to court 20, 30, 50 or even more years after the alleged crime was committed. Indeed, in passing the War Crimes Act 1991, Parliament intended that crimes committed during the Second World War should be prosecuted. A few prosecutions have been brought under this Act. For example, in *Sawoniuk*,[89] the defendant was tried for offences said to have been committed more than 50 years earlier.

---

[83] See D. Brown, *Reducing Delays in the Magistrates' Courts*, Home Office Research Findings No 131 (2000); J. Robins, 'The Speed of Fight' *Law Society Gazette* 3 August 2000, 24.

[84] See CJS, above n 82, 7.   [85] Ministry of Justice, *Judicial and Court Statistics 2008* (2009), 143.

[86] *Ibid.*, Table 6.15.   [87] Magistrates' Courts Act 1980, s 127.

[88] Though a few offences do have time limits attached to them, e.g. under Trade Descriptions Act 1968, s 19, prosecutions for indictable offences under the Act must be commenced within three years of the offence, or one year of its discovery, whichever is the earlier.

[89] [2000] 2 Cr App R 220.

A decision to prosecute an offence which occurred many years ago should obviously not be taken lightly. Quite apart from the difficulty of gathering reliable evidence, it may be argued that it is simply not right to hold someone to account for something that they did many years ago, given that their personality and circumstances may have changed completely during the intervening years. This is perhaps particularly pertinent where an adult is prosecuted for a crime committed during their youth. There is some recognition of this in the Code for Crown Prosecutors, which, among the public interest factors against prosecution, lists the situation where 'there has been a long delay between the offence taking place and the date of the trial.'[90] Of course, this should not always be a determining factor. Where, as in the case of war crimes, an offence is extremely serious, lapse of time by itself should not be a bar to prosecution. The CPS Code goes on to acknowledge counter-balancing factors, noting that staleness is not such a good reason against prosecution where 'the offence is serious; the delay has been caused in part by the defendant; the offence has only recently come to light; or the complexity of the offence has meant that there has been a long investigation.'[91] In the course of an inquiry into child abuse in children's homes the Home Affairs Committee considered whether a statute of limitations should be introduced to deal with the problems caused by delay.[92] It decided against it, and this seems right. Delay should not be an absolute bar to trial; it needs to be considered along with the counter-balancing factors in the individual case.

The primary concern of the courts in delay cases of this type is whether the defendant can have a fair trial, in the sense that he can adequately defend himself against the charges brought by the prosecution. There are two principal devices available to the courts to deal with this problem. The first is a warning to the jury about the difficulties caused by delay. The Judicial Studies Board has issued a specimen direction on the issue.[93] The gist of this is that the judge should ask the jury to consider the reasons for delay—for example, whether it reflects on the reliability of the complainant. The jury should also be told to make allowances for the fact that the passage of time may have made it difficult for the defendant to defend himself: he may have little memory of events many years ago, and evidence once available to him—such as an alibi—may no longer be.

In some cases the courts will go further than this. They may stay the prosecution on the grounds that it is an abuse of process. The relevant principles are summarized in *R v S*:

'(i)   Even where delay is unjustifiable, a permanent stay should be the exception rather than the rule;

(ii)   Where there is no fault on the part of the complainant or the prosecution, it will be very rare for a stay to be granted;

---

[90]   Para 6.5.   [91]   *Ibid.*

[92]   Home Affairs Committee, *The Conduct of Investigations into Past Cases of Abuse in Children's Homes*, Fourth Report 2001–2, paras 84–9.

[93]   Specimen Direction 37, available at www.jsboard.co.uk/criminal_law/cbb/index.htm. Cf *Brian M* [2000] 1 Cr App R 49.

(iii)   No stay should be granted in the absence of serious prejudice to the defence
        so that no fair trial can be held;

(iv)   When assessing possible serious prejudice, the judge should bear in mind
        his or her power to regulate the admissibility of evidence and that the trial
        process itself should ensure that all relevant factual issues arising from delay
        will be placed before the jury for their consideration in accordance with
        appropriate direction from the judge;

(v)   If, having considered all these factors, a judge's assessment is that a fair trial
        will be possible, a stay should not be granted.'[94]

These rather abstract principles give little insight into the practice of the courts, which
is inevitably fact-specific. It is therefore helpful to consider a few examples from the
case law. In *R v Telford Justices, ex parte Badhan*,[95] the defendant was prosecuted for a
sexual offence some 15 years after it was said to have occurred. The Divisional Court
held that proceedings should have been stayed, because it was not possible for the
defendant to receive a fair trial. Here, there was no abuse of process in the sense that
the prosecution was at fault: it had not caused the delay. The delay was due to the complainant not having come forward for many years, for reasons which the court seemed
to accept were good ones. Nevertheless, the feeling that the defendant was placed in a
very difficult position—'to investigate an alibi for an unknown Saturday evening in a
year commencing 16 years ago is a doomed enterprise'[96]—justified a stay. The case may
be contrasted with *Wilkinson*,[97] where the defendant was charged with sexual assaults
of his daughters some 15 to 30 years earlier. Although the Court of Appeal noted that
the defendant himself may have contributed to the delay—by swearing his daughters
to secrecy—it put most emphasis on the criterion of whether a fair trial was possible.
It was held that it was, the court noting that in this case the allegation did not relate
to a specific day, but to a continuing course of conduct. 'Accordingly, it is not a case
in which inability, after many years, to establish a particular alibi for a particular day
could have been an important factor.'[98] In *Sheikh*,[99] where there was no suggestion
that the prosecution was at fault, the fact that the 25-year delay meant that certain
documents relevant to D's defence were no longer available was held to be significant;
this meant that D could no longer receive a fair trial and proceedings should have
been stayed. *Ali* considers the question of missing material in more detail.[100] Here
there was some fault on the part of the prosecution; D was originally arrested in 1997,
but not charged. He was rearrested seven years later, after which proceedings ensued
promptly. The delay meant that certain documents were unavailable. While 'The mere
fact that missing material might have assisted the defence will not necessarily lead to

---

[94] [2006] EWCA Crim 756, [21]. S also notes that, contrary to what was said in some of the earlier cases,
the defendant does not bear a burden of proof to show that a fair trial would not be possible.

[95] [1991] 2 QB 78.   [96] *Ibid.*, at 91.   [97] [1996] 1 Cr App R 81.   [98] *Ibid.*, at 86.

[99] [2006] EWCA Crim 2625.

[100] [2007] EWCA Crim 691.

a stay', there should be 'sufficiently credible evidence, *apart from the missing evidence*, leaving the defence [*sic*] to exploit the gaps left by the missing evidence. The rationale for refusing a stay is the existence of credible evidence, itself untainted by what has gone missing.'[101] In this case, the missing material would have been important in assessing the complainants' credibility, and this counted in favour of a stay. However, the Court of Appeal suggested that careful judicial direction might have addressed the problem. The complainants had both made applications for compensation to the Criminal Injuries Compensation Authority. Documents showed that one application contained untruths, casting doubt on this complainant's general credibility, but the documents in relation to the other application were no longer available. The prejudice caused by the unavailability of this material 'could only have been cured…by directing the jury to assume that T's application was as mendacious as that of S.'[102] This is an interesting approach, but it is not clear that it would—or should—be extended beyond cases where the loss of evidence has been caused by the prosecution.

The difficulties posed for the courts by delay are well illustrated by the Court of Appeal's strange decision in *R v B*,[103] where the defendant had been convicted, in 2002, of sexually abusing his stepdaughter between 1968 and 1972. The Court of Appeal did not feel that any criticism could be made of the judge's decision to proceed with the case, and, indeed, to allow the case to go to the jury. Nevertheless, it decided to use what it referred to as its 'residual discretion to set aside a conviction if we feel it is unsafe or unfair to allow it to stand'.[104] The principal concern was the difficulty the defendant faced in defending himself: 'All that the defendant could do was to say that he had not committed the acts alleged against him…. [W]hen faced with allegations of the sort that were made here, "I have not done it" is virtually no defence at all.'[105] The decision is said to have caused some consternation among prosecutors,[106] and was quickly doubted by a differently constituted Court of Appeal in *R v E*, which commented that 'while juries continue to decide questions of guilt, we must have confidence that they will make allowances for the difficulties faced by a defendant who can only say "I didn't do it" as well as delay'.[107] However, the court in *E* also noted that the cases could be distinguished, in that in *E* there was some material on which the complainant could be cross-examined, which suggests that it might have regarded *B* as a case where the trial judge should have prevented the case from going to the jury.

Taking the lead from *E*, it might be suggested that the courts have sometimes been too ready to stop a case on the grounds that the lapse of time between the alleged offence and the trial has caused difficulties for the defence. After all, it is possible that

---

101 *Ibid.*, [29]–[30].

102 *Ibid.*, 38. There are parallels here with the problem of cases where the police have failed to set up an identification procedure; there too there is missing evidence and the question of what should be presumed about it. See Ch 5 and A. Roberts, 'Pre-trial Defence Rights and the Fair Use of Eyewitness Identification Procedures' (2008) 71 *MLR* 331.

103 [2003] EWCA Crim 319.   104 *Ibid.*, 27.   105 *Ibid.*, 28.

106 See Home Affairs Committee, *The Work of the Criminal Cases Review Commission* (2004), at Q75.

107 [2004] 2 Cr App R 36, [17].

in any case, even one brought to trial within weeks of the alleged offence, there will be missing evidence: witnesses die, forget things, evidence may be destroyed or simply go undiscovered. And whether or not there has been delay, consent defence rape cases are notorious for depending on one person's word against another's. On this view, unless the prosecution can be blamed for the loss of evidence, where a stay or the approach in *Ali* may be appropriate, the case should go to the jury, which should be trusted to take into account the difficulties caused by delay. Nevertheless, a case such as *B* may present extreme problems. There seems to have been very little evidence available with which to test the complainant's story. In a normal consent defence rape case, even one largely dependent on the complainant's word, it would be easier to test for consistency and explore possible reasons for fabrication. The argument then would be that the jury in a case like *B* would have no good basis for concluding that the case against the defendant was proved beyond reasonable doubt. A difficulty with this argument is that, as the Court of Appeal in *B* noted, whereas the law once required corroboration in cases of rape and sexual assault, the corroboration rules were abolished in 1994.[108] To decide that a prosecution should be stayed because a complaint is unsupported, then, would seem to undermine Parliament's decision that corroboration is not required for a conviction. Further, a judge should not refuse to let a case go to the jury just because he has doubts about the credibility of the witness. This is the rule in *Galbraith* (about which more will be said in the Chapter 11) that credibility is an issue for the jury. All the same, the argument that a prosecution should not proceed in a case such as *B* is not quite an argument for corroboration, so much as an argument that the jury should have some means of assessing the complainant's veracity beyond simple reliance on her testimony. Similarly, a refusal to let the case proceed does not reflect badly on the complainant's testimony, but merely acknowledges the difficulty faced by the jury in assessing it.

(B) CUSTODY TIME LIMITS

Article 5 of the ECHR protects the right to liberty. Pre-trial detention is permissible, but a defendant so detained is 'entitled to trial within a reasonable time or to release pending trial'. The European Court of Human Rights has held that that where the defendant is detained, the prosecution must act with 'special diligence' in bringing the case to trial.[109] Where indictable offences are concerned, English law has various provisions which help to ensure that defendants remanded in custody are brought to trial with reasonable dispatch. A defendant can only be remanded in custody for 28 days; after that period, a new decision must be taken. More importantly, the Prosecution of Offences Act 1985 and regulations issued under it contain provisions on custody time limits. Under these, for example, a defendant charged with an offence triable only

---

[108] See D. Birch, 'Corroboration: Goodbye to All That?' [1995] *Crim LR* 524.
[109] *Stögmüller v Austria* (1979) 1 EHRR 155, [5].

on indictment is entitled to trial within 182 days of his case being transferred to the Crown Court.[110] If a time limit expires, a defendant is entitled to be released on bail, but the prosecution may apply for extension of the time limit before it expires. Section 22(3) of the Act provides that an extension should not be granted unless the court is satisfied that there is good and sufficient cause (the section lists the illness or absence of a judge or important witness as good causes, among others), and that the prosecution has acted 'with all due diligence and expedition'.

On the whole, the courts take custody time limits seriously and are reluctant to extend them.[111] While the prosecution is to be judged by 'realistic, not impossible, standards and…should not in any event be refused an extension unless its lack of due diligence and expedition has in fact delayed the trial date',[112] the courts will not look favourably, when considering whether there has been due expedition, on 'pre-texts such as chronic staff shortages,…overwork, sickness, absenteeism or matters of that kind.'[113] Factors such as the complexity of the case and the cooperativeness of the accused are relevant, however. Delay caused by actors external to the prosecution may justify extension of a custody time limit: for example, delays caused by foreign prosecutors,[114] or by the late provision of phone logs by a mobile phone company.[115] Such factors are no fault of the prosecuting authorities; some cases will always take longer to come to trial than others, and so long as the prosecution has done all it can, an extension of the time limit seems appropriate. More controversial, though, is the decision in *R v Central Criminal Court, ex parte Johnson (Orleander)*.[116] Here, delay was caused by the Forensic Science Service. The court held that as this was not the prosecution's fault—again, it had done all it could to speed things up—the custody time limit could be extended. It refused to see the Forensic Science Service as being part of the prosecution for the purposes of the custody time limit rules. This is arguable: it seems clear that if delay is caused by unexceptional lack of court or judicial resources in a routine case, time limits should not be extended.[117] As it was put in *R (Miah) v Snaresbrook Crown Court*: 'it is for the executive, if it wishes the court system to try its citizens, to will the means to enable them to be tried in an expeditious manner.'[118] The Forensic Science Service, as the State's principal forensic science resource, should perhaps be seen in a similar manner.

In rare circumstances, a court may refuse both to extend a custody time limit and to release the person detained. This was the outcome in *R (O) v Harrow Crown Court*[119] where, under s 25 of the Criminal Justice and Public Order Act 1994, D, who had a previous conviction for rape, could not be granted bail on a charge of rape unless there were exceptional circumstances. The House of Lords held that in this situation there

---

[110] Prosecution of Offences (Custody Time Limits) Regulations 1987 (SI 1987 No 299), reg 5.
[111] See, generally, A. Samuels, 'Custody Time Limits' [1997] *Crim LR* 260.
[112] *R (O) v Harrow Crown Court* [2006] UKHL 42, [57].
[113] *R v Manchester Crown Court, ex p McDonald* [1990] 1 WLR 841, 847.   [114] As in *ibid.*
[115] *R (Thomas) v Central Criminal Court* [2006] EWHC 2138 (Admin).
[116] [1999] 2 Cr App R 51.   [117] See *R v Manchester Crown Court*, above n 113, 848.
[118] [2006] EWHC 2873 (Admin), [3].   [119] Above n 112.

was no breach of Article 5(3), because the lack of due diligence, which prevented an extension of the custody time limit, did not necessarily equate with the lack of 'special diligence' which triggers Article 5(3). It was thought that, despite the similarity in language, Strasbourg takes a more holistic view of the question of delay, often referring to the seriousness of the case and sometimes finding that delay can be remedied by an offer to expedite the case.

What if a custody time limit is about to expire, and the prosecutor replaces the original charge against the defendant with a new one? The literal effect of the time limit rules is that a new time limit will start to run with the introduction of the new charge; the obvious problem here is that this may allow the prosecutor to manipulate the rules. This situation was considered in *R v Leeds Crown Court, ex parte Wardle*.[120] The defendant had originally been charged with murder for causing death during a burglary. When the custody time limit was about to expire, the prosecution substituted the murder charge for one of manslaughter. On appeal to the Crown Court, the judge considered that, had the charge not been changed, an extension of the time limit would not have been granted: the prosecution had not acted with due expedition. Nevertheless, the effect of the new charge was to institute a new time limit, so the defendant lost his automatic right to release on bail. The defendant was, of course, free to make a new application for bail, but this was turned down because he had a previous history of offending on bail and of not surrendering. The case eventually reached the House of Lords. All of the judges expressed some concern about the way the rules allow a new charge to institute a new time limit, but a majority held that the law could not be interpreted in such a way as to allow the defendant's release in this situation. Nor could there be said to have been an abuse of process. Wardle applied to the European Court of Human Rights, claiming that his Article 5 rights had been breached, but his application was ruled inadmissible. The Court considered that there had been adequate judicial supervision of the decision to keep him in custody, and that the prosecution had acted with sufficient expedition.[121]

Wardle leaves the law in an unsatisfactory state. The case seems to have involved some shoddy performance on the part of the police and prosecutors. From the facts given in the various judgments, it is difficult to see why a charge of murder was ever considered appropriate. The victim, who had a weak heart, seems to have died from a combination of shock and minor injuries, facts which do not suggest any intention to kill or cause serious harm. One would have expected the charge to have been reduced at a much earlier stage. There is also the Crown Court judge's finding that the prosecution had not acted with much urgency in disclosing witness statements and in obtaining video evidence. The just result here would seem to involve blocking the start of a new time limit, and a minority in the House of Lords (Lord Nicholls and Lord Scott) did think that the rules could be read so as to achieve this. Another way of protecting the defendant would be to stay the proceedings for abuse of process. There was general

---

[120] [2002] 1 AC 754.   [121] *Wardle v United Kingdom* (2003) 4 EHRLR 459.

agreement in the House of Lords that this device might be used in extreme cases: where a new charge was substituted solely to introduce a new time limit. But that was not felt to be the case here, because the charge had also been altered for good reasons, in that the evidence did not support the murder charge. Staying the trial for abuse of process would certainly be a drastic step in *Wardle*, for it would more or less ensure that Wardle could not be tried for a serious crime, so it is no surprise that all the judges were cautious about this remedy. Given that a stay was not thought appropriate in *Wardle*, it seems unlikely that there will be many cases where it will be justified; it will not be often that a prosecutor introduces a new charge *solely* to extend a time limit.

(C) DELAY BETWEEN CHARGE AND TRIAL

There has been general acceptance in English and Commonwealth courts that there is a common law right to be tried without unreasonable delay or, to put the matter differently, that the courts have an inherent jurisdiction to prevent an abuse of their process where there has been unreasonable delay in bringing a case to trial.[122] This general right applies whether or not the defendant is in custody, and so can be distinguished from the issue of custody time limits discussed in the previous section. However, the English courts have insisted that the remedy of staying the prosecution for abuse of process should be invoked sparingly, and only where there has been clear fault on the part of the prosecution or where the delay has seriously prejudiced the defendant.[123] This approach prompts the question of the appropriate remedy for the general run of cases in which delay occurs and whether, in those circumstances, what we have is a right without a remedy. This difficult issue has been brought into sharp relief by the Human Rights Act and by several recent decisions of the European Court of Human Rights. Before returning to the question of remedies for breach, we consider the general approach of the Convention, and how the English courts have interpreted and applied it.

The European Convention provides various guarantees of timely decision making in criminal justice (e.g. Article 5.3, arrestee should be 'brought promptly before a judge'; Article 5.4, person detained 'entitled to take proceedings by which the lawfulness of his detention shall be decided speedily by a court'), but the most relevant for present purposes is the guarantee in Article 6.1—applicable equally to civil and criminal cases—of a 'fair and public hearing *within a reasonable time* by an independent and impartial tribunal'. It was established by the Court at an early stage that the rationale for this right is that individuals should not be allowed to remain 'too long in a state of uncertainty about their fate',[124] although subsequently the Court has emphasized

---

[122] See, e.g., the Privy Council in *Bell v DPP of Jamaica* [1985] AC 937, and the High Court of Australia in *Jago v District Court of New South Wales* (1989) 87 ALR 577.

[123] For magistrates' courts, see *R v Brentford JJ, ex p Wong* [1981] QB 445; for the Crown Court, see *Attorney-General's Reference No 1 of 1990* [1992] QB 630.

[124] *Stögmüller v Austria* (1979) 1 EHRR 155, 5.

more broadly 'the importance of rendering justice without delays which might jeopardise its effectiveness and credibility'.[125] We may identify four key questions about the extent and effect of this right—when time begins to run, to what decisions the right applies, what amounts to a breach, and what remedies should be given.

(i) When does time begin to run?

For the purposes of both Articles 5 and 6, it was established by the Strasbourg Court in *Deweer v Belgium*[126] that time begins to run from the point of charge, but that the term 'charge' has an autonomous meaning in this context which approximates to whether 'the situation of the [suspect] has been substantially affected'. The *Deweer* approach was applied by the Court in *Heaney and McGuinness v Ireland*,[127] holding that the applicants had been 'charged' for this purpose when served with a notice requiring them to account for their movements, prior to being formally charged with an offence.

However, in *Attorney-General's Reference (No 2 of 2001)*[128] Lord Bingham, with whom all their Lordships concurred on this point, held that time will usually begin to run from the point at which a person is charged (in the English sense) or summoned, adding mysteriously that this is not an inflexible rule. He referred to the Strasbourg decision in *Howarth v United Kingdom*,[129] where the Court held that time began to run from the point at which the applicant had been interviewed by the Serious Fraud Squad, some four and a half months before he was charged. Without engaging with that decision or the other Strasbourg jurisprudence, Lord Bingham commented that 'arrest will not ordinarily mark the beginning of that period. An official indication that a person will be reported with a view to prosecution may, depending on the circumstances, do so.'[130]

There are two obvious difficulties with the House of Lords' position. First, Lord Bingham appeared to depart from the Strasbourg approach without giving reasons for doing so—he is entitled to do this, but when s 2 of the Human Rights Act 1998 states that a British court 'must take into account' the Strasbourg jurisprudence one would expect a discussion of the relevant decisions and good reasons to be offered for taking a different approach. Secondly, Lord Bingham's speech leaves it unclear under what circumstances an English court may properly hold that time begins to run before the point of charge. This is manifestly unsatisfactory: should courts be guided by the Strasbourg decisions (such as *Deweer, Howarth* and *Heaney and McGuinness*), or is Lord Bingham signalling an approach that is more flexible from the prosecutor's point of view but different from the Convention jurisprudence?

(ii) To which stages of the criminal process does the guarantee apply?

The Strasbourg jurisprudence indicates that the 'reasonable time' guarantee applies from the time of arrest through to the final stage of appeals. Thus in *Howarth v United*

---

125 *H v France* (1990) 12 EHRR 74.   126 (1980) 2 EHRR 30.   127 (2000) 33 EHRR 264.
128 [2003] UKHL 68.   129 (2001) 31 EHRR 861.   130 [2003] UKHL 68, at [28].

Kingdom,[131] a two-year delay in dealing with an appeal was held to breach Article 6(1); in *Mellors v United Kingdom*,[132] a three-year delay between trial and appeal in Scotland was held unreasonable; and in *Reid v United Kingdom*,[133] the Court held that:

'The delays which appear in this case cannot be justified either by the complexity of the case or the exigencies of internal procedure. While one year per instance may be a rule of thumb in Art. 6(1) cases, Art. 5(4) concerning issues of liberty requires particular expedition.'

This contrast is not so much between the 'reasonable time' guarantees in the two Articles, as between whether the appellant was in custody or not—the Court has rightly insisted that custody cases call for greater expedition.

In *R (on the application of Lloyd) v Bow Street Magistrates' Court*,[134] the Divisional Court held that the guarantee covers the execution of a sentence or ancillary order made on conviction. Thus Dyson LJ found no difficulty in applying Article 6.1 to the enforcement of a confiscation order made on conviction for conspiracy to handle stolen goods: 'such proceedings are part and parcel of the confiscation proceedings, which in turn are part and parcel of the original criminal proceedings'.[135] It is therefore apparent that the question of unreasonable delay may be raised at any point between the initial charge (howsoever interpreted) and the final appeal or final act of enforcing orders of the court.

(iii) What amounts to a breach?

It is well established that the length of a delay must be considered in relation to the complexity of the case and the conduct of the public authorities (prosecution, court) and of the defendant.[136] As the Court put it in *Mellors v United Kingdom*:

'the reasonableness of the length of proceedings must be assessed in the light of the circumstances of the case and having regard to ... the complexity of the case, the conduct of the applicant and of the relevant authorities, and the importance of what is at stake for the applicant.'[137]

In that case the delay of three years and two weeks in dealing with the appeal was held unreasonable: the case was not unduly complex, and although the defence contributed in a small way to the delays, the major problem was one of listing the appeal. Similarly in *Ahmed v Birmingham Magistrates' Court and the CPS*,[138] a Divisional Court held that a delay of some three years in enforcing a summons for dangerous driving and bringing the case to court breached Article 6.1. This was too long 'for the trial of a very simple, uncomplicated case of dangerous driving'. The causes lay in the court's failure to notice that it was sending letters to the wrong address, and in certain periods of

---

[131] (2001) 31 EHRR 861.   [132] Judgment of 17 July 2003, App No 57836/00.

[133] (2003) 37 EHRR 211.   [134] [2004] *Crim LR* 136.

[135] The decision in *R v Chichester Justices, ex p Crowther* [1998] All ER (D) 457, which went the other way, has been challenged in Strasbourg and the application has been declared admissible by the Court.

[136] *Konig v Germany* (1978) 2 EHRR 170.

[137] Above n 132, at [28].   [138] [2003] EWHC 72 (Admin).

unexplained inactivity, and there was no evidence that the defendant was trying to avoid or escape trial.

In *R (on the application of Lloyd) v Bow Street Magistrates' Court* it had taken some five years for proceedings to be brought against the applicant to enforce the confiscation order in respect of the unpaid portion. Among other delays were two years during which the receiver appointed by the court did nothing, and a further year's delay before the final summons could be heard at Bow Street. Dyson LJ stated:

'Convicted criminals who are the subject of confiscation orders do not attract sympathy, and are not entitled to favoured treatment. But there is nothing surprising about the requirement that, if the prosecuting authorities/magistrates court seek to enforce a confiscation order, they should do so within a reasonable time. It is potentially very unfair on a defendant that he should be liable to be committed to prison for non-payment of sums due under a confiscation order many years after the time for payment has expired, and long after he has been released from custody and resumed work and family life.'[139]

This is important in the way that it brings the discussion back to the reasons for respecting the right to be tried without unreasonable delay—the effects on people's lives and decision making about their future.

(iv) What is the appropriate remedy for breach?

The House of Lords has accepted in *Porter v Magill*,[140] that the right to trial within a reasonable time is a free-standing right safeguarded by Article 6(1): it is no answer to a breach of this right that other rights guaranteed by Article 6, such as the right to a fair trial before an independent and impartial tribunal, have been respected. The more difficult question concerns remedies. The Strasbourg Court has acknowledged that breach of the right does not necessarily render the whole proceedings a nullity,[141] but because it operates after exhaustion of local remedies that Court has never had to consider the proper approach to a case which has been delayed so that the trial has not yet taken place. It has, however, held that each Contracting State must have in place a remedy or range of remedies for breach of the right which are effective in law and in practice.[142] What remedies English law offers was the principal question before the nine members of the House of Lords in *Attorney-General's Reference (No 2 of 2001)*.[143] The House of Lords held by a majority of 7–2 that it will rarely be appropriate to stay the proceedings if they have not yet begun, because there is a strong public interest in having charges tried. A court should therefore consider lesser remedies such as compensation or mitigation of sentence. Thus Lord Bingham held that:

'The appropriate remedy will depend on the nature of the breach and all the circumstances, including particularly the stage of the proceedings at which the breach is established. If the

---

[139] [2003] EWHC 2294 (Admin), at [25].   [140] [2002] 2 AC 357.
[141] *Bunkate v Netherlands* (1993) 19 EHRR 477.
[142] *Kudla v Poland*, judgment of 26 October 2000, App No 30210/96, at [158].   [143] [2003] UKHL 68.

breach is established before the hearing, the appropriate remedy may be a public acknowledgement of the breach, action to expedite the hearing to the greatest extent practicable and
perhaps, if the defendant is in custody, his release on bail. It will not be appropriate to stay
or dismiss the proceedings unless (a) there can no longer be a fair hearing or (b) it would
otherwise be unfair to try the defendant. The public interest in the final determination of
criminal charges requires that such a charge should not be stayed or dismissed if any lesser
remedy will be just and proportionate in all the circumstances. The prosecutor and the court
do not act incompatibly with the defendant's Convention right in continuing to prosecute
or entertain proceedings after a breach is established in a case where neither of conditions
(a) or (b) is met, since the breach consists in the delay which has accrued and not in the prospective hearing.'

Two judges delivered strong dissents to the majority decision, Lord Hope arguing
that the majority approach 'empties the reasonable time guarantee almost entirely of
content'.[144] However, in a later Privy Council decision, which provided an opportunity
to review more recent Strasbourg case law, the dissenting judges reconciled themselves to the majority view.[145]

It is clear from the decision in *Attorney General's Reference* that (b) is intended to be
a narrow category. It includes 'cases of bad faith, unlawfulness and executive manipulation', but may also go a little further than this. Lord Bingham accepted that there
may be cases 'where the delay is of such an order, or where a prosecutor's breach of professional duty is such ... as to make it unfair that the proceedings against a defendant
should continue.' *Darmalingum v The State*[146] was provided as an example of extreme
delay; that the delay in the case was 15 years from charge to the close of proceedings
suggests that this will be a narrow category. There remains, then, the question whether
'lesser remedies' than a stay are really sufficient in cases where there has been delay that
is neither that extreme nor involves a breach of professional duty by the prosecutor. If
the rationale of the right to a timely trial is that a defendant should not face excessive
uncertainty over his future, then there is a good argument that courts should be prepared to stay proceedings in more than just the narrow category indicated by (b).[147]

9.5 ENTRAPMENT

Many of the pre-trial issues we have considered in this chapter are connected to the
fairness of the trial: by regulating disclosure, and considering issues of delay, the
pre-trial process offers an opportunity to ensure that the coming trial is as fair as
possible. In extreme cases, as in those involving unreasonable delay, a stay for abuse
of process can be used to prevent the trial from taking place at all. Our final topic

---

[144] *Ibid.*, at [46].   [145] *Spiers v Ruddy* [2007] UKPC D2.   [146] [2000] 1 WLR 2303.
[147] See further J. Jackson and J. Johnstone, 'The Reasonable Time Requirement: An Independent and
Meaningful Right?' [2005] *Crim LR* 3.

in this chapter considers the use of pre-trial remedies as a response to entrapment. Here, the courts will sometimes prevent a trial from taking place because the police have gone beyond their law enforcement role by 'creating' the crime with which the offender is charged.

Although the majority of recorded offences are reported to the police by members of the public, there are a minority of cases in which the police decide to adopt proactive methods. Typically, these are crimes without direct victims, such as drug-related crimes, or those involving a form of conspiracy or other organization. Intelligence-led policing may take different forms,[148] and our concern here is with approaches that rely on the deployment of undercover officers or participant informers. We saw in Chapter 5 above that the use of surveillance may impinge on the target person's right to respect for private life, and that this is why the European Court of Human Rights has insisted on certain safeguards, which the Regulation of Investigatory Powers Act 2000 attempts to translate into English law.[149] Proactive methods of law enforcement such as undercover policing and the use of participant informers raise similar questions about the right to respect for private life and the prevention of arbitrary interference by State officials, but they also raise a deeper question about the right to a fair trial under Article 6 of the Convention. If the State, through the police or a police-instigated informant, engages in an operation to test whether a person will commit a crime in a given situation, there is a point at which this becomes State-created crime; and for the State to create a crime and then to prosecute a person for it would be a gross abuse of power. As we will see, the contention is that in this situation it would not be fair to try the defendant at all. This is how the point of principle was put in the leading English decision:

'It is simply not acceptable that the state through its agents should lure its citizens into committing acts forbidden by the law and then seek to prosecute them for doing so. That would be entrapment. That would be a misuse of state power, and an abuse of the process of the courts. The unattractive consequences, frightening and sinister in extreme cases, which state conduct of this kind could have are obvious. The role of the courts is to stand between the state and its citizens and make sure this does not happen.'[150]

This does not rule out all forms of proactive policing, as we will see. But it purports to set a limit to the exercise of police power and to create a realm of protection for citizens. It does so both because citizens should not be tempted by State officials in this way; if they are, the trial should be stayed in order to protect the defendant from

---

[148] For discussion, see M. Maguire, 'Policing by Risks and Targets: Some Dimensions and Implications of Intelligence-Led Policing' (2000) 9 *Policing and Society* 315, and R. Billingsley, T. Nemitz and P. Bean (eds), *Informers: Policing, Policy, Practice* (2001).

[149] For comments on the extent to which this has been achieved, see Ch 5.

[150] *Per* Lord Nicholls in *Attorney-General's Reference No 3 of 2000; Looseley* [2001] UKHL 53. For analysis of the decision, see A. Ashworth, 'Re-drawing the Boundaries of Entrapment' [2002] *Crim LR* 161.

unjust conviction. As the Strasbourg Court put it in the leading decision of *Teixeira de Castro v Portugal*:

'The Court concludes that the two officers' action went beyond those of undercover agents because they instigated the offence and there is nothing to suggest that without their intervention it would have been committed. That intervention and its use in the impugned criminal proceedings meant that, right from the outset, the applicant was definitively deprived of a fair trial.'[151]

Thus the leading decisions in both Strasbourg and London hold that the appropriate remedy for entrapment is that the proceedings should not take place at all—in England, this indicates a stay of the proceedings for abuse of process.

What form of activity by law enforcement agents amounts to entrapment and justifies this remedy? The House of Lords in *Looseley*[152] concluded that it would be acceptable for the police to target an individual if three conditions are fulfilled. First, they must have reasonable grounds to suspect that person of involvement in the offence or, more broadly, reasonable grounds for suspecting people who frequent a certain place of being thus involved. The notion of reasonable suspicion plays an important role in Article 5(1) of the Convention, in justifying restrictions of liberty such as arrest, and has been emphasized by Strasbourg in its various decisions on entrapment.[153] But the difficulty with *Looseley* is the extension of reasonable suspicion to places as well as people.[154] Since entrapment is not the only way of dealing with areas where it is known that offending is taking place but not who the offenders are—it might, for example, be possible to set up a surveillance operation in order to determine which individuals might reasonably be suspected of involvement in offences—it may be argued that this extension of the condition is not Convention-compliant. In fact, the later Court of Appeal decision in *Moon* goes some way towards accepting this criticism.[155] The police targeted a bus station where they believed drug dealing was taking place, and after some initial reluctance the defendant supplied heroin to an undercover officer. On appeal, the prosecution accepted that there was no reasonable suspicion that the defendant was anything other than an addict, and on this basis the Court of Appeal held that proceedings should have been stayed.

The second condition in *Looseley* is that the officers or informants should be duly authorized to carry out the operation in accordance with the Codes of Practice issued under the Regulation of Investigatory Powers Act 2000: this is a procedural requirement, and is intended to enhance supervision and to remove arbitrariness. For example, the Code of Practice makes it clear that proactive methods should not be used unless less intrusive methods of investigation are likely to be unsuccessful. And thirdly, if the first two conditions are fulfilled, the officer or participating informant

---

[151] (1999) 28 EHRR 101, at 39.   [152] Above n 150.

[153] *Vanyan v Russia* App No 53203/99 (2005); *Ramanauskas v Lithuania* App No 74420/01 (2008); *Milinenev Lithuania* App No 74355/01 (2008).

[154] See D. Ormerod and A. Roberts, 'The Trouble with *Teixeira*: Developing a Principled Approach to Entrapment' (2002) 6 *E & P* 38, at 51–2.

[155] [2004] EWCA Crim 2872.

must do no more than provide the suspect with an unexceptional opportunity to commit the offence. Formerly this was sometimes phrased in terms of passive rather than active involvement, but in practice, the officer or informant will often have to do some acts in order to provide the opportunity. The key factor is that the officer or informant should act normally, as a potential customer would do in a given situation, and not hold out any extra temptation.

While it is now clear that the courts will stay some prosecutions where there has been State instigation of crime, the theoretical basis for objecting to entrapment is less clear. Indeed, Squires has questioned whether there is any coherent basis for doing so.[156] After all, if a defendant such as Moon had been persuaded to supply heroin to a member of the public, and the police had stumbled upon the transaction, she would have had no defence in law and no claim to have proceedings stayed.[157] Part of Squires' argument, influenced by Seidman,[158] is that the distinction drawn between cases of impermissible entrapment and legitimate police investigations serves to protect the privileged from having their virtue tested (especially as most of us would actually succumb to temptation if a sufficiently attractive offer were made), while allowing the police to target those who already inhabit an environment where they encounter temptation to commit crime. Thus in *Director of Public Prosecutions v Willliams and O'Hare*,[159] the police parked a van in a street with its back doors unlocked, and cartons of cigarettes visible inside. On being confronted with this temptation, the defendants proceeded to take the cigarettes. The Divisional Court held that this was not entrapment, and in *Looseley* the House of Lords agreed that the prosecution was appropriate largely, it seems, because an area of high vehicle crime had been targeted. The 'fact that the defendants may not have previously been suspected or even thought of offending was their hard luck.'[160] Presumably, if the van had been left in a low-crime area, the courts would have found that there was impermissible entrapment.

While Squires' argument is intriguing, it is not entirely convincing. Insofar as his thesis claims to describe the practice of the courts, the decision in *Williams* is the strongest point in its favour. But many commentators doubt that *Williams* was correctly decided,[161] and the later decision in *Moon*, which emphasizes reasonable suspicion of an individual rather than of an area, undermines it. *Moon* itself is a decision which is hard to reconcile with Squires' view of the case law, for the defendant certainly inhabited an environment where she was surrounded by temptation to commit crime, yet the court found her prosecution illegitimate because there was no evidence that she was involved in dealing rather than using drugs. We would suggest, then, that a coherent doctrine of entrapment can be based on the idea that the police can

---

[156] D. Squires, 'The Problem with Entrapment' (2006) 26 *OJLS* 351.

[157] See K. Hofmeyr, 'The Problem of Private Entrapment' [2006] *Crim LR* 319.

[158] L. Seidman, 'The Supreme Court, Entrapment and Our Criminal Justice Dilemma' [1981] *Supreme Court Review* 111. See also Seidman's useful recent paper, 'Entrapment and the "Free Market" for Crime' in P. Robinson et al (eds), *Criminal Law Conversations* (2009).

[159] (1994) 98 Cr App R 206.   [160] Above n 150, [65].   [161] See Choo, above n 72, 149–50.

only legitimately target those who they reasonably suspect to be currently involved in criminal activity: *currently* is significant, because otherwise the police would be able to target anyone with previous convictions. At a more normative level, the argument would be that it is not legitimate for the State to seek to use criminal sanctions against those who are not committing crime; its role should be largely reactive. However, there are various difficulties with this defence of the entrapment doctrine, which we will address briefly.

Feinberg has defended the sort of position outlined above—that the State should not seek to lure non-criminals into crime—on the grounds that we should face no more than the 'natural odds' of being tempted to commit crime.[162] Some of us may be faced with temptation to commit crime in our normal lives; if we give in, we will be rightly prosecuted. The problem here is that the natural odds, under which some people face fewer temptations to commit crime than others, are not really natural. As Seidman points out,[163] they are the products of various political choices and reflect social inequality. This can be conceded, but so long as entrapment is used to target those who are currently committing crime, the entrapment doctrine is no more a tool for preserving social inequality than is the rest of the criminal law. It is true that entrapment could be used in the pursuit of a rather strange programme of equality, whereby the privileged could be faced with temptations to commit crime just as the underprivileged are, but surely the more sensible social programme would be to ameliorate the criminogenic environments that the underprivileged face.

A second difficulty an entrapment doctrine faces is how to respond to 'test purchase' cases. In *Amin* plain clothes police officers flagged down a taxi in an area not covered by its licence.[164] The driver was prosecuted for picking them up, and this was held not to be an abuse of process. Similar tactics are sometimes used to check whether shops are sticking to the terms of their licence.[165] There was no reasonable suspicion of the taxi driver in *Amin*, and while requiring suspicion might be appropriate in cases involving shopkeepers, it would be far more difficult in the *Amin* scenario. If it is felt important that the police should be able to test licensees without reasonable suspicion,[166] it might be possible to argue that those who take part in a regulated activity, such as driving a taxi or selling alcohol, are legitimate targets of virtue testing. A similar argument was used in respect of the privilege against self-incrimination in Chapter 5, though it should be noted that the argument is potentially unruly.

Finally, if reasonable suspicion plays a key role in setting the bounds of the entrapment doctrine, there is a difficult question about the extent to which reasonable suspicion may be supplied, or bolstered, after the defendant has been targeted. In *Moon*, the

---

[162] J. Feinberg, 'Criminal Entrapment' in *Problems at the Roots of Law: Essays in Legal and Political Theory* (2003).

[163] Seidman, 'Free Market', above n 158.

[164] *Nottingham City Council v Amin* [2000] 1 Cr App R 426.

[165] *Director of Public Prosecutions v Marshall* [1988] 3 All ER 683.

[166] See also *Stratford on Avon DC v Dyde*, Div Ct, 4 November 2009.

Court of Appeal remarked that a search of the defendant's apartment had uncovered evidence of personal use of drugs rather than of dealing. If the search had found drugs in quantities that indicated dealing, could this have been used to support the argument that Moon was a legitimate target of the police operation? In *Looseley*, the police initially targeted Looseley because they had been given his telephone number in a pub where they suspected heroin was being dealt from. They phoned the number and Looseley agreed to supply them with drugs, which he in fact did on three occasions. It might be argued that while the initial tip off was insufficient to provide reasonable suspicion that Looseley was currently engaged in drug dealing, the ease with which he procured drugs provided further evidence that he was a dealer. In *Williams*, it is possible, as acknowledged in *Looseley*, that the defendants had not even 'thought of' offending before being confronted with the easy opportunity of the unsecured cigarettes, and this gives strong grounds for arguing that they should not have been prosecuted. But might things have been different had the defendants smashed the window of a car in order to steal a wallet left on the front seat? This behaviour seems to display a rather higher level of commitment to offending, and might be taken to be evidence that the defendants were among those responsible for vehicle crime in the area. There are difficult questions here. One argument would be that, because the entrapment doctrine is intended to regulate police conduct, a decision to target a particular person cannot be justified after the fact. On the other hand, if the concern is about whether in fact the target was lured into committing a crime that he was not already committing, a wider enquiry may be appropriate.

FURTHER READING

QUIRK, H., 'The Significance of Culture in Criminal Procedure Reform: Why the Revised Disclosure Scheme Cannot Work' (2006) 10 *E & P* 42.

CHOO, A., *Abuse of Process and Judicial Stays of Criminal Proceedings*, 2nd ed, Oxford: Oxford University Press, 71–96 (on delay).

SQUIRES, D., 'The Problem with Entrapment' (2006) 26 *OJLS* 351.

Questions for Discussion

1. Does the prosecution disclose too little evidence and the defence too much?

2. Should the courts be less reluctant to stay proceedings for abuse of process in cases involving delay?

3. What, if anything, is wrong with entrapment?

10

PLEA

One of the key decisions for people who are prosecuted is how to plead. With the exception of special pleas such as *autrefois convict* and *autrefois acquit* in cases where the defendant pleads that he or she has previously been tried and cannot lawfully be re-tried for the offence,[1] and the rare plea of not guilty by reason of insanity, defendants have a choice of two: guilty or not guilty. In some cases the decision on plea may depend on the offence(s) charged, so that a plea of guilty may be offered to a lesser offence than the one charged or to only one or two offences where more offences are charged. In this connection, as we will see, the discussion of prosecutorial decision making in Chapter 7 above is particularly relevant. In some cases the decision on plea may depend on the mode of trial, i.e. the level of court in which the charge is likely to be heard. Summary offences are triable only in magistrates' courts, and indictable-only offences are tried in the Crown Court, but there is a large middle category of offences triable either way. In these cases defendants have a right to elect Crown Court trial: the Crown Court has a higher acquittal rate than the magistrates' courts, but there is a longer delay before the trial and, where a conviction results, sentences in the Crown Court tend to be higher than in the magistrates' courts. The incentives are therefore mixed for defendants, whereas prosecutors tend to wish to have as many either way offences as possible dealt with in the magistrates' courts. The system for determining mode of trial is now designed to ensure that as many cases as possible, in the triable either way category, are dealt with by magistrates. Thus the 'plea before venue' system in place since the Criminal Procedure and Investigations Act 1996 ensures that those who indicate an intention to plead guilty to an either way offence are dealt with in the magistrates' courts (subject to the possibility of committal to the Crown Court for sentence).

If the defendant pleads not guilty, the case goes to trial. If the defendant pleads guilty, there is no trial. Instead, the defence may submit a 'basis of plea', and the prosecution will always give a statement of facts in court; if there is disagreement about the facts on which sentence should be passed, the judge may have to hold a *Newton* hearing to resolve the matter.[2] The European Convention on Human Rights declares

---

[1] See the discussion of double jeopardy, below, Ch 11.

[2] See the leading case of *Newton* (1982) 4 Cr App R (S) 388, and discussion by A. Ashworth, *Sentencing and Criminal Justice* (5th ed, 2010), Ch 11.

that 'everyone is entitled to a fair and public hearing', that 'everyone charged with a criminal offence shall be presumed innocent until proven guilty according to law', and that everyone shall have the right 'to examine or have examined witnesses against him'.[3] A defendant who pleads guilty gives up these rights and does not put the prosecution to proof; as we describe below, the English criminal justice system contains an array of incentives designed to produce this outcome. In some countries those rights have been thought so fundamental that they cannot be waived, the unavailability of the guilty plea being regarded as a guarantee of defendants' rights.[4] In France, however, that rigid approach was called into question by the Delmas-Marty Commission,[5] and the French legislature has approved the introduction of guilty pleas coupled with the incentive of a lesser sentence.[6] In the Netherlands there seems to be an increasing gap between legal theory and legal practice: the theory is still that the ascertainment of guilt is for public officials to accomplish, not for defendants to concede, and the court must review and check the dossier; in practice there are various possibilities of bargaining, and more summary procedures for those who do not contest their guilt.[7] In Germany there is no guilty plea, but there are forms of 'plea bargain' in which a defendant may confess to the judge in order to gain a reduction in the sentence.[8] In Italy, a defendant who waives the right to trial and accepts judgment on the basis of the case papers is entitled to a sentence reduction of one-third.[9] Thus there is evidence of increasing Europe-wide recognition of guilty pleas coupled with reduced sentences. Any reduction in sentences seems to run counter to the trend for increasing severity against terrorism, organized crime and other serious types of offending; the suggestion is that pressures on resources are leading governments to find ways of reducing the number of trials taking place.

In England and Wales guilty pleas were relatively unusual in the eighteenth century and did not become common until the nineteenth century, when defence lawyers were allowed to play a fuller part.[10] Nowadays there may be some examination of the plea

---

[3] See Ch 2 above.

[4] M. Damaska, 'Evidentiary Barriers to Conviction and Two Models of Criminal Procedure: a Comparative Study' (1973) 121 *U Pa LR* 506.

[5] Commission Justice Pénale et Droits de l'Homme, *La Mise en Etat des affaires pénales* (1991), 10. See also the essay by Judge F. Tulkens, 'Negotiated Justice' in M. Delmas-Marty and J. R. Spencer (eds), *European Criminal Procedures* (2002).

[6] See 'Lawyers Protest as French MPs give police more powers' *The Guardian* 12 February 2004.

[7] See N. Jorg, S. Field and C. Brants, 'Are Inquisitorial and Adversarial Systems Converging?' in C. Harding et al, *Criminal Justice in Europe* (1995), esp 47–51.

[8] J. Herrmann, 'Bargaining Justice: a Bargain for German Criminal Justice?' (1992) 53 *U Pittsburgh LR* 755; L. Leigh and L. Zedner, *A Report on the Administration of Criminal Justice in the Pre-Trial Phase in France and Germany* (1992), 43; H. Jung, 'Plea-Bargaining and its Repercussions on the Theory of Criminal Procedure' (1997) 5 *Eur J of Crime, Criminal Law and Criminal Justice* 112.

[9] S. Maffei, 'Negotiations on Evidence and Negotiations on Sentence: Adversarial Experiments in Italian Criminal Procedure' (2004) 2 *J Int Crim J* 1050, at 1060.

[10] M. Feeley, 'Legal Complexity and the Transformation of the Criminal Process: the Origins of Plea Bargaining' (1997) 31 *Israel LR* 183; cf the analysis of the socio-political context of early plea-bargaining in the United States in M. Vogel, *Coercion to Compromise* (2007).

by a judge at plea and case management hearing, but not necessarily before passing sentence on a guilty plea. In essence, the guilty plea constitutes a waiver by the defendant of the right to a trial and to put the prosecution to proof. The law provides a strong incentive to plead guilty, in a provision that now appears in s 144 of the Criminal Justice Act 2003:[11]

'(1) In determining what sentence to pass on an offender who has pleaded guilty to an offence before that or another court a court must take into account:

(a) the stage in the proceedings for the offence at which the offender indicated his intention to plead guilty; and

(b) the circumstances in which this indication was given.'

The legislation does not state the amount of the discount, but sentencing guidelines now deal authoritatively with the details.[12] In brief, the discount ranges from one-third for a guilty plea at the earliest reasonable opportunity, downwards on a sliding scale to one-tenth for a change of plea at the door of the court. The guidelines make it clear that, if the offence is already close to the custody threshold, a guilty plea may have the effect of reducing the sentence to a non-custodial one.

This chapter begins with an inquiry into the percentage of defendants who plead guilty. It then considers some of the principal reasons for changes of plea, looking at charge bargains (where the defendant agrees to plead guilty in exchange for the prosecution reducing the level of the charge or the number of charges), at fact bargains (where the defendant agrees to plead guilty only on the basis that the prosecution will put forward a particular version of the facts), and at plea negotiation (where the change of plea is motivated by considerations of sentence). The tendencies evident in the English system are then evaluated in the light of defendants' rights and the supposed advantages to the public.

10.1 THE RATE OF GUILTY PLEAS

In the magistrates' courts the rate of guilty pleas is well over 90 per cent. Most of these are relatively minor matters, three-quarters being summary offences that almost always end in a fine. A contested trial in a magistrates' court is therefore fairly rare. Figures from the Crown Prosecution Service (CPS) show that in 2007–8 some 5.8 per cent of their cases[13] heard in the magistrates' courts were contested, and over one-third

---

[11] The section was originally enacted as s 48 of the Criminal Justice and Public Order Act 1994. The changes in its terms are not significant for present purposes.

[12] Sentencing Guidelines Council, *Reduction in Sentence for a Guilty Plea: Revised Guideline* (2007).

[13] Possibly a quarter of cases in the magistrates' courts are brought by other agencies, such as Trading Standards officers or the regulatory agencies: see G. Slapper, *Organisational Prosecutions* (2001). The CPS figures are therefore not comprehensive, but they are the best available.

of those (or 2.2 per cent of the total) were dismissed.[14] These are the figures for cases heard in the magistrates' courts, excluding the 9 per cent of cases discontinued by the CPS. If we turn to the Crown Court, some 12 per cent of cases were not proceeded with, 73 per cent resulted in a guilty plea, and 14.2 per cent of cases were contested, and of those over 45 per cent resulted in acquittal.[15]

However, interpretation of the statistics is not straightforward. As will be apparent from the CPS figures just quoted, it would be misleading to refer to 'the acquittal rate' in magistrates' courts or the Crown Court without making it clear how the rate has been calculated and, in particular, whether cases discontinued or otherwise withdrawn or dismissed are included. Thus the *Judicial Statistics 2008* record a guilty plea rate in the Crown Court that has increased from 60 per cent in 2004 to 70 per cent in 2008; during the same period the acquittal rate has increased from 50 to 60 per cent.[16] The figures in the *Judicial Statistics* are total acquittal rates: nearly two-thirds of them are cases discharged by the judge, perhaps because the prosecution wishes to offer no evidence (because a key witness has not attended court) or has agreed to bind the defendant over, and a further 7 per cent are acquittals directed by the judge (e.g. because the evidence is insufficient), so that of all acquittals in 2008 only 29 per cent were by a jury.[17] There are also longstanding variations according to region and type of offence. Thus for many years the North Eastern circuit has had a far higher guilty plea rate than other circuits, whereas in the London courts the figure has been constantly below the national average. No clear explanation for these divergences has been found, and the acquittal rate of those who plead not guilty seems to be roughly the same among the various circuits. One relevant difference may be the higher proportion of black defendants in London, it being established that such defendants are less likely to plead guilty (and also more likely to be acquitted at trial) than others.[18]

It is also noteworthy that the guilty plea rate differs according to the type of offence. Taking the total number of offenders sentenced in the Crown Court, some 86 per cent of them had pleaded guilty, but the rate was somewhat higher for burglary and for fraud (both 93 per cent), slightly lower for offences of violence, the largest group in the Crown Court, at 81 per cent, and significantly lower for sexual offences (only 62 per cent).[19] These lower guilty plea rates may be related, in part at least, to the difficulty of ensuring that witnesses testify.

Why do so many defendants plead guilty and forgo their right to be tried? In the early 1970s Bottoms and McClean conducted interviews with over 200 defendants who pleaded guilty either at a magistrates' court or at the Crown Court. When they asked why the defendant pleaded guilty, about two-thirds answered that it was because

---

[14] CPS, *Annual Report 2007–2008*, Annex B. As will be seen below, the *Judicial Statistics 2008* record a much higher acquittal rate in the Crown Court.

[15] *Ibid.*   [16] *Judicial Statistics 2008*, Tables 6.6 and 6.7.   [17] *Ibid.*, Table 6.8.

[18] See B. Bowling and C. Phillips, *Racism, Crime and Justice* (2002), Ch 7, and M. Tonry, *Punishment and Politics* (2004), Ch 4.

[19] *Sentencing Statistics 2007*, Table 2.19.

they were guilty. Indeed, some 70 per cent of these admitted to the police from the beginning that they were guilty.[20] A similar finding emerged from the later survey by Hedderman and Moxon, although 65 per cent of their respondents also said that the prospect of a lighter sentence was a reason for their decision.[21]

What about those who change their plea? There is little information about plea-changers in the magistrates' courts,[22] but for the Crown Court there are statistics on what are termed 'cracked trials'. A cracked trial is one that is listed as a not guilty plea, with court time set aside for a contested trial, and in which the defendant changes to a guilty plea after the case has been listed, i.e. at a fairly late stage. Some trials 'crack' on the day of the hearing, others a day or two before. Cracked trials cause unnecessary inconvenience and even anxiety to victims and other witnesses who are brought to court on what turns out to be a fruitless journey. They are also productive of inefficiencies in the criminal justice system, since they cause listing difficulties (even though there are usually one or two other trials waiting to come on) and consequently they may result in a wastage of scarce resources, namely court time, judicial time, and public money. The *Judicial Statistics 2008* record a 'cracked trial' rate of 41 per cent in 2008, meaning that two-fifths of cases listed for trial 'cracked' at the last minute—mostly (62 per cent) because the defendant entered a late plea of guilty, but alternatively because the defendant pleaded guilty to a lesser charge (19 per cent), or the prosecution dropped the case (17 per cent).[23] It appears that the introduction of plea and case management hearings has not yet brought any significant reduction in cracked trials. Thus the encouragement of earlier guilty pleas continues to form a major part of the official strategy for increasing 'efficiency' in the criminal process.

10.2 PLEADING NOT GUILTY

We have seen that around 6 per cent of defendants in magistrates' courts plead not guilty throughout, but that in the Crown Courts just over a quarter exercise their right to be tried. More do so in London, fewer in the North-East. Why do they persist in their pleas of not guilty, whilst others change their pleas? Once again, the most obvious answer is that they maintain that they are not guilty. It seems that around 60 per cent of defences involve a denial of the basic facts:[24] around one in six of these are alibi defences, and perhaps one-quarter are claims of mistaken identification.[25] The other 40 per cent of defences accept the basic facts but contest guilt on the basis of

---

[20] A. E. Bottoms and J. D. McClean, *Defendants in the Criminal Process* (1976), 115.

[21] C. Hedderman and D. Moxon, *Magistrates' Court or Crown Court? Mode of Trial Decisions and Sentencing* (1992), 24.

[22] J. Baldwin, *Pre-Trial Justice* (1986), 92–7.   [23] *Judicial Statistics 2008*, Table 6.11.

[24] *Ibid.*, 121.   [25] *Ibid.*, 75 and 92.

justification or lack of culpability. Some three-quarters of these seem to amount to a denial of *mens rea*, and almost all the remaining one-quarter claim self-defence.

Just as it seems likely that some people who are innocent eventually plead guilty, so it also seems likely that some who are guilty plead not guilty. They may do so for a variety of personal reasons, ranging from over-confidence to shame at the offence and an unwillingness to admit it publicly in any circumstances (e.g. with serious sexual offences). Some guilty defendants may be alive to the possibility that they have a chance of gaining an acquittal if prosecution witnesses fail to attend court to give evidence. Just as it is recognized that some defendants who change their pleas to guilty on the day of the trial do so because they see that the prosecution witnesses are at the court, so there may be others who, seeing that the prosecution witnesses have not arrived, persist in their plea of not guilty, with the result that the case collapses. While no study has identified the numbers involved, it seems entirely plausible that some defendants do benefit from windfalls of this kind. The Home Office mentioned the view that 'delayed guilty pleas are a tactic employed in the hope that witnesses will lose patience and decide not to testify'.[26] The usual official response to this is to reinforce the incentives to plead guilty and to enter that plea early in the process. The difficulty is how to distinguish between the not-guilty pleaders who are guilty and the not-guilty pleaders who are not guilty, a key issue to which we return later. Moreover, account must also be taken of a third group—those who have an arguable point, such as whether a taking was dishonest or whether force was used reasonably in self-defence, and who wish to have that decided by a court.

10.3 CHARGE BARGAINS

The term 'charge bargaining' is used here to encompass two distinct kinds of case. The first is where a defendant faces two or more charges and signifies an intention to plead not guilty to them. It is then possible for the prosecution to drop one or more of the others, in return for a plea of guilty to one charge. Either the prosecution or the defence may suggest this way of resolving the matter. Many of these are cases where several distinct offences are alleged, but some will be cases in which the prosecution has charged a person with both theft and handling stolen goods in the expectation that there would be a conviction of only one offence. The second kind of case is where the defendant faces a serious charge and signifies an intention to plead not guilty to it. It may be possible for the prosecution to drop the serious charge in exchange for a plea of guilty to a less serious charge. Much depends on the criminal law. At some points the law seems to be ready-made for this kind of charge bargain: for example, a defendant might intend to plead not guilty to grievous bodily harm with intent, contrary to

---

[26] Home Office, *Justice for All* (2002), 4.41.

s 18 of the Offences Against the Person Act 1861, but might be willing to plead guilty to the lesser offence of recklessly inflicting grievous bodily harm contrary to s 20 of the same Act. The same applies if the original charge is under s 20, and the defendant is willing to plead to the lesser offence under s 47, assault occasioning actual bodily harm. Elaine Genders has demonstrated the way in which many s 18 charges come to be downgraded, partly because of the problems of proving intent unless the injury was particularly serious.[27] In her sample only 19 per cent of those charged under s 18 were eventually convicted under that section. Similarly, Ralph Henham found that some 62 per cent of those charged under s 18 pleaded guilty to a lesser offence.[28] In Chapter 7.4(b) above, we noted evidence of some downgrading of charges of racially aggravated offences.

Apart from the specific types of offence just considered, in what proportion of cases do charge bargains take place? Most of the research focuses on the Crown Court, but charge bargains are by no means uncommon in magistrates' courts. Thus both Baldwin[29] and Mulcahy[30] found plenty of evidence of charges being reduced in number or in seriousness, followed by a change of plea to guilty. Such practices may be the result of a pre-trial review, whereby the defence lawyer discovers the likely strength of the prosecution case; or they may emerge by the usual processes of inter-action between prosecution and defence lawyers, either around the court or even by telephone contact. Mulcahy's interviews with a small number of defence and prosecution lawyers working in magistrates' courts led to the conclusion that trial avoidance is often thought desirable on both sides: if this is a fair representation of the general working culture,[31] to which there may of course be exceptions, then it is likely that there will be considerable pressure on some defendants in magistrates' courts to plead guilty. Similar findings emerge from the study of Health and Safety inspectors by Hawkins: although he found that there were some cases in which inspectors would not bargain, he discovered ample evidence of cases of 'pre-trial manoeuvring over number and type of charges'.[32] His conclusion, however, was that from the inspectors' point of view it was not simply a matter of speed and saving resources: 'while many of the bargains reveal a strong desire to expedite the matter, they also reveal a desire to achieve a commensurate penalty.'[33]

Turning to the Crown Court, as many as 77 of the 112 defendants in McCabe and Purves's sample who changed their plea at a late stage pleaded guilty to only part of

[27] E. Genders, 'Reform of the Offences Against the Person Act: Lessons from the Law in Action' [1999] Crim LR 689, at 691–3; see also A. Cretney and G. Davis, Punishing Violence (1995), 137–8.
[28] R. Henham, 'Further Evidence on the Significance of Plea in the Crown Court' (2002) 41 Howard JCJ 151, 153.
[29] J. Baldwin, Pre-Trial Justice (1986).
[30] A. Mulcahy, 'The Justification of "Justice": Legal Practitioners' Accounts of Negotiated Case Settlements in Magistrates' Courts' (1994) 34 BJ Crim 411.
[31] See also M. McConville et al, Standing Accused (1994), 194–8, and M. Travers, The Reality of Law (1997), Ch 5 on defence solicitors.
[32] K. Hawkins, Law as Last Resort (2003), 105.   [33] Ibid., 108.

the original indictment,[34] whereas in Baldwin and McConville's sample it was only 11 out of 121 late guilty pleaders[35] and in Bottoms and McClean's sample only three out of 68.[36] Most of the recent research on cracked trials does not provide details of the nature of any negotiation that took place, but some 51 per cent of those in Hedderman and Moxon's sample who changed their plea stated that they did so in the expectation that some charges would be dropped or reduced, resulting in a lighter sentence.[37] It may therefore be assumed that one or other form of charge bargain is a fairly frequent phenomenon.

What are the advantages and disadvantages for the prosecution? The chief benefit is that they are assured of at least one conviction, and do not have to risk the hazards of trial, more particularly in the Crown Court where as many as 60 per cent of contested cases end in an acquittal. In view of the possibility that witnesses may fail to turn up or may alter their story, or that the jury will be swayed by some non-legal factor, it is tempting for the prosecution to settle for the certainty of a conviction, albeit of a less serious offence (or fewer offences than charged). The Code for Crown Prosecutors (2010) states in paragraph 10.2 that in these cases:

'Prosecutors should only accept the defendant's plea if they think that the court is able to pass a sentence that matches the seriousness of the offending, particularly where there are aggravating features. Prosecutors must never accept a guilty plea just because it is convenient.'

This brief guidance reveals some of the conflicts besetting a prosecutor when taking a decision about accepting a lesser plea. The final words enjoin prosecutors not to give priority to 'convenience', but presumably this means their own personal convenience in getting a file off their desk. If we revert to the fuller description provided by the 1992 version of the Code, we find a more frank acknowledgement of the conflicting forces at work:

'Administrative convenience in the form of a rapid guilty plea should not take precedence over the interests of justice, but where the court is able to deal adequately with an offender on the basis of a plea which represents a criminal involvement not inconsistent with the alleged facts, the resource advantages both to the Service and to the courts generally will be an important consideration.'[38]

Shorn of its double negatives, this seems to suggest that it is proper to accept a plea of guilty to a lesser offence if the maximum sentence for that offence is not too low compared with the seriousness of what the defendant did. Thus, for example, if in the Crown Court a defendant enters a plea of not guilty to a s 18 charge of causing grievous bodily harm with intent (which carries a maximum sentence of life imprisonment), and the defendant then offers to plead guilty to the lesser s 20 offence of inflicting

---

[34] S. McCabe and R. Purves, *By-Passing the Jury* (1972).
[35] J. Baldwin and M. McConville, *Negotiated Justice* (1977), Ch 2.
[36] Bottoms and McClean, above n 18, 126–7.   [37] Hedderman and Moxon, above n 19, 24.
[38] Code for Crown Prosecutors (2nd ed, 1992), para 11.

grievous bodily harm (which carries a maximum sentence of five years' imprisonment), the prosecutor should reflect on whether the five-year maximum is appropriate
for what was done. However, this guidance is rather naïve when viewed in the light
of sentencing law. As Lord Bingham CJ stated, it is 'inconsistent with principle that a
defendant should be sentenced for offences neither admitted nor proven by verdict.'[39]
In the context of offences under ss 18 and 20, the maximum sentence of five years for
s 20 offences must be reserved for the worst conceivable cases, and it would only be
in rare cases that a sentence as far up the range as four years would be proper.[40] In
practice, therefore, a prosecutor who accepts a plea to s 20 on an indictment charging
s 18 would have to be satisfied that a sentence of two or three years would be adequate
on the facts.

What are the advantages and disadvantages of charge-bargaining from the defendant's point of view? These depend on whether the defendant has committed an offence
and, if so, what offence(s). It is easy to say that, if the defendant has really committed
the higher offence, a plea of guilty to a lesser offence brings a benefit to the defendant
in terms of a lower sentence. What is more debatable is the kind of case in which the
defendant may be said to have been overcharged in order to put pressure on him or her
to plead guilty to the lesser charge. In Chapter 7 we recorded evidence that this does
occur, despite injunctions to the contrary in the Code for Crown Prosecutors. To the
extent that it does happen, it means that some charge bargains hold no true advantage
for the defence and only for the prosecution. By appearing to reduce the charge(s), the
prosecutor obtains a plea of guilty to the offence that should really have been charged
in the first place.

Much worse is the position of the defendant who maintains innocence of all charges.
As we saw at the beginning of this chapter, English sentencing law holds out a massive
institutional temptation, stemming from three sources—pleading guilty to a lesser
charge should result in a lower sentence for the lesser offence, plus a further discount
for pleading guilty, and if the defendant indicates an intention to plead guilty when
brought before the magistrates on an either way charge the early plea may result in
the magistrates passing sentence or at least committing the case to the Crown Court
for sentence with a full discount. These institutional incentives may be known to the
defendant, but they may be all the more powerful when conveyed by a lawyer who
might be regarded as an expert. Thus if counsel's advice is that pleading guilty to a
lesser charge is likely to result in a non-custodial sentence whereas conviction after a
trial might result in custodial sentence, a defendant may well succumb to the pressure
to forgo a perfectly reasonable defence. The dependence of the defendant on his or her
legal representatives is considerable, and this brings issues of professional ethics to
the fore.[41]

---

[39] *Canavan and Kidd* [1998] 1 Cr App R (S) 243, at 247.
[40] Sentencing Guidelines Council, *Assault and other Offences against the Person* (2008).
[41] See Ch 3 above, and L. Bridges, ''Ethics of Representation on Guilty Pleas' (2006) 9 *Legal Ethics* 80.

10.4 FACT BARGAINS

In some cases the defendant changes the plea to guilty following negotiation with the prosecution about how the facts of the case should be stated. This informal process might begin with the defendant submitting a written basis of plea, or might involve the preparation of an agreed basis of plea by prosecution and defence. An agreement to minimise a particular aggravating feature, for example, or not to mention the part played by another (such as a friend or spouse) may be sufficient to persuade the defendant to plead guilty. Again, the principal advantage for the prosecution is that it secures a conviction in the case, even though the 'public interest' may be said to suffer a loss because the sentence is based on facts less serious than those that actually occurred. The judge is not bound to accept an agreed basis of plea. The defendant, on the other hand, stands to benefit from the favourable statement of the facts and the discount for pleading guilty, which will lower the sentence further—although it can only be counted as a benefit if he or she is actually guilty of a more serious version of the offence than that put to the court.

In *Beswick*,[42] there was evidence that the offender had bitten the victim's ear and crushed his nose with his knee during an altercation. The indictment was for wounding with intent, contrary to s 18 of the Offences Against the Person Act 1861. Just before the trial the prosecution agreed not only to accept a plea of guilty to s 20 wounding but also to accept that plea on the basis that he merely 'bit at' the victim's ear, without mention of the facial injury. The prosecution statement of facts conformed to that agreement, but the judge refused to sentence on that basis and insisted on a *Newton* hearing at which witnesses were heard in order to determine the true facts.[43] The Court of Appeal approved the course taken by the judge, and stated that:

'The prosecution should not lend itself to any agreement whereby a case is presented to the sentencing judge to be dealt with so far as that basis is concerned on an unreal and untrue set of facts concerning the offence to which a plea of guilty is to be tendered.'

There remain cases where the judge takes control when the prosecution appear not to dispute a basis of plea submitted by the defendant.[44] The Criminal Procedure Rules, which now govern 'basis of plea' cases, make it clear that the judge has the power to decide whether or not to accept the basis of plea and, if not, to hold a *Newton* hearing.[45]

In cases where the defendant wishes to put forward a plea of guilty on a version of facts that the prosecution is unable to accept, the Code for Crown Prosecutors states

---

[42] [1996] 1 Cr App R (S) 343.   [43] On *Newton* hearings, see n 2 above.

[44] For a recent example, see *Elicin and Moore* [2009] 1 Cr App R (S) 561; see also *Attorney-General's Reference No 44 of 2000 (Peverett)* [2001] 1 Cr App R 416 (discussed in Part 5 below), where part of the bargain was that the defendant's (less serious) version of the facts should be accepted (see the report at 418–19).

[45] Criminal Procedure Rules (2009 amendment), IV45.10–45.14, applying *Underwood* [2005] 1 Cr App R (S) 90.

that 'the court should be invited to hear evidence to determine what happened, and then sentence on that basis.'[46] The CPS is also pledged to deal with any defence mitigation that 'contains unjust criticism of the character of the victim,' by stating its rejection of what has been said and inviting the court (where necessary) to hear evidence on the point.[47] In both instances, therefore, the judge should be asked to hold a *Newton* hearing. If the evidential findings at that hearing go against the defendant, 'some or even the whole of any discount to which he might otherwise have been entitled by reason of his plea of guilty' may be forfeited.[48]

10.5 PLEA BARGAINS

One of the main reasons for dealing first with charge bargains and fact bargains is that it leaves for separate consideration those cases in which the defendant begins by signifying a plea of not guilty to the charge and subsequently alters the plea to guilty. These are cases where there is no question of reducing the number or level of the charges, and no bargain about the factual basis on which the case will be put forward. The bargain, in effect, is with the law: it is only a bargain because the law holds out the incentive of a reduced sentence to those who plead guilty, starting from a one-third reduction for a guilty plea entered at the earliest reasonable opportunity. The essence is that the defendant trades a chance of acquittal for a lower sentence than would have been received in the event of conviction after a trial. There are six major ways in which the institutional incentives to plead guilty may have an impact on the defendant: the sentence discount itself, advance indication of sentence, plea discussions in serious fraud cases, the 'plea before venue' system, plea and case management hearings, and lawyer's advice. Together they amount to formidable pressure, but they will be examined separately at first. Most of the discussion here relates to the Crown Court, but the 'guilty plea discount' applies equally in magistrates' courts.

(A) THE SENTENCE DISCOUNT

At the beginning of this chapter the wording of s 144 of the Criminal Justice Act 2003, on reduction of sentence for pleading guilty, was set out. Its broad and unqualified wording has now been the subject of guidelines from the Sentencing Guidelines Council: the discount applies to all courts (including magistrates' courts) and to all forms of sentence (including fines and community sentences). The provision also requires courts to state that they have reduced a sentence under that provision. The

[46] Code, para 10.4; the guidance is qualified by the clause, 'where this may significantly affect sentence'.
[47] CPS, *The Treatment of Victims and Witnesses*, para 3.6.
[48] *Elicin and Moore* [2009] 1 Cr App R (S) 561.

early evidence was that compliance with that requirement was variable,[49] but it is increasingly recognized as good sentencing practice to state how much of a reduction in sentence has been given for the guilty plea.[50] Insofar as this practice is followed, it amounts to an authoritative form of communication to offenders and their lawyers, which is likely to heighten the influence of the discount.

To what extent are sentence reductions given in practice? Evidence shows that the overall differences in the Crown Court are considerable: thus in 2007 some 67 per cent of indictable offenders pleading not guilty who were convicted received custodial sentences, compared with 55 per cent of those pleading guilty. This is a considerable difference, which surely demonstrates that a plea of guilty can make the difference between custody and community—a critical distinction, capable of exerting enormous pressure on defendants. For those sent to custody, the average lengths of sentence were 42 months for those convicted on a not guilty plea and 24 months for the guilty pleaders.[51] It is important to note that these are gross figures which take no account of previous convictions or mitigating factors.[52] The 2007 figures are presented in Table 10.1 on pp 304–5.

The 2007 differentials between the average sentence lengths for guilty pleaders and those convicted after a trial are variable and, intriguingly, for motoring offences the gap is small. One possible explanation for this is that persons prosecuted for causing death by dangerous driving might only plead guilty if persuaded that there is really no point in contesting the case because the offence was such a bad one, whereas those who do contest it are those whose offence is at the lower end of the scale, who may hope for the offence to be reduced to one of causing death by careless driving.

The result of this discussion is that there is both statutory authority for, and broad empirical confirmation of, a significant discount for pleading guilty. Insofar as the discount is known to defendants or is brought to their attention by lawyers, it is likely to exert a considerable pressure towards pleading guilty. That, of course, is the purpose of the relevant law. It was formerly thought that the sentence discount did not apply in magistrates' courts, but the law is now clear and the *Magistrates' Court Sentencing Guidelines* remind benches that a timely plea should result in a sentence reduction.

---

[49] R. Henham, 'Bargain Justice or Justice Denied? Sentence Discounts and the Criminal Process' (1999) 63 *MLR* 515; cf also his discussion of a small project in magistrates' courts, R. Henham, 'Reconciling Process and Policy: Sentence Discounts in the Magistrates' Courts' [2000] *Crim LR* 436. For criticisms of the methodology and conclusions of these projects, see A. Sanders and R. Young, *Criminal Justice* (3rd ed, 2006), 392.

[50] See the Sentencing Guidelines Council, *Reduction of Sentence for Guilty Plea* (Revised Guideline, 2007) This was also the view of the High Court of Australia in *Cameron v R* (2002) 209 CLR 339.

[51] *Sentencing Statistics 2007*, Table 2.19.

[52] When Hood took account of previous convictions and mitigating factors, a difference of ten months was reduced to one of three months: R. Hood, *Race and Sentencing* (1992), 125.

(B) ADVANCE INDICATION OF SENTENCE

The screw is further turned by the new procedures for advance indication of sentence recommended in the Auld Report. The Court of Appeal in *Goodyear*[53] decided to overrule the previous authority (*Turner*)[54] and to give what it termed 'guidelines' on the circumstances in which a judge might give an 'advance indication of sentence' to a defendant who is pleading not guilty but wishes to know the likely sentence on a guilty plea. The guidelines are detailed, but essentially a defendant may ask the judge (usually at a plea and case management hearing) whether the judge could give an indication of the maximum sentence that would be given based on the prosecution case papers, were the plea to be one of guilty, but before taking account of mitigation; the judge may decline to give such an indication; but if an indication is given, this binds the judge and any subsequent judge dealing with the case.[55] The Auld Report thought such a procedure both desirable and acceptable, asking 'What possible additional pressure, unacceptable or otherwise, can there be in the judge, whom [the defendant] has requested to tell him where he stands, indicating more precisely the alternatives?'[56] The court in *Goodyear*, which included Lord Woolf CJ and Judge LJ, likewise concluded that if the defendant seeks the judge's view, 'we do not see why a judicial response to a request for information from the defendant should automatically be deemed to constitute improper pressure on him.' The difference, of course, lies between defence counsel's prediction and the authoritativeness of the judicial indication: the element of roulette has gone, but the judge's indication may impose enormous pressure on the defendant, particularly where the indicated sentence on a change of plea to guilty does not involve immediate imprisonment. The *Goodyear* procedure, in combination with the guideline on reduction of sentence for a guilty plea, imposes considerable pressure on the guilty and innocent alike.

The court's approach in *Goodyear* was probably influenced by Schedule 3 to the Criminal Justice Act 2003, which provides for the introduction of advance indication of sentence in the magistrates' courts. In the event, those provisions have not been brought into force; and it is not clear whether *Goodyear* can be taken to apply by analogy to summary proceedings. When proposing the provisions that may be found in Schedule 3, the Home Office recognized the danger to innocent defendants, and seemed to think that this is adequately covered by leaving it to the defence to make the request for sentence indication.[57] It must be doubted whether that procedural difference would outweigh the substantial incentive arising if magistrates then indicated that the sentence on a guilty plea would be non-custodial.

---

[53] [2006] 1 Cr App R (S) 23.
[54] [1970] 2 QB 321, extensively discussed in the previous edition at pp 280–2.
[55] See further *Asiedu* [2009] 1 Cr App R (S) 420.   [56] Auld (2001), 434–44.
[57] Home Office, *Justice for All* (2002), para 4.43.

Table 10.1 Persons sentenced[1] for indictable offences at the Crown Court: Plea,[2] immediate custody and average sentence length, 2007

England and Wales

Sex and offence group	Total number sentenced			Number of persons, percentages and average sentence length (months)						
				Immediate custody					Average length of sentence[3]	
	Guilty plea	Not guilty plea	Percentage pleading guilty	Guilty plea	Percentage of guilty pleas	Not guilty plea	Percentage of not guilty pleas		Guilty plea	Not guilty plea
Males										
Indictable offences										
Violence against the person	10,878	2,557	81.0	5,397	49.6	1,719	67.2		22.4	36.3
Sexual offences	2,090	1,283	62.0	1,370	85.6	1,073	83.6		39.4	58.8
Burglary	5,160	392	92.9	3,526	68.3	279	71.2		26.7	33.5
Robbery	4,173	749	84.8	3,358	80.5	635	84.8		33.2	44.4
Theft and handling stolen goods	4,063	510	88.8	1,642	40.4	225	44.1		13.6	24.6
Fraud and forgery	3,920	280	93.3	2,773	70.7	150	53.6		11.8	25.0
Criminal damage	1,035	132	88.7	440	42.5	73	55.3		24.3	39.3
Drug offences	6,875	895	88.5	4,327	62.9	711	79.4		35.9	59.0
Other (excluding motoring) offences	7,417	891	89.3	3,263	44.0	509	57.1		15.8	28.5
Motoring offences	1,197	195	86.0	557	46.5	82	42.1		10.5	11.2
Total	46,808	7,884	85.6	26,653	56.9	5,456	69.2		24.5	42.8
Females										
Indictable offences										
Violence against the person	1,135	236	82.8	289	25.5	106	44.9		21.6	32.5
Sexual offences	28	11	71.8	9	32.1	7	63.6		20.0	59.1
Burglary	252	20	92.6	113	44.8	10	50.0		21.2	39.6
Robbery	371	54	87.3	203	56.1	33	61.1		26.1	32.0

Theft and handling stolen goods	738	84.2	139	23.0	170	27.3	38	13.3	23.0
Fraud and forgery	1,354	91.4	128	45.2	612	29.7	38	9.7	20.3
Criminal damage	172	92.0	15	30.2	52	33.3	5	31.8	34.5
Drug offences	967	89.1	118	43.1	417	66.1	78	34.5	54.2
Other (excluding motoring) offences	797	88.8	101	22.8	182	45.5	46	11.9	21.4
Motoring offences	45	72.6	17	28.9	13	29.4	5	10.5	8.2
Total	5,859	87.5	839	35.2	2,065	43.6	366	19.6	33.9
All persons									
Indictable offences									
Violence against the person	12,013	81.1	2,793	47.3	5,686	65.3	1,825	22.4	36.0
Sexual offences	2,118	62.1	1294	65.1	1,379	83.5	1,080	39.2	58.8
Burglary	5,412	92.9	412	67.2	3,639	70.1	289	26.6	33.7
Robbery	4,544	85.0	803	78.5	3,566	83.2	668	32.7	43.7
Theft and handling stolen goods	4,801	88.1	649	37.7	1,812	40.5	263	13.5	24.4
Fraud and forgery	5,274	92.8	408	64.2	3,385	46.1	188	11.4	24.1
Criminal damage	1,207	89.1	147	40.8	492	53.1	78	25.0	39.0
Drug offences	7,842	88.6	1,013	60.5	4,744	77.9	789	35.8	58.6
Other (excluding motoring) offences	8,214	89.2	992	41.9	3,445	55.9	555	15.6	27.8
Motoring offences	1,242	85.4	212	45.9	570	41.0	87	10.5	11.1
Total	52,667	85.8	8,723	54.5	28,718	66.7	5,822	24.2	42.2

[1] Excludes persons sentenced after summary conviction.
[2] Final plea recorded on completion of trial.
[3] Excludes life and indeterminate sentences.

(C) PLEA DISCUSSIONS IN SERIOUS FRAUD CASES

In 2009 the Attorney General introduced a new procedure for plea discussions in cases of serious or complex fraud, and this is now incorporated into the Criminal Procedure Rules.[58] One purpose of this procedure is to encourage defendants in these cases to reach an agreement that avoids the need for a lengthy and costly trial. It therefore follows that there may be concessions on both sides. The idea is that, where the defendant intends to plead guilty, the defence and prosecution will work on an agreed basis of plea, combined with sentencing submissions, which would then be submitted to the judge (ideally seven days before the hearing date). The basis of plea should be accompanied by material provided by the prosecution to the defence, and any documents in support of mitigating factors relied upon by the defence. The sentencing submissions should identify the relevant range in the sentencing guidelines, and should also deal with ancillary orders. As with any case involving a basis of plea, the judge remains in control and has the power to reject either the basis of plea or the sentencing submission or both, adopting the appropriate procedural response (such as a *Newton* hearing). The defendant may wish to ask for an advance indication of sentence before engaging in this procedure, and so the comments made in (b) above may apply here too. The English scheme has been drawn up with a view to avoiding some of the excesses encountered in the United States,[59] but its practical impact remains to be assessed, not least because it requires a full admission from the defendant.

(D) PLEA BEFORE VENUE

There is widespread recognition of the principle that, the earlier an intention to plead guilty is made known, the larger the sentence reduction should be. This follows from the rationale for the sentence discount, stated by the Sentencing Guidelines Council:

'A reduction in sentence is appropriate because a guilty plea avoids the need for a trial (thus enabling other cases to be disposed of more expeditiously), shortens the gap between charge and sentence, saves considerable cost, and, in the case of an early plea, saves victims and witnesses from the concern about having to give evidence. The reduction principle derives from the need for the effective administration of justice and not as an aspect of mitigation.'[60]

Putting this sentencing principle into practice means that the courts should reserve the maximum discount for those who indicate a plea of guilty at the earliest possible stage. Under the 'plea before venue' procedure, all defendants who are charged with triable either way offences are brought before magistrates and asked whether

---

[58] Criminal Procedure Rules (2009 amendment), IV.45.16–45.28. For broader discussion, see R. Julian, 'Judicial Perspectives in Serious Fraud Cases' [2008] *Crim LR* 764, esp at 776–8.

[59] E.g. those revealed in *McKinnon v United States of America* [2008] UKHL 59; see N. Vamos, 'Please Don't Call it Plea-Bargaining' [2009] *Crim LR* 617.

[60] Sentencing Guidelines Council, *Reduction in Sentence for a Guilty Plea* (Revised Guideline, 2007), para 2.2.

they intend to plead guilty. If they decline to intimate an intention to plead guilty, they may elect to be tried in the Crown Court or, if not, the magistrates will have the decision whether to commit them to the Crown Court for trial or to deal with the case themselves. However, the real incentive is for those who intimate an intention to plead guilty. The magistrates have the power to sentence them, if they decide that the case falls within their sentencing powers,[61] and this might mean a smaller and swifter sentence for the offender. However, that outcome is not certain, since the magistrates also have the power to commit the case to the Crown Court for sentence.

It appears that the purpose of the procedure—to avoid late changes of plea and to have more cases dealt with cheaply in the magistrates' courts—has been met in part. The number of committals to the Crown Court for trial has declined, although there has recently been a relatively sharp rise in the number of offenders committed to the Crown Court for sentence (from 30,000 in 2004 to over 41,000 in 2008). However, 'plea before venue' places great pressure on defendants to plead guilty very early, perhaps before they have had disclosure from the prosecution and therefore properly grounded legal advice. In order to secure the maximum sentence reduction of one-third, a defendant has to plead guilty at the 'first reasonable opportunity', a phrase elaborately defined in an Annex to the guideline and which goes even earlier than 'plea before venue' to encompass statements made in the police station.[62] Whether a discount of more than one-third for pleading guilty is ever justifiable is a question to be discussed in the concluding part of this chapter.

(E) PLEA AND CASE MANAGEMENT HEARINGS

In the early 1980s some magistrates' courts began to hold pre-trial reviews of contested cases, with a view to facilitating an exchange of information between prosecution and defence, identifying issues so as to save time and perhaps bring about pleas of guilty. Research suggested that they had modest advantages in cost-benefit terms: Brownlee, Mulcahy and Walker found that they had little overall effect on the speed of case disposal, and resulted in relatively few changes of plea to guilty, but they still argued that there were overall cost-savings because the reviews were relatively inexpensive.[63] It seems that pre-trial reviews are now rare in magistrates' courts, and that effectively the plea before venue procedure has displaced them.

Turning to the Crown Court, the Auld Review identified four different types of pre-trial hearing, and was critical of this multiplicity of arrangements and also of the rigidity and bureaucracy sometimes associated with them. Auld's recommendation

---

[61] It was held in R v Warley Justices, ex p DPP [1998] 2 Cr App R 307 that the magistrates' courts limit of six months' imprisonment for one offence could be used for cases that might justify a sentence of nine months at the Crown Court, if taking account of the discount meant that six months was the appropriate sentence.

[62] Sentencing Guidelines Council (above n 60).

[63] I. Brownlee, A. Mulcahy and C. P. Walker, 'Pre-Trial Reviews, Court Efficiency and Justice: a Study in Leeds and Bradford Magistrates' Courts' (1994) 33 Howard JCJ 109; for earlier discussion, see J. Baldwin, Pre-Trial Justice (1986).

was for a more flexible single system, and the result is the plea and case management hearing.[64] This has many of the functions of the former plea and directions hearing, in terms of taking the defendant's plea, assessing the readiness of prosecution and defence, and so forth. But there is an additional emphasis on active case management by the judge; and, of course, the plea and case management hearing gives an opportunity to a defendant whose current plea is not guilty to ask the judge for an advance indication of sentence, were the plea to change to guilty.

(F) NEGOTIATED DIVERSION

The focus of this discussion of plea bargains has been upon defendants whose decision to plead guilty is influenced by the sentence reduction. However, another form of bargain is where the possibility of a criminal charge acts as an incentive to participate in some scheme of diversion. An example of this, mentioned in Chapter 6, is the new system of conditional cautions, under which the CPS may agree conditionally not to prosecute a person if he or she agrees to certain conditions for a caution. Those conditions can impose some obligations, such as participation in a programme of work or treatment, and the threat of prosecution is suspended conditionally on compliance with the agreed terms. Thus the defendant may avoid a criminal conviction by agreeing to the terms for a conditional caution. As we noted,[65] one of the conditions for such a caution must be a free admission of guilt, but earlier research suggests that innocent persons can be tempted to agree to a caution rather than face the threat of something more serious. This type of bargain therefore holds the same advantages and disadvantages as plea-bargaining more generally.

(G) PLEA BARGAINS: THE BALANCE OF ADVANTAGES

What is the balance of advantages of plea bargains for the Crown? They contribute to the smooth running of the system by bringing speed and a reduction of the cost and resources needed to deal with the cases. They ensure a conviction, and avoid the hazards of trial which produce an overall acquittal rate of around 60 per cent in the Crown Court. In the present system these advantages come at the price of a sentence reduction: it could be claimed that offenders who benefit from the sentence discount are receiving a lower sentence than they deserve (on the basis of harm and culpability), purely for reasons of speed and cost. Those who believe that sentencing should be based on preventive grounds, such as deterrence or incapacitation, would also regard the discount as detracting from its primary purpose. It would be difficult to calculate whether these losses to the system are justified by the advantages, because that would

[64] See Criminal Procedure Rules (2009), 3.5 and 3.11.
[65] Above, Ch 6.4; simple police cautions offer the same possibilities for bargains.

also involve a calculation of how many defendants would persist in a not guilty plea if there were no sentence discount for pleading guilty.

What is the balance of advantages for victims? In general guilty pleas spare victims the anxiety of having to give evidence in court, and the unpleasantness of hearing all the details of the crime analysed at length in public. For those victims who do give evidence (a minority, because of the large numbers of guilty pleas), the process is often stressful.[66] However, research for the Sentencing Advisory Panel found that some rape victims resented the discount given for pleading guilty and said they would have been prepared to give evidence, if they had been given the choice, in order to ensure that substantial mitigation was not based on this factor.[67] It is not known whether a majority of victims feel this way, but the evidence is sufficient to raise questions about what some see as undeserved mitigation based on this ground—compounded, in some cases, by a reduction in the level of charge. In these cases it is particularly important that the victim or victim's family should be notified of such a significant step, but this does not always happen.[68]

What is the balance of advantages for defendants? The primary benefit is the discount for pleading guilty, which in general promises a substantial reduction in the length of a custodial sentence and (as the statistics in Table 10.1 strongly suggest) may in some cases result in the passing of a non-custodial rather than a custodial sentence. Such sentence reduction may be magnified by the defence lawyer's speech in mitigation: in general, it is much easier to construct a convincing mitigation for someone who has pleaded guilty than for someone who has contested guilt. It has often been said to be a further advantage that a defendant who was remanded in custody and who intended to plead guilty could delay the plea in order to benefit from the better conditions and more frequent visits available to remand prisoners,[69] but the recent emphasis on larger discounts for early pleas may have lessened the attraction of this course.

These, however, are only advantages for the guilty defendant. From the point of view of other defendants, these may be regarded as disincentives to a justifiable challenge to the prosecution case. There are undoubtedly some innocent defendants who feel pressure to plead guilty, because they believe there is a risk that they may not obtain an acquittal and it might appear best to 'cut their losses' in the hope of receiving a non-custodial sentence. Estimates of the number of innocent defendants who take this course vary: Zander and Henderson's figures suggested that up to 11 per cent of guilty pleaders claim innocence,[70] and earlier research suggested that an even higher

---

[66] E.g. J. Morgan and L. Zedner, *Child Victims* (1992), 141–3; J. Shapland, J. Willmore and P. Duff, *Victims in the Criminal Justice System* (1985), 63–7.

[67] Sentencing Advisory Panel, *Advice to the Court of Appeal on Rape* (2002), at 41. The Panel drew attention to the possibility of making a Victim Personal Statement to this effect.

[68] For what should happen, see the *Code of Practice for Victims of Crime* (2006).

[69] Cf the discussion in the Auld Review (above, n 56), 434–44.

[70] Zander and Henderson, above n 21, 138–42.

percentage of guilty pleaders were 'possibly innocent' of one or more charges.[71] Not enough is known about the mental processes of people placed in this position, but the research on false confessions should be sufficient to dispel any initial reluctance to believe that people could indeed plead guilty when they are innocent.[72] Moreover, the concept of innocence also needs careful attention: a defendant may have a perfectly arguable defence and should, one might contend, have a right to put the prosecution to disproof of the defence. Yet such a defendant may be advised that running the defence is not worth the risk and the consequent loss of discount, especially if this may make the difference between a custodial and a non-custodial sentence. The sentencing discount positively discourages defendants from putting the prosecution to proof of guilt, not least because it can be as much as a one-third reduction or even the avoidance of a custodial sentence.

The defence lawyer's ethical duty is not to place any pressure on the defendant but to give a frank appraisal of the prospects and of the advantages and disadvantages of continuing with a plea of not guilty. Peter Tague has argued, on the basis of discussions with London barristers, that there are three good reasons for maintaining a not guilty plea—the high chance of acquittal, the relative smallness of the sentence discount (which some would dispute), and the possibility of an appeal in the event of conviction.[73] Tague further argues that the fee structure does not create perverse incentives for barristers to prefer guilty pleas to trials, and that barristers who repeatedly advised lay clients to plead guilty when they and their solicitors preferred to plead not guilty would find themselves being briefed less frequently.[74] However, it remains true that the framework of criminal justice described in paragraphs (a) to (f) above, based on a substantial sentencing discount, contains strong incentives for those who are innocent to plead guilty, and that it is the lawyer's duty to explain that.[75]

10.6 POLICIES AND PRINCIPLES

There is much that is unsatisfactory in the rules and practices described in this chapter. Charge bargains are an unavoidable aspect of any system that includes graduated criminal offences (more serious, less serious) and that allows multiple charging. Graduated offences are right in principle,[76] and it is often justifiable to charge more

---

[71] See the summary by P. Darbyshire, 'The Mischief of Plea Bargaining and Sentencing Rewards' [2000] *Crim LR* 895, at 903.

[72] See Royal Commission on Criminal Justice (1993), para 4.32, on false confessions of guilt.

[73] P. Tague, 'Tactical Reasons for Recommending Trials rather than Guilty Pleas in the Crown Court' [2006] *Crim LR* 23.

[74] P. Tague, 'Barristers' Selfish Incentives in Counselling Defendants over Choice of Plea' [2007] *Crim LR* 3.

[75] For a forthright critique, see M. McConville, 'Plea Bargaining: Ethics and Politics' in S. Doran and J. Jackson (eds), *The Judicial Role in Criminal Proceedings* (2000), at 81–5, and Bridges, n 41 above.

[76] Cf A. Ashworth, *Principles of Criminal Law* (6th ed, 2009), Ch 3, esp 75–80.

than a single offence. But the result is to place pressure on defendants to plead guilty to something, as a kind of compromise. Fact bargains also seem to have an element of inevitability: defendants may only be prepared to plead guilty on a particular version of the facts, and the prosecution may be persuaded that this is right or acceptable. Plea bargains in the Crown Court operated for many years in a kind of half-light, with the *Turner* rules being flouted so frequently by barristers and trial judges that the Court of Appeal had to use strong language on several occasions in condemning the culture of disobedience.[77] At that time counsel had to predict the sentence that the judge was likely to give, particularly if the judge had declined to see counsel privately. Now the system has brought these matters more into the open, notably with advance indication of sentence and with plea discussions in serious fraud cases. This may make matters clearer to the defendant and the defence lawyer, when a defendant is considering a change of plea to guilty; but the amount of pressure is very great, particularly where there is a difference between a custodial and non-custodial outcome. From the public point of view, all of this may result in two kinds of unwanted consequences—the conviction (by guilty plea) of some people who are innocent, and the manipulation of criminal justice by some people who are guilty and who 'play the system', for example by waiting until the day of trial in order to see whether key witnesses attend before signifying their plea.

The movement in recent years has therefore between towards greater incentives and greater openness about what is on offer to defendants who are currently pleading not guilty. In 2002 the Government stated its objective of getting more defendants to plead guilty and to do so earlier, by means of a 'clearer tariff of sentence discount, backed up by arrangements whereby defendants could seek advance indication of the sentence they would get if they pleaded guilty.'[78] The benefit to witnesses and victims was acknowledged, but savings of court time and public money also loomed large: 'if more defendants pleaded guilty early in the process, the courts and other agencies within the CJS would be able to concentrate on the remaining contested cases.'[79] Many of the measures originated in the report of the Auld Review, which recommended a clear set of graduated sentence discounts and a new system of advance indication of sentence, initiated by the defendant.[80] In reaching his conclusions, Auld LJ took account of a number of concerns raised in the second edition of this book, relating to the difficulty of reconciling the various incentives to plead guilty with the framework of rights to which the UK is a signatory. The Royal Commission on Criminal Justice of 1993 spectacularly failed to make any reference to these rights. The Auld Review did so, but concluded that they do not stand in the way of the recommendations made.

---

[77] E.g. in *Pitman* [1991] 1 All ER 468 and in *Attorney General's Reference No 44 of 2000 (Peverett)* [2001] 1 Cr App R 416.

[78] Home Office, *Justice for All* (2002), para 4.42.   [79] *Ibid.*, para 4.41.

[80] Auld Review, above n 56, 443–4.

The argument here is that the sentence discount for pleading guilty runs contrary to the spirit of at least four of the rights recognized under the European Convention on Human Rights, and possibly counter to their letter too. This argument starts by considering the rights of a defendant charged with a criminal offence, rather than starting with the objective of making the criminal justice system operate as smoothly and as cost-effectively as possible. The four rights to be considered are: the presumption of innocence, the privilege against self-incrimination, the right not to be discriminated against in the exercise of Article 6 rights, and the right to a fair and public hearing.

(A) THE PRESUMPTION OF INNOCENCE

Article 6(2) of the European Convention on Human Rights declares that 'everyone charged with a criminal offence shall be presumed innocent until proved guilty according to law'. One implication of this seems to be that a defendant has a right to put the prosecution to proof. No one should be recorded as guilty of an offence until the prosecution has proved that guilt, and 'any doubt should benefit the accused'.[81] The question is whether this right can be waived and, if so, under what conditions. The first part of the question may be answered by reference to a rather old decision of the European Commission on Human Rights, which held in 1972 that the possibility of pleading guilty does not infringe Article 6(2) so long as there are adequate safeguards against abuse, and that the judge is satisfied that the accused understands the effect of his plea.[82] The second part of the question is more difficult to answer, and the authorities indicate that the presence of a substantial incentive to give up the right to be tried—one-third or more off the sentence for the offence(s)—needs to be reviewed in Strasbourg.

In an early case entitled *X v United Kingdom*,[83] the trial judge had observed when passing sentence that a guilty plea would have constituted a mitigating circumstance. The applicants argued in Strasbourg that this amounted to the imposition of a heavier sentence on the grounds that they had contested the charge, and accordingly that the sentence was in breach of Article 6. In rejecting the application as manifestly ill-founded the Commission observed:

'It is clear from the statements by the trial judge that he did not increase the applicants' sentence on the ground that they had affirmed their innocence throughout the trial, but rather refrained from reducing what he deemed to be the proper sentence, having regard to the gravity of the offences concerned.'

This is consistent with the theory behind the guilty plea discount in English law,[84] even though it remains true that exercising one's right to be tried has a cost in the

---

[81] *Barbera, Messegue and Jabardo v Spain* (1989) 11 EHRR 360, para 33.
[82] *X v United Kingdom* (1972) 40 CD 64, at 67, discussed by B. Emmerson, A. Ashworth and A. Macdonald (eds), *Human Rights and Criminal Justice* (2nd ed, 2007), 697.
[83] (1975) 3 DR 10, at 16.   [84] See, e.g., *Harper* [1968] 1 QB 108.

sense that the sentence passed in the event of conviction will be higher (possibly 50 per cent higher)[85] than the sentence on a guilty plea. Does the compatibility of a discount for pleading guilty depend on the extent of the inducement involved? In *Deweer v Belgium*,[86] the Court found a violation of Article 6 where the applicant had been offered the choice between paying a relatively modest fine by way of 'compromise' or facing lengthy criminal proceedings. If he had chosen to contest the charge his butcher's shop would have remained closed by administrative order, thus depriving him of income. The Court held that a procedure under which an accused can waive the right to a hearing on payment of a penalty is not necessarily inconsistent with Article 6, but that such a settlement must be free from 'constraint'. In the present case there was such disproportionality between the moderate fine and the substantial collateral consequences of contesting the proceedings that the settlement was tainted by constraint and therefore in breach of Article 6. In English cases the discount on a custodial sentence can be up to one-third,[87] and it is clear that a plea of guilty may make the difference between a custodial sentence and a community sentence.[88] Is a decision to plead guilty made in those circumstances sufficiently free from 'constraint', in the sense applied in *Deweer v Belgium*?

The magnitude of the English discount may suggest that it is not. It is one thing to offer a small inducement to plead guilty, in order to reinforce the proposition that those who are guilty should plead guilty and not try to 'play the system'. It is quite another thing if the extent of the inducement is so great as to 'drown out' that proposition and induce those who are not guilty to change their plea. Auld LJ, in his report, recognized the risk that some innocent defendants might be induced to plead guilty and commented that no system can guarantee that this will not happen. But his primary concern seemed to be that a sentencing system should not be tailored to encourage a defendant who knows he is guilty to 'try his luck', and this is why the sentence discount—and, on his view, a substantial one—is necessary.[89] In our view, this approach ignores the force of the presumption of innocence and sacrifices it too readily to expediency.

The 1993 Royal Commission sought to deal with the problem of innocent defendants thus:

'Provided that the defendant is in fact guilty and has received competent legal advice about his or her position, there can be no serious objection to a system of inducements designed to encourage him or her so to plead. Such a system is, however, sometimes held to encourage defendants who are not guilty of the offence charged to plead guilty to it nevertheless... This risk cannot be wholly avoided and, although there can be no certainty as to the precise

---

[85] If the sentence after conviction is three years, and the sentence after an early guilty plea is two years (applying the one-third discount), then the former is 50 per cent higher than the latter.
[86] (1980) 2 EHRR 439.
[87] Sentencing Guidelines Council, *Reduction in Sentence for a Guilty Plea* (Revised Guideline, 2007).
[88] *Ibid.*; see also *Howells* [1999] 1 Cr App R (S) 335, *per* Lord Bingham CJ at 337.
[89] Auld Report, above, n 56, 439–40.

numbers... it would be naive to suppose that innocent persons never plead guilty because of the prospect of the sentence discount.'[90]

The only relevant point made subsequently is that 'against the risk that defendants may be tempted to plead guilty must be weighed the benefits to the system and to defendants of encouraging those who are in fact guilty to plead guilty. We believe that the system of sentence discounts should remain.'[91] This kind of 'balancing' argument, which appears to assign no particular weight to the presumption of innocence or any other recognized right, is quite unacceptable. Certainly it would be wrong for the advocates of rights to argue that it behoves us to take *every possible* step to ensure that innocent persons are never convicted. That would result in an immense investment of resources into criminal trials that might cripple the economy. But to dismiss that extreme position is not enough. As Dworkin argues, there is a strong case for maintaining that at all stages of the criminal process our procedures should put the proper value on the fundamental harm of wrongful conviction.[92] What the proper value is may be a matter for debate, but the argument here is that to hold out a substantial sentence discount as a standing incentive for defendants to waive their right to trial goes too far. It fails to give any special weight to the presumption of innocence, whereas its position as a fundamental right ought surely to require this.

(B) THE PRIVILEGE AGAINST SELF-INCRIMINATION

Although this privilege is not declared expressly in the European Convention on Human Rights, it is now established that the privilege and the related right of silence are implied rights that form part of the right to a fair trial in Article 6 of the Convention.[93] Leading Strasbourg decisions describe the privilege against self-incrimination as a 'generally recognized international standard' which lies 'at the heart of the notion of fair procedure under Article 6', and the same applies to the right of silence.[94] Both rights have been held to: 'presuppose that the prosecution in a criminal case seek to prove their case against the accused without resort to evidence obtained through methods of coercion or oppression in defiance of the will of the accused. In this sense the right is closely linked to the presumption of innocence contained in Article 6(2) of the Convention.'[95]

As we discuss elsewhere, the concept of coercion has been quite widely drawn by the Court.[96] The question here is whether the sentence discount for pleading guilty amounts to coercion in an analogous sense.

Two points may be made briefly. The first is that a substantial discount, of a third or more, may well amount to an inducement of the same magnitude as the financial

---

[90] Royal Commission on Criminal Justice, *Report*, para 7.42.   [91] *Ibid.*, para 7.45.

[92] R. M. Dworkin, 'Principle, Policy, Procedure' in C. Tapper (ed), *Crime, Proof and Punishment* (1981), 212.

[93] See Ch 2 above.

[94] E.g. *Murray v United Kingdom* (1996) 22 EHRR 29 and *Saunders v United Kingdom* (1997) 23 EHRR 313, both drawing on Art 14 of the International Covenant on Civil and Political Rights.

[95] *Saunders, ibid.* at para 68.   [96] Above, Ch 5.6.

penalties considered in cases such as *JB v Switzerland*[97] to infringe the privilege against self-incrimination. The second point is that there is a considerable literature on false confessions, as the Royal Commission on Criminal Justice recognized.[98] Difficult as it may be to imagine, some people who are innocent may be induced to plead guilty by the prospect of a non-custodial sentence and no further fuss. Just as the law holds that a confession should not be admitted if it was obtained in consequence of anything said or done which was likely, in the circumstances existing at the time, to render it unreliable, so one might argue that *pari passu* a plea of guilty should not be upheld if it was obtained in consequence of what might be described as a substantial inducement. Indeed, the argument would be that the legal system should not provide such an inducement, whereas English law, through its sentencing discount, clearly does.

(C) THE RIGHT NOT TO BE DISCRIMINATED AGAINST IN THE EXERCISE OF ARTICLE 6 RIGHTS

Article 14 of the European Convention on Human Rights declares that the rights in the Convention 'shall be secured without discrimination on any ground such as sex, race, colour'. Would this principle be breached, either in the letter or in the spirit, if it were found that the operation of the criminal justice system routinely discouraged members of a particular ethnic minority from disputing their guilt?

Consider the available evidence in England and Wales. All studies that have included data on defendants' plea show that both persons from an African-Caribbean background and those from an Asian background tend to plead not guilty at a higher rate than whites. It also appears that African-Caribbeans are more likely to be acquitted, which may be regarded as vindicating their pleas.[99] The John Report found that 'defendants from African Caribbean and Asian ethnic groups are more likely to be acquitted than white defendants,'[100] suggesting that some of them are prosecuted when they should not be—which may explain the higher not guilty plea rate. Roger Hood found that not only do African-Caribbeans tend to plead not guilty more frequently than whites but that, when convicted, they tend to receive longer sentences largely because they have forfeited the discount for pleading guilty.[101] This can be regarded as a form of indirect discrimination: a general principle (the sentence discount) has a disproportionate impact on members of ethnic minorities simply because they exercise a right (the right to be tried and to be presumed innocent until convicted). The Royal Commission seemed to recognize this, but merely expressed its support for 'the recommendation made by Hood that the policy of offering sentence discounts should be kept under review'.[102] In fact, Hood argued that 'it is time [i.e. now] to consider all the implications of a policy which favours

---

[97] [2001] *Crim LR* 748.   [98] Royal Commission on Criminal Justice, *Report*, para 4.32.

[99] For a summary of the early research, see M. Fitzgerald, *Ethnic Minorities and the Criminal Justice System* (1993), 26.

[100] Gus John Partnership, *Race for Justice* (2003), para 37.

[101] R. Hood, *Race and Sentencing* (1992), 125.

[102] Royal Commission on Criminal Justice, *Report*, para 7.58.

316 THE CRIMINAL PROCESS

so strongly those who plead guilty'.[103] The Auld Review recognized that 'it is important to discover why one group of defendants, distinguished only by their ethnicity, should behave differently from others when faced with the same choices,'[104] and called for research to determine why this is so and whether the discount for pleading guilty was relevant to this. However, it appears that Auld was sceptical of these arguments, and took the general position that if members of ethnic minorities sought to exercise their right to be tried, they should take the consequence of a more severe sentence if found guilty. This overlooks the powerful argument about indirect discrimination, an argument that strongly favours the abolition (or substantial diminution) of the guilty plea discount.[105]

(D) THE RIGHT TO A 'FAIR AND PUBLIC' HEARING

Article 6(1) of the European Convention declares that 'everyone is entitled to a fair and public hearing', and goes on to describe the limited situations in which 'the press and public may be excluded from all or part of the trial'. One characteristic of cases in which there is a guilty plea is that there is no real public hearing. An added characteristic of cases in which there is a plea bargain is that the crucial negotiation takes place in the absence not only of the public but also of the accused. The High Court of Australia spoke out strongly against these private meetings between judge and counsel, disapproving even the limited contact allowed by the *Turner* rules on the ground that this is inconsistent with 'the common law rule which requires a court to administer justice in public',[106] and there is good reason to believe that a case determined in this way would not satisfy Article 6(1) of the Convention. Of course it may be replied that there is always some form of public hearing, at which the defendant pleads guilty, prosecution and defence speeches are made, and the judge decides on sentence. But if it can be established that the defendant's fate was determined by words spoken in private, of which only some were relayed to the defendant by counsel, this might cause some reconsideration of the Strasbourg approach.[107]

10.7 CONCLUSIONS

From the point of view of principle there are powerful arguments in favour of re-assessing the sentence discount for those who plead guilty. It is certainly against the spirit of the four fundamental rights and freedoms recognized in the European Convention on Human Rights—the presumption of innocence, the privilege against

---

[103] Hood, above n 101, 182.   [104] Auld Review, above n 56, 441.
[105] In M. Tonry, *Punishment and Politics* (2004), 75 and 87, it is argued that this reasoning should lead to the abolition of the guilty plea discount.
[106] *Tait and Bartley* (1979) 24 ALR 473, at 488.
[107] See the case of *X v United Kingdom* at n 98 above, and accompanying text.

self-incrimination, the right to equal treatment in the exercise of rights, and the right to a fair and public hearing—and is probably against the letter of two of them. The sentence discount sustains a number of perverse incentives that are liable to distort both the pursuit of truth and the protection of rights, in the context of charge, fact, and plea bargains.

One major difficulty is the size of the sentence discount: it can be as much as one-third (although less for a late change of plea), and can certainly make the difference between immediate custody and a non-custodial sentence.[108] These are formidable incentives, applicable both to those who are guilty and to those who are innocent. It has been argued here that discounts of this kind are so great that they place unfair pressure on those who maintain their innocence and wish to put the prosecution to proof—a strong temptation to 'cut one's losses' and plead guilty in exchange for a lesser sentence, particularly if it is non-custodial. A fairer system (assuming that the discount is to be retained) would be to offer a small incentive of no more than a 10 per cent reduction, aimed at preserving the freedom of choice of someone who maintains innocence and at ensuring that the exercise of the right to be presumed innocent until proved guilty does not have a significant cost.[109]

During the first decade of the new century there have been significant steps towards increasing the openness of plea negotiations, with a greater involvement of judges. Both advance indication of sentence and the new plea discussions in serious fraud cases are significant moves in that direction. The increased number of sentencing guidelines—now covering most offences—should increase the predictability of sentencing. But there remains the question whether increased transparency and increased judicial involvement do not amount to increased pressure on the guilty and the innocent alike. The Royal Commission of 1993 concluded that a system in which the judge gave such a sentence indication would amount to placing undue pressure on defendants, largely because the involvement of a judge made the pressure greater than simply the prediction of counsel. But Auld LJ disagreed:

'That comparison is precisely what a defendant considering admitting his guilt wants to know. He knows and will, in any event, be advised by his lawyer that a plea of guilty can attract a lesser sentence and broadly what the possible outcomes are, depending on his plea. So what possible additional pressure, unacceptable or otherwise, can there be in the judge, whom he has requested to tell him where he stands, indicating more precisely the alternatives?'[110]

Such a system of sentence indication may succeed in reducing the element of uncertainty, but it surely imposes additional pressure through the involvement of the authoritative figure of the judge. Given the magnitude of the possible difference between the

---

[108] Sentencing Guidelines Council, *Reduction in Sentence for Guilty Plea* (Revised Guideline, 2007).

[109] Of course, any reduction in the amount of the discount would have to form part of a general re-appraisal of sentence levels and approaches to sentencing. We are certainly not arguing for any overall increase in the severity of sentences: other adjustments would have to be made.

[110] Auld Review, above n 56, Ch 10, para 112.

two sentences, the real question is whether the pressure is so great as to impinge on the defendant's freedom of choice in the exercise of fundamental rights. If such an inducement were made to someone before he or she confessed a crime to the police, the prevailing principle is that the confession should be ruled inadmissible.[111] False confessions do occur. Our submission is that the same considerations should apply in the context of changes of plea from not guilty to guilty.

Could the greater involvement of the judge be turned into an advantage for defendants, as a means of protecting the defendant's rights rather than imposing undue pressure? In Philadelphia, the fourth largest city in the US, there is no principle of sentence discount for pleading guilty. The result is that most defendants in felony cases do opt for trial, many of these being 'bench trials' by judge alone, which can be dealt with fairly quickly. This shows that, even in a country in which plea-bargaining has come to be regarded as endemic, it is in fact merely a policy choice.[112] It could be eliminated or reduced substantially. That might entail costs, but it throws down the challenge to simplify criminal procedure generally. When the US Federal Sentencing Guidelines were introduced they were designed to reduce the discount for pleading guilty and to place controls on plea negotiation: Schulhofer and Nagel concluded from their research that in the vast majority of cases (some 65 to 80 per cent) there was compliance with the guidelines and plea negotiations were not used as a means of circumventing them.[113] Alschuler, who has studied plea-bargaining in the US extensively over a long period, argues that changes in criminal procedure could make for a fairer system that afforded the opportunity of trial to every defendant.[114]

No examination of these possibilities appears to have been conducted in this country. The overriding assumption is that it is necessary to increase the proportion of guilty pleas and of early guilty pleas, and any reference to the greater involvement of judges in assessing case papers and in ascertaining that innocent defendants were not being pressured into pleading guilty would probably be dismissed as too costly. But even if this is true—and until it has been thoroughly investigated, it would be unwise to make the assumption—then the question is plainly one of expense rather than respect for rights. In this chapter we have noted the strong structural incentives to plead guilty and to enter that plea at the earliest opportunity, and we have argued that these incentives undermine safeguards for the innocent. Stephen Schulhofer has advanced the same view in powerful terms:

'Contractual exchange, under appropriate conditions, can leave both parties better off. But the converse is also true. When the conditions necessary for welfare-enhancing transactions

---

[111] It would be inconsistent to create an exception for the sentence discount: see the discussion in Ch 4 above.

[112] S. J. Schulhofer, 'Is Plea Bargaining Inevitable?' (1984) 97 *Harv LR* 1037.

[113] S. J. Schulhofer and I. Nagel, 'Plea Negotiations under the Federal Sentencing Guidelines: Guideline Circumvention and its Dynamics in the Post-*Mistretta* Period' (1997) 91 *Northwestern ULR* 1284.

[114] Among his many writings, see particularly A. Alschuler, 'Implementing the Criminal Defendant's Right to Trial' (1983) 50 *U Chi LR* 931.

are not met, contractual exchange can leave both parties worse off. In criminal justice, pervasive structural impediments to efficient, welfare-enhancing transactions have produced just this situation. With trials in open court and deserved sentences imposed by a neutral factfinder, we protect the due process right to an adversarial trial, minimize the risk of unjust conviction of the innocent, and at the same time further the public interest in effective law enforcement and adequate punishment of the guilty. But plea negotiation simultaneously undercuts all of these interests. The affected parties are represented by agents who have inadequate incentives for proper performance; prospects for effective monitoring are limited or non-existent; and the dynamics of negotiation can create irresistible pressure for defendants falsely to condemn themselves. As a result, plea agreements defeat the public interest in effective law enforcement at the same time that they deny defendants the benefits of a vigorous defence and inflict undeserved punishment on innocents who could win acquittal at trial.'[115]

These words were written in an American context, and the somewhat optimistic description of trials seems rather overdone. Indeed, this point is taken up by Robert Scott and William Stuntz, who ask whether it is really desirable to push more innocent people to trial, on the basis that some of them will be convicted and will then receive harsher sentences than they would have done if they had pleaded guilty:

'This result stands every known theory of distributional justice on its head. We would think it common ground that losses, equally unjust losses, are better spread than concentrated, all else being equal. Schulhofer, like most critics of plea bargaining, seems to prefer a few innocent defendants serving long prison terms to a larger number serving a few years apiece.'[116]

Their view is certainly contestable: if all known theories of distributional justice point in the direction of more convictions of the innocent, then that is a good reason for not subscribing to them. From the rights perspective, the right of innocent persons not to be convicted ought to be recognized as a strong right with a high value, not something to be traded off simply for supposed efficiency gains. Scott and Stuntz would insist that, in a world where there are going to be convictions of innocent people, we must face the choice to which they refer, and not avoid it. Their approach, in the leading article on which Schulhofer was commenting, is to eschew both extremes—to argue both against the existing system of plea negotiation, and against the abolition of all plea negotiations—and to press the case for reconfiguring the bargaining process in order to make it fairer. They start from the position that modern criminal justice systems are so demanding of resources that, in most countries, there is an 'inability to test innocence claims at acceptable cost'.[117] Recent reforms in this country, in the form of advance indication of sentence and plea discussions in serious fraud cases, appear to have moved towards the greater information for defendants on the choice to be made, and clearer sentencing guidance to enhance predictability, that Scott and

[115] S. J. Schulhofer, 'Plea-Bargaining as Disaster' (1992) 101 *Yale LJ* 1979, at 2008–9.
[116] R. E. Scott and W. J. Stuntz, 'A Reply: Imperfect Bargains, Imperfect Trials and Innocent Defendants' (1992) 101 *Yale LJ* 2011, at 2013.
[117] R. E. Scott and W. J. Stuntz, 'Plea Bargaining as Contract' (1992) 101 *Yale LJ* 1909, at 1951.

Stuntz recommend. However, as argued above, the size of the discount available in England and Wales is too great, the pressure it exerts on defendants is too much, the effect on innocent defendants (especially those from certain racial minorities) is unacceptable, and the system as a whole fails to place a sufficiently high value on preventing wrongful convictions.[118] Recent governments have failed to give priority to avoiding undue pressure on the innocent in their search for ways of achieving the efficiencies they desire.

FURTHER READING

McConville, M., 'Plea Bargaining: Ethics and Politics' in S. Doran and J. Jackson (eds), *The Judicial Role in Criminal Proceedings*, Oxford: Hart Publishing, 2000.

Lord Justice Auld, *Review of the Criminal Courts of England and Wales: Report*, London: The Stationery Office, 2001, 434–44.

Tonry, M., *Punishment and Politics*, Cullompton: Willan, 2004, Ch 4.

Questions for Discussion

1. Are charge bargains inevitable?

2. Is the procedure for advance indication of sentence a worthwhile innovation?

3. Are the rights-based arguments against the sentence discount for pleading guilty convincing at the level of principle? Even if they are, would there be insuperable problems in devising a practical system that took them into account?

---

[118] Cf the argument of Dworkin, above n 92 and accompanying text.

11

THE TRIAL

The trial is the focal point of criminal procedure. Case preparation in the earlier stages of the process will be carried out in the light of the possibility that the case may go to court. The rules governing trials therefore shape decisions made by police and prosecutors. While it is true that the majority of defendants plead guilty, and that the system encourages trial avoidance in this manner, the trial remains of importance because defendants' decisions on whether or not to plead guilty are often informed by what they believe to be the probability of conviction. Furthermore, in those cases where defendants do not plead guilty, a decision has to be made on whether or not the defendant is actually guilty. The mechanism for making this crucial decision deserves close consideration.

Many aspects of the trial can only be understood through detailed consideration of the rules of evidence and fact-finding processes. Such a study is beyond the scope of the present work. We will merely present an overview of courtroom processes and consider some of the rules of evidence which are most closely connected to issues of procedural fairness. Before proceeding to this, we briefly consider theoretical perspectives on the trial.

It goes without saying that a primary function of the trial, as of the criminal process as a whole, is accurate decision making. The trial is an attempt to sort the innocent from the guilty and to determine the level of wrongdoing of the guilty, though it is constrained by the high standard of proof (beyond reasonable doubt) which protects the innocent from wrongful conviction. For some writers, there is little more to the trial than this; although other values might in theory play a role in the trial, they are not sufficiently compelling to outweigh the strong interest in accurate fact-finding.[1] As a description of actual trial practices, this view has little to be said for it (which hints that it is deficient as a theory, too). Anglo-American jurisdictions (as well as the regime under the European Convention on Human Rights (ECHR) recognize the importance of a fair trial, where fairness comprises more than accuracy. In England and Wales, the abuse of process jurisdiction, discussed in Chapter 9, is a good example of this. The exclusion of improperly obtained evidence, discussed in this chapter, is a further example. Thus there is widespread agreement that the criminal trial is not

---

[1] See L. Laudan, *Truth, Error and Criminal Law: An Essay in Legal Epistemology* (2006).

a purely instrumental process. Saying just what it is in addition to an instrumental process, however, is more difficult and here there is less agreement.

The simplest way to incorporate values other than accuracy in a theory of the trial is to depict the trial as a side-constrained instrumental process, where things such as the need to respect the defendant's rights restrain the pursuit of truth. In contrast, a more complex theory would argue that values other than accurate fact-finding are an intrinsic part of the trial, and thus should not be seen as constraints on accuracy but as an integral part of the trial's aims. One way of grounding this vision of the trial is provided by Duff and his co-authors who have argued that the trial should be seen as a communicative process in which the defendant is called to answer for alleged wrong-doing, and to account for that wrongdoing should it be proved.[2] Because, for Duff et al, the trial is a process or moral engagement with the accused, accuracy is no longer a primary aim, but is intertwined with moral values. This is an ambitious theory, and there may be questions about the extent to which the criminal trial should be mod-elled as a process of moral dialogue when it involves the application of State power to an individual.[3] A slightly different, and influential, way of acknowledging the integral position of values other than accuracy to the criminal trial is to stress the need for criminal verdicts to be legitimate.[4] At one level, it is hard to disagree with this—who would argue that trial verdicts should be illegitimate? But unpacking the notion of legitimacy is not straightforward; advocates of legitimacy have tended to explain legit-imacy in terms of public confidence, but public attitudes are sufficiently fickle that they offer no guarantee that the trial would respect the defendant's rights or result in more than a largely instrumental trial process. Legitimacy therefore probably needs some objective grounding, but explaining just why certain actions of the State—such as the unlawful deportations in *Mullen*[5] and *Bennett*[6]—should affect the legitimacy of the trial remains difficult.

The difference between these various theories should not be over-stated. Indeed, the distinction between side-constrained instrumentalism and intrinsic theories may be one with no practical difference.[7] Most theorists who reject pure-instrumentalism share a broadly similar vision of the trial—though we will point up possible disagree-ments about certain cases below. As we explained in Chapter 2, our own vision of the trial, and of the wider criminal process to which it is central, emphasizes respect for dignity and rights. We located important rights as internal values in criminal process, so, for what it is worth, these values are properly seen as intrinsic to the trial rather than as side constraints. While we are cautious about the language of legitimacy, this account could be translated into legitimacy terms by suggesting that respect for rights

    [2] A. Duff et al, *The Trial on Trial Volume 3: Towards a Normative Theory of the Criminal Trial* (2007).
    [3] See M. Redmayne, 'Theorizing the Criminal Trial' (2009) 12 *New Crim LR* 287.
    [4] A view taken in I. Dennis, *The Law of Evidence* (3rd ed, 2007), and P. Roberts and A. Zuckerman, *Criminal Evidence* (2004).
    [5] [2000] QB 520.   [6] *R v Horseferry Road Magistrates' Court, ex p Bennett* [1995] 1 Cr App R 147.
    [7] See Redmayne, above n 3.

is a primary objective constraint on legitimacy.[8] However, while this makes it clear that respect for rights is an important part of the account of the trial, it says little about what makes trials distinctive as processes which involve rights and what particular rights and values a trial might engage. This is a complex topic, and we will do no more at this point than note that one important aspect of the trial is its association with the rule of law.[9] As Waldron explains, when someone is accused of breaking the law:

'they should have an opportunity to request a hearing, make an argument, and confront the evidence before them prior to the application of any sanction associated with the norm. The Rule of Law is violated when the institutions that are supposed to embody these procedural safeguards are undermined. In this way the Rule of Law has become associated with political ideals such as the separation of powers and the independence of the judiciary.'[10]

Criminal trials might also engage the rule of law in another way. Trials are constrained by the demand that 'citizens be protected from oppression and their dignity respected';[11] more ambitiously, they provide an opportunity to examine the actions of the State in prosecuting crime—calling the State to account, as it has been put.[12] This helps to explain why close scrutiny of the legality of police actions in investigating crime may become an important part of a criminal trial.

11.1 MODES OF TRIAL

(A) MAGISTRATES' COURT AND CROWN COURT

There are two different levels of court with substantial differences in the trials that take place in them. The least serious cases are tried in the magistrates' courts and the more serious ones in the Crown Court; in practice, the vast majority of cases—at least 95 per cent—are dealt with in the magistrates' court. The principal distinction between the two courts is that cases in the Crown Court are tried by a professional judge sitting with a jury, and cases in the magistrates' court are tried by lay magistrates, or by a judge sitting alone. Lay magistrates are unpaid and hear cases on a part-time basis, usually sitting in court for half a day every week;[13] they typically sit in benches of three and are advised on legal points by a clerk. There is considerable debate

---

[8] This seems to be Choo's position: A. Choo, *Abuse of Process and Judicial Stays of Criminal Proceedings* (2nd ed, 2008), 190.

[9] See Duff et al, above n 2, 94–6.

[10] J. Waldron, 'The Concept and the Rule of Law' (2008) 43 *Georgia L Rev* 1, 8.

[11] Duff et al, above n 2, 95.

[12] H. Ho, 'Book Review: The Trial on Trial' (2008) 6 *International Commentary on Evidence* (www.bepress.com/ice/).

[13] The standard requirement is a half day sitting each fortnight, but many magistrates sit more often than this, making the national average closer to a half day each week. There is considerable variation, however. See R. Morgan and N. Russell, *The Judiciary in the Magistrates' Courts* (2000), 18–19.

about the relative merits of the two types of trial, and it is important to understand something about these issues before considering the way in which cases are allocated between the different courts.

The first point to make is that there is nothing unusual about having two levels of court. Most jurisdictions have more elaborate procedures for trying the more serious cases.[14] Given limited resources, this is entirely appropriate. Accurate adjudication is more important in serious than non-serious cases, because the cost of error (of either mistaken conviction or mistaken acquittal) is greater. This does not, of course, mean that trials in the lower tier of court should be cursory, or that defendants tried there should face an undue risk of mistaken conviction. One of the concerns about the magistrates' court is that defendants do in fact face an unacceptable risk of false conviction. It is often remarked that the conviction rate is higher in the magistrates' court than in the Crown Court. According to Crown Prosecution Service (CPS) statistics, 62 per cent of defendants in contested trials in the magistrates' courts are convicted, compared with 54 per cent in the Crown Court.[15] This is a significant and recurring difference, but it is not obvious how to interpret it. In the inevitable absence of knowledge of the proportion of innocent and guilty defendants in each court, it is impossible to say whether one court is more accurate, or even lenient, than the other. It should also be noted that the cases dealt with in each court have different characteristics. Those tried in the Crown Court are more complex, and many summary offences have no *mens rea* element; it may therefore be that cases heard in the magistrates' courts are simply easier to prove.[16]

Moving beyond acquittal rates, there is a general perception among defendants and lawyers that trials in the Crown Court are fairer than magistrates' trials.[17] There are several reasons why Crown Court trial may be fairer. Juries typically come fresh to a case; they are not 'case hardened' in the way magistrates may be. Trial by judge and jury is also an effective way of keeping certain information—such as the fact that the defendant has previous convictions—away from the fact-finder.[18] Juries tend to be more representative of the general population than magistrates, and in some circumstances this may make them superior fact-finders, for they will have a wider

---

[14] Details of various jurisdictions can be gleaned from N. Osner, A. Quinn and G. Crown, *Criminal Justice Systems in Other Jurisdictions* (1993).

[15] *CPS Annual Report 2008–2009*, Annex B. Both figures include cases where judge or magistrates found no case to answer.

[16] See P. Darbyshire, 'For the New Lord Chancellor—Some Causes for Concern About Magistrates' [1997] *Crim LR* 861, 869–72. We do know that at Crown Court the conviction rate is considerably higher for summary offences than for indictable offences (97 per cent versus 78 per cent), which lends some support to this argument, but as these figures include guilty pleas they are not quite on point. *Criminal Statistics England and Wales 2007* (2008), Table 2.14.

[17] See C. Hedderman and D. Moxon, *Magistrates' Court or Crown Court? Mode of Trial Decisions and Sentencing* (1992), 20, where 62 per cent of defendants and 70 per cent of solicitors are said to support the statement 'magistrates are on the side of the police'. See also Darbyshire, above n 16, 869.

[18] On the problems of achieving this in the magistrates' court, see M. Wasik, 'Magistrates' Knowledge of Previous Convictions' [1996] *Crim LR* 851; P. Darbyshire, 'Previous Misconduct and the Magistrates' Courts—Some Tales from the Real World' [1997] *Crim LR* 105.

range of life experiences.[19] In referring to these as good reasons for thinking that jury trial is fairer, it is suggested that these reasons are connected to the reason for having trials in the first place, which is, primarily, to make accurate decisions. There are of course other reasons why jury trial is thought to be fair, but there is likely to be more debate about the merits of such reasons. For example, juries are able to exercise 'jury equity' by reaching a verdict in defiance of the law. A case often used to illustrate this is the acquittal of Clive Ponting, who was charged with leaking information in breach of the Official Secrets Act for reasons which many would have regarded as reflecting the public interest. Although he had no defence in law, he was acquitted by the jury.[20] Jury equity is controversial, because it seems to undermine the rule of law.[21] However, one of the values associated with the rule of law in the view of writers such as Waldron and MacCormick,[22] is that legal decisions are contestable and open to argument; in this way, jury equity may be less threatening to legal values than is sometimes supposed. As a deliberate decision to disapply the law, jury equity is likely to be rare; however, jury decision making is probably characterized by discretion and moral judgement to a greater degree than judicial decision making,[23] and this is to some extent encouraged by the criminal law, which often uses open-textured standards such as reasonableness to define criminal liability. Jury trial is often praised for helping to ensure that the defendant is tried by his peers, but this probably adds little to the points just made.

It should be noted that jury trial has merits beyond those associated with the interests of defendants. The jury is, in various ways, a democratic institution. Jury trial gives citizens some input into the application of the criminal law.[24] The institution of the jury helps to ensure that the criminal law is expressed in terms comprehensible to ordinary people, and it also serves an educational and social function which, a recent survey suggests, should not be underestimated.[25] Bringing lay people into the courtroom means that the pursuit of criminal justice is not a closed shop, dominated by lawyers and other professionals. It makes trials genuinely public and helps to prevent the State abusing its power. However, not all of these merits are the exclusive preserve of the jury; the use of lay magistrates also helps to keep the law simple and serves a civic function. Whatever the merits of the arguments of principle about the jury, though, there is little doubt that it is an institution that holds much public confidence. Indeed,

---

[19] See M. Redmayne, 'Theorizing Jury Reform' in A. Duff et al, *The Trial on Trial: Volume 2. Judgment and Calling to Account* (2006).

[20] See G. Drewry, 'The *Ponting* Case—Leaking in the Public Interest' [1985] *PL* 203.

[21] For a variety of perspectives on jury equity, or 'nullification', see J. Kleinig and J. Levine (eds), *Jury Ethics: Juror Conduct and Jury Dynamics* (2006).

[22] See Waldron, above n 10; N. MacCormick, 'Rhetroic and the Rule of Law' in D. Dyzenhaus (ed), *Recrafting the Rule of Law* (1999).

[23] See N. Finkel, 'Jurors' Duries, Obligations and Rights: The Ethical/Moral Roots of Discretion' in Kleinig and Levine, above n 21.

[24] See *ibid.*

[25] See R. Matthews, L. Hancock and D. Briggs, *Jurors' Perceptions, Understanding, Confidence and Satisfaction in the Jury System: A Study in Six Courts* (2004), 64–6.

in surveys the 'right' to trial by jury is seen as more important than various other rights, such as the right not to be detained more than a week before charge.[26]

As well as these general points about the respective institutional merits of magistrates' and jury trial, there is research on magistrates' trials which does lend some support to the criticism that this is a cursory form of justice. Some time ago McBarnet commented on the 'ideology of triviality'[27] which she found prevailing in the magistrates' courts: the presumption that the cases dealt with there were not important and that full due process protections were not appropriate. McConville et al were also critical of the quality of justice in magistrates' courts, commenting that defendants in the lower courts, rather than benefiting from a presumption of innocence, typically face an uphill struggle in persuading the court that the prosecution case is not made out.[28] In Morgan and Russell's study, only 30 per cent of regular court users professed to having 'a great deal' or 'a lot' of confidence in lay magistrates, as compared to nearly 90 per cent with this level of confidence in professional magistrates.[29] At the same time, only 8 per cent said they had 'no' or 'very little' confidence in the lay magistracy.

The differences between the two types of trial make the allocation of cases between them an important issue. From the point of view of the Government, the question of case allocation is particularly critical because it has significant resource implications. A typical trial in the magistrates' courts costs around ten times less than a Crown Court trial.[30] Measures that will keep more cases at the lower level therefore have the potential to make considerable savings. The primary tool for case allocation is the classification of offences into three types: summary, either way and offences triable only on indictment. The first and last categories are straightforward. Summary offences, the least serious criminal offences, can only be tried in the magistrates' court. Offences triable only on indictment, a category comprising the most serious offences, can only be tried in the Crown Court. Things are more complicated with either way (also referred to as 'indictable') offences. This large category comprises some common offences such as theft and assault occasioning actual bodily harm. Here, a decision must be taken as to where the case will be tried. The decision is for the magistrates, and is taken at a mode of trial hearing. At the hearing, the magistrates decide whether or not to try the case themselves; the decision will be based primarily on how serious and complex the case is, but a Practice Direction details various other considerations which are relevant to the mode of trial decision.[31] Magistrates have limited sentencing powers (no more than six months' imprisonment or a £5,000 fine for a single offence), so the more serious either way offences are best dealt with in the Crown Court, where

---

[26] J. Roberts and M. Hough, *Public Opinion and the Jury: An International Literature Review* (2009).

[27] D. McBarnet, *Conviction: Law, the State and the Construction of Justice* (1983), 144.

[28] M. McConville et al, *Standing Accused: The Organization and Practices of Criminal Defence Lawyers in Britain* (1994), Ch 9.

[29] Above n 13, 60.

[30] Home Office, *Digest 4: Information on the Criminal Justice System in England and Wales* (1999), 69.

[31] See Consolidated Criminal Practice Direction, Pt V, available at: www.justice.gov.uk/criminal/procrules_fin/contents/practice_direction/pd_consolidated.htm.

they can be sentenced appropriately. As noted above, even disregarding sentencing powers, the more elaborate fact-finding procedures of Crown Court trial should be used in the most serious cases. If the magistrates decide to send the case to the Crown Court, the case will be dealt with there. If, however, the decision is to retain the case in the summary jurisdiction, that is not an end to the matter. The defendant may override this decision by choosing to be tried in the Crown Court. A complicating factor is that if the magistrates try the case themselves and find the defendant guilty, they may commit the case to the Crown Court for sentencing if, on reflection, they conclude that their sentencing powers are not sufficient. In practice, the vast majority (about 90 per cent) of either way offences sent to the Crown Court are sent because magistrates decline jurisdiction.[32] The prosecution's arguments on appropriate venue are usually the dominant factor in mode of trial hearings.[33]

Over the years, a number of steps have been taken to ensure that as many cases as possible are tried summarily. Some either way offences have been reclassified as summary, for example, common assault, driving whilst disqualified and criminal damage up to a value of £5,000. The Practice Direction on mode of trial decision making is now drafted so as to create a presumption in favour of summary trial, unless the court considers that the case contains an aggravating feature (various such features are listed in the guidelines), and that its sentencing powers are insufficient.[34] Moreover, in 1997 the 'plea before venue' arrangement was introduced.[35] This allows defendants to indicate whether or not they intend to plead guilty before the magistrates make the mode of trial decision. The idea here is that, if the defendant indicates that he intends to plead guilty, the magistrates will be more prepared to deal with the case themselves. Only if they consider that their sentencing powers are inadequate, after factoring in the sentence discount for a guilty plea at this early stage, will they commit the case for sentence in the Crown Court.[36] The immediate result of this reform was a decline of some 15,000 cases a year committed to the Crown Court for trial, off-set in part by a rise of some 10,000 cases a year committed to the Crown Court for sentence.[37] Since then, the number of offences committed for sentence has dropped, although there has been some increase during the last few years.[38] But there is an increasing trend for magistrates to decline jurisdiction and commit for trial, which has drawn the concern of the Justice Secretary.[39]

In addition to these policies, there has been one proposal about mode of trial decision making that has proved very controversial. In 1993 the Royal Commission on Criminal Justice suggested that defendants should no longer have the right to elect Crown Court trial in either way cases; this reform would mean that, in the absence

---

[32] CPS, above n 15, Annex B.

[33] See S. Cammiss, 'Deciding Upon Mode of Trial' (2007) 46 *Howard J CJ* 372.

[34] Above n 31.   [35] See Ch 10.   [36] See *R v Warley Justices, ex p DPP* [1998] 2 Cr App R 307.

[37] *Criminal Statistics, England and Wales 2002*, Figure 3.2.

[38] *Criminal Statistics England and Wales 2007* (2008), Table 2.13.

[39] *Ibid.*, Table 2.13; Jack Straw, Speech to Magistrates' Association AGM, 14 November 2009 (at www.justice.gov.uk/news/speeches-nov09.htm).

of agreement between defence and prosecution, the magistrates' decision would be determinative.[40] In support of this proposal, it was argued that many defendants who elect Crown Court trial go on to plead guilty. They thus do not benefit from the arguably fairer trial procedures in the Crown Court, but are likely to be sentenced more harshly than they would have been in the magistrates' court. In this way, abolition of the right to elect could be said to be in the interests of defendants. This argument, however, has been disputed: there are no precise figures on the proportion of those electing Crown Court trial who go on to plead guilty. Even if many do, this may be the result of a charge bargain[41] offered by the prosecution which would not have been offered had the case remained in the magistrates' jurisdiction. Another argument used to support the reform was that it simply is not appropriate for defendants to choose trial venue; this allocative decision should be based on case characteristics which are suitably assessed by the magistrates.

The Royal Commission's proposal was immediately controversial, and the then Conservative Government did not attempt to introduce this particular reform; plea before venue was introduced instead as a means of reducing the number of indictable offences committed for Crown Court trial. It was eventually a Labour administration that attempted to remove the right to elect jury trial in either way cases. The proposal attracted considerable opposition.[42] Some of this was based on broad propositions about a right to jury trial. But there were also concerns about whether the mode of trial decision could be taken fairly by magistrates. The proposed legislation would have allowed defendants to argue their preference for jury trial before the magistrates. In making their decision, magistrates were to take into account the possible effect of a conviction on a defendant's livelihood and reputation. This might have involved considering whether the defendant had previous convictions, and therefore whether he had a reputation to protect which might have made a stronger case for jury trial. While it is something of a caricature, the thinking here seems to be that jury trial is especially valuable for middle class defendants charged for the first time with an offence such as theft. Unsurprisingly, such arguments are potentially socially divisive. In the event, such was the controversy that the original Mode of Trial Bill failed to win Parliamentary support. It was withdrawn, to be replaced by a Criminal Justice (Mode of Trial) (No 2) Bill, which did not allow magistrates to take the defendant's reputation into account. This drew criticism from some of the supporters of the original bill[43] and, for various reasons, the second bill did not succeed either.[44]

It seems most unlikely that a government will attempt to remove the right to elect again in the foreseeable future. Misleading though they may be, headlines about the

---

[40] Royal Commission on Criminal Justice, *Report* (1993), 87.   [41] See Ch 10.

[42] A good account of the mode of trial saga is Windlesham, *Responses to Crime Volume 4: Dispensing Justice* (2001), Ch 7.

[43] Most notably Michael Zander, who had been a member of the Royal Commission on Criminal Justice: see M. Zander, 'Why Jack Straw's Jury Reform Has Lost the Plot' (2000) 150 *NLJ* 723.

[44] See Windlesham, above n 42.

abolition of the right to jury trial do too much political damage. In the wake of the failure of the mode of trial bills, the Labour Government put provisions in the Criminal Justice Act (CJA) 2003 which would have provided a different way of keeping more cases in the magistrates' court. The Act doubled magistrates' custodial sentencing powers from a maximum of six months for any one offence to a maximum of 12 months.[45] At the same time, magistrates' power to commit defendants to the Crown Court for sentencing in cases where they have accepted jurisdiction was removed.[46] Connected to this, defendants in cases where the magistrates have accepted jurisdiction would be able to ask the magistrates for an indication of whether a custodial sentence would be passed if they pleaded guilty at that stage.[47] A defendant who received an indication that the sentence would be non-custodial, would have considerable incentive to plead guilty at that stage, for then the magistrates would be bound by their indication. The Criminal Justice Act also provided that magistrates should be informed of a defendant's previous convictions when determining mode of trial.[48] However, these reforms have not been implemented. The increase in sentencing power was bound up with 'Custody plus', an initiative aimed partly at reducing the number of short sentences handed down by the courts. But it now seems that Custody plus will not be brought in, and so it is likely that the reforms just described will not come into effect either.[49]

Previous editions of this book have examined the debate about mode of trial and the right to elect Crown Court trial in some detail.[50] Now that the issue has moved out of the political spotlight, there is less need to examine the issues in depth. Briefly, however, there remains a reasonable argument for removing the right to elect jury trial in either way cases. Relatively few jurisdictions allow defendants a comparable choice,[51] and there is nothing like a right to choose trial venue in the European Convention on Human Rights. The argument that the decision is one for the courts, to be taken primarily on grounds of case seriousness, is a strong one. While there is something to the argument that certain types of case are especially suited to jury trial, regardless of their seriousness (an example is theft, which can involve the broad evaluative issue of dishonesty, defined in the case law in terms of the standards of ordinary and reasonable people[52]), there is a danger that in practice this argument will become the one that certain people (such as those without previous convictions) have a greater claim to jury trial than others, a contention that should be resisted. To say this is not to say that there is a strong case for removing the right to elect.

---

[45] CJA 2003, s 154.   [46] CJA 2003, Sch 3 para 22 et seq.   [47] CJA 2003, Sch 3, para 6.

[48] CJA 2003, Sch 3, para 5, inserting a new s 19 into the Magistrates' Courts Act 1980.

[49] See S. Cammiss and C. Stride, 'Modelling Mode of Trial' (2008) 48 *Brit J Criminol* 482, 493 n 15; see also comments by Jack Straw, to the effect that short prison sentences should not be abandoned: 'Issues in Criminal Justice Lecture', University of Birmingham, 29 October 2009 (at www.justice.gov.uk/news/speeches-oct09.htm).

[50] See Ch 8 of the second edition.

[51] An exception is New Zealand: N. Cameron, S. Potter and W. Young, 'The New Zealand Jury' (1999) 62 *Law & Contemporary Problems* 103.

[52] *Ghosh* [1982] QB 1053.

Pressure for reform has been driven by the desire for efficiency, and there are reasons to regard efficiency-based arguments with caution. To the extent that jury trial is valuable—and above we have very briefly sketched some reasons for thinking that it is—any proposal to reduce the number of jury trials should be viewed sceptically. It should be noted, however, that jurors themselves consider that many of the cases they hear are too trivial to justify the disruption to their lives involved in hearing them.[53] That view counts for something and suggests the need to reflect carefully on where and how we draw the line between summary and Crown Court jurisdictions, free of the rhetorical bombast about the right to jury trial that has dominated much of the debate.[54]

(B) TRIAL BY JUDGE AND JURY AND TRIAL BY JUDGE ALONE

Crown Court trial has traditionally been trial by judge and jury. But there have recently been various attempts to allow certain cases in the Crown Court to be tried by a judge sitting alone. The Criminal Justice Act 2003 allows for trial without jury in cases where there is evidence of jury-tampering.[55] The Act also contains provisions on trial by judge alone in cases of serious fraud,[56] but these cannot be implemented without further legislation.[57] A Fraud (Trials Without a Jury) Bill was introduced in 2007, but the bill failed and there have been no further moves to legislate on this issue.[58] The original version of the Criminal Justice Bill also included provisions on jury waiver, allowing defendants to opt for trial by judge alone rather than jury trial,[59] but this clause of the Bill was controversial and was dropped during the legislative process.

In the previous section we reviewed some of the arguments in favour of jury trial, and drew comparisons between jury trial and magistrates' trial. A slightly different question is now relevant: what are the key differences between trial by judge and trial by jury? While we saw that magistrates have a higher conviction rate than jurors, it is not clear that in the Crown Court judges would convict more defendants than juries would. As the prospect of trial by judge alone is so recent,[60] there are no comparative statistics available for England and Wales. In Northern Ireland, a system of Diplock courts where trial is by judge alone has existed since 1973. Here, jury acquittal rates have generally been slightly higher than that of Diplock judges.[61] However, jury

[53] See Matthews et al, above n 25, 63.

[54] See, e.g., B. Houlder, 'The Importance of Preserving the Jury System and the Right of Election for Trial' [1997] *Crim LR* 875.

[55] CJA 2003, ss 44–6.   [56] CJA 2003, s 43.   [57] CJA 2003, s 330(5)(b).

[58] For the background to the Bill, see M. Peck, *The Fraud (Trials Without a Jury) Bill 2006–07*, House of Commons Research Paper 06/57.

[59] Clause 36 of the original Bill, available at: www.publications.parliament.uk/pa/cm200203/cmbills/008/2003008.htm.

[60] So far, only one trial has been cleared to proceed without a jury: see *R v Twomey* [2009] 2 Cr App R 25. The trial began in January 2010.

[61] See J. Jackson and S. Doran, *Judge Without Jury* (1995), 35.

acquittal rates in Northern Ireland may be higher than elsewhere,[62] and the Diplock acquittal rates are close, on average, to those of juries in England and Wales. In the United States judicial acquittal rates are generally higher than those of juries. In the Federal jurisdiction, for example, the difference is marked: between 1989 and 2002 the average jury conviction rate was 84 per cent, compared to 55 per cent in judge trials.[63] Some of this may be explained by the different characteristics of the cases dealt with in each mode of trial, but the difference is certainly very marked and does suggest that juries and judges approach cases differently.[64] Puzzlingly, though, a different research method points in the other direction. When judges are asked how they would have decided jury cases which they have presided over, they tend to report that they would have convicted in more cases than the actual juries did. In a recent study from the US, judges report that they would convict in about 7 per cent more cases than juries did.[65] After examining various case characteristics that might explain the difference, the researchers concluded that juries were more likely to acquit than judges in cases with significant defence evidence, where the defendant had no prior record and claimed to have rejected a plea bargain on grounds of being innocent. As the authors note, these variables are consistent with an explanation that jurors look more closely for evidence of innocence than do judges. At a more qualitative level, Jackson and Doran's study of Diplock courts found that the trials in them had a different atmosphere to jury trials; in jury trials more emotive arguments might be used. These authors also noted the difficulty of involving the judge both in managing the trial and in bearing responsibility for the verdict, in that this might at least appear to compromise judicial independence.[66]

As noted above, of the three exceptions to jury trial originally included in the Criminal Justice Bill, the only one to have become law is the exception for cases where there is a risk of interference with the jury. In *R v Twomey* the Court of Appeal considered the operation of this provision.[67] Twomey's trial was underway when the judge received information that members of the jury had been approached with a view to putting pressure on them. The judge discharged the jury, but refused to continue the trial sitting by himself (an option under s 46 of the Criminal Justice Act 2003) because he had seen inadmissible and prejudicial material. He also refused to rule that a new trial should take place without a jury on the grounds that it would be possible to put in place measures to protect the jury. The Court of Appeal disagreed with both decisions. In a judgment which put considerable emphasis on resource issues, it held that

---

[62] See J. Jackson, K. Quinn and T. O'Malley, 'The Jury System in Contemporary Ireland' (1999) 62 *Law & Contemporary Probs* 202, 227.

[63] A. Leipold, 'Why are Federal Judges so Acquittal Prone?' (2005) 83 *Washington ULQ* 151.

[64] See *ibid*.

[65] D. Givelber and A. Farrell, 'Judges and Juries: The Defense Case and Differences in Acquittal Rates' (2008) 33 *Law & Social Inquiry* 31.

[66] Above n 61. See further J. Jackson, S. Doran and M Seigel, 'Rethinking Adversariness n Non-Jury Criminal Trials' (1995) 23 *Am J Crim L* 1.

[67] *R v Twomey* [2009] 2 Cr App R 25.

a judge in the position of the judge in *Twomey* should ordinarily continue the trial sitting alone.[68] It found that the proposed protective measures could not effectively guard against threats to the jurors' families, and that even if they could: 'it would be unreasonable to impose that package with its drain on financial resources and police manpower on the police, and, no less important, it would be totally unfair to impose the additional burdens consequent on the deployment of this package on individual jurors.'[69] It also noted that protective measures might prejudice the jury against the defendant.

While we have suggested that jury trial incorporates certain important values, jury trial should not be insisted on at any cost. There is a good case to be made for allowing non jury trial in cases where jurors would otherwise be put at risk; jurors have rights as well as defendants (e.g. under Articles 5 and 8 ECHR). Given that much of the evidence in *Twomey* was secret, it is impossible to judge whether the case for non jury trial was made out on the facts. What is problematic, though, is the Court of Appeal's insistence that in this situation a part heard trial should normally be continued by the presiding judge. If jurors are likely to be prejudiced by being subject to protective measures, then surely there is a substantial risk that the judge, who in the course of the hearing to discharge the jury will have heard detailed evidence about attempts to intimidate jurors, will also be prejudiced.[70] If, as was the case in *Twomey*, the evidence of intimidation is partly withheld from the defence, the situation is in tension with the decision in *Edwards and Lewis v United Kingdom*, where lack of adversarial argument on matters of 'determinative importance'[71] was found to be problematic: in the *Twomey* scenario, the judge will be privy to unchallenged information that may colour the determinative decision whether to convict. If there is concern about the wasted resources involved in stopping the trial part way through, one solution would be to have the application to discharge the jury heard by a judge other than the one conducting the trial.

When it comes to serious fraud cases, arguments for departing from the norm of jury trial have been more controversial, and it now seems that we will not see juryless fraud trials in the near future. The principal argument for reform in this area is that certain trials involve issues so complex that they are not well suited to lay fact-finding. Connected to this is the argument that fraud trials could be made to run more speedily were there no need to explain complex issues to the jury and that long trials place undue demands on jurors; jurors in the Jubilee Line case sat for nearly two years, and while they report having been pleased to be involved in the trial, the lengthy proceedings placed a heavy cost on their lives, especially in terms of employment.[72] The argument that juries cannot understand fraud cases has very little empirical support.[73]

---

[68] *Ibid.*, [20].   [69] *Ibid.*, [33].

[70] See A. Wistrich, C Guthrie and J. Rachlinski, 'Can Judges Ignore Inadmissible Information? The Difficulty of Deliberately Disregarding' (2005) 153 *U Pennsylvania L Rev* 1251.

[71] (2005) 40 EHRR 24, [57].

[72] See S. Lloyd-Bostock, *Report on Interviews with Jurors in the Jubilee Line Case* (2006).

[73] See, e.g., T. Honess, M. Levi and E. Chapman, 'Juror Competence in Processing Complex Information: Implications from a Simulation of the Maxwell Trial' [1998] *Crim LR* 763; R. Lempert, 'Civil Juries and

It seems that in practice a jury of 12 will include individuals who are perfectly capable of understanding the issues involved and of explaining them, where need be, to other jurors.[74] Further, the complexity of a trial is not fixed: measures can be taken to educate jurors about business practices and to explain things to them simply and clearly, and cases might be split into separate trials of distinct issues. With a new protocol on the management of fraud trials in place, judges are reasonably confident that fraud trials can be made to run more efficiently.[75] If this means that fraud trials can be made to exact less of a cost on jurors, then the case for juryless fraud trials is not made out.

The Criminal Justice Act 2003 originally contained a provision on 'jury waiver'. This would have allowed defendants in the Crown Court to opt for trial by judge alone. The choice of juryless trial could only have been refused in exceptional cases. This provision was removed from the Act at a late stage in the legislative process.[76] Letting defendants waive jury trial is, at first sight, an appealing idea.[77] But it is in fact potentially very radical. It would have allowed defendants effectively to bring the institution of trial by jury to an end: all it would take would be for every defendant to decline jury trial. Of course, it is extremely unlikely that this would happen: jury trial is often thought to be in the interests of defendants, and it is probable that sufficient numbers of defendants share this view that trial by judge alone would have remained exceptional.[78] All the same, the theoretical possibility of *de facto* jury abolition should prompt us to look carefully at the jury waiver proposal.

The superficially appealing logic behind jury waiver is that, to the extent that jury trial is justified as being in the interests of defendants, there can be no objection to allowing defendants to forego it in favour of some other appropriate trial arrangement. There is no denying that defendants have legitimate interests in the means by which they are tried: interests in impartial and accurate fact-finding arrangements which adequately weight the presumption of innocence. But these things are also in the interests of the courts and of society as a whole. It is more difficult to find legitimate interests defendants might have in a particular form of trial which are not shared in this manner. Perhaps there are some cases where defendants have a legitimate concern about jury trial: if, for example, the case is one likely to arouse strong emotions,[79] or if the defence case will raise complex issues which the jury may have difficulty

Complex Cases: Taking Stock After Twelve Years' in R. Litan (ed), *Verdict: Assessing the Civil Jury System* (1993); N. Vidmar, 'The Performance of the American Civil Jury: An Empirical Perspective' (1998) 40 *Arizona L Rev* 849.

74 This seems to have been the situation in the Jubilee Line case: see Lloyd-Bostock, above n 72.

75 R. Julian, 'Judicial Perspectives in Serious Fraud Cases' [2008] *Crim LR* 764.

76 See 'Blunkett Furious as Lords Throw out Reform of Jury Trial' *The Guardian* 20 November 2003.

77 See S. Doran and J. Jackson, 'The Case for Jury Waiver' [1997] *Crim LR* 155.

78 An opinion poll in England found that a quarter of respondents would opt for trial by judge rather than by jury: Roberts and Hough, above n 26, 32. See also M. Zander and P. Henderson, *Crown Court Study* (1993), 172: 30 per cent of defendants said they would not choose jury trial.

79 See N. Vidmar, 'Generic Prejudice and the Presumption of Guilt in Sex Abuse Trials' (1997) 21 *Law & Human Behavior* 5.

understanding[80] (though, as noted above, we should be wary of accepting that certain issues are too complex for jury trial), it may be appropriate to allow trial by judge alone. But a problem with the provision in the Criminal Justice Act was that, with very limited exceptions, it simply left the decision to the defendant, with no acknowledgement that decisions about mode of trial affect the community's interests in the trial system as well.[81] In some jurisdictions which allow waiver of jury trial, the prosecution is allowed to make representations on the issue,[82] and this seems appropriate.

(C) RACE AND MODE OF TRIAL

So far we have not considered the implications of the defendant's race in the debates about mode of trial. Race is a complicating factor for many of the issues discussed so far. Defendants from minority ethnic groups may feel that a tribunal with members from their, or another, racial minority will afford them a fairer trial. To what extent should mode of trial decisions take this into account?

Something should first of all be said about how representative, in terms of race, the various forms of tribunal are. The magistracy as a whole seems to be racially representative of the country's population. That is, the percentage of black and Asian magistrates (to concentrate on the two largest groups) is more or less the same as that of the national population. However, this picture breaks down when one looks at particular areas. As a rule, in urban areas where there is a large minority ethnic population, the local benches are unrepresentative.[83] A study by Hood, Shute and Seemungal found that 35 per cent of benches in the three urban areas they studied had at least one minority ethnic magistrate, thus the majority had none.[84] Where professional magistrates (District Judges) are concerned, 5 per cent were found to be from a minority ethnic group.[85] In the Crown Court, many fewer judges are from minorities: 1 per cent in the Hood et al study.[86] Just as with magistrates, the fact that the jury is a multi-member body makes it far more likely to contain minority ethnic members. A very detailed study by Thomas, confirming earlier research,[87] found that jury pools were a good representation of the ethnic make up of the communities from which they were drawn.[88] However, because juries are in principle selected randomly, there is no guarantee that a black or Asian defendant will be tried by a jury including a juror from a minority ethnic group. The Crown Court Study found that nationally 65 per cent of juries were all white. While Thomas found

---

[80] An example might be *R v Adams* [1996] 2 Cr App R 467.   [81] See n 59 above.

[82] See Jackson and Doran, above n 61.

[83] Morgan and Russell, above n 13, 14–15. On race and the magistracy, see also G. Davies and J. Vennard, 'The Experience of Ethnic Minority Magistrates' (2006) 45 *Howard JCJ* 485.

[84] R. Hood, S. Shute and F. Seemungal, *Ethnic Minorities in the Criminal Courts: Perceptions of Fairness and Equality of Treatment* (2003), 23.

[85] *Ibid.*   [86] *Ibid.*

[87] M. Zander and P. Henderson, *Crown Court Study* (1993), 241; Matthews et al, above n 25, 19–20.

[88] C. Thomas, *Diversity and Fairness in the Jury System* (2007).

that during her study period juries at Blackfriars Crown Court were always ethnically mixed, reflecting the diversity of the local population, this was not the case
in courts in less ethnically mixed areas. About half of juries in Reading and one
Manchester site had minority ethnic representation.[89] In other areas, which Thomas
terms 'Low Ethnicity', the chance of minority ethnic representation was lower still.
This, Thomas suggests, is potentially problematic in areas where the local population contains pockets of 'High Ethnicity':

'For instance, Nottingham Crown Court's juror catchment area has such a low BME [Black
and minority ethnic] population level (6.5%) that summoning is unlikely to produce any
substantial numbers of BME jurors, but the existence of high concentrations of ethnic
minorities in parts of the catchment area means that juror ethnicity is still very likely to be
a relevant issue in relation to both defendants and victims…[and] is likely to generate an
expectation among court users and the public that ethnic minorities will be serving on juries in these courts.'[90]

This situation has led to a proposal, made by both the Royal Commission on Criminal
Justice and by the Auld Review, that defendants in cases involving a minority ethnic
dimension should be able to request minority ethnic representation on the jury.[91] This
proposal has never found favour with policy-makers. In some cases, judges have tried
to manipulate jury selection to increase the chances of minority representation, but
the Court of Appeal has held that this should not occur.[92] The case for reform is not
very strong. There is some evidence that more minority ethnic representation would
increase confidence in the courts: Hood et al found that some minority ethnic defendants complained of jury bias (20 per cent of the black defendants tried by jury, though
14 per cent of white defendants were also 'unhappy with jury'), but only 4 per cent
of Crown Court defendants identified an increase in the number of minority ethnic
jurors as something to be done to increase confidence (the call for more minority ethnic judges was far more common).[93] Opinion polls have found that blacks and Asians
have concerns about the racial make up of the jury, but it is not clear what to read into
this finding (as we have seen, minority ethnic groups are not under-represented).[94]
At a more abstract level, it is sometimes argued that a defendant should be tried by
his peers,[95] but one has to ask just what is meant by peers in this context, and why
it is thought that only our peers are well placed to judge us. More practically, it is
not clear how the relevant cases would be chosen, nor how appropriate jurors would
be selected. The manipulation of jury selection might undermine the confidence of

---

[89] *Ibid.*, 148.   [90] *Ibid.*, 68.

[91] Royal Commission on Criminal Justice, above n 40, 133; Auld LJ, *Review of the Criminal Courts of
England and Wales: Report* (2001), 156–9. See also B. Bowling and C. Phillips, *Racism, Crime and Justice*
(2002), 187–8.

[92] *R v Ford* [1989] 3 All ER 445; *R v Smith* [2003] 1 WLR 2229.

[93] Above n 84, 34, 39, 116. Cf Bowling and Phillips, above n 91.

[94] Roberts and Hough, above n 26, 27.

[95] H. Fukurai and R. Krooth, *Race in the Jury Box: Affirmative Action in Jury Selection* (2003), 138–48.

society as a whole in the system.[96] It might also change the dynamics of jury delibera-
tion: jurors who know that they have been chosen specifically because a case involves a
racial dimension might come to see their role differently—as representing a particular
point of view, rather than the views of society as a whole.[97]

There is some empirical evidence on race and jury decision making. Thomas conducted research using jurors from Blackfriars Crown Court. She found evidence that
individual jurors decided a staged case differently depending on their ethnicity—an
effect she termed 'same race leniency' (though it might equally be termed 'other race
harshness'). Specifically, 'BME [black and minority ethnic] defendants were less likely
to be found guilty than White defendants, while the White defendant was much more
likely to be found guilty by BME jurors than White jurors.'[98] But any such bias could
not be detected in decisions of the jury as a whole (as the jury literature sometimes
puts it, in a group of 12, bias 'washes out'). Further, and in line with earlier research
from the US,[99] Thomas found that where a racial issue was made salient in the case
presented to the jury, differential treatment could not be detected in individual juror
votes.[100] However, Thomas's research involved ethnically mixed juries drawn from the
diverse area surrounding Blackfriars Crown Court. What we do not know, and what
might make a case for some departure from random selection, is whether the all white
juries which Thomas found to be predominant in areas such as Nottingham might
exhibit a different pattern of decision making to those at Blackfriars.

Racial issues are not only relevant to jury composition. The magistrates' and Crown
Court benches should as far as possible reflect the social characteristics of society as
a whole, if only because everyone should have an equal opportunity of sitting on the
bench. However, when we come to look at the choice between magistrates' and Crown
Court, and between trial by jury and trial by judge alone, race raises more complex
issues. In some cases, minority ethnic defendants may have concerns about possible
jury bias. There are reported cases where jurors are said to have made racially discriminatory remarks, and, because of the basic rule that jury deliberations should remain
secret, the courts have found it difficult to deal with this situation.[101] If a defendant
fears that the jury which tries him may be biased, then this is just the sort of situation
where there is a case for jury waiver: the defendant may well prefer trial by a judge,
where the verdict will be supported by reasons.

---

[96] N. King, 'The Effects of Race-Conscious Jury Selection on Public Confidence in the Fairness of Jury
Proceedings: An Empirical Puzzle' [1994] *Am Crim LR* 1177; L. Ellis and S. Diamond, 'Race, Diversity, and
Jury Composition: Battering and Bolstering Legitimacy' (2003) 78 *Chicago-Kent L Rev* 1033.

[97] See J. Abramson, *We the Jury: The Jury System and the Ideal of Democracy* (1994), Ch 3.

[98] Above n 88, 164.

[99] S. Sommers and P. Ellsworth, 'How Much Do We Really Know About Race and Juries? A Review of
Social Science Theory and Research' (2003) 78 *Chicago-Kent L Rev* 997.

[100] Above n 88, 166–7.

[101] *R v Quereshi* [2002] 1 WLR 518; *R v Connor, R v Mirza* [2004] UKHL 2. See generally R. Pattenden and
G. Daly, 'Racial Bias and the English Criminal Trial Jury' [2005] 64 *CLJ* 678.

When it comes to the choice between magistrates' court and Crown Court, concerns about racial discrimination provide some support for the right to elect Crown Court trial. There is evidence that black defendants are more likely to elect Crown Court trial than are whites.[102] This should make us cautious about removing the right to elect jury trial, because it may indirectly discriminate against black defendants. At its strongest, the argument is this: there is evidence that black suspects are charged by the police at lower standards of evidence than are white suspects.[103] As they enter the system, then, the cases against blacks tend to be weaker, and to be charged at a higher level than is merited (see Chapters 7 and 10). Black defendants may, therefore, choose Crown Court trial for the better chance of acquittal offered there, and also because the CPS are more likely to reduce charges in order to secure a guilty plea once the case has gone to Crown Court. Removing the right to elect would thus deny black defendants a means of protecting themselves against discriminatory police charging practices. There is empirical research to support this view of the merits of the right to elect,[104] but there is also evidence which cautions against over-simplifying the situation. As we saw above, Hood et al found that some black defendants were worried about jury bias; they also found that, overall, slightly more black defendants complained about unfair treatment in the Crown Court than in the magistrates' court.[105]

The possibility of indirect discrimination is a reason against removing the right to elect jury trial, at least until more is known about why minority ethnic defendants might favour this mode of trial. It also points to the importance of ensuring that proceedings in the magistrates' courts are as fair as possible. In the Hood et al study, around a third of minority ethnic defendants, when asked what could be done to improve things, pointed to the need for more minority ethnic District Judges and magistrates; magistrates themselves took the same view.[106] The authors suggest organizing magistrates' rotas so that, 'in those areas where a substantial proportion of defendants are from minority ethnic backgrounds, at least one magistrate from such a background will be sitting on the Bench'.[107] Random selection has never been the principle in the magistrates' court, therefore this proposal deserves serious consideration.

(D) PROFESSIONAL AND LAY MAGISTRATES

A final issue about the way in which cases are allocated between different decision makers concerns the balance between lay and professional magistrates ('District Judges'). There are around 100 full time District Judges in England and Wales, with around half

---

[102] See M. Fitzgerald, *Ethnic Minorities and the Criminal Justice System* (1993), 21, 45. Cammiss and Stride, above n 49, found some evidence that minority ethnic defendants were more likely to be sent to the Crown Court by the magistrates.

[103] See C. Phillips and D. Brown, *Entry into the Criminal Justice System: A Survey of Police Arrests and Their Outcomes* (1998), 183–6.

[104] See L. Bridges, 'Taking Liberties' *Legal Action* 6 July 2000, 6.

[105] Above n 84, 31–5. The position was reversed for Asian defendants.   [106] *Ibid.*, 117, 131.

[107] *Ibid.*, 135.

of these sitting in London. Indeed, in London the majority of court appearances may be heard by District Judges.[108] There are significant differences between professional and lay magistrates: District Judges command more confidence from court users, they work more quickly, are less likely to grant adjournments, and sentence more harshly.[109] They are also less representative of the general population in terms of race and gender. In economic terms, there is probably not an awful lot to choose between lay and professional magistrates. Whereas District Judges are salaried, the fact that they work more quickly and rarely require advice from a clerk probably means that each mode of trial is equally efficient. At least, that is the case in terms of court work; to the extent that District Judges use custody more frequently than lay magistrates, they perhaps will impose greater costs on the criminal justice system.[110]

Despite the differences between the two types of magistrate, there is little formal policy on how cases should be allocated between them. In practice, District Judges tend to deal with the more complex and serious cases, and there is some potential here for resentment from their lay colleagues, who are apt to feel that they are missing out on the most interesting cases.[111] But there is no hard and fast rule and, especially in London, District Judges deal with considerable numbers of routine cases. Morgan and Russell comment:

'What is unique about England and Wales is the way in which, within any one courthouse, the choice between adjudicators may be random.... We know of no jurisdictions other than England and Wales where moderately serious cases are allocated randomly within the same court tier between lay and professional judges.'[112]

An official policy of reserving the most serious cases for District Judges would probably face considerable opposition from lay magistrates. But the current *laissez-faire* policy is questionable in terms of principle. It also raises a more difficult question: should moderately serious cases, in which defendants can lose their liberty, be dealt with by single decision makers? Morgan and Russell's impression was that, while many other jurisdictions use the single judge model, it tends to be confined to less serious cases than in England and Wales.[113] There is evidence that the public have more confidence in group decision making than in decision making by a single individual.[114] An alternative model would be for the more serious cases in the magistrates' courts to be heard by a panel of two lay magistrates sitting with a District Judge.[115] Such a system would involve the identification of a threshold of seriousness, or perhaps a sentencing limit, for the allocation of cases between the two types of magistrates' trial. A more radical proposal is for

---

[108] Morgan and Russell, above n 13, 26.   [109] *Ibid.*, 48–54.   [110] *Ibid.*, viii.

[111] *Ibid.*, 26–9.

[112] *Ibid.*, 100. See also P. Seago, C. Walker and D. Wall, *The Role and Appointment of Stipendiary Magistrates* (1995), 143–5.

[113] *Ibid.*, 103.

[114] *Ibid.*, 78–9; A. Sanders, *Community Justice: Modernising the Magistracy in England and Wales* (2001), 24–5.

[115] R. Morgan, 'Magistrates: The Future According to Auld' (2002) 29 *JLS* 308.

all trials in the magistrates' courts to be heard by such panels.[116] Whatever is thought of the merits of these various proposals,[117] the principal point is that we should be prepared to think imaginatively about modes of trial. The choice is not just between decision making by a single professional adjudicator and decision making by a lay panel; the option of adopting small mixed panels should not be dismissed.

11.2 CROWN COURT TRIAL: JUDGE AND JURY

Crown Court trial involves a division of responsibility between judge and jury. Generally speaking, questions of law are for the judge and questions of fact are for the jury. But this division is not rigid. The judge will often make factual evaluations when deciding whether or not evidence is admissible.[118] Judges also play a role in guarding against false conviction by ensuring that a weak case does not go to the jury. We came across this in Chapter 7 where, in discussing the role of the CPS, it was noted that around a third of acquittals are on the basis of an order or direction from the judge to the jury, rather than because the jury has acquitted of its own accord. Judges also have some influence in cases that do go to the jury. At the end of the trial the judge sums up on the facts, and can emphasize aspects of the evidence which he or she deems to be important. Convictions are occasionally quashed because a judge has gone too far and given a one-sided summing up.[119] Many cases nowadays will involve the judge giving some direction to the jury on fact-finding: perhaps a warning about suspect evidence, or a direction on how to draw an inference from a particular factual scenario. The growing volume of standard directions published by the Judicial Studies Board attests to the importance of the judge's role in guiding the jury.[120] There are some hints that the European Court of Human Rights regards such directions as an important component of the right to a fair trial: given that the jury does not give reasons for its decision, carefully stated judicial warnings are the best guarantee that the jury has taken important factors into account.[121]

---

[116] See Sanders, above n 114; A. Sanders, 'Core Values, the Magistracy and the Auld Report' (2002) 29 *JLS* 324.

[117] Germany uses mixed panels, and the view there appears to be that the professional judges dominate proceedings. See S. Machura, 'Interaction Between Lay Assessors and Professional Judges in German Mixed Courts' (2002) 72 *International Rev Penal Law* 451; C. Renning, 'Influence of Lay Assessors and Giving Reasons for the Judgement in German Mixed Courts' (2002) 72 *International Rev Penal Law* 481. However, in England and Wales, where there is a tradition of independent decision making by magistrates, things might work out differently.

[118] See, generally, R. Pattenden, 'Pre-Verdict Judicial Fact-Finding in Judicial Trials with Juries' (2009) 29 *OJLS* 1; R. Pattenden, 'The Proof Rules of Pre-Verdict Judicial Fact-Finding in Criminal Trials by Jury' (2009) 125 *LQR* 79.

[119] *R v Wood* [1996] 1 Cr App R 207; *R v Bryant* [2005] EWCA Crim 2079.

[120] See www.jsboard.co.uk/criminal_law/index.htm.

[121] See *Condron v United Kingdom* (2001) 31 EHRR 1.

The principles underlying the division of roles between judge and jury are well illustrated by the debates surrounding the test the judge should apply in deciding whether there is a case to go to the jury. The leading case is *Galbraith*, which clarified conflicts in the case law. Under *Galbraith*, the judge should direct a verdict of acquittal if evidence to prove any element of the prosecution case is lacking. That much is relatively simple; things are more difficult 'where there is some evidence but it is of a tenuous character'. Here, the court identified two principles:

'(a) Where the judge comes to the conclusion that the prosecution case, taken at its highest, is such that a jury properly directed could not properly convict upon it, it is his duty, upon a submission being made, to stop the case. (b) Where however the prosecution evidence is such that its strength or weakness depends on the view to be taken of a witness's reliability, or other matters which are generally speaking within the province of the jury and where on one possible view of the facts there is evidence upon which a jury could properly come to the conclusion that the defendant is guilty, then the judge should allow the matter to be tried by the jury.'[122]

A crucial issue is what is meant by the prosecution case 'taken at its highest'. The rest of the quotation implies that the judge should assume that the witness is 'reliable', and apply the test on that basis. Of course, the defendant may suggest that the witness is lying or mistaken, but that is a matter for the jury. The usual criticism of this approach is that it affords insufficient protection to defendants. The judge may have serious misgivings about the reliability of a key witness, but unless the witness's evidence is self-contradictory,[123] the case should still be left to the jury. It is often pointed out that it seems odd that the trial judge should apply this test, while the Court of Appeal when reviewing the safety of a conviction applies a much broader test of whether the conviction is 'unsafe'. While the Court of Appeal shows great deference to the jury when applying this test, the 'unsafe' test does allow it to quash a conviction because of doubts about a witness.[124] The defence of *Galbraith* involves arguing that it is important to reserve some questions for the jury, and to avoid so far as possible the judge encroaching on the jury's domain. This policy, whereby issues of witness credibility are reserved for the jury, in fact underlies considerable parts of the law of evidence.[125]

The thin nature of the distinction involved here can be seen by examining the facts of *Hill*.[126] In this case, the defendant had been observed selling a 'small dark substance' to customers. Tried for supplying cannabis, *Hill* argued that the observations of the police officers were insufficient to make out a case for him to answer. The Court of Appeal agreed, and quashed his conviction. Without suggesting that there is anything wrong with this decision, it is not easy to articulate why the prosecution case, taken at its highest, did not warrant a conviction while, on slightly different facts, it would have done. If, for example, Hill's customer had testified that he had purchased from

---

[122] [1981] 1 WLR 1039, 1042. See also *R v P* [2008] 2 Cr App R 6.   [123] *Slippey* [1988] *Crim LR* 767.
[124] A good example is *R v B* [2003] EWCA Crim 319, discussed in Ch 9.
[125] See, e.g., *R v Turner* [1975] QB 834; *R v H* [1995] 2 AC 596.   [126] (1993) 96 Cr App R 456.

Hill a substance that was cannabis, the case would almost certainly have been strong enough to go to the jury.[127] No matter what doubts the judge had about the witness, he could not, within the confines of the *Galbraith* rule, have stopped the case. To answer that questions of credibility are for the jury is not immediately convincing: why, one might ask, should the nature of the substance which police officers saw Hill selling not be an issue for the jury? If there is a difference between the scenarios, it lies not in credibility, but in the degree of risk to which the defendant is exposed in leaving the case to the jury.

The *Galbraith* rule appears even harder to support when one notes that there are a number of exceptions to it.[128] There are some credibility issues which judges do decide, and where a decision against the prosecution may bring the case to a halt. We have already come across examples: s 76 of the Police and Criminal Evidence Act 1984 (PACE) can result in the exclusion of a confession where the prosecution cannot convince the judge of its reliability (see Chapter 4), and the *Turnbull*[129] rule can result in a case depending substantially on poor quality eyewitness evidence being withdrawn from the jury (see Chapter 5). The Court of Appeal has also held that unconvincing confessions from a mentally handicapped defendant should be withdrawn from the jury, even where the case does not raise a s 76 issue.[130] The Criminal Justice Act 2003 requires judges to direct an acquittal where the prosecution case is based on a statement made out of court which is thought to be unconvincing.[131] In practice, too, *Galbraith* is sometimes ignored: cases depending on the testimony of child witnesses are sometimes stopped when a judge has doubts about the witness's evidence.[132] It is possible to reinterpret *Galbraith* so as to reconcile these seeming exceptions with it: the situations just described, it might be argued, relate to doubts about the reliability of testimony, rather than about the sincerity of the witness (in the sense of whether the witness is deliberately lying). Although *Galbraith* itself seemed to raise both types of issue, it might be argued that the issue which really needs to be reserved to the jury is that of whether or not the witness is lying. There may be a policy reason for this distinction, though not, perhaps, a terribly convincing one in the criminal setting: judges are doubtless reluctant to say that they think a witness may be lying.[133] It is rather more diplomatic to leave this sort of decision to the secrecy of the jury room.

Galbraith involves an important issue: it determines just when a defendant will be put at risk of criminal conviction. It is difficult to find convincing reasons for the current rule, and the case law, as we have seen, recognizes a number of exceptions to it. The Criminal Cases Review Commission, a body with considerable experience of the possible causes of false conviction, has noted that 'Judges sometimes allow cases go to

---

[127] The courts are prepared to recognize lay expertise in drug identification: *R v Chatwood* [1980] 1 WLR 874.

[128] See I. Dennis, *The Law of Evidence* (3rd ed, 2007), 113–14.   [129] [1977] QB 224.

[130] *Mackenzie* (1993) 96 Cr App R 98.   [131] CJA 2003, s 125.

[132] See G. Davis et al, *An Assessment of the Admissibility and Sufficiency of Evidence in Child Abuse Prosecutions* (1999), 47–8.

[133] Cf Judicial Studies Board, *Civil Bench Book*, para 10.4.

the jury for decision where the prosecution evidence can hardly be said to support a conviction beyond reasonable doubt.... Trial judges should be more vigorous in ruling that there is no case to answer'.[134] It would be better, both in terms of consistency and of protecting defendants, to allow a judge to stop a case whenever it is thought that a conviction would be unsafe.[135]

Galbraith concerns the question of when the judge should direct the jury to acquit. But what about the converse situation, where the prosecution case is strong and the defence has no answer to it? Here we see an example of the asymmetry of criminal procedure.[136] As the House of Lords confirmed in *Wang*,[137] a judge is never permitted to direct a jury to convict. If the defendant has no good defence in law, the judge can make this very plain to the jury, but the jury must never be told that it has to convict. The justification for this is jury equity. Controversially, the principle is that a jury should always have the power to acquit a defendant in defiance of the law.

11.3 THE EXCLUSION OF UNFAIRLY AND ILLEGALLY OBTAINED EVIDENCE

Where the police have obtained evidence against a suspect by unfair or illegal means, the courts face a difficult question: whether or not to admit the evidence. Sometimes, a decision to exclude such evidence will result in the collapse of the case against the defendant, and where the crime involved is a serious one, such as murder or rape, the court may be extremely reluctant to take this course. The issues involved here are complex, and to make any headway in considering them a number of distinctions must be drawn.

The police may engage in conduct which affects the reliability of the evidence against the accused. The most obvious examples here involve confessions. The police might, for instance, put undue pressure on a suspect by bullying him, lying to him, denying him legal advice or, in the case of a juvenile, denying access to an appropriate adult. The police might also question a suspect outside the police station, so evading the protections offered by the PACE regime. Depending on the circumstances, these actions might affect the reliability of a resulting confession. For example, we saw in Chapter 4 that vulnerable suspects may confess falsely where they are bullied (as in the case of *Miller*[138]). A juvenile or an adult might feel overwhelmed by the experience of being detained, and without access to independent advice, might confess falsely. Where a suspect is questioned outside the police station, there may be no definitive record of what was said and so the very claim that a confession was made may be disputed. Where unreliability is the concern, there are good reasons for excluding the relevant

---

[134] Memorandum to Home Affairs Committee, HC 1703, 2005–6, para 3.1.
[135] This was the recommendation of the Royal Commission on Criminal Justice: above n 40, 59.
[136] For further discussion, see Ch 13.   [137] [2005] UKHL 9.   [138] (1992) 97 Cr App R 99.

confession. Section 76 of PACE, discussed in Chapter 4, provides a legal basis for doing so; it mandates the exclusion of confessions obtained in consequence of anything said or done which was likely to render the confession unreliable. The exclusion of unreliable evidence is not especially controversial (though it is certainly not easy to say just how unreliable evidence should be before it is a target for exclusion), and we will give little further attention to it in this chapter. That allows us to concentrate on the more difficult question of whether a confession, or other evidence, should be excluded where there are no doubts about its reliability. A defendant wrongly denied access to legal advice might be an intelligent adult, and might even admit the truth of the confession. Should the confession then be excluded? The first distinction to be drawn, then, is that between cases where reliability is a concern and those where it is not.

The examples given above allow further distinctions to be made. Where the police deny a suspect access to legal advice, they will usually be acting in breach of s 58 of PACE, which requires a suspect to be given access to legal advice except in very exceptional circumstances. But problematic behaviour may not always be a clear breach of a rule. For example, in *Mason*,[139] the police lied to the suspect about the existence of incriminating information. The usual objection to such conduct is not that it is in breach of the rules for conducting criminal investigations, but the rather vaguer complaint that it is somehow unfair.[140] Another example of unfairness, which we came across in Chapter 9, is entrapment. The principal objection to entrapment is not that it is in breach of any particular rules, but that involves inappropriate action on the part of the State. However, entrapment often will involve a breach of the criminal law. Where an undercover police officer asks a person to supply him with heroin, he will be committing a criminal offence: usually the inchoate offence of incitement, and perhaps also a drug possession offence. Other police practices will also involve breaches of the criminal law. In *Khan*,[141] the police placed a bugging device on the outside of a house in order to obtain incriminating information. This probably involved the commission of criminal damage—although the damage was minor. The bugging operation also involved the breach of the right to privacy in Article 8 ECHR, and the interference could not be justified by reference to the prevention of crime because there was no legal framework regulating such police operations, as Article 8(2) requires. As in most of the examples above, improper investigative action will usually involve problematic treatment of the *defendant*. But this will not always be the case. In *Khan*, it was not the defendant, Khan's, property that was damaged, but that of a third party whose house he was visiting. In *A v Home Secretary*,[142] the question was whether certain information, which might have been obtained from a third party by means of torture, was admissible, even if it was

---

[139] [1988] 1 WLR 139.

[140] It was argued in Ch 4, however, that deception during questioning should be ruled out on reliability grounds. For more detailed discussion of why deception may be unacceptable, see A. Ashworth, 'Should the Police be Allowed to Use Deceptive Practices?' (1998) 114 *LQR* 108.

[141] [1996] 3 All ER 289.   [142] [2005] UKHL 71.

reliable. These various examples enable us to make the following distinctions: there may be an objection to police conduct because it breaches a statutory rule designed to protect suspects (e.g. denial of legal advice); because it is thought to be somehow unfair (e.g. lying to a suspect); because it breaches the criminal law (e.g. criminal damage); because it breaches a broad human rights norm (e.g. the right to privacy); or because it involves improper treatment of a third party (e.g. the breach of a third party's right not to be tortured). We will return to the possible significance of these distinctions in the discussion to follow.

In order to understand the arguments surrounding the exclusion of unfairly and illegally obtained evidence, it is useful to follow the literature in distinguishing four different approaches that the courts might adopt. The first is the disciplinary approach. The idea here is that evidence is excluded in order to deter future misconduct by the police. If the police gain a confession after improperly denying the suspect legal advice, then the court should exclude the confession in order to teach the police a lesson. The police will be less likely to deny legal advice in future cases if they are aware that any evidence they obtain from the suspect by questioning him cannot be used against him in court. However, this last assumption is questionable, and herein lies a common objection to the disciplinary approach. Just as there are doubts about the deterrent effects of punishing criminals, there are doubts about the deterrent effect of excluding improperly obtained evidence. In future cases, the police may not be deterred if they are unaware of the relevant rules, if they think that the misconduct will not come to light, if they think that the suspect will plead guilty, or if for any other reason gathering evidence for use at trial is not what is motivating their conduct (the literature on policing makes it clear that much police conduct is motivated primarily by the goal of 'order maintenance').[143] While acknowledging this, it should be recognized that in some situations deterrence may be effective. The right to legal advice before questioning is an example. In the early days of PACE, the police frequently ignored this right. Judgments of the Court of Appeal, which in some cases overturned convictions based on confessions obtained after denial of legal advice, probably played a role in changing this situation.[144] The exclusion of evidence may have been particularly effective here because police questioning is usually centred on obtaining evidence rather than on other goals, such as order maintenance, and because the police station is a relatively well regulated area where rules can be enforced and misconduct is quite likely to come to light (contrast decisions to stop and search). In the United States, where deterrence is the primary justification for the exclusionary rule in search and seizure cases, there has been considerable debate about whether exclusion of evidence deters police misconduct.[145] It is obviously difficult to

---

[143] See, e.g., R. Reiner, *The Politics of the Police* (3rd ed, 2000).

[144] Brown found that after the Court of Appeal decision in *Samuel* [1988] 1 QB 615, the power to delay access to legal advice was regarded as a 'dead letter' by detectives. D. Brown, *Investigating Burglary: The Effects of PACE* (1991), 76. See also D. Brown et al, *Changing the Code: Police Detention Under the Revised PACE Codes of Practice* (1992).

[145] For a sceptical view of deterrence, see C. Slobogin, 'Why Liberals Should Chuck the Exclusionary Rule' (1999) *U Illinois L Rev* 363.

conduct empirical research on this area. Quantitative studies have often failed to find that significant exclusionary judgments have had an impact. But there is considerable evidence at a more anecdotal level that, as a reaction to judicial policy, the police have taken constitutional rights more seriously.[146]

A second approach to illegally and improperly obtained evidence is the protective or remedial approach.[147] If the focus of the deterrence rationale is on the wrongdoer (the police), then the focus of the remedial approach is on the victim of the police misconduct: usually the defendant, against whom the prosecution seeks to introduce illegally or improperly obtained evidence. By excluding evidence under the remedial rationale, the courts seek to put the defendant back in the position he would have been in had his rights not been breached. This may involve a question of causation: if a suspect was denied access to legal advice, and then confessed, it will be legitimate to ask whether the confession came about as a result of the denial of legal advice. If the suspect would have confessed anyway, then excluding the confession will not restore the status quo. This may be a very difficult judgement to make. It is worth noting at this stage a substantial difference between the deterrent and protective rationales. Suppose that the police breach the defendant's rights, but do so in good faith. For example, they may rely on a legal decision which is later overturned.[148] If this means that the defendant has been disadvantaged by a breach of his rights then, under the remedial approach, any evidence obtained in consequence of the breach should be excluded. But this would not be the outcome under a deterrence rationale. The police could not have known that they were acting illegally, so deterrence would not be effective. In this vein, in the United States, if a wrongful arrest is the result of isolated negligence rather than systemic error or recklessness—as in *Herring v United States*,[149] where the police relied on information that there was a warrant for the defendant's arrest, but the information was mistaken owing to an administrative error—resulting evidence will not be excluded under the deterrence rationale. The courts accept the argument that sanctions are unlikely to reduce the number of such errors.

A common criticism of the remedial approach is that it is insensitive to 'comparative reprehensibility',[150] in that it leads to exclusion where there is a breach of a minor right when investigating a major crime. Suppose that a defendant who has been denied access to legal advice confesses to a series of murders. Excluding the confession might lead to the collapse of the case against him, something many people would feel very

---

[146] See Y. Kamisar, 'In Defense of the Search and Seizure Exclusionary Rule' (2003) 26 *Harvard J Law & Public Policy* 120; A. Alschuler, 'Studying the Exclusionary Rule: An Empirical Classic' (2008) 75 *U Chicago L Rev* 1365.

[147] A. Ashworth, 'Excluding Evidence as Protecting Rights' [1977] *Crim LR* 723; J. Norton, 'The Exclusionary Rule Reconsidered: Restoring the Status Quo Ante' (1998) 33 *Wake Forest L Rev* 261; W. Schroeder, 'Restoring the Status Quo Ante: The Fourth Amendment Exclusionary Rule as a Compensatory Device' (1983) *George Washington L Rev* 633.

[148] E.g. *R v Forbes* [2001] 1 Cr App R 430.

[149] 555 US __ (2009).

[150] Y. Kamisar, '"Comparative Reprehensibility" and the Fourth Amendment Exclusionary Rule' (1987) 86 *Michigan LR* 1.

uncomfortable about. The deterrence approach might have the same effect. A third way of justifying the exclusion of illegally or unfairly obtained evidence avoids such outcomes by taking comparative reprehensibility as its central element. This is the moral legitimacy or integrity rationale.[151] There are different ways of theorizing this approach.[152] One, which reflects the legitimacy theory of the trial sketched in the introduction to this chapter, is to appeal to the need for the verdicts of courts to appear legitimate in the eyes of the public. Citizens will not have faith in the courts if judges too easily overlook wrongdoing by the authorities; but nor will citizens be comfortable if they see serious criminals going free because of relatively minor wrongdoing. Judges should therefore bear in mind both the importance of convicting the guilty and the importance of sanctioning official wrongdoing when deciding whether or not to exclude improperly obtained evidence. As we have noted, a possible difficulty with this approach is that it puts too much emphasis on the reaction of the public. In crimes which attract widespread revulsion, such as the sexual abuse of children, the public might be perfectly happy to see the use of tortured confessions.[153] Most advocates of the integrity approach therefore distance themselves from 'public attitude integrity'. For example, the Canadian Charter of Rights and Freedoms provides for the exclusion of evidence obtained in breach of Charter rights where its admission 'would bring the administration of justice into disrepute'.[154] Aware of the dangerously emotive nature of this test, the Supreme Court has held that the test 'does not focus on immediate reaction to the individual case. Rather, it looks to whether the overall repute of the justice system, viewed in the long term, will be adversely affected by admission of the evidence. The inquiry is objective. It asks whether a reasonable person, informed of all relevant circumstances and the values underlying the *Charter*, would conclude that the admission of the evidence would bring the administration of justice into disrepute.'[155]

Under the theory of the trial developed by Duff and his co-authors, the idea of legitimacy, or integrity, is taken in a slightly different direction.[156] Rather than stressing public reaction to the verdict, more emphasis is put on the trial as a process of moral communication with the defendant. The argument is that if a court admits improperly obtained evidence, it will undermine its moral standing to try the defendant, because if the defendant is convicted the court will at once be both condoning wrongdoing and condemning it. However, a process of balancing is still central. Not just any wrongdoing will result in exclusion. As one purpose of the trial is to vindicate the wrong done

---

[151] See I. Dennis, *The Law of Evidence* (3rd ed, 2007), 49–58, 86–107, Ch 8; and discussion in P. Mirfield, *Silence, Confessions and Improperly Obtained Evidence* (1997), 23–8.

[152] For further discussion, see A. Ashworth, 'Exploring the Integrity Principle in Evidence and Procedure' in P. Mirfield and R. Smith (eds), *Essays for Colin Tapper* (2003).

[153] P. Mirfield, above n 151, 23–8, 364–70.   [154] Section 24(2).

[155] *R v Grant* (2009) SCC 32, [68]. Previously the court had said that the test involves thinking of the reaction of the 'average person in the community, but only when that community's current mood is reasonable'. *Collins* [1987] 1 SCR 265, [44].

[156] Above n 2, Ch 8.

to the victim of the crime, a court should be aware of the costs of excluding significant evidence. But whether under the moral standing or legitimacy approach, it is not obvious quite how this balancing process should proceed. In a serious case, how are we to tell whether moderate wrongdoing by the police would bring the administration of justice into disrepute in the eyes of a reasonable person, or whether it would fatally undermine the moral standing of the court? In general, a legitimacy or moral standing approach is prone to exclude evidence in fewer cases than the remedial approach. But in the situation in *A v Home Secretary*, where it is a third party whose right has been breached, the remedial approach cannot justify exclusion, whereas a legitimacy approach might well do.

A fourth approach, which might be termed the 'external' approach, would hold that the exclusion of improperly obtained evidence is never appropriate.[157] So long as the relevant evidence is reliable, the argument would go, the court should use it in its primary task of fact-finding. This is not to say that the police were right to beat the defendant up, or deny him a solicitor, or bug his house; nor is it to say that such impropriety should be overlooked. The argument is simply that a response to the impropriety should take place in a venue external to the present trial. The police could be prosecuted for assault, or disciplined for breaking the PACE rules, and in the bugging case an action for damages might be brought under the Human Rights Act. One difficulty with this argument, however, is that often those other remedies will be insufficient. There have been long-standing problems with police disciplinary proceedings, and if the authorities decide not to institute them there is little the victim can do. And while it is possible to prosecute the police for assault, this would involve further legal proceedings; there is something to be said, in terms of efficiency, for responding to the wrongdoing in the initial criminal trial.

The way the courts approach the exclusion of improperly or illegally obtained evidence can be evaluated on another dimension: that of the width of discretion given to the courts. On its face, there is little discretion involved under the remedial rationale. Once it is decided that the defendant's rights have been breached, any resulting evidence should be excluded. Exclusion is automatic. Exclusion under the deterrence rationale also tends to be automatic: police wrongdoing must be punished. These two approaches will tend to result in clearer exclusionary rules. This is not the case with the integrity rationale, for here a difficult balancing exercise is central to the rule. This contrast should not be overstated. Under the protective rationale the courts will have considerable leeway in deciding whether the evidence in question was obtained as a result of police wrongdoing, and the integrity approach can gain structure through the development of case law or the use of multi-factor tests to constrain decision making.[158] Discretion can also be added to the protective and disciplinary rationales by

---

[157] For this argument in the context of the Fourth Amendment to the US Constitution, see A. Amar, 'Fourth Amendment First Principles' in *The Constitution and Criminal Procedure* (1997). For further discussion of the external, or 'separation' approach, see Ashworth, above n 152, 113–15.

[158] As in Canada and New Zealand: see below.

allowing exceptions to be made in certain cases. Nevertheless, the basic distinction here is important in evaluating the approaches. The more one dislikes leaving considerable leeway to judges, the more one will favour the stricter rule-based approaches.

There is much more to say about these theoretical approaches to the exclusion of evidence. We will discuss them further after saying something about the case law that has developed on these matters in England and in other jurisdictions.

(A) THE ENGLISH CASE LAW

The approach of the English courts to illegally and unfairly obtained evidence has changed since the introduction of the Police and Criminal Evidence Act 1984. The old common law approach was, basically, unsympathetic to the exclusion of such evidence. The words of Crompton J in *Leatham* are often quoted to illustrate the position: 'It matters not how you get it; if you steal it even, it would be admissible in evidence.'[159] There are dicta in some post-war cases which suggest that judges might have a discretion to exclude improperly obtained evidence, but these dicta are obscure, and there are very few decisions where courts did use the discretion to exclude evidence.[160]

Section 78 of PACE provides that:

'In any proceedings the court may refuse to allow evidence on which the prosecution proposes to rely to be given if it appears to the court that, having regard to all the circumstances, including the circumstances in which the evidence was obtained, the admission of the evidence would have such an adverse effect on the fairness of the proceedings that the court ought not to admit it.'

This vaguely worded provision has led to a change in the way the courts have approached illegally and unfairly obtained evidence. There is a considerable amount of case law, and it is not easily summarized. Indeed, guidance from the higher courts is conspicuous for its absence. The Supreme Courts of Canada and New Zealand have given very detailed consideration to questions of general policy in this area, and to the factors that point towards or away from exclusion.[161] When faced with issues under s 78, however, the House of Lords and Court of Appeal have tended to focus on the facts of the immediate case, and to give little general guidance. Despite this, various observations can be made about the English case law.

PACE introduced a number of provisions regulating the treatment of suspects in the police station and the way in which evidence is gathered. The courts have been prepared to exclude evidence where these provisions have been breached, but exclusion is by no means automatic. A preliminary question is often whether the breach is 'significant and substantial'. A breach of s 58—the right to legal advice—for example, will be

---

[159] (1861) 8 Cox CC 498, 501.

[160] For good summaries of the pre-PACE position, see Dennis, above n 151, 296–301; D. Ormerod and D. Birch, 'The Evolution of the Discretionary Exclusion of Evidence' [2004] *Crim LR* 767.

[161] *Grant*, above n 155; *Williams* [2007] 3 NZLR 207.

considered significant and substantial. But other breaches may be regarded as merely technical. In *Blackwell*, for example, there were various breaches of PACE Code C: among other things, the defendant was not reminded of his right to legal advice at the beginning of one of several interviews, and had been given breakfast and a light lunch but was not offered a main meal; these were described as technical breaches.[162] That a breach is significant and substantial is not determinative of the admissibility issue. The courts put considerable importance on the question whether the defendant was disadvantaged by the breach of his rights. In *Samuel*,[163] for example, there was a wrongful denial of legal advice, and the defendant's solicitor testified that had he given advice it would have been to say nothing in the interview in which Samuel in fact confessed. But in *Alladice*, the defendant who was wrongly denied legal advice admitted that he was fully aware of his rights, and the court therefore found that allowing legal advice would have made little difference to him.[164] The confession in *Samuel* was excluded, but the one in *Alladice* admitted. Many other cases take this approach.[165] Another factor which has been held to have some relevance is the question of bad faith. That the police breached PACE or the Codes in good faith will not necessarily prevent exclusion, but it has been said that bad faith is more likely to lead to exclusion.[166]

The case law discussed so far relates to breaches of PACE and the Codes of Practice. The rules involved are fairly clear and are generally designed to protect defendants. The judiciary seems to have adopted these rules and to be happy to enforce the rights contained in them. The wording of s 78 is far broader than the protection of such procedural rights; it refers simply to fairness. The courts are prepared to use s 78 in other situations, but it is probably fair to say that they are more cautious in doing so. One example is *Mason*,[167] where the defendant and his solicitor were falsely informed that Mason's fingerprints had been found at the crime scene. Mason's confession was excluded; the court emphasized the fact that his solicitor was subject to the deception, so it may be that the exclusionary reaction here was connected to the court's desire to protect access to legal advice (what good is legal advice, after all, if that advice can be manipulated by deception?) In other cases involving more passive forms of deception, exclusion has generally not followed. In *Bailey*,[168] *Roberts*,[169] and (a different) *Mason*,[170] for example, suspects were encouraged to make incriminating admissions while in bugged cells. The admissions were not excluded, though in the latter case the court did call for clearer guidance on what was acceptable.[171] As for other sorts of deception, there are dicta suggesting that s 78 might be used in cases involving

---

162 [1995] 2 Cr App R 625.   163 [1988] 1 QB 615.

164 (1998) 87 Cr App R 380. For other examples of the difficult causal decision involved, see *Oliphant* [1992] *Crim LR* 40; *Law-Thompson* [1997] *Crim LR* 674.

165 See, e.g., *R v Miller* [2007] EWCA Crim 1891; *R v Shillibier* [200] EWCA Crim 793; *H v DPP* [2007] EWHC 2192 (Admin).

166 *Samuel*, above n 163; *Walsh* (1990) 91 Cr App R 161.   167 [1988] 1 WLR 139.

168 [1993] 3 All ER 513.   169 [1997] 1 Cr App R 217.   170 [2002] 2 Cr App R 38.

171 For further discussion of this sort of deception, see Ashworth, above n 140.

entrapment,[172] though, as we have seen, in such cases the more usual remedy is a stay for abuse of process.

There are also cases where the exercise of s 78 has been considered in relation to breaches of the European Convention on Human Rights. The best known example is *Khan*.[173] Here, the police covertly recorded incriminating statements made by the defendant. The House of Lords seemed prepared to accept that this involved a breach of Article 8 of the Convention, which protects the right to privacy. This was held to be relevant to, though not determinative of, the s 78 question. The significance of the fact that the police have broken a law (here, the placing of the device may have involved criminal damage), or Convention right, would be determined by 'its effect, taken as a whole, upon the fairness or unfairness of the proceedings'.[174] In this case it was held that the trial judge had been within his discretion to decide that the evidence should not be excluded. The issues in *Khan* were considered by the European Court of Human Rights, which confirmed that there had been a breach of Article 8, but also held that relying on the evidence at trial did not breach the right to a fair trial in Article 6.[175] The Court of Appeal has considered a similar issue in the wake of the introduction of the Human Rights Act 1998, and reached the same conclusion: although a breach of Article 8 is relevant to the s 78 question, evidence obtained in breach of that Article need not be excluded.[176]

But where breach of a more fundamental human rights norm is involved, the reaction has been very different. One question in *A v Home Secretary* was whether evidence obtained by torture was admissible before the Special Immigration Appeals Tribunal—a body not subject to the ordinary law of evidence (and thus not subject to PACE, s 78).[177] The allegation was that some intelligence being relied on by the Home Secretary to justify the applicants' detention had been obtained by torture of a third party in a foreign State. The House of Lords unequivocally held that while the Home Secretary was free to consider evidence gained by torture when making executive decisions (the Home Secretary can 'read whatever he likes'[178]), such evidence was inadmissible in any English court under the common law (though this was somewhat undercut by a decision to place the burden of proof in respect of whether torture had been used on the defence). The judges did allow, however, that 'fruit of the poisoned tree'—evidence obtained as an indirect result of torture, such as real evidence discovered via a tortured confession—would be admissible, reflecting a 'pragmatic compromise'.[179]

The European Court of Human Rights (ECtHR) has taken a similar view. In *Jalloh v Germany*, it held that evidence obtained by torture should never be used against the victim, irrespective of the seriousness of the offence.[180] However, in *Jalloh* itself, the maltreatment (forcible administration of an emetic to obtain drugs from the defend-

172 *Smurthwaite and Gill* (1994) 98 Cr App R 437; *R v Looseley* [2001] UKHL 53, [16], [43].
173 [1996] 3 WLR 162.   174 *Ibid.*, 175.
175 *Khan v United Kingdom* (2001) 31 EHRR 45. See also *Heglas v Czech Republic* (2009) 48 EHRR 44.
176 *Mason* [2002] 2 Cr App R 38.   177 Above n 142.   178 *Ibid.*, [93].
179 *Ibid.*, [16], [161].   180 (2007) 44 EHRR 32.

ant's stomach) was characterized as inhuman and degrading treatment rather than as torture (still a breach of Article 3). While the Court held that on the facts the admission of this evidence had breached Article 6, it would not rule out the possibility that such evidence should be admissible in a more serious case. As for 'fruit of the poisoned tree', the position is more complex. In *Gäfgen v Germany*, the applicant had been threatened with violence unless he revealed the whereabouts of a kidnap victim.[181] This was classified as inhuman treatment. The fact that Gäfgen had quickly revealed where the victim's body could be found was excluded by the German courts, and the ECtHR found that this restoration to the 'status quo ante' was sufficient remedy for the breach of Article 3. But use of information discovered as a result of the confession might be compatible with Article 6:

'there is a strong presumption that the use of items of evidence obtained as the fruit of a confession extracted by means contrary to Article 3 renders a trial as a whole unfair in the same way as the use of the extracted confession itself. It is thus necessary for the Court to determine the fairness of the proceedings against the applicant in the light of all the circumstances of the case, having regard, in particular, to the circumstances established by untainted evidence, to the weight attached to the impugned items of evidence and to whether the applicant's defence rights were respected, notably the opportunity for him to challenge the admission and use of such evidence at his trial.'[182]

In the event, it was found that the proceedings at issue in *Gäfgen* had been fair.

Returning to domestic case law, the discussion so far suggests that there has been a fair degree of consensus about the operation of s 78, at least so far as the courts are concerned. There are, however, significant differences of approach in the case law. In *Chalkley*, the Court of Appeal read s 78 as simply restating the old common law.[183] The result of this would be that, except in the case of confessions, s 78 would not enable evidence to be excluded unless the reliability of that evidence was in question. What was not appropriate, it was said, was for a judge to use the exclusionary discretion to express disapproval of the way in which evidence had been obtained—in *Chalkley*, by secretly placing a bugging device in the accused's flat. If such factors were to be considered, this should be in the context of the discretion to stay proceedings for abuse of process, not in the context of s 78.

The decision in *Chalkley* has been controversial.[184] It is not easy to reconcile with much of the other case law on the section, nor with the later decisions of the House of Lords in *Looseley* and *A v Home Secretary*.[185] As a matter of law, it is probably best disregarded. Nevertheless, one should at least try to appreciate why a narrow reading of s 78 might be attractive. The key question under the section is whether admission

---

[181] (2009) 48 EHRR 13.   [182] *Ibid.*, [105].

[183] [1998] QB 848. A similar view of s 78 (as only applying to potentially unreliable evidence) can be found in other cases, e.g. *Cooke* [1995] 1 Cr App R 318.

[184] For cogent criticism, see Dennis, above n 151, 96–100. See also A. Choo and S. Nash, 'What's the Matter with Section 78?' [1999] *Crim LR* 929.

[185] *Attorney General's Reference (No 3 of 2000)*; *R v Looseley* [2001] 1 WLR 2060.

of evidence would have an adverse effect on the fairness of the proceedings. Unless evidence is unreliable, it might be argued that a decision to admit it cannot render the proceedings unfair. If there are no doubts about the reliability of the confession obtained through deception in *Mason*,[186] or the confession in *Samuel*,[187] or the covertly obtained statements in *Khan*,[188] just how can admitting them make the proceedings unfair?[189] Mason may have been treated unfairly when he and his solicitor were deceived, but that unfairness precedes the trial and is not caused by a decision to admit the evidence. There is, then, a certain logic to reading s 78 as being solely concerned with reliability. Against this view, one can argue that the key question is whether the proceedings—interpreted broadly as extending beyond the trial—are fair. Section 78 might be thought to give the courts the power to ensure that the proceedings as a whole are fair by refusing to admit evidence that has been improperly obtained. Indeed, in *Sanghera* the Court of Appeal stated that 'Section 78 allows the court to ensure the fairness of the trial process, and indeed to ensure the fairness of the prosecution process.'[190] Admitting the evidence might be said to amplify the original unfairness. The European Convention on Human Rights is also relevant here: the Strasbourg Court views trial fairness as incorporating the fairness of pre-trial procedures.[191] Moving away from the wording of the section itself, the distinction might be put in terms of a distinction which is drawn in the abuse of process case law,[192] between whether the defendant can have a fair trial, and whether it is fair to try him. A defendant can have a fair trial so long as he is not exposed to an inappropriate risk of false conviction, such as might be produced by the admission of unreliable evidence; but it may not be fair to try a defendant where the authorities have acted unjustly towards him, even if he can receive a fair trial in the sense just described. When thinking about trial fairness, it is easy to get confused by moving between the fair trial/fair to try questions, and this may explain some of the ambiguity in the s 78 case law. In summary, the wording of s 78 is deeply ambiguous; similar ambiguity can be found in the normative question underlying the section (what makes a trial fair?). The issues raised in *Chalkley*, then, illustrate the difficulty of questions about the exclusion of evidence, and their controversial nature.

To point up some of the more controversial issues, we might consider the question of how the seriousness of the crime with which the defendant is charged relates to the s 78 exclusionary discretion. *Nathaniel* is an excellent example.[193] Here, the defendant was convicted of rape. The case against him relied on DNA identification evidence; however, the DNA in question had been retained by the police in breach of the then rules governing the retention of DNA profiles. The Court of Appeal quashed

---

[186] [1998] 1 WLR 139.   [187] Above n 163.   [188] Above n 173.

[189] For this view, see L. Laudan, above n 1, Ch 7; B. Robertson, 'The Looking Glass World of Section 78' (1989) *NLJ* 1223; N. Walker, 'What Does Fairness Mean in a Criminal Trial?' (2001) *NLJ* 1240.

[190] (2001) 1 Cr App R 20, [17].

[191] E.g. *Teixeira de Castro v Portugal* (1999) 28 EHRR 101; *Jalloh v Germany* (2007) 44 EHRR 32.

[192] *R v Beckford* [1996] 1 Cr App R 94.   [193] [1995] 2 Cr App R 565.

his conviction. It put some emphasis on the fact that when Nathaniel's DNA profile had originally been taken, he was informed that it would only be used in connection with the crime he was then charged with, which was not the rape he was eventually convicted of, and this 'breach of promise' might be thought to add a significant dimension to the case.[194] Nevertheless, the decision in *Nathaniel* draws divergent reactions. Dennis, who supports an integrity-based theory of the exclusionary rule, is critical, arguing that the rule in question does not reflect a fundamental norm. His reasoning reflects an appreciation of the seriousness of the crime with which Nathaniel was charged.[195] However, Grevling, who appears to adopt a remedial theory, approves of the decision in *Nathaniel*.[196]

Cases such as *Nathaniel*, which involve cogent real evidence and serious offences, are interesting test cases for the exclusionary discretion. For this reason, it is worth saying something about the decision in *Attorney General's Reference (No 3 of 1999)*,[197] even though it raises somewhat different issues. At the relevant time, the rules in PACE on the retention of DNA profiles were that where a DNA sample had been taken from a defendant in relation to an offence of which he was acquitted, the sample and any information derived from it should be destroyed as soon as practicable. Further, under PACE, s 64(3), in this situation information derived from the sample 'shall not be used (a) in evidence against the person [entitled to its destruction]; or (b) for the purposes of any investigation of an offence.' In the case giving rise to the reference, as in *Nathaniel*, the sample had not been destroyed when it should have been. The defendant was then connected to a violent rape through the DNA sample; he was arrested and a new DNA sample was obtained from him. It was this new sample that was used against him at trial. Because it was a new sample, its use did not fall foul of rule (a) above. The question for the House of Lords was whether rule (b) meant the DNA evidence should have been excluded from the trial. It held that it did not, because (b) does not refer to what the consequences of its breach should be; it says nothing about whether evidence should be excluded when a DNA sample is wrongly used to investigate an offence. In the House of Lords, argument was restricted to this issue of statutory interpretation. For this reason, there was little discussion of whether s 78 should be used to exclude evidence obtained in breach of rule (b). But Lord Hutton hinted heavily that, given the seriousness of the offence and the need to protect society, he would not have exercised the discretion in favour of the defendant.[198] We will return to the question of whether this is the right way to conceive of the exclusionary discretion; for now, it is worth making a further point about the decision. The interpretation of PACE given by the House of Lords has a certain literal logic to it: it is right that rule (b) says nothing about

---

[194] Cf *R v Croydon Justices, ex p Dean* [1993] QB 769.

[195] Above n 151, 314. For a similar view, see M. Hirst, *Andrews and Hirst on Criminal Evidence* (4th ed, 2001), para 14.22.

[196] K. Grevling, 'Fairness and the Exclusion of Evidence Under Section 78(1) of the Police and Criminal Evidence Act' (1997) 113 *LQR* 667, 683.

[197] [2001] 2 AC 91.   [198] *Ibid.*, at [43].

the effects of its breach. But it is nevertheless an odd interpretation of the rules. It is not what the Court of Appeal and the trial judge thought the provisions meant. Moreover, if (b) is not interpreted as being a rule of strict inadmissibility, it makes a mockery of (a), as the House of Lords later went some way to acknowledging.[199] There can be little point in saying that evidence obtained from a wrongly retained DNA sample cannot be used in evidence if the police can circumvent the rule by obtaining a new sample which is not covered by the exclusionary rule. The general lesson to draw from this is that the courts can be very sceptical of strict exclusionary rules when they are regarded as having undesirable results. Here, PACE is subjected to a strained interpretation in order to avoid such results.

Moving beyond these DNA cases, there is relatively clear authority that crime seriousness is relevant to the exercise of the s 78 discretion. We find this in the bugging cases mentioned earlier.[200] And in *Khan*, Lord Nolan, while not expressly addressing this point, commented that 'it would be a strange reflection on our law if a man who has admitted his participation in the illegal importation of a large quantity of heroin should have his conviction set aside on the grounds that his privacy has been invaded.'[201] It is significant that these comments are found in cases dealing with abstract fairness, rather than breach of the PACE rules. When one looks at the PACE cases, one finds that the courts will say that 'fairness' in s 78 includes fairness to the prosecution as well as to the defence.[202] It is hard to tell just what is meant by this, but it may simply imply that reliable prosecution evidence should not be excluded without good reason. Apart from this, the PACE cases generally do not suggest that the seriousness of the crime at issue is a factor to consider in deciding whether to exclude evidence. The comments in the *Attorney General's Reference* are of course an exception to this, to which we will return.

(B) OTHER COMMONWEALTH JURISDICTIONS

A detailed analysis of exclusionary rules in other jurisdictions is beyond the scope of this work, but it is worth looking briefly abroad to gain a wider perspective, before returning to discuss the strengths and weaknesses of the approach of the courts in England and Wales.[203]

The legal position in the United States is complex, because much of the case law has been developed by the Supreme Court in the context of different constitutional

---

[199] The distinction drawn in the case 'did not reflect well on the law', according to Lord Steyn in *R v CC South Yorkshire, ex p LS/Marper* [2004] UKHL 39, [33].

[200] See *Mason* (2002), above n 170 at 70, quoting with approval from *Bailey*, above n 168. See also *Latif and Shahzad* [1996] 1 WLR 104.

[201] Above n 173, 175.

[202] Eg *R v Sanghera* (2001) 1 Cr App R 20. See also *DPP v Meakin* [2006] EWHC 1067 (Admin).

[203] A very useful survey is A. Choo and S. Nash, 'Improperly Obtained Evidence in the Commonwealth: Lessons for England and Wales?' (2007) 11 *E & P* 75.

provisions:[204] there is no equivalent to s 78 of PACE which, as we have seen, can be used in a wide range of circumstances. Concentrating on the Fourth Amendment, which guarantees security against unreasonable searches and seizures, the key decision is perhaps *Mapp v Ohio*, which extended the exclusionary rule from the Federal jurisdiction to the States.[205] Deterrence has become the main justification for the rule, though dissenters in the recent Supreme Court decision in *United States v Herring* have argued for a 'more majestic conception' of the rule, referring to legitimacy concerns.[206] While the exclusionary rule is strict in that there is no balancing process, there are a number of exceptions to the rule that evidence obtained in violation of the Fourth Amendment is inadmissible. Improperly obtained evidence need not be excluded if the police obtained an invalid search warrant in good faith,[207] or if the evidence would inevitably have been discovered by lawful means in due course,[208] and exclusion only applies to the prosecution's case in chief: the evidence can be used to rebut the defendant's evidence at trial.[209] It is often said, too, that strictness of the exclusionary rule leads trial courts to ignore breaches of the Fourth Amendment, for example by making a finding of fact that the police did have good grounds for conducting a search, and that it has led the Supreme Court to narrow down the Fourth Amendment.[210]

Outside the US, a number of jurisdictions apply some version of the integrity rationale for the exclusion of illegally and unfairly obtained evidence. In Canada, for example, a number of rights are recognized in the Canadian Charter of Rights and Freedoms. Section 24(2) of the Charter provides that where evidence has been obtained in breach of a Charter right, it should be excluded from a criminal trial if its admission would bring the administration of justice into disrepute. At one time the Supreme Court drew a distinction between 'conscriptive evidence'—evidence produced via the participation of the defendant—and other evidence. However, in *R v Grant* it responded to concerns that the exclusionary rule had become automatic in conscriptive cases, emphasizing that a broad balancing approach should be taken in all cases.[211] The factors to consider are the seriousness of the breach of the Charter, which includes questions of good faith on the part of the police; the impact of the breach on the defendant's protected interests; and society's interests in an adjudication on the merits of the case. As regards the latter, while the 'view that reliable evidence is admissible regardless of how it was obtained' is to be eschewed,[212] reliability is still an important factor in the balancing process. The seriousness of the offence, however, is a more equivocal factor, because while society has a greater interest in adjudication on the merits in serious cases, it also 'has an interest in a justice system that is above

---

[204] Good overviews are C. Bradley, 'United States' in C. Bradley (ed), *Criminal Procedure: A Worldwide Study* (1999); Mirfield, above n 151, 319–39.

[205] 367 US 643 (1961). For a detailed analysis of decisions on exclusion under the Fourth Amendment, see J. Dressler and A. Michaels, *Understanding Criminal Procedure, Vol 1: Investigations* (4th ed, 2006), Ch 20.

[206] Above n 149.   [207] *US v Leon* 468 US 897 (1984).   [208] *Nix v Williams* 467 US 431.

[209] *US v Havens* 446 US 620 (1980).   [210] Mirfield, above n 151, 322.   [211] Above n 155.

[212] *Ibid.*, [80].

reproach, especially where the penal stakes for the accused are high.'[213] Guidance was also given on particular types of evidence. On the facts of *Grant*, where the accused had been found to be in possession of a firearm during an illegal street detention, the balancing process was said to be close, but the police error was understandable and the evidence cogent, thus admissible. The Supreme Court decided *R v Harrison* on the same day.[214] Here, an illegal detention which led to the discovery of a large quantity of cocaine was held to involve a more blatant disregard for Charter rights. The evidence was held inadmissible: 'to appear to condone wilful and flagrant charter breaches that amounted to a significant incursion on an accused's rights does not enhance the long-term repute of the administration of justice... it undermines it.'[215]

In Australia, it was recognized in *Bunning v Cross* that evidence can be excluded on grounds of 'public policy'.[216] The balancing test adopted by the High Court in this case has been adopted in the Evidence Act 1995, which states that illegally and improperly obtained evidence should not be admitted unless 'the desirability of admitting the evidence outweighs the undesirability of admitting evidence that has been obtained in the way in which the evidence was obtained.'[217] The Act goes on to list a series of factors to be taken into account, including the probative value and importance of the evidence, the difficulty of obtaining it without impropriety, and the nature of the offence for which the defendant is on trial. While the general approach is similar to that in Canada, the consensus is that Australian courts are reluctant to exclude improperly obtained evidence.[218] The absence of human rights legislation may be significant here, but while Victoria has recently adopted a Charter of Rights, commentators suspect that this will make little difference to the exclusion of evidence.[219]

The New Zealand position is closer to that in Canada. While the New Zealand Bill of Rights, unlike the Canadian Charter, does not contain a provision on the exclusion of evidence obtained through its breach, the courts at one point adopted a 'prima facie' exclusionary rule, whereby there was a presumption of inadmissibility when a right in the Bill had been breached.[220] While this rule has been abandoned,[221] the courts still take breaches of the Bill of Rights seriously. The framework for exclusion is now found in s 30 of the Evidence Act 2006, which requires the court to determine 'whether or not the exclusion of the evidence is proportionate to the impropriety by means of a balancing process that gives appropriate weight to the impropriety but

---

[213] *Ibid.*, [216].   [214] [2009] SCC 34.   [215] *Ibid.*, [39].   [216] (1978) 141 CLR 54.

[217] Evidence Act 1995 (Australia) s 138. There is an identical provision under s138 of the Evidence Act 1995 (New South Wales) and s 138 of the Evidence Act 2008 (Victoria).

[218] See J. Gans and A. Palmer, *Australian Principles of Evidence* (2004), 430–5; B. Presser, 'Public Policy, Police Interest: A Re-Evaluation of the Judicial Discretion to Exclude Improperly or Illegally Obtained Evidence' (2001) 25 *Melbourne UL Rev* 757; C. Williams, 'An Analysis of Discretionary Rejection in Relation to Confessions' (2008) 32 *Melbourne U L Rev* 302.

[219] J. Gans, 'Evidence Law Under Victoria's Charter: Remedies and Responsibilities' (2008) 19 *Public Law Review* 285.

[220] *Goodwin* [1993] 2 NZLR 153.

[221] R. Mahoney, 'Abolition of New Zealand's *Prima Facie* Exclusionary Rule' [2003] *Crim LR* 607. For more detail, see P. Rishworth et al, *The New Zealand Bill of Rights* (2003), Ch 28.

also takes proper account of the need for an effective and credible system of justice.' The court should take into account the importance of any right breached, whether any impropriety was in bad faith, the seriousness of the offence and the quality of the evidence. These factors more or less replicate the pre-existing law, and are unlikely to result in any significant change of approach.[222] The New Zealand courts are far more prone to exclude improperly obtained evidence than their Australian counterparts, even when the police have acted in good faith.[223] While the courts have given detailed guidance on the balancing exercise—specifying, for example, that a mark of seriousness is whether an offence carries a custodial sentence of four years or more[224]—there is some unpredictability in the case law.[225]

(C) EVALUATING THE APPROACHES

The foregoing discussion has illustrated a number of different approaches to the exclusion of illegally and unfairly obtained evidence, and highlighted many salient issues which need to be considered when analysing this area of the law. We are now in a position to say a little more about the pros and cons of the various positions on the exclusionary rule. We approach the question by looking more closely at what the English courts have been doing and evaluating this critically.

The first thing to say is that the English courts do not much refer to theories of exclusion when justifying their admissibility decisions. The most significant statement one can find is a negative one: that the courts do not see their role as being to discipline the police.[226] Despite this, there does seem to be an overall pattern to the case law, one that is perhaps more coherent than it looks at first sight. When it comes to breaches of the PACE rules, the rationale appears to be remedial. The courts are concerned to ensure that defendants are not disadvantaged by breach of their rights, and the exclusionary rule is relatively strict. Thus the courts put considerable emphasis on the question whether, for example, a defendant would have confessed even if his rights had not been breached. Of course, the protective rationale here involves a difficult question of fact: in determining whether the defendant was disadvantaged, the court must ask a 'what if?' question, and this opens the door to a certain amount of discretion in the decisions.[227] But this discretion is probably unavoidable: discretion features in some way in any version of the exclusionary rule, as the US experience shows. But once the question of fact has been decided, the protective rationale does give a clear answer to

---

[222] See *R v Williams* [2007] 3 NZLR 207, [149]–[50].

[223] For recent examples, see *R v Rock* [2008] NZCA 81; *R v Horsfall* [2008] NZCA 449. Cf admissibility in a case involving a 'technical' breach in *R v Javid* [2007] NZCA 232.

[224] *Williams*, above n 222, [135].

[225] Contrast *Rock* and *Horsfall*, above n 223, with *R v Taylor* [2006] NZCA 76.

[226] Mirfield, above n 151, 139. Cf *R v Marcus* [2004] EWCA Crim 3387 at [24]: 'If this appeal is dismissed that position might be replicated in other cases.'

[227] For this reason the New Zealand Court of Appeal has cautioned against putting too much weight on the question of 'inevitable discovery': *Williams*, above n 222, [129].

the admissibility question: if evidence has been obtained as a result of breach of rights, it should be excluded.

A problem with the protective rationale is often said to be that it would allow exclusion of evidence after a technical breach of minor rights. One way of responding to this point is to suggest that the remedial approach is not intended to meet the breach of just any rule with the exclusion of evidence; only those offering significant protections to suspects should be treated in this way. Another response is that, in practice, the problem of technical breaches is overcome by stressing that exclusion is only required where evidence has been obtained as a result of a breach of the defendant's rights. Thus, in *Blackwell*,[228] where the PACE codes were breached because the defendant had only been given a light lunch, exclusion would not be appropriate because the defendant would presumably have confessed whatever size of meal he had had.[229] Things might be different had this been one of a number of breaches which had plausibly worn Blackwell down so that he could not resist confessing. In that situation, exclusion would be appropriate.

A significant problem with this remedial reading of the case law is that the courts identify bad faith as a factor to take into account when deciding whether or not to exclude evidence. However, although several cases make this point, it may be less significant when it comes to the actual decisions made by the courts. We are not aware of any decision under s 78 where evidence is obtained in breach of a PACE right but is admitted owing to the absence of bad faith. Bad faith might operate to widen the scope of exclusion, in other words to sanction malpractice even where it is not clear that the defendant was disadvantaged as a result of the impropriety. This suggests that the integrity rationale may also play a role in the case law, a point we expand on below.

The case law discussed so far does not make a decisive case for the protective rationale. It could be explained as well under some version of the legitimacy principle, especially one which emphasizes respect for rights.[230] Where the two approaches are most likely to differ is in a case such as *Nathaniel*, where what might look to be a relatively trivial breach of the PACE rules results in the exclusion of cogent evidence of a serious crime. *Nathaniel* is in fact a very useful test case for thinking about the exclusionary rule. From the legitimacy perspective, the argument for admissibility would be that the court will undermine its legitimacy or moral standing if it excludes the evidence. The remedial argument against admissibility is that Nathaniel had a right not to have the evidence used to connect him to a crime. The only way to give that right significant force is to exclude evidence obtained in breach of it, and here the seriousness of

---

[228] Above n 162.

[229] This helps to explain why decision under the Road Traffic Act—where the courts have often excluded evidence following minor breaches of the provisions (see M. Hirst, 'Excess Alcohol, Incorrect Procedures and Inadmissible Evidence' (1995) 54 *CLJ* 600)—are problematic. The breaches would usually have had no effect on the breath or blood sample or its quality.

[230] See Choo, above n 8, 190.

the crime is not relevant.[231] It may be that the moral values underlying the PACE rule here are not especially weighty ones—the interference with privacy involved in the retention of DNA profiles is minor—but what matters here are the rules set down by Parliament. It is not for the courts to rethink them, and to decide which deserve protection and which do not.

The legitimacy based argument for admissibility would proceed by pointing out that the rules in *Nathaniel* have been breached and that we have learned something very significant as a result: that Nathaniel committed a serious crime. We cannot now discard this knowledge,[232] and it would be wrong for the court to attempt to do so by excluding the crucial evidence. Although this argument has its attractions, close analysis suggests that there is something unsatisfactory about it. No one wants a rapist to go unpunished, but this was in fact an inevitable consequence of the rules on the destruction of DNA profiles in force at the time of the decision. If the police were applying the PACE rules at all, then, by destroying DNA profiles, they presumably ensured that large numbers of people could not be linked to all sorts of crimes, including rape and murder. That is undesirable, but Parliament presumably thought it an appropriate price to pay when it specified the circumstances in which DNA profiles should be destroyed. This argument has been criticized on the grounds that, when Parliament passed the law, it would have known that there was no strict exclusionary rule in place, thus a law requiring destruction of DNA profiles cannot be equated with a decision to exclude them as evidence.[233] But a value judgement has still been made at the legislative level that the profiles should not be used in the criminal process, and that should surely be taken seriously. The same reasoning applies to *Attorney General's Reference No 3 of 1999*.[234] In that case, even accepting the interpretation of s 64 of PACE made by the House of Lords, the DNA evidence should probably have been excluded under s 78.[235] Presumably, the integrity theorist would argue against this by claiming that the fact that we have a defendant before us who we know has committed a serious crime should make the difference. But it is difficult to see why so much weight should be put on our clear knowledge of guilt in the case in front of us. Just why should this override the value judgement made by Parliament? It seems to us that the integrity theorist who objects to the exclusion of the DNA evidence in *Nathaniel* and *Attorney General's Reference* is really arguing that Parliament's policy choice was wrong. That is a respectable position to take, but it is slightly odd that those who argue for admissibility in breach of rights do not concentrate on wider arguments about the merits of the underlying law, but instead focus their criticisms on what is

---

[231] On the inappropriateness of taking seriousness into account, see further A. Ashworth, *Human Rights, Serious Crime and Criminal Procedure* (2002), 108–18.

[232] See P. Roberts and A. Zuckerman, *Criminal Evidence* (2004), 152.

[233] *Williams*, above n 222 at 117. [234] Above n 197.

[235] A complication is that, on the facts of the case, there was an argument that the law did allow retention. Because the defendant had given a false name on arrest, the police did not realise that they had the power to retain his DNA profile on the grounds of his past offending history. Arguably, then, the status quo to be restored is one in which the police could have retained the DNA profile.

really far less significant—the importance of convicting the guilty defendant in the immediate case.[236]

In the earlier discussion, the PACE case law was distinguished from a series of decisions under s 78 which involve wider issues of fairness, such as the use of deception (as in *Mason*) or breach of the right to privacy in Article 8 of the ECHR. Here, it is more difficult to argue that the courts are following a remedial rationale, and the absence of detailed provisions enacted with the intention to protect suspects perhaps makes arguments about the policy choices made by Parliament less relevant. A legitimacy or integrity based approach may be more appropriate here. There are hints in the case law in decisions such as *Khan* that the courts see legitimacy as the exclusionary framework for s 78. Legitimacy language is far more explicit in abuse of process cases, and it is prominent in the House of Lords decision on torture evidence in *A v Home Secretary*. A key criticism of legitimacy as a criterion is its vagueness. As we have seen, courts in both Australia and New Zealand refer to legitimacy, but exclusion of evidence is rare in the former and common in the latter, which suggests that there is nothing in the concept of legitimacy in itself to determine its application to particular cases. Nevertheless, there is a reasonable amount of consistency within each jurisdiction; in New Zealand this has been achieved through the detailed guidance given by the courts, which shows that the vagueness in the theory need not lead to marked inconsistency when it comes to the case law. This is fortunate, because to the extent that different courts come to different decisions, legitimacy itself will be undermined.

We would argue that, where a regime such as PACE has been set up, which lays out clear rules for the protection of suspects, a remedial approach to exclusion is appropriate, and, indeed, is largely consistent with the English case law. This means that the seriousness of the offence with which the defendant is charged and the question of whether the police were acting in good faith should not feature in arguments to exclude the evidence. If the defendant has not been disadvantaged by the breach, however, these factors might feature in an argument to exclude evidence on legitimacy grounds, or to stay the trial as in *Grant*,[237] where the police recorded privileged conversations between Grant and his lawyer but gained no useful information.

A critical question remains how breaches of the ECHR should be dealt with. We have seen that the Strasbourg Court itself has accepted the notion of balancing, even implying that evidence gained via inhuman and degrading treatment might be admissible in a serious enough case. The Canadian and New Zealand approach is preferable to that currently adopted by the English courts, as the structured balancing processes in those jurisdictions ensures that particular attention is paid to breaches of rights guaranteed by human rights documents. But there is a good case for going further, and applying a strict, remedial approach to ECHR breaches. The rights in the ECHR are intended to constrain State action in spheres where important interests are at

---

[236] Some commentators did address their criticisms to the underlying law: see M. Zander, 'All the Evidence Suggests that we Should Change our Minds over DNA' *The Times* 30 May 2000.

[237] [2005] EWCA Crim 1089.

stake. The consequence of accepting rights is that sometimes the State will not be able to pursue the greater good. Evidence should simply not be gained by subjecting suspects to inhuman treatment, and if it is a court should not admit it: not because this would somehow taint or defile the court, to use the language of *A v Home Secretary*, or because it might undermine public confidence in the courts, but because the State should be bound to accept the price of rights by being placed in the position it would be in had it not broken the right. Some may say that if exclusion causes the case to fail, the State fails to vindicate the wrong done to the victim, but it is plain that many cases go unsolved which might have been pursued to conviction were the State not constrained in its choice of investigative methods. To argue, as the ECtHR has done, that the seriousness of the crime involved might justify admission, is to invite the argument that crime seriousness can justify inhuman treatment in the first place. While these arguments have been made in the context of Article 3, they apply equally to Article 8, although there of course the State is in the first place less constrained because a process of balancing is already built into the scope of Article 8 through the 'necessary in a democratic society' wording.

If legitimacy is to be used as a criterion for admissibility in some cases, then some response to the 'separation thesis' is needed.[238] Under the separation thesis, because the courts are independent of law enforcement agencies, a decision to admit improperly obtained evidence need not be seen as condonation of the improper behaviour, and thus as undermining the legitimacy of the court. Indeed, a court could roundly condemn the police and even call for disciplinary action to be taken against them. There are several responses to the separation thesis. Insofar as the admission of evidence encourages police lawlessness, it would be rather hypocritical of a court to take this stance, just as a person cannot condemn the evils of the drug trade while using trafficked drugs himself. Given that the police rarely face disciplinary action for breaches of PACE and the like, it is the courts who are best placed to deter police malpractice. While many writers are sceptical of the deterrence theory, the evidence from the United States is mixed, and, especially when it comes to behaviour in the police station, it is likely that court decisions have some effect. This link between deterrence and legitimacy is nicely brought out by the comments of the Court of Appeal in *R v Marcus*, where it excluded evidence gained in breach of Code D: 'If this appeal is dismissed that position might be replicated in other cases. The court would have validated in principle, or might be taken to have done so, the use of a procedure which violated the Code.'[239]

A second response to the separation thesis is that, as a matter of historical fact, it is unrealistic. In England and Wales the courts have simply taken responsibility for oversight of the police, as when, long before PACE, they drew up the Judges' Rules to govern the treatment of suspects in police detention.[240] This shared responsibility for

---

[238] See Ashworth, above n 152.   [239] Above n 226, [24].
[240] See S. Sharpe, *Judicial Discretion and Criminal Litigation* (1998), 29–36.

criminal justice may make it difficult for the courts to distance themselves from the actions of the police. Further, it was suggested in the introduction to this chapter that trials are intimately connected to the rule of law, and provide an opportunity to call the State to account for its conduct. This may make it especially important for courts to mark illegality with exclusion. Finally, it is possible that even if a decision to admit evidence does not condone the conduct which produced it, the court will still be compromised. On the facts of *A v Home Secretary*, the separation thesis is at its strongest. With the alleged misconduct being by an agent of a foreign State, there is little possibility of deterrence, and the English courts could hardly be said to have a responsibility for the conduct of investigations in that State. But one striking thing about the language of the House of Lords in *A* is the use of the metaphor of contamination: admission of evidence gained by torture would 'defile an English court whatever the nationality of the torturer';[241] and 'abuse or degrade the proceedings and involve the state in moral defilement'.[242] While evidence gained by torture is an extreme example, Bilz has reported empirical evidence of subjects' reactions to scenarios involving illegally obtained evidence which suggests that this idea of contamination may be part of the thinking behind legitimacy.[243]

11.4 CONFRONTATION

As stated in the introduction to this chapter, a detailed consideration of the law of evidence is outside the scope of this work. In this final section, we briefly examine one area of the law of which, like the exclusion of improperly obtained evidence, is closely tied to processual norms: the law relating to hearsay and the confrontation of witnesses.

Article 6(3) of the ECHR gives a defendant the right to 'examine or have examined witnesses against him'. It is convenient to refer to this as the right of confrontation. In recent years, courts in England and Wales have been faced with difficult questions about the extent to which law and practice conflicts with this right. Key questions concern the extent to which out of court statements can be presented at trial in lieu of the presence of the witness who made them, and in what circumstances witnesses can be allowed to give evidence anonymously.

As regards out of court statements, the primary rule has long been that such 'hearsay' statements are inadmissible. The person who made the statement should attend trial, where they can be cross-examined. However, exceptions to the rule against hearsay have been expanded over time, with significant changes to the law being introduced by the Criminal Justice Act 2003.[244] If a witness has made a statement

---

[241] Above n 142, [91].   [242] *Ibid.*, [150].

[243] K. Bilz, 'Integrity or Deterrence: The Psychology of the Exclusionary Rule' (forthcoming).

[244] See, generally, J. Spencer, *Hearsay Evidence in Criminal Proceedings* (2008).

prior to trial—typically, but not necessarily, to the police—that statement may now be presented in court in certain circumstances. Under s 116 of the CJA the circumstances are that the witness is unavailable to attend the trial: because she is dead; is physically or mentally unfit to attend; is outside the United Kingdom and attendance is not practical; cannot be found, despite attempts having been made; or because the witness will not give evidence through fear. Where fear is the reason for non-attendance, s 116 requires that an interests of justice test be satisfied before the out of court statement is admitted, which includes considering the 'risk that its admission or exclusion will result in unfairness to any party to the proceedings (and in particular to how difficult it will be to challenge the statement if the relevant person does not give oral evidence)'. But the interests of justice are relevant to the other grounds of unavailability as well, because of the applicability of s 78 of PACE.[245]

If a witness statement is admitted against the defendant under s 116, will this be incompatible with the confrontation right in Article 6(3)? There is a large Strasbourg case law on the interpretation of this right,[246] and while the case law is not entirely consistent, it is clear that the answer to this question will depend on various issues, prominent among them the extent to which the defendant was able to challenge the statement, and whether the statement is the 'sole or decisive' evidence against the defendant. The following passage is indicative of the Strasbourg approach:

'evidence must normally be produced at a public hearing, in the presence of the accused, with a view to adversarial argument. There are exceptions to this principle, but they must not infringe the rights of the defence. As a general rule, paragraphs 1 and 3 (d) of Article 6 require that the defendant be given an adequate and proper opportunity to challenge and question a witness against him, either when he makes his statement or at a later stage … where a conviction is based solely or to a decisive degree on depositions that have been made by a person whom the accused has had no opportunity to examine or to have examined, whether during the investigation or at the trial, the rights of the defence are restricted to an extent that is incompatible with the guarantees provided by Article 6'.[247]

The English courts have tended to be sceptical of the requirements laid down in the Strasbourg cases,[248] and there has now been a successful challenge to the English approach in *Al-Khawaja and Tahery v United Kingdom*.[249] In *Al-Khawaja* the complainant had died after making a statement to the police; in *Tahery*, the witness declined to give evidence through fear (though the defendant, Tahery, does not seem to have done anything to cause the fear; the witness was scared of the reaction from other members of the Iranian community). In both cases the witness statements were admitted at trial. The ECtHR found that the statements were a decisive basis for the applicants'

---

[245] CJA, s 126(2)(a).
[246] For detailed analysis, see S. Maffei, *The European Right to Confrontation in Criminal Proceedings* (2006).
[247] *Luca v Italy* (2003) 36 EHRR 46, [39]–[40].
[248] See *R v M(KJ)* (2003) 2 Cr App R 322; *R v Sellick and Sellick* [2005] EWCA 651.
[249] (2009) 49 EHRR 1.

convictions. The Government largely conceded this, but relied on the argument that the applicants had still been able to challenge the statements, and that this should be considered to counterbalance the absence of the witnesses. Among the means of challenge were that in *Al-Khawaja* the defence could have pointed out inconsistencies in the applicant's statements, and in *Tahery* it could have called other witnesses who might have cast doubt on the statement. It is unclear to what extent the Court accepted that such means of challenge might counterbalance the inability to examine the witness. While 'the Court doubt[ed] whether any counterbalancing factors would be sufficient to justify the introduction in evidence of an untested statement which was the sole or decisive basis for the conviction of an applicant',[250] this is not an absolute statement, and the Court does seem to have taken the Government's counterbalancing argument seriously by examining it on its merits. On the facts, however, it was not convinced by the argument. As regards *Tahery*, this may be right; it seems that all of the potential witnesses to the crime were reluctant to give information, which only left Tahery's own testimony, something unlikely to carry much weight. The conclusion is more debatable in *Al-Khawaja*: the Court noted that the inconsistencies in the complainant's accounts were minor, and that her allegation corresponded with that of another complainant, with whom collusion could be ruled out. But surely the issue is the *potential* for challenge provided by these other items of evidence, not the fact that they happen not to support the defence case; otherwise the prosecution is put in a worse position to the extent that the impugned evidence is reliable.

The Court of Appeal has now responded to Strasbourg's ruling by arguing that, for various reasons, it is wrong. In *Horncastle* it reads the ECtHR as having laid down an absolute rule that where the evidence of an absent witness is the sole or decisive basis for conviction, counterbalancing factors, such as the ability to challenge the statement through other evidence, cannot make up for the absence of confrontation.[251] As we suggested in the previous paragraph, the judgment in *Al-Khawaja* may not support such a reading. Be that as it may, the Court of Appeal argues that such an absolutist position is not supported by previous ECtHR decisions, nor is cogent as a matter of principle. For the Court of Appeal, the question is 'whether the evidence can be assessed and tested so that it is safe to rely upon it'; the absolutist position presumes 'that all hearsay evidence which is critical to a case will be potentially unreliable in the absence of testing in open court [and that] the fact-finder cannot be trusted to assess the weight of such evidence.' 'The importance of the evidence within the case is an entirely separate issue from its reliability.'[252] The court goes on to give various examples of hearsay evidence which it thinks would be reliable enough to determine a case standing alone.

It is obvious that in *Horncastle* the Court of Appeal is interpreting the concern over confrontation as one that is focused purely on reliability. But this is not the only way to

---

[250] *Ibid.*, [37].
[251] *Ibid.*, 41. The Court of Appeal's decision was endorsed by the Supreme Court in *R v Horncastle* [2009] UKSC 14.
[252] *Ibid.*, [58], [60], [64].

understand confrontation. The sixth amendment to the US Constitution guarantees the defendant's right 'to be confronted with the witnesses against him'.[253] The confrontation right has recently been invigorated by the Supreme Court which, in *Crawford v Washington*,[254] held that evidence that was admissible under reliability based exceptions to the hearsay rule might still be inadmissible on grounds of violation of the confrontation right. At one point it observed that 'Dispensing with confrontation because testimony is obviously reliable is akin to dispensing with jury trial because a defendant is obviously guilty.'[255] One interpretation of this is that confrontation is a 'dignitarian' right, i.e. it reflects respect for human dignity rather than the need to protect defendants from false conviction. As it was put, if rather mysteriously, in *Coy v Iowa*: 'there is something deep in human nature that regards face-to-face confrontation between accused and accuser as essential to a fair trial in a criminal prosecution'.[256] In the United States, confrontation is interpreted as a strong right. It will result in the exclusion of evidence even if that evidence is not the 'sole or decisive' element of the State's case, and there is no question of counterbalancing through rebuttal evidence. However, the right only applies to 'testimonial' evidence: broadly speaking, evidence given in contemplation that it might be used in a criminal prosecution. Thus in *Davis v Washington* statements made during an emergency call to the police, when the caller's mind would have been preoccupied with getting help, were admissible in the absence of the witness.[257] Further, the confrontation right can be forfeited by the defendant if, for example, he kills or frightens the witness with the intention of preventing her from testifying.[258] Strasbourg has hinted that it would recognize some sort of forfeiture doctrine.[259]

On the current Strasbourg jurisprudence, it is not clear whether the ECtHR views the European confrontation right as being, in whole or in part, dignitarian. The concerns expressed in *Al-Khawaja* are mainly focused on the ability of the defence to demonstrate the unreliability of the evidence. We do not know how Strasbourg would respond to a case where the disputed testimony is 'obviously reliable'—whether it would still insist on confrontation. But it is true that the dignitarian case for confrontation is not an easy one to make; the cases where there is intuitively the strongest case for confrontation—'testimonial' cases, in the US terminology—are usually ones where there are also reliability concerns, and it may be this that drives the feeling that confrontation is such an important right. If we rule out a dignitarian basis for confrontation, then the Court of Appeal's argument of principle in *Horncastle* appears plausible. However, although it gives various examples of hearsay evidence which is both reliable and decisive, the examples are problematic: they tend either not to involve

---

[253] For analysis, and comparison with the ECHR approach, see R, Friedman, 'The Confrontation Right Across the Systemic Divide' in J. Jackson, M. Langer and P. Tillers (eds), *Crime, Procedure and Evidence in a Comparative and International Context* (2008).

[254] 541 US 36 (2004).   [255] *Ibid.*, 62.   [256] 487 US 1012 (1988), 1017.

[257] 547 US 813 (2006).   [258] *Giles v California* 554 US __ (2008).

[259] See *Al-Khawaja*, above n 249, [37].

'testimonial' statements, and thus not to make the strongest case for confrontation,[260] or to be underdescribed. Examples of testimonial hearsay evidence that could convict a defendant standing alone are probably very rare. The more significant part of the Court of Appeal's argument is that counterbalancing factors can justify the admission of decisive hearsay by providing some equivalent of cross-examination. And here, there is a good argument for admissibility on the facts of *Al-Khawaja*. There, the victim's death does not raise suspicions about the motive for the witness not wanting to face the defendant in court (as might be present in a case of a witness who refuses to attend court, as in *Tahery*), and was not foreseeable, so the prosecution could not have been expected to arrange some sort of confrontation prior to trial.[261] Further, the evidence in the case allowed some checking for consistency, providing an—albeit very approximate—substitute for cross-examination, and some reassurance that the evidence was not moulded by the police[262] (the victim had initially complained spontaneously to a neighbour).

The cases discussed so far involve the defence being unable to question a prosecution witness. The Strasbourg case law also deals with the situation where the defence can question a witness, but is handicapped by not knowing the identity of the witness. Anonymity may seriously limit the ability to cross examine: often the defence will not be able to explore potential reasons for giving false testimony. Genuine confrontation—the ability to examine the witness—may be lost. In various cases the English courts have allowed witnesses to testify anonymously, shielding their identity by allowing them to give evidence from behind a screen. In a welcome change from the usual minimalist response to Convention rights, in *R v Davis* the House of Lords held that in the absence of legislative authority this practice was not permissible;[263] indeed, the House of Lords admonished the Court of Appeal for giving too little weight to rights and resorting too readily to a process of balancing.[264] Davis had been 'gravely impeded'[265] in his cross-examination of witnesses: his defence was that the witnesses who identified him were part of a conspiracy led by an embittered ex-girlfriend, but in court he could not even be sure which of the witnesses was the ex-girlfriend and so could not question her effectively.

It is clear that the use of anonymous witnesses is permissible under the ECHR, but Strasbourg requires that certain conditions are met. Significantly, the case law

---

[260] There is some suggestion in the Strasbourg case law that something like the 'testimonial' requirement may operate before the confrontation right is triggered: see *X v United Kingdom* (1992) 15 EHRR CD 113, finding an application 'manifestly ill-founded' where the complaint was against the use of anonymous witnesses whose evidence did not 'implicate' the defendant, but provided evidence of the background to events.

[261] Contrast the facts of *R v Cole, R v Keet* [2008] 1 Cr App R 5, where the slow onset of dementia might have afforded this opportunity.

[262] A concern in some of the confrontation literature: W. O'Brien, 'The Right of Confrontation: US and European Perspectives' (2005) 121 *LQR* 481.

[263] [2008] UKHL 38.   [264] *Ibid.*, [16], [34].   [265] *Ibid.*, [32].

recognizes that there is a need to balance the rights of defendants and witnesses in this area, stating in *Doorson v The Netherlands*:

'It is true that Article 6 does not explicitly require the interests of witnesses in general, and those of victims called upon to testify in particular, to be taken into consideration. However, their life, liberty or security of person may be at stake, as may interests coming generally within the ambit of Article 8 of the Convention. Such interests of witnesses and victims are in principle protected by other, substantive provisions of the Convention, which imply that Contracting States should organise their criminal proceedings in such a way that those interests are not unjustifiably imperilled. Against this background, principles of fair trial also require that in appropriate cases the interests of the defence are balanced against those of witnesses or victims called upon to testify.'[266]

In *Doorson* itself the Court found that there had been no breach of Article 6. There were counterbalancing factors in place, in that the defence was able to point to factors undermining the credibility of the anonymous witnesses, and their evidence was not the 'sole or decisive' basis for conviction. As with absent witnesses, the 'sole or decisive' criterion appears significant: 'it should be recalled that, even when 'counterbalancing' procedures are found to compensate sufficiently the handicaps under which the defence labours, a conviction should not be based either solely or to a decisive extent on anonymous statements'.[267]

The Government quickly responded to *Davis* by passing emergency legislation. The Criminal Evidence (Witness Anonymity) Act 2008 permitted witnesses to give evidence anonymously, subject to various conditions. The Act is now replaced by provisions in the Coroners and Justice Act 2009, but there is little change to the initial provisions. The legislation lays down three conditions for anonymity:[268] (a) anonymity must be necessary to protect a person or prevent serious damage to property or 'real harm' to the public interest; (b) anonymity must be consistent with a fair trial for the defendant; (c) anonymity must be in the interests of justice because the witness's testimony is important and she would not testify otherwise. The Act goes on to specify various considerations to be taken into account when assessing whether (a)–(c) are satisfied.[269] These include the defendant's right to know the identity of a witness; the extent to which the witness's credibility will be an issue; whether the witness's evidence can be tested under anonymity; and whether the witness's evidence might be the sole or decisive evidence implicating the defendant. Anonymity orders have been made in a significant number of trials. According to the CPS, 129 applications for witness anonymity were granted between the legislation coming into force in July 2008 and December of that year (this would have involved a smaller number of trials, as many trials would involve multiple anonymous witnesses).[270]

---

[266] (1996) 22 EHRR 330, [70].   [267] *Ibid.*, [76].   [268] Section 88.   [269] Section 89.
[270] Human Rights Joint Committee, *Eighth Report 2008–9 (Legislative Scrutiny: Coroners and Justice Bill)*, para 1.119.

The original legislation was given detailed consideration by the Court of Appeal in *R v Mayers*.[271] The court made various significant points, for example noting the crucial importance of prosecution investigation and disclosure in order to give the defence as full a basis as possible for cross-examination. It considered alternative measures to protect witnesses, but noted that protections such as witness relocation constitute a 'tumultuous' interference with a witness's life, as well as with that of their family.[272] It found that the witness's fear need not be caused by he defendant. In one of the cases in this conjoined appeal it put considerable weight on the fact that the victim had been attacked in public, in full view of onlookers, and found that this would give a sound basis for the witnesses to be afraid of the consequences of testifying without anonymity.[273] In two of the four cases the Court of Appeal concluded that the defendants had received a fair trial. But in one the conviction was quashed because there were doubts about the credibility of the witness, and the available evidence did not allow a proper opportunity for her evidence to be tested. In another it held that there is no provision for anonymous hearsay, i.e. for an anonymous witness statement to be presented in court.

Most significantly, perhaps, *Mayers* confirms what is implicit in the legislation: that whether the evidence of an anonymous witness is the sole or decisive evidence is only a factor to be considered when making an anonymity order. If anonymous evidence is the mainstay of the prosecution case, that will not prevent an order being made, nor render the trial unfair.[274] Moreover, when considering whether anonymous evidence is sole or decisive, it appears that each witness is to be considered individually: if there is more than one anonymous witness then anonymous evidence is not sole or decisive.[275] This does not seem to be the way Strasbourg interprets the test. A key question about anonymity orders, then, is whether they will survive challenge in Europe. While, as noted above, *Doorson* states that anonymous evidence cannot be the decisive basis for conviction, Lord Mance in *Davis* noted that Strasbourg has never been confronted with a test case on this issue: where a trial has been found to be unfair this has usually been because of multiple problems. There is a good argument here that sole or decisive should not be a strict criterion. One of the cases in *Mayers* involved undercover police officers who had made several visits to a nightclub in order to test whether drugs could be bought. They were allowed to give evidence anonymously, on the grounds that revealing their identities would make them ineffective as undercover workers. As the Court of Appeal noted, in this situation knowing the identity of the officers, who are unlikely to have a personal grudge against the defendant, is probably not crucial to effective cross-examination. But in other cases, there must be considerable doubt as to whether a conviction on the basis of a single anonymous witness could be fair.

---

[271] [2009] 1 Cr App R 30.   [272] *Ibid.*, [9].   [273] See also *R v Powar* [2009] EWCA Crim 594.
[274] Above n 271, [23].   [275] *Ibid.*, [25], [75].

FURTHER READING

DUFF A. et al, *The Trial on Trial Volume 3: Towards a Normative Theory of the Criminal Trial*, Oxford: Hart Publishing, 2007, esp Ch 8 on the exclusion of improperly obtained evidence.

REDMAYNE, M., 'Theorizing the Criminal Trial' (2009) 12 *New Crim LR* 287.

ABRAMSON, J., *We the Jury: The Jury System and the Ideal of Democracy*, New York: Basic Books, 1994.

O'BRIEN, W., 'The Right of Confrontation: US and European Perspectives' (2005) 121 *LQR* 481.

Questions for Discussion

1. How should we decide which cases should be tried by jury? If it is accepted that jury trial is appropriate in some cases, should there be exceptions to the principle that jurors are selected at random?

2. What is the rule in *Galbraith*? Is it appropriate?

3. When, if ever, should improperly obtained evidence be excluded from a criminal trial?

4. Should defendants have an absolute right to confront the witnesses against them? If not, what exceptions should there be?

12

APPEALS

The appeals system serves many purposes. From the legal system's point of view, perhaps the most important purpose is the development and clarification of the law. A common law system could hardly exist unless appeals offered a means of reviewing the law. In performing this role, appeals allow the higher courts to exert some control over the lower courts. These are important functions of appeals and add much to an understanding of the forces shaping the appeals system. We can also consider appeals from the point of view of litigants, for whom appeals offer a chance to challenge a result they are unhappy with. Such challenges have provided the criminal justice system with some of its most memorable images: the photographs of victims of long-running miscarriages of justice, such as the 'Guildford Four' and the 'Birmingham Six', celebrating their freedom on the steps of the Court of Appeal have a dramatic resonance. However, like much media coverage of the criminal justice system, such images, if taken to be representative of what the appeals system is all about, are apt to mislead. For one thing, it is not only the Court of Appeal that hears criminal appeals. Further, while the criminal appeals system does play an important role in securing the acquittal of those who dispute the facts on which they were found guilty, the majority of appeals do not revolve around questions of fact. Most appeals involve legal issues. The legal issues vary: in a large number of appeals the question is solely about whether the sentence given by the court was correct.[1] Other appeals involve questions about the criminal law: whether, for example, the court applied the correct definition of some legal concept such as 'intention'. We will not consider such appeals in this chapter. The focus will be on the atypical, but important, appeals on questions of fact. We will also look at some appeals on questions of law, but only where the legal questions involve the defendant's procedural rights. These 'due process appeals' have given rise to difficult questions about when the courts should quash the convictions of the factually guilty. These appeals might be said to perform a third function of the appeals system. As we saw in the previous chapter, the criminal courts offer an opportunity to review, and on occasion to condemn, executive action, and this scrutiny is at its most prominent in appeal courts.

---

[1] In 2008 the Court of Appeal heard 2,094 sentence appeals and 438 conviction appeals: *Judicial Statistics 2008*, Table 1.7.

Before moving on to consider these issues, it will be helpful to offer a brief overall sketch of the criminal appeals system. As well as the distinctions just mentioned, there is also a difference in the way prosecution and defence appeals are treated by the system: in general, prosecution appeals are more restricted than defence appeals, albeit that recent reforms have diminished this distinction. Bearing this in mind, both prosecution and defence have rights of appeal from decisions of the magistrates' courts. The defence can appeal on questions of fact; here, appeal is to the Crown Court, which hears the appeal as a specially constituted panel of two judges sitting with a magistrate. This type of criminal appeal is unique in that it involves a rehearing of the case: the witnesses will be heard again, and their evidence assessed afresh. In most other appeals the court will hear argument from the parties, but it is rare for an appeal court to hear evidence from witnesses. Both prosecution and defence are also able to appeal from the magistrates' court on questions of law. Here, appeal is by way of 'case stated' to the Administrative Court, a division of the High Court. The magistrates are asked to supply a statement of the facts of the case as they have found them, as well as their legal conclusions; this will provide the basis on which the court hears the appeal. Both parties are also able to challenge the magistrates' decision on legal grounds by way of judicial review;[2] these appeals are again heard by the Administrative Court. From the Administrative Court, further appeal is possible to the House of Lords: leave will only be granted for points of law of general public importance. The Administrative Court also hears appeals from the Crown Court when it sits as a court of appeal for appeals from the magistrates' court; these appeals may be by way of case stated or by judicial review.[3]

From the Crown Court as a court of first instance, a defendant is able to appeal against a finding of guilt on grounds of either fact or law. Appeal is to the Court of Appeal, from where either party may appeal to the House of Lords. The prosecution has fewer appeal rights. Since 1987, it has been able to appeal certain pre-trial rulings to the Court of Appeal; this jurisdiction was originally confined to serious fraud cases, but was enlarged in 1996 to include all lengthy or complex cases.[4] The Criminal Justice Act 2003 now allows prosecution appeals on rulings made by the judge during the trial; if the prosecution is not successful in the Court of Appeal the effect will often be the acquittal of the defendant. These prosecution appeals involve points of law. Until recently, the situation was that the prosecution was not able to appeal against an acquittal in the Crown Court.[5] One (so far unused) exception to this rule

[2] The judicial review procedure would occasionally allow a decision of fact to be challenged, where the magistrates can be shown to have drawn an unreasonable conclusion.

[3] The Law Commission has suggested that all appeals from the Crown Court should be to the Court of Appeal: *The High Court's Jurisdiction in Relation to Criminal Proceedings: A Consultation Paper* (2007).

[4] Under Criminal Justice Act 1987, s 9 and Criminal Procedure and Investigations Act 1996, ss 35–6. Section 309 of the Criminal Justice Act 2003 has added 'seriousness' to the criteria for appeal from preparatory hearings under the Criminal Procedure and Investigations Act 1996.

[5] The Attorney General is able to obtain a ruling on a point of law arising in a case in which the defendant was acquitted, but this is not a true appeal as the defendant's acquittal is unaffected. The power is found in the Criminal Justice Act 1972, s 36.

was introduced in 1996, when the prosecution was given the power to challenge an acquittal that was tainted by, for example, threats of violence to jurors or witnesses.[6] In 2003 the Criminal Justice Act took things further, allowing appeals against acquittals in serious cases where significant new evidence of guilt emerges after the trial. With both these exceptions to the 'double jeopardy' principle there is a fairly complex process designed to ensure that an acquittal is not too easily challenged.

12.1 RESTRICTIONS ON APPEAL RIGHTS

The foregoing sketch is one-dimensional in that it illustrates the various avenues of appeal but says nothing about the conditions for appeal. A very important aspect of the appeal process is the way in which appeals are restricted and discouraged. All appeals from the Crown Court sitting as a court of first instance involve some sort of leave, either from the trial judge or from the Court of Appeal itself. This important filtering exercise will be discussed further below. Where the prosecution is concerned we have already seen that appeal rights are on the whole less generous. Although the Criminal Justice Act (CJA) 2003 extends prosecution appeal rights by allowing interlocutory appeals from legal rulings by a Crown Court judge, prosecutors may well be discouraged from exercising this right by the possibility that, if they lose the appeal, the defendant will be acquitted.[7] Where defendants are concerned, there are also disincentives. For example, in the magistrates' court the appeal avenue to the Divisional Court by way of case stated or as an application for judicial review will generally only allow parties to appeal questions of law. A defendant who contends that the magistrates have made a factual mistake can appeal to the Crown Court. Although this right of appeal initially looks to be generous—the defendant does not need leave to appeal—there is a disincentive in that the Crown Court can increase his sentence. According to Pattenden, the power to increase sentence 'is not used very often'; however 'this fact is probably not well known'.[8] The power may well dissuade defendants from exercising their right of appeal; indeed, some commentators suspect that it exists partly for this purpose.[9] Another restriction on appeal to the Crown Court is that the right can only be exercised by those who have pleaded not guilty.[10] As we saw in Chapter 10, the vast majority of convictions at summary trial are achieved by way of guilty plea. This might not be troubling were it not for the fact that the guilty plea is not always a reliable

---

[6] Criminal Procedure and Investigations Act 1996, s 54.

[7] Though in this respect contrast ss 58 and 62 of the CJA 2003. These provisions are discussed in more detail below.

[8] R. Pattenden, *English Criminal Appeals 1844–1994* (1996), 219. Cf *R v St Albans Crown Court, ex p Cinnamond* [1981] 2 WLR 681, where a period of driving disqualification was increased from three to 18 months.

[9] *Ibid.*; J. Sprack, *Emmins on Criminal Procedure* (9th ed, 2002), 458.

[10] Magistrates' Courts Act 1980, s 108.

indicator of guilt. The Crown Court has gone some way towards mitigating this rule by allowing a case where a guilty plea can be shown to be 'equivocal', or to have been made under duress, to be remitted to the magistrates for reconsideration. This, however, probably does not cover the situation where a defendant has pleaded guilty for a tactical reason (for example, because he thought his case was weak and he wanted to benefit from the sentence discount), or after 'forceful' persuasion from his lawyer which does not amount to duress.[11]

Turning to consider appeal to the Court of Appeal from trial in the Crown Court, we find a similar disincentive. Although the Court of Appeal does not have the power to increase sentence on a defence appeal, it can achieve something very similar. It may take several months for a defendant's appeal to be heard by the Court of Appeal. Many defendants will have spent this time in custody, and normally the time served in custody up to the failure of an appeal will be counted as part of their sentence. The Court of Appeal, however, has the power to rule that time served will not be subtracted from the sentence.[12] Effectively, then, the time served is treated as an additional punishment for defendants who are thought to be wasting the court's time. While it seems that this power was used rarely, the Court of Appeal has recently made clear that it will use it against applications that are considered to be without merit. The power appears to be being used more frequently, and in *R v Fortean* the court ordered 42 days loss of time, considerably longer than what seemed in practice to have been the limit of 28 days. It commented:

'This court is coping, with considerable effort, with over 6,000 applications each year for leave to appeal. It is anxious to deal promptly with those which raise properly arguable grounds of appeal, whether in the end they are successful or not. It is an important feature of this jurisdiction, unlike some others, that the trial process is concluded with sentence. An appeal is not built into the trial process but must be justified on properly arguable grounds. This also means that the sentence is operative pending appeal. That reinforces the need to attend promptly to those who have appeals of arguable substance. The court's ability to do that is significantly hampered by meritless applications such as the present.... We make it clear that this power may be exercised in *any* meritless application which should never have been pursued after due warning. That counsel or solicitors have associated themselves with such a renewal will be relevant, but it will not necessarily avoid such an order if there was no justification for continuing the case.'[13]

To bring the possibility of loss of time to the attention of prospective appellants, the judges who first consider whether to grant leave to appeal have started to indicate whether loss of time is likely if a rejected application for leave to appeal is renewed by the appellant. This has apparently had an impact on appeals against sentence (fewer applications are being renewed), though not yet on appeals against conviction.[14]

---

[11] 'Forceful' advice on plea is permitted under the Bar Code of Conduct. See the general discussion of guilty pleas in Ch 10.

[12] Criminal Appeal Act 1968, s 29.

[13] [2009] EWCA Crim 437, [10], [17]. See also *R v Hart* [2006] EWCA Crim 3239.

[14] Court of Appeal Criminal Division, *Review of the Legal Year 2007/2008*, para 10.3.

The loss of time rule and the power to increase sentence in the Crown Court are disturbing. Rather like the sentence discount for a guilty plea, their effect is to discourage defendants from pursuing their legal rights. As with the sentence discount, the justification for this is that such powers are necessary in order to prevent the courts from being overwhelmed by unmeritorious cases. In both areas this claim is difficult to assess: with the sentence discount there is some evidence to suggest that the flood of newly contested cases would not be that great.[15] With the loss of time rule, it appears that when the court's intention to use the power was announced in a Practice Direction,[16] the number of appeals was halved.[17] What cannot be known, of course, is how many meritorious appeals are deterred. While in *Fortean* the Court of Appeal justifies tougher use of the loss of time rule on the grounds that it is overwhelmed, the number of applications to it by defendants has been decreasing in the last ten years. Further, in the Court of Appeal the arguments are complicated by the system of leave to appeal. Leave offers a means of filtering out the weakest cases before they result in a full court hearing, and this might be thought to be a more rational way of dealing with the possible flood of appeals than the threat of extra punishment. Of course, even the initial filtering process requires judicial resources, which, by all indications, are stretched, but it is doubtful that the current system makes the best use of judicial resources.[18]

The loss of time rule has been challenged before the European Court of Human Rights (ECtHR). The Court held that the rule did not infringe Article 6 (fair trial) nor, more surprisingly, Article 5(1) (right to liberty and security of person). The exception in Article 5(1)(a), which allows 'lawful detention of a person after conviction by a competent court', was held to apply to the loss of time rule. This, it must be said, is puzzling. The ECtHR acknowledged that this exception does not permit just any lawful detention after conviction: there must be some rational connection between the conviction and the detention. Given that the time added to the sentence through the loss of time rule is not part of the punishment for the offence for which the defendant was convicted, it is not easy to see what this connection could be. The Court's explanation was that:

'Whilst the loss of time ordered by the Court of Appeal is not treated under domestic law as part of the applicants' sentences as such, it does form part of the period of detention which results from the overall sentencing procedure that follows conviction. As a matter of English law, a sentence of imprisonment passed by a Crown Court is to be served subject to any order which the Court of Appeal may, in the event of an unsuccessful application for leave to appeal, make as to loss of time.'[19]

The difficulty here is that this reasoning could be used to justify any further detention ordered after conviction: if, after an unsuccessful appeal, it was the practice of

[15] M. Tonry, *Punishment and Politics* (2004), 87.   [16] [1970] 1 All ER 119.
[17] See *Monnell and Morris v United Kingdom* (1988) 10 EHRR 205, 30.
[18] See J. Spencer, 'Does our Present Criminal Appeals System Make Sense?' [2006] *Crim LR* 677.
[19] *Ibid.*, 46.

the Court of Appeal to toss a coin as a means of deciding whether or not to double the appellant's sentence, this too could be said to be one of the conditions understood to be imposed by a Crown Court sentence. Subsequent decisions of the ECtHR have taken a rather tougher line to the use of detention as a means of controlling appeals processes, and the decision in *Monnell* might now be subject to rethinking.[20]

As has been pointed out, the requirement for leave to appeal is in principle a more rational way of dealing with the problem of a flood of appeals. The system works as follows. A convicted defendant needs to obtain leave before his appeal will be heard by the Court of Appeal. This can be obtained from the judge who tried him, but, as the appeal will often involve some criticism of the judge, it is more common for appellants to apply to the Court of Appeal for leave to appeal. When an application is made, it will first be considered by a single judge. If the application is unsuccessful at this stage, it can be renewed; the renewed application is considered by the 'full court': a panel of two or three judges sitting in open court. If leave to appeal is granted, the appeal proceeds to a full hearing by the Court of Appeal. Table 12.1 gives a breakdown of the success rate at the various stages of this process for appeals against conviction over the last five years. In proportional terms, in 2008 about 2.5 per cent of all those convicted in the Crown Court sought leave to appeal against their convictions. Thirteen per cent of applications for leave were granted by the single judge. Of the 87 per cent that were refused, around half (51 per cent) made a renewed application to the full court. On this renewed attempt to get leave, a third were successful. From the 1,588 original applications, this gives an overall success rate in obtaining leave of 23 per cent. Of the 438 appeals heard by the full court in 2008, 42 per cent were successful. Of the original 1,588 applicants, then, about 10 per cent would finally succeed in having their convictions quashed.

Table 12.1 Success rates for appeals against conviction

		2004	2005	2006	2007	2008
Applications for leave Received		1,782	1,661	1,596	1,508	1,588
Single judge	Leave granted	348	360	291	288	212
	Leave refused	1,187	1,111	843	881	774
Applications renewed to full court		545	557	481	520	400
	Leave granted	144	141	137	125	146
Appeal heard by full court	Appeal allowed	240	228	181	196	188

Source: Judicial and Court Statistics 2008

---

[20] B. Emmerson, A. Ashworth and A. Macdonald, *Human Rights and Criminal Justice* (2nd ed, 2007), 723–5.

It is not obvious what to make of these figures: there is no telling whether or not 10 per cent is a reasonable overall success rate. What is perhaps significant is that many who have their applications turned down by the single judge persist and have a reasonable chance of success on the renewed application to the full court. This suggests that the initial stage, where the application is considered by a single judge, is somewhat haphazard. Other evidence supports this. JUSTICE, a body with considerable experience of miscarriage of justice cases, suggests that the process 'is regarded as particularly susceptible to inconsistency'.[21] It provides the following anecdote about one appeal against sentence: a solicitor mistakenly sent in two sets of appeal papers in the same case. 'Two single judge decisions followed, one granting and one refusing leave. Both decisions had been made, at different times, by the same judge.'[22] In his review of the criminal courts, Lord Justice Auld drew attention to some of the problems with the system: the single judge is required to consider applications for leave 'out of normal court sitting hours and in addition to preparatory work for each day's sitting.... The norm is that they are done in the evenings, sometimes over the weekend and during vacation periods.'[23] It seems that the system is not properly resourced, and it is therefore not surprising that inconsistent decisions are made at the initial stage.

Returning to appeals from the magistrates' court to the Crown Court, it is worth looking at the available figures to see how they compare with those for the Court of Appeal. In 2008 the Crown Court heard 13,251 appeals against conviction: this represents about 1 per cent of all those found guilty in the magistrates' courts. In 39 per cent the appeal was allowed.[24] It is obvious that the rate of appeal is very low, and it is likely that some innocent defendants do not pursue an appeal.[25] This may in part be due to the fear of an increased sentence and perhaps also to poor legal advice, but it may also be due to defendants simply not perceiving it worthwhile to appeal against a conviction, especially if the punishment has been slight. Beyond these figures, and the inferences that can be drawn from them, little is known about the appellate process in the Crown Court. This remains an under-researched area of the criminal process.

12.2 CHALLENGING JURY VERDICTS

Our focus now turns to the Court of Appeal, where it will remain for the rest of the chapter. When the Royal Commission on Criminal Justice reported in 1993, considerable critical attention was focused on the Court of Appeal. The court was seen to have played a key role in the long-running miscarriage of justice cases that were finally

---

[21] *Remedying Miscarriages of Justice* (1994), 8.   [22] *Ibid.*
[23] Auld LJ, *Review of the Criminal Courts of England and Wales: Report* (2001), 639.
[24] *Judicial and Court Statistics 2008*, Table 6.10.
[25] See K. Malleson and S. Roberts, 'Streamlining and Clarifying the Appellate Process' [2002] *Crim LR* 272, 274.

rectified in the late 1980s and early 1990s. The Birmingham Six and Guildford Four had both had appeals dismissed by the court soon after their convictions; the Birmingham Six had also had a second appeal turned down in 1986. There was a widespread perception that the Court of Appeal had been unduly sceptical of claims of miscarriage of justice during the 1980s, and that some defendants had had their appeals dismissed unjustly.[26] Connected to this complaint that the court has been over-sceptical is a criticism that it has tended to show too much deference to jury verdicts, in other words, that the court is reluctant to interfere with a jury's decision to convict a defendant. There is a good deal of truth in the claim that the court shows considerable deference to the jury.[27] But, as Pattenden observes, the Court of Appeal is also reluctant to overturn findings of fact by a trial judge (as when a judge makes a preliminary finding of fact when making an admissibility decision).[28] Indeed, the Court of Appeal even shows considerable deference to its own previous decisions when a defendant appeals his conviction for a second time.[29] There seems to be a general reluctance to challenge the factual (as opposed to legal) decisions of criminal courts, whereas civil appeal courts play a more interventionist role. There are various possible reasons for the reluctance on the criminal side; some of these apply more to jury decisions than to the decisions of judges. First, the Court of Appeal is at a disadvantage in relation to the trial court. The trial court will have seen and heard the witnesses in the case, whereas the Court of Appeal will only have access to the transcript of the original trial. While the court may hear some live evidence, its role is restricted to that of reviewing the case, rather than rehearing it. Further, the jury does not give reasons for its decisions, thus the Court of Appeal lacks access to the precise reasons why the jury became convinced of the defendant's guilt. Secondly, the jury plays a crucial role in the criminal justice system, deciding whether or not defendants are guilty in the most serious contested cases. The criminal justice system puts considerable trust in the jury to make these decisions, as it does in judges to conduct trials properly. If the Court of Appeal interfered with trial verdicts too readily, it would put itself in the uncomfortable position of questioning the ability of trial courts to reach correct verdicts: it might be thought to be undermining the very system which it oversees. A third reason why the court may be reluctant to interfere with decisions of trial courts, and its own previous decisions, is finality: there is some value in seeing the verdict as an authoritative ruling on a disputed issue; this allows interested parties to get on with their lives with a clear view of what their legal position is. If verdicts are too readily overturned, then this sense of finality will be eroded. Finally, as we have already seen, the Court of Appeal is very conscious of the

---

[26] On the appeal of the Birmingham Six, see C. Mullin, *Error of Judgement* (1990), Chs 41–4. More generally, see J. Rozenberg, 'Miscarriages of Justice' in E. Stockdale and S. Casale, *Criminal Justice under Stress* (1992); A. Zuckerman, 'Miscarriage of Justice and Judicial Responsibility' [1991] *Crim LR* 492.

[27] This is made plain in *Pendleton* [2001] UKHL 66.

[28] R. Pattenden, 'The Standard of Review for Mistake of Fact in the Court of Appeal, Criminal Division' [2009] *Crim LR* 15.

[29] See *R v Stock* [2008] EWCA Crim 1862.

finite resources in the criminal justice system. If verdicts were overturned too readily, there might be more appeals.

It is not surprising, then, to find the Royal Commission on Criminal Justice commenting that:

'In its approach to the consideration of appeals against conviction, the Court of Appeal seems to us to have been too heavily influenced by the role of the jury in Crown Court trials. Ever since 1907, commentators have detected a reluctance on the part of the Court of Appeal to consider whether a jury has reached a wrong decision. This impression is underlined by research conducted on our behalf. This shows that most appeals are allowed on the basis of errors at the trial, usually in the judge's summing up. We are all of the opinion that the Court of Appeal should be readier to overturn jury verdicts than it has shown itself to be in the past.'[30]

In the aftermath of the Royal Commission's report, there were a number of changes to the appeals system. A new body, the Criminal Cases Review Commission, was established to take over the role of the Home Office in investigating miscarriages of justice and referring cases back to the Court of Appeal where defendants have exhausted their normal appeal rights. There were also modifications to the Criminal Appeal Act 1968, which governs the powers of the Court of Appeal. The Act now provides that the Court of Appeal 'shall allow an appeal against conviction if they think the conviction is unsafe' and shall 'dismiss such an appeal in any other case'.[31] The Act also made changes to the court's power to hear 'fresh' evidence. As noted above, the Court of Appeal is basically a court of review: it does not rehear cases. But sometimes new evidence will emerge after the conclusion of a trial, throwing doubt on the original verdict. Here, the question arises whether the Court of Appeal should hear such 'fresh' evidence. There is some concern that a defendant will simply fail to call important evidence at his initial trial, knowing that, should he be convicted, he will be able to challenge the verdict on appeal by revealing the evidence then. For this reason, the reception of fresh evidence is not automatic; the court will be very reluctant to admit it if it could have been adduced at the original trial. The Royal Commission criticized the Court of Appeal for being too reluctant to admit fresh evidence, and the Criminal Appeal Act now provides in s 23 that the court should hear fresh evidence where this is 'necessary or expedient in the interests of justice', having regard to a number of factors such as 'whether the evidence appears to the court to be capable of belief' and 'whether there is a reasonable explanation for failure to adduce the evidence' at the original trial.[32]

The legal framework described in the previous paragraph obviously leaves considerable discretion to the Court of Appeal. Before examining how the court approaches

---

[30] Royal Commission on Criminal Justice, *Report* (1993), 162.

[31] Criminal Appeal Act 1968, s 2(1). The amendments were introduced by the Criminal Appeal Act 1995.

[32] Criminal Appeal Act 1968, s 23. For recent decisions refusing to admit fresh evidence where it could have been presented at trial, see *R v Diamond* [2008] EWCA Crim 923; *R v Hill* [2008] EWCA Crim 76.

conviction appeals, one more aspect of its powers needs to be mentioned. If the court decides that a conviction is unsafe, that does not necessarily mean that the appellant will go free. Since 1964 the court has had the power to order a retrial.[33] Thus, if there remain doubts about the appellant's guilt, he can be retried by a new jury. This will not always be appropriate: there may have been such a lapse of time since the original trial that a retrial is no longer practical. In some cases, there will have been such media attention around the case that there will be doubts about the fairness of a new trial.[34] Currently, retrials are used with some frequency, being ordered in around 40 per cent of the appeals allowed in 2007 and 2008.[35]

As we have seen, the Royal Commission urged the Court of Appeal to overturn jury verdicts more readily. One way of trying to assess whether there has been any change in the court's attitude since 1993 is to look at the statistics. At this level, there has been little change. In the early 1990s, about a third of applications were granted leave to appeal. Once in front of the full court, about 43 per cent of appeals were allowed. Today, slightly fewer get leave (23 per cent), but there is a similar success rate once in front of the court.

When it comes to the introduction of fresh evidence, it again seems that the Court of Appeal's working practices have changed little. Roberts has replicated research carried out for the Royal Commission, by examining appeals heard by the court in 2002. She found that fresh evidence was a ground of appeal in slightly more cases than it had been in 1990: 23 grounds of appeal from 300 cases in 1990 involved fresh evidence, compared with 37 from 300 cases in 2002.[36] Given that all of these cases had passed the leave stage, it suggests that the court is, in some sense, being more receptive to fresh evidence (this issue is very hard to be precise about, because the court sometimes hears fresh evidence 'de bene esse', i.e. without specifying whether it passes the test in s 23, but may then declare the fresh evidence unconvincing). Against this, however, Roberts found that fresh evidence was a slightly less successful ground of appeal in 2002 than in 1990 (a 27 per cent success rate as compared to 35 per cent in 1990). Perhaps the court is hearing more fresh evidence but remains no more receptive to it as a ground for overturning a conviction.

It is obvious that an argument from fresh evidence is a relatively rare ground of appeal, making up only around 7 per cent of grounds. As the Royal Commission noted, appeals are far more likely to be successful where it is argued that a (legal) error was made at trial. It is especially difficult for a defendant to mount a successful appeal when he can point to no error at trial and has no fresh evidence. Such appeals are often referred to as 'lurking doubt' appeals.[37] The appellant is basically arguing that

---

[33] The history of this reform is described in R. Nobles and D. Schiff, *Understanding Miscarriages of Justice* (2000), 62–4.

[34] On the approach to this, see *Stone* [2001] *Crim LR* 465.

[35] *Judicial and Court Statistics 2008*, Table 1.7.

[36] S. Roberts, 'The Royal Commission on Criminal Justice and Factual Innocence' (2004) 1 *JUSTICE Journal* 86, 91. There was a general growth in the number of grounds of appeal.

[37] See L. Leigh, 'Lurking Doubt and the Safety of Convictions' [2006] *Crim LR* 809.

the jury made a mistake on the evidence as it was presented to it at trial, and here one would expect the court to be most sensitive about its role in relation to that of the jury. Roberts found this ground of appeal referred to in seven of the 300 appeals from 2002, and in only one of these was it successful.[38] We briefly discussed a case of this sort in Chapter 9. In R v B, the court quashed a conviction for sexual abuse which was alleged to have occurred some thirty years before the trial.[39] There was no reference either to lurking doubt or to the Criminal Appeal Act; the court simply justified its decision by referring to a 'residual discretion to set aside a conviction if we feel it is unsafe or unfair to allow it to stand.'[40] The ambivalence here (was the conviction unsafe or was the trial unfair?) indicates the difficulty lurking doubt cases can cause. If the prosecution case was demonstrably weak, then the appeal would not be a lurking doubt one but a challenge to the judge's (legal) decision to allow the trial to proceed after a submission of no case to answer.[41] In a lurking doubt case the court is invited to quash a conviction without, perhaps, being able to explain exactly why it is doing so. As the lurking doubt test is described in Cooper: 'the court must in the end ask itself a subjective question, whether we are content to let the matter stand as it is, or whether there is not some lurking doubt in our minds which makes us wonder whether an injustice has been done. This is a reaction which may not be based strictly on the evidence as such: it is a reaction which can be produced by the general feel of the case as the court experiences it'.[42] The lurking doubt test seems to push the court beyond its ability to justify its decision with reasons, and it is therefore not surprising that it is reluctant to resort to it. What may happen, however, is that a feeling of lurking doubt will make the Court of Appeal more ready to allow the appeal on some legal ground. This can be seen in R v B: 'unfair' hints at a legal ground for allowing the appeal, something rather more substantial than the court's unease about the conviction on purely factual grounds.

In a fresh evidence appeal, an appellant is on slightly firmer ground. His argument is not that the jury simply got it wrong, but that there is evidence, never heard by the jury, which makes the conviction unsafe. This raises the question of how the Court of Appeal should react to the fresh evidence. The issue was considered by the House of Lords in Pendleton.[43] The question is sometimes said to involve a choice between a 'jury impact' test, which considers whether the fresh evidence might have had an impact on the trial jury, and a test whereby the Court of Appeal concentrates on its own reaction to the evidence. The previous authority, Stafford, had rejected the jury impact test. The court, it was held, should not ask whether the new evidence might have made a difference to the jury, but come to it its own view of the significance and credibility of the evidence. It is not always easy to see the difference between these two approaches. The sort of difference the test might make is alluded to in Stafford, where it was noted that the appellant had 'urged that the court should recognise that reasonable men can come to different conclusions on contested issues of fact and

[38] Above n 36.   [39] [2003] EWCA Crim 319.   [40] Ibid., [27].
[41] Galbraith [1981] 1 WLR 1039, discussed in Ch 11.   [42] Cooper [1969] 1 QB 267, 271.
[43] [2001] UKHL 66.

that, although the court came to the conclusion that the fresh evidence raised no reasonable doubt as to the guilt of the accused, they should nonetheless quash the conviction if they thought that a jury might reasonably take a different view.[44] That there is an issue worth arguing about here is also hinted at by the Royal Commission, which contended that *Stafford* was open to criticism 'insofar as it concerns a decision by the court to hear and evaluate itself the fresh evidence and despite it to reject the appeal. In our view, once the court has decided to receive evidence that is relevant and capable of belief, and which could have altered the outcome of the case, it should quash the conviction and order a retrial unless that is not practicable or desirable.'[45] Presumably evidence can be capable of belief even if the court itself does not believe it. Under the Royal Commission's approach, it seems that the court would avoid taking a view on the credibility of a witness called to present fresh evidence (rather along the lines of *Galbraith*[46]). Where, however, a retrial is impracticable, the Commission thought that the only approach was to follow *Stafford*, and to allow the court to decide the issue for itself.

The simplest thing to say about *Pendleton* is that it rejects the criticisms of the Royal Commission and follows *Stafford*. The outcome is that the court should come to its own view of the safety of the conviction, and therefore the question of the practicality of a retrial does not arise until it is decided whether or not the conviction should be quashed. The appellant had argued that this approach undermined the role of the jury: only the jury impact test truly recognized the centrality of the jury in trial on indictment. The response of the House of Lords was that this got things the wrong way round: the real way to respect the jury was to be rather more reluctant to overturn its verdict. According to Lord Hobhouse, 'it is the appellant's argument which is unprincipled since it is he who is seeking to escape from the verdict of a jury merely upon the possibility ... that the jury might have returned a different verdict.'[47] Lord Hobhouse distanced himself from the jury impact test.[48] Lord Bingham's judgment, however, with which the other judges expressed agreement, is more equivocal. While endorsing *Stafford*, Lord Bingham suggested that the jury impact test might have some use:

'First, it reminds the Court of Appeal that it is not and should never become the primary decision-maker. Secondly, it reminds the Court of Appeal that it has an imperfect and incomplete understanding of the full processes which led the jury to convict. The Court of Appeal can make its assessment of the fresh evidence it has heard, but save in a clear case it is at a disadvantage in seeking to relate that evidence to the rest of the evidence which the jury heard. For these reasons it will usually be wise for the Court of Appeal, in a case of any difficulty, to test their own provisional view by asking whether the evidence, if given at the trial, might reasonably have affected the decision of the trial jury to convict. If it might, the conviction must be thought to be unsafe.'[49]

---

[44] *Stafford v Director of Public Prosecutions* [1973] 3 All ER 763, 765.   [45] Above n 30, 175.
[46] [1989] 1 WLR 1039; see discussion in Ch 11.   [47] Above n 43, [36].   [48] *Ibid.*, [32].
[49] *Ibid.*, [19].

Evidently, *Pendleton* leaves some uncertainty over the question of what approach should be taken to fresh evidence cases. It is therefore unsurprising to find varying approaches in the later Court of Appeal case law. One of the first cases to consider *Pendleton* was *Hakala*,[50] which associated itself with the more restrictive approach of Lord Hobhouse rather than the jury impact dicta of Lord Bingham. *Pendleton* was interpreted as simply confirming the decision in *Stafford*. But in other cases it has been said that after *Pendleton* the test is whether the jury would inevitably have convicted.[51] That view echoes the jury impact line, but lies in stark contrast to Auld LJ's statement in *Maloney* that: 'The issue is not whether the Court considers, in the light of the proposed fresh evidence, that a jury might conceivably have reached a different decision if it had heard it. So, ... the Court should beware against adopting, consciously or unconsciously, a train of thought that unless they can be certain the jury would have convicted had they heard the proffered fresh evidence, the conviction must be unsafe.'[52]

Pendleton was considered by the Privy Council in *Dial v Trinidad*. The majority judgment (with which, significantly, Lord Bingham agreed), stressed that *Pendleton* had decided that the Court of Appeal should take its own view of cases involving fresh evidence:

'Where fresh evidence is adduced on a criminal appeal it is for the Court of Appeal, assuming always that it accepts it, to evaluate its importance in the context of the remainder of the evidence in the case. If the court concludes that the fresh evidence raises no reasonable doubt as to the guilt of the accused it will dismiss the appeal. The primary question is for the court itself and is not what effect the fresh evidence would have had on the mind of the jury. That said, if the court regards the case as a difficult one, it may find it helpful to test its view "by asking whether the evidence, if given at the trial, might reasonably have affected the decision of the trial jury to convict".'[53]

Despite the decision in *Dial* (which the Lord Chief Justice has gone so far as to draw to the attention of the Criminal Cases Review Commission),[54] in the later Court of Appeal case law one can still find references to the proper test being the possible impact of the fresh evidence on the jury.[55]

One might wonder how much is at stake here. Commentators presume that the jury impact approach is more liberal, and more likely to result in a successful appeal, but the difference between the approaches can seem very thin: as it was put in *Pendleton*: 'If the Court has no reasonable doubt about the verdict, it follows that the Court does not

---

[50] [2002] EWCA Crim 730.

[51] See *Gray* [2003] EWCA 1001 at 13; *Ward* [2003] EWCA Crim 3191 at 9.

[52] [2003] EWCA Crim 1373, at 45.

[53] *Dial and Another v State of Trinidad and Tobago* [2005] UKPC 4, at [31], quoting *Pendleton*.

[54] See L. Elks, *Righting Miscarriages of Justice? Ten Years of the Criminal Cases Review Commission* (2008), 68–9.

[55] E.g. *R v Carter* [2009] EWCA Crim 1739; *R v F* [2008] EWCA Crim 2014; *R v Kennedy* [2007] EWCA Crim 3132.

think that the jury could have one; and, conversely, if the Court says that a jury might in the light of the new evidence have a reasonable doubt, that means that the Court has a reasonable doubt.'[56] There are, however, cases where *Pendleton* has been used to justify a decision which might not otherwise have been made. An appeal in *Mills and Poole* had been heard by the Court of Appeal in 1996 and dismissed. In 2002 the Criminal Cases Review Commission (CCRC) referred the case back to the court, giving as one of its reasons for doing so the recent decision in *Pendleton*. In considering the new appeal, which was allowed, *Pendleton* appears to have made the court particularly cautious about making its own judgements as to the credibility of witnesses.[57] In *R v Criminal Cases Review Commission, ex parte Farnell*,[58] an application for judicial review of a decision by the CCRC not to refer a case to the Court of Appeal was successful; *Pendleton* was again used to justify the decision. The case in question involved a claim of provocation. The Commission had expressed the view that the Court of Appeal was unlikely to find the defendant's actions excusable, but the High Court called attention to passages in *Pendleton* where the Court of Appeal was warned not to trespass on the jury's territory. It seems the Commission should have asked whether the Court of Appeal might find that *a jury* could consider Farnell's actions excusable.

This review of the Court of Appeal's case law in the aftermath of *Pendleton* might suggest that all is chaos. There is something to that view. Certainly the Court of Appeal, as well as the House of Lords, have found it difficult to explain how they approach fresh evidence. Beneath the conflicting dicta, however, there is probably a reasonable degree of consistency. Much depends on the overall strength of the case against a defendant. If the court has some doubt about the safety of the conviction, then, as in *Mills and Poole*, *Pendleton* may be used as a justification for allowing the appeal. Where there is less doubt, the court may feel no need to consider the jury's view of things. It may also feel able to decide for itself a reasonably self-contained issue, such as whether new expert evidence is convincing. But some appeals raise wider issues: in *Pendleton*, the defendant's defence had never been put before the jury, and in *Mills and Poole* there were questions about several aspects of the prosecution case. Here, the court is likely to be aware of its role as a court of review: it cannot easily make judgements about witnesses it has never seen, or about how new lines of defence affect the case as a whole. Reference to the jury's perspective is a means of explaining this difficulty. 'It all depends on the facts' is often an unsatisfactory way of summarizing a complex area of case law, but there is considerable truth in it here.

This leaves a question at a more conceptual level. The debate about *Stafford* and *Pendleton* is partly a theoretical one. Lord Devlin was highly critical of the decision in *Stafford* because he believed it undermined the role of the jury.[59] We saw earlier that the Royal Commission on Criminal Justice, too, thought the *Stafford* approach wrong. But, unless the wide use of retrials is advocated—and they will often be impractical

---

[56] Above n 43, [15].   [57] See *R v Mills and another (No 2)* [2004] 1 Cr App R 7 at 79, 83.

[58] [2003] EWHC 835.   [59] Devlin, *The Judge* (1979), 148–76.

or, worse, put an innocent defendant in jeopardy—it is hard to see how the Court of
Appeal deciding the case on its own view of the merits undermines the jury. The original jury cannot be asked for its opinion, so a decision has to be made somehow. The
argument might be that, because we do not know why the jury convicted, we should
presume that the fresh evidence might have made a difference. That seems to be an
argument that the defendant should be given the benefit of any doubt. But the law only
requires that defendants be given the benefit of reasonable doubt, and whether there
is a reasonable doubt is precisely the question the Court of Appeal, under *Stafford*
and *Dial*, should be asking itself. There is no reason of principle for adopting the jury
impact test; indeed, to adopt it on grounds of respect for the jury would seem to rule
out allowing appeals on the basis of lurking doubt when there is no new evidence, and
we would not advocate that. But where the jury impact test may be useful is in guarding against the sort of approach the Court of Appeal took to notorious cases such
as the Birmingham Six appeals, where it would do its best to explain away any flaw
revealed in the prosecution evidence.[60] In *Dial*, Lord Steyn ended his dissenting judgment with a rhetorical flourish, criticizing the judge who had upheld the defendants'
convictions: 'It is always important for a judge to bear in mind what Learned Hand J
in his famous address during the Second World War, in Central Park, New York City,
called the spirit of liberty. He said that the spirit of liberty is the spirit which is not too
sure that it is right. The need for such an approach is immeasurably increased where
the issue at stake is killing a man by the cruel and barbaric punishment of the death
penalty. This spirit is not evident in the judgment of de la Bastide CJ. Instead his judgment is expressed in certainties and absolutes with some questionable and speculative
assumptions in favour of the State.'[61]

When judging the performance of the Court of Appeal in the years since the Royal
Commission reported, the question whether the court is taking an unduly sceptical
attitude to fresh evidence seems the better one to ask then whether it should adopt a
jury impact or some other test. Whether the court is being too sceptical is very difficult to judge. The court might be criticized for building considerable flexibility into
its approach to appeals, flipping between *Dial* and *Pendleton* as it sees fit. But it is not
so easy to say whether this leads it to uphold convictions that it should not. However,
in at least one recent appeal there are signs of the court taking the sort of attitude
criticized by Lord Steyn. *Stock* involved a long running allegation of miscarriage of
justice.[62] Stock had been convicted of robbery in 1970. His case was considered by the
Court of Appeal for the fourth time in 2008, this being the second time that it had
been referred to the Court of Appeal by the Criminal Cases Review Commission. The
Court of Appeal put considerable weight on its earlier judgments, and on occasion

[60] See R. Nobles and D. Schiff, *Understanding Miscarriages of Justice* (2000), Ch 5.
[61] Above n 53, [64].
[62] [2008] EWCA Crim 1862. See also *R v Pinfold* [2009] EWCA Crim 2339, though there the Court of
Appeal's decision is perhaps less open to criticism.

indulged in some rather speculative interpretations of the evidence.[63] The fact that evidence relied on by the appellant involved events being recollected that took place a long time before was held against him.[64] Elks, a former member of the CCRC, suggests that the decision in *Stock* echoes the sort of attitude to miscarriages of justice evident in cases such as the Birmingham Six.[65] It would be too hasty to conclude that the Court of Appeal has slipped back to the dark days of the 1980s, but given its track record, its judgments in appeals against conviction require constant and critical scrutiny. *Stock* is a worrying sign.

12.3 DUE PROCESS APPEALS

In the previous section we concentrated on cases where the appellant's argument is basically that he is innocent, and that the jury came to a mistaken factual conclusion. In this section we discuss another type of appeal, where the defendant's principal contention is that there has been a failure of due process at trial and that, because of this, his conviction should be quashed whether or not he is guilty. Appeals of this type are dealt with under the same statutory framework as the 'fact' appeals considered above: in other words, the Court of Appeal should quash the conviction if it is 'unsafe'. This is a slightly strange test to apply to due process appeals. Before 1995, the test was in terms of whether the conviction was 'unsafe *or unsatisfactory*'. The new wording came about as a result of a recommendation of the Royal Commission and was intended to simplify the language of the statute. It was not intended to change the practice of the Court of Appeal which had previously been prepared to allow due process appeals.[66] In the event, however, the new test led to some uncertainty about the Court of Appeal's powers. The tensions in the case law reflect not just differing views on the statutory language, but also deeper matters of principle. The questions here are similar to ones we discussed in Chapter 11 when looking at the power of the courts to exclude illegally or improperly obtained evidence.

The issues are well illustrated by the facts and decision in *Chalkley and Jeffries*.[67] The defendants were charged with conspiracy to rob. The principal evidence against them was a tape recording of their conversations, which had been obtained by placing a bugging device in Chalkley's home after he had been arrested on a pretext. The trial judge refused to exclude this evidence, and this led the defendants to plead guilty. On appeal it was held that, even if the trial judge's ruling as to the admissibility of the evidence had been wrong, the convictions were not unsafe. One of the issues here concerns the effect of a guilty plea on an appeal against conviction. It was held that,

---

[63] *Ibid.*, [55]–[56].   [64] *Ibid.*, [46].   [65] L. Elks, *R v Stock* (2008) 9 *Archbold News* 3.

[66] J. Smith, 'The Criminal Appeal Act 1995: Appeals Against Conviction' [1995] *Crim LR* 920; D. Schiff and R. Nobles, 'Criminal Appeal Act 1995: The Semantics of Jurisdiction' (1996) 59 *MLR* 573.

[67] [1998] 2 Cr App R 79.

unless it could be shown that a mistaken decision by the judge left the accused with no alternative in law but to plead guilty, a guilty plea would normally preclude a successful appeal.[68] (The caveat—'normally'—is aimed at cases where a plea was made by mistake or without intention to admit the truth of the charge.) A further issue concerned the interpretation of the Criminal Appeal Act following the 1995 amendments. Auld LJ's conclusion was that: 'The Court has no power under the substituted section 2(1) to allow an appeal if it does not think the conviction unsafe but is dissatisfied in some way with what went on at the trial.'[69] Thus what we are here referring to as 'due process appeals' should, on Auld's view, no longer be allowed.

Chalkley, then, gives a simple answer to the question we are considering. However, other cases take a different view of the Court of Appeal's powers under the amended Criminal Appeal Act, and the consensus now seems to be that *Chalkley* was wrongly decided.[70] For example, in *Mullen* the Court of Appeal held that the defendant's trial had involved an abuse of process and that, whether or not he was guilty, his conviction should be quashed.[71] Similarly, in *Davis, Johnson and Rowe* it was recognized that: 'A conviction may be unsafe even where there is no doubt about guilt but the trial process has been "vitiated by serious unfairness…".'[72] There are many other dicta to like effect. But *Chalkley* is significant in that it highlights the tensions in this area, between respect for due process and the need for accurate verdicts.

It is accepted, then, that the Court of Appeal should allow due process appeals and that the Criminal Appeal Act permits it to do so. However, what is not clear is just when it should quash a conviction on due process grounds. What can be said with a good deal of certainty is that if the original trial was vitiated by an abuse of process, then an appeal will be successful. However, 'abuse of process' is a relatively narrow category. It covers cases where a defendant has been entrapped, where he has been prejudiced by undue delay between charge and trial, cases of disguised extradition (as in *Mullen*), situations where the prosecution has reneged on an agreement, and various other things. As we saw in Chapter 9, with the example of delay, the Court of Appeal is anxious to restrict the use of stays for abuse of process as far as possible, and they will only be available in cases where the prosecutor's conduct falls seriously below acceptable standards, as in the situations just described. This prompts the question: where a trial has been unfair in some way that does not amount to an abuse of process, should the defendant's conviction nevertheless be quashed? While statements such as the one made in *Davis*, quoted above, suggest that the answer to this question is 'yes', the case law has not yet made it clear just when unfairness short of abuse of process results in 'unsafety', nor is there agreement among commentators as to how this question should be answered.[73]

---

[68] *Ibid.*, 94. On the approach to guilty pleas, see further *R v Kelly and Connolly* [2003] EWCA Crim 2957.
[69] *Ibid.*, 98.   [70] *Hakala*, above n 50 at [5], states that *Chalkley* is not to be followed on this point.
[71] (1999) 2 Cr App R 143.
[72] [2001] 1 Cr App R 115, 132, quoting *Smith* (1999) 2 Cr App R 238.
[73] See I. Dennis, 'Fair Trials and Safe Convictions' (2003) 56 *CLP* 211; N. Taylor and D. Ormerod, 'Mind the Gap: Safety, Fairness and Moral Legitimacy' [2004] *Crim LR* 266.

A complicating factor here is Article 6 of the European Convention on Human Rights (ECHR), brought into English law by the Human Rights Act 1998. Article 6 guarantees the right to a fair trial, and the precise content of that right is determined largely by the judges in Strasbourg rather than by the English judiciary. This means that the Court of Appeal is no longer able to define trial fairness in such a way that its own conception of unfairness coincides with just those cases where it is prepared to quash a conviction irrespective of guilt. The Court of Appeal has, as it were, lost control of the definition of fairness. And, to complicate things further, the ECHR demands that a remedy be provided to anyone whose rights—including fair trial rights—are infringed.[74] An obvious remedy would be the quashing of a conviction. If this approach were taken, the concept of unsafety in the Criminal Appeal Act would be identical to the ECHR concept of fairness: whenever a trial was unfair under Article 6, the Court of Appeal would quash a defendant's conviction. At first sight, this is an attractive approach. The courts have flirted with it: in *Togher* it was said that 'if a defendant has been denied a fair trial, it will be almost inevitable that the conviction will be regarded as unsafe.'[75] In *R v A* it was said that the 'guarantee of a fair trial under Article 6 is absolute: a conviction obtained in breach of it cannot stand'.[76] But it is now clear that these observations are not good law. Even where an appellant has had a judgment in his favour from the European Court of Human Rights, establishing a breach of Article 6, the Court of Appeal will not necessarily find a conviction unsafe.[77] As noted, the Convention does require a remedy be given for a breach of Article 6, but the remedy need not be the quashing of a conviction: it can be an award of damages, a reduction in sentence, or merely an acknowledgment that a right has been breached.[78] However, it may be that such remedies will not always be a sufficient response to a breach of Article 6, or some other procedural right. Taylor and Ormerod suggest that using these remedies to respond to an Article 6 breach 'fails to elevate human rights to their proper status in the overall context in which decisions are to be made'.[79] On this view, the court should be prepared to quash some convictions gained in breach of Article 6 even if the defendant is plainly guilty. This brings us back to the question asked earlier: in which cases should this occur?

It will be obvious that what is at stake in due process appeals is very similar to the issues surrounding the exclusion of illegally and improperly obtained evidence. In both contexts there is a tension between the role of the courts as fact-finders, and their role in upholding the moral integrity of the criminal process. We will not revisit all the issues discussed in Chapter 11; suffice it to say that in developing a framework for considering when unfair convictions should be quashed and when upheld we are not attracted

---

[74] ECHR, Art. 13.   [75] *R v Togher and others* [2001] 3 All ER 463, 33.

[76] [2002] 1 AC 45, 25.

[77] *R v Lewis* [2005] EWCA Crim 859; *Dowsett v Criminal Cases Review Commission* [2007] EWHC 1923 (Admin).

[78] Dennis, above n 73; Emmerson, Ashworth and Macdonald, above n 20, 17, 36–8.

[79] Above n 73, 279.

by solutions which put significant weight on such vague concepts as legitimacy and moral integrity, unless more is said about exactly what these terms mean. Our approach would be the one we took to the exclusion of improperly obtained evidence: a protective, or remedial approach. Defendants should not be disadvantaged by breach of their rights. Where a conviction is gained via a breach of Article 6, therefore, that conviction should be held to be unsafe and quashed. Key here, as it was with improperly obtained evidence, is a causal question. The court will have to ask whether, if Article 6 had not been breached, the defendant would have been convicted. As before, this will sometimes prove difficult to answer. There will doubtless be a temptation to find, in cases where defendants have obviously committed serious crimes, that the Article 6 breach did not cause the conviction. In some cases a retrial will be possible, and that offers a way out of some of the more difficult dilemmas the court may face.

We doubt whether the explicit adoption of the remedial approach to breaches of Article 6 will greatly change the practice of the Court of Appeal. The most significant change would be in cases, such as *Chalkley* and *Togher*, where the defendant has pleaded guilty. The guilty plea in *Chalkley* was obviously caused by the judge's decision to admit the challenged evidence. Were this decision to be found in breach of Article 6, or to infringe the domestic conception of fairness under s 78, then on our account the conviction should be quashed. This would result in the factually guilty walking free, but if our commitment to fair trials is to mean anything, that is surely an appropriate outcome: it is what would have happened had the defendants' rights been respected in the first place. In *Togher* the decision is not so straightforward: there would be a difficult decision as to whether the undisclosed material, which went to the credibility of prosecution witnesses, might have caused the jury to acquit. If it might have, the conviction would, on our account, be unsafe. In *Togher*, unlike in *Chalkley*, a retrial would probably be a viable option.

If the remedial approach is an appropriate way of marking the gravity of Article 6 breaches, it is not so obvious that it provides a solution to all due process appeals. In *Clarke and McDaid* the House of Lords decided that the defendants' convictions should be quashed because of a technical error: the bill of indictment had not been signed by an officer of the court.[80] This decision raises slightly different issues to the ones we have been discussing so far. As a matter of statutory interpretation, it was held that the signature was an essential step for there to be a valid trial. The error did not disadvantage the defendants in any material sense; the trial would have proceeded to conviction in exactly the same way had the indictment been signed. It might therefore seem odd that the convictions were quashed. However, there is probably a class of procedural errors that should be seen as invalidating a conviction regardless of whether they disadvantage a defendant, as when a court simply has no jurisdiction: if a summary offence is tried in error by the Crown Court, for example.[81] Seen in

---

[80] [2008] UKHL 8.
[81] See J. Spencer, 'Quashing Convictions for Procedural Irregularities' [2007] *Crim LR* 835.

this light, *Clarke* might not be such a problematic decision. A further difficulty for our account is a case involving far more serious malpractice. In *Mullen*, the defendant had been illegally deported from Zimbabwe, in order to avoid proper extradition procedures.[82] It may be that he suffered no real disadvantage through this, in that he could have been deported through legal means, albeit in a more protracted process. In cases like *Mullen*, involving serious abuse of power by the executive, the conviction should still be quashed. As we noted in our discussion of the exclusion of improperly obtained evidence, legitimacy must play some role in decisions to exclude evidence and to stay proceedings for abuse of process, and here it provides one explanation for why Mullen's conviction should have been quashed.

For those who think that the courts should never acquit those who have committed serious crimes (Mullen was convicted of conspiracy to cause explosions), *Mullen* is a controversial decision. This was certainly the Government's view, and in 2006 it published a 'consultation' paper (on which views were only canvassed on *how*, not whether, to change the law), proposing to prevent the Court of Appeal from quashing convictions in cases where defendants are plainly guilty.[83] The proposals were widely condemned by the legal establishment,[84] and a modified provision was included in the Criminal Justice and Immigration Bill. This would have specified that a conviction is not unsafe where there is no reasonable doubt about guilt, with a proviso that an appeal could be allowed if it would 'seriously undermine the proper administration of justice to allow the conviction to stand'. This probably did little more than state the position the Court of Appeal had already come to (though it might have prevented the decision in *Clarke and McDaid*), but was still controversial. The Government dropped the provision in order to ensure passage of the rest of the Bill through Parliament.

12.4 POST-APPEAL REVIEW OF CONVICTIONS: THE CRIMINAL CASES REVIEW COMMISSION

Many defendants will find that their appeal is unsuccessful. Others will not appeal; after a certain time (28 days where appeals against conviction in the Crown Court are concerned), their right to appeal will lapse. In these situations, normal appeal rights have been exhausted. However, that is not quite an end to the matter. It is possible to have a conviction referred back to the Crown Court or Court of Appeal.[85] This may occur where, for example, new evidence emerges to throw doubt on the conviction. The system used to be that a decision on whether or not to refer a case back to the Court of Appeal was made by the Home Secretary, on advice from civil servants in

---

[82] [1999] 2 Cr App R 143.   [83] Home Office, *Quashing Convictions* (2006).
[84] See Elks, above n 54, 47–9.
[85] There also remains the possibility of a pardon. See Pattenden, above n 8, 378–84.

the Home Office.[86] In the wake of the Royal Commission on Criminal Justice, a new body was set up to take over this role. The Criminal Cases Review Commission started work in 1997.

The CCRC investigates claims of miscarriage of justice and refers cases back to the appropriate appeal court. Although the Commission's powers involve both magistrates' and Crown Court cases,[87] and challenges to sentence as well as verdicts, we here concentrate on the most common situation, where an application is made to have a conviction referred back to the Court of Appeal. The usual procedure is that an application will be made to the CCRC.[88] The Commission will consider whether the application is eligible: it may only exceptionally make a reference if the applicant did not appeal at the time of his original conviction, and many applications are rejected because the applicant did not.[89] If eligible, the application will be investigated. In some cases this can be done fairly rapidly, but others will involve considerable work. The Commission has the power to initiate police investigations. At the end of the process, a decision is made whether or not to refer a case to the Court of Appeal. If a preliminary decision is made not to make a referral, the applicant or his lawyer will usually be informed of the proposed reasons for non-referral and invited to comment. The Criminal Appeal Act 1995 sets out the criteria for making a referral, which should not be made unless 'the Commission consider that there is a real possibility that the conviction...would not be upheld'. The grounds on which the conviction would not be upheld must involve 'an argument, or evidence, not raised in the proceedings which led to it or any appeal or application for leave to appeal against it', unless there are exceptional circumstances.[90]

It is obvious that at the centre of the Commission's task is a predictive exercise. It should not make a referral just because it thinks there has been a miscarriage of justice, but only if it believes that the Court of Appeal may quash the conviction. Thus its decision must be informed by the Court of Appeal's working practices. The Criminal Appeal Act underlines this by requiring a new argument or evidence, but even without this provision something new would generally be needed, because that is what the Court of Appeal itself demands. The referral criteria have been discussed by the Divisional Court, in a case involving judicial review of a CCRC decision.[91] Significantly, the judgment was given by Lord Bingham, who was then Lord Chief Justice. The 'real possibility test' he explained, 'plainly denotes a contingency which in the Commission's judgment is more than an outside chance or bare possibility but

---

[86] See Pattenden, above n 8, Ch 10.

[87] Referrals of convictions in the magistrates' courts are rare. See K. Kerrigan. 'Miscarriages of Justice in the Magistrates Court: The Forgotten Power of the CCRC' [2006] *Crim LR* 143.

[88] For useful description of the CCRC's working methods, see D. Kyle, 'Correcting Miscarriages of Justice: The Role of the Criminal Cases Review Commission' (2004) 52 *Drake L Rev* 657.

[89] Criminal Appeal Act 1995, s 13. Criminal Cases Review Commission, *Annual Report 2002–2003*, 13: about a quarter of applications are found to be ineligible.

[90] Criminal Appeal Act 1995, s 13.

[91] *R v Criminal Cases Review Commission, ex p Pearson* [2000] 1 Cr App R 141.

which may be less than a probability or likelihood or racing certainty'.[92] In cases concerning fresh evidence, 'the Commission must ask itself a double question: do we consider that…there is a real possibility that the Court of Appeal will receive the fresh evidence? If so, do we consider that there is a real possibility that the Court of Appeal will not uphold the conviction?'[93] A little more guidance is available to the Commission in the form of statements made by the court itself in referral cases. The court has on occasion been critical of the Commission for referring to it cases which it regards as a waste of its time.[94] Less bluntly, the court has been prepared to give the Commission a lesson on the law, commenting in *Sharp*, a case that apparently came 'nowhere near' the criteria for the admissibility of fresh evidence, that 'had the Commission had its attention drawn to the authorities that we have set out in this judgment, which it does not appear to have had before it, it would have taken a very different view of Mr Sharp's application'.[95]

As will be obvious from the material already covered in this chapter, the Commission's predictive task is not an easy one. There is a fair degree of unpredictability in the Court of Appeal's approach to appeals, especially as regards the test to be applied in fresh evidence cases. Despite this, the Commission is reasonably good at predicting what the court will do: about 70 per cent of its referrals are successful.[96] As with many of the statistics in this chapter, there is no good way of judging whether this is too high, too low, or about right.[97] One can be reasonably sure, however, that were the success rate to fall far below 50 per cent the Court of Appeal, mindful of being 'burdened with a mass of hopeless appeals',[98] would use its criticisms of referrals to prompt a more careful approach from the Commission. Some think that the success rate indicates that the Commission is too conservative; unsurprisingly, the Commissioners themselves deny the criticism that the CCRC is a 'handmaid' of the Court of Appeal, adopting an uncritical approach to miscarriages of justice.[99] The decision to refer *Stock* to the Court of Appeal for a second time, a referral that involved criticism of the court's interpretation of the evidence in the previous referral, is some testament to the CCRC's independence. As for the Commission's case load, this is not negligible: since

---

[92] *Ibid.*, 149.   [93] *Ibid.*, 150.

[94] *R v Ellis* [2003] EWCA Crim 3930; *R v Gerald* [1999] *Crim LR* 315.

[95] [2003] EWCA Crim 3870 at 33. See also the criticism of the Commission at 26.

[96] Criminal Cases Review Commission, *Annual Report and Accounts 2008/09*, 4.

[97] The Commission view it as about right, but others think it too high: see Home Affairs Committee, *The Work of the Criminal Cases Review Commission, Oral and Written Evidence Tuesday 27 January 2004*, Q 27, 74; cf the Memorandum submitted to the Home Affairs Committee by the Criminal Appeal Lawyers Association. Similar criticisms of the CCRC for being too conservative appear in submissions to the more recent investigation by the Home Affairs Committee (HC 1703, 2005–6). See further R. Nobles and D. Schiff, 'The Criminal Cases Review Commission: Reporting Success?' (2001) 64 *MLR* 280.

[98] *Ex p Pearson*, above n 91, 149.

[99] See Kyle, above n 88; Elks, above n 54, 345–7; slightly more ambivalently, Jessell, 'Turning a Blind Eye' *The Guardian* 13 July 2004. An interesting perspective from a former member of the Scottish CCRC is P. Duff, 'Straddling Two Worlds: Reflections of a Retired Criminal Cases Review Commissioner' (2009) 72 *MLR* 693. On criticism of the CCRC and the test for referral to the Court of Appeal, see H. Quirk, 'Identifying Miscarriages of Justice: Why Innocence in the UK is Not the Answer' (2007) 70 *MLR* 759.

1997 it has considered in the region of 11,000 applications, and referred about 420 cases to the Court of Appeal (around 4 per cent).[100] It refers more cases to the Court of Appeal than the Home Office did.[101]

The CCRC appears to have a reputation for careful investigation and to do its job well.[102] While some have hoped that the Commission would come to play a vocal role in criminal justice debates, using its expertise to propose general lessons about the causes of miscarriages of justice, it has not found this easy. But some general lessons can be drawn from various comments by commissioners. It seems that allegations of police corruption and malpractice are now rare in the applications in it receives, only featuring in cases from the 1980s and earlier.[103] Kyle gives a useful flavour of the sort of case the CCRC now investigates:

'From the Commission's perspective, cases that result in referral tend to fall into two broad categories. The first is cases in which relevant new evidence appears, occasionally if rarely being wholly exculpatory, but more often being of a nature that, had it been heard by the jury, might reasonably have caused them to come to a different verdict. This includes cases, quite often encountered, in which new psychiatric evidence supports the argument that an applicant should have been convicted of manslaughter by reason of diminished responsibility or provocation, rather than murder. The second category, more closely aligned to the types of issues raised by applicants themselves, involves some flaw in the investigation, prosecution, or trial process not brought about by malice but rather, in plain terms, because someone has not done his or her job properly—and this may well be something to which the defence lawyers have contributed.'[104]

On a more detailed level, a memorandum from the CCRC, submitted to the Home Affairs Committee, identified the following problematic areas: (1) historic sex abuse cases, which often involve limited and old evidence. The trial judge can stop the trial as an abuse of process in some situations, but this happens rarely. (2) Rape and other sexual offences: 'Our experience, and that of the courts, does not support the proposition that complaints of rape or similar assaults are always reliable and truthful'. (3) Expert Evidence: in a small number of cases, there are doubts about the ability of the jury to cope with controversial issues. (4) Case to answer and abuse of process: 'Trial judges should be more vigorous in ruling that there is no case to answer or that the prosecution should be stopped as amounting to an abuse of process.'[105]

The CCRC has been one of the most positive additions to the criminal justice landscape in the last twenty years. It cannot be expected to perform miracles: its ability to correct miscarriages of justice is limited by the Court of Appeal's interpretation of

---

[100] CCRC, above n 96, 4.   [101] Nobles and Schiff, above n 97, 282–3.

[102] See A. James, N. Taylor and C. Walker, 'The Criminal Cases Review Commission: Economy, Effectiveness and Justice' [2000] *Crim LR* 140.

[103] See Kyle, above n 88, 672; Zellick, response to Q70, Home Affairs Committee (05/06), above n 97.

[104] Above n 88, 672.

[105] Memorandum to Home Affairs Committee, above n 97, para 3.1. The CCRC also notes the problems caused by the law of Homicide; reform of homicide is now underway, with a report from the Law Commission and reform of the partial defences in Part 2 of the Coroners and Justice Act 2009 .

its own powers. Its role is also limited by the budget it gets from central Government. In the early years it seems to have been underfunded.[106] The situation improved, but recent budget cuts have meant that the number of Commissioners has been reduced.[107] Administrative reforms have meant that it has still been able to reduce its case backlog and thus waiting times for review,[108] but it is crucial that it continues to receive adequate support from government.

12.5 PROSECUTION APPEALS

We saw above that the structure of the appeals process reveals a marked asymmetry between prosecution and defence appeal rights. Prosecutors have fewer opportunities to appeal than defendants. Where prosecutors do have appeal rights, as in the magistrates' court, these tend to be restricted so as to allow appeals on points of law, rather than challenges to fact-finding. Recently, however, the appeal rights of prosecutors have been extended: the Criminal Justice Act (CJA) 2003 gives the prosecution ways of challenging decisions as to points of law made by judges in the Crown Court. Most significantly, the same act allows the reopening of jury acquittals when they are challenged on factual grounds. The creation of this exception to the double jeopardy principle has been controversial. Even with these developments, however, the picture remains asymmetrical. In order to understand the law in this area, then, we need to begin by thinking about the reasons for this asymmetry.[109] Because double jeopardy raises particular issues of principle, we discuss it separately in the next section.

We want the courts to make good decisions: to find facts accurately, to interpret the law properly and apply it to the facts in an appropriate manner. In general, appeals offer a means of enhancing these values: the trial court's conclusions can be checked and reassessed. Where questions of law are concerned, the process also allows appeal courts to develop and clarify the law, for the benefit of all trial courts. There are reasons for restraining and filtering appeals: appeal courts cannot work effectively if overloaded, trial courts need to retain some independence, and there is value in coming to a final decision reasonably quickly. While nothing in this picture yet explains why we should want appeal rights to be asymmetrical, the last point mentioned—that there are reasons for restraining appeals—does point us towards an explanation. Because mistaken convictions are much more serious than mistaken acquittals, the need to rectify a mistaken conviction carries far more weight in overcoming the reasons for restraining appeals. Nevertheless, this insight does not provide a very clear picture of how an appeals process might be structured: it explains why we might find asymmetry in an appeals system, but does not *require* asymmetry. If, for example, we decided that

---

[106] James et al, above n 102, 145.   [107] Memorandum, above n 105.
[108] Annual Report, above n 96, 4.
[109] Cf L. Laudan, *Truth, Error and Criminal Law: An Essay in Legal Epistemology* (2006), Ch 8.

the restraint reasons were not very compelling, we might want to give prosecutors and defendants equal appeal rights. This position would be perfectly compatible with an acknowledgment that there are better reasons to permit defence appeals than prosecution appeals. There is, however, one further reason for asymmetry, which applies particularly to jury trial. Jury equity, or jury nullification, is the practice whereby a jury acquits a guilty defendant for reasons of principle. Jury equity is seen by some as being an important value in jury trial. Allowing appeals against jury acquittals might allow prosecutors to undermine jury equity.[110] This argument will not persuade everyone;[111] as we saw in Chapter 11, jury equity is controversial. There might also be some way of distinguishing nullification cases from others, and allowing appeals in the latter but not the former. Another argument that often emerges in the debates around appeals is that prosecution appeals should be avoided because they subject defendants to stress and uncertainty. While this point should not be overlooked, again it does not give us a very clear picture of how we should structure appeal rights. As a matter of practice, it is not taken to rule out all prosecution appeals. Even when a defendant appears to have secured a victory, as in having his acquittal quashed in the Court of Appeal, he may still face a retrial or further appeal to the House of Lords. Further, defence appeals too may impose stress and uncertainty on victims, or even on an 'alternative suspect' who may fear that, once the conviction is overturned, he will be prosecuted for the crime.[112]

It is not surprising, then, to find that the asymmetry in appeal rights is unstable, and that new avenues of prosecution appeal are being created. The foregoing discussion suggests that the best way to assess these changes is to examine them individually. The discussion here will focus on the issues in broad outline, rather than the technical detail. The Criminal Justice Act 2003 for the first time gives prosecutors rights of appeal during trial on indictment. Previous appeal rights, which themselves were recent creations, were restricted to preparatory hearings in serious and lengthy cases. Under s 58, the appeal can relate to any ruling made up to the start of the summing up, including a submission of no case to answer. However, the Act has found a practical way of restricting such appeals to rulings which severely affect the prosecution case. If the Court of Appeal confirms the judge's ruling, the outcome will be the acquittal of the defendant; the prosecution must also agree to the defendant's acquittal if it abandons the appeal or if leave is refused. As this implies, prosecution appeals, like defence appeals, require leave, either from the trial judge or the Court of Appeal. The Court of Appeal cannot allow the appeal just because it disagrees with the judge's exercise of a

---

[110] See P. Westen and R. Drubel, 'Towards a General Theory of Double Jeopardy' [1978] *Supreme Court Review* 81.

[111] See J. Spencer, above n 18, 687–8.

[112] As in the case of the murder of Wendy Sewell, for which Stephen Downing had his conviction quashed in 2001: see 'Guilty Secret of Town with Blood on its Hands' *The Observer* 11 February 2001; 'Bakewell Killer Hunt Reopens After 25 Years' *The Observer* 14 April 2002. Cf 'Cleared of Murder—But Still the Sole Suspect' *The Guardian* 28 February 2003.

discretion: the decision must be wrong in law or unreasonable.[113] A practical problem with allowing 'interlocutory' appeals—appeals during the course of a trial—is that proceedings will be suspended, creating delay and prolonging the defendant's stress. Provisions allow for the more urgent appeals to be expedited,[114] but in practice a jury, once empanelled, cannot be kept waiting for very long. The usual result of a successful prosecution appeal, then, will be that the Court of Appeal will order a retrial, but it may only do so if this is in the interests of justice.

A more wide-ranging power of appeal is to be found in s 62 of the Act, although this section is not yet in force and no implementation date has been set. Section 62 only applies to certain serious offences, such as rape, murder, robbery and arson.[115] It allows the prosecution to challenge any evidential ruling, and here an unsuccessful appeal does not result in acquittal. It would be unsatisfactory if the trial could be put on hold over just any ruling with which the prosecution disagrees—a decision not to allow an inference from silence, for example—and the act has a solution of sorts to this problem. The evidentiary ruling must 'significantly weaken' the prosecution case.

Section 58 has proved reasonably popular. There were 29 appeals under it in 2007–8.[116] The case law emphasizes that the only condition for an appeal under s 58 is whether the prosecution is prepared to agree to the defendant's acquittal should it be unsuccessful:[117] the ruling it challenges need not be one that significantly undermines its case, although this will usually be so in practice if the prosecution is prepared to give the acquittal undertaking. Further, the fact that s 62 refers to 'evidentiary' rulings does not mean that the prosecution cannot challenge a decision to exclude evidence under s 58.[118] Now that the width of s 58 has been recognized, it may be that there is little point in implementing s 62.

In principle, there is little to object to in these powers: widening prosecution appeal rights serves the ends of justice by allowing the scrutiny of the decisions of trial judges. It may also be of use in avoiding the situation where the law develops in a lopsided manner. If only defendants can appeal legal rulings, an anti-defendant bias in the application of the law may be prevented, but a pro-defendant bias may remain hidden. There have been some concerns about the new powers, however. The Law Commission, when reviewing this area of the law, was initially cautious about creating prosecution rights of appeal, and would not have allowed appeal against a successful submission of no case to answer.[119] It expressed the concern that the defence

---

[113] CJA 2003, s 67.   [114] CJA 2003, s 64.

[115] Schedule 4, Part 1 contains a list of around 30 serious offences.

[116] Court of Appeal Criminal Division, *Review of the Legal Year 2007/2008*, section 4.

[117] *R v R* [2007] EWCA Crim 370.

[118] *R v Y* [2008] EWCA Crim 10. Case management decisions can also be challenged: *R v C* [2007] EWCA Crim 2352.

[119] Law Commission, *Prosecution Appeals Against Judges' Rulings*, Consultation Paper No 158 (2000). This stance was modified in Law Commission, *Double Jeopardy and Prosecution Appeals*, Law Com No 267 (2001), in which it was proposed that appeals be allowed on the first, but not the second, limb of *Galbraith*

might be discouraged from making such a submission by the fear that, if successfully appealed, there would be a new trial and thus a loss of any tactical advantage gained during the original trial. This emphasis on tactical factors did not impress commentators.[120] The Commission also expressed some concern over equality of arms, noting that given that the defence has no interlocutory appeal rights, it might seem odd to provide the prosecution with them. One response to this is that prosecution interlocutory appeals are the equivalent of defence appeals after the jury verdict, which prosecutors do not possess; however, it may be questioned whether it is right to make defendants wait until they have been convicted before they can challenge a ruling which is obviously wrong.[121]

The principal objection to the new appeals in the Criminal Justice Act may well turn out to be practical. Dealing at the moment largely with defence appeals post-trial, we have seen that the Criminal Division of the Court of Appeal is stretched in terms of resources, and that this may affect the quality of decision making at the leave stage, and encourage loss of time orders. Prosecution appeals put further pressure on the court. Linked to this is the question of delay. Compared to its European counterparts, English criminal procedure has generally resolved criminal matters speedily. This is due partly, no doubt, to the 'concentrated' nature of criminal proceedings in this jurisdiction, with the key stage being the trial.[122] Interlocutory appeals are a threat to this tradition. The net result may well be defendants spending longer on remand, and in a state of uncertainty about the outcome of the proceedings against them.

Reform of criminal procedure rarely stands still for long. Now that we have prosecution appeals during the trial, attention may well turn to prosecution appeals post verdict, which might involve a challenge to the judge's directions to the jury on the substantive law. Indeed, if interlocutory appeals under ss 58 and 62 of the CJA come to disrupt trials by regularly throwing them into hiatus, it may well be argued that the appropriate place for those appeals is at the end of the trial. The Law Commission saw no case for post-verdict prosecution appeals,[123] but Lord Justice Auld did raise the question of the power to appeal 'perverse' jury verdicts (this turned out to be one of the most controversial proposals in his report).[124] Some jurisdictions—Canada is an example[125]—allow the prosecution to appeal points of law after a jury acquittal. Although such appeals raise difficult issues, they should not be ruled out of contemplation.

(i.e. on a decision whether there is no evidence to support part of the prosecution's case, but not on whether such evidence as there is, taken at its highest, is sufficient to convict).

[120] See R. Pattenden, 'Prosecution Appeals Against Judges' Rulings' [2000] *Crim LR* 971; I. Dennis, 'Prosecution Appeals and Retrial for Serious Offences' [2004] *Crim LR* 619.

[121] See Spencer, above n 18. It would, however, be difficult to find a way of limiting defence appeals: there is no obvious equivalent of the prosecution's acquittal undertaking.

[122] M. Damaška, *Evidence Law Adrift* (1997), Ch 3.

[123] Law Commission, above, n 119.   [124] Auld, above n 23, 636–7.

[125] See K. Roach, 'Canada' in C. Bradley, *Criminal Procedure: A Worldwide Study* (1999), 77.

12.6 DOUBLE JEOPARDY

The traditional double jeopardy principle meant that jury acquittals were final, as were acquittals by the magistrates once the appeals process was over. In addition, the principle protects defendants from retrial for an offence of which they have already been convicted. The law here involves some technical issues, because it needs to establish when a new charge is the 'same' as one for which the defendant has already stood trial.[126] In simple terms, if the new trial involves substantially the same facts as a prior one, the defendant will not be retried, either because he has a 'plea in bar' of trial or because the trial should be stayed as an abuse of process. We will not discuss these technical points; as before we concentrate on the arguments of principle.

In 1996 an exception to the double jeopardy principle was introduced, allowing an acquittal to be quashed and a new trial to take place in cases where the acquittal is found to be 'tainted' by the commission of an 'administration of justice offence involving interference with or intimidation of a juror or witness'.[127] This power has never been used.

The Criminal Justice Act 2003 goes much further. It creates a 'fresh evidence' exception to the double jeopardy principle.[128] The basic idea is that, where new evidence emerges throwing doubt on an acquittal, an application can be made to the Court of Appeal to quash the acquittal and order a new trial. The court should only do so if there is 'new and compelling' evidence.[129] 'New' is defined in terms of whether it was adduced in the proceedings resulting in the acquittal, and 'compelling' in terms of whether the evidence is substantial, reliable, and 'in the context of the outstanding issues [i.e. the issues in dispute at the trial], it appears highly probative of the case against the acquitted person'.[130] If this test is satisfied, the acquittal will not necessarily be quashed: first, an interests of justice test must be considered. The considerations here include whether a fair trial is possible (it may not be, owing to, for example, media coverage or delay), and 'whether it is likely that the new evidence would have been adduced in the earlier proceedings against the acquitted person but for a failure by an officer or by a prosecutor to act with due diligence or expedition.'[131] A very significant point about the power to quash acquittals is that it is retrospective: it applies to acquittals secured before the new power is implemented as well as those secured after implementation. The power is also restricted to a number of serious offences, including murder, manslaughter and serious sexual and drug offences.[132] New Zealand, and various Australian jurisdictions, have followed England's lead and introduced new evidence exceptions to the double jeopardy rule.[133]

---

[126] See *Connelly* [1964] AC 1254; *Beedie* [1998] QB 356 and, generally, A. Choo, *Abuse of Process and Judicial Stays of Criminal Proceedings* (2008), 21–56.
[127] Criminal Procedure and Investigations Act 1996, s 54.
[128] CJA 2003, Part 10. [129] CJA 2003, s 78. [130] CJA 2003, s 78(3)(c).
[131] CJA 2003, s 79(2)(c). [132] Schedule 5, Part 1 contains a list of 29 'qualifying offences'.
[133] Reform is also being considered in Scotland: Scottish Law Commission, *Discussion Paper on Double Jeopardy* (2009).

The first thing to say about the new double jeopardy provision is that, in the opinion of the Joint Committee on Human Rights, it probably conflicts with the UK's international human rights obligations.[134] The International Covenant on Civil and Political Rights (ICCPR) does not permit 'retrial' after an acquittal. In exceptional circumstances, however, 'reopening' of a trial will be acceptable. The distinction is that reopening would involve new evidence, not evidence that was available to the prosecutor at the original trial. The position under the ECHR is less clear: Article 4 of Protocol 7, which the UK has declared its intention to sign, permits a retrial on evidence of 'new or newly discovered' facts. It is not clear whether this would allow the use of evidence known to be available at the time of the first trial. While the provisions in the Criminal Justice Act allow the Court of Appeal to refuse to quash a conviction under the interests of justice test if the new and compelling evidence was originally available, as the Joint Committee argued, it does not appear acceptable to rely on discretion to protect human rights.

There are, of course, much deeper issues at stake here than whether or not the new law is compatible with the ICCPR. Reform of the law was controversial;[135] we need to ask whether any change to the double jeopardy provision can be justified. Put another way: what is the value of the double jeopardy principle? Most people would share the intuition that it is wrong for the State to have unlimited power to question acquittals. If a defendant is acquitted, the State should not be permitted to have another go, to see whether on the next occasion a conviction can be achieved. What is not so obvious, however, is exactly why this is regarded as wrong, nor whether there should be exceptions to the general principle. The intuition presumably has something to do with the importance of having limits on State power, but this idea needs a good deal of unpacking. The State is powerful in all sorts of ways. To pick one comparison which is particularly germane to the present discussion, there is no limitation on the number of times a person can be tried for different crimes. If a person is acquitted of burglary, there is nothing to stop the State from immediately charging him with burglary again, so long as the charge relates to a different burglary. In this way, a person's life could be made a constant misery by serial prosecution. It is true that where the new charge is for exactly the same crime, the prosecution will find it easier to bring the case: having established a case to answer once, it could easily put the defendant in genuine jeopardy of conviction again. But, especially when one bears in mind the possibility that the State can manufacture evidence, this distinction is not sufficiently absolute to rob the comparison of its force. In thinking abut double jeopardy, then, it is worth asking why we object to that rather than to serial jeopardy.

---

[134] Joint Committee on Human Rights, Eleventh Report 2002–3, *Criminal Justice Bill: Further Report*, 27–38.

[135] See in particular P. Roberts, 'Double Jeopardy Law Reform: A Criminal Justice Commentary' (2002) 65 *MLR* 393.

Some of the reasons given for the double jeopardy principle are not especially convincing.[136] It is true that, in general, repeated prosecution increases the risk of false
conviction.[137] However, this applies to serial jeopardy as much as to double jeopardy.
What is more, the risk can be controlled by devices such as the requirement for 'compelling' new evidence. It is also suggested that the new trial will cause distress to the
accused,[138] but we are prepared to accept such distress when ordering retrials after
successful appeals and, again, serial jeopardy surely causes equal distress. Finality is
perhaps a more promising value to draw on in order to support the double jeopardy
principle.[139] There is value to the parties, and to society as a whole, in accepting that a
contested issue has been resolved. We are prepared to put aside concerns about finality when there is evidence that an innocent person has been convicted, but this can
be seen to reflect the fact that, as explained above, the conviction of the innocent is a
much more serious wrong than acquittal of the guilty. While there is much to be said
for this explanation, it would not rule out the creation of exceptions to the double
jeopardy principle. Finality might sometimes be thought worth sacrificing in order to
secure the conviction of the guilty.

Ian Dennis has made much of this last point.[140] He cautiously supports the new
evidence exception to the double jeopardy principle, and justifies it by appeal to the
value of legitimacy, which he takes to be the controlling value of, if not the whole of
the criminal process, at least the trial. On his account, when new evidence emerges
to throw doubt on an acquittal, the verdict risks losing its legitimacy. Verdict legitimacy can be restored, however, by a new trial. The strength of Dennis's account is that
it recognizes that the criminal process does not exist just to protect the interests of
defendants. However, the key role that legitimacy plays here is at least questionable.
As we have observed before, legitimacy is a rather vague value. An opponent of double
jeopardy reform could as easily argue that the value of finality is such that it is never
appropriate to reopen an acquittal (while eschewing the language of legitimacy, this,
in effect, is Paul Roberts' argument against the reform).[141]

We think an argument for the double jeopardy principle can be put in slightly different terms than the ones explored so far. When the State invokes the machinery of
criminal process against a defendant, it puts him at risk of conviction; in some cases,
of false conviction. In order to have the moral authority to do this, the State should
consider its trial procedures to be generally reliable; to the extent that it thinks they
are not, it lacks the moral authority to use them to put people in jeopardy of conviction.[142] This suggests that the State is bound by the verdicts of its trial procedures; it is,

---

[136] For further discussion, see P. Roberts, 'Justice for All? Two Bad Arguments (and Several Good
Suggestions) for Resisting Double Jeopardy Reform' (2002) 6 *E & P* 197.

[137] Law Commission, *Double Jeopardy*, Consultation Paper No 156 (1999), 37.   [138] *Ibid.*, 37–8.

[139] *Ibid.*, 35–8.

[140] I. Dennis, 'Rethinking Double Jeopardy: Justice and Finality in Criminal Process' [2000] *Crim LR*
933; Dennis, above n 120.

[141] Above n 135.

[142] For something like this argument, see R. Nozick, *Anarchy, State and Utopia* (1974), 102–8.

we might say, estopped from calling them into question. To demand that a defendant face the jeopardy of conviction a second time is for the State to admit that its trial procedure is unreliable, and this undermines its authority to demand that the defendant stand trial again. This does not, of course, prevent defendants from calling a verdict into question: there is no inconsistency when this occurs.

We suggest that this account has some value in explaining the contours of the double jeopardy principle. The brief discussion of the ICCPR framework, above, implies that there is particular antipathy towards retrying an acquitted defendant by using evidence that was in the possession of the prosecution at the original trial. In this situation, the estoppel principle should bite with full force. Where new evidence emerges after the trial—by chance, as it were—there is perhaps an argument that things are different. The failure in the trial procedure might be said to be outside the State's responsibility. There is reason to be cautious about this argument: one can always imagine future technological breakthroughs that will give us new evidence, and in that sense trials will never be as reliable as they could be. Nevertheless, courts have to operate within the realm of present day possibility; the State should not be able to distance itself from trial verdicts by saying that things may be different in the future. In the same way, when new evidence does emerge to throw doubt on an acquittal, it might be argued that the State should not be able to revisit the acquittal.

We saw above that the initial exception to the double jeopardy principle in England and Wales was the 'tainted acquittal' procedure introduced by the Criminal Procedure and Investigations Act. On the account sketched above, this is none too objectionable. Where the trial process has been undermined in some way, especially by the defendant, it could be said that the State has less reason to be committed to the verdict. It is worth noting that the New Zealand Law Commission, which examined the double jeopardy rule around the time that the Law Commission for England and Wales was doing so, concluded that only an exception along the lines of the tainted acquittal procedure was acceptable.[143] Its proposals were in some ways narrower than the English provisions: the exception would only apply where the accused himself had tainted the acquittal. But in other respects they were wider: perjury at the original trial would be included among the administration of justice offences that can trigger reopening of the verdict. In terms of theoretical coherence, there is a lot to be said for reform along these lines. In the event, however, the New Zealand legislature adopted a reform which went further, creating a new evidence exception much like that in England and Wales.[144]

We hope that the account sketched here goes some way to capturing the basic value of the double jeopardy protection. We would not claim that it shows the Criminal Justice Act reforms to be unacceptable: things are rarely so neat when it comes to theoretical defences of supposedly fundamental principles. We hope, however, that it

---

[143] New Zealand Law Commission, Report 70, *Acquittal Following Perversion of the Course of Justice* (2001).

[144] Crimes Amendment Act (No 2) 2008, s 6.

underscores the sort of objection that can be made about the new law. In the final analysis, much must depend on how the new provisions are used in practice. Prosecutors
have now made a number of attempts to reopen acquittals, but the Court of Appeal
has been reasonably cautious about quashing acquittals. In two cases involving a co-
defendant who, on being convicted, offered to give evidence against his acquitted
co-accused, the court thought that the co-defendant's mixed motives (he might gain
favourable treatment by helping the authorities) meant that the new evidence could
not be classified as 'compelling'. In one of these cases, *R v G*, it suggested the new
evidence would have to meet a very high standard: it should be 'evidence which cannot realistically be disputed.' It observed that 'the exercise which we have undertaken
is quite different from the question which any jury might address if this former co-
accused were to be a witness, on any topic, whose evidence had to be considered. We
are not here to say whether his evidence might or might not properly be accepted; we
are addressing the considerably more exacting test of whether it is compelling in the
sense used by section 78.'[145] The court has also suggested that a test based on whether
an acquittal in the light of the new evidence would be 'perverse' is appropriate,[146] but
that is probably putting it too high. In *Andrews*, the case in which the 'perverse' standard was mentioned, a more accurate description of the evidence was that it was 'strong
supporting evidence...the evidence that the respondent was guilty of the rape...is
now significantly more powerful than it was. In our judgment if it had been available
at the first trial, or if it now were to be deployed at a second trial, the high probability is
that the respondent would have been or will be convicted.'[147] This was held to be sufficient to justify quashing the acquittal. In *R v Celaire*, a high probability of conviction
also seems to have been the standard applied.[148]

   While the Court of Appeal is currently applying a high standard to applications
to quash an acquittal, it is not so exacting that it might not apply to a large number of cases. As Hamer notes, the new evidence exception to the double jeopardy
rule may have a far wider field of application than many have thought.[149] Under a
'high probability of conviction' standard, it is quite possible that a good number
of convictions could be challenged on the basis of bad character evidence that has
been rendered admissible by the Criminal Justice Act 2003. As the boundaries of
the new evidence exception are still being established, it is difficult to tell just how
significant a reform it is. We have already seen the first media campaign to reopen
an acquittal.[150] It may be that in the near future acquittals will be seen as much less
final than they once were.

---

[145] *R v G* [2009] EWCA Crim 1207, [5]. See also *R v B* [2009] EWCA Crim 1036; *R v Miell* [2008] 1 WLR 627.
[146] *R v Andrews* [2008] EWCA Crim 2908, [28].   [147] *Ibid.*, 38.
[148] [2009] EWCA Crim 633.
[149] D. Hamer, 'The Expectation of Incorrect Acquittals and the "New and Compelling Evidence"
Exception to Double Jeopardy' [2009] *Crim LR* 63.
[150] See 'Should Wendell Wilberforce Baker be Tried Again for Rape?' *The Times* 28 July 2009, reporting
on a documentary, *Double Jeopardy*, broadcast on BBC1, 30 July 2009.

FURTHER READING

SPENCER, J., 'Does our Present Criminal Appeals System Make Sense?' [2006] *Crim LR* 677.

DENNIS, I., 'Prosecution Appeals and Retrial for Serious Offences' [2004] *Crim LR* 619.

QUIRK, H., 'Identifying Miscarriages of Justice: Why Innocence in the UK is Not the Answer' (2007) 70 *MLR* 759.

Questions for Discussion

1. What criteria should courts use to decide whether to quash a conviction?

2. With exceptions to double jeopardy and the ability to appeal pre-trial rulings, do prosecutors now have too many appeal rights?

13

CIVIL PREVENTIVE ORDERS

The focus of the preceding chapters has been on the process by which criminal cases are dealt with. In Chapters 6 and 7 we noted the possibility of diverting criminal cases from the formal criminal process, by means of an array of out-of-court disposals. Subsequent chapters have examined key stages in the process of cases that are prosecuted as criminal offences, including pre-trial remand, plea-bargaining, trial and appeal. However, one notable feature of the English legal system is the development over the last decade of civil preventive orders—orders that may be made by a court sitting as a civil court, orders that contain prohibitions created by the court as a response to conduct by the defendant, and orders the breach of which amounts to a criminal offence. It will therefore be seen that the civil preventive order involves a kind of hybrid or two-step process (first, the making of the order according to civil procedure, and secondly, criminal proceedings in the event of breach), and this has several implications for the criminal process and for the rights of defendants.

13.1 THE CORE OF CRIMINAL PROCEDURE

In Chapter 2 we noted that the European Convention on Human Rights declares that, before a person can be convicted of a criminal offence, that person is entitled to a fair trial with a range of procedural safeguards. It is significant that these rights are additional to those declared for civil trials. Thus, according to Article 6(1) of the Convention, defendants in civil and criminal trials are entitled to 'a fair and public hearing within a reasonable time by an independent and impartial tribunal.' But, according to Articles 6(2) and 6(3), defendants in criminal trials have additional rights including the presumption of innocence, the right to legal assistance and the right to confront witnesses; and, as we have seen, the Strasbourg Court has expanded that list of additional rights by recognizing certain rights (such as equality of arms, and the privilege against self-incrimination) as 'implied' into Article 6. The purpose of these additional safeguards is to provide fundamental guarantees against arbitrary State conduct and potential misuse of its authority, an authority that is considerable when the public censure of conviction and State punishment are at stake.[1] As Duff, Farmer, Marshall and Tadros have argued, the criminal trial is a process of considerable social importance, required to determine whether the accused should be held accountable and criminally liable for certain conduct, and in order to achieve this the State must establish the legitimacy of its own claim to hold the defendant to account, by observing 'norms that require defendants to be treated as citizens of a liberal polity, not as mere subjects of power'.[2]

One feature of legislative activity in the last 12 years has been the expansion of the criminal law through the creation of around 3,000 additional offences. Whatever view one takes of that development, each of those offences is subject to criminal procedure, in some form or other. Thus, in principle, if the government wishes a new crime to be created, it must accept that the additional safeguards of criminal procedure will apply to it.

13.2 ANTI-SUBVERSION DOCTRINES IN EUROPEAN HUMAN RIGHTS LAW

Because of the importance attached to additional safeguards in criminal cases, the Strasbourg Court has developed two anti-subversion doctrines to restrict the ability of governments to re-label new measures as civil, administrative or regulatory in order to place them outside the criminal law. What the Strasbourg Court has done is to give an 'autonomous meaning' to certain terms in the Convention: this means that only the Court's definition of those terms is authoritative, and that the classification of a measure in domestic law as 'civil' or 'disciplinary' is not determinative. Thus the Court has insisted that the term 'criminal charge' in Article 6 is interpreted autonomously, so that a measure (howsoever labelled in domestic law) may be regarded as criminal if it involves a fault requirement and/or if it provides for the imposition of punishment.[3] There is an extensive European case law on this, which has resulted in legal measures from several countries being held to be 'criminal' in substance, despite their domestic designation.[4] It has also insisted that the term 'penalty' in Article 7 has an autonomous meaning, so that even if a measure is preventive in purpose, it may nevertheless be considered to be punitive in effect and therefore to be a 'penalty' to

---

[1] See A. Ashworth and L. Zedner, 'Preventive Orders: a Problem of Under-Criminalization?' in R. A. Duff et al, *Criminalization* (forthcoming, 2010).

[2] A. Duff, L. Farmer, S. Marshall and V. Tadros, *The Trial on Trial: volume 3: Towards a Normative Theory of the Criminal Trial* (2007), 288.

[3] The leading cases are *Engel v Netherlands* (1979) 1 EHRR 647 and *Benham v United Kingdom* (1996) 22 EHRR 293.

[4] E.g. *Garyfallou AEBE v Greece* (1999) 28 EHRR 344 (regulatory penalties), and *Ravnsborg v Sweden* (1994) 18 EHRR 38 (contempt of court); see generally B. Emmerson, A. Ashworth and A. Macdonald (eds), *Human Rights and Criminal Justice* (2nd ed, 2007), Ch 4.

which the non-retroactivity principle applies.[5] These judicial doctrines have the effect of constraining governmental attempts to circumvent the additional safeguards in criminal cases, by insisting that if a measure is in substance a criminal charge or a penalty, designating it as some other kind of legal form cannot be permitted. If it is held to be a 'criminal charge' or 'penalty', the relevant safeguards must apply.

13.3 CIVIL PREVENTIVE ORDERS AND THE ORIGINS OF THE ASBO

The Anti-Social Behaviour Order (ASBO) is now a well-known feature of English law. It was introduced by s 1 of the Crime and Disorder Act 1998, and was a flagship measure of the then New Labour government. Its origins lay in various Labour Party documents of the mid-1990s, which made it clear that nuisance behaviour by neighbours was significantly detrimental to the quality of life of many people, not least those living in public or low-cost housing.[6] It was also believed that the criminal process was not effective in dealing with such behaviour, partly because a criminal offence focuses on a particular event without capturing the full effects of a course of conduct, and partly because the victims of such conduct were often unwilling to give evidence in court against people with whom they had to mix every day. It was against this background that the notion of a civil preventive order was developed, a legal form that would allow evidence to be given according to civil procedure, if necessary by public officials who had witnessed or been told of the objectionable conduct, and which would then enable a court to make an order containing various prohibitions.

According to s 1 of the 1998 Act, a court may make an ASBO where it finds that the defendant has acted in an anti-social manner, that is, 'in a manner that caused or was likely to cause harassment, alarm or distress', and where it finds that the order is necessary to protect persons from further such behaviour. The court may then make an order 'which prohibits the defendant from doing anything described in the order' for a minimum of two years. If the defendant breaches the terms of the order without reasonable excuse, a criminal offence is committed and the maximum penalty is five years' imprisonment. Most cases are brought to a magistrates' court by the local authority or the police. In the early years there was little enthusiasm for applying for ASBOs in most areas of the country, so that between January 1999 and the end of 2002

---

[5] The leading cases are *Welch v United Kingdom* (1995) 20 EHRR 247 and *Ibbotson v United Kingdom* (1999) 27 EHRR CD 332; for further analysis, see Emmerson, Ashworth and Macdonald, *Human Rights and Criminal Justice*, 699–703.

[6] For detailed discussion, see E. Burney, *Making People Behave: Anti-Social Behaviour, Politics and Policy* (2nd ed, 2009); P. Squires and D. E. Stephen, *Rougher Justice: Anti-Social Behaviour and Young People* (2005); for shorter discussions, see A. Ashworth, 'Social Control and Anti-Social Behaviour: the Subversion of Human Rights?' (2004) 120 *LQR* 263 and S. Macdonald, 'A Suicidal Woman, Roaming Pigs and a Noisy Trampolinist: Refining the ASBO's Definition of Anti-Social Behaviour' (2006) 69 *MLR* 183.

only about 1,000 ASBOs were made across the whole country. Since then it has become possible for a criminal court to make an ASBO as a supplement to a sentence imposed on a convicted offender,[7] and it seems that ASBOs made in this way now account for the majority of orders made.[8] Even so, the available statistics show that 3,440 were made in 2004, 4,090 in 2005 and 2,822 in 2006. The breach rate is 47 per cent, and around half of those found to have breached an ASBO receive a custodial sentence.[9]

We have noted that the ASBO was created in order to deal with what was believed to be a widespread social problem—nuisance behaviour that has a significant negative impact on the quality of everyday life. There are some criminological links here to the 'broken windows' thesis that influenced policing in New York and some other areas of the United States. The thesis is that visible policing which deals with minor disorder and other sources of insecurity (such as broken windows left unrepaired) can have the effect of reducing the amount of more serious crime, as well as increasing the sense of security in communities.[10] The theory and its empirical foundations have been subjected to strong and detailed criticism,[11] but it has nonetheless had some adherents in policy circles in this country and may have played some role in sustaining the government's belief in ASBOs despite the reluctance of many local authorities to apply for them. Thus the current Home Office website states that:

'Anti-social behaviour doesn't just make life unpleasant. It holds back the regeneration of disadvantaged areas and creates an environment where more serious crime can take hold.'[12]

This suggests a commitment to the 'broken windows' thesis, despite the absence of convincing evidence that it works.

What is anti-social behaviour? The Home Office website currently lists:

'Rowdy and noisy behaviour; yobbish behaviour; vandalism, graffiti and fly-posting; dealing or buying drugs in the street; fly-tipping rubbish; aggressive begging; street drinking; setting off fireworks late at night.'[13]

Some of this behaviour is non-criminal (similarly, teenagers hanging around on street corners, people kicking over dustbins), some of it amounts to quite serious criminal offending—as in the case of dealing in drugs, and also repeated criminal damage or burglary, which have been alleged in some cases. This is a curious process whereby several forms of crime and disorder 'have been re-problematised as anti-social behaviour, thereby lending a spurious new integrity to the politics of exclusion, to intolerance and to inequality.'[14] It seems, therefore, that the term 'anti-social behaviour' is now used to cover a wide spectrum of activities, including some fairly serious crimes. Why has this

---

[7] The power was introduced by s 64 of the Police Reform Act 2002.   [8] Burney, *op cit*, 171.

[9] www.homeoffice.gov.uk/anti-social-behaviour.

[10] The thesis was originally put forward by J. Q. Wilson and G. Kelling, 'Broken Windows' (1982) *Atlantic Monthly* (March), 29.

[11] Most notably by B. Harcourt, *Illusion of Order: the False Promise of Broken Windows Policing* (2002).

[12] www.homeoffice.gov.uk/anti-social-behaviour.   [13] *Ibid*.

[14] Squires and Stephen, *Rougher Justice*, 7.

happened, and why is it that ASBOs have attracted such strong and persistent criticism from many quarters? In essence, the answer to both questions lies in the broad scope of the powers given to the authorities and the paucity of safeguards for defendants. This can be elaborated through the following critical observations.

First, s 1 of the 1998 Act delegates a wide rule-making discretion to the courts. The effect of this, given the other features of the ASBO, is that a court acting under civil procedure is constituted as a body able to make criminal laws for this defendant—i.e. to impose conditions restricting his or her behaviour, on pain of conviction and punishment. The decision to make an ASBO or other preventive order is therefore 'a form of criminalization: an *ex ante* prohibition, not an *ex post facto* verdict', and the power thus conferred on the civil court is of enormous width and potency.[15]

Secondly, the court is able to impose extensive prohibitions on the defendant, going well beyond the scope of the anti-social behaviour proved. The judiciary has attempted to impose a framework on the making of orders and their contents,[16] and if followed that framework should reduce the force of this objection. Thus there are Court of Appeal decisions insisting that orders should be clear and precise in their requirements, should not be imposed merely to increase the sentence range for a particular type of offence, and should not impose prohibitions so numerous that they make compliance difficult.[17] However, the requirement that each of the prohibitions be 'necessary' for the protection of others from anti-social behaviour has not been enforced rigorously.[18] It is not clear how far a court may go in framing the order so as to prohibit a person, not merely from doing an anti-social act, but also from putting himself in a position where he may be able to indulge in anti-social behaviour: many prohibitions of enormous width have been approved, such as banning a person from the whole of the Tyneside Metro system as a means of stopping him from spraying graffiti on trains.[19] The minimum period for an order is two years, and although all prohibitions do not need to last for that minimum period, there have been cases where an order lasting ten years has passed without comment in the Court of Appeal (even where the defendant was only 18).[20]

Thirdly, just under a half of those receiving ASBOs are young people, despite the government's original declaration that the measure was not aimed at the young, and some orders have been made on mentally disturbed persons. There has been little provision of support for those subjected to ASBOs, even though they are likely to be

---

[15] See the argument of A. P. Simester and A. von Hirsch, 'Regulating Offensive Conduct through Two-Step Prohibitions', in A. von Hirsch and A. P. Simester (eds), *Incivilities: Regulating Offensive Behaviour* (2006).

[16] Judicial Studies Board, *Anti-Social Behaviour Orders: a Guide for the Judiciary* (3rd ed, 2007).

[17] The leading decisions are *Boness, Bebbington and others* [2006] 1 Cr App R (S) 690, *H Stevens and Lovegrove* [2006] 2 Cr App R (S) 463, and *W and F* [2006] 2 Cr App R (S) 724.

[18] On this and other aspects of section 1, see P. Ramsay, 'What is Anti-Social Behaviour?' [2004] *Crim LR* 908.

[19] *Lamb* [2006] 2 Cr App R (S) 11.   [20] *Verdi* [2005] 1 Cr App R (S) 197.

people who may need support.[21] The measure fails to tackle the causes of the behaviour, although it is fair to say that in some parts of the country an application for an ASBO is usually brought after some lesser measure such as an 'Acceptable Behaviour Contract' has been tried. An ABC is a less formal agreement between a young person and the local authority, whereby the young person agrees not to do certain things (e.g. not to swear, not to hang around a particular shopping centre, not to associate with a particular person); breach has no formal consequence, but stronger measures (such as applying to a court for an ASBO) may then be taken.[22] In practice, ABCs are made in considerable numbers: in 2005–06 some 7,500 ABCs were made, much higher than the number of ASBOs.[23] Nonetheless, Squires and Stephen use their empirical research to argue that many young people on ABCs (as well as those on ASBOs) lack practical support for the many problems that they have, and that policies place greater emphasis on punishment and restrictions than on support and development.[24]

Fourthly, the maximum penalty for the offence of breaching a prohibition in an ASBO is five years, higher than the maximum penalty for many other offences (such as assault, affray, assaulting a police officer), even though the substance of the offence is the breach of a civil order; and, as noted earlier, around a half of those convicted of breaching an ASBO receive a custodial sentence. These penalties can be questioned on proportionality grounds, especially when the original order has been made according to civil rather than criminal procedure.

Fifthly, linking the first and fourth objections, there is a particular concern about the anti-democratic effect of the ASBO when it is applied to conduct that is criminal but which the democratically elected legislature has made non-imprisonable. The two prime examples of this are begging, and soliciting for prostitution, both of which Parliament decided to make non-imprisonable in 1982.[25] When Parliament took those decisions, it clearly held that such offenders should not be liable to imprisonment for such minor offences, no matter how many times they were repeated. Yet this democratic decision can now be subverted if a court decides to make an ASBO that contains a prohibition on begging or on soliciting for prostitution,[26] breach of which may result in a sentence of imprisonment, and indeed a sentence of up to five years. This possibility demonstrates the far-reaching effects of the ASBO legislation.

In view of the high maximum penalty and the other objections just set out, can it be said that the ASBO is compatible with European human rights law, or is it in substance a penalty or criminal charge, despite being labelled a civil preventive order?

---

[21] A court should consider making a parenting order where a person under 18 is subjected to an ASBO; the court may also make an Individual Support Order, although these seem fairly infrequent.

[22] Squires and Stephen, *Rougher Justice*, 127–9.

[23] Statistics taken from a government website in 2007, and noted by the Sentencing Advisory Panel, *Sentencing for Breach of an Anti-Social Behaviour Order: Advice to the Sentencing Guidelines Council* (2008), n 3.

[24] Squires and Stephen, *Rougher Justice*, 199–200.

[25] Criminal Justice Act 1982, ss 70 and 71.

[26] E.g. *Chief Constable of Lancashire v Potter* [2003] EWHC 2272 (Admin).

This question has not been considered by the Strasbourg Court. When it was considered by the British courts, the argument that the ASBO is in substance a criminal charge was rejected. The House of Lords held that the two stages or steps in the ASBO are distinct, and each of them complies with the necessary procedural safeguards.[27] The first step is entirely civil, when the court determines whether to make an ASBO and what prohibitions to insert into it. At this stage there is no question of a conviction being registered: the order is simply preventive. The second step only occurs if the order is breached. That is a criminal offence, and criminal procedure applies in its entirety to the breach proceedings. The only concession made by the House of Lords was to hold that the standard of proof in the initial civil proceedings should be high, equivalent to the standard in criminal proceedings (beyond reasonable doubt), in view of the possible consequences of breach of the order. The gist of this concession marks some acknowledgement of the opposite argument—that to consider the two steps in civil preventive orders as entirely separate is to privilege form over substance, when the proper approach (as evident in the anti-subversion doctrines of the Strasbourg Court) is to look to the substance of the measure. That substance might be different if the penalty for breach of an ASBO were more moderate. But, since the penalty may involve not only imprisonment but a substantial custodial sentence of up to five years, that should certainly be enough to insist that the two stages of the civil preventive order should be considered as two parts of the whole, and not as separate. This would mean that all the safeguards for criminal cases should be available at the stage of making the civil preventive order, including legal assistance and the right to confront witnesses.

There remains a considerable gulf, however, between the liberal critique of ASBOs and other civil preventive orders elaborated above, and the position of many policy-makers, law enforcement officers and members of the public. We have noted that there is some government support for the 'broken windows' theory, and that historically the legal structure of the ASBO grew out of dissatisfaction with the criminal law (and, partly, with the protections that it accords to accused persons). Can the ASBO and similar orders derive support from any normative theory? Peter Ramsay argues that traditional liberal critiques, such as the one presented above, fail to take account of the argument that as citizens we have the duty to assure others that we will respect their interests. Thus the autonomy of the individual is a fundamental element of the good life, but each person's autonomy is 'intrinsically vulnerable to the spontaneous self-interested preferences of others', which supplies a reason why 'behaviour which fails to reassure [should be] controlled by a preventative order.'[28] He argues that reasoning of this kind underlies the promotion of the ASBO and other civil preventive orders. He does not conclude that this theory of vulnerable autonomy is a convincing

---

[27] *Clingham v. Royal Borough of Kensington and Chelsea; R (on behalf of McCann) v Crown Court at Manchester* [2003] 1 AC 787.

[28] P. Ramsay, 'The Theory of Vulnerable Autonomy and the Legitimacy of Civil Preventative Orders' in B. McSherry, A. Norrie and S. Bronitt (eds), *Regulating Deviance* (2009), 131.

rationale, but argues that it has some legitimacy in the context of prevailing political ideologies.[29]

13.4 THE RANGE OF CIVIL PREVENTIVE ORDERS

Having set out various objections to the ASBO as currently constituted, we now return to the fact that those objections have not yet been recognized by the courts, and that the Government has pressed ahead with what it regards as a successful new legal form. The civil preventive order is a hybrid order, with the first (civil) stage determining the contents of the prohibitions in the order, and the second (criminal) stage resulting in conviction and sentence of those who breach the order. At least 12 varieties of this model of the civil preventive order have now been introduced, as follows:

- Anti-social behaviour orders[30]
- Restraining orders[31]
- Non-molestation orders[32]
- Exclusion from licensed premises orders[33]
- Football spectator banning orders[34]
- Travel restriction orders[35]
- Sexual offences prevention orders[36]
- Foreign travel orders[37]
- Risk of sexual harm orders[38]
- Drinking banning orders[39]
- Serious crime prevention orders[40]
- Violent offender orders[41]

The essence of all these orders is that they are procedurally civil, and are ostensibly preventive in purpose. However, as already noted, there is a ferocious sting in the tail when one of the orders is breached: that is a criminal offence of staggering breadth (e.g. 'doing anything which he is prohibited from doing by an anti-social behaviour order'), which imposes strict liability, although on 'reasonable excuse' the defendant bears

[29] *Ibid.*, 138–9.   [30] Crime and Disorder Act 1998, s 1 (as amended).
[31] Protection from Harassment Act 1997, s 5.   [32] Family Law Act 1996, s 42A.
[33] Licensed Premises (Exclusion of Certain Persons) Act 1980, s 1.
[34] Football Spectators Act 1989, s 14A.   [35] Criminal Justice and Police Act 2001, s 33.
[36] Sexual Offences Act 2003, s 104.   [37] *Ibid.*, s 114.   [38] *Ibid.*, s 123.
[39] Violent Crime Reduction Act 2006, s 1.   [40] Serious Crime Act 2007, s 1.
[41] Criminal Justice and Immigration Act 2008, s 98.

only the evidential burden, and the prosecution must disprove the excuse.[42] With the exception of three of the orders, the maximum penalty for breach is five years' imprisonment, and in around half the ABSO cases the defendant is sent to prison.[43] Non-molestation orders in family cases were previously enforced through contempt of court proceedings, with a maximum penalty of two years' imprisonment; the effect of integrating them into the scheme of civil preventive orders was to more than double the maximum penalty to five years. Risk of sexual harm orders, like all the other civil preventive orders, do not depend on proof that the subject has committed any sexual offences: so long as evidence is presented that the person has done a specified act in relation to a child on at least two occasions, on the basis of which a court can conclude that it is necessary to make the order for the purpose of protecting one or more child from that person, it may make an order that prohibits the person from doing anything described in the order for a minimum of two years.[44]

Even more serious are the violent offender order and the serious crime prevention order. The former applies only to a restricted group of people—those who have been convicted of a specified offence (essentially, an offence contrary to s 20 of the Offences Against the Person Act 1861 or worse, for which a sentence of at least 12 months' imprisonment was imposed). If a chief constable persuades the court that the person has 'acted in such a way as to give reasonable cause to believe that it is necessary' for the order to be made, for the purpose of protecting the public from serious harm, then the court may make a violent offender order. It may run from two to five years, and may include prohibitions, restrictions or conditions on matters such as not going to certain places or not having contact with certain people. Turning to the serious crime prevention order, this can be made by a court that is satisfied that a person has been involved in serious crime, including 'conducting himself in a way that was likely to facilitate the commission by him or another of a serious offence', and where the court has reasonable grounds to believe that the order would protect the public by preventing, restricting or disrupting the person's involvement in serious crime. The order may contain prohibitions, restrictions or requirements that are appropriate for the above purposes, such as prohibitions on certain property or financial dealings, on travel, or on the use of certain premises. The legislation includes certain procedural protections, but the sanction for breach is a prison sentence of up to five years, and there are further powers on breach such as forfeiture of assets.

Closely related to the 12 civil preventive orders listed above are control orders under the Prevention of Terrorism Act 2005. After the events of September 11, 2001, the British legislature passed the Anti-Terrorism, Crime and Security Act 2001, which

---

[42] *Charles* [2009] EWCA Crim 1570.

[43] The three exceptions are: drinking banning order (maximum penalty is a fine on level 4), exclusion from licensed premises order (maximum, imprisonment for one month), and football banning order (maximum, imprisonment for six months).

[44] See further S. Shute, 'New Civil Preventative Orders: Sexual Offences Prevention Orders; Foreign Travel Orders; Risk of Sexual Harm Orders' [2004] *Crim LR* 417.

contained a number of provisions that the Government justified as necessary to protect
the country against terrorism. One of the measures was the indefinite detention without trial of suspected international terrorists. This was implemented, but its compatibility with the European Convention on Human Rights was challenged in the courts.
In *A and others v Secretary of State for the Home Department*[45] the House of Lords
declared these powers of detention without trial to be incompatible with Convention
rights. Clearly the powers breached the right to liberty declared by Article 5, but the
Government relied on its derogation from Article 5 as a justification. This justification was scrutinized by their Lordships, who held *inter alia* that the derogation could
not be supported under Article 15 since it was restricted to suspected *international*
terrorists.

As a result of this ruling, the Government abandoned the power of indefinite detention without trial and invented the control order.[46] This was presented as another
attempt to deal with the problem of persons who could not be deported because the
potential receiving country was one that might use torture against the person, and
whom it was thought inadvisable to prosecute in this country because that might lead
to the secret processes of the security services becoming known. In essence, this new
power authorizes the executive (the Home Secretary) to place certain persons under
the restrictions of a control order. Broadly speaking,[47] the order confines its subject
to a particular apartment or house for a certain number of hours each day, and seeks
to control the use by that person of the telephone and internet and to control whom
the person may meet during the hours of liberty each day. As with other civil preventive orders, the consequence of a breach is conviction and a maximum sentence
of five years' imprisonment. Control orders were also challenged in the courts, on
the ground that in substance they amounted to a deprivation of liberty contrary to
Article 5, whereas the Government's view was that this was merely a restriction on
liberty, which therefore did not engage Article 5. This challenge brought into focus
a third form of anti-subversion doctrine, the autonomous meaning given by the
Strasbourg Court to the term 'deprivation of liberty'. As that Court had declared in
Guzzardi v Italy,[48] it is for the Court to determine whether in substance a particular restriction amounts to a deprivation of liberty or not. In *JJ v Secretary of State
for the Home Department* (2007)[49] the House of Lords had to consider whether the
particular restrictions imposed by a certain control order (including confinement to
a particular apartment for 18 hours per day, no use of telephone or internet, no pre-
arranged meetings with others during the hours of liberty except with approval, and
so on) were such as to amount, in substance, to a deprivation of liberty contrary to

---

[45] [2004] UKHL 56; see now *A v United Kingdom* (2009) 49 EHRR 625.
[46] See generally L. Zedner, Preventive Justice or Pre-Punishment? The Case of Control Orders' (2007)
59 *CLP* 174.
[47] The precise details of derogating and non-derogating control orders are not discussed here: see Zedner,
ibid.
[48] (1981) 3 EHRR 333.   [49] [2007] UKHL 45.

Article 5. By a majority the House of Lords held that it did amount to a deprivation of liberty, but the House made it clear that some reduction in the constraints would bring the control order back into the realm of a mere restriction on liberty, which would be outside Article 5.

13.5 RE-ASSESSING THE AMBIT OF THE CRIMINAL PROCESS

Since the opening chapter of the book we have drawn attention to the considerable expansion of the criminal law in recent years, stemming from the tendency of the government to create a new criminal offence whenever a social problem achieves high profile in the media. Rampant criminalization this may be, but at least the creation of a crime brings with it the additional procedural safeguards for which Articles 6(2) and 6(3) provide, so that a person cannot be convicted of that crime unless certain protections are accorded during the criminal process. In Chapters 6 and 7 we noted the rapid growth of out-of-court penalties in the last few years: the power to impose (or, some would say, offer) such penalties lies with either the Crown Prosecution Service (in the case of conditional cautions) or with the police or other law enforcement agency (in the case of all the other out-of-court penalties), but respect for the additional safeguards available for criminal charges is retained by the opportunity that the ticketed person has to refuse the out-of-court penalty and to insist on the matter being heard in court. Article 6 of the Convention is satisfied, the Strasbourg Court has held,[50] so long as the ticketed person can insist on having a court hearing—even though, as we noted, there may be powerful pressures to accept the out-of-court penalty.

Although there are grounds for questioning the form that out-of-court disposals take in English law, and the degree of power they place in the hands of enforcement officers, we noted in Chapter 6 that there may be good reasons of proportionality (as well as efficiency and economy) to deal with some minor cases without bringing them to court. Similarly, it can be said that there may be good reasons for dealing with some types of social problem through regulatory, civil, or other non-criminal channels, rather than resorting to the criminal law—indeed, this is implicit in the criticism of 'rampant criminalization' over the last decade. Thus in this chapter we have charted the progress of a further development in the criminal process, in which the Government and Parliament have sought to use a form of hybrid or two-step civil preventive order to deal with certain types of social problem. Now when it is argued that there is good sense in trying to use non-criminal methods of dealing with social problems, this may attract considerable support. It may suggest an attempt to tackle the causes of the problem, rather than simply to punish its manifestations after the

---

[50] *Ozturk v Germany* (1984) 6 EHRR 409.

event. However, what we have observed, in the development of the ASBO and several other civil preventive orders, is the imposition of one or more prohibitions on an individual with a view to preventing nuisance or harm, reinforced by the frequent use of sentences of imprisonment for breach. Thus the recent development of the civil preventive order cannot really be supported by those who argue in favour of greater use of the civil law instead of the criminal law, since the civil preventive order has what we have described as a ferocious sting in the tail—the maximum sentence of five years' imprisonment for breach. It has been argued here that this high maximum penalty colours the whole approach of the civil preventive order, aligning it much more with the criminal law and certainly calling for greater safeguards at the (civil) stage of drafting and imposing the prohibitions than are currently required. In our view, the House of Lords was wrong to treat the two steps of the ASBO as separate,[51] and to conclude that the first stage of proceedings is not criminal in substance, and indeed its concession that the standard of proof at the first stage of the proceedings should be as high as the criminal standard seems to recognize the importance of the severity of the possible consequences.

Nevertheless, the House of Lords decision represents the law, and the civil preventive order operates in the way that the Government intends—which is why so many new civil preventive orders have been created in recent years. The effect is to emasculate the protections of criminal procedure: of course they are applicable when an individual is charged with breaching a civil preventive order, but those proceedings are relatively peremptory. The major question is whether the individual breached a prohibition in the order, since breach is a strict liability offence (unless there is a 'reasonable excuse'), and so the matter becomes one of sentencing. There are sentencing guidelines applicable in most of these cases,[52] but those guidelines are framed within the statutory structure and are therefore relatively severe. The courts' use of civil preventive orders has been relatively low—certainly compared with out-of-court penalties—but when they are used they are powerfully constraining and privative.

Granted that the civil preventive order currently stands outside criminal procedure in English law, what are the limits of the technique? It has been argued elsewhere that the civil preventive order seems to fall into 'a jurisprudential black hole,'[53] in which there is no presumption of innocence, no ban on retrospectivity and no prospect of the additional safeguards that are available in criminal cases. Whether there are any operative restraining principles is difficult to divine. The English courts have insisted on standards of certainty and specificity (avoiding over-breadth) in the framing of prohibitions,[54] and the Strasbourg jurisprudence offers some support for three

---

[51] In the *Clingham* decision, see n 27 above and accompanying text.

[52] Sentencing Guidelines Council, *Sentencing for Breach of a Protective Order* (2006); Sentencing Guidelines Council, *Breach of an Anti-Social Behaviour Order* (2008).

[53] A. Ashworth, 'Criminal Law, Human Rights and Preventative Justice' in B. McSherry, A. Norrie and S. Bronitt (eds), *Regulating Deviance* (2009), 100.

[54] See the decisions listed in n 17 above.

restraining principles—the principle of necessity, that it must be established that the restrictions are necessary to prevent the harm; the principle of subsidiary, that less intrusive measures must have been considered and adjudged to be insufficient; and the principle of proportionality, that the measures taken must not be out of proportion to the danger apprehended, taking account of any relevant rights of the individual (such as the right to respect for private life under Article 8 of the Convention).[55] However, even if these restraining principles were recognized and enforced, it is unlikely that they would do more than structure the decisions of the courts on imposing particular prohibitions in particular cases. It seems unlikely that they would require alterations in the legislation on civil preventive orders.

It therefore seems that the British Government, perhaps relying on a version of the theory of vulnerable autonomy,[56] remains free to use civil preventive orders as a method of social control without the need to respect the protections accorded to defendants in criminal cases. While this may spur criminal lawyers to question whether the criminal law and criminal process cannot be refined to deal more effectively with the type of case in which civil preventive orders are now being used, the trend is distinctly in the opposite direction.

FURTHER READING

ASHWORTH, A. and ZEDNER, L., 'Preventive Orders: a Problem of Under-Criminalization?' in R. A. Duff et al, *Criminalization* (forthcoming, 2010).

SIMESTER, A. P. and VON HIRSCH, A., 'Regulating Offensive Conduct through Two-Step Prohibitions' in A. von Hirsch and A. P. Simester (eds), *Incivilities: Regulating Offensive Behaviour*, Oxford: Hart Publishing, 2006.

RAMSAY, P., 'The Theory of Vulnerable Autonomy and the Legitimacy of Civil Preventative Orders' in B. McSherry, A. Norrie and S. Bronitt (eds), *Regulating Deviance*, Oxford: Hart Publishing, 2009.

Questions for Discussion

1. Are there good social reasons for the Government to make greater use of civil or hybrid orders, for the purpose of social control?

2. How strong are the objections to the favoured model of the civil preventive order in English law?

---

[55] Two relevant decisions supporting these principles are *Witold Litwa v Poland* (2001) 33 EHRR 1267 and *Enhorn v Sweden* (2005) 41 EHRR 643.

[56] See text at nn 28–9 above.

14

CRIMINAL PROCESS VALUES

Chapters 4 to 12 of the book have discussed various key stages of decision making in the criminal process, making reference to issues of policy and principle in the relevant law and practices. It is time now to reflect more generally upon the values that appear to dominate the English criminal process, the values that ought to dominate it, and how change might be brought about. We start by offering some general observations about the criminal process.

Early in Chapter 1, a distinction was drawn between three types of decision at the pre-trial stage: processual decisions, which are concerned with the progress of the case from arrest through to court, or as far as the case goes; dispositive decisions, which divert a case from the process of prosecution and trial and which may dispose of the case through some kind of undertaking or penalty; and the temporizing decision, remand, which determines whether or not the defendant should be at liberty between first court appearance and trial. While there is often a tendency to regard these decisions as discrete rational determinations, it will have become apparent that they cannot be assessed properly without having regard to the system or process of which they form part. Thus, for example, each decision is shaped by the flow of information to the decision maker and by the way in which 'facts' and opinions are selected, constructed and communicated—all of which may be influenced as much by power relations between the parties as by the law. Additionally, each decision maker may be not only subject to rules or guidelines, as the case may be, but also influenced by an occupational culture and by the expectations of others both within and outside the system. It is therefore important not to neglect the serial view of decisions, noting that decisions by the public and by ordinary police officers or by the personnel of regulatory agencies may have considerable implications for later determinations; that decisions on charge may have implications for mode of trial; that decisions on mode of trial may have implications for remand and for plea; and so forth. Moreover, events which occur early in the process—a mistaken identification, a false confession—can have profound implications later on. The fragility of various types of evidence should caution us to view claims about the 'facts' of cases, or about innocence and guilt, with a degree of scepticism.

Little has been said, in the foregoing chapters, about the differences between accusatorial and inquisitorial systems of criminal justice. The English criminal process is fundamentally accusatorial in orientation, eschewing the idea of an impartial inquiry into the case by a neutral official in favour of the notion that a fair result emerges from an adversarial process in which the prosecution constructs a case for convicting the defendant and the defendant attempts to undermine or discredit that case. One reason for not dwelling on this contrast is the complexity of the adversarial/ inquisitorial distinction, both in theory and in practice.[1] Another reason may be found in what may be termed the 'theory of convergence'—suggesting that the trend in Europe has been away from a clear dichotomy of approaches and towards a unified framework.[2] The convergence is said to have been assisted by the European Convention on Human Rights (ECHR). However, the dynamics here are not straightforward. Jackson has suggested that the model promoted under the Convention is distinctive rather than an amalgam of features associated with accusatorial and inquisitorial systems. Further, it is unlikely that a single model of proof will emerge under the Convention because differences between jurisdictions mean that ECHR requirements will be implemented in different ways in different jurisdictions: 'we may be witnessing a realignment of the two existing models of proof rather than simply a convergence of the two but one which gives plenty of scope for diverse application in different institutional and cultural settings.'[3] Independently of the Convention, one can point to aspects of particular legal systems which appear to be influenced by elements of a foreign procedural tradition. Thus we saw in Chapter 9 that in England and Wales the Criminal Procedure Rules have led the courts to criticize certain adversarial tactics by defendants, especially those associated with 'ambushing' the prosecution. In Chapter 10 we noted that forms of plea-bargaining have been introduced in France and Germany, and in Italy there has been a bold experiment in procedural reform involving the introduction of elements associated with adversarial systems.[4] But it is still problematic to talk of convergence, in part because the legal traditions and cultures of the various jurisdictions still play a powerful role in the way that these developments evolve, as the literature on the Italian reforms demonstrates.[5] Perhaps the better lesson to draw from these various developments is that it is problematic in the first place to measure actual legal systems against an ideal type of the accusatorial or inquisitorial system.[6] Do the changes

---

[1] The best-known work is by M. Damaška, *The Faces of Justice and State Authority* (1976), and 'Evidentiary Barriers to Conviction and Two Models of Criminal Procedure: a Comparative Study' (1973) 121 *U Penn LR* 506.

[2] For further discussion, see N. Jorg, S. Field and C. Brants, 'Are Inquisitorial and Adversarial Systems Converging?' in C. Harding et al, *Criminal Justice in Europe* (1995); M. Delmas-Marty and J. Spencer (eds), *European Criminal Procedures* (2002).

[3] J. Jackson, 'The Effects of Human Rights on Criminal Evidentiary Processes: Convergence, Divergence or Realignment?' (2005) 68 *MLR* 737, 740.

[4] See V. Grevi, 'The New Italian Code for Criminal Procedure: a Concise Overview' in A. Pizzorusso, *Italian Studies in Law* (1994).

[5] S. Maffei, 'Negotiations on Evidence and Negotiations on Sentence: Adversarial Experiments in Italian Criminal Procedure' (2004) 2 *J Int Crim J* 1050; E. Grande, 'Italian Criminal Procedure: Borrowing and Resistance' (2000) 48 *Am J Comp L* 227.

[6] See further the essays in Part 1 of J. Jackson, M. Langer and P. Tillers (eds), *Crime, Procedure and Evidence in an International and Comparative Context* (2008).

to English criminal procedure inspired by the Criminal Procedure Rules make it less accusatorial? If party control of proceedings is the essence of the accusatorial system, then it must be recognized that there is no pure accusatorial system, because ethical duties to the court and exclusionary rules have always limited the ability of the parties to conduct proceedings how they want. Further, a claim that the English system is becoming less accusatorial often seems to convey a value judgement: that important defence rights are being eroded, for example. But this requires careful assessment in the individual case, not comparison with some non-existant ideal type. Much the same could be said when it comes to deployment of Packer's models.

14.1 THE AVOIDANCE OF CRIMINAL TRIALS

In the course of this book it has become evident that, whereas the rhetoric of English criminal procedure tends to place emphasis on trial by jury according to the laws of evidence, the practice is otherwise. Most cases are heard in magistrates' courts, not in the Crown Court with a jury. The vast majority of cases—over 90 per cent in magistrates' courts and some two-thirds in the Crown Court—proceed on a plea of guilty, which means that no trial of guilt ever takes place. In no sense is this a 'natural' or 'unavoidable' phenomenon: the system is structured so as to produce it. There are incentives towards the avoidance of trials, incentives that do not exist in some other legal systems. The most notable of these is the sentence discount for a plea of guilty, up to one-third off the sentence that would otherwise be given for the offence. There are also disincentives to appealing against court decisions, introduced for similar reasons. For some time there have been increasing fiscal pressures towards having fewer cases dealt with in the Crown Court and more in the magistrates' courts, manifested in such changes as the reclassification of certain offences as 'summary only' in 1988, and the introduction of the 'plea before venue' system in 1997. However, in addition to these structural factors there are also cultural influences pulling in the same direction. We have noted evidence that defence lawyers and prosecutors may act cooperatively at some stages, particularly in plea negotiations, to the extent of subverting the ethics of client representation.[7] What ought to be different ethical orientations may thus become submerged beneath the working practices and occupational cultures of the local groups of professionals.

It is not only for cases that are pursued to conviction that the system tends strongly towards trial-avoidance. The trend towards diversion is designed to take cases out of the formal criminal process and to dispose of them separately. Prominent among these dispositive decisions are the police caution, conditional cautions, penalty notices for

---

[7] See Ch 3 above, and M. McConville, 'Plea Bargaining: Ethics and Politics' in S. Doran and J. Jackson (eds), *The Judicial Role in Criminal Proceedings* (2000); L. Bridges, 'Ethics of Representation on Guilty Pleas' (2006) 9 *Legal Ethics* 80.

disorder (PNDs), and the various warnings and compounded penalties used by the 'regulatory' agencies. The Crime and Disorder Act 1998 introduced a more rigid statutory regime for the diversion of offenders under 18, by way of reprimands and final warnings. Under that statute and by other means, various forms of restorative justice have also become available as means of diverting cases by agreement between victim, offender and 'community'.[8] The continued vitality of diversion, despite a generally repressive penal climate, seems to stem from the confluence of some very different arguments—that the painful consequences of being prosecuted may themselves be too severe a response to some forms of wrongdoing; that there is scant evidence that formal court processes are more effective in preventing re-offending; that encounters with the court system may create stigma and disadvantage that makes future law-abidance more difficult; that diversion is far less expensive and time consuming than court proceedings; and that it is an effective way of closing the 'justice gap' by clearing up more offences. Although some may suspect that considerations of cost and clear up rates weigh most heavily with policy-makers, the result may also be to advance the other arguments in favour of diversion.

It would be wrong, however, to overlook the disadvantages. On a general plane, a widely used discretion not to prosecute may be regarded as undermining the principle of legality and the idea of the rule of law. For example, the Sexual Offences Act 2003 creates several offences that criminalize perfectly normal acts of friendly touching between teenagers:[9] the Government's response is that no prosecutions will be brought for such conduct, and the Crown Prosecution Service (CPS) has drawn up guidelines to that end.[10] The official view is that these broad offences are needed to catch the minority of wicked sexual predators, but the counter-argument is that if guidelines for prosecutors can be drawn up, then the law itself should be drafted so as to decriminalize normal and non-predatory acts. The law should not give such discretion to prosecutors to determine the effective ambit of a widely cast law, and citizens should not have to trust prosecutors not to criminalize them inappropriately.[11] That there has been at least one very problematic prosecution under the Sexual Offences Act is testament to this.[12] On a more specific plane, existing methods of diversion are often inseparable from incentives for the suspect or defendant to accept them. Rather like the discount for pleading guilty, the incentive to accept a PND or caution may prove a powerful practical inducement to terminate one's involvement with the criminal justice system quickly and without the anxiety of a court appearance. However, the European Court has insisted, and English law generally provides, that anyone who does not wish to accept diversion can decline and invite the prosecution to bring the case before a court.[13] This has some importance now that cautions, PNDs, conditional cautions, reprimands and final warnings are recorded nationally

---

[8] See the discussion in Ch 6.

[9] J. Spencer, 'The Sexual Offences Act 2003: Child and Family Offences' [2004] *Crim LR* 347.

[10] See www.cps.gov.uk.   [11] See V. Tadros, 'Crimes and Security' (2008) 71 *MLR* 940.

[12] *R v G* [2008] UKHL 37.   [13] *Ozturk v Germany* (1984) 6 EHRR 409.

and are liable to be cited in court if the defendant is subsequently convicted of an offence. Proper safeguards, such as access to legal advice, should be made available, and there should be a principle that any sentence the court passes on a subsequent finding of guilt should not be significantly more onerous than the penalty voluntarily rejected by the defendant.

These remarks are at a general level, and the practical operation of the system may vary to some extent according to the type of crime alleged. In the previous chapters we have noted the special difficulties arising in certain types of case: for example, the problems of investigating and prosecuting offences of 'domestic' violence and serious sexual assaults have led to changes in law and in practice that may be said to create special sub-systems for such cases.[14] There is certainly a sub-system for cases of serious fraud, following the Criminal Justice Act 1987 and the operations of the Serious Fraud Office. With the introduction of plea negotiation in the wake of the Fraud Review, this sub-system is becoming even more distinct.[15] While in principle it is right to contemplate separate procedural approaches to circumvent practical difficulties arising in certain types of case, there is a danger that the social concerns (sometimes expressed in terms of victims' interests or rights) motivating these changes may lead to a neglect of fundamental rights for suspects and defendants, and that once special measures are justified in one area they will become 'normalized' and spread to other areas of the criminal process.[16] Politicians are particularly fond of claiming that a new method of combating a particular type of crime is called for, and that the best approach is to curtail the rights of suspects and defendants, which they then purport to justify as being in the greater public interest or for public protection.[17] This form of assertion is most frequently encountered in the context of the 'war against terrorism', with the provisions of the Anti-Terrorism, Crime and Security Act 2001 being a prime example. More recently this style of reasoning has been used in the context of organized crime, with coercive powers to obtain information from witnesses contained in the Serious Organised Crime and Police Act 2005. Such reasoning may also be found outside the context of serious crime, as in recent extensions to powers of arrest and search, where the consultation document contained not one reference to human rights.[18] We have argued in Chapter 2 that it is quite wrong for a country that has signed the European Convention on Human Rights to make such proposals without a thorough analysis of the rights implications; that this does not mean that there may not be situations of vivid danger where public interest arguments may justify some curtailment of a right under Article 5 or 6 (but no more than absolutely necessary, and preserving the essence of the right); but that the factual premise needs to be established by clear evidence, rather than

---

[14] See particularly Ch 7.   [15] See Ch 10.5(c).

[16] See O. Gross, '"Control Systems" and the Migration of Anomalies' in S. Choudhry (ed), *The Migration of Constitutional Ideas* (2007).

[17] See the discussion of such arguments in Chs 1 and 2 above.

[18] Home Office, *Policing: Modernising Police Powers to meet Community Needs* (2004).

assuming that reducing the rights of offenders or increasing the rights of victims will necessarily be effective.

Implicit in those arguments is the principle that there are general norms of the criminal process which apply to all offences, and therefore that any difference of legal framework for particular types of case calls for justification. In Chapters 6 and 7 we argued that the English criminal process lacks an overall strategy for pre-trial justice. Different agencies continue to operate in different ways: the police and the CPS may be converging in their operations, but the regulatory agencies continue to follow their differing paths and priorities. These variations, not to mention the discretionary powers that go with them, leave open the possibility of differences of approach that may discriminate on improper grounds such as class, social position, race and gender. What is absent from pre-trial justice is a common starting point for all types of case: there is no conception that people who commit offences of similar seriousness should receive similar responses (unless there are strong grounds for doing otherwise), and no real attempt to provide guidance on the relative seriousness of the various types of offence. The so-called regulatory agencies have policies that are markedly different from those of the police, not to mention the differences among the different agencies, and this means that offences of a similar degree of seriousness may receive different responses according to the context (in a public place, on company premises, in a shop, in a customs shed at a channel port, and so forth). The responses differ at the point of enforcement and investigation, and also in the various forms of diversion used. Like sentencing, diversion decisions are dispositive. Unlike sentencing, there are no open hearings and there are no general principles applicable across the diverse contexts of tax, customs, health and safety, pollution, and so on.

The absence of an aspiration to promote general norms and consistency of treatment is also manifest in local variations of policy. We saw in Chapter 6 that, despite national standards, the statistics show the persistence of variations among police force areas in the use of police cautions, most of which follows longstanding patterns. To what extent the introduction of conditional cautions will follow the same pattern remains to be seen: in organizational terms the CPS is a national agency with a national hierarchy, but working alongside the police in a local criminal justice culture may have the effect of reproducing traditional patterns. Local variations in stop and search rates, remand decisions, plea rates, mode of trial decisions and in the practices of some regulatory agencies are also longstanding. Some policy initiatives even promote local variation, for example 'community impact statements' are being piloted, which the CPS will consider when making charging decisions.[19] It is true that several worthwhile innovations in the criminal process have originated in local schemes (e.g. bail information systems, Public Interest Case Assessment schemes), and the ability to experiment should be preserved in some form. What should not be tolerated are declarations of local independence in matters of criminal justice policy. It is unjust that a person who

---

[19] Criminal Justice System, *Engaging Communities in Criminal Justice* (2009), 3.

is (rightly or wrongly) suspected of a certain offence in one area should be treated in a significantly different way from a similar person in another area. Local variations in practice should be monitored and local variations in policy should only be permitted if clear justifications can be found: this would expose the unwarranted whilst enabling experimental schemes to be introduced.

Both processual and dispositive decisions, as we have seen, tend towards the avoidance of trials. One feature of pre-trial processes that has become evident from the foregoing chapters is the tendency of some decisions to be taken in anticipation of the decisions of other agencies. There are, in fact, several influences flowing in different directions. Almost all the 'input' received by the CPS has come from the police, who have therefore exerted considerable practical influence through their construction of case files, and this is unlikely to be much diminished by the collocation of police and CPS. We have noted how some of the working practices of the CPS (in relation to bail and mode of trial decisions, for example) may be shaped by local magistrates or justices' clerks or the local judiciary. Equally some defence solicitors will tailor their approach on bail and other matters to the particular prosecutor, justices' clerk or bench of magistrates. Magistrates may sometimes defer to the police or to the CPS rather than applying their judgement independently on remands or mode of trial. It is not always easy to be sure of the existence of undue influence in these relationships: it is sometimes theoretically possible that two different parties are applying the same test and reaching the same conclusion, but the research cited on prosecutions (Chapter 7), on remands (Chapter 8) and on mode of trial (Chapter 11) is strongly suggestive of other, less ethical approaches.

Two people who have less central roles than may be thought appropriate are the defendant and the victim. We have seen that, under existing practice in both the Crown Court and magistrates' courts, the defendant is excluded from plea negotiations and has to depend on the mediated words of legal representatives.[20] Direct information for the defendant at this often crucial stage is relatively rare, and this places much emphasis on the quality of legal representation. There is growing evidence that this is variable, and that it is not always motivated by a desire to secure the defendant's rights but is sometimes diluted by a desire to curry favour with the police, or to obtain the maximum fee for the minimum work, or not to 'pull the stops out' for a client deemed unworthy.[21] In the face of strong structural and cultural pulls towards trial avoidance and negotiated outcomes, an independent and ethical approach from the defence lawyer is vital to protect the suspect-defendant.

Victims, too, may be marginalized as the criminal process moves forward. Although it has long been known that the flow of information to victims about 'their' cases has not been good, efforts to improve it have not been wholly successful. Decisions on prosecution and non-prosecution, bail and acceptance of pleas are not always communicated to the victim. However, as argued in Chapter 2, while the case for greater

[20] J. Baldwin, *Pre-Trial Justice* (1986); A. Mulcahy, 'The Justifications of Justice' (1994) 34 *BJ Crim* 411.
[21] M. McConville et al, *Standing Accused* (1994), 273 and 281; M. Travers, *The Reality of Law* (1997), Ch 5.

support and information for victims is a strong one, the arguments for victim involvement in decision making are not.

14.2 THE PRINCIPLED APPROACH

The scourge of many debates about criminal justice policy is the concept of 'balance'. As it is often expressed, notably in the report of the 1993 Royal Commission, the 'balancing' of conflicting interests is presented as if there is no particular weighting of or priority among the interests. They are all matters to be taken into consideration, and somehow a 'balance' emerges. Sometimes the process is given an apparent respectability by quoting probabilities that a certain consequence will ensue—for example, the low risk of innocent people being convicted. The existence of a low risk on one side of the equation may be presented as if it tips the scales in that direction. However, as argued in Chapter 2 above, this would be to short-circuit the course of reasoning and to ignore the strength of some of the authoritatively recognized rights. It is time, now, to re-state the argument in the light of the material in the intervening chapters.

The principled approach to criminal justice—unlike Packer's two models—is explicitly normative. The purpose of the criminal process is to bring about accurate determinations through fair procedures. The approach therefore emphasizes various rights and principles that ought to be safeguarded: some rights, such as the right not to be wrongly convicted, may be defended on a philosophical basis, but the rights declared by the European Convention on Human Rights are recognized authoritatively and indeed brought into English law by the Human Rights Act 1998. The European Convention is largely about fair procedures, and its rights are designed to eliminate arbitrariness and to promote fairness rather than to achieve particular outcomes. The effect of the 1998 Act may therefore be described as the constitutionalization of the criminal process, insofar as the Act recognizes the fundamental status of Convention rights in English law through, for example, the courts' duty to take decisions compatibly with the Convention (s 6) and to interpret statutes 'so far as possible' compatibly with Convention rights (s 3). Thus the Act has had significant effects on the shape of the English criminal process, in matters such as disclosure and public interest immunity, adverse inferences from silence, pre-trial remands, the use of various forms of surveillance, entrapment and so on. However, it was argued in Chapter 2 that the British courts and some politicians have paid insufficient attention to the differing strengths of the Convention rights, and have made the mistake of treating rights under Article 6 as if they were qualified in the same way as those in Articles 8 to 11. Rectification of this mistake, which has led to the importation of broad 'balancing' notions into fair trial guarantees by way of a modified concept of proportionality, should lead to a further sharpening of the human rights approach.

None of this is to suggest that the Convention should be regarded as a solution to the ills of the criminal process. Both in Chapter 2 and subsequently, attention has been drawn to various shortcomings of the Convention. Its coverage of rights is incomplete and patchy: if one were drawing up such a document for the new millennium, there would be several obvious candidates for inclusion that find no place in the 1950 Convention—for example, victims' rights, protection for witnesses, special rights for young people and for women (whether as defendants, victims or witnesses), fault requirements for criminal convictions, and so on. The Convention has been treated by the Strasbourg Court as a living instrument, so that the Court has developed certain implied rights—such as the privilege against self-incrimination and the principle of equality of arms—and has applied other rights in a creative fashion. There have also been Protocols that have added rights to the Convention on matters such as double jeopardy, capital punishment and the right to personal property. But the document as a whole is much less comprehensive than, say, the Charter of Fundamental Rights of the European Union; and the future of that charter deserves careful attention.

14.3 DISCRIMINATION AND NON-DISCRIMINATION

The principle of equality before the law, or non-discrimination, ought to be respected as a fundamental element in the administration of justice. In its present form, the Convention does not declare it to be so: Article 14 declares a right not to be discriminated against in the exercise of other Convention rights, but only the declaration and ratification of a new Protocol on Non-Discrimination will achieve the wider recognition of the principle. It would then be necessary to use the principle as the basis for positive obligations that would recognize the case for special treatment of certain groups. We have noted in previous chapters that special procedures to protect the mentally disordered must be introduced to assist and to protect them in the criminal process.[22] The same should apply to members of minority ethnic groups, in respect of whom we have noted evidence that people from an African-Caribbean background may be disadvantaged in decisions to prosecute or caution and in the process of plea negotiation.[23] Increases in the number of people from ethnic minorities in the legal profession and the various criminal justice agencies are necessary, but they are unlikely to solve the above problems, at least in the short term. The extent of discrimination on grounds of gender is unclear, and some might argue that the discrimination favours rather than disfavours women. However, studies of sentencing suggest that it would be unwise to take at face value the apparently lenient treatment of women and girls, and remand decisions appear to bear this out.[24]

In relation to young suspects and defendants, a case for positive discrimination has long been recognized. However, the special procedures introduced for child

---

[22] See Ch 6 on diversion.   [23] See Chs 7 and 10.

[24] Prison Reform Trust, *Justice for Women: the Need for Reform* (2000), paras 5.4–5.13; E. Player, 'Remanding Women in Custody: Concerns For Human Rights' (2007) 70 *MLR* 402.

defendants after the decision in *V and T v United Kingdom*[25] and for child witnesses under the Youth Justice and Criminal Evidence Act 1999 stand in contrast to the increasingly tough rhetoric used in relation to young defendants. ASBOs, with their stripped down procedural protections, are a major concern here, for they are much used against young people (see Chapter 13). In this country the spirit underlying the United Nations Convention on the Rights of the Child does not pervade Government pronouncements on youth justice, and the desire for vote-winning headlines seems to be thought more important.[26]

A further source of discrimination, discussed at several points in the foregoing chapters, may be found in factors connected with social class or wealth. It is evident from Chapters 6 and 7 that any systematic examination of the prosecution policies of the police compared with those of the so-called regulatory agencies would reveal a diversity of approaches, amounting in general to a less formal, less public and less severe response to law-breaking by employers, taxpayers and others in established ways of life. It is hardly surprising that statistics about the social background of offenders show a predominance of those from the lower socio-economic groups when the enforcement process is skewed against those groups and in favour of those from the higher occupational categories. However, changing this would present a structural problem of immense proportions for the English criminal justice system. Those who adopt a desert or retributive approach would probably argue that the first task should be to decide on the relative seriousness of all these offences, whether 'white-collar', 'normal', 'financial', 'commercial', 'domestic' or however they may be labelled. The second task might then be to ensure that the criminal law may only be invoked at a certain level of seriousness, whatever the context of the offence, and not below that level. This would represent an attempt to achieve equality before the law, in the hope of preventing the use of the criminal process (or anti-social behaviour orders) for relatively minor offences by impecunious or poorly connected defendants when at the same time ensuring that corporate or wealthy defendants do not benefit from a less vigorous approach where their offences are serious. That change of emphasis would not be easy to achieve, however, for many reasons—the need for a significant shift of resources to allow equivalent enforcement of regulatory offences, the need to reconsider the ways in which certain regulatory offences are drafted, and the possibility that wealthy or corporate 'deviants' might deploy their considerable resources to devise means of 'creative compliance' with the law.[27]

An alternative approach would be to adopt a form of restorative justice, abandoning the search for equivalent measures of punishment and instead requiring

---

[25] (2000) 30 EHRR 121; cf *SC v United Kingdom* [2005] *Crim LR* 130, where a further breach was found.

[26] M. Tonry, *Punishment and Politics* (2004), esp Ch 2; R. Reiner, *Law and Order: An Honest Citizen's Guide to Crime and Control* (2007), 136.

[27] See D. McBarnet and C. Whelan, 'The Elusive Spirit of the Law: Formalism and the Struggle for Legal Control' (1991) 54 *MLR* 848.

corporations who offend to make due reparation to those harmed by their offending behaviour.[28] This approach is premised not only on a rejection of the retributive paradigm for punishment but also on the difficulty and expense involved in holding companies responsible according to traditional criminal procedures and doctrines. Thus Braithwaite and Fisse argue that companies should be served with a notice that presumes liability and requires them to state what remedial measures they propose to take, in respect of both any individual victims and the wider community. In their scheme this would release resources otherwise devoted to prosecuting corporate crime and enable law enforcement agencies to devote more resources to dealing fairly with other forms of crime.[29] Thus companies would be taken out of the criminal process and their offences dealt with by different procedures, not so much on principle but rather as a means of controlling scarce resources. An alternative might be to keep companies within the criminal process and to raise the threshold for dealing with individual offenders, putting fewer inadequate and minor offenders in prison.

Important as it is to tackle unfair discrimination in the criminal law, in the enforcement process, and in criminal procedure, it remains supremely difficult to do so within a society many of whose institutions and practices may be said to lean towards unfair discrimination. The criminal process should not be regarded as something separate from wider social issues and capable of separate treatment. Discrimination on grounds of race, gender, age and other criteria will be hard to remove from the criminal process for so long as its manifestations are present in everyday social life.[30] This is not to deny the importance of efforts to remove discrimination from the criminal process, but it is to argue that there are structural factors that make it likely that some discriminatory effects might be found even if law enforcers were scrupulously fair in their own actions.

14.4 PROMOTING THE PRINCIPLES

How should the principled approach outlined in Chapter 2 and in this chapter be put into practice? Lawyers would tend to look to a network of rules or to a system of legal regulation as the means of advancing the desired principles. It has often been remarked that many stages in the criminal process are characterized by wide swaths of little-regulated discretion, from which it is assumed that the path of reform involves restrictions on or the complete removal of discretion. However, this would be naïve. It would be to assume that the existence of rules eliminates the practices that discretion

[28] B. Fisse and J. Braithwaite, *Corporations, Crime and Accountability* (1993).
[29] For which the authors also have proposals based on restorative justice, reinforced by strong sanctions: J. Braithwaite and P. Pettit, *Not Just Deserts: A Republican Theory of Criminal Justice* (1990), discussed critically in A. von Hirsch and A. Ashworth (eds), *Principled Sentencing* (2nd ed, 1998), Ch 7.
[30] Cf the argument of J. Chan, 'Changing Police Culture' (1996) 36 *BJ Crim* 109.

allows. There are plenty of examples of rules being circumvented or neutralized, for instance by the police (Chapters 3 and 4), by crown prosecutors (Chapter 7) and by counsel and judges (Chapter 10). Thus the mere enactment of rules in primary legislation should not be regarded as sufficient, or even as more effective than discretion complemented by guidelines. Working practices need to be changed, and this is where questions of ethics and of training come to the fore.

We noted in Chapter 1 that the origins of many of the miscarriage of justice cases of recent years lie in the early parts of the criminal justice system, particularly the stage of investigation by police and forensic scientists. One of the most welcome developments has been the creation of the Criminal Cases Review Commission, discussed in Chapter 12 above. The Commission is, however, currently a remedial rather than a preventive mechanism,[31] and it remains necessary to focus attention on the working practices of the police and other law enforcement agencies, and also the CPS and defence lawyers, at the early stages in the process. The criminal process in England and Wales has made significant advances in the treatment of certain fragile forms of evidence—notably confessions and eyewitness evidence—but further improvements should be made to eyewitness identification procedures, and thought needs to be given to new issues such as voice identification. Good legal advice should be available in these early stages, and this means ensuring that the system of payment for defence solicitors rewards early advice and case preparation appropriately,[32] and that the Public Defender Service develops along the right lines.

Moreover, it is not just the prosecution of some weak cases that is a cause for concern, or unwarranted arrests followed by detention. The attrition rate is also in need of constant scrutiny, and may embody miscarriages of justice of a different kind inasmuch as guilty people are not prosecuted or are acquitted because the system is organized in a way that fails to prevent that result. Thus there is a need to review procedures for witness protection and for encouraging witnesses to give evidence by the increased availability of video links and other mechanisms, subject to proper safeguards for the defence. Unfortunately, however, some of the recent changes to criminal procedure savour more of reducing the rights of the defence for symbolic reasons rather than of improving the position of victims: as argued in Chapter 2, the Government's notion of 're-balancing the system in favour of victims' is utterly flawed.

What should happen when a breach of one or more pre-trial procedures is uncovered? Much has been made, by some academics[33] and even by some British judges,[34] of the 'integrity principle'. The argument is that the integrity of the court, or more

---

[31] The Commission has frequently stated that it will use its experience of miscarriage of justice cases to make recommendations for improving the criminal process. It has found it difficult to do so but some of its general observations are reported in Ch 13.

[32] See House of Commons Constitutional Affairs Committee, *Draft Criminal Defence Service Bill* (Fifth Report of Session 2003/4).

[33] E.g., I. Dennis, *Criminal Evidence* (3rd ed, 2007), Ch 2E.

[34] E.g., Lord Lowry in *R v Horseferry Road Magistrates' Court, ex p Bennett* [1994]1 AC 42, and Lord Nicholls in *R v Looseley* [2001] UKHL 53. See also the judgments in *A v Home Secretary* [2005] UKHL 71.

widely of the criminal justice system, would be compromised if it were to act on evidence that had been obtained as a result of a departure from proper procedure. At one level the argument is persuasive, and the imagery of 'tainting' or 'the fruit of the poisoned tree' seems apposite. Yet in other respects, as argued in Chapter 11, the integrity principle leaves certain questions unanswered. Should every departure from procedure, no matter how small or inconsequential, be regarded as calling into question the integrity of a court or the whole system? If not, by what criteria can we tell whether integrity is compromised? Questions of this kind raise a doubt whether the integrity principle can be a satisfactory operating standard for the courts: attractive as it is in clear and gross cases, it needs considerable refinement if it is to be suitable for the general run of situations.[35] More relevant to the objective of promoting a principled approach to criminal justice is the protective principle: that a court should not act on evidence if that would deprive the defendant of a protection that should have been assured. In other words, a deviation from procedures may only be overlooked if the evidence in question was not obtained as a result of its breach. The defendant should not be disadvantaged by an investigator's non-observance of the procedures.

Of course, that leaves the question of just what procedures are proper. Once we move away from the rules in the Police and Criminal Evidence Act 1984 which give suspects various rights, there are a host of difficult questions: when, if ever, is deception, or covert recording, or entrapment, proper? There is simply no avoiding the fact that, in general, an evaluation of the criminal process involves difficult questions about what values should be respected. Other examples are questions such as: When might a breach of the privilege against self-incrimination be appropriate? When is it appropriate to keep a suspect's DNA profile on a database? How wide should arrest powers be? When is jury trial appropriate? Are there exceptions to the right of confrontation? Human rights documents will not always provide clear, or convincing, answers to such questions, and there is room for reasonable disagreement on them. But our argument is that any attempt to answer these questions must involve careful analysis of the values at stake. All too often this does not happen.

The promotion of a principled approach requires not only the provision of appropriate remedies in cases where the principles are not put into practice, but also programmes of training and supervision and guidance for the professionals concerned. No doubt it would be argued that there are professional organizations to take care of such matters, and the role of the Law Society and the Bar Council will be cited. However, the discussion of occupational cultures which began in Chapter 3 and continued in subsequent chapters makes it plain that there is, at the very least, a risk not only that simply changing the rules will fail but also that leaving the task of changing practices to the professional organizations is unlikely to succeed. The risk of failure would be greatest where the particular occupational culture is adverse and strong.

---

[35] For fuller analysis, see A. Ashworth, 'Exploring the Integrity Principle in Evidence and Procedure' in P. Mirfield and R. Smith (eds), *Essays for Colin Tapper* (2003).

It is therefore necessary to attempt to reshape the occupational cultures of some of those working within the criminal process. As a first step, more detailed ethical principles need to be drawn up which spell out the role responsibilities of prosecutors and defence lawyers, and the constraints on their pursuit of these goals. The ethical principles should ideally be supported by examples of situations in which they are intended to bite. This would be a means of challenging occupational cultures in a direct way. In order to do that, of course, it would be necessary to have a reasonably accurate impression of the operation of occupational cultures in practice, and the available research (discussed in previous chapters) provides some evidence of unethical practices (without suggesting that all members of the various groups follow these practices). Ideas such as 'society expects us to fight crime with our hands tied behind our backs' must be carefully and persuasively unpicked. Thus it is vital to incorporate into training the reasons for respecting rights, and to reorient professional goals and official performance indicators in a way that reveres and rewards respect for rights over the mere obtaining of convictions.

None of this means that convicting the guilty is unimportant; rather, it emphasizes that this worthy goal should be achieved by fair processes. This is not just a matter of ensuring that Parliament, the courts and public authorities uphold Convention rights, although that is constitutionally important after the Human Rights Act. There is also evidence that people in general regard fair procedures as an essential element in a criminal justice system. To set against the belief of some politicians that public confidence in the system would be threatened by thoroughgoing respect for human rights (not that it is often thus expressed) are the findings of social psychologists such as Tom Tyler that people place as much emphasis on the fairness of procedures (notably, having a fair hearing) as on their outcomes.[36] Although some of Tyler's conclusions may seem overblown,[37] there is good reason to accept his fundamental point that fair processes matter.

14.5 THE CRIMINAL PROCESS OF THE FUTURE

Any detailed reform proposals such as those advanced in this book are likely to have a modest effect if other aspects of the criminal justice system remain little changed, and any changes in the criminal justice system may have a modest effect if various social structures and policies remain little changed. Moreover, considerations of cost and public expenditure must be taken into account by anyone who forsakes the cover

---

[36] T. Tyler, *Why People Obey the Law* (1990); T. Tyler and Y. Huo, *Trust in the Law: Encouraging Public Cooperation with the Police and Courts* (2002). See also R. Moorhead, M. Sefton and L. Scanlan, *Just Satisfaction? What drives Public and Participant Satisfaction with Courts and Tribunals?* (2008).

[37] E.g., at 101: 'if people receive fair procedures, outcome is not relevant to their reactions. If they do not, it is.'

of academic discussion to venture some policy proposals. Recognizing cost as a constraint does not, however, argue against fundamental change. A decade and a half ago, the Report of the 1993 Royal Commission was a missed opportunity in criminal justice reform—not only because of its abject failure to discuss Convention rights and their implications for criminal justice, but also because it considered expenditure in relation to discrete stages in the process rather than the whole. A more creative approach would be to take the annual budget of the whole system—including police, prosecutors, courts, legal aid, prisons, and so forth—and to consider a five-year reorientation of expenditure which would enhance human rights to the greatest extent without increasing the overall budget.[38] Rather than resorting to the imagery of 'balance' at each stage of the process, the challenge would be to ensure or maximize respect for rights while enhancing convictions of the guilty, looking critically at the roles of the various professional groups, at their powers, and at their practices. In addition to debating the rights of victims, the approach would be to examine wider social methods of preventing crime that promise fewer victims (and fewer offenders), such as the increased availability of pre-school education, improved housing, and other changes in social policy. It is unlikely that changing the criminal process itself will make much difference to crime rates and the safety of citizens: altering the rules of the criminal process is attractive to governments, not least because it is much easier than tackling fundamental issues of social policy, but also because the symbolic effects of appearing 'tough on crime' are expected to have favourable electoral consequences.

Thus one obvious feature of debates on the criminal process in the last decade is their increased politicization. A Government that began in 1997 by advocating evidence-based changes quickly forsook that approach in favour of announcing changes that appear tough and anti-defendant and thus court no danger of losing the political initiative to the opposition.[39] In this climate there is a dire need for an attractive replacement discourse if rights—also advocated by this Government in its early days, prior to the enactment of the Human Rights Act—are to be respected properly in the criminal process. We have witnessed an unfortunate backsliding on human rights, to the extent that recent Home Office policy papers have rarely even discussed the issue in the context of new proposals for 'reform'. Occasionally, the Government has been openly hostile to rights, as in its attack on, and misrepresentation of, the European Court of Human Rights decision in *Chahal v United Kingdom*,[40] discussed in Chapter 2. The Government might also have been said to have been hostile to the rule of law, as seen in its attempt to prevent judges from overturning convictions gained through serious executive malpractice.[41] More recently, however, it has been

---

[38] As argued in previous editions, the inquiry must necessarily take in spheres of expenditure other than criminal justice. Even if the debate could be confined within criminal justice, this approach would place the benefits of, say, pre-trial legal advice in a proper perspective rather than simply seeing it as an extra expense. See also K. Roach, 'The Criminal Process' in P. Cane and M. Tushnet (eds), *Handbook of Legal Studies* (2003).

[39] See Reiner, above n 26, Ch 5.   [40] (1997) 23 EHRR 413.

[41] See *Quashing Convictions* (2006), discussed in Ch 12.

more conciliatory towards human rights. The Green Paper *Rights and Responsibilities* states that the Government is proud to have introduced the Human Rights Act.[42] The document floats ideas for inclusion in a UK Bill of Rights, but does not propose altering Convention rights in the area of criminal justice, though it does suggest that a Bill of Rights might explicitly recognize victims' rights. In the likely prospect of a Conservative administration taking power in 2010, however, things are less certain. The Conservatives are committed to repeal of the Human Rights Act and its replacement with a Bill of Rights. Exactly what would be included in the Bill of Rights is uncertain;[43] there is mention of time limits on detention (though detention is already constrained under Article 5 of the ECHR) and the right to jury trial. Given that the vast majority of cases are heard in the magistrates' court, it is unclear how the latter right might be framed so as to make it meaningful.[44] Lurking behind Conservative dissatisfaction with the Human Rights Act is what may be a more sinister policy; there are concerns that the Human Rights Act has inhibited law enforcement: 'The rights of criminals have been put before the rights of law abiding citizens'.[45] A Bill of Rights, it is said, would enable the UK to rebalance laws in favour of public protection. As we have argued throughout this book, such rhetoric is antagonistic to respect for rights.

The human rights approach to criminal justice advocated in Chapter 2 of this book therefore runs counter to much contemporary policy, although it has its basis in the UK's international obligations (notably the Convention). However, neither the Convention nor other international instruments—nor, it may be added, any known general theory—provides a comprehensive set of principles for the criminal process. In practice there will always be some choices to be made, and some trade-offs to be agreed. What is distinctive about the approach advocated here, and elaborated in Chapter 2 is that it insists on a weighted approach, with justifications given for the different priority given to different rights. It also insists on evidence rather than rhetoric, and on evidence of actual enhancements in prevention or protection rather than evidence of reductions in the risk people believe they face.[46]

---

[42] *Rights and Responsiibilities: Developing Our Constitutional Framework* (2009), 10.
[43] See M. Amos, 'Problems with the Human Rights Act 1998 and How to Remedy Them: Is a Bill of Rights the Answer?' (2009) 72 *MLR* 883, 906–7.
[44] See the cautious discussion of such a right in *Rights and Responsibilities*, above n 42, 35–7.
[45] 'News Story', 7 October 2009, at www.conservatives.com/.
[46] For recent argument to the same effect on criminal justice policy and sentencing, see Tonry, above n 26.

BIBLIOGRAPHY

ABRAMSON, J. (1994), *We, The Jury: The Jury System and the Ideal of Democracy*, New York: Basic Books.

ALLEN, R. (2008), 'Theorizing About Self-Incrimination', *Cardozo L Rev*, 30: 751.

ALSCHULER, A. (1983), 'Implementing the Criminal Defendant's Right to Trial', *U Chi LR*, 50: 931.

——(1997), 'Constraint and Confession', *Denver U L Rev*, 74: 957.

——(2008), 'Studying the Exclusionary Rule: An Empirical Classic', *U Chicago L Rev*, 75: 1365.

AMAR, A. (1997), *The Constitution and Criminal Procedure*, New Haven, CT: Yale University Press.

AMERICAN BAR ASSOCIATION (1980), *Standards Relating to the Prosecution Function and the Defense Function*, Chicago: American Bar Association.

AMOS, M. (2009), 'Problems with the Human Rights Act 1998 and How to Remedy Them: Is a Bill of Rights the Answer?', *MLR*, 72: 883.

ASHWORTH, A. (1977), 'Excluding Evidence as Protecting Rights', *Crim LR*, 723.

—— (1998), 'Should the Police be Allowed to Use Deceptive Practices?', *LQR*, 114: 108.

—— (2002), *Human Rights, Serious Crime and Criminal Procedure* London: Sweet & Maxwell.

—— (2002), 'Re-drawing the Boundaries of Entrapment', *Crim LR*, 161.

—— (2002), 'Responsibilities, Rights and Restorative Justice', *BJ Crim*, 43: 578.

——(2003), 'Exploring the Integrity Principle in Evidence and Procedure' in Mirfield and Smith, eds, qv.

——(2004), 'Social Control and "Anti-Social Behaviour": the subversion of Human Rights?', *LQR*, 120: 263.

—— (2004), 'Criminal Justice Reform: Principles, Human Rights and Public Protection', *Crim LR*, 516.

—— (2007), 'Security, Terrorism and the Value of Human Rights' in Goold and Lazarus, eds, qv.

——(2008), 'Self-Incrimination in European Human Rights Law—A Pregnant Pragmatism?', *Cardozo L Rev*, 30: 751.

—— (2009), 'Criminal Law, Human Rights and Preventative Justice' in McSherry, Norrie and Bronitt, eds, qv.

—— (2009), *Principles of Criminal Law*, 6th ed, Oxford: Oxford University Press.

—— (2010), *Sentencing and Criminal Justice*, 5th ed, London: Butterworths.

—— and FIONDA, J. (1994), 'The New Code for Crown Prosecutors: Prosecution, Accountability and the Public Interest', *Crim LR*, 894.

——and STRANGE, M. (2004), 'Criminal Law and Human Rights', *EHRLR*, 121.

——and WASIK, M., eds (1998), *Fundamentals of Sentencing Theory*, Oxford: Oxford University Press.

—— and ZEDNER, L. (2008), 'Defending the Criminal Law: Reflections on the Changing Character of Crime, Procedure and Sanctions', *Crim Law & Phil*, 2: 21.

—— and —— (2010), 'Preventive Orders: a Problem of Under-Criminalization?' in Duff, Farmer, Marshall and Tadros, eds, qv (forthcoming).

AUDIT COMMISSION (1996), *Misspent Youth: Young People and Crimes*, London: Audit Commission.

AULD, R. E. (2001), *Review of the Criminal Courts of England and Wales; Report*, London: The Lord Chancellor's Department.

AUSTIN, R. C. (2007), 'The New Powers of Arrest', *Crim LR*, 459.

BAILEY S. and TAYLOR, N. (2009), *Civil Liberties: Cases, Materials and Commentary*, 6th ed, Oxford: Oxford University Press.

BALDWIN, J. (1986), *Pre-Trial Justice*, Oxford: Oxford University Press.

—— (1992), *The Supervision of Police Investigations in Serious Criminal Cases*, Royal Commission on Criminal Justice Research Study No 4, London: HMSO.

—— (1993), 'Legal Advice at the Police Station', *Crim LR*, 371.

—— (1997), 'Understanding Judge Ordered and Directed Acquittals in the Crown Court', *Crim LR*, 536.

—— and MCCONVILLE, M. (1977), *Negotiated Justice*, Oxford: Martin Robertson.

BALDWIN, R. (2004), 'The New Punitive Regulation', *MLR*, 67: 351.

—— and HAWKINS, K. (1984), 'Discretionary Justice: Davis Reconsidered', *PL*, 570.

BARCLAY, G. C., ed (1999), *Digest 4: Information on the Criminal Justice System in England and Wales*, London: Home Office.

—— and MHLANGA, B. (2000), *Ethnic Differences in Decisions on Young Defendants Dealt With by the Crown Prosecution Service*, Section 95 Findings 1, London: Home Office.

BILLINGSLEY, R., NEMITZ, T. and BEAN, P., eds (2001), *Informers: Policing, Policy, Practice*, Cullompton: Willan Publishing.

BILZ, K. (2010), 'Integrity or Deterrence: The Psychology of the Exclusionary Rule' (forthcoming).

BIRCH, D. (1995), 'Corroboration: Goodbye to All That?', *Crim LR*, 524.

—— (1999) 'Suffering in Silence: a Cost-Benefit Analysis of Section 34 of the Criminal Justice and Public Order Act 1994', *Crim LR*, 769.

BITTNER, E. (1967), 'The Police on Skid Row: a Study in Peacekeeping', *American Sociological Review*, 32: 699.

BLAKE, M. and ASHWORTH, A. (1998), 'Some Ethical Issues in Prosecuting and Defending Criminal Cases', *Crim LR*, 16.

—— and —— (2004), 'Ethics and the Criminal Defence Lawyer', *Legal Ethics*, 7: 167.

BLANDON-GITLIN, I., SPERRY, K. and LEO, R. (2010), 'Jurors Believe Interrogation Tactics are not Likely to Elicit False Confessions: Will Expert Witness Testimony Inform them Otherwise?', *Psychology, Crime and Law*, 16 (forthcoming).

BLOCK, B., CORBETT, C. and PEAY, J. (1993), *Ordered and Directed Acquittals in the Crown Court*, Royal Commission on Criminal Justice Research Study No 15, London: HMSO.

BOTTOMS, A. K. and MCCLEAN, J. D. (1968), 'The Granting of Bail: Principles and Practice', *MLR*, 31: 40.

—— and MCCLEAN, J. D. (1976), *Defendants in the Criminal Process*, London: Routledge.

BOWLING, B. and PHILLIPS, C. (2002), *Racism, Crime and Justice*, Harlow: Longman.

—— and —— (2007), 'Disproportionate and Discriminatory: Reviewing the Evidence on Police Stop and Search', *MLR*, 70: 936.

BRADLEY, C. (1993), 'The Emerging International Consensus as to Criminal Procedural Rules', *Michigan J Int Law* 14: 171.

—— (1999), *Criminal Procedure: a Worldwide Study*, Durham, NC: Carolina Academic Press.

BRADLEY, C. (1999), 'United States' in Bradley, ed, qv.

BRADLEY, K. (2009), *The Bradley Report: Lord Bradley's Review of People with Mental Health Problems or Learning Disabilities in the Criminal Justice System*, London: Department of Health.

BRAITHWAITE, J. and PETTIT, P. (1990), *Not Just Deserts: a Republican Theory of Criminal Justice*, Oxford: Oxford University Press.

BRANTS, C. and FIELD, S. (1995), 'Discretion and Accountability in Prosecution', in Fennell, Harding, Jörg and Swart, eds, qv.

BRIDGES, L. (2000), 'Taking Liberties' *Legal Action*, 6 July.

—— (2006), 'Ethics of Representation on Guilty Pleas', *Legal Ethics*, 9: 80.

—— and CAPE E. (2008), *CDS Direct: Flying in the Face of the Evidence*, London: Centre for Crime and Justice Studies, King's College London.

—— and CHOONGH, S. (1998), *Improving Police Station Legal Advice*, London: Law Society.

BROOKE, D., TAYLOR, C., GUNN, J. and MADEN, A. (2000), 'Substance Misuse as a Marker of Vulnerability Among Male Prisoners on Remand', *BJ Psychiatry*, 177: 248.

BROOKMAN, F. and PIERPOINT, H. (2003), 'Access to Legal Advice for Young Suspects and Remand Prisoners', *Howard JCJ*, 42: 452.

BROWN, D. (1991), *Investigating Burglary: The Effects of PACE*, London: HMSO.

—— (1997), *PACE Ten Years On: A Review of the Research*, Home Office Research Study 155, London: Home Office.

—— (2000), *Reducing Delays in the Magistrates' Courts*, Home Office Research Findings No 131, London: Home Office.

—— and ELLIS, T. (1994) *Policing Low-Level Disorder*, Home Office Research Study 135, London: Home Office.

——, LARCOMBE, K. and ELLIS, C. (1993), *Changing the Code: Police Detention under the Revised PACE Codes of Practice*, Home Office Research Study 129, London: HMSO.

BROWNLEE, I. (2004), 'The Statutory Charging Scheme in England and Wales: Towards a Unified Prosecution System?', *Crim LR*, 896.

—— (2007), 'Conditional Cautions and Fair Trial Rights: Form versus Substance in the Diversionary Agenda', *Crim LR*, 129.

——, MULCAHY, A. and WALKER, C. P. (1994), 'Pre-Trial Reviews, Court Efficiency and Justice: a Study in Leeds and Bradford Magistrates' Courts', *Howard JCJ*, 33: 109.

BUCKE, T. and BROWN, D. (1997), *In Police Custody: police powers and suspects' rights under the revised PACE codes of practice*, Home Office Research Study 174, London: Home Office.

——, STREET, R. and BROWN, D. (2000), *The Right of Silence: the Impact of the Criminal Justice and Public Order Act 1994*, Home Office Research Study 199, London: Home Office.

BURNEY, E. (2009), *Making People Behave: Anti-Social Behaviour, Politics and Policy*, 2nd ed, Cullompton: Willan Publishing.

—— and PEARSON, G. (1995), 'Mentally Disordered Offenders: Finding a Focus for Diversion', *Howard JCJ*, 34: 291.

—— and ROSE, G. (2002), *Racist offences— How is the Law Working?*, Home Office Research Study 244, London: Home Office.

BURROWS, P., HENDERSON, P. and MORGAN, P. (1994), *Improving Bail Decisions: the Bail Process Project*, London: Home Office Research and Planning Unit.

BURTON, M. (2001), 'Reviewing Crown Prosecution Service Decisions not to Prosecute', *Crim LR*, 374.

BUXTON, R. (2009), 'The Private Prosecutor as Minister of Justice', *Crim LR*, 427.

CAMERON, N., POTTER, S. and YOUNG, W. (1999), 'The New Zealand Jury', *Law & Contemporary Problems*, 62: 103.

CAMMISS, S. (2007), 'Deciding Upon Mode of Trial', *Howard JCJ*, 46: 372.

—— and STRIDE, C. (2008), 'Modelling Mode of Trial', *Brit J Criminol*, 48: 482.

CANE, P. and TUSHNET, M., eds (2003), *Oxford Handbook of Legal Studies*, Oxford: Oxford University Press.

CAPE, E. (1999), 'Sufficient Evidence to Charge?', *Crim LR*, 874.

—— (2003), 'The Revised PACE Codes of Practice: A Further Step Towards Inquisitorialism', *Crim LR*, 355.

—— (2004), 'The Rise (and Fall) of a Criminal Defence Profession', *Crim LR*, 408.

—— (2006), *Defending Suspects at Police Stations*, 5th ed, London: Legal Action Group.

—— (2006), 'Rebalancing the Criminal Justice Process: Ethical Challenges for Criminal Defence Lawyers', *Legal Ethics*, 9: 56.

—— (2007), 'Modernising Police Powers— Again?', *Crim LR*, 934.

—— and YOUNG, R., eds (2008), *Regulating Policing: the Police and Criminal Evidence Act 1984, Past, Present and Future*, Oxford: Hart Publishing.

CARLILE, A. (2009), *Report on the Operation in 2008 of the Terrorism Act 2000 and of Part I of the Terrorism Act 2006*, London: Home Office.

CARSON, D. (1989), 'Prosecuting People with Mental Handicaps', *Crim LR*, 87.

CHAN, J. (1996), 'Changing Police Culture', *BJ Crim*, 36: 109.

CHOO, A. (2008), *Abuse of Process and Judicial Stays of Criminal Proceedings*, 2nd ed, Oxford: Oxford University Press.

—— and NASH, S. (2007), 'Improperly Obtained Evidence in the Commonwealth: Lessons for England and Wales?', *E & P*, 11: 75.

—— and —— (1999), 'What's the Matter with Section 78?', *Crim LR*, 929.

CHOONGH, S. (1998), 'Policing the Dross: a Social Disciplinary Model of Policing', *BJ Crim*, 38: 623.

CHOUDHRY, S., ed (2007), *The Migration of Constitutional Ideas*, Cambridge: Cambridge University Press.

CLARE, I., GUDJONSSON, G. and HARARI, M. (1998), 'Understanding of the Current Police Caution (England and Wales)', *J Community & Applied Social Psychology*, 8: 323.

CLARKE, C. and MILNE, R. (2001), *National Evaluation of the PEACE Investigative Interviewing Course*, London: Home Office.

CLARKSON, C., CRETNEY, A., DAVIS, G. and SHEPHERD, J. (1994), 'Assaults: the Relationship between Seriousness, Criminalisation and Punishment', *Crim LR*, 4.

COMMISSION FOR RACIAL EQUALITY (1992), *Juvenile Cautioning: Ethnic Monitoring in Practice*, London: CRE.

COMMISSION JUSTICE PÉNALE ET DROITS DE L'HOMME (1991), *La Mise en Etat des Affaires Pénales*, Paris: la Documentation Francaise.

CORRE, N. and WOLCHOVER, D. (2004), *Bail in Criminal Proceedings*, 3rd ed, Oxford: Oxford University Press.

COUNCIL OF EUROPE (1987), *The Simplification of Criminal Justice*, Recommendation R(87)18 (1987), Strasbourg: Council of Europe.

—— (2000), *Crime and Criminal Justice in Europe*, Strasbourg: Council of Europe.

COURT OF APPEAL (2006), *Protocol for the Control and Management of Unused*

Material in the Crown Court, London: Ministry of Justice.

CRAIG, P. (2004), 'Grounds for Judicial Review: Substantive Control over Discretion' in Feldman, ed, qv.

CRANSTON, R. (1979), *Regulating Business*, Oxford: Oxford University Press.

CRETNEY, A. and DAVIS, G. (1995), *Punishing Violence*, London, New York: Routledge.

CRIMINAL CASES REVIEW COMMISSION (2003), *Annual Report 2002–2003*, Birmingham: Criminal Cases Review Commission.

CRIMINAL JUSTICE SYSTEM (2007), *Delivering Simple, Speedy, Summary Justice: An Evaluation of the Magistrates' Courts Tests*, London: Criminal Justice System.

—— (2009), *Engaging Communities in Criminal Justice*, London: Criminal Justice System.

CRIMINAL LAW REVISION COMMITTEE (1972), *Eleventh Report: Evidence (General)*, Cmnd 4991, London: HMSO.

CROWN PROSECUTION SERVICE (1996), *Code for Crown Prosecutors: Explanatory Memorandum*, London: CPS.

—— (2004), *Annual Report 2003–04*, London: CPS.

—— (2007), *The Director's Guidance on Conditional Cautioning*, 5th ed, London: CPS.

—— (2009), *Annual Report 2008–09*, London: CPS.

—— (2009), *Care and Treatment of Victims and Witnesses*, www.cps.gov.uk.

—— (2009), *Supporting Victims and Witnesses with Mental Health Issues*, www.cps.gov.uk.

—— (2009), *The Public Prosecution Service— Setting the Standard*, London: CPS.

CUTLER, B. and PENROD, S. (1995), *Mistaken Identification: The Eyewitness, Psychology and the Law*, New York: Cambridge University Press.

DAMAŠKA, M. (1973), 'Evidentiary Barriers to Conviction and Two Models of Criminal Procedure: a Comparative Study', *U Pa LR*, 121: 506.

—— (1976), *The Faces of Justice and State Authority*, New Haven, CT: Yale University Press.

—— (1997), *Evidence Law Adrift*, New Haven, CT: Yale University Press.

DARBYSHIRE, P. (1997), 'For the New Lord Chancellor: Some Causes for Concern about Magistrates', *Crim LR*, 861.

—— (1997), 'Previous Misconduct and the Magistrates' Courts—Some Tales from the Real World', *Crim LR*, 105.

—— (2000), 'The Mischief of Plea Bargaining and Sentencing Rewards', *Crim LR*, 895.

DAVIES, F. G. (1995), 'CPS Charging Standards: a Cynic's View', *JP*, 159: 203.

—— (1997), 'Ten Years of the Crown Prosecution Service: the Verdict', *JP*, 161: 207.

DAVIES G. and VENNARD, J. (2006), 'The Experience of Ethnic Minority Magistrates', *Howard JCJ*, 45: 485.

DAVIS, G., HOYANO, L., KEENAN, C., MAITLAND, L. and MORGAN, R. (1999), *An Assessment of the Admissibility and Sufficiency of Evidence in Child Abuse Prosecutions*, London: Home Office.

DAW, R. (1994), 'The CPS Code—a Response', *Crim LR*, 904.

DE SCHUTTER, O. and RINGELHEIM, J. (2008), 'Ethnic Profiling: A Rising Challenge for European Human Rights Law', *MLR*, 71: 358.

DELMAS-MARTY, M. and SPENCER, J. R., eds (2002), *European Criminal Procedures*, Cambridge: Cambridge University Press.

DEMPSEY, M. (2009), *Prosecuting Domestic Violence*, Oxford: Oxford University Press.

DENNIS, I. (2000), 'Rethinking Double Jeopardy: Justice and Finality in Criminal Process', *Crim LR*, 933.

—— (2003), 'Fair Trials and Safe Convictions', *CLP*, 56: 211.

—— (2004), 'Prosecution Appeals and Retrial for Serious Offences', *Crim LR*, 619.

—— (2007), *The Law of Evidence*, 3rd ed, London: Sweet & Maxwell.

DENYER, R. (2009), 'The Defence Statement', *Crim LR*, 340.

DERSHOWITZ, A. (2006), *Pre-Emption*, New York: W. W. Norton.

DEVLIN, P. (1976), *Report to the Secretary of State for the Home Department of the Departmental Committee on Evidence of Identification in Criminal Cases*, London: HMSO.

—— (1979), *The Judge*, Oxford: Oxford University Press.

DHAMI, M. (2002), 'Do Bail Information Schemes Really Affect Bail Decisions?', *Howard JCJ*, 41: 245.

—— (2004), 'Conditional Bail Decision-Making in the Magistrates' Court', *Howard JCJ*, 43: 27.

—— (2005), 'From Discretion to Disagreement: Explaining Disparities in Judges' Pre-Trial Decisions', *Behavioural Sciences and the Law*, 23: 367.

DINGWALL, G. and HARDING, C. (1998), *Diversion in the Criminal Process*, London: Sweet & Maxwell.

DIXON, D. (1997), *Law in Policing: Legal Regulation and Police Practices*, Oxford: Oxford University Press.

—— (1990), 'Safeguarding the Rights of Suspects in Police Custody', *Policing & Society*, 1: 115.

—— (2008), 'Authorise and Regulate: A Comparative Perspective on the Rise and Fall of a Regulatory Strategy' in Cape and Young, eds, qv.

—— and TRAVERS, G. (2007), *Interrogating Images: Audio-Visually Recorded Police Questioning of Suspects*, Sydney: Sydney Institute of Criminology.

DOHERTY, C. and EAST, R. (1985), 'Bail Decisions in Magistrates' Courts', *BJ Crim*, 25: 251.

DOLINKO, D. (1986), 'Is there a Rationale for the Privilege Against Self-Incrimination?', 33 *UCLA L Rev*, 33: 1063.

DORAN, S. and GLENN, R. (2000), *Lay Involvement in Adjudication*, Belfast: The Stationery Office.

—— and JACKSON, J. D. (1997), 'The Case for Jury Waiver', *Crim LR*, 155.

—— and ——, eds (2000), *The Judicial Role in Criminal Proceedings*, Oxford: Hart Publishing.

DOWNES, D. and MORGAN, R., (2007), 'No Turning Back: the Politics of Law and Order into the Millennium', in Maguire, Morgan and Reiner, eds, qv.

DRESSLER, J. and MICHAELS, A. (2006), *Understanding Criminal Procedure, Vol 1: Investigations*, 4th ed, Newark, NJ: LexisNexis.

DREWRY, G. (1985), 'The Ponting Case—Leaking in the Public Interest', *PL*, 203.

DRIZIN, S. and LEO, R. (2004), 'The Problem of False Confessions in the Post-DNA World', *North Carolina L Rev*, 82: 891.

DROR, I. and FRASER-MACKENZIE, P. (2009), 'Cognitive Biases in Human Perception, Judgment, and Decision Making: Bridging Theory and the Real World' in Rossmo, ed, qv.

—— and ROSENTHAL, R. (2008), 'Meta-Analytically Quantifying the Reliability and Biasability of Forensic Experts', *J Forensic Sciences*, 53: 900.

DUFF, P. (2009), 'Straddling Two Worlds: Reflections of a Retired Criminal Cases Review Commissioner', *MLR*, 72: 693.

—— and HUTTON, N., eds (1999), *Criminal Justice in Scotland*, Aldershot: Ashgate.

DUFF, R. A. (1986), *Trials and Punishments*, Cambridge: Cambridge University Press.

—— (2005), 'Strict Liability, Legal Presumptions and the Presumption of Innocence' in Simester, ed, qv.

——, FARMER, L., MARSHALL, S. and TADROS, V., eds (2006), *The Trial on Trial: Volume 2. Judgment and Calling to Account*, Oxford: Hart Publishing.

——, ——, —— and ——, eds (2007), *The Trial on Trial: Volume 3. Towards a Normative Theory of the Criminal Trial*, Oxford: Hart Publishing.

——, ——, —— and ——, eds (2010), *Criminalization* (forthcoming).

DWORKIN, R. M. (1981), 'Principle, Policy, Procedure', in Tapper, ed, qv.

DYZENHAUS, D., ed (1999), *Recrafting the Rule of Law*, Oxford: Hart Publishing.

ELKS, L. (2008), 'R v Stock', *Archbold News* 9: 3.

—— (2008), *Righting Miscarriages of Justice? Ten Years of the Criminal Cases Review Commission*, London: JUSTICE.

ELLIS, L. and DIAMOND, S. (2003), 'Race, Diversity, and Jury Composition: Battering and Bolstering Legitimacy', *Chicago-Kent L Rev*, 78: 1033.

ELLISON, L. (2007), 'Promoting Effective Case-Building in Rape Cases: a Comparative Perspective', *Crim LR*, 691.

EMMERSON, B., ASHWORTH, A. and MACDONALD, A. (2007), *Human Rights and Criminal Justice*, 2nd ed, London: Sweet & Maxwell.

EVANS, R. (1993), 'Comparing Young Adult and Juvenile Cautioning in the Metropolitan Police District', *Crim LR*, 572.

—— (1993), 'Evaluating Young Adult Diversion Schemes in the Metropolitan Police District', *Crim LR*, 490.

—— (1996), 'Challenging a Police Caution using Judicial Review', *Crim LR*, 104.

—— and ELLIS, R. (1997), *Police Cautioning in the 1990s*, Home Office Research Findings No 33, London: Home Office.

—— and WILKINSON, C. (1990), 'Variations in Police Cautioning', *Howard JCJ*, 29: 155.

FEELEY, M. (1979), *The Process is the Punishment*, New York: Russell Sage Foundation.

—— (1997), 'Legal Complexity and the Transformation of the Criminal Process: the Origins of Plea Bargaining', *Israel LR*, 31: 183.

—— and SIMON, J. (1994), 'Actuarial Justice: the New Emerging Criminal Law' in Nelken, ed, qv.

FEILZER, M. and HOOD, R. (2004), *Differences or Discrimination?*, London: Youth Justice Board.

FEINBERG, J. (2003), 'Criminal Entrapment' in Feinberg, ed, qv.

—— (2003), *Problems at the Roots of Law: Essays in Legal and Political Theory*, Oxford: Oxford University Press.

FELDMAN, D. J. (2009) (ed), *English Public Law*, 2nd ed, Oxford: Oxford University Press.

FENNELL, C. (2003), *The Law of Evidence in Ireland*, 2nd ed, Dublin: LexisNexis.

FENNER, S., GUDJONSSON, G. and CLARE, I. (2002), 'Understanding of the Current Police Caution (England and Wales) Among Suspects in Police Detention', *J Community & Applied Social Psychology*, 12: 83.

FIELD, S. (2008), 'Early Intervention and the "New" Youth Justice: a Study of Initial Decision-making', *Crim LR*, 177.

FIELDS, P. (2008), 'Clarke and McDaid: A Technical Triumph', *Crim LR*, 612.

FINDLEY, K. and SCOTT, M. (2006), 'The Multiple Dimensions of Tunnel Vision in Criminal Cases', *Wisconsin L Rev*, 2: 291.

FINKEL, N. (2006), 'Jurors' Duties, Obligations and Rights: The Ethical/Moral Roots of Discretion' in Kleinig and Levine, eds, qv.

FIONDA, J. (1995), *Public Prosecutors and Discretion: a Comparative Study*, Oxford: Clarendon Press.

FISHER, H. (1977), *Report of an Inquiry by the Hon. Sir Henry Fisher into the circumstances leading to the trial of three persons on charges arising out of the death of Maxwell Confait and the fire at 27 Doggett Road, London SE6*, London: HMSO.

FISSE, B. and BRAITHWAITE, J. (1993), *Corporations, Crime and Accountability*, Sydney: University of Sydney Press.

FITZGERALD, M. (1993), *Ethnic Minorities and the Criminal Justice System*, Royal Commission on Criminal Justice Research Study No 20, London: HMSO.

——(1999), *Final Report into Stop and Search*, London: Metropolitan Police Service.

FOOTE, C. (1954), 'Compelling Appearance in Court: the Administration of Bail in Philadelphia', *U Pa LR*, 102: 1031.

FOSTER, J. (2003), 'Police Cultures' in Newburn, qv.

——, NEWBURN, T. and SOUHAMI, A. (2005), *Assessing the Impact of the Stephen Lawrence Inquiry*, London: Home Office.

FREED, D. J. and WALD, P. (1964), *Bail in the United States*, New York: Vera Institute of Justice.

FRIEDMAN, R. (2008), 'The Confrontation Right Across the Systemic Divide' in Jackson, Langer and Tillers, eds, qv.

FUKURAI, H. and KROOTH, R. (2003), *Race in the Jury Box: Affirmative Action in Jury Selection*, Albany, NY: State University of New York Press.

GANS, J. (2008), 'Evidence Law Under Victoria's Charter: Remedies and Responsibilities', *Public Law Review*, 19: 285.

—— and PALMER, A. (2004), *Australian Principles of Evidence*, Sydney: Cavendish.

GARDNER, J. (1998), 'Punishment—in Proportion and in Perspective' in Ashworth and Wasik, qv.

GENDERS, E. (1999), 'Reform of the Offences Against the Person Act: Lessons from the Law in Action', *Crim LR*, 689.

GIVELBER, D. and FARRELL, A. (2008), 'Judges and Juries: The Defense Case and Differences in Acquittal Rates', *Law & Social Inquiry*, 33: 31.

GLIDEWELL, I. (1998), *Review of the Crown Prosecution Service: a Report*, Cm 3960, London: The Stationery Office.

GOLDKAMP, J. and GOTTFREDSON, M. R. (1985), *Policy Guidelines for Bail: an Exercise in Court Reform*, Philadelphia, PA: Temple University Press.

GOOLD, B. and LAZARUS, L., eds (2007), *Security and Human Rights*, Oxford: Hart Publishing.

——, —— and SWINEY, G. (2007), *Public Protection, Proportionality and the Search for Balance*, London: Ministry of Justice.

GOTTFREDSON, M. and HIRSCHI, T. (1990), *A General Theory of Crime*, Stanford, NJ: Stanford University Press.

GRANDE, E. (2000), 'Italian Criminal Procedure: Borrowing and Resistance', *Am J Comp L*, 48: 227.

GREENAWALT, K. (1981), 'Silence as a Moral and Constitutional Right', *William & Mary L Rev*, 23: 15.

GREVI, V. (1994), 'The New Italian Code of Criminal Procedure: a Concise Overview' in Pizzarusso, qv.

GREVLING, K. (1997), 'Fairness and the Exclusion of Evidence Under Section 78(1) of the Police and Criminal Evidence Act', *LQR*, 113: 667.

GRIFFITHS, A. and MILNE, B. (2006), 'Will it All End in Tiers? Police Interviews with Suspects in Britain' in Williamson, ed, qv.

GROSS, O. (2007), '"Control Systems" and the Migration of Anomalies' in Choudhry, ed, qv.

GUDJONSSON, G. (2003), *The Psychology of Interrogations and Confessions: A Handbook*, Chichester: Wiley.

—— (2007), 'Investigative Interviewing' in Newburn, Williamson and Wright, eds, qv.

GUS JOHN PARTNERSHIP (2003), *Race for Justice*, London: CPS.

HALLIDAY, S. and SCHMIDT, P., eds (2004), *Human Rights Brought Home: Socio-Economic Perspectives on Human Rights in the National Context*, Oxford: Hart Publishing.

HAMER, D. (2009), 'The Expectation of Incorrect Acquittals and the "New and Compelling Evidence" Exception to Double Jeopardy', *Crim LR*, 63.

HARCOURT, B. (2002), *Illusion of Order: the False Promise of Broken Windows Policing*, Cambridge, MA: Harvard University Press.

—— (2007), *Against Prediction: Profiling, Policing and Punishing in an Actuarial Age*, Chicago, IL: University of Chicago Press.

HARDING, C., FENNELL, P., JÖRG, N. and SWART, B., eds (1995), *Criminal Justice in Europe*, Oxford: Clarendon Press.

HARRIS, D. and JOSEPH, S., eds (1995), *The International Covenant on Civil and Political Rights and United Kingdom Law*, London: Butterworths.

——, O'BOYLE, M. and WARBRICK, C. (2009) *Law of the European Convention on Human Rights*, 2nd ed, Oxford: Oxford University Press.

HARRIS, J. and GRACE, S. (1999), *A Question of Evidence?*', Home Office Research Study 196, London: Home Office.

HARTWIG, M, ANDERS GRANHAG, P., STRÖMWALL, L. and VRIJ, A. (2005). 'Detecting Deception via Strategic Disclosure of Evidence', *Law & Human Behavior*, 29: 469.

——, ——, —— and KRONKVIST, O. (2006), 'Strategic Use of Evidence During Police Interviews: When Training to Detect Deception Works', *Law & Human Behavior* 30: 603.

HAWKINS, K. (1984), *Environment and Enforcement*, Oxford: Oxford University Press.

——, ed (1992), *The Uses of Discretion*, Oxford: Oxford University Press.

—— (2003), *Law as Last Resort*, Oxford: Oxford University Press.

HEALTH AND SAFETY EXECUTIVE (2009), *Enforcement Policy Statement*, www.hse.gov.uk.

HEATON-ARMSTRONG, A., SHEPHERD, E. and WOLCHOVER, D., eds (1999), *Analysing Witness Testimony*, London: Blackstone Press.

——, WOLCHOVER, D. and MAXWELL-SCOTT, A. (2006), 'Obtaining, Recording and Admissibility of Out-of-Court Witness Statements' in Heaton-Armstrong, Shepherd, Gudjonsson and Wolchover, eds, qv.

——, SHEPHERD, E., GUDJONSSON, G. and WOLCHOVER, D., eds (2006), *Witness Testimony: Psychological, Investigative and Evidential Perspectives*, Oxford: Oxford University Press.

HEDDERMAN, C. and HOUGH, M. (1994), *Does the Criminal Justice System Treat Men and Women Differently?*, Home Office Research Findings No 10, London: Home Office.

—— and MOXON, D. (1992), *Magistrates' Court or Crown Court? Mode of Trial Decisions and Sentencing*, Home Office Research Study 125, London: Home Office.

HEINZ, W. (1989), 'The Problems of Imprisonment', in Hood, qv.

HELMHOLZ, R., GRAY, C., LANGBEIN, J., MOGLEN, E., SMITH, H. and ALSCHULER, A. (1997), *The Privilege Against Self Incrimination: Its Origins and Development*, Chicago, IL: University of Chicago Press.

HENHAM, R. (1999), 'Bargain Justice or Justice Denied? Sentence Discounts and the Criminal Process', *MLR*, 63: 515.

—— (2000), 'Reconciling Process and Policy: Sentence Discounts in the Magistrates' Courts', *Crim LR*, 436.

—— (2002), 'Further Evidence on the Significance of Plea in the Crown Court', *Howard JCJ*, 41: 151.

HERRMANN, J. (1974), 'The Rule of Compulsory Prosecution and the Scope of Prosecutorial Discretion in Germany', *U Chi LR*, 41: 468.

—— (1992), 'Bargaining Justice: a Bargain for German Criminal Justice?', *U Pittsburgh LR*, 53: 755.

HILSON, C. (1993), 'Discretion to Prosecute and Judicial Review', *Crim LR*, 639.

HIRST, M. (1995), 'Excess Alcohol, Incorrect Procedures and Inadmissible Evidence', *CLJ*, 54: 600.

—— (2001), *Andrews and Hirst on Criminal Evidence*, 4th ed, Bristol: Jordan.

HM CROWN PROSECUTION SERVICE INSPECTORATE (1998), *Cases Involving Domestic Violence, Thematic Report*, London: HMCPSI.

—— (1999), *Adverse Cases*, London: HMCPSI.

—— (1999), *Central Casework Section*, London: HMCPSI.

—— (2000) *The Inspectorate's Report on the Thematic Review of the Disclosure of Unused Material*, London: CPS.

—— (2002), *Report of a Joint Inspection into the Investigation and Prosecution of Cases involving Allegations of Rape*, London: HMCPSI.

—— (2002), *Report on the Thematic Review of Casework Having a Minority Ethnic Dimension*, London: HMCPSI.

—— (2003), *Streets Ahead: A Joint Inspection of the Street Crime Initiative*, London: HMCPSI.

—— (2004), *A Follow Up Review of CPS Casework with a Minority Ethnic Dimension*, London: HMCPSI.

—— (2007), *Discontinuance*, London: HMCPSI.

—— (2008), *Disclosure: A Thematic Review of the Duties of Disclosure of Unused Material Undertaken by the CPS*, London: HMCPSI.

—— (2008), *Inspection of CPS Direct*, London: HMCPSI.

—— and HM INSPECTORATE OF CONSTABULARY (2004), *Violence at Home: A Joint Thematic Inspection of the Investigation and Prosecution of Cases Involving Domestic Violence*, London: HMCPSI and HMIC.

—— and —— (2008), *Joint Thematic Review of the New Charging Arrangements*, London: HMCPSI and HMIC.

HM INSPECTORATE OF CONSTABULARY (2002), *Under the Microscope Refocused: A Revisit to the Thematic Inspection Report on Scientific and Technical Support*, London: HMIC.

HO, H. (2008), 'Book Review: The Trial on Trial', *International Commentary on Evidence*, 6.

HODGSON, J. (1994), 'Adding Injury to Injustice: The Suspect at the Police Station', *J Law & Soc*, 21: 85.

—— (2002), 'Human Rights and French Criminal Justice' in Halliday and Schmidt, qv.

—— (2003), 'Codified Criminal Procedure and Human Rights: Some Observations on the French Experience', *Crim LR*, 165.

HOFMEYR, K. (2006), 'The Problem of Private Entrapment', *Crim LR*, 319.

HOME AFFAIRS COMMITTEE (2002), *The Conduct of Investigations into Past Cases of Abuse in Children's Homes*, 4th Report, HC 836.

—— (2004), *The Work of the Criminal Cases Review Commission*, HC.

HOME OFFICE (1997), *No More Excuses: a New Approach to Tackling Youth Crime in England and Wales*, London: Home Office.

—— (1998), *Speaking Up for Justice*, London: Home Office.

—— (1999), *Digest 4: Information on the Criminal Justice System in England and Wales*, London: Home Office.

—— (1999), *Interception of Communications in the United Kingdom*, Cmnd 4368, London: Home Office.

—— (2002), *Justice for All*, Cmnd 5563, London: Home Office.

—— (2003), *Crime in England and Wales 2002/2003*, London: Home Office.

—— (2004), *Policing: Modernising Police Powers to Meet Community Needs*, London: Home Office.

—— (2006), *Delivering Simple, Speedy, Summary Justice*, London: Home Office.

—— (2006), *Quashing Convictions*, London: Home Office.

—— (2006), *Rebalancing the Criminal Justice System in Favour of the Law-Abiding Majority: a consultation paper*, London: Home Office.

—— (2008), *Government Proposals in Response to the Review of the Police and Criminal Evidence Act 1984*, London: Home Office.

—— (2009), *DNA Retention Policy: Re-Arrest Hazard Rate Analysis*, London: Home Office.

—— (2009), *Keeping the Right People on the DNA Database: Science and Public Protection*, London: Home Office.

—— (2009), *Operation of Police Powers Under the Terrorism Act 2000 and Subsequent Legislation*, London: Home Office.

—— (2009), *Regulation of Investigatory Powers Act 2000: Consolidating Orders and Codes of Practice: A Public Consultation Paper*, London: Home Office.

—— (2009), *Written Ministerial Statement: DNA and Fingerprint Retention*, London: Home Office.

HONESS, T., LEVI, M. and CHAPMAN, E. (1998), 'Juror Competence in Processing Complex Information: Implications from a Simulation of the Maxwell Trial', *Crim LR*, 763.

HOOD, R. G., ed (1989), *Crime and Criminal Policy in Europe: Proceedings of a European Colloquium*, Oxford: Centre for Criminological Research.

—— (1992), *Race and Sentencing*, Oxford: Oxford University Press.

——, SHUTE, S. and SEEMUNGAL, F. (2003), *Ethnic Minorities in the Criminal Courts: Perceptions of Fairness and Equality of Treatment*, Lord Chancellor's Department Research Series No 2/03, London: Lord Chancellor's Department.

HOULDER, B. (1997), 'The Importance of Preserving the Jury System and the Right of Election for Trial', *Crim LR*, 875.

HOUSE OF COMMONS CONSTITUTIONAL AFFAIRS COMMITTEE (2004), *Draft Criminal Defence Service Bill*, HC 746-I, London: TSO.

HOUSE OF COMMONS JUSTICE COMMITTEE (2009), *The Crown Prosecution Service: Gatekeeper of the Criminal Justice System*, London: HMSO.

HOYANO, A., HOYANO, L., DAVIS, G. and GOLDIE, S. (1997), 'A Study of the Impact of the Revised Code for Crown Prosecutors', *Crim LR*, 556.

HOYLE, C. (1998), *Negotiating Domestic Violence*, Oxford: Oxford University Press.

HUCKLESBY, A. (1996), 'Bail or Jail? The Practical Operation of the Bail Act 1976', *JLS*, 23: 213.

—— (1997), 'Court Culture: an Explanation of Variations in the Use of Bail by Magistrates' Courts', *Howard JCJ*, 36: 129.

—— (1997), 'Remand Decision Makers', *Crim LR*, 269.

—— (2004), 'Not Necessarily a Trip to the Police Station: the Introduction of Street Bail', *Crim LR*, 803.

HUMAN GENETICS COMMISSION (2009), *Nothing to Hide, Nothing to Fear? Balancing Individual Rights and the Public Interest in the Governance and Use of the National DNA Database*, London: Central Office of Information.

HUMPHREYS, C. (1955), 'The Duties and Responsibilities of Prosecuting Counsel', *Crim LR*, 739.

HUTTER, B. (1988), *The Reasonable Arm of the Law*, Oxford: Oxford University Press.

INDEPENDENT POLICE COMPLAINTS COMMISSION (2009), *Police Complaints: Statistics for England and Wales 2008/09*, London: Independent Police Complaints Commission.

INTERNATIONAL ASSOCIATION OF PROSECUTORS (2006), *Standards for Prosecutors: an Analysis of the United Kingdom National Prosecuting Agencies*, The Hague: International Association of Prosecutors.

IP, J. (2008), 'The Rise and Spread of the Special Advocate', *PL*, 717.

IRVING, B. (1980), *Police Interrogation: A Study of Current Practice*, London: HMSO.

—— and DUNNIGHAN, C. (1993), *Human Factors in the Quality Control of CID Investigations*, Royal Commission on Criminal Justice Research Study No 21, London: HMSO.

JACKSON, J. D. (2001), 'Silence and Proof: Extending the Boundaries of Criminal Proceedings in the United Kingdom' *E & P*, 5: 145.

—— (2003), 'Justice for All: Putting Victims at the Heart of Criminal Justice?', *JLS*, 30: 309.

—— (2005), 'The Effects of Human Rights on Criminal Evidentiary Processes: Convergence, Divergence or Realignment?', *MLR*, 68: 737.

—— (2006), 'Ethical Implications of the Enhanced Role of the Crown Prosecutor', *Legal Ethics* 9: 35.

—— (2009), 'Re-Conceptualizing the Right of Silence as an Effective Fair Trial Standard', *ICLQ*, 58: 835.

—— and DORAN, S. (1995), *Judge without Jury*, Oxford: Oxford University Press.

—— and JOHNSTONE, J. (2005), 'The Reasonable Time Requirement: An Independent and Meaningful Right?', *Crim LR*, 3.

——, LANGER, M. and TILLERS, P., ed (2008), *Crime, Procedure and Evidence in a Comparative and International Context*, Oxford: Hart Publishing.

——, —— and SEIGEL, M. (1995), 'Rethinking Adversariness in Non-Jury Criminal Trials', *Am J Crim L*, 23: 1.

——, QUINN, K. and O'MALLEY, T. (1999), 'The Jury System in Contemporary Ireland', *Law & Contemporary Probs*, 62: 202.

——, WOLFE, M. and QUINN, K. (2000), *Legislating Against Silence: The Northern Ireland Experience*, Belfast: Northern Ireland Office.

JAMES, A., TAYLOR, N. and WALKER, C. (2000), 'The Criminal Cases Review Commission: Economy, Effectiveness and Justice,' *Crim LR*, 140.

JEFFERSON, T. and WALKER, M. (1992), 'Ethnic Minorities in the Criminal Justice System', *Crim LR*, 83.

JEREMY, D. (2008), 'The Prosecutor's Rock and Hard Place', *Crim LR*, 925.

JOHNSTONE, G. (2001), *Restorative Justice*, Devon: Willan Publishing.

—— (2003), *A Restorative Justice Reader*, Devon: Willan Publishing.

JOINT COMMITTEE ON HUMAN RIGHTS (2003), *Criminal Justice Bill: Further Report, HC 724*, London: TSO.

—— (2009), *Legislative Scrutiny: Coroners and Justice Bill, HC 362*, London: TSO.

—— (2009) *Legislative Scrutiny: Policing and Crime Bill (gangs injunctions)*, London: TSO.

JONES, P. R. (1985), 'Remand Decisions at Magistrates' Courts', in Moxon, qv.

—— and GOLDKAMP, J. S. (1991), 'Judicial Guidelines for Pre-Trial Release: Research and Policy Developments in the United States', *Howard JCJ*, 30: 140.

JORG, N., FIELD, S. and BRANTS, C. (1995), 'Are Inquisitorial and Adversarial Systems Converging?', in Harding, Fennell, Jörg and Swart, eds, qv.

JUDICIAL STUDIES BOARD (2007), *Anti-Social Behaviour Orders: a Guide for the Judiciary*, 3rd ed, London: Judicial Studies Board.

JULIAN, R. (2008), 'Judicial Perspectives in Serious Fraud Cases', *Crim LR*, 764.

JUNG, H. (1993), 'Criminal Justice: a European Perspective', *Crim LR*, 237.

—— (1997), 'Plea-Bargaining and its Repercussions on the Theory of Criminal Procedure', *European Journal of Crime, Criminal Law and Criminal Justice*, 5: 112.

JUSTICE (1970), 'The Prosecution Process in England and Wales', *Crim LR*, 668.

—— (1994), *Remedying Miscarriages of Justice*, London: JUSTICE.

—— (1998), *Under Surveillance*, London: JUSTICE.

KAMISAR, Y. (1987), 'Comparative Reprehensibility and the Fourth Amendment Exclusionary Rule', *Michigan LR*, 86: 1.

—— (2003), 'In Defense of the Search and Seizure Exclusionary Rule', *Harvard J Law & Public Policy*, 26: 120.

KASSIN, S. M. (2003), 'Behavioral Confirmation in the Interrogation Room: On the Dangers of Presuming Guilt', *Law & Human Behavior*, 27: 187.

—— and FONG, C. (1999), '"I'm Innocent": Effects of Training on Judgments of Truth and Deception in the Interrogation Room', *Law & Human Behavior*, 23: 499.

—— and GUDJONSSON, G. (2004), 'The Psychology of Confessions: A Review of the Literature and Issues', *Psychological Science in the Public Interest*, 5: 33.

—— and McNALL, K. (1991), 'Police Interrogation and Confession: Communicating Promises and Threats by Pragmatic Implication', *Law & Human Behavior*, 5: 233.

——, GOLDSTEIN, C. C. and SAVITSKY, K. (2003), 'Behavioral Confirmation in the Interrogation Room: On the Dangers of Presuming Guilt' 27 *Law & Human Behavior* 187.

——, DRIZIN, S., GRISSO, T., GUDJONSSON, G, LEO, R. and REDLICH, A. (2010), 'Police-Induced Confessions: Risk Factors and Recommendations', *Law & Human Behavior*, 34 (forthcoming).

KAYE, D. and SMITH, M. (2004), 'DNA Databases for Law Enforcement: The Coverage Question and the Case for a

Population-Wide Database' in Lazer, ed, qv.

KAYE, T. (1991), *'Unsafe and Unsatisfactory'? Report of the Independent Inquiry into the Working Practices of the West Midlands Serious Crime Squad*, London: Civil Liberties Trust.

KELLOUGH, G. and WORTLEY, S. (2002), 'Remand for Plea: Bail Decisions and Plea Bargaining as Commensurate Decisions', *BJ Crim*, 42: 186.

KEMP, V. and BALMER, A. (2008), *Criminal Defence Services: Users' Perspectives (Interim Report)*, London: Legal Services Commission.

KENNEDY, M., TRUMAN, C., KEYES, S. and CAMERON, A. (1997), 'Supported Bail for Mentally Vulnerable Defendants', *Howard JCJ*, 36: 158.

KERRIGAN. K. (2006), 'Miscarriages of Justice in the Magistrates Court: The Forgotten Power of the CCRC', *Crim LR*, 143.

KERSHAW, C., NICHOLAS, S. and WALKER, A., (2008) *Crime in England and Wales 2007–2008*, London: Home Office.

KING, N. J. (1994), 'The Effects of Race-Conscious Jury Selection on Public Confidence in the Fairness of Jury Proceedings: An Empirical Puzzle', *Am Crim LR*, 31: 1177.

KLEINIG, J. and LEVINE, J., eds (2006), *Jury Ethics: Juror Conduct and Jury Dynamics*, Boulder, CO: Paradigm Publishers.

KRAINA, C. and CARROLL, L. (2006), *Penalty Notices for Disorder: Review of Practice across Police Forces*, London: Office for Criminal Justice Reform.

KYLE, D. (2004), 'Correcting Miscarriages of Justice: The Role of the Criminal Cases Review Commission', *Drake L Rev*, 52: 657.

KYMLICKA, W. (2002), *Contemporary Political Philosophy: An Introduction*, 2nd ed, Oxford: Oxford University Press.

LANGER, M. (2004), 'From Legal Transplants to Legal Translations: the Globalization of Plea-Bargaining and the Americanization Thesis in Criminal Procedure', *Harvard Int LJ*, 45: 1.

LAUDAN, L. (2006), *Truth, Error and Criminal Law: An Essay in Legal Epistemology*, Cambridge: Cambridge University Press.

LASSITER, G., SLAW, R., BRIGGS, M. and SCANLAN, C. (2006), 'The Potential for Bias in Videotaped Confessions', *J Applied Social Psychol*, 22: 1838.

LAW COMMISSION (1999), *Double Jeopardy*, Consultation Paper No 156, London: Stationary Office.

—— (2000), *Prosecution Appeals Against Judges' Rulings*, Consultation Paper No 158, London: Stationery Office.

—— (2001), *Bail and the Human Rights Act 1998*, Consultation Paper No 157, London: Stationery Office.

—— (2001), *Double Jeopardy and Prosecution Appeals*, Report No 267, London: Stationery Office.

—— (2007), *The High Court's Jurisdiction in Relation to Criminal Proceedings: A Consultation Paper*, London: Stationary Office.

LAW SOCIETY (2008), *Criminal Procedure Rules: Impact on Solicitors' Duties to the Client*, London: Law Society.

LAZER, D., ed (2004), *DNA and the Criminal Justice System: The Technology of Justice*, Cambridge, MA: The MIT Press.

LEA, S., LANVERS, U. and SHAW, S. (2003), 'Attrition in Rape Cases', *BJ Crim*, 43: 583.

LEGAL SERVICES COMMISSION (2005), *Code for the Criminal Defence Service*, London: Legal Services Commission.

—— (2008), *Evaluation of CDS Direct First Phase Expansion*, London: Legal Services Commission.

LEIGH, L. (2006), 'Lurking Doubt and the Safety of Convictions', *Crim LR*, 809.

—— (2007), 'Private Prosecutions and Diversionary Justice', *Crim LR*, 289.

—— and ZEDNER, L. (1992), *A Report on the Administration of Criminal Justice In the Pre-Trial Phase in France and Germany*, Royal Commission on Criminal Justice Research Study No 1, London: HMSO.

LEIPOLD, A. (2005), 'Why are Federal Judges so Acquittal Prone?', *Washington ULQ*, 83: 151.

LEMPERT, R. (1993), 'Civil Juries and Complex Cases: Taking Stock After Twelve Years' in Litan, ed, qv.

LENG, R. (1993), *The Right to Silence in Police Interrogation*, Royal Commission on Criminal Justice Research Study No 10, London: HMSO.

—— (2000), 'The Exchange of Information and Disclosure' in McConville and Wilson, eds, qv.

LENSING, H. and RAYAR, L. (1992), 'Notes on Criminal Procedure in the Netherlands', *Crim LR*, 623.

LEVI, M. (1993), *The Investigation, Prosecution and Trial of Serious Fraud*, Royal Commission on Criminal Justice Research Study No 14, London: HMSO.

LIEBLING, A. and KRARUP, H. (1993), *Suicide Attempts and Self-Injury in Male Prisons*, Cambridge: Institute of Criminology.

LIPPERT-RASMUSSEN, K. (2006), 'Racial Profiling Versus Community', *J Applied Philosophy*, 23: 191.

LITAN, R., ed (1993), *Verdict: Assessing the Civil Jury System*, Washington, DC: The Brookings Institution.

LLOYD-BOSTOCK, S. (2006), *Report on Interviews with Jurors in the Jubilee Line Case*, London: HMCPSI.

LOADER, I. (2006), 'Fall of the Platonic Guardians: Liberalism, Criminology and Responses to Crime in England and Wales', *Brit J Criminol*, 46: 561.

LOFTUS, B. (2008), 'Dominant Culture Interrupted', *BJ Crim*, 48:756.

—— (2009), *Police Culture in a Changing World*: Oxford, Oxford University Press.

LUBAN, D. (1993), 'Are Criminal Defenders Different?', *Mich LR*, 91: 1729.

LUSTGARTEN, L. (2002), 'The Future of Stop and Search', *Crim LR*, 603.

MACCORMICK, N. (1999), 'Rhetoric and the Rule of Law' in Dyzenhaus, ed, qv.

MACDONALD, S. (2006), 'A Suicidal Woman, Roaming Pigs and a Noisy Trampolinist: Refining the ASBO's Definition of Anti-Social Behaviour', *MLR*, 69: 183.

—— (2008), 'Constructing a Framework for Criminal Justice Research: Learning from Packer's Mistakes', *New Criminal LR*, 11: 257.

MACHURA, S. (2002), 'Interaction Between Lay Assessors and Professional Judges in German Mixed Courts', *International Rev Penal Law*, 72: 451.

MACNAIR, M. (1990), 'The Early Development of the Privilege Against Self-Incrimination', *OJLS*, 10: 66.

MACPHERSON, SIR W. (1999), *The Stephen Lawrence Inquiry: Report of an Inquiry*, Cm 4261, London: Stationery Office.

MCBARNET, D. (1983), *Conviction: Law, the State and the Construction of Justice*, London: Macmillan.

—— and WHELAN, C. (1991), 'The Elusive Spirit of the Law: Formalism and the Struggle for Legal Control', *MLR*, 54: 848.

MCCABE, S. and PURVES, R. (1972), *By-Passing the Jury*, Oxford: University of Oxford Penal Research Unit.

MCCARTNEY, C. (2006), *Forensic Identification and Criminal Justice:*

Forensic Science, Justice and Risk, Cullompton: Willan Publishing.

McCONVILLE, M. (1992), 'Videotaping Interrogations: Police Behaviour on and off Camera', *Crim LR*, 532.

—— (1993), *Corroboration and Confessions: The Impact of a Rule Requiring that No Conviction Can Be Sustained on the Basis of Confession Evidence Alone*, London: The Stationery Office.

—— (2000), 'Plea Bargaining: Ethics and Politics' in Doran and Jackson, eds, qv.

—— and BALDWIN, J. (1981), *Prosecution, Courts and Conviction*, Oxford: Oxford University Press.

—— and HODGSON, J. (1993), *Custodial Legal Advice and the Right of Silence*, Royal Commission on Criminal Justice Research Study No 16, London: HMSO.

—— and WILSON, G., eds (2002), *The Handbook of the Criminal Justice Process*, Oxford: Oxford University Press.

——, SANDERS, A. and LENG, R. (1991), *The Case for the Prosecution*, London: Routledge.

——, HODGSON, J., BRIDGES, L. and PAVLOVIC, A. (1994), *Standing Accused*, Oxford: Oxford University Press.

McKENZIE, I., MORGAN, R. and REINER, R. (1990), 'Helping the Police with their Enquiries: the Necessity Principle and Voluntary Attendance at the Police Station', *Crim LR*, 22.

McMAHON, M. (1990), 'Net-Widening: Vagaries in the Use of a Concept', *BJ Crim*, 30: 121.

McSHERRY, A., NORRIE, A. AND BRONITT, S., eds (2009), *Regulating Deviance*, Oxford: Hart Publishing.

MAFFEI, S. (2004), 'Negotiations on Evidence and Negotiations on Sentence: Adversarial Experiments in Italian Criminal Procedure', *J Int Crim J*, 2: 1050.

—— (2006), *The European Right to Confrontation in Criminal Proceedings*, Groningen: Europa Law Publishing.

MAGUIRE, M. (2000), 'Policing by Risks and Targets: Some Dimensions and Implications of Intelligence-Led Policing', *Policing and Society*, 9: 315.

—— (2007), 'Crime Data and Statistics' in Maguire, Morgan and Reiner, eds, qv.

—— and JOHN, T. (1996), 'Covert and Deceptive Policing in England and Wales: Issues in Regulation and Practice', *European Journal of Crime, Criminal Law and Criminal Justice*.

—— and NORRIS, C. (1992), *The Conduct and Supervision of Criminal Investigations*, Royal Commission on Criminal Justice Research Study No 5, London: HMSO.

——, MORGAN, R. and REINER, R., eds (2007), *Oxford Handbook of Criminology*, 4th ed, Oxford: Oxford University Press.

MAHONEY, R. (2003), 'Abolition of New Zealand's *Prima Facie* Exclusionary Rule', *Crim LR*, 607.

MALLESON, K. and ROBERTS, S. (2002), 'Streamlining and Clarifying the Appellate Process,' *Crim LR*, 272.

MATTHEWS, R., HANCOCK, L. and BRIGGS, D. (2004), *Jurors' Perceptions, Understanding, Confidence and Satisfaction in the Jury System*, Research Development and Statistics Directorate, Findings 177, London: Home Office.

METROPOLITAN POLICE AUTHORITY (2007), *Counter-Terrorism: The London Debate*, London: Metropolitan Police Authority.

MIDDLETON, D. (2005), 'The Legal and Regulatory Response to Solicitors Involved in Serious Fraud', *BJ Crim*, 45: 810.

MILLER, J., BLAND, N. and QUINTON, P. (2000), *The Impact of Stops and Searches on Crime and the Community*, Police Research Series, Paper 127.

MINISTRY OF JUSTICE (2008), *Offender Management Caseload Statistics 2007*, London: Ministry of Justice.

—— (2008), *Punishment and Reform: our Approach to Managing Offenders*, London: Ministry of Justice.

—— (2009), *Judicial and Court Statistics 2008*, London: Ministry of Justice.

—— (2009), *Statistics on Race and the Criminal Justice System 2007/8*, London: Ministry of Justice.

MIRFIELD, P. (1997), *Silence, Confessions and Improperly Obtained Evidence*, Oxford: Oxford University Press.

—— and SMITH, R., eds (2003), *Essays for Colin Tapper*, London: LexisNexis.

MOECKLI, D. (2007), 'Stop and Search Under the Terrorism Act 2000', *MLR*, 70: 654.

MOORHEAD, R., SEFTON, M. and SCANLAN, L. (2008), *Just Satisfaction? What drives Public and Participant Satisfaction with Courts and Tribunals?*, London: Ministry of Justice.

MORENO, Y. and HUGHES, P. (2008), *Effective Prosecution*, Oxford: Oxford University Press.

MORGAN, D. and STEPHENSON, G., eds (1994) *Suspicion and Silence: The Right to Silence in Criminal Investigations*, London: Blackstone Press.

MORGAN, J. and ZEDNER, L. (1992), *Child Victims*, Oxford: Oxford University Press.

MORGAN, P.M. (1992), *Offending Whilst on Bail, Research and Planning Unit Paper 65*, London: Home Office.

—— and HENDERSON, P. (1998), *Remand Decisions and Offending on Bail*, Home Office Research Study 184, London: Home Office.

MORGAN, R. (1996), 'The Process is the Rule and the Punishment is the Process', *MLR*, 59: 306.

—— (2001), 'International Controls on Sentencing and Punishment' in Tonry and Frase, eds, qv.

—— (2002), 'Magistrates: The Future According to Auld', *JLS*, 29: 308.

—— (2008) *Summary Justice: Fast—But Fair?*, Centre for Crime and Justice Studies, King's College: London.

—— and RUSSELL, N. (2000), *The Judiciary in the Magistrates' Courts*, Home Office and LCD Occasional Paper 66, London: Home Office.

MORRIS, A. (2002), 'Critiquing the Critics: a Brief Response to Critics of Restorative Justice', *BJ Crim*, 42: 578.

MORRIS, N. and TONRY, M. (1990), *Between Prison and Probation*, New York: Oxford University Press.

MOSTELLER, R. (1986), 'Discovery Against the Defense: Tilting the Adversarial Balance', *California L Rev*, 74: 1567.

MOSTON, S. and STEPHENSON, G. (1993), *The Questioning and Interviewing of Suspects outside the Police Station*, Royal Commission on Criminal Justice Research Study No 22, London: HMSO.

MOTT, J. (1983), 'Police Decisions for Dealing with Juvenile Offenders', *BJ Crim*, 23: 249.

MOXON, D., ed (1985), *Managing Criminal Justice*, London: HMSO.

—— and HEDDERMAN, C. (1994), 'Mode of Trial Decisions and Sentencing Differences between Courts', *Howard JCJ*, 33: 97.

MULCAHY, A. (1994), 'The Justifications of "Justice": Legal Practitioners' Accounts of Negotiated Case Settlements in Magistrates' Courts', *BJ Crim*, 34: 411.

MULLIN, C. (1990), *Error of Judgement*, Dublin: Poolbeg Press.

MVA and MILLER, J. (2000), *Profiling Populations Available for Stops and*

Searches, Police Research Series, Paper 131, London: Home Office.

NANCE, D. (1994), 'Civility and the Burden of Proof', *Harvard J Law & Public Policy*, 17: 647.

NAREY, M. (1997), *Review of Delay in the Criminal Justice System ('The Narey Report')*, London: Home Office.

NASH, R. and WADE, K. (2009), 'Innocent But Proven Guilty: Using False Video Evidence to Elicit False Confessions and Create False Beliefs', *Applied Cognitive Psychology*, 23: 624.

NATIONAL AUDIT OFFICE (1997), *The Crown Prosecution Service*, London: National Audit Office.

—— (2006), *Crown Prosecution Service: Effective Use of Magistrates' Courts Hearings*, London: National Audit Office.

NATIONAL POLICING IMPROVEMENT AGENCY (2009), *National Investigative Interviewing Strategy*, London: National Policing Improvement Agency.

NELKEN, D., ed (1994), *The Futures of Criminology*, London: Sage.

NEW ZEALAND LAW COMMISSION (2001), *Acquittal Following Perversion of the Course of Justice*, Report No 70, Wellington: New Zealand Law Commission.

NEWBURN, T., ed (2003), *Handbook of Policing*, Cullompton: Willan Publishing.

——, WILLIAMSON, T. and WRIGHT, A., eds (2007), *Handbook of Criminal Investigation* (2007).

NEWTH, T. (2008), *HMRC Investigations and Enquiries*, Haywards Heath: Tottel Publishing.

NEYROUD, P. (2003), 'Policing and Ethics' in Newburn, eds, qv.

—— (2006), 'Ethics in Policing: Performance and the Personalization of Accountability in British Policing and Criminal Justice', *Legal Ethics*, 9: 16.

NICOLSON, D. and WEBB, J. (1999), *Professional Legal Ethics*, Oxford, New York: Oxford University Press.

NISSMAN, C. M. and HAGEN, E. (1982), *The Prosecution Function*, Washington, DC: Lexington.

NOBLES, R. and SCHIFF, D. (2000), *Understanding Miscarriages of Justice*, Oxford: Oxford University Press.

—— and —— (2001), 'The Criminal Cases Review Commission: Reporting Success?', *MLR*, 64: 280.

NORTON, J. (1998), 'The Exclusionary Rule Reconsidered: Restoring the Status Quo Ante', *Wake Forest L Rev*, 33: 261.

NOZICK, R. (1974), *Anarchy, State and Utopia*, New York: Basic Books.

NUFFIELD COUNCIL ON BIOETHICS (2007), *The Forensic Use of Bioinformation: Ethical Issues*, London: Nuffield Council on Bioethics.

O'BRIEN, W. (2005), 'The Right of Confrontation: US and European Perspectives', *LQR*, 121: 481.

O'CONNOR, P. (1992), 'Prosecution Disclosure: Principle, Practice and Justice', *Crim LR*, 464.

OFFICE FOR CRIMINAL JUSTICE REFORM (2007), *Out-of-court Disposals for Adults: a Guide to Alternatives to Prosecution*, London: Office for Criminal Justice Reform.

OFSHE, R. and LEO, R. (1997), 'The Decision to Confess Falsely: Rational Choice and Irrational Action', *Denver University L Rev*, 74: 979.

ORMEROD, D. (2001), 'Sounds Familiar?— Voice Identification Evidence', *Crim LR*, 595.

—— and BIRCH, D. (2004), 'The Evolution of the Discretionary Exclusion of Evidence', *Crim LR*, 767.

—— and ROBERTS, A. (2003), 'The Police Reform Act 2002', *Crim LR*, 141.

—— and —— (2002), 'The Trouble with *Teixeira*: Developing a Principled Approach to Entrapment', *E & P*, 6: 38.

OSNER, N., QUINN, A. and CROWN, G. (1993), *Criminal Justice Systems in Other Jurisdictions*, The Royal Commission on Criminal Justice, London: HMSO.

PACKER, H. (1968), *The Limits of the Criminal Sanction*, Stanford, CA: Stanford University Press.

PADFIELD, N. (1993), 'The Right to Bail: a Canadian Perspective', *Crim LR*, 510.

PARKER, H., SUMNER, M. and JARVIS, G. (1989), *Unmasking the Magistrates*, Milton Keynes: Open University Press.

PATTENDEN, R. (1996), *English Criminal Appeals, 1844–1994*, Oxford: Oxford University Press.

—— (2000), 'Prosecution Appeals Against Judges' Rulings', *Crim LR*, 971.

—— (2009), 'Pre-Verdict Judicial Fact-Finding in Judicial Trials with Juries', *OJLS*, 29: 1.

—— (2009), 'The Proof Rules of Pre-Verdict Judicial Fact-Finding in Criminal Trials by Jury', *LQR*, 125: 79.

—— (2009), 'The Standard of Review for Mistake of Fact in the Court of Appeal, Criminal Division', *Crim LR*, 15.

—— and DALY, G. (2005), 'Racial Bias and the English Criminal Trial Jury', *CLJ*, 64: 678.

—— and SKINNS, L. (2000), 'Choice, Privacy, and Publicly Funded Legal Advice at Police Stations', *MLR*, 73 (forthcoming).

PEARSE, J. and GUDJONSSON, G. (1996), 'Police Interviewing Techniques at Two South London Police Stations', *Psychology, Crime & Law*, 3: 63.

PEAY, J. (2002), 'Mentally Disordered Offenders' in Maguire, Morgan and Reiner, eds, qv.

PECK, M. (2006), *The Fraud (Trials Without a Jury) Bill 2006–07*, House of Commons Research Paper 06/57, London: House of Commons Library.

PHILLIPS, C. and BOWLING, B. (2007), 'Ethnicities, Racism, Crime and Criminal Justice' in Maguire, Morgan and Reiner, eds, qv.

—— and BROWN, D. (1998), *Entry into the Criminal Justice System: A survey of Police Arrests and Their Outcomes*, Home Office Research Study No 185, London: Home Office.

PHILLIPS, M., McAULIFF, B., KOVERA, M. and CUTLER, B. (1999), 'Double-blind Photoarray Administration as a Safeguard Against Investigator Bias', *J Applied Psychology*, 84: 940.

PHILPOTTS, G. J. O. and LANCUCKI, L. B. (1979), *Previous Convictions, Sentence and Reconvictions*, Home Office Research Study 53, London: HMSO.

PIKE, G., BRACE, N. and KYNAN, S. (2002), *The Visual Identification of Suspects: Procedures and Practice* (Home Office Briefing Note 2), London: Home Office.

PIZZARUSSO, A., ed (1994), *Italian Studies in Law, vol. II*, Dordrecht: Martinus Nijhoff.

PLAYER, E. (2007), 'Remanding Women in Custody: Concerns for Human Rights', *MLR*, 70: 402.

——, ROBERTS, J., JACOBSON, J., HOUGH, M. and ROBOTTOM, J. (2010), 'Remands in Custody', *Howard Journal of Criminal Justice* (forthcoming).

PLOTNIKOFF, J. and WOOLFSON, R. (2001), 'A Fair Balance'? Evaluation of the Operation of Disclosure Law, London: Home Office.

PLUGGE, E., DOUGLAS, N. and FITZPATRICK, R. (2006), *The Health of Women in Prison*,

Oxford: Department of Public Health, University of Oxford.

POLICE COMPLAINTS AUTHORITY (2004), *Stop and Search Complaints 2000–2001, Summary Report*, London: Police Complaints Authority.

PRATT, J. (2007), *Penal Populism*, London: Routledge.

PRESSER, B. (2001), 'Public Policy, Police Interest: A Re-Evaluation of the Judicial Discretion to Exclude Improperly or Illegally Obtained Evidence', *Melbourne ULR*, 25: 757.

PRISON REFORM TRUST (2000), *Justice for Women: the Need for Reform*, London: Prison Reform Trust.

QUINTON, A., ed (1967), *Political Philosophy*, Oxford: Oxford University Press.

QUINTON, P., BLAND, N. and MILLER, J. (2000), *Police Stops, Decision-Making and Practice*, Police Research Series, Paper 130.

QUIRK, H. (2006), 'The Significance of Culture in Criminal Procedure Reform: Why the Revised Disclosure Scheme Cannot Work', *E & P*, 10: 42.

—— (2007), 'Identifying Miscarriages of Justice: Why Innocence in the UK is Not the Answer', *MLR*, 70: 759.

RAIFERTAIGH, U. (1997), 'Reconciling Bail Law with the Presumption of Innocence', *OJLS*, 17: 1.

RAINE, J. and WILLSON, M. (1996), 'The Imposition of Conditions in Bail Decisions', *Howard JCJ*, 35: 256.

—— and —— (1997), 'Police Bail with Conditions', *BJ Crim*, 37: 593.

RAMSAY, P. (2004), 'What is Anti-Social Behaviour?', *Crim LR*, 908.

—— (2009), 'The Theory of Vulnerable Autonomy and the Legitimacy of Civil Preventative Orders' in McSherry, Norrie and Bronitt, eds, qv.

REDMAYNE, M. (2004), 'Disclosure and its Discontents', *Crim LR*, 441.

—— (2006), 'Theorizing Jury Reform', in Duff, Farmer, Marshall and Tadros, qv.

—— (2007), 'Rethinking the Privilege Against Self-Incrimination', *OJLS*, 27: 209.

—— (2008), 'English Warnings', *Cardozo L Rev*, 30: 1047.

—— (2009), 'Theorizing the Criminal Trial', *New Crim LR*, 12: 287.

REID, K. (2009), 'Race issues and Stop and Search: Looking Behind the Statistics', *J Crim L*, 73: 165.

REINER, R. (2000), *The Politics of the Police*, 3rd ed, Hemel Hempstead: Wheatsheaf.

—— (2007), *Law and Order: An Honest Citizen's Guide to Crime and Control*, Cambridge: Polity Press.

RENNING, C. (2002), 'Influence of Lay Assessors and Giving Reasons for the Judgement in German Mixed Courts', *International Rev Penal Law*, 72: 481.

RICHARDSON, G., OGUS, A. and BURROWS, P. (1982), *Policing Pollution*, Oxford: Oxford University Press.

RISHWORTH, P., HUSCROFT, G., OPTICAN, S. and MAHONEY, R. (2003), *The New Zealand Bill of Rights*, Auckland: Oxford University Press.

RISSE, M. and ZECKHAUSER, R. (2004), 'Racial Profiling', *Philosophy & Public Affairs*, 32: 131.

ROACH, K. (1999), 'Canada', in Bradley, qv.

—— (1999), *Due Process and Victims' Rights: the New Law and Politics of Criminal Justice*, Toronto: UTP.

—— (2003), 'The Criminal Process', in Cane and Tushnet, eds, qv.

ROBERTS, A. (2008), 'Pre-Trial Defence Rights and the Fair Use of Eyewitness Identification Procedures', *MLR*, 71: 331.

ROBERTS, D. (1993), 'Questioning the Suspect: the Solicitor's Role', *Crim LR*, 368.

ROBERTS, J. and HOUGH, M. (2009), *Public Opinion and the Jury: An International Literature Review*, London: Ministry of Justice.

ROBERTS, P. (2002), 'Double Jeopardy Law Reform: A Criminal Justice Commentary', *MLR*, 65: 393.

—— (2002), 'Justice for All? Two Bad Arguments (and Several Good Suggestions) for Resisting Double Jeopardy Reform', *E & P*, 6: 197.

—— and SAUNDERS, C. (2008), 'Introducing Pre-Trial Witness Interviews—a Flexible New Fixture in the Crown Prosecutor's Toolkit', *Crim LR*, 831.

—— and ZUCKERMAN, A. (2004), *Criminal Evidence*, Oxford: Oxford University Press.

ROBERTSON, B. (1989), 'The Looking Glass World of Section 78', *NLJ*, 1223.

——, DELL, S., GROUNDS, A. and JAMES, K. (1992), 'Mentally Disordered Remand Prisoners', *Home Office Research Bulletin*, 32: 1.

ROBINS, J. (2000), 'The Speed of Fight', *Law Society Gazette*, 3: 24.

ROBINSON, P. (2001), 'Punishing Dangerousness: Cloaking Preventive Detention as Criminal Justice', *Harvard LR*, 114: 1429.

——, GARVEY, S. and FERZAN, K., eds (2009), *Criminal Law Conversations*, Oxford: Oxford University Press.

ROCK, P. (1993), *The Social World of an English Crown Court*, Oxford: Clarendon Press.

—— (2004), *Constructing Victims' Rights: the Home Office, New Labour and Victims*, Oxford: Clarendon Press.

ROGERS, J. (2006), 'Restructuring the Exercise of Prosecutorial Discretion in England', *OJLS*, 26: 775.

—— (2008), 'The Boundaries of Abuse of Process in Criminal Trials', *Current Legal Problems*, 289.

ROLLOCK, N. (2009), *The Stephen Lawrence Inquiry 10 Years On: A Critical Review of the Literature*, London: The Runnymede Trust.

ROORDING, J. (1996), 'The Punishment of Tax Fraud', *Crim LR*, 240.

ROSSMO, K., ed (2008), *Criminal Investigative Failures*, London: CRC.

ROYAL COMMISSION ON CRIMINAL JUSTICE (1993) (chair: Viscount Runciman), *Report*, Cmnd 2263, London: HMSO.

ROYAL COMMISSION ON CRIMINAL PROCEDURE (1981) (chair: Sir Cyril Phillips), *Report*, Cmnd 8092, London: HMSO.

ROZENBERG, J. (1992), 'Miscarriages of Justice', in Stockdale and Casale, eds, qv.

RUTHERFORD, A. (1993), *Criminal Justice and the Pursuit of Decency*, Oxford: Oxford University Press.

SAMUELS, A. (1997), 'Custody Time Limits', *Crim LR*, 260.

SANDERS, A. (1985), 'Class Bias in Prosecutions', *Howard JCJ*, 24: 176.

—— (1988), 'The Limits to Diversion from Prosecution', *BJ Crim*, 28: 513.

—— (2001), *Community Justice: Modernising the Magistracy in England and Wales*, London: IPPR.

—— (2002), 'Core Values, the Magistracy and the Auld Report', *JLS*, 29: 324.

—— (2008), 'Can Coercive Powers be Effectively Controlled or Regulated? The Case for Anchored Pluralism' in Cape and Young, eds, qv.

—— and BRIDGES, L. (1990), 'Access to Legal Advice and Police Malpractice', *Crim LR*, 494.

—— and YOUNG, R. (2007), *Criminal Justice*, 3rd ed, London: Butterworths.

—— and —— (2007), 'From Suspect to Trial', in Maguire, Morgan and Reiner, eds, qv.

——, HOYLE, C., MORGAN, R. and CAPE, E. (2001), 'Victim Impact Statements: Can't Work, Won't Work', *Crim LR*, 447.

SAURON, J.-L. (1990), 'Les Vertus de l'Inquisitoire, ou l'Etat au Service des Droits', *Pouvoirs*, 55: 53.

SCHIFF, D. and NOBLES, R. (1996), 'Criminal Appeal Act 1995: the Semantics of Jurisdiction', *MLR*, 59: 573.

SCHROEDER, W. (1983), 'Restoring the Status Quo Ante: The Fourth Amendment Exclusionary Rule as a Compensatory Device', *George Washington L Rev*, 51: 633.

SCHULHOFER, S. (1984), 'Is Plea Bargaining Inevitable?', *Harv LR*, 97: 1037.

—— (1992), 'Plea Bargaining as Disaster', *Yale LJ*, 101: 1979.

—— and NAGEL, I. (1997), 'Plea Negotiations under the Federal Sentencing Guidelines', *Northwestern ULR*, **91**: 1284.

SCOTT, R. E. and STUNTZ, W. J. (1992), 'Plea Bargaining as Contract', *Yale LJ*, 101: 1909.

—— and —— (1992), 'A Reply: Imperfect Bargains, Imperfect Trials and Innocent Defendants', *Yale LJ*, 101: 2011.

SCOTTISH LAW COMMISSION (2009), *Discussion Paper on Double Jeopardy*, Edinburgh: Scottish Law Commission.

SCOULAR, J. and O'NEILL, M. (2007), 'Regulating Prostitution: Social Inclusion, Responsibilization and the Politics of Prostitution Reform', *BJ Crim*, 47: 764.

SEAGO, P., WALKER, C. and WALL, D. (1995), *The Role and Appointment of Stipendiary Magistrates*, London: CCJS Press and Lord Chancellor's Department.

SEDLEY, S. (2001), 'Wringing Out the Fault: Self-Incrimination in the 21st Century', *NILQ*, 52: 107.

SEIDMANN D. and STEIN, A. (2000), 'The Right to Silence Helps the Innocent', *Harvard L Rev* 114: 430.

SEIDMAN, L. (1981), 'The Supreme Court, Entrapment and Our Criminal Justice Dilemma', *Supreme Court Review*, 111.

—— (2009), 'Entrapment and the "Free Market" for Crime' in Robinson, Garvey and Ferzan, eds, qv.

SELIH, A. (2000), 'The Prosecution Process' in Council of Europe, qv.

SENTENCING ADVISORY PANEL (2002), *Advice to the Court of Appeal on Rape*, London: Sentencing Guidelines Secretariat.

——(2008), *Sentencing for Breach of an Anti-Social Behaviour Order: Advice to the Sentencing Guidelines Council*, London: Sentencing Guidelines Secretariat.

SENTENCING GUIDELINES COUNCIL (2006), *Sentencing for Breach of a Protective Order* (2006), London: Sentencing Guidelines Secretariat.

——(2007), *Reduction in Sentence for a Guilty Plea*, London: Sentencing Guidelines Secretariat.

—— (2008), *Assault and Other Offences Against the Person*, London: Sentencing Guidelines Secretariat.

—— (2008), *Breach of an Anti-Social Behaviour Order*, London: Sentencing Guidelines Secretariat.

SHAPLAND, J., DUFF, P. and WILLMORE, J. (1985), *Victims in the Criminal Justice System*, Aldershot: Gower.

SHARPE, S. (1998), *Judicial Discretion and Criminal Litigation*, 2nd ed, Oxford: Clarendon Press.

SHEPHERD, E. and MILNE, R. (1999), 'Full and Faithful: Ensuring Quality, Practice and Integrity of Outcome in Witness Interviews' in Heaton-Armstrong, Shepherd and Wolchover, eds, qv.

—— and —— (2006), '"Have you Told Management about this?": Bringing

Witness Interviewing Into the Twenty-First Century' in Heaton-Armstrong, Shepherd, Gudjonsson and Wolchover, eds, qv.

SHUTE, S. (2004), 'New Civil Preventative Orders: Sexual Offences Prevention Orders; Foreign Travel Orders; Risk of Sexual Harm Orders', *Crim LR*, 417.

SIMESTER, A. P. (2005), *Appraising Strict Liability*, Oxford, Oxford University Press.

——and VON HIRSCH, A. (2006), 'Regulating Offensive Conduct through Two-Step Prohibitions', in von Hirsch and Simester eds, qv.

SIMMONS, J. and DODD, T. (2003), *Crime in England and Wales 2002–2003*, London: Home Office.

SIMON, W. H. (1993), 'The Ethics of Criminal Defense,' *Mich LR*, **91**: 1703.

SILVESTRI, A., OLDFIELD, M., SQUIRES, P. and GRIMSHAW, R. (2009), *Young People, Knives and Guns*, London: Centre for Crime and Justice Studies, KCL.

SKINNS, L. (2009), 'I'm a Detainee; Get me Out of Here', *Brit J Criminol*, **49**: 399.

—— (2009), ' "Let's Get it Over With": Early Findings on the Factors Affecting Detainees' Access to Custodial Legal Advice', *Policing and Society*, **19**: 58.

SKOLNICK, J. (1966), *Justice without Trial*, New York: Wiley.

SLAPPER, G. (2001), *Organisational Prosecutions*, Aldershot: Ashgate.

——and TOMBS, S. (2000), *Corporate Crime*, London: Longman.

SLOBOGIN, C. (1999), 'Why Liberals Should Chuck the Exclusionary Rule', *U Illinois L Rev*, 363.

SMITH, J. C. (1994), 'The right to life and the right to kill in law', *New LJ*, 144: 354.

—— (1995), 'The Criminal Appeal Act 1995: Appeals against Conviction', *Crim LR*, 920.

SOMMERS, S. and ELLSWORTH, P. (2003), 'How Much Do We Really Know About Race and Juries? A Review of Social Science Theory and Research', *Chicago-Kent L Rev*, 78: 997.

SOUKARA, S., BULL, R., VRIJ, A., TURNER, M. and CHERRYMAN, J. (2009), 'What Really Happens in Police Interviews of Suspects? Tactics and Confessions', *Psychology, Crime & Law*, 15: 493.

SOOTHILL, K. (2009), 'Keeping the DNA Link', *NLJ*, 159: 1021.

——, WAY, C. and GIBBENS, T. (1980), 'Rape Acquittals', *MLR*, 43: 159.

SPENCER, J. R. (2004), 'The Sexual Offences Act 2003: Child and Family Offences', *Crim LR*, 347.

—— (2006), 'Does our Present Criminal Appeals System Make Sense?', *Crim LR*, 677.

—— (2007), 'Arrest for Questioning', *CLJ*, 66: 282.

—— (2007), 'Quashing Convictions for Procedural Irregularities', *Crim LR*, 835.

—— (2008), *Hearsay Evidence in Criminal Proceedings*, Oxford: Hart Publishing.

SPRACK, J. (2002), *Emmins on Criminal Procedure*, 9th ed, London: Blackstone Press.

SQUIRES, D. (2006), 'The Problem with Entrapment', *OJLS*, 26: 351.

SQUIRES, P. and STEPHEN, D. E. (2005), *Rougher Justice: Anti-Social Behaviour and Young People*, Cullompton: Willan.

STEBLAY, N., DYSART, J., FULERO, S. and LINDSAY, R. (2001), 'Eyewitness Accuracy Rates in Sequential and Simultaneous Lineup Presentations: A Meta-Analytic Comparison', *Law & Human Behavior*, 25: 459.

STEPHEN, H. (1926), *The Conduct of an English Criminal Trial*, London: University of London Press.

STOCKDALE, E. and CASALE, S., eds (1993), *Criminal Justice Under Stress*, London: Blackstone Press.

STONE, C. (1988), *Bail Information for the Crown Prosecution Service*, London: Vera Institute of Justice.

STONE, V. and PETTIGREW, N. (2000), *The Views of the Public on Stops and Searches*, Police Research Series Paper 129, London: Home Office.

TADROS, V. (2008), 'Crimes and Security', *MLR*, 71: 940.

TAGUE, P. (2006), 'Tactical Reasons for Recommending Trials rather than Guilty Pleas in the Crown Court', *Crim LR*, 23.

—— (2007), 'Barristers' Selfish Incentives in Counselling Defendants over Choice of Plea', *Crim LR*, 3.

TAK, P. J. P. (1986), *The Legal Scope of Non-Prosecution in Europe*, Helsinki: HEUNI.

TAPPER, C., ed (1981), *Crime, Proof and Punishment*, London: Butterworths.

TAYLOR, N. and ORMEROD, D. (2004), 'Mind the Gap: Safety, Fairness and Moral Legitimacy', *Crim LR*, 266.

TEMKIN, J. (2000), 'Prosecuting and Defending Rape: Perspectives from the Bar', *J Law & Soc*, 27: 219.

—— (2002), *Rape and the Legal Process*, 2nd ed, Oxford: Oxford University Press.

—— and KRAHE, B. (2008), *Sexual Assault and the Justice Gap: a Question of Attitude*, Oxford: Hart Publishing.

THOMAS, C. (2007), *Diversity and Fairness in the Jury System*, London: Ministry of Justice.

TONRY, M. (2004), *Punishment and Politics*, Cullompton: Willan.

—— and FRASE, R., eds (2001), *Sentencing and Sanctions in Western Countries*, Oxford: Oxford University Press.

TRAVERS, M. (1997), *The Reality of Law*, Aldershot: Ashgate.

TULKENS, F. (2002), 'Negotiated Justice' in Delmas-Marty and Spencer, eds, qv.

TYLER, T. (1990), *Why People Obey the Law*, New Haven, CT: Yale University Press.

—— and HUO, Y. (2002), *Trust in the Law: Encouraging Public Cooperation with the Police and Courts*, New York: Russell Sage Foundation.

VALENTINE, T. (2006), 'Forensic Facial Identification' in Heaton-Armstrong, Shepherd, Gudjonsson and Wolchover, eds, qv.

—— and HEATON, P. (1999), 'An Evaluation of the Fairness of Police Lineups and Video Identifications', *Applied Cognitive Psychology*, 13: 59.

——, DARLING, S. and MEMON, A. (2006), 'Do Strict Rules and Moving Images Increase the Reliability of Sequential Identification Procedures?', *Applied Cognitive Psychology*, 21: 933.

VAMOS, N. (2009), 'Please Don't Call it Plea-Bargaining', *Crim LR*, 617.

VAN BUEREN, G. (2005) *Commentary on the U.N. Convention on the Rights of the Child*, Leiden: Martinus Nijhoff Publishers.

VAN ZYL SMIT, D. and ASHWORTH, A. (2004), 'Disproportionate Sentences as Human Rights Violations', *MLR*, 67: 541.

VICTIM SUPPORT (1995), *The Rights of Victims of Crime*, London: Victim Support.

VIDMAR, N. (1997), 'Generic Prejudice and the Presumption of Guilt in Sex Abuse Trials', *Law & Human Behavior*, 21: 5.

—— (1998), 'The Performance of the American Civil Jury: An Empirical Perspective', *Arizona L Rev*, 40: 849.

VOGEL, M. (2007), *Coercion to Compromise*, Oxford: Oxford University Press.

VON HIRSCH, A. and ASHWORTH, A., eds (1998), *Principled Sentencing: Readings in Theory and Policy*, 2nd ed, Oxford: Hart Publishing.

VON HIRSCH, A. and ASHWORTH, A. (2005), *Proportionate Sentencing*, Oxford: Oxford University Press.

—— and SIMESTER, A. P., eds (2006), *Incivilities: Regulating Offensive Behaviour*, Oxford: Hart Publishing.

WADDINGTON, P. A. J. (1999), 'Police (Canteen) Culture: an Appreciation', *BJ Crim*, 39: 286.

——, STENSON, K. and DON, D. (2004), 'In Proportion: Race, and Police Stop and Search', *B J Criminol*, 44: 889.

WALDRON, J. (2003), 'Security and Liberty: the Image of Balance', *J Political Philosophy*, 11: 191.

—— (2008), 'The Concept and the Rule of Law', *Georgia L Rev*, 43: 1.

WALKER, C. (2004), 'Terrorism and Criminal Justice—Past, Present and Future', *Crim LR*, 311.

—— (2007), 'The Treatment of Foreign Terror Suspects', *MLR*, 70: 427.

WALKER, N. (2001), 'What Does Fairness Mean in a Criminal Trial?', *NLJ*, 1240.

WARBURTON, H., MAY, T. and HOUGH, M. (2005), 'Looking the Other Way: the Impact of Reclassifying Cannabis on Police Warnings', *BJ Crim* 45: 113.

WARD, A. and PEERS S., eds (2004), *The EU Charter of Fundamental Rights*, Oxford: Hart Publishing.

WARD, T. and GARDNER, P. (2003), 'The Privilege Against Self Incrimination: In Search of Legal Certainty', *European Human Rights L Rev*, 387.

WASIK, M. (1996), 'Magistrates: Knowledge of Previous Convictions', *Crim LR*, 851.

WELLS, G. (2006), 'Eyewitness Identification: Systemic Reforms', *Wisconsin L Rev* 615.

—— and OLSON, E. (2003), 'Eyewitness Identification', *Annual Review of Psychology*, 54: 277.

——, MEMON, A. and PENROD, S. (2006), 'Eyewitness Evidence: Improving its Probative Value', *Psychological Science in the Public Interest*, 7: 45.

WESTEN, P. and DRUBEL, R. (1978), 'Towards a General Theory of Double Jeopardy', *Supreme Court Review*, 81.

WHITE, R. (2006), 'Investigators or Prosecutors or, Desperately Seeking Scotland: Re-Formulation of the "Philips Principle"', *MLR*, 69: 143.

WILLIAMS, C. (2008), 'An Analysis of Discretionary Rejection in Relation to Confessions', *Melbourne U L Rev* 32: 302.

WILLIAMSON, T., ed (2006), *Investigative Interviewing: Rights, Research, Regulation*, Cullompton: Willan.

—— (2006), 'Towards Greater Professionalism: Minimizing Miscarriages of Justice' in Williamson, ed, qv.

WILSON, J. Q. and KELLING, G. (1982) 'Broken Windows', *Atlantic Monthly* (March), 29.

WINDLESHAM, LORD (2001), *Responses to Crime, Volume 4: Dispensing Justice*, Oxford: Oxford University Press.

WISTRICH, A., GUTHRIE C. and RACHLINSKI, J. (2005), 'Can Judges Ignore Inadmissible Information? The Difficulty of Deliberately Disregarding', *U Pennsylvania L Rev* 153: 1251.

WOLCHOVER D. (2008), 'Viper Disappointments in the PACE Review', *Archbold News*, 10: 4.

—— and HEATON-ARMSTRONG, A. (2004), 'Ending the Farce of Staged Street Identifications', *Archbold News*, 3: 5.

—— and —— (2006), 'Improving Visual Identification Procedures Under PACE Code D' in Heaton-Armstrong, Shepherd, Gudjonsson and Wolchover, eds, qv.

WOOLF, H. and TUMIN, S. (1991) 'Prison Disturbances April 1990: Report of an Inquiry', Cmnd 1456, London: HMSO.

YOUNG, R. (2008) 'Street Policing after PACE: the Drift to Summary Justice' in Cape and Young, eds, qv.

—— and SANDERS, A. (2004), 'The Ethics of Prosecution Lawyers', Legal Ethics, 7: 167.

—— and WILCOX, A. [2007] 'The Merits of Legal Aid in the Magistrates' Courts Revisited', Crim LR, 109.

ZANDER, M. (2000), 'Why Jack Straw's Jury Reform Has Lost the Plot', NLJ, 150: 723.

——and HENDERSON, P. (1993), Crown Court Study, Royal Commission on Criminal Justice Research Study No 19, London: HMSO.

ZEDNER, L. (2005), 'Securing Liberty in the Face of Terror', J Law & Society, 32: 507.

—— (2007), 'Preventive Justice or Pre-Punishment? The Case of Control Orders', CLP, 59: 174.

—— (2007), 'Seeking Security by Eroding Rights: the Side-stepping of Due Process' in Goold and Lazarus, eds, qv.

ZUCKERMAN, A. A. S. (1989), The Principles of Criminal Evidence, Oxford: Oxford University Press.

—— (1991), 'Miscarriage of Justice and Judicial Responsibility', Crim LR, 492.

INDEX

THE CRIMINAL PROCESS